Mike Meyers'
CompTIA Security+®
Certification Guide
Second Edition

(Exam SY0-501)

Mike Meyers
Scott Jernigan

Mc
Graw
Hill
Education

New York   Chicago   San Francisco
Athens   London   Madrid   Mexico City
Milan   New Delhi   Singapore   Sydney   Toronto

Library of Congress Cataloging-in-Publication Data

Names: Meyers, Mike, 1961- author. | Jernigan, Scott, author.
Title: Mike Meyers' CompTIA security+ certification guide, (exam SY0-501) /
   Mike Meyers, Scott Jernigan.
Other titles: CompTIA security+ certification guide, (exam SY0-501)
Description: Second edition. | San Francisco : McGraw-Hill Education, [2018]
   | Includes index.
Identifiers: LCCN 2017051849 | ISBN 9781260026375 (set/package : alk. paper)
Subjects: LCSH: Computer security—Examinations—Study guides. | Computer
   networks—Security measures—Examinations—Study guides. | Computer
   technicians—Certification—Study guides. | Electronic data processing
   personnel—Certification—Study guides.
Classification: LCC QA76.9.A25 M4876 2018 | DDC 005.8—dc23 LC record available at
https://lccn.loc.gov/2017051849

McGraw-Hill Education books are available at special quantity discounts to use as premiums and sales promotions, or for use in corporate training programs. To contact a representative, please visit the Contact Us pages at www.mhprofessional.com.

Mike Meyers' CompTIA Security+® Certification Guide, Second Edition (Exam SY0-501)

6 7 8 9   LCR   21 20 19

ISBN: Book p/n 978-1-260-02635-1 and CD p/n 978-1-260-02636-8
of set 978-1-260-02637-5

MHID: Book p/n 1-260-02635-3 and CD p/n 1-260-02636-1
of set 1-260-02637-X

Sponsoring Editor Timothy Green	**Technical Editor** Matt Walker	**Production Supervisor** James Kussow
Editorial Supervisor Janet Walden	**Copy Editor** William McManus	**Composition** Cenveo Publisher Services
Project Managers Dipika Rungta and Radhika Jolly, Cenveo® Publisher Services	**Proofreader** Claire Splan	**Illustration** Cenveo Publisher Services
Acquisitions Coordinator Claire Yee	**Indexer** Karin Arrigoni	**Art Director, Cover** Jeff Weeks

A mi amiga, Marisol Galindo. Espero con ansias el día en que bebemos margaritas en tu casa en Cancún.

—Mike

A mi esposa, Katie. Te amo.

—Scott

ABOUT THE AUTHORS

Mike Meyers, CompTIA A+®, CompTIA Network+®, CompTIA Security+, MCP, is the industry's leading authority on CompTIA certifications and the best-selling author of nine editions of *CompTIA A+ Certification All-in-One Exam Guide* (McGraw-Hill). He is the president and founder of Total Seminars, LLC, a major provider of PC and network repair seminars for thousands of organizations throughout the world, and a member of CompTIA.

Scott Jernigan, CompTIA IT Fundamentals, CompTIA A+, CompTIA Network+, CompTIA Security+, MCP, is the author or co-author (with Mike Meyers) of over two dozen IT certification books, including *CompTIA IT Fundamentals Certification All-in-One Exam Guide* (McGraw-Hill). He has taught seminars on building, fixing, and securing computers and networks all over the United States, including stints at the FBI Academy in Quantico, Virginia, and the UN Headquarters in New York City, New York.

About the Technical Editor

Matt Walker is currently working as a member of the Cyber Defense and Security Strategy team within DXC Technology. An IT security and education professional for more than 20 years, he has served as the director of the Network Training Center and a curriculum lead/senior instructor for Cisco Networking Academy on Ramstein AB, Germany, and as a network engineer for NASA's Secure Network Systems (NSS), designing and maintaining secured data, voice, and video networking for the agency. Matt also worked as an instructor supervisor and senior instructor at Dynetics, Inc., in Huntsville, Alabama, providing on-site certification-awarding classes for (ISC)², Cisco, and CompTIA, and after two years he came right back to NASA as an IT security manager for UNITeS, SAIC, at Marshall Space Flight Center. He has written and contributed to numerous technical training books for NASA, Air Education and Training Command, and the U.S. Air Force, as well as commercially, and he continues to train and write certification and college-level IT and IA security courses.

Becoming a CompTIA Certified IT Professional Is Easy

It's also the best way to reach greater professional opportunities and rewards.

Why Get CompTIA Certified?

Growing Demand

Labor estimates predict some technology fields will experience growth of more than 20% by the year 2020. (Source: CompTIA 9th Annual Information Security Trends study: 500 U.S. IT and Business Executives Responsible for Security.) CompTIA certification qualifies the skills required to join this workforce.

Higher Salaries

IT professionals with certifications on their resume command better jobs, earn higher salaries, and have more doors open to new multi-industry opportunities.

Verified Strengths

Ninety-one percent of hiring managers indicate CompTIA certifications are valuable in validating IT expertise, making certification the best way to demonstrate your competency and knowledge to employers. (Source: CompTIA Employer Perceptions of IT Training and Certification.)

Universal Skills

CompTIA certifications are vendor neutral—which means that certified professionals can proficiently work with an extensive variety of hardware and software found in most organizations.

 **Learn**  **Certify**  **Work**

Learn more about what the exam covers by reviewing the following:

- Exam objectives for key study points.

- Sample questions for a general overview of what to expect on the exam and examples of question format.

- Visit online forums, like LinkedIn, to see what other IT professionals say about CompTIA exams.

Purchase a voucher at a Pearson VUE testing center or at CompTIAstore.com.

- Register for your exam at a Pearson VUE testing center.

- Visit pearsonvue.com/CompTIA to find the closest testing center to you.

- Schedule the exam online. You will be required to enter your voucher number or provide payment information at registration.

- Take your certification exam.

Congratulations on your CompTIA certification!

- Make sure to add your certification to your resume.

- Check out the CompTIA Certification Roadmap to plan your next career move.

Learn More: Certification.CompTIA.org/securityplus

CompTIA Disclaimer

CONTENTS AT A GLANCE

CONTENTS

ACKNOWLEDGMENTS

In general, we'd like to thank our amazing teams at McGraw-Hill Education and Cenveo for such excellent support and brilliant work editing, laying out, and publishing this edition. Special shout out to our friend Joachim Zwick, who proved an invaluable sounding board for many ideas and concepts. Your knowledge helped so much!

We'd like to acknowledge the many people who contributed their talents to make this book possible:

To **Tim Green, our acquisitions editor at McGraw-Hill**: Always such a pleasure to do a project with you!

To **Matt Walker, technical editor**: You caught some excellent oops! and added so many great anecdotes and ideas. It's a much better book with your input.

To **Bill McManus, copy editor**: Awesome work smoothing dual voices and helping turn some awkward phrases into silky prose. You're the best!

To **Claire Yee, acquisitions coordinator at McGraw-Hill**: Thanks for keeping track of everything and reminding Scott when *he* forgot things.

To **Dipika Rungta and Radhika Jolly, project managers at Cenveo**: Such a pleasure to work with you, Dipika, for most of the book. And thanks also, Radhika, for coming in at the 11th hour for the final stretch. Seamless transition and we look forward to the next project with you.

To **Claire Splan, proofreader**: You did a super job, thanks you so mich!

To **Karin Arrigoni, indexer** extraordinaire: Well done!

To **Cenveo, compositors**: The layout was excellent, thanks!

To **Janet Walden, editorial supervisor at McGraw-Hill**: Wow, you caught some mistakes at the last minute and I am so thrilled that you did! Thank you.

To **Jim Kussow, production supervisor at McGraw-Hill**: Thanks for waving that magic wand of yours and making so much happen as smoothly as possible.

INTRODUCTION

Most societies teem with a host of networked devices, from servers to smartphones, that provide the backbone for much of modern life. People and companies use these devices to produce and sell products and services, communicate around the globe, educate at every level, and manage the mechanisms of governments everywhere. Networked devices and the complex networks that interconnect them offer advances for humanity on par with, or perhaps beyond, the Agricultural and Industrial Revolutions. That's the good news.

The bad news is the fact that reliance on these devices creates a security risk to the resources placed on them. Networks can lose critical data and connections, both of which equate to loss of energy, confidence, time, and money. To paraphrase a few words from the American statesman, James Madison, if humans were angels, there'd be no need for security professionals. But humans are at best negligent and at worst petty, vindictive, and astoundingly creative in pursuit of your money and secrets.

Networked devices and the networks that interconnect them need security professionals to stand guard. The need for security professionals in Information Technology (IT) far outstrips demand, and we assume that's why you picked up this book. You see the trend and want to take the first step to becoming an IT security professional by attaining the acknowledged first security certification to get CompTIA Security+.

This introduction starts with an overview of the goals of security, to put a framework around everything you're going to learn. Second, we'll discuss the CompTIA Security+ certification and look at exam details. Finally, this introduction details the overall structure of the book, providing a roadmap for studying for the exam.

Goals of Security

Traditional computer security theory balances among three critical elements: functionality, security, and the resources available to ensure both. From a *functionality* standpoint, systems must function as people need them to function to process the data needed. Users and other systems need to interface with systems and data seamlessly to get work done. Don't confuse functionality with free rein. Allowing users to do whatever they wish with systems and data may result in loss, theft, or destruction of systems and data. Therefore, functionality must balance with security.

From the *security* standpoint, however, increasing the levels of protection for systems and data usually *reduces* functionality. Introducing security mechanisms and procedures into the mix doesn't always allow users to see or interact with data and systems the way they would like. This usually means a reduction in functionality to some degree.

Figure I-1
Balancing
functionality,
security, and
resources

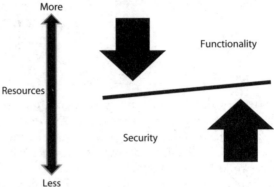

To add another wrinkle, the *resources* expended toward functionality and security, and the balance between them, are finite. No one has all the money or resources they need or as much functionality or security as they want. Keep in mind, therefore, that the relationship between functionality and security is inversely proportional; that is to say, the more security in place, the less functionality, and *vice versa*. Also, the fewer resources a person or organization has, the less of either functionality or security they can afford. Figure I-1 illustrates this careful balancing act among the three elements of functionality, security, and resources.

Security theory follows three goals, widely considered the foundations of the IT security trade: confidentiality, integrity, and availability. Security professionals work to achieve these goals in every security program and technology. These three goals inform all the data and the systems that process it. The three goals of security are called the *CIA triad*. Figure I-2 illustrates the three goals of confidentiality, integrity, and availability.

 NOTE The CIA triad is put into practice through various security mechanisms and controls. Every security technique, practice, and mechanism put into place to protect systems and data relates in some fashion to ensuring confidentiality, integrity, and availability.

Confidentiality

Confidentiality is the goal of keeping systems and data from being accessed, seen, read, or otherwise interacted with by anyone who is not authorized to do so. Confidentiality is a characteristic met by keeping data secret from people who aren't allowed to have it or interact with it in any way, while making sure that only those people who do have the right to access it can do so. Confidentiality is met through various means, including the use of permissions to data, encryption, and so on.

Figure I-2
The CIA triad

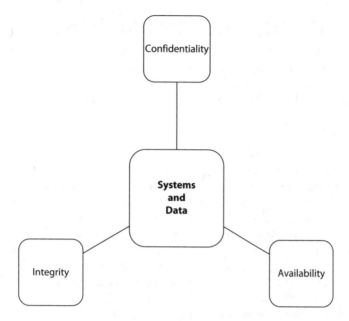

Integrity

Meeting the goal of *integrity* requires maintaining data and systems in a pristine, unaltered state when they are stored, transmitted, processed, and received, unless the alteration is intended due to normal processing. In other words, there should be no unauthorized modification, alteration, creation, or deletion of data. Any changes to data must be done only as part of authorized transformations in normal use and processing. Integrity can be maintained by the use of a variety of checks and other mechanisms, including data checksums, comparison with known or computed data values, and cryptographic means.

Availability

Maintaining *availability* means ensuring that systems and data are available for authorized users to perform authorized tasks, whenever they need them. Availability bridges security and functionality, because it ensures that users have a secure, functional system at their immediate disposal. An extremely secure system that's not functional is not available in practice. Availability is ensured in various ways, including system redundancy, data backups, business continuity, and other means.

During the course of your study, keep in mind the overall goals in IT security. First, balance three critical elements: functionality, security, and the resources available to ensure both. Second, focus on the goals of the CIA triad—confidentiality, integrity, and availability—when implementing, reviewing, managing, or troubleshooting network and system security. The book returns to these themes many times, tying new pieces of knowledge to this framework.

CompTIA Security+ Certification

The CompTIA Security+ certification has earned the reputation as the first step for anyone pursuing a career in the highly complex, highly convoluted, and still very much evolving world of IT Security. Let's start with a description of CompTIA, then look at the specifics of the certification.

CompTIA

The *Computing Technology Industry Association (CompTIA)* is a nonprofit, industry-wide organization of just about everyone in the IT industry. The different aspects of CompTIA's mission include certification, education, and public policy.

As of this writing, CompTIA offers around 18 vendor-neutral certifications covering a wide range of information technology areas. Examples of some of these areas and certifications include CompTIA Linux+ (focusing on the Linux operating system), CompTIA A+ (which focuses on computer technology support fundamentals), CompTIA Network+ (covering different network technologies), and, of course, CompTIA Security+.

CompTIA certifications are considered the *de facto* standard in the industry in some areas. Because they are vendor neutral, almost all of CompTIA certifications cover basic knowledge of fundamental concepts of a particular aspect of IT. CompTIA works hard to develop exams that accurately validate knowledge that professionals must have in that area. This enables employers and others to be confident that the individual's knowledge meets a minimum level of skill, standardized across the industry.

The CompTIA Security+ Exam

Let's state up front that CompTIA does not have any requirements for individuals who want to take the CompTIA Security+ exam. There are no prerequisites for certification or definitive requirements for years of experience. CompTIA does have several recommendations, on the other hand, including knowledge that might be validated by other CompTIA certifications such as the CompTIA Network+ certification. In other words, the level of networking knowledge you are expected to have before you take the CompTIA Security+ exam is the level that you would have after successfully completing the CompTIA Network+ certification. Here are CompTIA's recommendations:

- Network+ certification
- Two years of experience in network or server administration, with a focus on security

You should have experience in several areas, such as networking knowledge, basic information security concepts, hardware, software (both operating systems and applications), cryptography, physical security, and so on. The next few sections cover specific exam objectives that you need to know.

Table I-1 shows the six domains in the CompTIA Security+ Certification Exam Objectives document for exam SY0-501. Each of these domains has very detailed exam objectives.

Domain	Name	Percent of Exam
1.0	Threats, Attacks and Vulnerabilities	21
2.0	Technologies and Tools	22
3.0	Architecture and Design	15
4.0	Identity and Access Management	16
5.0	Risk Management	14
6.0	Cryptography and PKI	12

Threats, Attacks and Vulnerabilities

Domain 1.0 is all about the attacks, from malware to application attacks. It's critical you know your keyloggers from your RATs, and your buffer overflows from your cross-site scripting. In addition, you should recognize the threat actors, from script kiddies to evil governments to incompetent users. Along with the threats and attacks, you should understand different types of vulnerabilities that enable these attacks to thrive and the two main tools you use to minimize those vulnerabilities, vulnerability assessments and penetration testing.

Technologies and Tools

Domain 2.0 is all about the hardware, protocols, and utilities that are critical and intrinsic to networks. For starters, you should understand the functions and features of not only more common devices such as switches, routers, and WAPs, but also less commonly used devices such as load balancers and SSL decryptors. Next are the many utilities used in IT security. You need to know simple tools, such as ping and netstat, and more complex tools, such as nmap and netcat. (This also means that if you're not yet using Linux, you will be by the time you're taking the exam.) Also, make sure you're very comfortable with secure protocols and how they work.

Architecture and Design

Domain 3.0 extends the ideas in the previous domain, requiring you to know how to use security devices, protocols, and tools. This domain covers the frameworks that enable secure IT, the design concepts such as defense-in-depth and benchmarks used to measure security. This domain covers technologies to defend networks, such as VLANs, DMZ, and wireless designs. In addition, this domain covers the design of secure applications and security for embedded systems. Domain 3.0 also covers physical security controls, such as fencing and fire prevention.

Identity and Access Management

Domain 4.0 goes into great detail about three terms you'll get to know very well: authentication, authorization, and accounting. It expects you to know authentication and the many identity and access services such as LDAP and Kerberos. The domain addresses authorization via user groups and accounts and the tools and methods used to control them.

Risk Management

Domain 5.0 defines critical concepts in risk management, such as events, exposures, incidents, and vulnerability. You're expected to know risk-related tools, such as business impact analysis, assessments, incident response, and disaster recovery/business continuity. There's even a subdomain on forensics.

Cryptography and PKI

Domain 6.0 details cryptography. What are clear text, ciphertext, and a cryptographic algorithm? What is the difference between a symmetric algorithm and an asymmetric algorithm? What are the differences between different cryptographic algorithms such as RC4 and AES? Where do we use them, and why? This domain also covers hashing, from the definition, to how to use it, to the different hash algorithms available. This domain also deals with how to use cryptography in authentication, and the authentication protocols used today. Domain 6.0 requires that you understand public key infrastructure, from digital signatures and certificates, to how these power tools keep data safe.

Getting Certified

This book covers everything you'll need to know for CompTIA's Security+ certification exam. The book is written in a modular fashion, with short, concise modules within each chapter devoted to specific topics and areas you'll need to master for the exam. Each module covers specific objectives and details for the exam, as defined by CompTIA. We've arranged these objectives in a manner that makes fairly logical sense from a learning perspective, and we think you'll find that arrangement will help you in learning the material.

 NOTE Throughout the book, you'll see helpful Exam Tips and Notes. These elements offer insight on how the concepts you'll study apply in the real world. Often, they may give you a bit more information on a topic than what is covered in the text or expected on the exam. And they may also be helpful in pointing out an area you need to focus on or important topics that you may see on the test.

End of Chapter Questions

At the end of each chapter you'll find questions that will test your knowledge and under-standing of the concepts discussed in the modules. The questions also include an answer key, with explanations of the correct answers.

Using the Exam Objectives Map

The Exam Objectives map included in Appendix A has been constructed to help you cross-reference the official exam objectives from CompTIA with the relevant coverage in the book. References have been provided for the exam objectives exactly as CompTIA has presented them—the module that covers that objective, the chapter, and a page refer-ence are included.

Media

The media (optical disc or direct download for the digital edition) accompanying this book features the Total Tester exam software that enables you to generate a complete practice exam or quizzes by chapter or by exam domain. See Appendix B for more information.

Study Well and Live Better

We enjoyed writing this book and hope you will enjoy reading it as well. Good luck in your studies and good luck on the CompTIA Security+ exam. If you have comments, questions, or suggestions, tag us:

Mike: desweds@gmail.com
Scott: jernigan.scott@gmail.com

CHAPTER 1

Risk Management

I am first and foremost a nerd. Not only a nerd, but an IT nerd. Not only an IT nerd, but an IT security nerd. I'm amazingly good at locking down firewalls and setting up secure VPNs. And on the other side, I can crack most 802.11 networks in a surprisingly short time. (*And Mike is startlingly modest! – Editor*)

Technical security skills like these are great (and fun), but when you look at IT security in general, "screwdriver techs" are *the least important part* of any IT security organization. Surprised? Well, it's true!

Proper IT security requires organization. That organization takes many forms:

- People
- Equipment
- Operating systems
- Applications
- Security processes

Organizing all these things enables you to protect your organization from harm.

This organization is based on the concept of risk management. *Risk management* is the science of identifying and categorizing risks and then systematically applying resources to these risks to minimize their impact on an organization. Risk management is a massive topic. Many fine universities around the world offer advanced degrees in risk management. Without risk management as the cornerstone of organizing a discussion on IT security, we're reduced to nothing more than reacting to security problems as they come. Knowing this, CompTIA dedicates an entire Security+ domain to risk management.

This chapter tours IT risk management in eight modules:

- Defining Risk
- Risk Management Concepts
- Security Controls
- Risk Assessment
- Business Impact Analysis
- Data Security and Privacy Policies

- Personnel Risks
- Third-Party Risk

Module 1-1: Defining Risk

This module covers the following CompTIA Security+ objective:

- **1.3** Explain threat actor types and attributes

In IT security, *risk* implies a lot more than the term means in standard English. Let's start with a jargon-filled definition, then examine each term in the definition. We'll review the definition with some examples at the end of the module.

> *Risk is the probability of a threat actor taking advantage of a vulnerability by using a threat against an IT system asset.*

This definition of risk includes five jargon terms that require further explanation:

- Probability
- Threat actor
- Vulnerability
- Threat
- Asset

Defining each jargon word or phrase relies at least a little on understanding one or more of the other jargon phrases. Let's give it a shot, starting with assets and then covering the other phrases in order.

Asset

An *asset* is a part of an IT infrastructure that has value. You can measure value either tangibly or intangibly. A gateway router to the Internet is an example of an asset with tangible value. If it fails, you can easily calculate the cost to replace the router.

What if that same router is the gateway to an in-house Web server? If that Web server is no longer accessible to your customers, they're not going to be happy and might go somewhere else due to lack of good faith or good will. Good faith doesn't have a measurable value; it's an intangible asset.

 NOTE *People* are an important intangible asset.

Here are a few more examples of assets:

- **Servers**   The computers that offer shared resources
- **Workstations**   The computers users need to do their job
- **Applications**   Task-specific programs an organization needs to operate
- **Data**   The stored, proprietary information an organization uses
- **Personnel**   The people who work in an organization
- **Wireless access**   Access to the network that doesn't require plugging into an Ethernet port
- **Internet services**   The public- or private-facing resources an organization provides to customers, vendors, or personnel via the Web or other Internet applications

We will cover assets in much greater detail later in this chapter.

Probability

Probability means the likelihood—over a defined period of time—of someone or something damaging assets. Here are a couple of examples:

- The company expects about five or six attacks on its Web server daily.
- Hard drives will fail after three years.

You will also hear the term *likelihood* as a synonym for probability.

Threat Actor

A *threat actor* can hurt stuff. A threat actor can be a malicious person, such as a classic hacker bent on accessing corporate secrets. But a threat actor can take different guises as well, such as programs automated to attack at a specific date or time. A threat actor could be a respected member of an organization who has just enough access to the IT infrastructure but lacks the knowledge of what *not* to do. The word *actor* here means simply someone or something that can initiate a negative event.

The CompTIA Security+ exam covers six specific types of threat actor:

- Hacktivists
- Script kiddies
- Insiders
- Competitors
- Organized crime
- Nation state/APT

A *hacktivist* is a hacker and an activist. These threat actors have some form of agenda, often political or fueled by a sense of injustice. Hacktivism is often associated with sophisticated yet loosely associated organizations, such as Anonymous.

Save the whales!

Script kiddies are poorly skilled threat actors who take advantage of relatively easy-to-use open-source attacking tools. They get the derogatory moniker because they don't have skills that accomplished hackers possess. Their lack of sophistication makes them notoriously easy to stop, most of the time.

Insiders are people within an organization. Since they are part of the targeted organization, these threat actors have substantial physical access and usually have user accounts that give them substantial access to assets. They are often motivated by revenge or greed.

Competitors are outside organizations that try to gain access to the same customers as the targeted company. Modern laws and law enforcement have made competitor attacks less common today than in the past, but given competitors are in the same business, they would know more precisely the type of secure information they want.

Organized crime groups use extra-legal methods to gain access to resources. Organized crime is a huge problem today. These groups are sophisticated, well-funded, and cause tremendous damage to vulnerable systems worldwide to make money.

A *nation state* as a threat actor refers to government-directed attacks, such as the United States sending spies into Russia. Whereas organized crime commonly uses threats specifically to make money, nation states take advantage of vulnerabilities to acquire intelligence. Nation states have the resources—people and money—to collect *open-source intelligence (OSINT)* successfully, information from media (newspapers, television), public government reports, professional and academic publications, and so forth.

Nation state threat actors are easily the best funded and most sophisticated of all threat actors. Nation states often use *advanced persistent threats (APTs)*. An APT is when a threat actor gets long-term control of a compromised system, continually looking for new data to steal.

 NOTE   Many nation states use organized crime to do the attacks against other nation states.

Vulnerability and Threat

The terms vulnerability and threat go hand-in-hand, so it makes sense to talk about both at the same time. A *vulnerability* is a weakness inherent in an asset that leaves it open to a threat. A *threat* is an action a threat actor can use against a vulnerability to create a negative effect. You can't have a threat without a vulnerability.

Vulnerabilities and their associated threats exist at every level of an organization. Not changing the default password on a router is a vulnerability; someone taking control of your router by using the default password is the threat. Giving a user full control to a shared folder (when that user does not need nor should have full control) is a vulnerability. That same user having the capability to delete every file in that folder is a threat.

Oh no!

Threats do not have to originate only from people or organizations. Forces of nature like earthquakes and hurricanes (a big deal here in Houston, Texas) can also be threats.

The IT industry aggressively looks for vulnerabilities and their associated threats. Virtually every company or organization that provides hardware, software, services, or applications has some form of bug bounty program. These programs reward people who report vulnerabilities with money, swag, and acclaim (Figure 1-1).

Figure 1-1   Facebook vulnerability reporting

Figure 1-2   NIST National Vulnerability Database

Governments also actively pursue vulnerability reporting. One of the most important is the National Institute of Standards and Technology's National Vulnerability Database (Figure 1-2).

As you might imagine, dealing with threats by minimizing vulnerabilities is a core component of risk management. The chapter will develop this in detail.

NOTE   You will see two other terms associated with the jargon phrases covered in this section, attack and incident. An *attack* is when a threat actor actively attempts to take advantage of a vulnerability. When the target recognizes an attack, it is called an *incident*. Both attacks and incidents go beyond the concept of risk and are covered in Chapter 10.

Circling Back to the Risk Definition

Now that we have explored each jargon term in some detail, let's look at the definition of risk again and follow it with an example.

> *Risk is the probability of a threat actor taking advantage of a vulnerability by using a threat against an IT system asset.*

Here's an example of a risk:

There's a 15 percent chance in the next month that Sally the hacktivist will guess correctly John's password on the important company server to gain access to secret documents.

The probability is 15 percent over the next month. The threat actor is Sally the hacktivist. John's lame password is a vulnerability; the threat is that Sally will get that password and use it to access the server. The assets are both the server and the secret documents. Got it? Let's move on.

The Risk "Formula"

Many IT security professionals use pseudo-math functions when describing risk, such as the following:

Risk = Probability × Vulnerability × Threat

Sometimes an addition sign is used, or different elements are emphasized:

Risk = Vulnerability + Threat + Asset

The problem with these pseudo math functions is that there is no math involved, nor is there any "one" formula that has broad consensus. They can, however, help you remember what the different risk terms mean.

Look at the first pseudo formula listed. A vulnerability makes a threat possible, but it doesn't really say anything about the risk other than the risk exists. The probability is the only aspect that makes this "formula" work. In fact, if risk requires a vulnerability/threat, we could arguably reduce the pseudo equation to nothing more than the following:

Risk = Probability

That equation isn't very useful. Yet there is one more term we can add that should make all this more accurate: impact.

This module already made a reference to impact in the context of how assets have a tangible or an intangible value that can be negatively impacted by an attack. *Impact* is the effect of an attack on a single asset. Impact is measured in different ways, such as financial (value, repair), life (as in human lives), and reputation (good will, mentioned earlier).

Impact is incredibly important to keep in mind when discussing risk. You can use impact to help decide how much time and energy to put into mitigating any one given threat. Try this pseudo equation:

Risk = Probability × Impact

Consider the following threat/vulnerabilities scenarios. What is the impact of a (small, not one of those end-of-the-world varieties) meteor hitting your facility? The impact is big. It will probably take out the whole building! But the probability of that meteor strike is pretty small. So, putting all this into a pseudo formula:

Risk of meteor threat = (very low probability) × (high impact)

Given the very low likelihood of a meteor impact, you won't try to reduce your vulnerability to this threat (anyone got a spare *Star Wars* ion cannon?).

Let's try this one more time with the threat of malware getting into a network via e-mail. Malware from e-mail is a huge problem, but generally not very hard to clean up, so:

Risk of malware through e-mail = (very high probability) × (moderate impact)

In this case, the very high probability suggests the need to mitigate this vulnerability by adding e-mail anti-malware to systems used for e-mail.

Unwelcome passenger!

Risk and Threat Mitigation

IT security professionals use a lot of tools to combat risk. These tools get lumped together under the term risk management. Primarily, the tools reduce the impact of—*mitigate*—threats posed to an organization. Module 1-2 explores risk management concepts; later modules expand on the toolsets available. Let's leave Module 1-1 with a definition of the job of an IT security professional:

> *IT security professionals implement risk management techniques and practices to mitigate threats to their organizations.*

Module 1-2: Risk Management Concepts

This module covers the following CompTIA Security+ objective:

- **3.1** Explain use cases and purpose for frameworks, best practices, and secure configuration guides

Module 1-1 ended with a pithy job description: IT security professionals implement risk management techniques and practices to mitigate threats to their organizations. To get to the "implement" stage requires knowledge, naturally, and the term "risk management" is loaded with meaning. This module explores four aspects of risk management: infrastructure, security controls, risk management frameworks, and industry-standard frameworks and reference architectures. Later modules build on this information to get you to the "implement" step.

 EXAM TIP IT risk management is 14 percent of the CompTIA Security+ exam!

Infrastructure

In IT risk management, the term *infrastructure* applies to just about every aspect of an organization, from the organization itself to its computers, networks, employees, physical security, and sometimes third-party access.

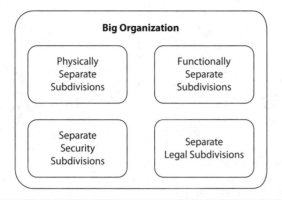

Figure 1-3 What's your organization?

Organization

At its most basic, an organization is who you work for: your company, your corporation, your non-profit, your governmental department. These are good potential examples of an organization, but in some cases, you might need more details. A single organization, for example, might look like a collection of smaller organizations in terms of risk management (Figure 1-3).

The big difference here is how autonomous your IT management is in relation to the overall organization. The more decisions the main organization lets a smaller group handle, the more the smaller group should look at itself as an organization. A smaller organization might be a single physical location in a different city or perhaps a different country. It might be a division of a corporation, or a regional governmental agency.

NOTE   A quick way to determine the scope of any IT infrastructure is to identify the bigwigs. A single IT infrastructure would never have more than one chief security officer, for example.

Systems

Computers and network equipment are part of an IT infrastructure, but there are many more components. People matter, such as IT managers, IT techs, human resources, governance (chief security officer, chief information officer), and legal staff; even individual users are part of the IT infrastructure. See Figure 1-4.

Physical Security

Physical security is also an important part of an IT infrastructure. Fences, cameras, and guards protect your infrastructure just as well as they protect the rest of your organization.

Third-Party Access

Third parties that your organization contracts with are part of your IT infrastructure. Have an intranet that enables suppliers to access your equipment? Then those suppliers are part of your IT infrastructure. Have a maintenance contract on all your laser printers?

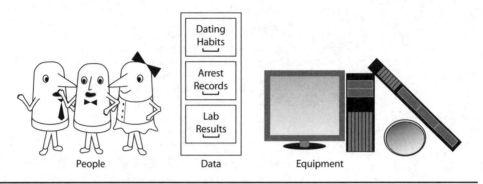

People   Data   Equipment

Figure 1-4   We are your infrastructure.

There's another part of your infrastructure. The company that hosts all your Web servers? Yes, they are part of your IT infrastructure as well.

Security Controls

The action of strengthening a vulnerability to reduce or eliminate the impact is called a *security control*. A security control is a directed action you place on some part of your infrastructure. Security controls don't say how to perform the steps needed to mitigate a threat, only that they must be performed.

Here is an example of a security control:

> *All user account passwords on Windows systems must meet Microsoft complexity requirements.*

IT security professionals locate vulnerabilities and apply security controls. It's what we do.

As you might imagine, the typical infrastructure probably has thousands, if not tens of thousands, of security controls that need to be applied. How does a lone IT security pro create this list of controls? The answer is, you don't. You use a bit of magic called a risk management framework.

Risk Management Framework

A framework is a description of a complex process, concentrating on major steps and the flows between the steps. A *risk management framework (RMF)* describes the major steps and flows of the complex process of applying security controls in an organized and controlled fashion.

Easily the most popular RMF available comes from the National Institute of Standards and Technology (NIST). See Figure 1-5. This RMF is described in NIST Special Publication 800-37, Revision 1, "Guide for Applying the Risk Management Framework to Federal Information Systems: A Security Life Cycle Approach." Originally designed as an RMF expressly for U.S. federal organizations, the NIST RMF has been adopted as the de facto RMF by the IT security industry.

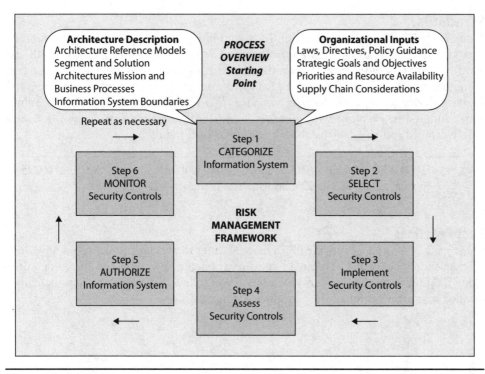

Figure 1-5 NIST RMF

The NIST RMF begins with two major inputs, Architecture Description and Organizational Inputs. Architecture Description covers the design and organization of the information systems being used by the organization. The architecture alone defines a huge number of security controls. Something as simple as an air-gapped Ethernet network wouldn't need a firewall or intrusion detection. Choosing a Windows Active Directory domain will give you robust single sign-on for all systems.

Organizational Inputs is far more interesting. This describes the many sources where less-obvious security controls come from. This includes sources such as laws, standards, best practices, and security policies.

Laws

Many *laws* affect how and what types of security controls your organization may use. In the United States, two laws stand out as important for IT security. First is the *Health Insurance Portability and Accountability Act (HIPAA)* of 1996. HIPAA provides data privacy and security provisions for safeguarding medical information. These include provisions for who may have access to patient records and how to properly store records. Second is the *Sarbanes–Oxley Act (SOX)* of 2002. This act has many provisions, but the one that is most important to many companies is the requirement for private businesses to retain critical records for specific time periods. Both HIPAA and SOX are discussed in more detail in Module 1-6.

Standards

A *standard* is a ruleset voluntarily adopted by an industry to provide more uniform products and services. It might be more accurate to replace the word *voluntarily* with the word *voluntold,* because many standards are often required for participation in certain industries. Easily the most far-reaching standard from the standpoint of IT security is the *Payment Card Industry Data Security Standard (PCI-DSS).* This industry-specific framework, adopted by everyone who processes credit card transactions, provides for several highly detailed security controls to mitigate credit card fraud.

 EXAM TIP The CompTIA Security+ exam will test your knowledge of U.S. laws such as HIPAA and SOX, and standards such as PCI-DSS.

Best Practices

A *best practice* is a ruleset provided by a manufacturer to give you guidance on how their product should be used. The entire IT industry is filled with vendor-specific guides, providing best practices that vendors recommend you follow. Microsoft provides incredibly detailed best practices for all their products (Figure 1-6).

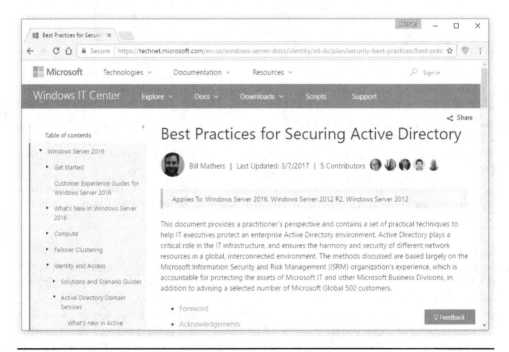

Figure 1-6 Best practices for a Microsoft product

Security Policies

A security policy is a document that organizations generate to declare what actions and attitudes they will take for certain critical aspects of their infrastructure. An organization may have hundreds of policies, but, generally, policies most commonly define security controls for the trickiest assets in every organization—the people. Later modules will delve deeply into policies; for now, let's look at one of the most common, an acceptable use policy.

An *acceptable use policy* defines exactly what users may or may not do on systems in the organization. Here are a few lines from an example pulled from one of many free boilerplates available on the Web:

- Users must not attempt to access any data, documents, e-mail correspondence, and programs contained on systems for which they do not have authorization.

- Users must not share their account(s), passwords, personal identification numbers (PIN), security tokens (i.e., smart card), or similar information or devices used for identification and authorization purposes.

- Users must not use non-standard shareware or freeware software without the appropriate management approval.

- Users must not engage in activity that may degrade the performance of Information Resources; deprive an authorized user access to resources; obtain extra resources beyond those allocated; or circumvent computer security measures.

- Users must not download, install or run security programs or utilities such as password cracking programs, packet sniffers, or port scanners that reveal or exploit weaknesses in the security of a computer resource unless approved by the CISO (chief information security officer).

 NOTE You can find the acceptable use policy in this example at www.cio.ca.gov. The specific document to search for is ACCEPTABLEUSEPOLICYTEMPLATE.doc.

These inputs generate blocks of security policies, but you apply these policies in a very specific manner. NIST SP 800-37 outlines the following steps.

Step 1: Categorize the Information System   Look at your assets and determine the impact of losing them.

Step 2: Select Security Controls   Select an initial set of baseline security controls for the information system based on the security categorization.

Step 3: Implement the Security Controls   Actually apply the security controls.

Step 4: Assess the Security Controls   Test/assess the security controls to verify they're doing the job you want them to do.

Step 5: Authorize Information System Authorize the now-strengthened information system to operate.

Step 6: Monitor the Security Controls Monitor the information system on an ongoing basis, checking for new vulnerabilities and overall performance.

Industry-Standard Frameworks and Reference Architectures

IT security is complicated and it interacts with every aspect of a business. Accomplished IT security professionals need to step out of the trenches and diagram all the systems that interact to secure their organization's IT infrastructure from current and future threats. They need to create an *enterprise information security architecture (EISA)* to accomplish this task. The EISA analyzes security systems in place. It encompasses industry-standard frameworks, such as the NIST RMF discussed previously. The EISA accounts for regulatory and non-regulatory influences—laws and standard operating procedures—and how compliance manifests. That includes national and international laws and practices.

The lists and charts of functions, departments, products, and security practices create a common vocabulary that IT and management can use to discuss current and future success. That common vocabulary, the *reference architecture*, helps to structure exceedingly complicated, interrelated aspects of the organization.

The CompTIA Security+ exam touches lightly on the concepts of industry-standard frameworks and reference architectures, going little more than defining these terms. More advanced IT security certifications go far deeper. The EU-based Information Technology Infrastructure Library (ITIL) certifications focus on best practices for developing complex yet complete EISA for any type and any size organization.

Module 1-3: Security Controls

This module covers the following CompTIA Security+ objectives:

- **3.1** Explain use cases and purpose for frameworks, best practices, and secure configuration guides
- **5.7** Compare and contrast various types of controls

The previous module covered the concept of security controls and even showed you a few examples. This module delves deeply into the organization of security controls. This organization makes it easier to consider the types of controls available and to classify them into specific groups based on what they do to mitigate threats.

Phase Controls

Thus far, the book has defined a security control as an action performed on a vulnerability to mitigate the impact of a risk. But what form of action can a control take? At first glance you might be tempted to look at a security control as an action to block an attack.

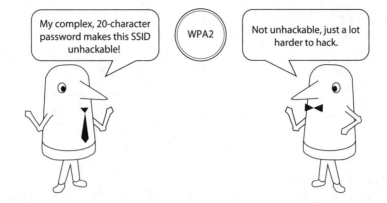

Figure 1-7
Mitigation isn't
perfection.

It's tempting, for example, to think of placing 20-character, complex WPA2 passwords on all the wireless access points (WAPs) in an organization as a security control that will stop anyone from hacking the 802.11 network. This is a strong security control no doubt, but it can't absolutely stop a determined attacker. Even long passwords can be hacked, although the probability of a successful attack is greatly reduced (Figure 1-7).

Mitigation doesn't mean stopping an attack. Attacks happen. Therefore, it's helpful to categorize security controls based on when they work relative to the phase of an attack. A security control might work before, during, or after an attack. These are generally known as *activity phase control types*. You need to know five phase control types for both essential skills and the CompTIA Security+ exam: deterrent, preventative, detective, corrective, and compensating.

Deterrent Control

A *deterrent control* is designed to deter a potential attacker from even attempting an attack. Good lighting around your building might deter an intruder from entering. Not building a server building near a fault line is another example. Figure 1-8 shows the welcome banner from a Secure Shell (SSH) server. Surely that will deter any potential hacker!

Preventative Control

A *preventative control* attempts to keep an active attack from succeeding. The earlier example of using a 20-character password on WPA2 is a great example of a preventative control. Putting a lock on the server room door is another example of a preventative control. Doing thorough background checks on potential new employees would be a third example.

NOTE Most security controls are preventative phase controls.

Figure 1-8
Mike's SSH
warning

```
login as:root

Welcome to Mike's SSH server!

*******************************************
* WARNING! AUTHORIZED USERS ONLY!        *
*                                         *
* YOUR IP ADDRESS IS BEING TRACKED!      *
*                                         *
*******************************************
root@10.11.12.101's password:_
```

Detective Control

A *detective control* works during an attack. As the name implies, these controls actively look for an attack and alert security professionals to the presence of an active, ongoing attack. An intrusion detection system, for example, watches a network for activity that indicates an intrusion attack. A security camera detects someone trying to go into a place he or she does not belong.

 EXAM TIP Some security controls cross phases. A security guard can be classified as a deterrent control, preventative control, or detective control, for example, depending on the role that the security guard is playing at any given moment.

Corrective

A *corrective control* applies after an attack has taken place and fixes/mitigates the result of the incident. Restoring data from backups is probably the most common example of a corrective control.

Compensating

Sometimes you need to provide a temporary solution to a vulnerability that's less than optimal. Perhaps someone tried to drive through a fence and you need to hire an extra guard for a short time. Maybe all users have to log into a system as root until a completely new system comes online, so you add extra logs to track usage more closely. These are *compensating controls*. You use compensating controls to keep going until a better control is available or possible.

Control Types

Another way to separate controls is by who or what they affect. In this case, we break security controls into technical, administrative, and physical.

Technical Controls

Technical controls are security controls applied to technology. If you specify a security control that states, "All edge routers must be able to communicate on SNMPv3," then you've made a technical control.

Administrative Controls

Administrative controls are applied to people. If you have a security control that states, "All users must log off their workstations every time they leave their office, regardless of length of time," then you've made an administrative control.

EXAM TIP Some industries (notably healthcare) require extensive frameworks that describe best practices and procedures for technical and administrative controls. These frameworks usually specify essential user training for proper security.

Physical Controls

Physical controls are applied to secure physical areas from physical access by unauthorized people. Fences, door locks, elevator floor blockers, and biometric retinal scanners are all examples of physical controls.

NOTE It's common to combine these two organizations of security controls. For example, a locked door is a great example of a physical, preventative security control.

Security Control Strategies

A well-applied security control is good, but if you combine security controls to work together, you get better security. The secret is to understand how security controls might be applied together.

Defense in Depth/Layered Security

Every IT infrastructure might be looked at as a series of concentric shells. The location of these shells depends on the types of threats you are mitigating. Consider the diagram of Total Seminars' small office (Figure 1-9). In this case, we're defending against physical

Figure 1-9
Physical defense
in depth

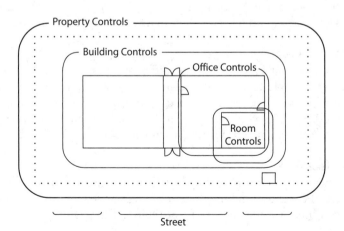

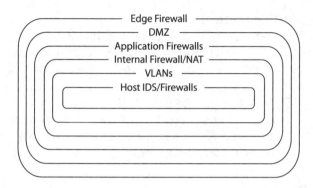

Figure 1-10
Network defense
in depth

intrusion. Each shell works together to reduce the threat of physical intrusion. This is an example of *defense in depth*, essentially, *layered security*.

Let's go through this exercise again except this time let's consider network intrusions. We redraw the shells to reflect the firewalls, DMZs, VLANs, and other security controls to protect individual systems from network intrusion (Figure 1-10).

Vendor Diversity

Every infrastructure uses several vendors to supply equipment and services. When IT professionals find a vendor they like and know, they tend to stick with that vendor. While using a single vendor has conveniences, it also creates a single point of failure that needs to be considered. Should that one vendor close up shop, the company might have trouble. If an equipment manufacturer should fail, hardware will continue to work but without support. This is inconvenient, but not an immediate impact in most cases. Single-vendor services are another story. It's far too easy to use a single cloud vendor, single firewall, or single operating system. In these cases, if a vendor closes shop, it could mean the loss of online presence, backup, firewall updates … this list is as long as your vendor list. The only way to avoid this vulnerability is through *vendor diversity*. This doesn't mean that every other router is purchased through a different vendor, nor does it mean you need to fire up an Amazon AWS server for every Microsoft Azure VM you create. It does mean that your staff should have freedom to diversify in R&D and production as they see fit.

Control Diversity

Control diversity means to combine different types of controls to provide better security. A classic example of control diversity is combining an administrative control such as requiring complex passwords with a technical control like adding a Windows complex password policy to your domain. In this case, you are using a technical tool to require users to adhere to an administrative control (Figure 1-11).

User Training

Your users are one of the greatest weaknesses in any infrastructure. You can reduce this vulnerability via user training. User training starts when a person joins your organization and continues throughout their association. User training covers critical issues such as

Figure 1-11
Windows
Domain com-
plexity policy

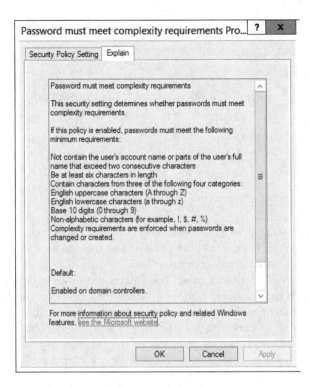

password usage, personal security, and, probably most importantly, the ability to recognize attacks.

Module 1-4: Risk Assessment

This module covers the following CompTIA Security+ objective:

- **5.3** Explain risk management processes and concepts

Previous modules discussed risk and the security controls used to mitigate risk. So,
you might think that risk management is nothing more than an ongoing process of identifying each vulnerability and then applying some form of security control to mitigate the
risks that vulnerability exposes. Applying security controls is important, but the actual
step of applying a security control is the end of a complex process. Risk management is
much more nuanced.

This nuance comes from the fact that every risk has a different vulnerability and
impact. A risk with very low impact might not be worth the cost of mitigation. Equally,
a risk with very low impact might motivate you to ignore the risk. Also, consider the fact
that IT security teams have a limited amount of money, time, and resources to apply to
addressing all the risks.

Figure 1-12
Probably not
worth it

Consider the risk of a meteor hitting your facility (Figure 1-12). If you could get a *Star Wars* ion cannon for the low, low price of $47 trillion, how would you feel about sending that bill to your accounting department?

These variables require a good IT security professional to develop a *risk assessment*, which is a carefully organized plan, more nuanced than simply trying to mitigate everything. A good risk assessment uses several tools and methods to enable the IT security professional to react to all threats in a realistic and practical way. This module starts by defining some of the main concepts and tools of risk assessment. The module describes existing frameworks you can use to help you perform a comprehensive risk assessment.

Concepts of Risk Assessment

Risk assessment brings a lot of jargon into play to describe specific aspects or nuances in security. This section defines risk assessment methods, threat sources, likelihood of occurrence, and impact.

Risk Assessment Methods

In addition to hiring knowledgeable and experienced risk management personnel, organizations can also implement and follow a formalized process or methodology in assessing risk. Developing this process can be quite an undertaking, but, fortunately, organizations can use existing methods that have been created by experts in the risk management profession. One such common method of conducting risk assessments is NIST Special Publication 800-30, Revision 1, "Guide for Conducting Risk Assessments." Another assessment methodology comes from ISACA, a professional association devoted to risk management, auditing, and security controls management. This methodology is *The Risk IT Framework*. Both methodologies describe detailed processes for conducting risk assessments, and both can be adapted for any organization to use.

NIST SP 800-30, Rev. 1, prescribes a four-step risk assessment process:

1. Prepare for assessment.

2. Conduct assessment:

    A. Identify threat sources and events.

    B. Identify vulnerabilities and predisposing conditions.

    C. Determine likelihood of occurrence.

    D. Determine magnitude of impact.

    E. Determine risk.

3. Communicate results.

4. Maintain assessment.

After initial preparation, the IT security professional begins the assessment. First, identify threat actors (sources) and threat events, and then identify vulnerabilities associated with assets and other risk factors. You then calculate likelihood and impact values, which define the risk. Communicating the risk assessment results means reporting the assessment to management, so that risk response options can be carefully considered. Maintaining the assessment means implementing the response options and closely monitoring the risk, periodically reassessing it to ensure the effectiveness of the response options and to determine whether the risk has changed.

NOTE Although you likely will not be tested on either the NIST or ISACA methodologies, they're good to know for use on the job, especially if you are assigned any type of risk assessment duties for your organization.

Identifying Threat Sources/Events

The first step in *threat assessment* is to identify the threat sources and to categorize them into groups. The process of categorizing threats may seem daunting, but NIST and ISACA provide some good basic categories to begin the process. Referencing NIST SP 800-30, Rev. 1, Table D-2, one possible categorization might look something like Figure 1-13.

You're not required to use this categorization. Some organizations simply break all threat sources into no more than the following four categories. Compare these to similar categories listed in Figure 1-13 to get an idea as to how different organizations can use totally different categories to cover the same types of threats.

- **Environmental**   Natural disasters outside the control of humans
- **Manmade**   Any threat that is not environmental
- **Internal**   Threat generated by internal sources, usually an insider to the organization
- **External**   Threat generated from outside your infrastructure

Likelihood and Impact

Once you have collected all the different data on threats, vulnerabilities, and assets, you can assess likelihood of occurrence and impact. *Likelihood of occurrence* is the probability that a threat actor will initiate a threat or the probability that a threat could successfully exploit a given vulnerability. *Impact* is the degree of harm or damage caused to an

TABLE D-2: TAXONOMY OF THREAT SOURCES

Type of Threat Source	Description	Characteristics

ADVERSARIAL
- Individual
  - Outsider
  - Insider
  - Trusted Insider
  - Privileged Insider
- Group
  - Ad hoc
  - Established
- Organization
  - Competitor
  - Supplier
  - Partner
  - Customer
- Nation-State
	Individuals, groups, organizations, or states that seek to exploit the organization's dependence on cyber resources (i.e., information in electronic form, information and communications technologies, and the communications and information-handling capabilities provided by those technologies).	Capability, Intent, Targeting

ACCIDENTAL - User - Privileged User/Administrator	Erroneous actions taken by individuals in the course of executing their everyday responsibilities.	Range of effects

STRUCTURAL
- Information Technology (IT) Equipment
  - Storage
  - Processing
  - Communications
  - Display
  - Sensor
  - Controller
- Environmental Controls
  - Temperature/Humidity Controls
  - Power Supply
- Software
  - Operating System
  - Networking
  - General-Purpose Application
  - Mission-Specific Application
	Failures of equipment, environmental controls, or software due to aging, resource depletion, or other circumstances which exceed expected operating parameters.	Range of effects

ENVIRONMENTAL
- Natural or man-made disaster
  - Fire
  - Flood/Tsunami
  - Windstorm/Tornado
  - Hurricane
  - Earthquake
  - Bombing
  - Overrun
- Unusual Natural Event (e.g., sunspots)
- Infrastructure Failure/Outage
  - Telecommunications
  - Electrical Power
	Natural disasters and failures of critical infrastructures on which the organization depends, but which are outside the control of the organization.
	
	Note: Natural and man-made disasters can also be characterized in terms of their severity and/or duration. However, because the threat source and the threat event are strongly identified, severity and duration can be included in the description of the threat event (e.g., Category 5 hurricane causes extensive damage to the facilities housing mission-critical systems, making those systems unavailable for three weeks).
		Range of effects

Figure 1-13   Example taxonomy of threat sources (from NIST SP 800-30, Rev. 1)

asset or the organization. Both can be viewed in either subjective or objective terms. In a subjective expression, both elements may be termed qualitatively, or using a range of descriptions on a scale. Objectively, likelihood or impact could be expressed in terms of numerical values. These two ways of expressing likelihood and impact are the two risk assessment methods discussed in the upcoming sections: *qualitative* (subjective) and *quantitative* (objective or numerical) assessment methods.

Risk Register

A *risk register* is a scatter-plot graph that compares probability to impact. Risk registers are handy tools for detecting otherwise easily missed risks.

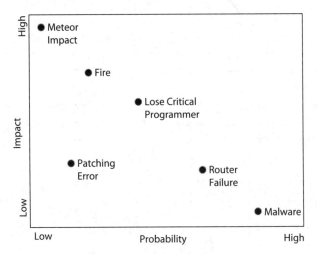

Taxonomy of Threat Sources

Quantitative Assessment

A *quantitative risk assessment* is based on objective data—typically, numerical data. A quantitative assessment is objective in that the data fed into it is measurable and independently verifiable. For example, cost expressed as a dollar value is a measurable and concrete piece of data often used to perform quantitative analysis. Other types of numerical data may include statistical analysis of different aspects of likelihood, for instance.

Quantitative risk assessments are used when an organization requires exact figures on risk that can be equated to likelihood and impact. Exact dollar values, for instance, can be used to describe impact or loss of an asset. Quantitative risk assessments require that the organization measure and obtain certain pieces of data, because the assessment depends upon the accuracy and completeness of the data fed into it. In the next few sections, we'll look at some of the different data elements that are necessary to perform a quantitative assessment. Note that these are very simplistic data elements; in more complex assessments, other data elements might be required as well.

Asset Value and Exposure Factor

The asset's value is the first data on which to perform a quantitative analysis. This may seem to be the easiest piece of data to obtain, since it could be as simple as determining an asset's replacement cost. Some organizations may need to consider depreciation values over time, however, which would reduce the amount of money they may have available to replace an asset. Another consideration is repair cost versus replacement cost. If an asset simply needs to be repaired to be brought back to an operational condition, then different costs for different components required to repair the asset may have to be considered. (See Module 1-5 for more on component failure measurements.)

Beyond cost to replace or repair the asset, you must also look at the revenue the asset generates. For example, let's say that you have determined that the replacement cost of a server is $5000. And the amount of revenue that the server brings in every day, due to the data that's processed on it, is $3000. So even if you pay the $5000 to order a new server, if the vendor can't get it to you and installed within four days, you've lost $12,000 in revenue in addition to the cost of the server. Those considerations may require you to reevaluate the value of the asset. Remember that it's not only about the cost of replacement for the asset itself, but also how much value it gives to the organization.

NOTE   When valuing an asset, consider not only the replacement cost, but also the revenue the asset generates, as this will be lost as well if the asset is not available.

Another factor you should consider with asset valuation is the *exposure factor*, the percentage of an asset that could be lost during a negative event. Realistically, you will not always lose 100 percent of the asset; you may lose only 30 percent or 50 percent, for example. Exposure factor considers the percentage of the asset (or the revenue derived from the asset) lost in the event of an incident.

You can use exposure factors when performing risk assessments to determine realistically how much of a loss your organization may suffer during an incident. This in turn affects how much money or other resources you should devote to budgeting for risk response. Exposure factors are normally expressed mathematically as a decimal number. An exposure factor of 0.4, for example, is a 40 percent loss, and an exposure factor of 1 is a 100 percent loss.

Single Loss Expectancy

The *single loss expectancy (SLE)* is a value that's computed simply by multiplying the asset's value (in dollars) by the exposure factor (percentage of loss). Use this simple formula as the initial step in describing risk from a quantitative point of view. The SLE indicates what the loss would be in a single circumstance of a negative incident affecting the asset. The formula can also be described as follows:

SLE (single loss expectancy) = AV (asset value) × EF (exposure factor)

Given this formula, suppose you had an asset worth $5000, and during a single loss event such as a fire, you'd expect to lose 50 percent of that asset. This would be expressed as:

SLE = $5000 (AV) × 0.50 (EF) = $2500

Obviously, this is a very simple scenario. When calculating SLE, you must look at other aspects of the loss, such as the event that might cause the loss, its likelihood, revenue generated from the asset, and so on. Additionally, exposure factor can be a difficult value to nail down as well. You might use statistical analysis, or even the "best guess" by a committee of experts, to determine exposure factor for different assets.

EXAM TIP Know the formula for single loss expectancy:
SLE = AV (asset value) × EF (exposure factor)

Annualized Rate of Occurrence

The *annualized rate of occurrence (ARO)* is how many times per year you would expect a particularly negative event to occur, resulting in a loss of the asset. This value relates more to likelihood than impact and serves to establish a baseline of how likely a specific threat is to occur, affecting the asset.

This value can result from several different sources. First, you could look at historical trends. For example, let's say that your business is in an area prone to tornadoes. You can gather information from the National Weather Service on how many tornadoes normally occur in your region every year. This would be the ARO for that threat. Obviously, other events would have other rates of occurrence. Some of these would be difficult to quantify without more in-depth information. For instance, obtaining the ARO for attacks from hackers would be problematic, since that would not necessarily be limited to a geographical area. You might have to gather data and perform statistical analysis to determine how often serious attacks occur, given specific circumstances, attack methods, level of attack, and so on, with regard to your type of industry or business. Some of this data might come from published industry trends, and some information may come from law enforcement or intelligence sources that provide aggregate analysis of this particular type of data. In the end, this might simply be an educated guess, based upon the best data you have available to you. In any case, what you're after is an end number that you can use as a factor in determining how often a particular threat might occur on an annual basis. You'll use this number during the next calculation, the ALE.

Annualized Loss Expectancy

The *annualized loss expectancy (ALE)* essentially looks at the amount of loss from the SLE and determines how much loss the organization could realistically expect in a one-year period. Viewing potential loss on an annual basis makes it easier to craft budgets and allocate resources toward risk management, since most organizations function on a fiscal-year basis. Additionally, this allows the organization to project how many times in a given year a particular event may occur. The formula for ALE is also quite simple:

ALE (annualized loss expectancy) = SLE × ARO

Let's use an example to make this formula clear.

The Bayland Widget corporation has a data center in Totoville, Kansas. Totoville averages about seven major tornados a year. The ARO of a tornado is therefore 7. A serious tornado hit to the $2,000,000 facility would likely cause about 20 percent damage. Put those numbers together to create the SLE:

SLE = AV ($2,000,000) × EF (20% or 0.2)
SLE = $400,000

If all seven major tornadoes that occurred during the year actually hit and caused this level of damage to the facility, then the ALE would be $400,000 (SLE) × 7 (ARO) = a *potential* loss of $2,800,000 (ALE). This would be the worst-case scenario. Realistically, since all seven are not likely to hit the facility, you can lower the ARO to a lesser number.

Obviously, this is a very simplistic (and most likely remote) scenario; the object here is to show you the different data elements and demonstrate how the formulas work. These simple formulas don't take into account realistic values or other risk factors that may affect likelihood and impact. However, they do demonstrate the basics of how you might calculate these two risk elements. You'll find that these particular formulas are prevalent throughout the Security+ exam as well as other higher-level information security exams, such as the CISSP.

 EXAM TIP   Understand the formula for computing the annualized loss expectancy:
ALE = SLE (single loss expectancy) × ARO (annualized rate of occurrence)

Qualitative Assessment

Quantitative risk assessments seem to be, on the surface, the way to go if an organization wants a very accurate, data-driven view of risk. Quantitative analysis, however, has a couple of weak points. First, a lack of data can force organizations to use incomplete or subjective numerical values. Second, even exact numbers can be misleading, simply because of the different methods people and organizations use to arrive at numerical values. Yet another issue is the fact that even when you're talking about exact numbers, they can still be subjective. People, because of their own opinions or limitations of their data collection and analysis processes, sometimes have to make educated guesses about numerical values. These issues can cause data to be incomplete, inexact, or simply incorrect. Another big shortfall with quantitative analysis is that many other types of data cannot be easily quantified or measured. Some of these pieces of data are also subjective. In other words, they are dependent upon the point of view of the person collecting and analyzing the data. This is why a qualitative analysis is often preferred.

A *qualitative risk assessment* doesn't necessarily use numerical values; it relies on descriptive elements derived from opinion, trend analysis, or best estimates. For example, what would the impact be to an organization if it suffered a loss of reputation in the marketplace? Reputation cannot be easily quantified numerically. But it can be assigned a descriptive value, such as low, medium, or high. Those are typically the values (or some similar range of descriptive values) that qualitative analysis uses. In the case of loss of reputation, the impact might be designated as *high*, for instance. Even risk elements that could normally be assigned a numerical value can be expressed qualitatively. The likelihood of a threat exploiting a vulnerability could be expressed in a range of descriptive values, such as very low, low, medium, high, and very high. The same could be said for impact. Of course, these values are subjective; what one person believes to be a *high* likelihood, another may believe to be a *very high* likelihood. In qualitative analysis, the organization must come to consensus over what qualitative values mean and the relationships among values.

TABLE D-3: ASSESSMENT SCALE – CHARACTERISTICS OF ADVERSARY CAPABILITY

Qualitative Values	Semi-Quantitative Values		Description
Very High	96–100	10	The adversary has a very sophisticated level of expertise, is well resourced, and can generate opportunities to support multiple successful, continuous, and coordinated attacks.
High	80–95	8	The adversary has a sophisticated level of expertise, with significant resources and opportunities to support multiple successful coordinated attacks.
Moderate	21–79	5	The adversary has moderate resources, expertise, and opportunities to support multiple successful attacks.
Low	5–20	2	The adversary has limited resources, expertise, and opportunities to support a successful attack.
Very Low	0–4	0	The adversary has very limited resources, expertise, and opportunities to support a successful attack.

Figure 1-14   Qualitative and semi-qualitative values (from NIST SP 800-30, Rev. 1)

Despite the subjective nature of qualitative analysis, this type of assessment can be very meaningful and accurate. The organization can develop a method of calculating risk based upon the relative values of impact and likelihood, even given descriptive values. In Figure 1-14, taken from NIST SP 800-30, Rev. 1, risk can be calculated from a qualitative perspective using descriptive likelihood and impact values.

It's also worth mentioning here that another type of scale could be used, one that does use numeric values. You could have a scale that uses values from 1 to 10, for example. In this case, the scale will be referred to as *semi-quantitative*, because these numbers could be averaged together to get aggregate values. Since it is still a subjective measurement, however, it is really a qualitative type of analysis.

Putting It All Together: Determining Risk

Although qualitative risk analysis is probably most often used because it can accept a wide variety of data including elements that are not easily quantifiable, most organizations use a combination of qualitative and quantitative analysis. To calculate the impact, for example, the organization might use quantitative assessments. To calculate likelihood, they may go with a qualitative approach. For some risk scenarios, either one or both may be more appropriate. Which method an organization uses depends upon what type of data they have and what type of data they want to obtain from the analysis.

Also, although risk scenarios typically revolve around a single threat, vulnerability, and asset at a time taken together in context, these risks are usually calculated and then rolled up into a larger level of risk that applies to the entire organization. Figure 1-15, also taken from NIST SP 800-30, Rev. 1, illustrates how the use of qualitative values can be used to describe overall risk. At first glance, Figure 1-15 seems almost identical to Figure 1-14, but read the descriptions. Figure 1-14's description is concerned with the attacker, whereas the description in Figure 1-15 describes the risk in terms of how it might affect infrastructure.

TABLE D-4: ASSESSMENT SCALE – CHARACTERISTICS OF ADVERSARY INTENT

Qualitative Values	Semi-Quantitative Values		Description
Very High	96–100	10	The adversary seeks to undermine, severely impede, or destroy a core mission or business function, program, or enterprise by exploiting a presence in the organization's information systems or infrastructure. The adversary is concerned about disclosure of tradecraft only to the extent that it would impede its ability to complete stated goals.
High	80–95	8	The adversary seeks to undermine/impede critical aspects of a core mission or business function, program, or enterprise, or place itself in a position to do so in the future, by maintaining a presence in the organization's information systems or infrastructure. The adversary is very concerned about minimizing attack detection/disclosure of tradecraft, particularly while preparing for future attacks.
Moderate	21–79	5	The adversary seeks to obtain or modify specific critical or sensitive information or usurp/disrupt the organization's cyber resources by establishing a foothold in the organization's information systems or infrastructure. The adversary is concerned about minimizing attack detection/disclosure of tradecraft, particularly when carrying out attacks over long time periods. The adversary is willing to impede aspects of the organization's missions/business functions to achieve these ends.
Low	5–20	2	The adversary actively seeks to obtain critical or sensitive information or to usurp/disrupt the organization's cyber resources, and does so without concern about attack detection/disclosure of tradecraft.
Very Low	0–4	0	The adversary seeks to usurp, disrupt, or deface the organization's cyber resources, and does so without concern about attack detection/disclosure of tradecraft.

Figure 1-15 Qualitative assessment of risk (from NIST SP 800-30, Rev. 1)

NOTE Remember the difference between qualitative and quantitative assessment methods. Qualitative methods used descriptive terms, while quantitative methods primarily use numerical values.

Risk Response

After you've identified and analyzed risk for assets and the organization, you must then decide how to respond to the risks produced as a result of the analysis. Responding to risk means to attempt to minimize its effects on the organization. *Risk response techniques* fall into four categories:

- Mitigate
- Transfer
- Accept
- Avoid

An organization chooses risk mitigation, risk transference, risk acceptance, or risk avoidance depending on several factors, including cost, effectiveness, and what value it places on the asset in question. Often, risk responses could include implementing technologies or controls that cost more than the asset is worth, and the organization has to decide whether it is worth it to deal with the risk.

Risk mitigation is an attempt to reduce risk, or at least minimize its effects on an asset. This may mean reducing the likelihood of occurrence, reducing or eliminating the exposure of the vulnerability, or reducing the impact if a negative event does occur. Mitigation usually involves adding security controls to protect an asset against a threat, reducing likelihood, exposure, or impact in some way.

Be aware that most risk management theory states that risk can never be completely eliminated; it can only be reduced or mitigated to an acceptable level. The acceptable level may be an extremely low likelihood of occurrence or an extremely low impact if the risk were to be realized.

Risk transference (also sometimes called *risk sharing*) deals with risk by sharing the burden of the risk, especially the impact element. In risk transference, an organization contracts with another party to share some of the risk, such as the cost to the organization if the threat were realized.

The standard example of risk transference you will often hear about in the security community is the use of insurance. Buying insurance to protect a business in the event of a natural disaster, for example, alleviates the burden to the business by reducing the impact of cost if a natural disaster occurs. The insurance pays the business if equipment or facilities are damaged, reducing the impact. Note that this doesn't lessen the likelihood of the threat occurring; it only lessens the financial impact to the business.

Another example of risk sharing is through the use of third-party service providers, such as those that provide infrastructure or data storage services. In this example, the business contracts with a third party to store and protect the business's data in a different location. Such an arrangement could be beneficial to the business because it might reduce the likelihood of a threat from occurring that would destroy data (by providing additional security controls and data redundancy, for example) as well as the impact.

 NOTE Transferring risk does not also mean transferring legal responsibility or liability from the organization. Ultimately, the responsibility for protecting data and following legal governance still belongs to the organization.

Risk acceptance means the organization has implemented controls and some risk remains. It does not mean simply accepting an identified risk without taking any action to reduce its effects on the organization. Risk acceptance isn't the act of ignoring risk.

Risk acceptance occurs when an organization has done everything it can do to mitigate or reduce risk inherent to an asset, yet finds that some small level of risk remains even after these efforts (called *residual risk*). Remember that risk can never be *completely* eliminated; it may simply be reduced to a very unlikely level or to a very insignificant impact. As an example, suppose that an organization believes there is significant risk to one of its most valuable information technology assets, a critical server that processes real-time financial transactions. If this server costs $20,000 to replace, the organization may spend $3000 in security controls to protect the server. After it has spent this money, the organization may find that the risk is reduced to a very small level. The residual risk is very unlikely, and even if it were to occur, it would have only a very slight impact. The organization could reduce the risk even more by spending an additional $2000 on more controls, but if the risk is very small, would spending the additional money be worth it? At this point, the organization has to decide whether to spend the additional money or simply accept the residual risk.

Risk avoidance means that the organization could choose not to participate in activities that cause unnecessary or excessive risk. Note that this doesn't mean that the risk is ignored and that the organization does not take steps to reduce it. In some cases, a business pursuit or activity may be too risky to undertake, for example. The organization may perform a risk analysis on a proposed activity and simply decide that the risk is not worth the potential negative effects to the asset or organization.

Often, an organization will use a combination of these responses to address the many and varied risks it encounters; there is no one perfect response solution that fits all organizations, assets, and activities. The decision of how to respond to a particular risk scenario involves many complex factors, which include cost, effectiveness of the response, value of the asset, and the ability of the organization to implement a particular response successfully. Additionally, as risk factors and conditions change over time, the organization must continually monitor and revisit risk responses from time to time to ensure that they are still effective.

 EXAM TIP   Remember the four possible risk responses: risk mitigation, risk transference, risk acceptance, and risk avoidance, as well as their definitions.

Module 1-5: Business Impact Analysis

This module covers the following CompTIA Security+ objective:

- **5.2**   Summarize business impact analysis concepts

A good risk assessment requires analysis of the impact of incidents against the IT infrastructure. You should consider the impact of an incident in terms of how it affects the work of an organization. To do this, security professionals perform a *business impact analysis (BIA)* that predicts both the consequences of incidents and the time and resources needed to recover from incidents.

This module starts with an overview of the steps involved with performing a BIA, using my company, Total Seminars, as an example. The rest of the module focuses on three important BIA functions: types of impact, location of critical resources, and calculating impact.

 NOTE   A business impact analysis is designed to mitigate the effects of an incident, not to prevent an incident.

BIA Basics

NIST SP 800-34, Revision 1, "Contingency Planning Guide for Federal Information Systems," offers a detailed, three-stage BIA (Figure 1-16):

1. ***Determine mission/business processes and recovery criticality.*** *Mission/Business processes supported by the system are identified and the impact of a system disruption to those processes is determined along with outage impacts and estimated downtime.*

    My interpretation: Make sure you know which workflows and processes your organization depends on to operate, in other words, the *mission-essential functions.* Determine the types of impact and consider the impact of the failure of each of these workflows and processes. Estimate how long it takes to bring those workflows and processes up to speed.

2. ***Identify resource requirements.*** *Realistic recovery efforts require a thorough evaluation of the resources required to resume mission/business processes and related interdependencies as quickly as possible.*

    My interpretation: What are the critical tools your organization uses to do these workflows and processes? Where are they? How do they work? In other words, a BIA provides *identification of critical systems.*

3. ***Identify recovery priorities for system resources.*** *Based upon the results from the previous activities, system resources can be linked more clearly to critical mission/business processes and functions. Priority levels can be established for sequencing recovery activities and resources.*

    My interpretation: Once you understand all the resources that together make a particular workflow/process work, determine the priority of bringing them back up to speed if they fail.

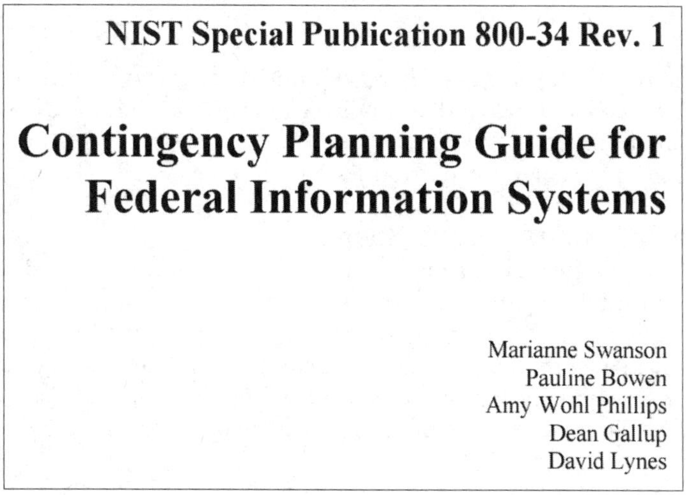

Figure 1-16
NIST Special
Publication
800-34 (Rev. 1)

NIST Special Publication 800-34 Rev. 1

Contingency Planning Guide for Federal Information Systems

Marianne Swanson
Pauline Bowen
Amy Wohl Phillips
Dean Gallup
David Lynes

NOTE A BIA is part of a broader field of study in IT security called *contingency planning (CP)*. CP covers almost everything an IT security person needs to consider to keep an infrastructure humming in the face of an incident. CP goes way beyond the scope of the CompTIA Security+ exam, but note for future studies that the two go together.

A typical small business provides an excellent example for a BIA in action. Total Seminars (or Totalsem, for short) writes books, generates online content, builds test banks, and makes lots of videos (shameless plug: check out hub.totalsem.com).

Determine Mission/Business Processes and Recovery Criticality

Totalsem has three critical workflows:

- The online store (www.totalsem.com) for selling products
- Internet access for R&D and customer communication
- Video production facility consisting of workstations and a few critical local servers

The three workflows differ in what the company can do to protect them. Amazon Web Services hosts the Web site and store, so there is little to do to mitigate the impact of AWS going down, other than wait. Internet access has two components. The cable company provides the pipe—not much to do there, just like with AWS—and Totalsem techs control access to the Internet for each workstation. Video production, while important, can go down for a day or two without too much impact (unless you're waiting for my next video!).

Now, let's sort these workflows by priority.

1. Internet access
2. Video production
3. Web store

The Web store generates company profits and, from a business sense, should have top priority. Because Totalsem has no direct control over the store, however, it drops to the bottom of this list.

Once you've determined priorities, move to the next BIA stage.

Identify Resource Requirements

At the second stage, you should analyze all the resources required for each mission/process outlined in the first stage. Total Seminars' Internet access provides a good example.

Total Seminars' Internet access isn't very complex. A single ISP provides a cable modem that's owned by the ISP. Locally, Totalsem has a midrange edge router (Cisco ASA) that supports a public-facing DNS server. The Totalsem internal network moves through a second NAT router (with a built-in switch) to individual systems.

The resources for Internet access therefore consist of a cable modem, a server, and a couple of routers/switches.

After outlining all resource needs for each mission/process, move to the next stage.

Identify Recovery Priorities for System Resources

At the final stage, prioritize recovery steps. If Totalsem completely lost Internet access, for example, the priority would be (other people may have a different opinion as to this order):

1. Repair/restore/replace cable modem (must have for Internet).

2. Repair/restore/replace edge router (need the protection for DNS server).

3. Repair/restore/replace DNS server (critical to access certain systems).

4. Repair/restore/replace NAT router (for workstations).

At this stage, you should identify recovery priorities for system resources that support every mission/process outlined in stage one.

Types of Impact

To analyze the impact of an incident, focus first on the consequences in terms of business processes supported by the affected resources. A typical BIA looks at (at least) five types of impact:

- Financial
- Reputation
- Property
- Safety/life
- Privacy

Financial

Financial impact manifests in several ways. It might mean lost or delayed sales. It might also lead to increased expenses, such as overtime, outsourcing, and fines. The one good aspect of financial impact is that it has a quantitative dollar value.

EXAM TIP The CompTIA Security+ exam objective uses the noun, *finance*, rather than the adjective, *financial*, used here. The impact is the same.

Reputation

How does a potential customer feel if he or she heads to www.totalsem.com only to find the Web site down (Figure 1-17)? Reputation is an important impact to consider, but it's also difficult to quantify. There are studies that can give a financial estimate of loss of reputation, but even these are very specific (such as sales loss due to lost customers due to a data breach).

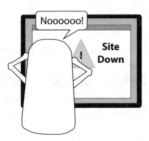

Figure 1-17
Reputation is
critical.

Property

Property impact encompasses both physical elements and less tangible ones as well. A fire in the building could render the video production stations useless, for example. Damage to the building is clearly physical property impacted. Second, intellectual property is also property. If I were to lose all the chapters, outlines, and graphics of this book—the intellectual property—the impact would damage my company substantially.

Safety/Life

The most serious impact is loss of safety or life. An incident that causes harm to humans may have catastrophic impact that includes all of the impact types. We tend not to think about IT as a dangerous occupation, but many ancillary aspects of our work—using ladders, getting shocked by electricity, being struck by objects—kill something in the region of nearly 100 non-construction workers per year in the United States.

Privacy Impact

Any organization that keeps individuals' personal information takes on several risks with serious legal and financial impacts, both to itself and to the individuals whose data is being stored. The next module, Module 1-6, goes into great detail on the concept of privacy. I'll save the details until then but address the concept of privacy impact here.

An organization performs a *privacy impact assessment (PIA)* to determine the impact on the privacy of the individuals whose data is being stored, and to ensure that the organization has sufficient security controls applied to be within compliance of applicable laws or standards.

To create a PIA, an organization performs a *privacy threshold assessment (PTA)* on its infrastructure to locate personal information, determine what personal information is stored, and from whom the personal information is collected. Once the PTA is complete, the PIA can then be applied.

Locating Critical Resources

Analyzing critical resources as part of a BIA can reveal unexpected vulnerabilities. Resources needed for Totalsem's Internet access provides a good example.

Total Seminars' Internet access relies on four basic resources:

- Cable modem
- Edge router

- DNS server
- NAT router

The BIA clearly shows several *single points of failure*: if any one of these resources fails, Totalsem loses its business process of Internet access. The impact of losing this process could cause negative financial consequences for the company: pretty much every employee stops working.

You should mitigate single points of failure if possible. In the case of resources needed for Internet access, for example, several actions could mitigate the problems:

- **Cable modem**   Add a second ISP into the mix. This could act as a failover if the primary ISP fails.

- **Edge router**   Cisco produces very reliable routers, but a quick check of the Cisco Web site shows the router model used by Totalsem accepts dual power supplies. This will help increase the MTBF (see the next section) significantly.

- **DNS server**   A single DNS server is never a good idea. Totalsem could add a second DNS server or create a secondary lookup zone on a cloud server.

- **NAT router**   Totalsem uses a low-quality router, but has spares ready to go. There will be a time impact to install the replacement, but having the spare onsite is far better than running to the store.

Calculating Impact

The process of calculating impact has the same problem that calculating risk in earlier modules had: is it qualitative or quantitative? The CompTIA Security+ exam touches only on qualitative, and only on a few well-known factors: MTBF, MTTF, and MTTR.

The *mean time between failures (MTBF)* factor, which typically applies to hardware components, represents the manufacturer's best guess (based on historical data) regarding how much time will pass between major failures of that component (Figure 1-18). This

	Capacity	
	Routing table size	512 entries (IPv4), 256 entries (IPv6)
	MAC address table size	16384 entries
Reliability	**MTBF (years)**	52.79
Environment	**Operating temperature**	23°F to 113°F (-5°C to 45°C)
	Operating relative humidity	10% to 90%, noncondensing
	Nonoperating/Storage temperature	-40°F to 158°F (-40°C to 70°C)

Figure 1-18   Router datasheet showing MTBF

is, of course, assuming that more than one failure will occur, which means that the component will be repaired rather than replaced. Organizations should take this risk factor into account because it may affect likelihood and impact of the risks associated with critical systems.

The *mean time to failure (MTTF)* factor indicates the length of time a device is expected to last in operation. In MTTF, only a single, definitive failure will occur and will require that the device be replaced rather than repaired.

Lastly, the *mean time to recovery (MTTR)* is the amount of time it takes for a hardware component to recover from failure.

 EXAM TIP   You should understand the difference between mean time between failures (MTBF), mean time to failure (MTTF), and mean time to recovery (MTTR) measurements for hardware failure.

Calculating Downtime

When systems go down, they affect other systems as well. The *recovery time objective (RTO)* is the maximum amount of time that a resource may remain unavailable before an unacceptable impact on other system resources occurs. The *recovery point objective (RPO)* defines the amount of time that will pass between an incident and recovery from backup. If a company backed up yesterday, for example, the RPO is 24 hours. If data changes so rapidly that any backup more an hour old requires calling customers or other extra ordinary actions (an accounts receivable database, for example) then the RPO is one hour. The RTO and RPO help IT professionals calculate how much an organization can or will lose if a system goes down before backup systems can be brought online.

Module 1-6: Data Security and Privacy Policies

This module covers the following CompTIA Security+ objective:

- **5.8**   Given a scenario, carry out data security and privacy practices

IT security professionals protect data. Proprietary data is the lifeblood of many companies. Those companies put a premium on securing that data (Figure 1-19).

Figure 1-19
Data is precious.

The challenge of data security is its complexity. Data manifests throughout an infrastructure in so many ways: from a single user's personal folders containing a few Word documents to massive multi-terabyte databases, accessed by hundreds or even thousands of users.

Access and control of data is equally complex. Every database program, every operating system, and many Internet services offer impressively fine control on what the users and groups who access the data may do. But how do we control that access? How do we look at the data and determine the amount of access any given entity receives? We'll answer these questions in Chapter 3.

There are huge legal and privacy issues with data. Serious financial, moral, and legal ramifications face the organization that doesn't protect its data aggressively. If your databases contain individuals' private medical information, customers' personal credit card numbers, or even a young offender's rap sheet, you are under tremendous pressure to maintain that privacy (Figure 1-20).

This module covers the basics of data security and privacy. The module starts by covering common methods of data organization, then delves into legal compliance and privacy. The module closes by covering data destruction, getting rid of data you no longer need (and no, deleting files isn't enough!).

Organizing Data

The first step to dealing with data security is organization. Analyze individual chunks of data, such as databases, spreadsheets, access control lists, and so on. Then determine the importance—the *sensitivity*—of that data. After accomplishing both tasks, sort the data into different classifications based on sensitivity. These classifications help security professionals to determine the amount of security control to apply to each data set.

The dynamic nature of data requires more than just classification of the data. Every piece of data needs people to administer that data set. The roles of the people who manage the data and the users who access that data need classification as well.

NOTE The NIST Federal Information Processing Standards (FIPS) Publication 199, "Standards for Security Categorization of Federal Information and Information Systems," is considered by many sources as the de facto framework for IT data classification.

Figure 1-20
Storing personal data brings heavy responsibilities.

Data Sensitivity

IT security professionals need to apply appropriate security controls for data, making decisions based on the sensitivity of that data. There's a dizzyingly large number of security controls that can be applied to data. Some data sets need stringent security controls. Other data sets need less complex security controls. Not all data in an organization has the same sensitivity. The more sensitive the data, the more controls we apply to ensure its security.

Organizations spend a lot of time thinking about their data and coming up with labels that enable them to classify and handle their data by sensitivity. One way to consider sensitivity is by the impact of an incident that exposes the data. NIST FIPS 199 provides one way to consider the impact by looking at the CIA of security and breaking the impact into three levels: low, moderate, and high (Figure 1-21). It's also very common to differentiate between commercial and government/military to classify data.

Security Objective	POTENTIAL IMPACT		
	LOW	MODERATE	HIGH
Confidentiality Preserving authorized restrictions on information access and disclosure, including means for protecting personal privacy and proprietary information. [44 U.S.C., SEC. 3542]	The unauthorized disclosure of information could be expected to have a **limited** adverse effect on organizational operations, organizational assets, or individuals.	The unauthorized disclosure of information could be expected to have a **serious** adverse effect on organizational operations, organizational assets, or individuals.	The unauthorized disclosure of information could be expected to have a **severe or catastrophic** adverse effect on organizational operations, organizational assets, or individuals.
Integrity Guarding against improper information modification or destruction, and includes ensuring information non-repudiation and authenticity. [44 U.S.C., SEC. 3542]	The unauthorized modification or destruction of information could be expected to have a **limited** adverse effect on organizational operations, organizational assets, or individuals.	The unauthorized modification or destruction of information could be expected to have a **serious** adverse effect on organizational operations, organizational assets, or individuals.	The unauthorized modification or destruction of information could be expected to have a **severe or catastrophic** adverse effect on organizational operations, organizational assets, or individuals.
Availability Ensuring timely and reliable access to and use of information. [44 U.S.C., SEC. 3542]	The disruption of access to or use of information or an information system could be expected to have a **limited** adverse effect on organizational operations, organizational assets, or individuals.	The disruption of access to or use of information or an information system could be expected to have a **serious** adverse effect on organizational operations, organizational assets, or individuals.	The disruption of access to or use of information or an information system could be expected to have a **severe or catastrophic** adverse effect on organizational operations, organizational assets, or individuals.

Figure 1-21   Impact table for data (FIPS 199)

Commercial Labels   Labeling data using commercial labels works well for most private-sector organizations. Most security pros in the nongovernmental sector start with some variation of the following list:

- **Confidential**   Information that one party offers to a second party. Usually secured via a nondisclosure agreement (NDA). A common example is internal company information used by its employees.

- **Private**   Information that specifically applies to an individual, such as a Social Security number.

- **Proprietary**   Information owned by a company that gives the company certain competitive advantages. The secret formula to Coca-Cola is an example.

- **Public**   Information that is not sensitive. The prices of all the products on eBay is one example.

NOTE   Public information may not have confidentiality, but it still needs integrity and availability.

Government/Military Labels   If you enjoy spy novels, most government/military labels should sound familiar. In fact, these types of labels predate computers to a time when paper documents literally had physical labels (or stamps) signifying their sensitivity. Experts disagree on exactly what these labels mean, although not as much as with commercial labels. Here in the United States, security professionals refer to Executive Order 13526 of December 29, 2009, "Classified National Security Information," which defines the labels as follows:

- "Top Secret" shall be applied to information, the unauthorized disclosure of which reasonably could be expected to cause exceptionally grave damage to the national security that the original classification authority is able to identify or describe.

- "Secret" shall be applied to information, the unauthorized disclosure of which reasonably could be expected to cause serious damage to national security that the original classification authority is able to identify or describe.

- "Confidential" shall be applied to information, the unauthorized disclosure of which reasonably could be expected to cause damage to the national security that the original classification authority is able to identify or describe.

Lots of Labels   While the commercial and government/military data classification labels just described cover everything you'll run into for the exam, keep in mind that every organization has different needs. It's normal for organizations to adopt their own labels that make sense for them. A few of these you might see are

- **Internet**   Data that is accessible to the public Internet. Your organization's Web page is a good example.

- **Internal Use**   Information that is only used internally by your organization. An internal phone directory is one type of internal-use information.

- **Restricted**   Information that is tied exclusively to a certain group within the organization. Starting salaries for new accountants is an example.

- **Sensitive**   A generic label that is often tied to both commercial and government/military label types.

Data Roles

Every data set needs some number of people with clearly defined roles who manage that data at various levels. Data roles help define both the various responsibilities and the responsible parties for the different jobs. Let's go through the data roles listed by the CompTIA Security+ exam objectives.

Data Owner   The data owner is the entity who holds the legal ownership of a data set. This includes any copyrights, trademarks, or other legal possession items that tie the data set to the entity. The data owner can rent, sell, or give away the data set as the owner sees fit. Data owners are almost always the organization itself and not an actual person. This entity has complete control over the data and will delegate responsibility for the management of that data set to persons or groups to handle the real work on that data.

Data Custodian   A data custodian ensures that the technical aspects of the data set are in good order. Data custodians are the folks who make sure the data is secure, available, and accurate. They audit the data and ensure they have both the appropriate storage capacity and proper backups.

Data Steward   A data steward makes sure that the data set does what the data is supposed to do for the organization. Data stewards interface with the users of the organization to cover data requirements, to define the metadata, and to make sure the data ties to company or industry standards. Data stewards update the data as needed to conform to needs. Data stewards also define how users access the data.

 NOTE   Data stewards and data custodians always closely interact.

Privacy Officer   When an organization has data that is subject to privacy laws and regulations (a big issue here in the United States), it will assign a privacy officer to oversee that data. Privacy officers perform the due diligence to make sure that the data's storage, retention, and use conform to any and all laws and regulations. We'll see more of this person in the next section.

Legal and Compliance

Most countries have laws, regulations, and standards designed to protect different forms of data. As introduced in Module 1-2, in the United States, the Health Insurance Portability and Accountability Act (HIPAA) and Sarbanes-Oxley Act (SOX) provide strict federal guidelines for the handling, storage, and transmission of data. In addition, the Payment Card Industry Data Security Standard (PCI-DSS), while not a law, has equally stringent guidelines for credit card data. In all these cases, the job of IT security changes from securing the IT infrastructure to making sure the organization doesn't get fined (and no one gets arrested!) for lack of compliance.

 NOTE The U.S. government has levied millions in fines and has imprisoned individuals for violations of both HIPAA and SOX. Credit card companies have revoked credit card processing from a huge number of stores for failure to comply with PCI-DSS standards.

Rather than break down these individual laws/standards, it's often better to concentrate on some of the more important aspects. Focus on personally identifiable information, protected health information, and data retention.

Personally Identifiable Information

Personally identifiable information (PII) is any information referencing an individual that either by itself or with other information could identify that individual, allowing persons to contact or locate that individual without their permission. The idea of PII has been around since the early 1970s, but came into stronger prominence with HIPAA in the mid-1990s. PII is also very important for PCI-DSS.

While there is no single definition of PII, NIST SP 800-122, "Guide to Protecting the Confidentiality of Personally Identifiable Information (PII)," (Figure 1-22) provides many examples:

- Name, such as full name, maiden name, mother's maiden name, or alias
- Personal identification numbers, such as Social Security number (SSN), passport number, driver's license number, taxpayer identification number, or financial account or credit card number
- Address information, such as street address or e-mail address
- Personal characteristics, including photographic image (especially of face or other identifying characteristic), fingerprints, handwriting, or other biometric data (e.g., retina scan, voice signature, facial geometry)
- Information about an individual that is linked or linkable to one of the above (e.g., date of birth, place of birth, race, religion, weight, activities, geographical indicators, employment information, medical information, education information, financial information)

Different laws and standards vary the definition of what entails PII. For example, here are a few examples of PII by PCI-DSS standards:

- Account number
- Cardholder name
- Expiration date

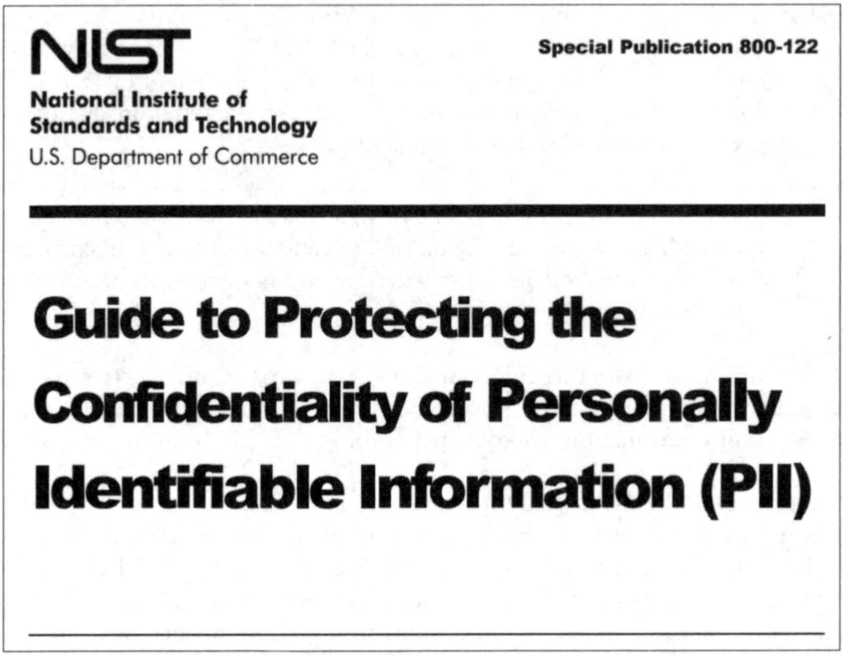

NIST

National Institute of
Standards and Technology
U.S. Department of Commerce

Special Publication 800-122

Guide to Protecting the Confidentiality of Personally Identifiable Information (PII)

Figure 1-22   NIST SP 800-122

- Magnetic strip or chip data
- PIN
- CVC/CVC2

Protected Health Information

Protected health information (PHI) is any form of personal health information (treatment, diagnosis, prescriptions, etc.) electronically stored or transmitted by any health provider, insurer, or employer. This health information must be tied to the individual's PII to be considered PHI. In other words, a blood pressure reading combined with age and race is alone not PHI. A blood pressure reading combined with a name or an address or SSN is PHI.

Data Retention

A number of laws and regulations require strict rules on how long different types of data is retained. The Sarbanes-Oxley Act is easily the most far-reaching law affecting the types of data public companies must retain and the length of time they must retain that data. In particular, IT departments must react to two parts of the law covered in Section 802(a):

> Whoever knowingly alters, destroys, mutilates, conceals, covers up, falsifies, or makes a false entry in any record, document, or tangible object with the intent to impede, obstruct, or influence the investigation ... shall be fined under this title, imprisoned not more than 20 years, or both.

Yipe! But at least it also gives some idea as to length of time companies need to retain records:

> Any accountant who conducts an audit of an issuer of securities … shall maintain all audit or review workpapers for a period of 5 years from the end of the fiscal period in which the audit or review was concluded.

It's not that hard to keep contracts, accounts, audits, and such for five years, but this also includes e-mail. Managing and storing e-mail for an entire company can be a challenge, especially because e-mail is usually under the control of individual users (ever deleted an e-mail?). SOX alone changed everything, requiring publicly traded companies to adopt standard practices outlined in the law, and making lots of storage providers very happy indeed!

Data Destruction

When it's time to get rid of storage media, you should also destroy the data stored on that media. But how do you destroy media in such a way to ensure the data is gone? Let's take a moment to talk about data destruction/media sanitization. NIST SP 800-88, Revision 1, "Guidelines for Media Sanitization," provides some great guidelines (Figure 1-23).

The CompTIA Security+ exam covers a number of different data destruction methods that apply to specific types of data. Stored data fits into one of two categories: legacy media (paper, film, tape, etc.) or electronic media (hard drives, SD cards, optical media, etc.). Each of these categories have different methods for data destruction.

 NOTE The terms data destruction, data sanitization, and data purging are interchangeable.

NIST Special Publication 800-88
Revision 1

Guidelines for Media Sanitization

Richard Kissel
Andrew Regenscheid
Matthew Scholl
Kevin Stine

Figure 1-23 NIST Special Publication 800-88 (Rev. 1)

Legacy Media

Given that most legacy media isn't completely erasable, the best way to eliminate the data is to destroy the media. Paper, film, and tape are all extremely flammable, so burning is an excellent method to destroy the data. For the more "green" organizations, pulping water-soluble media (paper) enables you to recycle the media and not pollute the environment.

Electronic Media

Almost all electronic media is erasable, so in many cases you can nondestructively remove the data. Simple erasing, even reformatting, isn't enough. A good forensic examiner can recover the original data from a hard disk that's been erased as many as nine times. You need to go through a specific wiping process that removes any residual data. NIST SP 800-88, Rev. 1, describes the ATA Secure Erase command built into PATA and SATA drives. Several programs can perform a secure erase. Figure 1-24 shows DBAN 2.3.0 (Darik's Boot and Nuke), a popular secure erase utility (and it's free!).

To ensure complete data destruction, destroy the media. A common method is degaussing the media through a degaussing machine. A degausser uses a powerful electromagnet both to wipe the data and make the media useless.

Pulverizing or shredding are great methods for destroying media as well. Pulverizing means to smash completely. Shredding works for both legacy media and electronic media. A classic shredder can shred paper, optical media, and many types of flash media. There are several types of shredding cuts (Figure 1-25).

Shredding doesn't stop with paper! There are machines available that shred (or pulverize, or crush) just about any media, reducing them to bits of metal for you to recycle. You'll see those machines, and much more about data sanitizing, in Chapter 5.

```
Darik's Boot and Nuke

Warning: This software irrecoverably destroys data.

This software is provided without any warranty; without even the implied
warranty of merchantability or fitness for a particular purpose. In no event
shall the software authors or contributors be liable for any damages arising
from the use of this software.  This software is provided "as is".

http://www.dban.org/

* Press the F2 key to learn about DBAN.
* Press the F3 key for a list of quick commands.
* Press the F4 key for troubleshooting hints.
* Press the ENTER key to start DBAN in interactive mode.
* Enter autonuke at this prompt to start DBAN in automatic mode.

boot: _
```

Figure 1-24   DBAN 2.3.0 (Darik's Boot and Nuke)

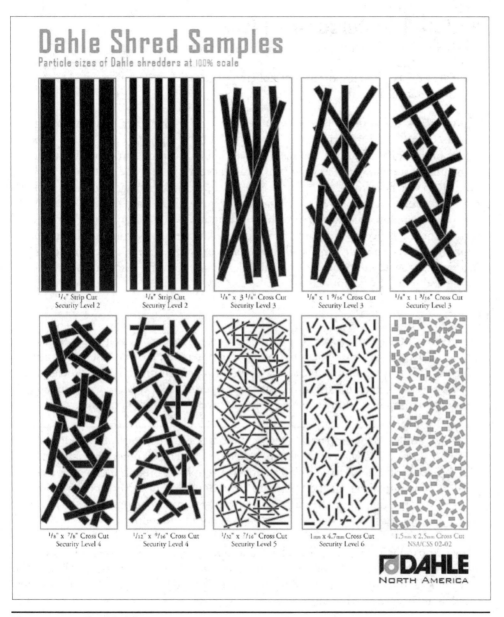

Figure 1-25 Shredded drive

Module 1-7: Personnel Risks

This module covers the following CompTIA Security+ objective:

- **5.1** Explain the importance of policies, plans, and procedures related to organizational security

Your users—the human beings who get their job done every day by using the resources of your IT infrastructure—are also one of the biggest IT risk issues faced by security professionals. Human actions, from accidental to innocent, from incompetent to downright criminal, keep security pros awake at night in fear and loathing.

But it doesn't have to be that way. A well-organized risk management plan includes security controls to mitigate risk brought on by personnel. This module explores the lifespan of an employee's relationship with an organization, from hiring day to exit day, and examines the risk concepts and security controls used to keep users from trashing the place.

Specifically, the module starts with hiring and onboarding, then goes into detail on personnel management policies. The module wraps up with discussions about user training and policies that apply to user habits.

Hiring

Personnel risk management starts before the new employee ever steps into the infrastructure. In today's security-conscious environment, a potential new hire is screened heavily. At the very least, it's common for someone in an organization to look at social media and do a general Web search. Many organizations perform *background checks* to look for potential issues, such as felony convictions, and to verify résumé statements.

 NOTE Many employers use credit reports as part of their background checks. Denying employment based on a bad credit report, however, is a serious legal issue called an adverse action. An organization needs a written adverse action policy to avoid problems. An *adverse action policy* communicates to the applicant why they were turned down for the job and provides him or her remedies for their credit situation.

Any company with substantial intellectual property will require new employees—and occasionally even potential candidates—to sign a *nondisclosure agreement (NDA)*. An NDA is a legal document that prohibits the signer from disclosing any company secrets learned as a part of his or her job.

Onboarding

Onboarding is the process of giving a new hire the knowledge and skills he or she needs to do the job, while at the same time defining the behaviors expected of the new hire within the corporate culture. A lot of onboarding has nothing to do with IT security, but this is the time where some part of onboarding process for new hires will be dedicated to helping them understand the expectations and attitudes towards IT security that are important to the organization. One of the biggest issues is their understanding of the organization's personnel management policies.

That Onboarding Moment

Personnel Management Policies

A *personnel management policy* defines the way a user works within the organization. An organization will invest in one or more personnel management policies to help mitigate a number of different types of personnel risks. Let's go through all of these personnel management policies to see how they work to make an infrastructure less vulnerable to risks.

Standard Operating Procedures

An important part of the onboarding process is making sure new hires understand the *standard operating procedures (SOPs)*—that is, how they do things according to the organization's best practices—for their job functions. Some SOPs that are particularly important for IT security include login procedures, usable data storage locations, use of security credentials, and procedures for lost or damaged equipment.

Necessary Knowledge

Mandatory Vacations

Many industries (for example, the U.S. banking industry) require all employees to take off work for a minimum of two weeks every year, a mandatory vacation. Mandatory vacations are an important security control mainly to make it harder to perpetuate embezzlement. Any embezzlement scheme usually requires the embezzler to monitor orders constantly, manipulate records, or deal with issues that might arise to keep themselves from being detected.

NOTE Mandatory vacations have benefits beyond IT security, but for the exam think "embezzlement."

Job Rotation

Job rotation involves periodically switching people around to work in different positions. This practice enables different people to become proficient in a variety of job roles so that the organization doesn't have to depend solely on one person to perform certain critical functions or tasks. If something were to happen to an individual occupying a critical position, for example, another person could step in to do the job.

When people become too comfortable with a job, they might believe that they can get away with performing actions they are not authorized to perform. Rotating people into different positions increases the potential to detect fraud or misuse in that position and can discourage or prevent nefarious activities.

Job rotation is difficult for many organizations, for the same reasons that organizations don't always implement mandatory vacations. A shortage of trained personnel as well as positions that require substantial training and commitment are two reasons why job rotation isn't always performed.

Separation of Duties

In the *separation of duties* concept, a single individual should not perform all critical or privileged-level duties. These types of important duties must be separated or divided among several individuals.

Separation of duties ensures that no single individual can perform sufficiently critical or privileged actions that could seriously damage a system, operation, or the organization. These critical or privileged actions can be split among two or more people, requiring some level of checks and balances. Security auditors responsible for reviewing security logs, for example, should not necessarily have administrative rights over systems. Likewise, a security administrator should not have the capability to review or alter logs, because he or she could perform unauthorized actions and then delete any trace of them from the logs. Two separate individuals are required to perform such activities to ensure verifiability and traceability.

Separation of duties is considered an administrative control, because it's related to policy. Closely related to the concept of separation of duties is the technique of using multi-person control to perform some tasks or functions.

Multi-person Control

Multi-person control means that more than one person is required to accomplish a specific task or function. An organization might implement multi-person controls, for example, to ensure that one person, by herself, could not initiate an action that would cause detrimental consequences for the organization, resulting in loss of data, destruction of systems, or theft.

Organizations implement multi-person control by dividing up critical tasks to require more than one person to accomplish those tasks. In a banking environment, for example, one person may be authorized to sign negotiable instruments, such as checks, for up to $10,000. Beyond the limit of $10,000, however, requires two signatures to process the transaction. This would help prevent one malicious person from stealing more than $10,000. Although it's conceivable that two people could conspire to use their assigned abilities to commit an unauthorized act, fraud in this case, separation of duties and multi-person control make this more difficult. In this case, counter-signing a check is a multi-person control. In an information security environment, multi-person control could be used to access sensitive documents, recover passwords or encryption keys, and so on.

Training

User training should take place at two very distinct points in the user's relationship with an organization: during the onboarding process to get the new hire to understand and subscribe to critical policies and good user habits, and, possibly even more importantly, as an ongoing continuing-education process.

User training differs according to the role an individual plays in an organization. *Role-based user awareness training* targets five broad categories: user, privileged user, executive user, system administrator, and data owner/system owner. Let's look at all five.

User

A *user* must understand how his or her system functions and have proper security training to recognize common issues (malware, unauthorized user at their system, etc.).

Privileged User

A *privileged user* has increased access and control over a system, including access to tools unavailable to regular users. Like a regular user, the privileged user needs a basic understanding of his or her system's functions; the privileged user must also have security awareness that ties to access level. A regular user may run anti-malware software, for example, but a privileged user may update the anti-malware program as well as run it.

Executive User

An *executive user* concentrates on strategic decisions including policy review, incident response, and disaster recovery.

System Administrator

The *system administrator* has complete, direct control over a system. His or her training would include best practices for adding and removing users, applying permissions, and doing system maintenance and debugging.

Data Owner/System Owner

From a role-based training aspect, these two otherwise slightly different functions are very similar in that in almost all cases the owner is the organization. In these cases, the main security role here is to know how to delegate security awareness to the proper authority. For data, this is usually the data custodian; for systems, it is usually the system administrator.

Policies

If people are going to use your organization's equipment, they need to read, understand, and, in most cases, sign policies that directly affect the user's experience. Two policy types handle this job: acceptable use policies and security policies.

Acceptable Use Policy/Rules of Behavior Policy

An *acceptable use policy (AUP)*, also called a *rules of behavior policy*, defines what a user may or may not do on the organization's equipment. These policies tend to be very detailed documents, carefully listing what users may and may not do. Some examples of issues covered in an AUP include

- Company data can only be used for company business uses.
- Users will not access illegal or unacceptable Internet sites.
- Users will not introduce malware into a system.
- Users will work aggressively to protect company systems and data.

General Security Policies

People use *social media networks* and *personal e-mail* to exchange information and photographs and keep in touch with family members and friends. Unfortunately, some people post way too much information on social media networks and through *social media applications*—hello, Snapchat—decreasing their (and others') level of privacy.

Although organizations may have very little control over what individual employees post to social media sites and send in their e-mail, it's a good idea to create a relevant policy and train users on what they should and should not post on social media or e-mail to others. For example, users should be briefed that they should not post any sensitive or proprietary information on their social media sites that would compromise the organization or result in any type of unauthorized access or breach of information.

User Habits

In addition to policy-related topics, topics that concern the actions and habits of users must be addressed in training programs. Many such items will also be set forth in policy, but that doesn't mean that users don't need training and reinforcement to break bad habits where they exist. We'll look at some of these bad habits in the next few sections and, where appropriate, discuss how they also may be established in policy and why they should be included in any organizational information security training program.

Password Behaviors

By now, you should be aware that password issues can pose serious problems in an organization. Users forget passwords, write them down where they can be easily discovered by others, share passwords, use simple passwords, and so on. These are the causes of most password security issues, and why users need training regarding how to create and use passwords properly in the organization. Following are some key points that should be emphasized:

- Users should create complex passwords.
- Users must try to create passwords that don't use dictionary words.
- Users should never share their passwords or write them down.
- Users should change their passwords *often* to thwart password attacks.

Of course, you should also use technical measures to reinforce some of these rules, including configuring systems to allow only complex passwords of a certain length, as well as password expiration rules. Periodically check around the users' work areas to make sure they haven't written down passwords, and ensure that multiple people aren't using the same accounts and passwords to log into systems. In addition, check to see if your password policies are being complied with by occasionally engaging in password cracking yourself—with the appropriate approval from management, of course. The problems associated with password behaviors, as well as the speed and ease with which passwords can be cracked by sophisticated attackers and systems, are the main reasons why organizations should consider multifactor authentication methods.

Clean Desk Policies

A clean desk policy isn't about asking employees not to leave old soda cans and candy wrappers on their desks! Instead, it creates a process for employees to clear sensitive data out of work areas so that it is stored securely at the end of the workday. Sensitive data must not be exposed to unauthorized people such as janitors, maintenance personnel, guards, and even other employees when an authorized employee is away from his or her desk.

A clean desk policy can apply to any time employees are using sensitive data at their desks and they need to leave the area. The goal is to make sure that sensitive data is not unattended and available. This policy should be developed and implemented as a formal written policy, and all employees should be trained on it.

Preventing Social Engineering Attacks

Users should be briefed on the general concepts of social engineering and how it works, and they should also be briefed on the specific types of attacks they may encounter, such as shoulder surfing, tailgating, dumpster diving, and so on. By being aware of these attacks, they can do their parts in helping to prevent them. Tailgating, in particular, exposes the organization and others to serious harm or danger if an unauthorized person is allowed to enter the facility. Users should be trained on how to spot potential social engineering attacks, including tailgaters, and how to respond to them by following organizational policies and procedures.

Personally Owned Devices

Users should get training on risks posed by bringing *personally owned devices* to work and how they might help prevent these risks. Using such devices in the organization can lead to a loss of privacy by the individual, as well as loss of both personal and organizational data if the device is lost or stolen. If the organization allows individuals to manage their own devices, while allowing their use in the organization to process the organization's data, then the organization incurs huge risk. Users must be trained on those risks and how serious their responsibilities are.

If the organization centrally manages mobile devices with *mobile device management (MDM)* software, the risk is significantly lowered because the organization can use remote capabilities to lock, encrypt, or wipe data on the device. Users should be briefed on these capabilities if they are used within the organization to manage devices, because users must accept organizational control of their devices and the policies that may be enforced on them.

Many companies around the globe have clear policies on *bring your own device (BYOD)*, the catchy phrase for incorporating employee-owned technology (such as laptops, tablets, and smartphones) in the corporate network. As the trend intensifies, just about every organization should have such policies.

Offboarding

When employees leave an organization, the organization must perform a number of important steps to ensure a tidy and professional separation. This process, called *offboarding*, varies among organizations, but includes several common steps:

- Termination letter
- Equipment return
- Knowledge transfer

Termination Letter/Exit Interview

An employee should provide a written *termination letter*, defining final day of employment. In many organizations, this is also the time to perform an exit interview. *Exit interviews* give the soon-to-be-separated employee an opportunity to provide insight to the employer about ways to improve the organization. Some example questions include

- What are your main reasons for leaving?
- What procedures can we improve upon?

Return of Equipment

All organizations should use a checklist to ensure that all equipment owned by the organization is returned by the departing employee. This includes computers, phones, and tablets, as well as any other issued equipment. Also, this is the time to return keys, ID cards, and other access tools.

Knowledge Transfer

Knowledge transfer is the process that makes sure a separating employee provides any and all knowledge needed by the organization. In some cases knowledge transfer may last weeks. In other cases it's no more than part of the exit interview.

Module 1-8: Third-Party Risk

This module covers the following CompTIA Security+ objective:

- **5.1** Explain the importance of policies, plans, and procedures related to organizational security

Every organization interacts with third parties. Every infrastructure has vendors, contractors, B2B intranets, partnerships, service providers—the list of third parties touching an infrastructure in one way or another is endless. The challenge with all these third parties is risk. What can IT security professionals do to mitigate risks potentially created by those outside the infrastructure? General security practices hold third parties to certain levels of security through several types of agreements (Figure 1-26). This module considers the concept of third-party risk and looks at some of the more common types of agreement used between parties.

What's the Risk?

It's said that the devil is in the details; this is definitely true when it comes to security considerations that involve multiple parties. When you negotiate a contract with a third-party provider or business partner, you must ensure that several considerations are specified in your business agreements. You should definitely have representatives from your security, privacy, and legal departments review any business agreements with third parties to ensure that certain security-related stipulations are included in the agreements and the day-to-day business transactions with outside entities. A few of these security considerations are discussed next.

Security Policy and Procedures

Although your organization should have its own security policies, procedures, and processes, third-party organizations usually have their own as well. Sometimes these policies and procedures conflict between the parties and have to be negotiated, resolving any differences between them, in advance. In some cases, contract agreements may specify security policies and procedures that both parties must follow regarding shared data or contracted services. This is true whether the third party is a service provider, business associate, subcontractor, or whatever other relationship your organization has with it.

Figure 1-26
It's all in the agreement.

For the most part, your organization shouldn't accept a third party's security policies if they cannot offer the level of protection required for your organization's data, since the data is just as critical and sensitive whether it's retained inside the organization or placed in the hands of an external entity. Security policies and procedures that are agreed upon in advance ensure that the external entities protect your organization's data to the level your organization would protect the data internally.

Privacy Considerations

Privacy is a serious consideration when exchanging data with any third party. If you contract services with a third party, make sure to agree on data privacy prior to entering into any business agreements. Privacy considerations include employee data privacy; privacy related to the type of data itself, such as financial data, personally identifiable information (PII), and protected health information (PHI); and how the third party will treat this data.

Legal or regulatory governance may provide you some protection, in that the third party has to obey laws with regard to data privacy, but you may find that your organization has additional requirements that need to be met by the third party. It's also possible that the agreement could be too restrictive in favor of the service provider, and your organization requires more flexible terms to ensure data privacy to your standards.

In any case, ensure that how private data is handled, including how it is stored, processed, accessed, and especially transmitted to other third parties, is specified in any agreements made between your organization and the third-party provider or business associate. For example, the HIPAA security regulations require that any third-party providers (referred to as "business associates" in HIPAA parlance) that could possibly have access to protected health information be subjected to strict access control and handling requirements for that type of data.

Risk Awareness

Another hot button with security in terms of third parties is risk awareness and management. Many organizations require that third-party providers or business associates have an established risk management program that includes threat and vulnerability assessments, risk mitigation strategies, and so on. This helps assure an organization that the third party has performed its due care and diligence in assessing and managing risk and is therefore able to reduce and mitigate it. The third party may be required to provide proof in the form of a risk assessment or risk analysis report that satisfies this requirement.

Unauthorized Data Sharing

Security policy set forth in third-party agreements should cover unauthorized data sharing and access control. In addition to setting forth minimum requirements for access control, which include administrative, technical, and operational controls, the agreement should set forth mechanisms that an organization must use in order to share data with other authorized parties, as well as conditions under which the third party must comply with the law in sharing data with government and law enforcement agencies. The agreement should also cover how the organizations will respond in the event of a data breach or unauthorized access.

Data Ownership

Organizations must define the types of data to which they claim ownership initially, and how they would classify that data in terms of its sensitivity and protection requirements. The organizations must also determine how they will decide on ownership of data that is created during the contract term and who will control it. Some third parties that process data for an organization specifically agree that any data created during the contract term still belongs to the originating organization, but other third-party providers may maintain that they have legal ownership over any data that is created on their systems, based upon their unique processes or proprietary methods. This issue must be resolved prior to engaging in business with a third party. Issues with data ownership can lead to disputes over copyrights and patents, as well as unauthorized disclosure issues between two parties that both claim to own the data produced.

Supply Chain Assessment

Supply chains, the processes by which organizations receive necessary goods and services from third parties, is a huge issue for any organization, especially in the manufacturing and distribution industries. From the standpoint of IT security, our biggest concern is availability of equipment, software, and online services. To that end, it's important for IT security folks to conduct a *supply chain assessment* to ensure those critical products are available as needed and to create alternative processes.

Agreement Types

When your organization enters into any type of business partnership or agreement with a third-party business partner or service provider, the agreements and contract documents created serve to protect both organizations from a legal perspective as well as establish the terms of the business relationship. You'll need to know several types of documents for the exam, covering various aspects of data protection, interoperability, interconnection, and so on. They basically define the interoperability relationship between the two (and sometimes more) parties. Obviously, these types of agreements will be negotiated by the business contracting and legal personnel in each organization, but advice and input should also come from other affected functions within the businesses, such as security, privacy, IT support, and so on. Let's take a look at a few of these types of business agreements.

Sales and Purchase Agreement (SPA)

A *sales and purchase agreement (SPA)* is a legal document obligating a buyer to buy and a seller to sell a product or service. SPAs are critical and common for large, complex purchases. An SPA not only defines prices, but payment amounts and time frames for deposits. On the seller's side, an SPA defines how and when the property is to be transferred to the seller, acceptable condition of the goods or services, and any details that might impede the transfer.

You'll often see SPAs used in the cabling industry. Pulling cable, especially in an existing building, is complex. A good SPA for cabling covers all of the issues, such as when the installation will take place, when it will be complete, what types of cabling will be used, where the cable runs will go, how the runs will be labeled, how technicians will enter your facility, and whether the vendor is payed at once or at certain completion points.

Service Level Agreement (SLA)

A *service level agreement (SLA)* is a legal document that defines the expectations for services that a third-party provider will guarantee to the organization. The provider guarantees the service they provide to be up and running and usable by the organization, either for a certain percentage of time or to a certain level of standards. If the provider is storing or processing data for the organization, the SLA may state that the data will be available in a particular format, through a particular application or system, in a specified format, and to authorized users within the organization. If the provider is offering a service such as outsourced network or Web-based transactional services, for example, the SLA states that the services will be available for authorized users whenever they need them. The SLA may describe technologies and redundant systems used to ensure availability for customer's data and services, as well as specify what actions the provider will take in the event of incidents that may affect availability of services, and how long they have to restore full access for the organization.

NOTE Time is an important element for an SLA—length of time of the agreement, uptime guarantees, and response time for problems.

Business Partners Agreement (BPA)

The *business partners agreement (BPA)* specifies what type of relationships the different parties will have, usually from a legal perspective. An entirely separate company may be established for the business venture, combining elements of both individual businesses; this is usually for long-term or large-scale ventures. Usually, however, legal agreements dictate the type of partnerships or customer-provider relationships. These partnerships are usually distinguished by scope, term length, and level of product, service, data access, and so forth provided to each party in the agreement.

NOTE A BPA rarely has a time frame but it will have clear methods for ending the partnership.

Memorandum of Understanding (MOU)

A *memorandum of understanding (MOU)*, sometimes called a *memorandum of agreement (MOA)*, is a document often used within a large business or government agency that establishes an agreement between two independently managed parties that may be working together on a project or business venture. In this type of agreement, a contract isn't necessarily in place (nor required), simply because both parties work for the same overall organization. An MOU is established so that each party will agree to provide certain services or functions to the other party. Since both parties may work for the same higher-level organization, money doesn't necessarily change hands, but it could in a fee-for-service model where funds are transferred from one party's account to another's within the same company, for example. An example of this type of MOU would be if a division of the company provides data center services to other divisions of the same company; this MOU would outline the division's responsibilities and guaranteed levels of services to another division that uses it for data storage and protection.

You'll also see an MOU type of agreement between different government agencies; a military base, for example, may agree to provide network infrastructure services for another nonmilitary government agency that resides on the base (think of NASA, for example, which may have divisions housed on various U.S. Army and U.S. Air Force bases throughout the world).

You could also see an MOU between two businesses, of course, as part of a larger contract agreement; this may simply serve to define functions and interactions between two lower-level functions or departments located in each organization that weren't specified in the overall contract. The MOU may be agreed to and signed off by the middle-level managers of each department.

Interconnection Security Agreement (ISA)

Telecommunication companies will use an *interconnection security agreement (ISA)* when connecting to each other's network to handle essential details about technology and personnel. An ISA is not a legal document used to cover technical issues between two parties. An ISA may detail how two independently owned and managed network infrastructures are connected to each other. The businesses that own each network may require interconnections to share and access each other's data, and may use this type of agreement to specify the technical details needed for the connections. The agreement may specify security requirements, such as firewall and VPN use, encryption levels and methods, authentication types, allowed protocols, and so forth. This may be an attachment or amendment to the overall contract between parties.

Verifying Compliance and Performance

Any agreement between business parties and providers should specify how each party can verify compliance and performance standards. You may specify certain common standards and performance levels that each party has to meet, as well as legal or governance compliance. Audits or periodic inspections may be used by either party to verify the other party's compliance and performance. Access control checks, data integrity checks, and review of availability mechanisms (such as backup and restore devices and processes) may be addressed in this part of the agreement. Performance and security metrics such as throughput, availability times, backup frequency, limits on data permissions, and so forth may be specified and used to measure whether or not each organization is adhering to compliance and performance standards. Details regarding noncompliance and failure to perform up to standards should also be addressed in such agreements, to give each party an avenue of redress against the other.

Questions

1. A script kiddie is a classic example of a(n) _____.

   A. attacker

   B. criminal

   C. threat

   D. threat actor

2. Risk is often considered formulaically as

   A. Risk = Probability × Threat

   B. Risk = Threat × Impact

   C. Risk = Vulnerability × Threat

   D. Risk = Probability × Impact

3. A company makes a document called "Acceptable Use" that defines what the company allows users to do and not do on their work systems. The company requires new employees to read and sign this. What is this type of document called?

   A. Standard

   B. Policy

   C. Procedure

   D. Control

4. A _____ is a description of a complex process, concentrating on major steps and the flows between the steps.

   A. law

   B. procedure

   C. framework

   D. control

5. A *No Trespassing* sign is an example of a _____ control.

   A. deterrent

   B. preventative

   C. detective

   D. corrective

6. A lock on the door of a building is an example of a _____ control.

   A. deterrent

   B. preventative

    C. detective

    D. corrective

7. An asset's exposure factor is measured in _____ .

    A. dollars

    B. percentages

    C. units

    D. reputation

8. Which of the following equations is correct?

    A. Single Loss Expectancy = Asset Value × Exposure Factor

    B. Annualized Rate of Occurrence = Asset Value × Exposure Factor

    C. Annualized Loss Expectancy = Asset Value × Exposure Factor

    D. Single Rate of Occurrence = Asset Value × Exposure Factor

9. Financial is one type of business impact. Which of the following names another?

    A. Pride

    B. Technical

    C. Device

    D. Reputation

10. Which of the following represents the component manufacturer's best guess (based on historical data) regarding how much time will pass between major failures of that component?

    A. MTTR

    B. MTBF

    C. MTMB

    D. MOAB

Answers

1. **D.** A script kiddie is a classic example of a threat actor.

2. **D.** Risk is often considered formulaically as Risk = Probability × Impact.

3. **B.** Policies are normally written documents that define an organization's goals and actions. Acceptable use policies are very common.

4. **C.** A framework is a description of a complex process, concentrating on major steps and the flows between the steps.

5. **A.** A deterrent control deters a threat actor from performing a threat. A *No Trespassing* sign is a good example.

6. **B.** A preventative control stops threat actors from performing a threat. Locks are a notable example.

7. **B.** Exposure factor is measured in terms of a percentage of loss to the value of that asset.

8. **A.** The only correct equation is Single Loss Expectancy = Asset Value × Exposure Factor.

9. **D.** Of the choices listed, only reputation is a common business impact.

10. **B.** Mean time between failures (MTBF) represents the component manufacturer's best guess (based on historical data) regarding how much time will pass between major failures of that component.

Cryptography

Every organization has private data, data accessible by authorized users and not accessible to outsiders. This data includes customer databases; e-mails with critical business strategies; file servers with proprietary recipes and manufacturing processes; cameras sending images of security gates; and Web sites where people type in their names, addresses, and credit card information. Organizations need to keep this data secure. Encryption gives organizations the tools to accomplish this goal.

Encryption is a reversible process of converting data such that to a third party the data is nothing more than a random binary string. Note the phrase *reversible process*. This means a good encryption method must make it easy for someone who knows something secret to encrypt the data, and to reverse the process to return the data from an encrypted to an unencrypted state. *Decrypting* makes encrypted data readable.

This chapter explores *cryptography*, the science of encrypting and decrypting data, in eight modules:

- Cryptography Basics
- Cryptographic Methods
- Symmetric Cryptosystems
- Asymmetric Cryptosystems
- Hashing Algorithms
- Digital Signatures and Certificates
- Public Key Infrastructure
- Cryptographic Attacks

Module 2-1: Cryptography Basics

This module covers the following CompTIA Security+ objectives:

- **6.1** Compare and contrast basic concepts of cryptography
- **6.2** Explain cryptography algorithms and their basic characteristics

Cryptography provides methods and technologies to enable people and systems to exchange information securely. Cryptography ensures *confidentiality*—the accurate data gets into the hands of only the intended recipient. Cryptography also affords *integrity*, so the recipient can know that the data came from the right person. To accomplish these tasks, developers and programmers have created immensely complicated and awesome systems … and those systems come with a ton of epic jargon and details.

This module begins the exploration into the systems that make up modern cryptographic methods. It starts with basic building block concepts, such as plaintext and ciphertext. You'll look at early cryptography to understand the methods with simple examples. The module finishes with an overview of the essential components of every cryptographic system.

Essential Building Blocks

Cryptography has terms that describe the state of data, tools used to affect that data, and the movement of data from one state to another. This section discusses these terms:

- Plaintext and ciphertext
- Code and cipher
- Data-at-rest, data-in-transit, data-in-process

Plaintext and Ciphertext

IT professionals use the terms *plaintext* and *ciphertext* to describe the current readability of data. Humans and machines can easily read plaintext. Ciphertext, on the other hand, is unreadable. The process of converting plaintext information into ciphertext information is called *encryption*. The goal of encryption is to obfuscate the plaintext—to make it unreadable, to look as though it were simply a random jumble of data. The reverse of encryption, converting ciphertext back into plaintext, is called *decryption*. Figure 2-1 shows the icons used here when discussing plaintext and ciphertext.

NOTE Don't mistake the "text" portion of the words *plaintext* and *ciphertext* to mean only letters of the alphabet. Any form of easily readable binary data is plaintext. Any form of encrypted binary data is ciphertext.

Figure 2-1
Plaintext and
ciphertext

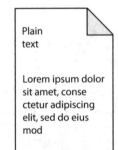
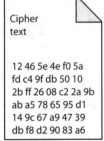

Plain
text

Lorem ipsum dolor
sit amet, conse
ctetur adipiscing
elit, sed do eius
mod

Cipher
text

12 46 5e 4e f0 5a
fd c4 9f db 50 10
2b ff 26 08 c2 2a 9b
ab a5 78 65 95 d1
14 9c 67 a9 47 39
db f8 d2 90 83 a6

Code and Cipher

IT professionals use the terms code and cipher to describe generically the ways tools encrypt and decrypt. A *code* is a representation of an entire phrase or sentence, whereas a *cipher* tends to represent text on a character-by-character basis. For example, a coded version of the phrase "We attack at dawn" might be "Mother bought some brown eggs at the store." Codes are not typically transformative; that is, there is usually no formal process to convert the true meanings of messages into their coded equivalents or back. Codes usually require a *codebook*, a predefined dictionary that translates codes to their plaintext messages and back. The need for a codebook limits the range of messages that can be sent and received via codes. Codes were common before computers, but are not at all common today.

Ciphers, on the other hand, use some form of formal, usually mathematical process to work instead of a fixed codebook. This makes the range of potential messages that can be sent using ciphers essentially unlimited, because these processes are usually done on the fly. Modern cryptographic methods with computers tend to use ciphers.

You may sometimes hear the terms *encode* (and *decode*), as well as *encipher* (and *decipher*) thrown around. Although they *don't* mean the same things, some IT people use them somewhat interchangeably. Don't be that kind of IT person! Since IT security focuses on ciphers, the book sticks to the terms that apply to ciphers, encrypt and decrypt.

 NOTE Codes are entire words and phrases; ciphers are individual characters. The cryptography methods discussed in this book focus on ciphers.

Data-at-Rest, Data-in-Transit, and Data-in-Process

Dealing with cryptography for computer data depends on the location of the data and the actions of that data at any given moment. The process of encrypting and decrypting data sitting on a hard drive, for example, differs from the process of encrypting and decrypting data moving wirelessly between a wireless access point and a wireless client. Three terms define the current state of data:

- Data-at-rest
- Data-in-transit
- Data-in-process

Data-at-Rest   *Data-at-rest* describes data that resides in storage. This data is not currently accessed, transmitted, or received, nor used by the computer. Data-at-rest is normally represented by data stored in static files on a hard drive or other storage media, when the device that holds that media is powered down. In other words, data on a laptop computer, powered down and sitting in Steve's bag, is data-at-rest. As soon as Steve logs into his computer at the airport lounge, that drive no longer holds data-at-rest; that applies to all the files and folders he's *not* accessing as well as those he *is* accessing.

Data-at-rest has high requirements for confidentiality. The thief of a company hard drive, for example, should not be able to access the data on that drive. Data-at-rest has very low requirements for integrity, because we know (in most cases) exactly where that data is stored and who may physically access it.

Data-in-Transit   *Data-in-transit* describes data currently in transport. This data is being transmitted or received from one person or host to another. Examples of data-in-transit include information moving over a network, over an Internet connection, from computer to computer over an Ethernet connection, or even over wireless networks. The data is not in storage; it has been transformed and formatted to be transmitted and received.

Data-in-transit has high requirements for confidentiality. It's relatively easy for bad guys to intercept transmitting data, so we need good encryption. Data-in-transit also has very high requirements for integrity. We don't know (in most cases) where the data came from or where it's going. Are we really talking to the actual person/server/WAP with whom we intend to communicate?

Data-in-Process   *Data-in-process* describes data currently in use by a computing device, and not at rest or in transit. Data in a computer's RAM and accessed by the computer's CPU, operating system, and applications is data-in-process. Operating systems and applications use data-in-process on a constant basis, transforming it, using it as input to processes, and so on. A Microsoft Word document Susan is currently editing is an obvious example.

Current technology makes data-in-process pretty much inaccessible to bad guys, at least in terms of cryptography. Times change and technology improves, however, so keep your skills current.

NOTE   Be comfortable with the three states of data and their sensitivity to confidentiality and integrity.

Outstanding! We've covered just enough terms to enable us to now briefly survey the history of cryptography. Pay attention here, as almost everything done hundreds of years ago is still used today on modern computers.

Early Cryptography

People throughout the past few thousand years have used cryptography to protect personal secrets, military troop movements, diplomatic messages, and so on. Historians have discovered several examples of the uses of crude, but effective, cryptographic methods, such as the Spartan *scytale*, which was a baton or stick with a strip of parchment wound around it several times, from one end of the stick to the other (Figure 2-2). On the parchment as it was wrapped on the baton, a person wrote a message, in plaintext. Once the parchment was removed from the stick, the words on the strip of parchment made no sense, since they were effectively encrypted. To "decrypt" the message, the receiver had

Figure 2-2
Author's home-
made scytale
(Attack at dawn)

to know the exact dimensions of the baton and have an identical one so that they could rewrap the parchment the exact same way around the baton and read the message.

Other historical uses of cryptography involved using different techniques to scramble letters of the alphabet so that only the sender and recipient would know how to unscramble and read them. Those methods are discussed in the next sections of the chapter. Still other, more modern ways of using cryptography involved the use of specially built machines to encrypt and decrypt messages. The classic example is the Enigma machine used by the Germans during World War II. This machine used encryption techniques that were considered unbreakable, until Dr. Alan Turing, a British mathematician, figured out how the machine worked and the methods it used to encrypt its information. Turing, now considered the father of modern cryptography and, to a large degree, computers, decrypted intercepted German messages. The ability of the British government to decrypt German military communications gave the Allies incredible insight to enemy troop movements, invasion plans, and so forth, effectively turning the tide of the war.

Alan Turing didn't invent cryptography, but many of the concepts used today were quantified by him in the huge number of academic papers Turing wrote. Turing clarified the ideas of substitution and transposition, the two pillars of cryptography.

Substitution

A *substitution* cipher swaps letters of the alphabet for other letters. To make a substitution cipher work, rotate the letters of the alphabet by some number of characters, then swap the letters that will substitute for them. A typical rotation shifts the alphabet 13 characters, called ROT13. Here's the standard alphabet:

ABCDEFGHIJKLMNOPQRSTUVWXYZ

And here's the same alphabet with ROT13 applied:

NOPQRSTUVWXYZABCDEFGHIJKLM

Note that the letter N replaces letter A. Letter G replaces letter T. Line the two up so you can see the full replacement scheme:

ABCDEFGHIJKLMNOPQRSTUVWXYZ
NOPQRSTUVWXYZABCDEFGHIJKLM

Now apply an example. The plaintext phrase, WE ATTACK AT DAWN, would change to JR NGGNPX NG QNJA in ROT13 encryption.

NOTE ROT13 is not the only ROT cipher. You can do ROT2, ROT10, ROT25, and so on.

This type of cipher is also called a *shift cipher* because it essentially shifts the entire alphabet down 13 spaces, and then starts over with the first letter. Still other methods of using substitution ciphers might use different words to begin the substitution alphabet, and then follow those words with the rest of the alphabet in normal order.

NOTE Julius Caesar used a substitution cipher in his military campaigns for sensitive communications. Thus, a substitution cipher is commonly referred to as a *Caesar cipher*.

More complex versions of substitution ciphers involve rearranging the words of the sentence into consistent groups of letters that have the same number of letters per group. This makes it more difficult to break the cipher, since you wouldn't have the ability to guess words based upon how many letters made up each word, particularly on easy words such as "a," "and," or "the," for example.

Yet another, more complex way of using substitution ciphers involves using multiple alphabets. This is called *polyalphabetic substitution*, and is sometimes called a *Vigenère cipher*. A Vigenère cipher works by using a series of letters, often simply a single word, as a *key* to change each position of the plaintext to a ROT code. Let's use the plaintext WE ATTACK AT DAWN once again. With the Vigenère cipher, apply a key—for this example we will use the word MIKE—repeatedly to the plaintext as follows:

WEATTACKATDAWN
MIKEMIKEMIKEMI

You can use the key to determine the ROT value. If the key letter is A, then use ROT0. If the key letter is B, then use ROT1. If the key letter is Z, then use ROT25. Here is the resulting Vigenère table:

A = ROT 0
B = ROT 1
C = ROT 2
…
Y = ROT 24
Z = ROT 25

This can be represented as a table (or a double entry grid) as shown in Figure 2-3. Vigenère ciphers were popular for centuries. Examples of substitution ciphers can be found in the standard word puzzle books you see on magazine racks in supermarkets and bookstores.

In cryptography, *confusion* means that every character in a key is used to make the ciphertext more random looking. Adding a key to change the ROT value of every character adds confusion, making a Vigenère cipher much harder to crack than a ROT.

Figure 2-3
Vigenère cipher table

	A	B	C	D	E	F	G	H	I	J	K	L	M	N	O	P	Q	R	S	T	U	V	W	X	Y	Z
A	A	B	C	D	E	F	G	H	I	J	K	L	M	N	O	P	Q	R	S	T	U	V	W	X	Y	Z
B	B	C	D	E	F	G	H	I	J	K	L	M	N	O	P	Q	R	S	T	U	V	W	X	Y	Z	A
C	C	D	E	F	G	H	I	J	K	L	M	N	O	P	Q	R	S	T	U	V	W	X	Y	Z	A	B
D	D	E	F	G	H	I	J	K	L	M	N	O	P	Q	R	S	T	U	V	W	X	Y	Z	A	B	C
E	E	F	G	H	I	J	K	L	M	N	O	P	Q	R	S	T	U	V	W	X	Y	Z	A	B	C	D
F	F	G	H	I	J	K	L	M	N	O	P	Q	R	S	T	U	V	W	X	Y	Z	A	B	C	D	E
G	G	H	I	J	K	L	M	N	O	P	Q	R	S	T	U	V	W	X	Y	Z	A	B	C	D	E	F
H	H	I	J	K	L	M	N	O	P	Q	R	S	T	U	V	W	X	Y	Z	A	B	C	D	E	F	G
I	I	J	K	L	M	N	O	P	Q	R	S	T	U	V	W	X	Y	Z	A	B	C	D	E	F	G	H
J	J	K	L	M	N	O	P	Q	R	S	T	U	V	W	X	Y	Z	A	B	C	D	E	F	G	H	I
K	K	L	M	N	O	P	Q	R	S	T	U	V	W	X	Y	Z	A	B	C	D	E	F	G	H	I	J
L	L	M	N	O	P	Q	R	S	T	U	V	W	X	Y	Z	A	B	C	D	E	F	G	H	I	J	K
M	M	N	O	P	Q	R	S	T	U	V	W	X	Y	Z	A	B	C	D	E	F	G	H	I	J	K	L
N	N	O	P	Q	R	S	T	U	V	W	X	Y	Z	A	B	C	D	E	F	G	H	I	J	K	L	M
O	O	P	Q	R	S	T	U	V	W	X	Y	Z	A	B	C	D	E	F	G	H	I	J	K	L	M	N
P	P	Q	R	S	T	U	V	W	X	Y	Z	A	B	C	D	E	F	G	H	I	J	K	L	M	N	O
Q	Q	R	S	T	U	V	W	X	Y	Z	A	B	C	D	E	F	G	H	I	J	K	L	M	N	O	P
R	R	S	T	U	V	W	X	Y	Z	A	B	C	D	E	F	G	H	I	J	K	L	M	N	O	P	Q
S	S	T	U	V	W	X	Y	Z	A	B	C	D	E	F	G	H	I	J	K	L	M	N	O	P	Q	R
T	T	U	V	W	X	Y	Z	A	B	C	D	E	F	G	H	I	J	K	L	M	N	O	P	Q	R	S
U	U	V	W	X	Y	Z	A	B	C	D	E	F	G	H	I	J	K	L	M	N	O	P	Q	R	S	T
V	V	W	X	Y	Z	A	B	C	D	E	F	G	H	I	J	K	L	M	N	O	P	Q	R	S	T	U
W	W	X	Y	Z	A	B	C	D	E	F	G	H	I	J	K	L	M	N	O	P	Q	R	S	T	U	V
X	X	Y	Z	A	B	C	D	E	F	G	H	I	J	K	L	M	N	O	P	Q	R	S	T	U	V	W
Y	Y	Z	A	B	C	D	E	F	G	H	I	J	K	L	M	N	O	P	Q	R	S	T	U	V	W	X
Z	Z	A	B	C	D	E	F	G	H	I	J	K	L	M	N	O	P	Q	R	S	T	U	V	W	X	Y

Vigenère ciphers have a weakness. Encrypt the plaintext WEATTACKATNOON with the MIKE key, but the key only affects the plaintext character directly underneath it. A better encryption should act in such a way that even the smallest change in the key makes for very different ciphertext. This is called *diffusion*. The Vigenère cipher lacks diffusion. Modern codes do not!

Transposition

A *transposition* cipher transposes or changes the order of characters in a message using some predetermined method that both the sender and recipient know. The sender transposes the message and sends it. The recipient applies the same transposition method in reverse, decrypting the message. There are a variety of different transposition methods, including columnar, rail fence, and route ciphers. Current computer-based cryptography uses both substitution and transposition together in wildly complex ways.

 EXAM TIP The CompTIA Security+ exam lumps substitution and transposition (along with XOR, which you'll see in a moment) together as examples of *obfuscation algorithms*. What that means in practical terms is that a hacker can look at something and not get any useful information about it.

Cryptanalysis

For as long as people have encrypted and decrypted data (or messages or whatever), others have tried to crack those messages. *Cryptanalysis* is the study of breaking encryption, the opposite of cryptography. You perform cryptanalysis on ciphertext data to reverse it to a plaintext state when you do not have access to the methods used to encrypt the data in the first place. Both security professionals and malicious actors perform cryptanalysis when attempting to decrypt ciphertext. There are hundreds if not thousands of methods for performing cryptanalysis, but many of them depend upon having a piece of plaintext that can be compared to its corresponding ciphertext, and vice versa, when you have some knowledge of the methods used to encrypt and decrypt the text. The next few modules discuss various methods of cryptanalysis.

Cryptography Components

Cryptography has several basic components that make the process work. These include algorithms, keys, XOR functions, shifts, rounds, and cryptosystems. While this module covers only the basics of these components, the remaining modules on cryptography discuss in depth how these different components work together.

Algorithms and Keys

Algorithms and keys work together to create cryptographic methods used to encrypt and decrypt messages. (They also can create cryptographic hash functions, used for digital signatures and more, a subject covered in depth in Module 2-5.)

Algorithms are mathematical constructs that define how to transform plaintext into ciphertext, as well as how to reverse that process during decryption. An individual algorithm might be very simple or very complex. A very simple algorithm used in a substitution cipher, for example, only requires shifting a letter several spaces to the right. Almost all the real-world algorithms used in IT encryption/decryption are extraordinarily complex. A single algorithm will contain a dizzying number of mathematical manipulations.

A *key* applies a variable used by the algorithm for the final cryptosystem (see the upcoming section "Cryptosystems"). In a ROT13 cryptosystem, ROT is the algorithm— to implement the encryption/decryption, shift letters of the alphabet. The 13 is the key or *cryptovariable* that defines how many letters to shift.

Algorithms often don't change. Keys change to keep bad guys guessing.

Keys are kept secret. Keys are typically not simplistic numbers. They are often complex, lengthy strings of numbers or characters. A key might also be a password, passphrase, personal identification number (PIN), code word, and so on. Algorithms and keys are used to encrypt or decrypt text, as illustrated in Figure 2-4.

Algorithms are generally well-known and tested, giving cryptographers and security professionals a level of confidence in their strength and ability to protect data. *Kerckhoffs' principle* states that the algorithm should not be the secret part of the cryptographic process or method used; the key should be kept secret, not the algorithm. Most security professionals follow this principle.

Key escrow grants knowledge or copies of keys to a third party. Businesses and other organizations use key escrow to store keys securely in the event they are lost, become corrupt, or an individual in the company with the only knowledge of the keys is terminated or quits. Key escrow provides an exception to Kerckhoffs' principle.

Figure 2-4
Algorithms
and keys

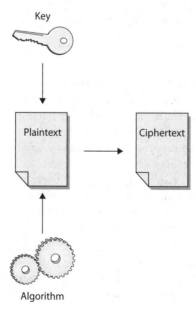

EXAM TIP An algorithm is a mathematical construct or rule that dictates how data will be encrypted and decrypted. Algorithms are generally well-known and not kept secret. Secret algorithms are not needed. Keys are the variables that algorithms use to ensure secrecy and randomness in the cryptographic process. Keys should be kept secret.

Block and Streaming Algorithms

Algorithms have a wide variety of characteristics that include mathematical foundation, strength, and how they operate on plaintext. Modules 2-3 and 2-4 go into detail about specific algorithms, but for now, let's discuss an important distinction within algorithms: block and streaming.

Remember the distinction between codes and ciphers and how they work with entire phrases (codes) or on individual characters (ciphers)? The algorithms discussed in this book work on binary digits (bits) of plaintext, either individually or in specified groups. A *block algorithm* operates on a predefined size of a group of bits, known as a *block*. Different block algorithms use different block sizes, but typical sizes are 16-, 64-, and 128-bit blocks. Most of the algorithms discussed in this book are block algorithms.

Streaming algorithms operate on individual bits, one bit at a time. Streaming algorithms don't work on blocks of text; instead they look at each individual bit and perform a mathematical operation on that bit, and then move on to the next bit. Streaming algorithms tend to work much faster than block algorithms and are used in cryptographic methods that support fast communications requirements, such as wireless technologies.

EXAM TIP Block algorithms work on predefined sizes of plaintext blocks, while streaming algorithms work on single bits of plaintext.

XOR Functions

Computing devices use binary data. Hard drives store Word documents in binary format. YouTube videos stream to a browser in binary format. Caesar ciphers use alphabets, not bits, so they don't readily apply to binary data. Computers need mathematical tools to encrypt, to transpose and substitute ones and zeros. The most commonly used binary math function used in cryptography is called *eXclusive OR (XOR)*. XOR compares two bits to determine difference.

With XOR, any bits that compare and are the same (two binary 0's, for example) yield a resultant bit of *false* (and produce a 0-bit as the output). Any bits that compare and are different (a binary 1 and a binary 0) produce a *true* value, and an output bit of 1 is generated. Figure 2-5 illustrates this process.

NOTE XOR results might seem a little weird at first. Keep in mind that XOR determines *differences* in compared data. A *true* result means that the compared data is *not* the same. A *false* result means the data is the same.

Figure 2-5
The XOR function
in action

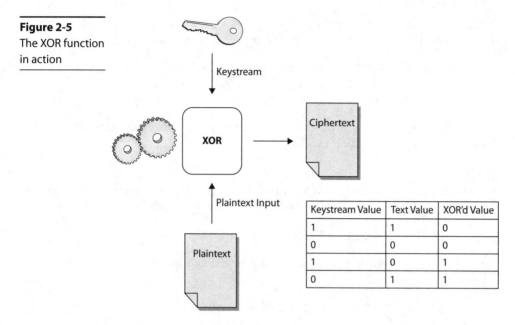

Keystream Value	Text Value	XOR'd Value
1	1	0
0	0	0
1	0	1
0	1	1

Here's an example of XOR in action, encrypting the *randomly selected* name, Mike, as the data:

MIKE

As a first step, convert these four letters into binary. For this example, we'll use ASCII code. ASCII converts every letter of the English alphabet in 8-bit binary values:

```
M = 01001101
I = 01001001
K = 01001011
E = 01000101
```

So, MIKE in binary is 01001101010010010100101101000101. This string of bits is the *plaintext*.

The XOR function compares two binary values, right? To encrypt with XOR requires another value to compare with the plaintext. To XOR encrypt this binary data, therefore, we need a binary key. Let's *arbitrarily* choose the ridiculously easy key of 0110. To encrypt, repeatedly place the key under the plaintext, as follows:

```
01001101010010010100101101000101 (plaintext)
01100110011001100110011001100110 (key repeated)
```

Now go one bit at a time, using XOR to encrypt:

```
01001101010010010100101101000101
01100110011001100110011001100110
00101011001011110010110100100011 (ciphertext)
```

Congrats! You've just done binary encryption, in this example using XOR. Want to decrypt the ciphertext? Just XOR it against the repeated key, as follows:

```
001010110010111100101101001000011 (ciphertext)
011001100110011001100110011001100110 (key repeated)
010011010100100101001011010001011 (plaintext)
```

Using XOR solely, especially with such a short key, creates an easily cracked ciphertext. Let's make it harder by adding a shift.

Shifts

As the name implies, a *shift* in binary means moving the ciphertext left or right. Let's shift the ciphertext four digits to the left. Here's the initial ciphertext:

```
001010110010111100101101001000011
```

Now, take the first four binary values on the far left and move them to the end on the far right, as follows:

```
101100101111001011010010000110010
```

Adding a shift increases the complexity involved in decrypting. You need the key, plus knowledge of the shift.

A simple shift makes better encryption, but a powerful computer can figure out this shifty trick in milliseconds! Let's enhance the encryption by doing the whole XOR/left-shift multiple times.

Rounds

Repeating the XOR/left-shift iteration more than once—such as five times—makes the encryption harder to crack. It also means it will take longer to encrypt and decrypt, because every encryption and decryption must repeat the iteration five times. (That's the price required for security.) Each of these XOR/left-shift iterations is called a *round*. Most modern algorithms use multiple rounds, repeating the process several times to ensure that the process is effective.

Cryptosystems

A *cryptosystem* includes everything in a cryptographic process, such as the algorithms, keys, functions, methods, and techniques. The example used here—the Mike Meyers Excellent Cryptosystem—includes four components:

- A four-bit key
- An XOR
- A four-digit left shift of the ciphertext
- The XOR/left-shift iteration repeated in five rounds

Cryptosystems use algorithms and keys as basic components to stir up the binary data, and also implement them in ways that enable the encryption/decryption to be faster, more efficient, or stronger.

Module 2-2: Cryptographic Methods

This module covers the following CompTIA Security+ objective:

- **6.1** Compare and contrast basic concepts of cryptography

Different aspects of cryptography are categorized in many ways. You've already learned how algorithms are generally divided up into block and streaming algorithms. Now we'll examine yet another way of dividing up cryptography into two different encryption methods—symmetric and asymmetric cryptography. These two types of cryptography focus more on the aspect of the keys used than the algorithms, although each type has its own algorithms, as discussed in later modules.

This module explores symmetric cryptography first, followed by asymmetric cryptography. The third section in the module describes a unique type of cryptography called hashing. The fourth section puts all three together in hybrid cryptography. The final section discusses what makes a perfect cryptosystem.

Symmetric Cryptography

Symmetric cryptography uses a single key that both encrypts and decrypts data. All parties that require access to a piece of encrypted data know that key. If someone encrypts a file or sends a secure message to another person, both persons must have the key used to encrypt the data to decrypt it.

Symmetric keys are sometimes called *secret* keys or *session* keys. Session keys, more specifically, are created and used for a single communications session. They are not reused after the communications session ends. If the parties want to communicate again using symmetric cryptography, new session keys are generated by either party or by the cryptosystem in use. Figure 2-6 shows how two parties use symmetric keys to exchange sensitive data.

 EXAM TIP Symmetric key cryptography uses a single key that both encrypts and decrypts data.

Symmetric key cryptography is both *low latency* (quick to respond) and good at handling large amounts of data, such as storage or transmission of large files. Symmetric keys require minimal computational overhead. Since only one key is involved, in communications limited to only two parties, symmetric key cryptography works great.

Symmetric key cryptography has a couple of weaknesses, in scaling and key exchange. First, when multiple parties require access to the same encrypted data (such as a group of friends or business associates), the exchange uses the same key. The more people

Figure 2-6
Symmetric keys
in use

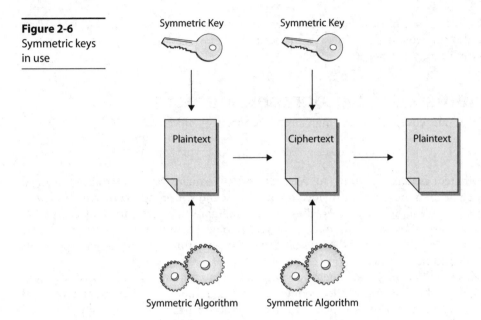

who have the key increases the chances that it will get inadvertently disclosed to an unauthorized person. Second, getting the key into the hands of only the desired users presents challenges.

Let's look at an example of the scaling problem. User Meghan wants to communicate with user Amy. Both need only one secret key. Adding more users, such as Tim, Bobby, and Dawn, means each must have the same key to access the encrypted data.

What if, however, Meghan wants only Amy to view a piece of data, and she doesn't want Tim, Bobby, and Dawn to be able to see it? Meghan must maintain separate symmetric keys for each party with whom she wants to communicate. Among a few people this scenario might be manageable. But imagine what happens if Meghan needs to maintain separate keys for 100 people? Meghan has a lot of keys!

Worse yet, what if each of the 100 people required secure, unique communication with every other user? How many total keys must be generated?

Math comes to the rescue here. The total number of keys required is equal to the number of people in the group, multiplied by that same number less 1, and then divided by 2. Here's the formula:

$$K = N \times (N - 1)/2$$

- K is the total number of keys required.
- N is the number of people in the group.

So: $K = 100 \times (100 - 1)/2 = 4950$. As you can see, with 100 users, a lot of keys must be generated, issued, and exchanged among each pair of users in the group who must securely communicate. Symmetric key cryptography does not scale very well in larger groups or entities that must securely communicate with one another.

Key exchange refers to the process used to exchange keys between users who send a message and those who receive it. Without the key, an authorized user or message recipient can't decrypt the message; the message will simply remain as ciphertext.

Since only one key is used in a symmetric communication, there must be a way to deliver the key securely to the right users, with an assurance that it won't be intercepted and compromised. E-mail is usually not the most secure way, although sometimes people send their secret keys via an e-mail message. Manual methods offer a little more security, such as giving someone a key stored on a USB memory stick.

Most of the time, especially in large organizations or when communicating with someone over greater distances, manual exchange isn't practical. The problem with key exchange, therefore, is getting the key to someone using a means that is considered secure—so that the key will not be intercepted and used by an unauthorized person, rendering the entire process useless. Symmetric key cryptography has problems with secure key exchange.

Key exchange has two terms to describe the exchange methods:

- In-band
- Out-of-band

In-band key exchange involves using the same communications channel you are using to send the message to send the key. This may not be the most secure way, since that channel may be monitored by a malicious person.

Out-of-band key exchange involves the use of a separate, independent channel, such as snail mail, USB stick, or even a different network connection, to send the key to the authorized users. In smaller groups of users that reside near each other, key exchange may not be much of a problem. In large organizations, however, in which users may be geographically separated, key exchange can be an issue, especially when using only symmetric key cryptography.

 EXAM TIP Symmetric key cryptography excels in speed, efficiency, and the ability to handle large amounts of data easily. The disadvantages primarily involve scalability and key exchange.

Asymmetric Cryptography

Asymmetric key cryptography uses two separate keys—a *key pair*—for secure communication. Data encrypted with one key requires the other key in the key pair for decryption.

In *public key cryptography*—the primary asymmetric implementation—these keys are called a *public key* and a *private key*. Each user is issued or generates a key pair for his or her own use. The user gives the public key to anyone, even posting it on the Internet. The user keeps the private key, on the other hand, secret. With public key cryptography, what one key encrypts, only the other key can decrypt, and vice versa. If the key in the pair is used to encrypt a message, it cannot decrypt the same message. This makes the cryptography process, particularly sending and receiving confidential messages, different from the process used in symmetric key cryptography.

 EXAM TIP Public key cryptography uses two mathematically related keys in a pair, a public key and a private key. What one key encrypts, only the other key in the pair may decrypt, and vice versa.

Jack and Jill want to communicate using public key cryptography. They need to follow specific steps. First, each must generate a unique key pair. Second, each user makes his or her public key readily available, such as posting it to the Internet.

Jack acquires Jill's public key, encrypts a message using that key, and sends it to Jill. Jill receives the message and decrypts it with her private key. Her private key is the only way to decrypt a message encrypted with her public key.

For Jill to send to Jack securely, she reverses the process. She gets his public key and uses it to encrypt the message. Upon receipt, Jack decrypts the message using his private key. It's an elegant system. Figures 2-7 and 2-8 demonstrate this process.

Asymmetric key cryptography has several advantages over symmetric key cryptography, the major one being key exchange. The process eliminates key exchange issues, since no one really has to exchange a key. Anyone can acquire the public key. The sending party encrypts the message with the receiving person's public key, and only the recipient who possesses the private key can decrypt it.

Asymmetric key cryptography has a couple of disadvantages as well. First, it's slower than symmetric key cryptography and more computationally intensive to generate keys. Second, it works well only with small amounts of data; it's not suited for bulk data encryption or transmission. Module 2-7 will discuss the primary uses of asymmetric key cryptography, which involve public key infrastructure, or PKI, and uses of digital certificates and signatures.

 EXAM TIP Asymmetric key cryptography does great key exchange, but features slower speed compared to symmetric key cryptography and doesn't handle large amounts of data very efficiently.

Figure 2-7
Distribution of public and private keys

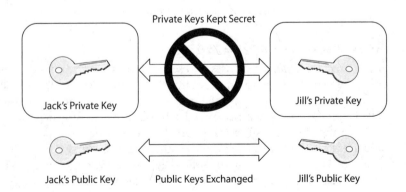

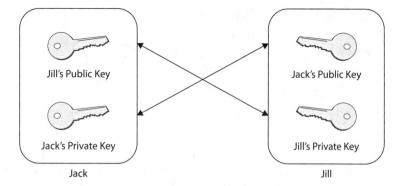

Figure 2-8
Using asymmetric
key cryptography

Hashing

Hashing provides integrity in the CIA of security by creating unique numbers for data and originators of information. Hashing helps verify that data came from a specific source and that the data did not change from what was sent.

In the hashing process, variable-length text, such as a document or spreadsheet, or even a password, is exposed to a cryptographic algorithm that produces a cryptographic sum, or *hash* (also sometimes called a *message digest*), of the document. This hash is only a representation of the text; it is not the same thing as the text itself. Think of a hash as a unique fingerprint that identifies a very specific piece of plaintext. The piece of plaintext can be any length, and it generally does not matter how large the input plaintext is. The resulting hash will always be a fixed-length piece of ciphertext, usually expressed in a hexadecimal format. An example of a typical hash is shown in Figure 2-9.

Unlike the encryption and decryption process, hashing was not designed to be reversible. In other words, you don't simply encrypt text with a hashing function with the expectation of decrypting it later. Hashing is a one-way mathematical function whose sole purpose is to produce the cryptographic sum of the input plaintext. Think of the hashing process as sort of a measuring process for the data, with the resultant hash being the actual measurement itself.

Although its purpose is not to decrypt text, the cryptographic sum produced by hashing has some uses. First, hashing is used to provide for integrity of data. A hash is unique to a particular piece of text. If one letter or word of the text is altered in any way, if even one binary digit changes, the resulting hash will differ from the original hash. Hashing assures

```
^  ˅  ×  CompTIA Security+
File  Edit  View  Terminal  Help
root@bt:~# md5sum testfile1
d24d7d237078f440d0a569afacd00823  testfile1
root@bt:~#
```

Figure 2-9   A hash value computed for a file

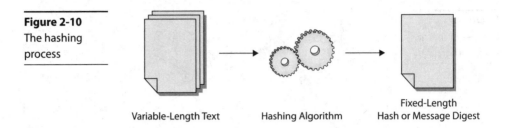

Figure 2-10
The hashing
process

Variable-Length Text   Hashing Algorithm   Fixed-Length
Hash or Message Digest

the integrity of a piece of plaintext, since any changes would produce an easily detected different sum. Figure 2-10 shows the hashing process.

Hashing enables integrity. Data transmitted over a network can be hashed before transmission and after reception, and the two resulting hashes can be compared. If the hashes match, you have unaltered data. If they differ, you can assume that the data has changed in some way during transmission. I'll discuss hashing in more depth in Module 2-5, with specific examples of hashing methods.

NOTE The term "message" generically refers to any piece of variable-length text, be it a password, text document, spreadsheet, picture file, or any other type of data.

Hybrid Cryptography

Many modern implementations of cryptography combine symmetric key and asymmetric key functions with hashing to create a highly secure mashup generically called *hybrid cryptography*. Symmetric key cryptography handles large data well, but is weak at key exchange. Asymmetric does key exchange well, but encrypts/decrypts more slowly than symmetric. Both pretty much *define* confidentiality, but lack integrity. Hashing provides the missing integrity aspect.

Here's an example of hybrid key cryptography in action. A common method of key exchange involves the creation of a "secret" between the two parties. This secret is then run through a hash to create the one-and-only unique, cannot-be-reversed (supposedly) key to be used on the symmetric side. Encrypt and send this hash via your asymmetric system and voilà! You've securely exchanged a viable key for your symmetric side.

Nothing is perfect, of course, and there are many variables—using certificates to identify each party; encryption streams within the exchange; and so on. But for the purposes of this discussion, just remember hybrid encryption means to use combinations of symmetric, asymmetric, and hashing to ensure better confidentiality and integrity.

EXAM TIP Hybrid cryptography leverages the advantages of both symmetric and asymmetric key cryptography together and eliminates their disadvantages.

The Perfect Cryptosystem

Cryptosystems should obfuscate any plaintext into what anyone who can't decrypt would see as nothing more than random data. This obfuscation makes data secure. *Security through obfuscation* is what cryptography is all about!

Proponents of *security through obscurity* argue that hiding how cryptosystems work hardens those systems. If you invent a great cryptosystem, full of interesting math using all kinds of substitutions, transpositions, and shifts over lots of rounds, and, in the implementation, count on the fact that no one else knows the algorithm, you have the perfect, uncrackable cryptosystem.

 NOTE Many IT security professionals argue that making a target appear uninteresting adds a level of protection. This differently nuanced definition of security through obscurity applies to situations such as a bank versus a would-be robber. The robber might spend all of his time on the vault door, so storing vital stuff in a simple locked janitor closet would work.

Security through obscurity misses one essential fact: every cryptosystem is crackable over time. What seems impossible today becomes child's play with tomorrow's technologies.

Rather than hiding how cryptosystems work, modern cryptography makes algorithms public. Making the systems available for everyone to attack exposes vulnerabilities and weaknesses that can be addressed. Make the underlying algorithm unassailable, as Kerckhoffs suggested, but keep the specific key used secret. Because of this attitude, new, more resilient cryptosystems come out every few years. The creators of these cryptosystems happily send them out for academic rigor, making sure the code has *high resiliency*, that it holds up against cracking.

Finally, that elusive perfect cryptosystem should hold up over time. In some cases, keys might be used for weeks, months, or even years perhaps. *Forward secrecy* means to protect a cryptosystem from one key giving away some secret that makes it easier to crack. If an algorithm achieves this, we call it *perfect forward secrecy*. There is no such thing as perfect forward secrecy other than using a key only once and throwing it away—a *one-time pad*.

Module 2-3: Symmetric Cryptosystems

This module covers the following CompTIA Security+ objective:

- **6.2** Explain cryptography algorithms and their basic characteristics

Developers have created and deployed numerous symmetric key cryptosystems over the years to provide fast and secure data communications. This module explores the six most common cryptosystems. Some of the data here is historical, but all of it informs modern cryptosystems. Let's look at these cryptosystems:

- DES
- 3DES

- AES
- Blowfish
- Twofish
- RC4

DES

The *Data Encryption Standard (DES)* is an older, now obsolete standard for commercial-grade encryption within the United States. DES uses an algorithm called Lucifer, developed by IBM. In the DES implementation, Lucifer has a 64-bit key size. Eight of those bits are used for computational overhead, so the true key size is only 56 bits. DES is a symmetric block algorithm and uses 64-bit block sizes. Blocks that are less than 64 bits in size are padded.

 EXAM TIP The CompTIA Security+ exam will quiz you on block sizes, so make notes throughout this module! Also, the CompTIA Security+ Acronyms list in the objectives incorrectly uses "Digital" rather than "Data" for the "D" in DES. Pay attention to the wording on any DES question.

DES works in *modes*, defined methods that determines how a plaintext block is input and changed to produce ciphertext. Each of these modes processes input blocks of text in different ways to encrypt the data. Modes also use certain mathematical functions to transform the data for stronger encryption. DES uses 16 rounds for each mode. So, for whichever mode is used, that process is repeated 16 times on a block of plaintext to produce the output ciphertext.

DES uses five different *cipher modes*:

- ECB
- CBC
- CFB
- OFB
- CTR

In the *Electronic Code Book (ECB)* mode, plaintext blocks of 64 bits are manipulated to produce ciphertext. With ECB mode, a given piece of plaintext will always produce the same corresponding piece of ciphertext. Unfortunately, this makes ECB mode very predictable, and it can easily be broken if an attacker has specific pieces of plaintext and ciphertext to compare.

The *Cipher Block Chaining (CBC)* mode produces much stronger encryption by XORing the previous block to the block being encrypted. The very first block gets an initialization vector (IV) into the process. This ensures that every block of plaintext input into the process produces a uniquely different piece of ciphertext. So even when the same block of plaintext is input repeatedly, the resultant ciphertext will not be identical to any previous outputs.

 NOTE Some cryptosystems use an arbitrary number—an *initialization vector (IV)*—along with a secret key for data encryption. (See *nonce* later in this chapter.)

Cipher Feedback (CFB) mode is like CBC except the plaintext is XORed into the IV after each round.

Output Feedback (OFB) mode is very similar to CFB mode, but instead of the previous block's ciphertext being the next block's IV, it takes the result of the previous encryption of the IV and key *before* the plaintext is XORed.

In DES, *Counter (CTR)* mode uses a random 64-bit block as the first IV, then increments a specified number or counter for every subsequent block of plaintext. CTR mode offers the best performance.

Figure 2-11 illustrates how complex even the simple ECB mode is in DES; this screenshot was taken from the freely available open-source CrypTool cryptography learning program (www.cryptool.org).

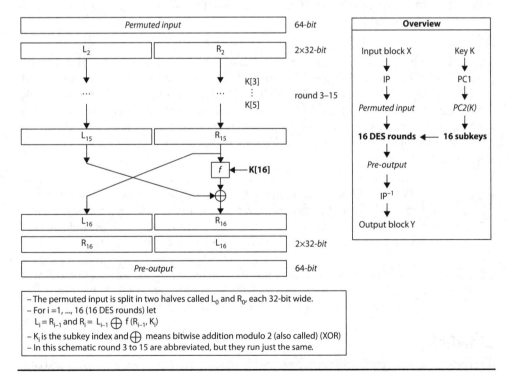

Figure 2-11   Illustration of how DES ECB mode works (screenshot from the CrypTool cryptography learning program)

EXAM TIP You need to know the different characteristics of DES for the exam—16 rounds of encryption, 64-bit blocks, 56-bit keys, and five cipher modes of operation.

3DES

Triple DES (3DES or TDES) is a later iteration of DES designed to fix some of the problems found in DES. It basically puts plaintext blocks through the same type of DES encryption process, but it does so in three distinct iterations. Where DES uses single 56-bit keys, 3DES uses three 56-bit keys. Many IT folks—and the CompTIA Security+ exam—combine the three keys, so describe 3DES as having a *168-bit key.*

3DES uses the same modes that DES uses, it just repeats them three times using three different keys. Other than the number of iterations, there are no differences between the two algorithms. This similarity causes 3DES to suffer from some of the same weaknesses as DES. These weaknesses motivated the industry to replace 3DES with more modern algorithms, particularly AES, discussed next.

 EXAM TIP 3DES made up for some of DES's weaknesses, but it did not significantly change the algorithm. It puts plaintext through more iterations than DES, but it still suffers from some of the same weaknesses.

AES

The Advanced Encryption Standard (AES) is a symmetric block cipher that can use block sizes of 128 bits, with key sizes of 128, 192, and 256 bits. It uses 10 rounds for 128-bit keys, 12 rounds for 192-bit keys, and 14 rounds for 256-bit keys. Like DES, AES can use different modes to encrypt and decrypt data. Most attacks on AES are theoretical in nature—referred to as *side-channel* attacks, which take advantage of ineffective implementations of the AES algorithm in the cryptosystem, versus the algorithm itself.

 EXAM TIP AES is the de jure encryption standard for the U.S. government and the de facto standard for private and commercial organizations. It is a block cipher that uses 128-bit block sizes, with 128-bit, 192-bit, and 256-bit keys. It uses 10, 12, and 14 rounds, respectively, for these keys.

AES supports all the modes listed under DES, but tends to use the much lower-latency mode called *Galois/Counter Mode (GCM)*. GCM starts with CTR mode, but adds a special data type known as a Galois field to add integrity.

Blowfish

Blowfish is a block cipher that accepts 64-bit blocks and has a wide range of variable key links, from 32 bits, all the way up to 448 bits. It uses 16 rounds of encryption, just as DES does. It is widely implemented in different software encryption solutions and is considered a good choice for a strong encryption algorithm, since there have been no more effective complete cryptanalysis solutions published to date.

Twofish

Twofish is a symmetric block algorithm that uses a 128-bit block size. It can use 128-bit, 192-bit, or 256-bit keys. Like DES, it uses 16 rounds of encryption. It is viewed as a successor to Blowfish. Although there have been some published partial theoretical attacks against Twofish, there are currently no publicly known attacks against it. Like Blowfish, Twofish has been placed in the public domain, making it freely available for anyone to use.

 EXAM TIP Although AES is the official U.S. standard, both Blowfish and Twofish are exceptionally good encryption algorithms. Both use 64-bit blocks and both perform 16 rounds of encryption. Blowfish can use key sizes from 32 to 448 bits, and Twofish uses key sizes of 128 bits, 192 bits, and 256 bits. Longer keys provide better key strength.

RC4

Rivest Cipher 4 (RC4) is a streaming symmetric algorithm (unlike the block algorithms discussed previously in the module). Because it is a streaming cipher, it uses only one round of encryption. RC4 can use key sizes from 40 to 2048 bits in length. It's a very fast protocol, as all streaming ciphers are. RC4 uses a key stream (stream of pseudo-random bits injected into the encryption process), which is then combined with plaintext using the XOR function to encrypt them into ciphertext.

RC4 is most popularly used in wireless encryption with the older, now obsolete and cryptographically broken Wired Equivalent Privacy (WEP) protocol. It can also be found in versions of the Secure Sockets Layer (SSL) and Transport Layer Security (TLS) protocols. RC4 has some documented weaknesses, which makes it unsuitable for future implementations. Current software vendors advise against its use, and the Internet Engineering Task Force's (IETF) RFC 7465 eliminated its use in TLS.

 EXAM TIP RC4 is likely the only example of a streaming cipher you will see on the exam. All the other symmetric algorithms discussed throughout this book are block ciphers.

Summary of Symmetric Algorithm Characteristics

Table 2-1 summarizes the characteristics of the different symmetric algorithms.

Symmetric Algorithm	Block or Streaming	Block Size	Rounds	Key Size	Notes
DES	Block	64-bit	16	56 bits (64 bits total, with 8 bits for parity overhead)	Uses five modes of operation: ECB, CBC, CFB, OFB, and CTR.
3DES	Block	64-bit	16	168 bits (three 56-bit keys)	Repeats DES process three times.
AES	Block	128-bit	10, 12, and 14 (based on key size)	128, 192, and 256 bits	Encryption standard for the U.S. government; GCM mode is popular.
Blowfish	Block	64-bit	16	32–448 bits	Public domain algorithm.
Twofish	Block	128-bit	16	128, 192, and 256 bits	Public domain algorithm.
RC4	Streaming	N/A	1	40–2048 bits	Used in WEP, SSL, and TLS; largely deprecated in current technologies.

Table 2-1   Summary of Symmetric Algorithms

Module 2-4: Asymmetric Cryptosystems

This module covers the following CompTIA Security+ objective:

- **6.2**   Explain cryptography algorithms and their basic characteristics

Developers have created and deployed numerous asymmetric key cryptosystems over the years to provide robust key exchange and secure data communications. This module explores the five most common asymmetric cryptosystems. Some of the data here is historical, but all of it informs modern cryptosystems. Let's look, in order, at these cryptosystems:

- RSA
- Diffie-Hellman
- PGP/GPG
- ECC
- ElGamal

RSA

RSA is used to create and use a public-private key pair. It generates keys based on the mathematical problem of the difficulty of factoring two very large prime numbers (each generally up to several hundred digits in length). RSA uses one round of encryption, and its typical key sizes range from 1024 to 4096 bits.

Although RSA is considered very secure, keys of smaller sizes have been broken in various published attacks. Still, these attacks are largely based upon faulty implementations of the protocol, rather than the protocol itself.

RSA is pretty much the de facto asymmetric algorithm used in most public key cryptography implementations today. Figure 2-12 demonstrates how RSA works, using very simple prime numbers in this instance, and the CrypTool learning program.

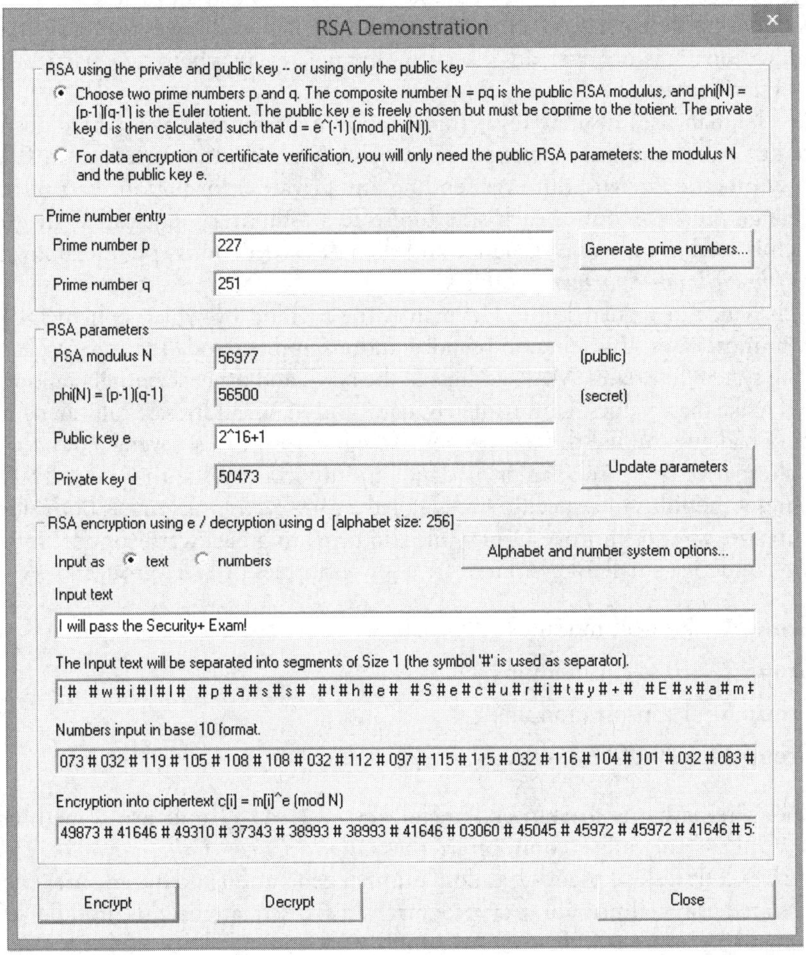

RSA Demonstration ×

RSA using the private and public key -- or using only the public key

○ Choose two prime numbers p and q. The composite number N = pq is the public RSA modulus, and phi(N) = (p-1)(q-1) is the Euler totient. The public key e is freely chosen but must be coprime to the totient. The private key d is then calculated such that d = e^(-1) (mod phi(N)).

○ For data encryption or certificate verification, you will only need the public RSA parameters: the modulus N and the public key e.

Prime number entry
Prime number p   227   Generate prime numbers...
Prime number q   251

RSA parameters
RSA modulus N   56977   (public)
phi(N) = (p-1)(q-1)   56500   (secret)
Public key e   2^16+1
Private key d   50473   Update parameters

RSA encryption using e / decryption using d [alphabet size: 256]

Input as ● text ○ numbers   Alphabet and number system options...
Input text

I will pass the Security+ Exam!

The Input text will be separated into segments of Size 1 (the symbol '#' is used as separator).

I# #w#i#l#l# #p#a#s#s# #t#h#e# #S#e#c#u#r#i#t#y#+# #E#x#a#m#

Numbers input in base 10 format.

073 # 032 # 119 # 105 # 108 # 108 # 032 # 112 # 097 # 115 # 115 # 032 # 116 # 104 # 101 # 032 # 083 #

Encryption into ciphertext c[i] = m[i]^e (mod N)

49873 # 41646 # 49310 # 37343 # 38993 # 38993 # 41646 # 03060 # 45045 # 45972 # 45972 # 41646 # 5

Encrypt   Decrypt   Close

Figure 2-12 Simple demonstration of the RSA algorithm (screenshot from the CrypTool cryptography learning program)

NOTE RSA is the de facto asymmetric protocol used for generating public-private key pairs. The name RSA reflects the first letters of its creators, Rivest, Shamir, and Adleman.

Diffie-Hellman

RSA is very secure, but requires a lot of computation and includes some robust but complex key exchange procedures. If you prefer speed over security, Diffie-Hellman is the asymmetric algorithm for you! *Diffie-Hellman (D-H)* is a set of asymmetric key exchange protocols that uses asymmetric key exchange to give both sides of a conversation a single symmetric key. D-H provides a secure key exchange to establish a secure communications session over an insecure channel, even when two parties have no previous relationship.

Diffie-Hellman uses discrete logarithms, modulo arithmetic, and prime numbers to generate key pairs randomly (as opposed to being permanently stored, as in RSA) that derive a symmetric key without ever sending any private information. Part of the D-H key exchange process requires each side to create a temporary key, called an *ephemeral key*, which is used in only one exchange and then discarded. This ephemeral key usage is called *Diffie-Hellman Ephemeral (DHE)*.

One challenge to regular Diffie-Hellman is the method by which ephemeral keys are derived. In most cases, this relies on pseudo-random number code that uses aspects of the underlying system like dates, MAC address of the NIC, and other seemingly random information to make these values. Unfortunately, dates and MAC addresses really aren't random; in theory, a bad guy can use this against you. To fight against this, several alternatives exist.

One alternative is to use a larger *modulus*: an important value that helps D-H derive keys. A preset modulus of a specific size is called a *D-H group*. As long as both sides agree to a group size, we can improve D-H while still providing backward support for systems that only can derive smaller keys. Here are a few examples of D-H groups:

- **Group 1** 768-bit modulus
- **Group 2** 1024-bit modulus
- **Group 5** 1536-bit modulus
- **Group 14** 2048-bit modulus

Another alternative is to skip ephemeral keys with D-H and use something more resilient. One of the most common is the *Elliptic Curve Diffie-Hellman Ephemeral (ECDHE)*. ECDHE skips pseudo-random number generation and instead uses ephemeral keys calculated using elliptic curve cryptography, discussed later in this module. ECDHE is negotiated by groups as well:

- **Group 19** 25-bit elliptic curve
- **Group 20** 384-bit elliptic curve
- **Group 21** 521-bit elliptic curve

NOTE Many applications (such as secure Web sites) use RSA for authentication and D-H for key exchange.

PGP/GPG

Pretty Good Privacy (PGP) is a cryptography application and protocol suite used in asymmetric cryptography. PGP can use both asymmetric and symmetric keys for a wide variety of operations, including bulk encryption, data-at-rest encryption (including both file and full disk encryption), key-pair generation, and key exchange. Unlike other public key cryptography schemes, PGP uses a *web-of-trust* rather than a public key infrastructure (both of which are described in detail in Module 2-7). Although PGP is considered a commercialized, proprietary version, it has an open source equivalent, GPG, which stands for Gnu Privacy Guard. The various versions of PGP comply with the OpenPGP standard, an IETF standard published as RFC 4880. GPG also complies with the standard.

EXAM TIP With PGP/GPG, think e-mail here. That's where you'll see these standards in play.

ECC

Elliptic curve cryptography (ECC) is an asymmetric method of cryptography based upon problems involving the algebraic structure of elliptic curves over finite fields. ECC has many uses, including variations that apply both to encryption and digital signatures.

ECC has special uses involving mobile devices. It requires low computational power and memory usage, so ECC has been widely implemented in smartphones and other low-power mobile devices.

ECC typically uses much smaller key sizes than other asymmetric algorithms, but these smaller-sized ECC keys are also harder to break. The largest known ECC key broken to date is only a 112-bit key, for example, compared to a 768-bit key size that has been broken with RSA.

ElGamal

ElGamal is an asymmetric algorithm that can be used for both digital signatures and general encryption. Taher ElGamal based his eponymous algorithm partially on Diffie-Hellman key exchange algorithms. It's widely used in open standards and cryptosystems, including PGP and GPG. The U.S. government's Digital Signature Algorithm (DSA) is based upon the ElGamal signature scheme. ElGamal uses mathematical problems related to computing discrete logarithms.

Module 2-5: Hashing Algorithms

This module covers the following CompTIA Security+ objective:

- **6.2** Explain cryptography algorithms and their basic characteristics

IT professionals use several hashing algorithms to ensure the integrity of data and source. This module starts with a brief discussion of how hashing works—a rehash of the introduction in Module 2-2, so to speak. [Insert groan here at bad pun.] Then we'll explore the four most common hashing algorithms:

- MD5
- SHA
- RIPEMD
- HMAC

Hashing Process

Encryption necessarily implies decryption. Plaintext transformed through encryption into an unreadable state can be decrypted and returned to a plaintext state.

Hashing does not encrypt text; it generates a representation of that text, which is the hash or message digest. A hash is not the plaintext itself, but rather a unique identifier for the text, like a fingerprint. Note that hashing does not use keys at all, only algorithms, also making it less like encryption and decryption.

Theoretically, an identical piece of plaintext will always produce the same hash value, assuming that the same hashing algorithm is used. Likewise, no two different pieces of plaintext should ever produce the same hash, given the same algorithm. These accidentally matching hashes are called *collisions*. If any given hash algorithm can be made to collide, then a bad guy could in theory generate a piece of data with the right hash to fool others as to its integrity. Figure 2-13 illustrates the collision process a bit more clearly.

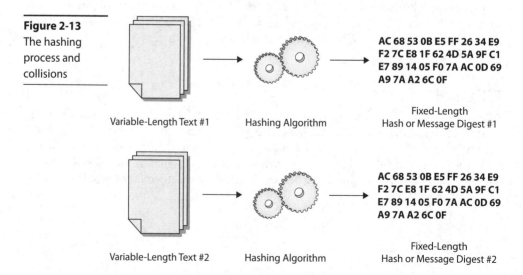

Figure 2-13 The hashing process and collisions

Variable-Length Text #1   Hashing Algorithm

AC 68 53 0B E5 FF 26 34 E9
F2 7C E8 1F 62 4D 5A 9F C1
E7 89 14 05 F0 7A AC 0D 69
A9 7A A2 6C 0F

Fixed-Length
Hash or Message Digest #1

Variable-Length Text #2   Hashing Algorithm

AC 68 53 0B E5 FF 26 34 E9
F2 7C E8 1F 62 4D 5A 9F C1
E7 89 14 05 F0 7A AC 0D 69
A9 7A A2 6C 0F

Fixed-Length
Hash or Message Digest #2

Several older hashing algorithms can produce collisions. As this module addresses the different hashing algorithms, I'll point out the older, collision-prone algorithms.

 NOTE Hashing is not the same thing as encryption and decryption. Hashes cannot be reversed or decrypted; they can only be compared to see if they match.

If the purpose of hashing isn't to encrypt a piece of text that can be decrypted, then what do we use it for? Hashing is used to provide confidentiality (in the case of hashing passwords, for instance) and integrity. For confidentiality, a password can be "hashed" and the resulting hash sent over an untrusted network, if needed, for authentication, so the actual password is not transmitted (Figure 2-14).

When the authenticating server receives the hash, it's not decrypted to reveal the password (hashes can't be decrypted, remember), but the server takes the password hash it has stored in the credentials database and compares it to the hash it received. If they match, the server knows that the user also knew the correct password, and it allows authentication. If the hashes don't match, the server refuses authentication, because the user obviously did not know the correct password, which in turn did not generate the correct hash.

Password hashes are sometimes encrypted during transmission using symmetric key cryptography, and then decrypted on the receiving end so that the hash is protected during transmission. This is because attackers can intercept a password hash as it travels over the network. They don't have the actual password at that point, of course, and can't reverse the hash to get it, but they can use various methods to perform the same type of hash comparisons against a list of potential passwords and generate an identical hash, letting them discover the original password. An encrypted hash blunts that capability.

Because identical pieces of plaintext always produce the same hash value, if the same hashing algorithm is used on both, it's very easy to tell if a piece of text has changed, even by one binary digit (bit). If even a single 1 or 0 bit changes in the text, the hash produced will be different from the original piece of text. In this way, comparing hashes of two supposedly identical pieces of plaintext can verify the integrity of the original. If the hashes match when compared, the samples of text are identical and have not been altered. If the hashes are different when compared, however, then one can assume there has been a change (no matter how slight) between the original text and what was received, violating integrity.

Figure 2-14
Sending a
password's hash
instead of the
password itself

EXAM TIP Hashing can be used to assure both confidentiality and integrity.

MD5

The *Message Digest version 5 (MD5)* hashing algorithm generates a 128-bit hash, 32 hexadecimal characters long, and it replaced an earlier version of the MD series, MD4. It was found to have weaknesses in it that showed the potential for collisions and has been proven again and again as unsuitable for further implementation—as early as 1996, and again most recently in 2007. It is still in widespread use, however, for low-security situations, but it should not be used in applications requiring serious security. MD5 is also used as part of other cryptographic methods, including the Extensible Authentication Protocol (EAP), as part of its EAP-MD5 implementation.

 EXAM TIP MD5 produces a 128-bit message digest, consisting of 32 hexadecimal characters, regardless of the length of the input text.

SHA

The *Secure Hash Algorithm (SHA)* is a series of hashing functions sponsored by NIST as a U.S. government standard. There have been several iterations of SHA, including SHA-0, SHA-1, SHA-2, and SHA-3. SHA-1 is a 160-bit algorithm, originally designed to be used as the standardized Digital Signature Algorithm for the United States. It produces 40-character hashes. SHA-1 was a contemporary of MD5 and had similar cryptographic flaws. SHA-2 is made up of two separate algorithms, SHA-256 and SHA-512, but each has minor versions that include SHA-224 and SHA-384. SHA-3 uses a hash function called Keccak that makes it different internally than SHA-1 and SHA-2. It has the same hash lengths as the SHA-2 versions.

 EXAM TIP SHA-1 and SHA-2 have been replaced by the latest iteration of SHA, known as SHA-3, which is an implementation of the Keccak hashing function. Also, you might see SHA on the exam as Secure *Hashing* Algorithm, so don't get confused. The exam means SHA.

RIPEMD

RACE Integrity Primitives Evaluation Message Digest (RIPEMD) is a hashing algorithm not often seen in practical implementation. It was developed in an open-standard type of environment, as opposed to SHA. RIPEMD comes in 128-, 160-, 256-, and 320-bit versions. Again, it is not in widespread use, despite the relatively stable and secure implementation of the RIPEMD-160 iteration, which is the most common.

HMAC

Hash Message Authentication Code (HMAC) is used in conjunction with a symmetric key both to authenticate and verify the integrity of the message. HMAC can use either MD5 or SHA series of hashing algorithms (and noted as HMAC-MD5 or HMAC-SHA1/2/3, respectively). The HMAC process produces a hash value, the *message authentication code (MAC)*, whose length and strength corresponds to whichever hashing algorithm was used to create it. Here's how it works.

You already know that a given piece of plaintext or message produces the same hash every time, as long as you use the same hashing algorithm. This can be used to verify integrity; however, anyone can send a message that can be verified in terms of integrity, if the hashes match. But you cannot verify the authenticity of the message—that is, who sent it—and you cannot verify who will be able to receive it.

HMAC uses a secret (symmetric) key with the hashing process, so that a given message produces a unique hash using that symmetric key. If someone does not have the key, she cannot reproduce the hash of the message, so that neither integrity nor authenticity can be verified. Only someone who has the secret key can successfully produce the same hash. This verifies not only integrity, but also authenticity, since only the person having the secret key could have produced that unique hash and sent the message.

 EXAM TIP   HMAC can use hashing functions and symmetric keys to produce a message authentication code (MAC), used to ensure both integrity and authenticity of a message.

Module 2-6: Digital Signatures and Certificates

This module covers the following CompTIA Security+ objective:

- **1.3**   Explain threat actor types and attributes

Asymmetric encryption relies heavily on trust. When you access a secure Web site to make a purchase, for example, you need to trust in the security of the connection between the Web server and your client before putting in a credit card number. Two related cryptographic functions create this security, digital signatures and digital certificates.

Digital Signatures

Secure Web sites use RSA keys for asymmetric encryption. Every connection to a secure Web site requires a key exchange. At the very least, the Web server provides its public key to the client so the client can encrypt messages securely. In some cases, the client will share its public key (Figure 2-15).

The challenge to key exchange isn't handing out the keys. The Web server and client can automatically share their public keys the moment they connect. The problem comes

Figure 2-15
Secure Web site,
Hello!

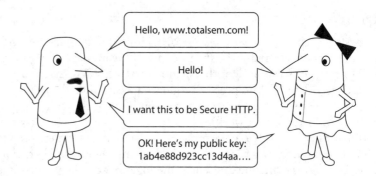

with the key itself. Imagine a scenario where a third party intercepts the data and tries to send a bogus public key to the client (Figure 2-16). Digital signatures address this scenario.

To send a message in a typical asymmetric encryption cryptosystem, the sender encrypts using the recipient's public key; the recipient decrypts using her private key. The reverse, however, can also work. The sender can encrypt with his *private* key; the only key that would enable decryption is his *public* key. This concept makes digital signatures possible. Here's the full process of creating a digital signature.

To prove that the public key your client receives came from the proper server, the Web server adds a digital signature. The Web server takes the current Web page and does the following:

1. Encrypts the page with the client's public key.

2. Hashes the page.

3. Encrypts the hash with the server's private key.

4. Sends the page, the public key, and the hash to the client.

Now it's the client's turn:

1. The client decrypts the hash using the server's public key to verify it really came from the server. (Only the server's public key can decrypt something encrypted with the server's private key.)

2. The client decrypts the message with the client's private key.

Figure 2-17 helps describe this process.

Figure 2-16
Third parties can
be evil!

Figure 2-17
Proof that the message came from the owner of the private key

The hash value encrypted with the private key and that accompanies the public key is a *digital signature*.

NOTE Digital signatures are one of the very few places where private keys are used to encrypt. Normally, public keys encrypt and private keys decrypt.

Digital signatures alone work great to verify the identity of a source. Successfully decrypting the message using the source's public key means the message could only have come from that source.

Digital Certificates

A digital signature is only good for verifying that the entity who sent you a public key is legitimately the one who possesses the corresponding private key. But how do you know that public key really came from the Web site, or the owner of that e-mail address, or the VPN service or whatever other thing you want to connect to that you need to know you can trust? You need something more than a digital signature (Figure 2-18).

You might at this point say, "I know I'm on the right Web site because it says so in the address bar" or, "I know this e-mail came from mike@totalsem.com, because that's who the e-mail said it came from." This is not acceptable. First, it's easy to make another Web site look just like one you know (Figure 2-19). Equally, it's easy to make another service—e-mail is a great example—look like it came from another source. This process is called *spoofing*. Simply relying on the fact that something looks like it's a legitimate source isn't good enough. (And how closely do most people look at URLs anyway?)

Worse, a bad guy can use Unicode to whack out URLs to the point where you could swear you knew where you were, but you were at a completely different URL.

To create trust in this scenario requires a *digital certificate*, an electronic file specifically formatted using industry standards that contains identifying information. That's a mouthful!

Figure 2-18 Who can you trust?

Think of a digital certificate like a Word document with a bunch of spaces to fill in with specific information. There are different digital certificate "forms" for different jobs (e-mail, Web servers, code signing, and many more). Any digital certificate will store a public key with a digital signature, personal information about the resource (URL, e-mail address, phone numbers, whatever), and a second digital signature from a third party you both trust (Figure 2-20).

Figure 2-19 It's easy to deceive.

Figure 2-20
A certificate
should have
a third-party
signature.

The rest of this module concentrates on the types of digital certificates and their formats, and tours a typical certificate on a PC.

 NOTE Module 2-7, "Public Key Infrastructure," goes into depth on maintaining digital certificates.

Touring a Certificate

Let's look at a digital certificate. In Windows, you can see your certificates by opening any Web browser's Settings and locating a certificates option. In Google Chrome, for example, click the icon with three vertical dots in the upper-right corner and choose Settings. Scroll down and click Advanced. Under HTTPS/SSL, click the Manage Certificates button to open the Certificates dialog box (Figure 2-21).

 NOTE All Web browsers have a certificate location. Take your time, you'll find it.

The Certificates dialog box features several tabs. For this module, pick any tab, select any certificate on that tab, and then click View (or whatever your system says) to see the certificate in detail. You should see something like Figure 2-22.

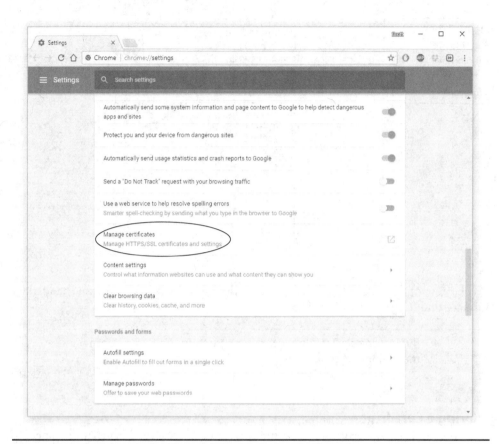

Figure 2-21 Getting to the Certificates dialog box in Google Chrome

Now click the Details tab at the top. On the Show pull-down menu, select Version 1 Fields Only to see something like Figure 2-23. Click each field as you read through the following descriptions to see what each value stores.

- **Version**   The common certificate format is *X.509*. It started with version 1. Modern certificates are version 3. This field shows the X.509 version of this certificate.
- **Serial number**   A unique number given to this certificate by the issuing body.
- **Signature algorithm**   The type of encryption and hash used by this certificate.
- **Signature hash algorithm**   Same as signature algorithm. (It's a Microsoft thing.)
- **Issuer**   X.509 formatted (CN, OU, O, C) name of issuer of this certificate.
- **Valid from**   Time the certificate was granted.
- **Valid to**   Time the certificate expires.
- **Subject**   To what this certificate is issued in X.509 format.
- **Public key**   The public key for the certificate.

Figure 2-22 Default certificate view in Windows

There's a lot more to see if you change Show: to <ALL>, but there are two fields that warrant note here:

- **Thumbprint**   The certificate's digital signature.
- **Authority Key Identifier**   The third party's digital signature.

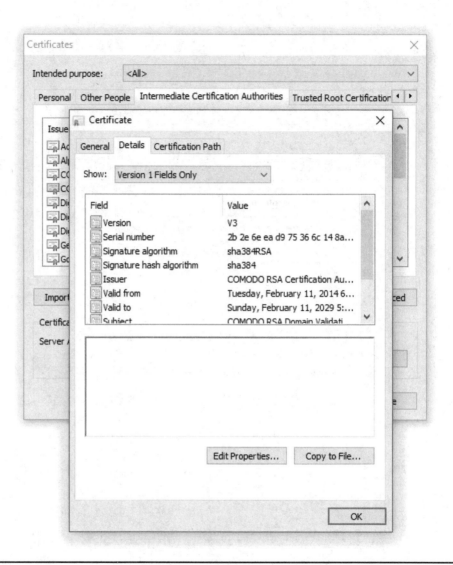

Figure 2-23   Typical certificate details in Windows

You'll be coming back to these settings in the next module as you go deeper into certificates.

Getting a Certificate

Virtually all cryptosystems that use asymmetric cryptography require a certificate. Probably the best example is a secure Web site. Let's say you want to set up a secure (HTTPS) Web server. You can spin up your own server and load some Web server software on your own, but if you want to use HTTPS, you'll need a certificate.

To get a certificate, submit information to some certificate issuing organization. There are a handful of these organizations, though four dominate the market: Comodo, Symantec (with its VeriSign branding), GoDaddy, and GlobalSign. Before you give them a credit card, you need to generate a Certificate Signing Request (CSR) on your Web server. Figure 2-24 shows part of this process in Microsoft Internet Information Services (IIS).

Once the CSR is created, there is usually some place to cut and paste this information into an online form. Depending on the certificate, you'll get your certificate sent via e-mail or through a Web interface. In most cases, the certificate installs itself. You can import if necessary.

NOTE You don't have to pay for third parties to sign certificates (https://letsencrypt.org is a popular free issuer). Self-signed certificates work just fine *within* your network for services that require certificates—applications and such on the corporate intranet, for example. There's no reason to pay for certificates for internal use. Make certain those self-signed or untrusted-signed certificates never see the rest of the world.

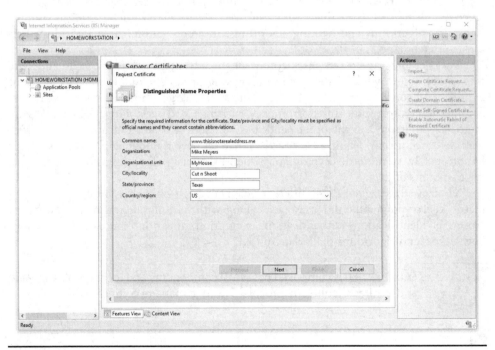

Figure 2-24   Creating a CSR in IIS

Module 2-7: Public Key Infrastructure

This module covers the following CompTIA Security+ objective:

- **6.4** Given a scenario, implement public key infrastructure

Public key infrastructure (PKI) implementations combine symmetric and asymmetric key cryptographic methods with hashing to create robust and secure systems. This module puts together all the information in Modules 1–6 of this chapter to describe these systems.

The module starts with keys, algorithms, and standards. The second section explores PKI services. The third section discusses digital certificates and PKI structures. We'll look at additional aspects of PKI next and then finish with trust models.

PKI puts cryptography into practical application. IT professionals use PKI to implement strong authentication and encryption schemes to protect data confidentiality and integrity, and ensure non-repudiation. Let's get started.

Keys, Algorithms, and Standards

I've already discussed all the different algorithms and key types that I'll mention here when discussing PKI. Note that PKI doesn't use only asymmetric algorithms; it also uses symmetric algorithms and hashing algorithms. In combination, these algorithms help make different aspects of PKI work.

Hybrid cryptographic systems incorporate the advantages of asymmetric and symmetric algorithms, while at the same time making up for the disadvantages each have. Symmetric algorithms are fast, and they can encrypt large amounts of data efficiently. Symmetric cryptography suffers from key exchange and scalability problems. Asymmetric cryptography, on the other hand, has no issues with key exchange. It's also very scalable, since it only requires that each individual have a public and private key pair. Unfortunately, asymmetric cryptography doesn't do very well with speed or encrypting large amounts of data.

PKI takes advantage of these different positive aspects of both asymmetric and symmetric key cryptography and uses each, along with hashing algorithms, for different aspects of identification, authentication, encryption, and non-repudiation. Let's look now at keys and algorithms that relate to PKI.

 EXAM TIP PKI is composed of several components and technologies, as well as the infrastructure and processes used to manage certificates.

Keys

In asymmetric cryptography, there is a public and private key pair. Both keys are mathematically related, but you cannot use one to derive the other. The keys are generated using various mathematical algorithms. What one key in a pair encrypts, only the other key in the same pair can decrypt. Public keys are given to anyone who wants them, and pri-

Figure 2-25
Communicating using public and private keys

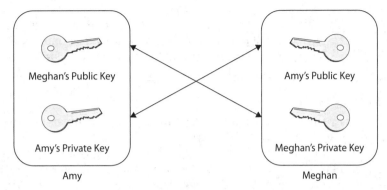

vate keys are kept confidential, protected by the individuals who own them. To exchange messages between two parties, each must have a public and private key pair. Each party must also possess the public key of the other party. When one person wants to send an encrypted message to the other, the sender encrypts the message using the receiver's public key. Then, the receiver decrypts it using her private key, since that's the only key in the pair that can decrypt what the public key encrypts. This is demonstrated in Figure 2-25.

Symmetric cryptography, on the other hand, uses only one key. Both parties must possess that same key to decrypt data. The problem, as I mentioned with symmetric key cryptography, is that key exchange can be an issue if keys can't be sent securely between parties. I discussed how messages can be sent back and forth between parties using public and private keys, but if the messages require speed or large volumes of data, public key cryptography isn't enough.

The hybrid approach is to generate a session key, using various key exchange methods, and get the key securely to both parties. The session key, once it is generated, can be encrypted using public keys and then sent on in encrypted format to the receiving party. The receiving party can then decrypt the encrypted session key with her own private key. After that, faster communications can take place using the symmetric session key.

Using this hybrid approach with asymmetric and symmetric keys ensures confidentiality, since both data and the session keys are encrypted. It doesn't, however, ensure authenticity or integrity of the message, nor does it provide for non-repudiation. That's why hashing algorithms are added into the process to help provide those services; I'll discuss those momentarily.

Algorithms

I've also already discussed the different algorithms, both symmetric and asymmetric, employed in PKI. These include symmetric algorithms such as AES and asymmetric algorithms such as RSA for key generation and Diffie-Hellman for key exchange. As you'll see shortly, hashing algorithms are also used in PKI; again, these algorithms are the same as those used for other hashing applications and include MD5, RIPEMD, and the SHA family of algorithms. Although a wide variety of different algorithms from each of these types can be used, different standardized PKI methods may require the use of algorithms specific for that method. I'll discuss some of the various PKI standards next.

NOTE PKI uses not only asymmetric algorithms and keys, but also symmetric algorithms and keys and hashing algorithms, all working together to perform different functions and provide services.

PKI Standards

PKI implementations use one of several standards. The primary standard is X.509; other standards apply to specific industries.

The International Telecommunication Union - Telecommunication Standardization Sector (ITU-T) *X.509* standard describes how digital certificates are constructed, including what information they will contain, their uses, and their formatting. The X.509 standard also describes processes involved with issuing certificates, as well as other processes in the certificate lifecycle.

Other standards that you will encounter in PKI come from different industry segments and are sometimes considered somewhat proprietary, although they are usually compliant with open standards. One set of these standards is the Public Key Cryptography Standards (PKCS), developed by RSA Security. The PKCS describe particulars about certificate construction and use. For instance, a PKCS #7 file is a digital certificate used to sign or encrypt messages, such as e-mail. A PKCS #12 file contains public and private keys and is encrypted for secure key storage.

Other vendors, such as Microsoft and Apple, for example, also have their own proprietary way of issuing and managing certificates throughout their lifecycle, although these standards are usually compliant with the X.509 standards.

EXAM TIP The primary standard used in PKI is the X.509 standard, which describes the certificate format and how it is used.

PKI Services

In addition to confidentiality, PKI provides for secure key exchange, message authentication and integrity, and non-repudiation. The next few sections discuss how PKI provides these different services. We'll also revisit digital signatures.

Key Generation and Exchange

PKI has technologies and methods built-in for several different processes. Among those are key generation and key exchange. *Key generation* is the process of creating a public and private key pair, which is then issued to an individual, based upon his or her confirmed identity. RSA is the most popular key generation algorithm, although there are others. *Key exchange* is a process, typically using Diffie-Hellman algorithms, which assists in the creation and secure exchange of symmetric keys, typically session keys used for one communications session only. After keys are generated, public and private keys are used to encrypt and decrypt session keys once they are transmitted and received, respectively, by both parties.

Non-repudiation

Non-repudiation means that a person cannot deny that he took a specific action. His identity has been positively verified, and any actions he takes are traced back to that identity.

PKI assures non-repudiation using public and private keys. As you will learn later when I discuss certificate authorities, an individual must be positively identified and authenticated to the certificate authority before a key pair is issued. Once a key pair is issued, the individual's digital certificate is digitally signed using the private key of the issuing organization. Signing a digital certificate by the entity that issues it means that the issuer confirms that they have validated the user's identity. Because only the issuing organization can sign with its private key, this verifies that the certificate came from a valid issuing organization.

Once an individual is in possession of a key pair, assuming he fulfills his responsibilities in protecting the private key, then any message he signs using his private key can be authenticated as originating from that individual. If a message is signed using a key pair owned by an individual, he cannot deny that he sent the message. This assures non-repudiation.

Message Integrity

PKI can provide message integrity through hashing algorithms. Using hashing algorithms such as SHA-512, for instance, you can hash messages to generate unique fingerprints, or hashes that can be checked both before transmission and after the message is received. If the hashes compare and match, you can be assured of data integrity. If they compare and do not match, you know that something (or someone) has changed the integrity of the message. Message integrity can be altered accidentally through simple "bit-flipping" during bad transmission conditions or intentionally by some malicious actor.

Message integrity is assured by also incorporating hashing algorithms into the PKI process. Although there are several possible ways to do this, the simplest way is to hash the message and encrypt both the message and the hash and send them on to the recipient, so that when the recipient gets the message, he can simply decrypt the message with his private key and then rehash the message to generate a hash that he can compare to the hash that was received. Obviously, the recipient doesn't really do all of this manually; PKI is an automatic set of processes that take care of all this at the application level.

Digital Signatures

PKI systems incorporate digital signatures to authenticate the source of a message. Encrypting a message with a private key assures the recipient of the source when the corresponding public key decrypts that message. Add in the hashing component of digital signatures and you've got a winning combination, as discussed back in Module 2-6.

Digital Certificates and PKI Structure

This section explores how a basic public key infrastructure organization works, describing some of the elements in a PKI, such as the certificate and registration authorities, as well as the certificate revocation list. First, however, we'll take another look at digital certificates and describe them in more detail.

Digital Certificates

As mentioned earlier, digital certificates are simple electronic files. The X.509 and PKCS standards determine the specific formats for digital certificates, as well as the file types and formats. Digital certificates come in a variety of file formats, including those with .cer and .pem file extensions. Additionally, there is a variety of types of certificate files, and each of these may fulfill a unique function in a PKI, such as a certificate request file. Digital certificates can be stored on several types of media, such as USB sticks, mobile devices, internal computer storage, and even centralized repositories on a network or the Internet.

Certificates are used for many purposes; you may see multipurpose certificates or certificates that are issued for very specific purposes. For example, a digital certificate may be issued for the purposes of signing and encrypting e-mails, or for network identification and authentication purposes, or even to identify servers or digitally sign software, verifying its authenticity from a publisher. Certificates typically contain a variety of information, including the public key of the individual and information that identifies that person, the issuing organization, and valid dates and functions for the certificate to be used. Figure 2-26 shows an example of a digital certificate file, as presented in a browser. Notice the different types of information that can be included with the certificate.

Figure 2-26

A digital certificate

Certificate Registration

The process of managing a digital certificate from issuance, through use, and finally disposal, is referred to as managing the certificate over its lifecycle. A digital certificate's lifecycle begins when a user registers to receive a certificate. The person requesting the certificate must register and provide valid identification to the *certificate authority*, the entity that issues and controls the digital certificates. *Registration* usually means the user must present identification that can be authenticated by the issuing organization. This confirms that the organization has verified the person's identity. Valid forms of identification that a requester may submit include her driver's license, birth certificate, passport, photographs, and any other identification that the issuing organization requires. Once a user has submitted the required identification, the certificate authority decides on whether to issue the certificate, and under what circumstances.

NOTE Before a certificate is issued to an individual, his or her identity must be positively verified.

Certificate Authority

A *certificate authority (CA)* issues and controls digital certificates. This might be a commercial organization, such as GoDaddy, or it could be the user's organization. Often, private organizations have their own internal certificate authorities that issue digital certificates used specifically within the logical bounds of the organization. The certificate authority also manages the certificate server (also sometimes referred to as the CA server), which is the actual host computer that generates keys and produces digital certificate files.

The certificate authority normally handles all user registration, identification, and validation processes, and it issues digital certificates to the user. In larger organizations, to help balance the workload for the CA, registration functions may be delegated to a separate registration authority (RA), which verifies user identities and then passes the information on to the actual CA for certificate generation.

The CA makes decisions on whether the certificate should be issued, under what circumstances, and with what caveats. When an entity requests a certificate, it submits a CSR as previously mentioned. The CA then reviews the *certificate signing request (CSR)*, which contains the information that will be embedded in the digital certificate, including the public key, organization name, common name, and so on. The CA then generates a certificate for the requesting entity. Once a certificate is generated, the CA is also responsible for performing actions on certificates, such as renewing, suspending, or revoking them, as needed. These actions are discussed later in the module.

EXAM TIP A certificate authority (CA) is the primary element in PKI.

Certificate Servers

Smaller organizations may use only one or two servers that manage all their certificate needs. Larger organizations, however, may have an entire hierarchy of servers. At the top of this hierarchy is the single master server, called the *root CA server*. The root issues its own self-signed certificate, unless the organization purchases and receives one from an external certificate provider.

The root can also issue certificates for any other use, but it typically issues trusted certificates only to other servers that can be set up and used as intermediate or subordinate servers. These intermediate servers may perform all the different certificate authority functions, or they may perform only very specific functions, depending upon the needs of the organization. Normally, once an organization has set up intermediate or subordinate servers, the root CA is taken offline to protect it against possible compromise. It may be brought back up online only occasionally for maintenance or to update certificate information. Figure 2-27 shows a typical arrangement of a hierarchy of certificate servers in an organization.

 NOTE The root CA is normally taken offline after intermediate and subordinate CAs are set up, to prevent compromise of the server and the root certificate. If this root certificate is compromised, all subordinate certificates that have been issued or signed by the root are also considered compromised and should be treated as no longer valid or trustworthy.

Certificate Revocation Lists

The CA publishes a *certificate revocation list (CRL)* that contains the certificates the entity has issued and subsequently revoked. Users can access this list to determine the validity of a certificate. If a certificate has been revoked, it is considered no longer valid and cannot be used. Certificate revocation lists can be published online, or they can be part of an automated process that application software checks from a centralized repository.

Figure 2-27
A hierarchy of
certificate servers

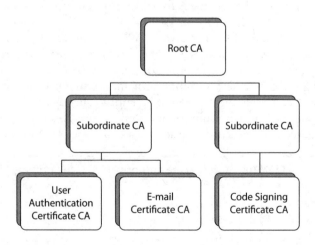

Similarly, the *Online Certificate Status Protocol (OCSP)* is used to automate certificate validation, making checking the status of certificates seamless and transparent to the user. Most modern browsers and other applications that use digital certificates can use OCSP to check CRLs automatically for certificate validity. A sample from a CRL, downloaded to a user's browser, is shown in Figure 2-28.

PKI Considerations

A digital certificate has a defined lifecycle. It begins with registering the user, validating his or her identity, generating a CSR and certificate, and issuing the certificate to the user. During its useful lifecycle, however, several events can take place that affect the validity of a certificate. We'll discuss those in this section, as well as other considerations with digital certificates such as recovery agents and key escrow.

Certificate Expiration, Suspension, and Revocation

Certificates do not last forever. Certificates remain valid only for a specific period of time, and after that time they expire. This is because, like passwords, certificates could be compromised. Expiring a certificate enables a user and the CA to monitor certificate

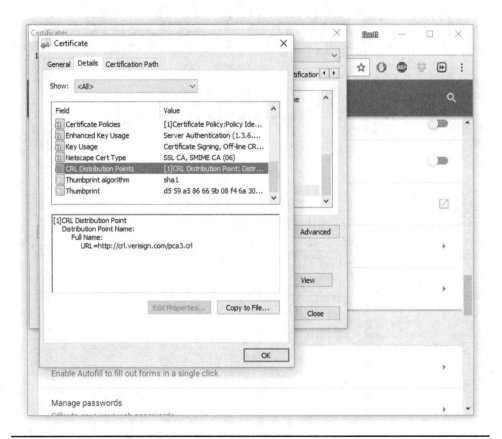

Figure 2-28   A small sample of a CRL entry from VeriSign

compromise and periodically reissue certificates to ensure that a compromised certificate isn't used over long periods of time.

CA rules determine certificate lifetimes. An average time might be three years, but it may be a longer or lesser period, depending upon the circumstances under which the certificate was issued. For example, a temporary employee might receive a digital certificate that's good for only a year. Before a certificate expires, the user and the issuing organization must take steps to revalidate the user, as well as their need for the certificate, and reissue it. A user cannot use an expired and thus invalid certificate. Most browsers and applications will display errors when trying to use or accept an expired certificate. Figure 2-29 gives an example of an expired certificate.

Certificates can lose their validity even before their expiration dates. This usually requires some intervention from the CA and is usually because of adverse circumstances. A certificate may be suspended, which renders it invalid for a temporary, indefinite time period. Normally a certificate would be suspended if the user is on extended leave, or during an investigation, for instance. *Suspending* a certificate means that it could be reinstated, allowing a user to continue using the certificate, but only if and when the CA makes a conscious decision to do so.

Figure 2-29

An expired certificate

Revoking a certificate, on the other hand, means that the certificate is permanently rendered invalid. Once a digital certificate has been revoked, it can't be reissued or reused. The CA might revoke a certificate if a user no longer needs it, if the user has been terminated or retires, or if the certificate has been misused or compromised in any way. If a certificate has been revoked, the CA must reissue a totally different certificate to the user if the CA determines that the user requires it.

OCSP permits users (through Internet browsers and other certificate-aware applications) to check for certificate expiration, suspension, and revocation before the certificate is accepted. In Figure 2-30, you can see an example of a revoked certificate, which in this case is a famous example of a certificate erroneously issued to a fraudulent party claiming to be Microsoft. The certificate was quickly revoked after the error was discovered.

 EXAM TIP   Suspended certificates can be reused after the organization determines it is safe to reactivate them. Revoked certificates are never reused, and are considered invalid forever.

Recovery Agent

A *recovery agent* is a designated person or entity who has the authority to recover lost keys or data in the event the person holding the keys is not available. Recovery agents can

Figure 2-30
A revoked certificate

work in a few different ways. One way requires the individual to store his private key in a secure area that a recovery agent can access, in the event the individual is terminated or unavailable to decrypt data, for example, that had been encrypted with his private key. This would be the least desirable way, however, since non-repudiation would suffer because private keys are supposed to be kept private and confidential, and accessible only by the user. Another, more common way would be to have the recovery agent maintain a different key that can decrypt any data encrypted by an individual.

Key Escrow

As you'll recall from Module 2-1, *key escrow* is the practice of maintaining private keys, sometimes by an independent third party, so that they can be accessed in the event individuals are not able or unavailable to use them to recover data that has been encrypted. Organizations should approach this practice with caution, however, because, as mentioned previously, this can create issues with non-repudiation. A secure, carefully executed, and transparent method of key escrow should be examined before being put into practice. An organization may want to implement key escrow to guard against the possibility that an individual will encrypt sensitive data, and then leave the company suddenly, without a way for the organization to recover the data.

Trust Models

Most commercial certificate authorities are generally trusted by most browsers and applications, since their root certificate is usually contained in the root certificate store of most devices. Private certificate authorities, however, such as an internal CA that might issue certificates only to its own employees, may not generally be trusted by outside organizations. This would render the certificates they have issued as untrusted by anyone outside their own organization. Because of this, some trust models have evolved over the years to allow organizations to take advantage of each other's digital certificates, permitting some level of trust between them. Let's look at three trust modules:

- Hierarchical trust
- Cross-trust
- Web-of-trust

Hierarchical Trust

A *hierarchical trust* is normally found within an organization, particularly a larger organization, and involves trust in digital certificates within organizational boundaries. Often, there are intermediate or subordinate CAs within a large organization that must trust each other. One subordinate CA may issue e-mail certificates, for example, and another may issue code-signing certificates. All the certificates, however, can be traced back and trusted through the originating root CA. This is possible with a hierarchical trust model, such that all subordinate and intermediate CAs trust each other because they trust the original root CA. Look again at Figure 2-27, shown earlier, as an example of a hierarchical trust model.

Cross-Trust

A *cross-trust* model is often found between two different organizations. In this trust model, organizations typically have their own certificate authorities and issuing servers. However, because of business partner arrangements, they must trust each other's certificates so that their personnel can authenticate to access resources in each other's security domains. A cross-trust model enables organizations to have their root CAs trust each other (and the certificates they generate) or even specific subordinate CAs trust each other. This type of trust can be open to any certificate or limited only to very specific certificates issued under particular circumstances.

Web-of-Trust

A *web-of-trust* model is not typically used in a PKI. You'll most often see this type of model used in smaller groups or organizations, typically in those that allow individual users to generate their own public and private key pairs. The use of Pretty Good Privacy (PGP) and Gnu Privacy Guard (GPG) between small groups of users is a prime example of a web-of-trust. In this model, there is no central issuing authority that validates user identities. It is left up to each individual user to trust another user's certificates. While this works well in small groups, where each user has some level of assurance of the identity of another user, it's typically not scalable to large groups of people or organizations.

Module 2-8: Cryptographic Attacks

This module covers the following CompTIA Security+ objectives:

- **1.2** Compare and contrast types of attacks
- **2.2** Given a scenario, use appropriate software tools to assess the security posture of an organization
- **6.1** Compare and contrast basic concepts of cryptography

Cryptanalysis, the science of breaking encryption, is as old as encryption itself. From Louis XVI at his palace in Versailles to the latest state-sponsored attacks, encryption has been successfully attacked many times. This module looks at some of the more common cryptographic attacks and the tools used to perform them. Understanding these attacks and their tools provides a better understanding on how to keep data secure. (Plus, it's really fun to crack stuff!)

The module starts with a general discussion of attack strategies and then examines attackable data. The second section explores password-oriented attacks and the tools commonly used in the attacks. The module finishes with a look at a few attacks that are not password related.

Attack Strategies

Let's begin by considering where we can attack any given cryptosystem. Every cryptosystem has an underlying algorithm, a key (or in the case of hashes, a digest), or some implementation of the cryptosystem itself, all of which the attacker understands. All cryptographic algorithms are known and rarely change, in accordance with Kerckhoffs' principle. Every cryptographic attack starts by careful inspection of the cryptosystem and aggressively probing and experimenting to find some form of weakness in one of those three aspects.

> **NOTE** Every cryptosystem currently in use has countries, universities, private organizations, and individuals who constantly experiment with them, looking for weaknesses. We need this research so that a weakness may be discovered and shared with others in IT security and adjustments may be made.

Attack the Algorithm

Every cryptographic algorithm is crackable given enough time to research. This is why organizations and agencies such as the National Security Agency (NSA) update encryption standards every few years. As of this writing, the only symmetric encryption algorithm that has not shown any substantial weakness is AES. The danger here is that many modern cryptosystems can use pre-AES encryptions. Transport Layer Security (TLS), the cryptosystem used in every secure (HTTPS) Web site, may optionally (and foolishly) use pre-AES encryptions such as RC4 or DES. In this case, skilled cryptographers can crack TLS by attacking the underlying algorithm.

> **NOTE** No secure Web server package will easily allow you to use non-AES encryptions.

Attack the Key

Given that virtually every cryptosystem uses some form of key, it's obvious that cryptanalysis will look at the key for weaknesses or, more importantly, attempt to determine the key simply by attacking at the ciphertext. One of the great weaknesses is key length. Modern increases in computing power make it easier to crack keys that were once considered too long to crack.

Consider a bike lock with only four wheels versus a bike lock with many more than four (Figure 2-31). Which of these is faster to crack? The same concept applies to keys. Taking a piece of ciphertext and trying every possible key until something that looks like plaintext appears is a brute-force attack. (More on those shortly.)

DES has an effective key length of only 56 bits. That means it has a *key space* (the total number of possible keys) of 2^{56} or 72,057,594,037,927,936 different combinations. This number seems like an impossibly large number of combinations, but specialized computing systems like the Electronic Freedom Federation's Deep Crack cracked a DES key in 22 hours ... back in 1998. Today, a high-end desktop computer's processing power isn't too far from that same power.

Figure 2-31
Two bike locks—
which is easier
to crack?

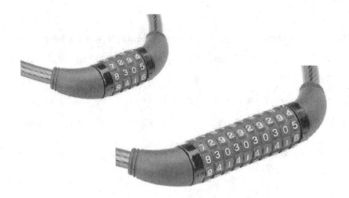

Attack the Implementation

Some implementations of new cryptosystems have some inherent flaw that causes an unanticipated weakness that is no fault of the underlying algorithm. The *Wired Equivalent Privacy (WEP)* was a complete 802.11 encryption cryptosystem, introduced with the first generation of 802.11 WAPs in 1999. Widely adopted, within a year it was discovered that WEP poorly implemented the way it used the underlying RC4 encryption. That flaw enabled a simple cryptanalysis to derive the key simply by collecting enough encrypted data.

Attackable Data

No cipher attack is going to work if you don't have access to something crackable. This crackable data can be divided into two different types: ciphertext or hashes. Before we go about attacking anything, let's first create two example scenarios: one with ciphertext and another with hashes. Then we'll attack.

Ciphertext Scenario

Let's use a single example of an 802.11 network encrypted with Wi-Fi Protected Access Pre-Shared Key (WPA-PSK). When a client connects to a WAP, they go through a simple handshake procedure that determines that each side stores the same PSK. This process does not transmit the key, but contains enough information to provide the key to a skilled hacker. Programmers have developed applications that can capture WPA handshakes. Figure 2-32 shows the popular Aircrack-ng program grabbing a handshake.

NOTE An online attack is executed against data-in-transit. An offline attack is done against data-at-rest.

Once this handshake is captured, the attacker has a value upon which he can apply a 128-bit key. If he places the correct 128-bit key, the attacker can determine the PSK.

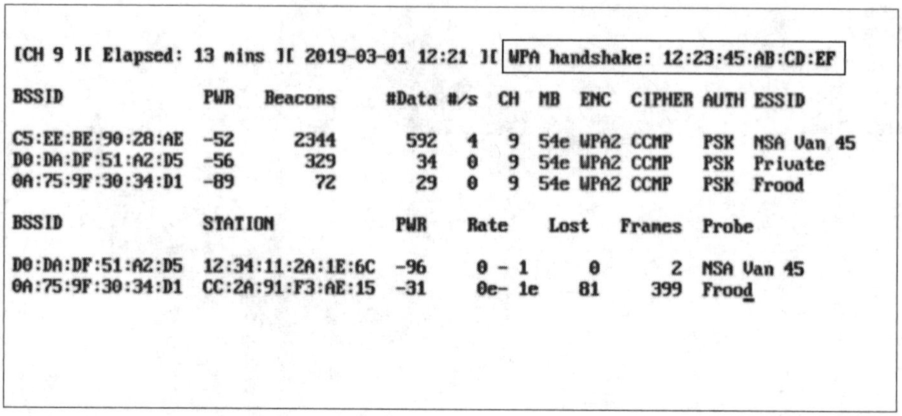

```
┌─────────────────────────────────────────────────────────────────────────────┐
│ [CH 9 ][ Elapsed: 13 mins ][ 2019-03-01 12:21 ][┌WPA handshake: 12:23:45:AB:CD:EF┐
│                                                                                │
│ BSSID              PWR    Beacons     #Data #/s  CH  MB  ENC  CIPHER AUTH ESSID │
│                                                                                │
│ C5:EE:BE:90:28:AE  -52     2344        592   4    9  54e WPA2 CCMP   PSK  NSA Van 45 │
│ D0:DA:DF:51:A2:D5  -56      329         34   0    9  54e WPA2 CCMP   PSK  Private │
│ 0A:75:9F:30:34:D1  -89       72         29   0    9  54e WPA2 CCMP   PSK  Frood  │
│                                                                                │
│ BSSID              STATION             PWR   Rate   Lost  Frames  Probe        │
│                                                                                │
│ D0:DA:DF:51:A2:D5  12:34:11:2A:1E:6C   -96   0 - 1     0       2  NSA Van 45    │
│ 0A:75:9F:30:34:D1  CC:2A:91:F3:AE:15   -31   0e- 1e   81     399  Frood         │
│                                                                                │
└─────────────────────────────────────────────────────────────────────────────┘
```

Figure 2-32   Aircrack-ng grabbing a WPA handshake

Hash Scenario

Many cryptographic attacks target cracking passwords. Let's start this scenario with a review of the where, how, and why of passwords.

A computer system or application that requires password authentication must contain a database or *table* of passwords. Because these password tables are potentially vulnerable to anyone with the technical knowledge to locate them and try to crack them, storing a plaintext password is dangerous. It is extremely common, therefore, not to store the password, but instead store a cryptographic hash of a user's password in the database.

The following is a sample of a hypothetical password list, consisting of four user names with their associated passwords stored as MD5 hashes. How can you tell they are MD5? Simply by counting the number of characters! This sample could be used for many applications. This example uses a text file; a password list could be a text file, a binary file, a cookie, or registry settings, depending on the application or the operating system that uses the passwords.

Mike, bd4c4ea1b44a8ff2afa18dfd261ec2c8
Steve, 4015e9ce43edfb0668ddaa973ebc7e87
Janet, 8cbad96aced40b3838dd9f07f6ef5772
Penny, 48cccca3bab2ad18832233ee8dff1b0b

Now that you have the hashes, you can hash every possible conceptual password to see if you can match the hash.

Attack Scenarios

The ciphertext and hash scenarios presented have common features. Both rely on a single data point: either ciphertext or a hash. Both have a clearly understood algorithm: WPA and MD5. Finally, you can use an attack to apply a key to obtain plaintext. But how do bad actors *perform* this attack? What tools do they use to read that ciphertext or hash and try to extract the plaintext key or password? Programs called *password crackers* or *password recovery tools* can perform these attacks. Password crackers come in a broad assortment of functions and interfaces. A Linux-based attacker, for example, uses Jack the Ripper or Hashcat (Figure 2-33). A Windows-based attacker might employ the venerable Cain & Abel (Figure 2-34).

In general, all these tools follow similar patterns. First, they grab the ciphertext or hashes you want to attack. Second, they analyze the data to determine the type of encryption (or they know the encryption by the source). Finally, they give you the option to attack in most, if not all, of the ways listed in this module.

Let's look at three common attack types that apply to these password-based scenarios:

```
root@et:~/hashcat# ./hashcat -m 15100 -a 3 -w 3 hash.txt ?l?l?l?l?l?lt
hashcat (v3.5.0) starting...

OpenCL Platform #1: NVIDIA Corporation
========================================
* Device #1: GeForce GTX 1080, 2026/8107 MB allocatable, 20MCU
* Device #2: GeForce GTX 1080, 2028/8114 MB allocatable, 20MCU
* Device #3: GeForce GTX 1080, 2028/8114 MB allocatable, 20MCU
* Device #4: GeForce GTX 1080, 2028/8114 MB allocatable, 20MCU

Hashes: 1 digests; 1 unique digests, 1 unique salts
Bitmaps: 16 bits, 65536 entries, 0x0000ffff mask, 262144 bytes, 5/13 rotates

Applicable optimizers:
* Zero-Byte
* Single-Hash
* Single-Salt
* Brute-Force

Watchdog: Temperature abort trigger set to 90c
Watchdog: Temperature retain trigger set to 75c

$sha1$20000$46487265$5EZZAHiEWP.Hwufke.kRNWOA.sg1:hashcat

Session..........: hashcat
Status...........: Cracked
Hash.Type........: Juniper/NetBSD sha1crypt
Hash.Target......: $sha1$20000$46487265$5EZZAHiEWP.Hwufke.kRNWOA.sg1
Time.Started.....: Wed Apr  5 11:37:22 2017 (2 mins, 8 secs)
Time.Estimated...: Wed Apr  5 11:39:30 2017 (0 secs)
Guess.Mask.......: ?l?l?l?l?l?lt [7]
Guess.Queue......: 1/1 (100.00%)
Speed.Dev.#1.....:   184.8 kH/s (91.44ms)
Speed.Dev.#2.....:   184.9 kH/s (91.24ms)
Speed.Dev.#3.....:   184.8 kH/s (91.30ms)
Speed.Dev.#4.....:   184.8 kH/s (91.53ms)
Speed.Dev.#*.....:   739.3 kH/s
Recovered........: 1/1 (100.00%) Digests, 1/1 (100.00%) Salts
Progress.........: 93716480/308915776 (30.34%)
Rejected.........: 0/93716480 (0.00%)
Restore.Point....: 0/11881376 (0.00%)
Candidates.#1....: harinat -> hmldcot
Candidates.#2....: waktltt -> wltxslt
Candidates.#3....: wkjytrt -> wqcduct
Candidates.#4....: wswsbut -> wwpfsit
HwMon.Dev.#1.....: Temp: 53c Fan:100% Util:100% Core:1936MHz Mem:4513MHz Bus:1
HwMon.Dev.#2.....: Temp: 59c Fan:100% Util:100% Core:1949MHz Mem:4513MHz Bus:1
HwMon.Dev.#3.....: Temp: 54c Fan:100% Util:100% Core:1949MHz Mem:4513MHz Bus:1
HwMon.Dev.#4.....: Temp: 55c Fan:100% Util:100% Core:1936MHz Mem:4513MHz Bus:1

Started: Wed Apr  5 11:37:17 2017
Stopped: Wed Apr  5 11:39:30 2017
```

Figure 2-33 Hashcat

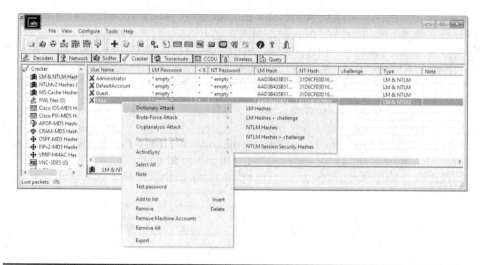

Figure 2-34   Cain & Abel

- Brute-force attack
- Dictionary attack
- Rainbow-table attack

NOTE   There is no such thing as a do-it-all single password cracker. There are hundreds of different password crackers, each with a different niche depending on your needs.

Brute-Force Attack

A *brute-force attack* is the simplest and least-efficient type of attack against known ciphertext/hashes. Brute-force attempts to derive a password or key by inspecting either ciphertext or a hash and then trying every possible combination of key or hash until it can decrypt the plaintext or generate a match. The challenge to brute force is the total number of iterations necessary to try every possible key combination. Consider a captured WPA handshake. The key is 128-bit, so it can go from 128 zeros to 128 ones, plus all the combinations in between.

So, how long does it take to try 2^{128} combinations? Longer means more combinations and therefore harder, so 2^{128} is equal to

$$3.4028236692093846346337460743176821456 \times 10^{38}$$

That's a huge number, but computers are powerful. A single, very high-end Intel Core i7 can process at half a *trillion* floating point operations per second (FLOPS), and you can readily source a computer with a lot of these CPUs. Additionally, password crackers

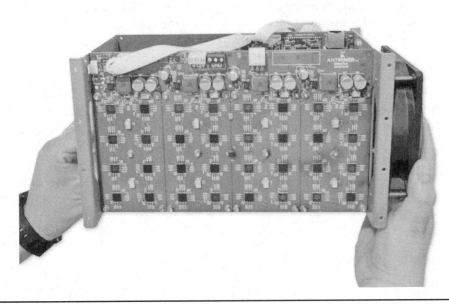

Figure 2-35   Typical ASIC

are carefully optimized to take advantage of all those FLOPS. In fact, the better crackers can even take advantage of powerful graphics processing units (GPUs) on video cards as well as special-purpose application-specific integrated circuit (ASIC) devices that work hundreds or even thousands of times faster than a CPU (Figure 2-35).

So, without spending outrageous text on the intricacies of CPUs, FLOPS, GPUs, and such, we can arguably say that a very high-end cracking system could process one trillion cracking attempts per second. It would take something like 10,790,283,070,806,014,188 years to try every possible key. If that seems like an impossibly long time to you, it is. Keep in mind that the key might be all zeros, which means you will get the WPA key on the very first try. Alternatively, the key might be all ones, which means you would have to try all 2^{128} combinations.

This might make you think that brute force is useless, and it is for relatively large keys. Shorter keys, however, can easily be cracked. For example, a 56-bit DES key can be cracked (using the preceding assumptions) in about 20 hours. As computing power increases, what was once a long key or hash becomes short. That's why keys and hashes get longer and longer over the years.

But even if we can run a brute-force attack in hours, why not come up with attacks that speed up the process? How can we narrow down the possible number of keys to try?

Dictionary Attack

Easily the weakest aspect to passwords is the fact that human beings create them. People produce passwords like this one:

Password123

This is a great password, right? It mixes upper- and lowercase with letters and numbers. Hmm … not so much when it comes to modern cryptographic attacks.

People rarely create a password that looks like this:

1x3^^7vEssde6)

That's a far more awesome password, but it's just not what typical people create.

With this thought in mind, we can tell our cracking program to read a text file filled with all the common words in the (in this case) English language—a *dictionary file*. The cracking software will then use this dictionary file instead of brute force in a *dictionary attack*. Here is a tiny, tiny piece of a dictionary file downloaded from the Internet:

A
AA
AAA
AAAA
a
aa
aaa
aaaa

As you can see, most dictionary files include lots of non-words as well. That's because non-words like "AAAA" or "QWERTY" or "NASA" are commonly used for passwords. A small dictionary file might only store a few million passwords. The largest dictionary files contain many millions of passwords.

Good dictionary attack tools don't try only passwords in the dictionary list. Check out the dictionary attack settings for Cain & Abel in Figure 2-36. Note the options that allow you to modify the dictionary. If your dictionary file has the word *cheese*, for example, Cain & Abel will let you

- Reverse the word: eseehc
- Double pass: cheesecheese
- Uppercase to lowercase: not applicable as cheese is all lowercase
- Lowercase to uppercase: CHEESE
- Number substitution: ch33s3
- Case permutations: Cheese, cHeese, etc.
- Add one or two numbers to the end: cheese1, cheese44

You can argue that these options add a brute-force aspect to a dictionary attack. A dictionary attack combined with brute-force options such as these is called a *hybrid attack*.

NOTE As a quick mental exercise, ask yourself this question: Would the Cain & Abel tool be able to derive any of the passwords you use?

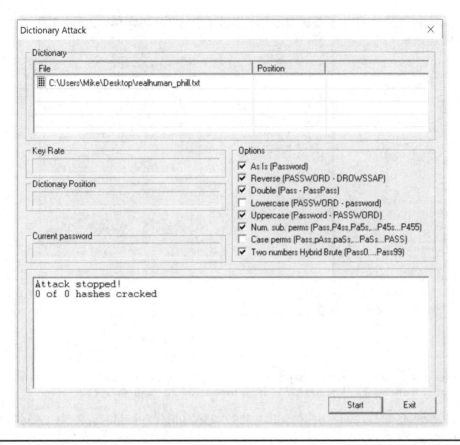

Figure 2-36 Cain & Abel dictionary options

Keep in mind there's a huge difference in the quality of dictionary files. I keep a set of dictionary files, accumulated over the years from many sources, sorted by length of password, lowercase/uppercase, special characters, numbers in front, and so forth. With good dictionary files, good understanding of the tools, and belief in the laziness of people to use poor passwords, I can crack most any offline password in a few hours.

What if you don't have any ciphertext to attack? What if you just want to try a few million passwords to try to log into a Web site? That's a classic *online attack* situation and it's no problem! There are plenty of online dictionary attack password crackers such as the popular Hydra (Figure 2-37). Online attacks are slow, but it's easy to start an attack and let it run for days or weeks.

Rainbow-Table Attack

The challenge to dictionary attacks, particularly when you are trying to crack hashed passwords, is the fact that you have to take a word in the dictionary, hash it, then compare the hash to the hash in the password file. You could include hash values for all the

Figure 2-37
Hydra in action

entries in a dictionary file using common hashing algorithms to increase the effectiveness of a dictionary attack. The SHA-256 hash for "password" will always be

$$5e884898da28047151d0e56f8dc6292773603d0d6aabbdd62a11ef721d1542d8$$

So, what if we edited our dictionary files to include the hash? Sure, it might take weeks to generate the billions of hashes and save them in our dictionary file, but once it's done we have a file that includes the dictionary word as well as the hash. Such a dictionary file would start like this:

a, ca978112ca1bbdcafac231b39a23dc4da786eff8147c4e72b9807785afee48bb
aa, 961b6dd3ede3cb8ecbaacbd68de040cd78eb2ed5889130cceb4c49268ea4d506
aaa, 9834876dcfb05cb167a5c24953eba58c4ac89b1adf57f28f2f9d09af107ee8f0
aaaa, 61be55a8e2f6b4e172338bddf184d6dbee29c98853e0a0485ecee7f27b9af0b4

Using such an inclusive dictionary file could make a dictionary attack brutally effective. Except there's a huge problem. Files like these are massive, potentially in the hundreds of petabytes range for dictionary files that include really long passwords. They are simply too big for practical use (Figure 2-38).

Math comes to the rescue! Well outside the scope of the CompTIA Security+ exam, complicated math can create a *rainbow table*, a dramatically reduced-sized dictionary file that includes hashed entries.

Figure 2-38
Simple dictionary
files with hashes
are too massive
for practical use.

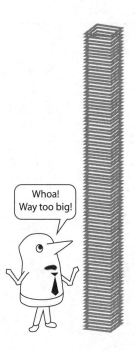

 NOTE Online vs. offline, which is better? You can run brute force, dictionary, and rainbow table attacks either way, but offline is faster if you have a key.

Rainbow tables are binary files, not text files. Figure 2-39 shows the contents of one set of rainbow tables, designed to help crack the old Windows XP–style List Manager passwords files. Rainbow tables for more advanced operating systems can be much larger, although always much smaller than a traditional dictionary file with hashes.

Rainbow tables were long the first choice for cracking passwords; such attacks are fast and generally very successful. Rainbow tables were so popular that you can find online services that let you load hashes to crack, and powerful systems will crack a password for just a few dollars (Figure 2-40). (Or, you can use GPU brute force, which is how modern hackers do it.)

Defending Password Storage

Between brute-force, dictionary, and rainbow attacks, traditional hash password storage has been under prolonged attack, making it important for cryptographers to come up with methods to make password storage more robust against these attacks. Salts and key stretching offer protections.

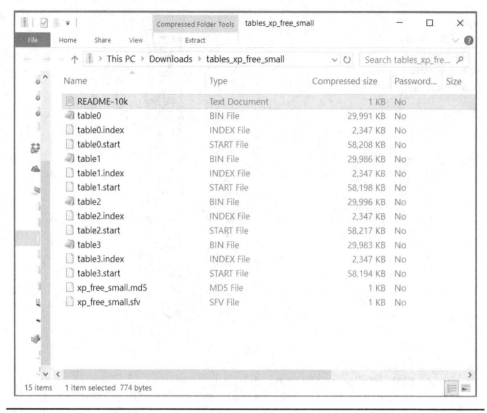

Figure 2-39 Rainbow tables for Windows XP passwords

Salts

A *salt* is an arbitrary value, usually created by the application or operating system storing passwords, added to the end of a password before it is hashed. If a user's password is 1234567, for example, a system might add an eight-character preset value, a salt, to the end of the password as such:

1234567akxcf3sf

When hashed (in this example SHA256), it looks like this:

a75f22d3cd5aea740f2a17b0275bfacd0c822aca

Salts defeat rainbow tables simply because (hopefully) there are no rainbow tables that include dictionary terms plus the string akxcf3sf. Salts are common in just about everything that stores passwords. The downside is that a salt must be stored. If someone had access to your hashes, they also have access to the salt. They can run dictionary attacks, but now they must add the salt every time and recalculate the hash, slowing cracking

Figure 2-40   One of many online cracking services

down immensely. Also, it is possible to grab a salt and re-create a rainbow table, although this is also a slow process.

> **NOTE**   All modern operating systems use salts in password storage.

A *nonce* is related to a salt, but differs in one key respect. A nonce is used once and then discarded.

Key Stretching

Another trick used to make cracking harder is key stretching. Keys are almost always generated from some plain English password. If we just hash the password, it doesn't take a lot of time for an attacker to pick a potential password, hash it, then compare the results to a password hash file. But what if we were to make the process by which a key is derived from a password more complex? We can do so with a *key derivation function*. What if, for example, we hashed an initial password five times to then derive the key? This would require the attackers to run not just one hash, but five hashes for every iteration. Using key derivation functions that intentionally slow this derivation of keys is *key stretching*.

There are several key stretching key derivation functions; two stand out and appear on the CompTIA Security+ exam: PBKDF2 and bcrypt.

Password-Based Key Derivation Function 2 (PBKDF2) combines adding a very long salt and a huge number of hashing iterations to make a key. PBKDF2 doesn't set the number of hash iterations. Some operating systems that employ PBKDF2 use 10,000 iterations!

bcrypt generates hashes based on the Blowfish cipher. In many ways similar to PBKDF2, it also has flexible hash iterations. bcrypt has a very long key derivation process and is considered stronger than PBKDF2.

 EXAM TIP bcrypt appears on the CompTIA Security+ exam with all caps, as *BCRYPT*.

Other Attack Options

Several types of cryptographic attacks deviate from the crack-the-password variety. This section explores three such attack types:

- Collision attacks
- Known-plaintext attacks
- Implementation attacks

Collision Attack

A *collision attack* exploits the fact that hashes have a finite size, and there will be times when two different values create the same hash, a *hash collision* (as described in Module 2-5). Given that hashes provide integrity, an attacker may take advantage of collisions to do harmful things. For example, if an attacker can create a collision with a digital signature, she doesn't need to know the actual private key, just a value to make an identical signature.

There's no magic to creating a collision. You use brute force on millions of hashes until you get one that collides. This is a big job, but there are some interesting aspects of hashes that make it a bit easier. The most well-known is the *birthday attack*.

It seems that every undergraduate statistics class begins with the teacher looking out at his or her class and saying, "There are 30 students in this classroom. What are the odds that two people share the same birthday?" They are surprisingly high; for 30 students, about 70 percent.

The same situation happens with hash collisions. A 64-bit hash has approximately 1.8×10^{19} different outputs. While this number is huge, the goal here is to find another identical hash. That's where the birthday statistic applies. It only takes roughly half (5.38×10^9) to generate a collision using brute force.

Known-Plaintext Attack

A *known-plaintext attack* isn't a true attack as much as it is an attack strategy. It you have both a known plaintext and the ciphertext, you can sometimes derive the key itself. Known-plaintext attacks have worked many times in the past. It's how the British cracked the Nazi Enigma code in World War II.

Attack the Implementation

Any cryptosystem has weaknesses or aspects that an attacker may use to help them. The most classic weak implementation attack is the infamous Wired Equivalent Privacy (WEP) weakness back in the early 2000s, but there are plenty of other examples.

Downgrade Attack   Almost all of today's cryptosystems give a client multiple ways to access a system. One of the best examples is TLS. A Web server using TLS supports several authentication and encryption methods to give flexibility for different Web browsers. In TLS, a client and a server traditionally request the most robust encryption. In a *downgrade attack*, the attack makes a legitimate request to the Web server to use a weak, deprecated algorithm that's easier to crack (Figure 2-41) in hopes of then successfully getting keys, passwords, and so forth.

 NOTE   A *deprecated algorithm* is an algorithm deemed obsolete or too flawed for use by the IT community. *Deprecated* means no one should use it in the future.

Replay Attack   In many situations, an attacker can *sniff* or capture traffic on a network, monitoring the different communications taking place. A *replay attack* is an attack where the attacker captures some type of legitimate traffic and resends it as needed to do something malicious. Here's an example:

> Bob: "Hey Joe, I need you to send the encryption keys for this session to me."
> Joe: "Okay, Bob, here you go."
> Bad Guy Mike: "Hey Joe, I need you to send the encryption keys for this session to me."
> Joe: "Okay, Bob. I thought I just did, but whatever. Here you go."
> Bad Guy Mike: "Mwuhuhahahahaha …."

Figure 2-41
Downgrade
attack against TLS

I offer 256-bit AES encryption!

Web Server

Can I just use DES?

Questions

1. Which of the following types of algorithms encrypts specified sizes of groups of text at a time?

   A. Asymmetric

   B. Symmetric

   C. Streaming

   D. Block

2. You must implement a cryptography system in your organization. You need to be able to send large amounts of data, quickly, over the network. The system will be used by a very small group of users only, and key exchange is not a problem. Which of the following should you consider?

   A. Asymmetric cryptography

   B. Symmetric cryptography

   C. Hybrid cryptography

   D. Key escrow

3. Which of the following asymmetric algorithms uses a maximum key size of 4096 bits?

   A. AES

   B. Diffie-Hellman

   C. RSA

   D. ECC

4. Which of the following asymmetric algorithms is widely used on mobile devices because of its low computational power requirements?

   A. ECC

   B. ElGamal

   C. Diffie-Hellman

   D. GPG

5. Which type of algorithm is typically used to encrypt data-at-rest?

   A. Symmetric

   B. Asymmetric

   C. Streaming

   D. Block

6. Which of the following places secrecy of the key versus secrecy of the algorithm as the most important factor in developing secure and reliable cryptosystems?

    A. Data Encryption Standard (DES)

    B. Advanced Encryption Standard (AES)

    C. Kerckhoffs' principle

    D. Digital Signature Algorithm (DSA)

7. Which of the following algorithms produces a 40-character message digest?

    A. MD5

    B. SHA-1

    C. RIPEMD-128

    D. Blowfish

8. If an individual encrypts a message with his own private key, what does this assure?

    A. Confidentiality

    B. Message authenticity

    C. Integrity

    D. Availability

9. Which of the following entities can help distribute the workload of the CA by performing identification and authentication of individual certificate requestors?

    A. Subordinate CA

    B. Root CA server

    C. Authentication authority

    D. Registration authority

10. Which of the following serves as the master certificate server in an organization?

    A. Intermediate CA server

    B. Root CA server

    C. Subordinate CA server

    D. Kerberos KDC

Answers

    1. D. Block algorithms encrypt entire groups of bits of text, usually of specific sizes.

    2. B. In this scenario, symmetric key cryptography would probably be the best choice, since the user group is very small and key exchange is not a problem. You also have the requirements of speed and efficiency, as well as the ability to send large amounts of data. All are advantages of using symmetric key cryptography.

3. C. RSA uses key sizes between 1024 and 4096 bits.

4. A. Elliptic curve cryptography (ECC) is an asymmetric algorithm widely found in use on mobile devices because it requires low amounts of computational power.

5. A. Symmetric algorithms are typically used to encrypt data that resides in storage.

6. C. Kerckhoffs' principle states that reliable cryptosystems should depend upon the secrecy of the key, rather than the secrecy of the algorithm.

7. B. SHA-1 is a 160-bit hashing algorithm that produces a 40-character hexadecimal message digest, or hash.

8. B. If an individual encrypts a message with his private key, this ensures message authenticity, since he is the only person who could have encrypted it.

9. D. The registration authority (RA) can help distribute the workload of the CA by performing identification and authentication of individual certificate requestors.

10. B. A root CA server is the master certificate server in an organization.

Identity and Access Management

Everything that is networking, everything that is the Internet, the whole reason to run cables, set up routers, configure firewalls and applications, and sit on the phone for hours with balky ISPs is really only to do one job: share resources. These resources are Web pages, e-mail messages, VoIP conversations, games .... The interconnected world has millions of resources for people to use to make work and leisure more convenient, more efficient, more inexpensive ... and more fun (Figure 3-1).

Resources are useless unless there's someone or something accessing and using the resources. A Web page has no value unless someone accesses it. A shared folder does nothing unless users read, modify, and delete files stored in those folders. E-mail messages sit on a server unread until you read them. Users must run client software to use those resources.

Offering a resource for anyone to use has major pitfalls. Users are at best ignorant, often nosy, and at worst, downright evil (Figure 3-2). IT professionals manage how users access the many resources.

This chapter dives deeply into *identity and access management*: using methods and technology to control who accesses resources and what they can do on those resources once they have access (Figure 3-3).

There are six modules in this chapter, each covering a very distinct aspect of access control. The first module defines critical terms and concepts such as authentication and authorization. The two modules that follow discuss the tools used to control access, and then managing user accounts and groups. The rest of the chapter examines specific access management systems, such as point-to-point authentication, network authentication, and the specialized authentications used with Internet applications.

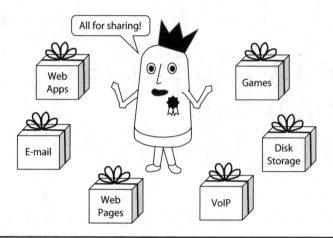

Figure 3-1   Lots of resources!

Figure 3-2   Unmanaged access to resources is foolhardy.

Figure 3-3
Controlling
resources

Module 3-1: Understanding Authentication

This module covers the following CompTIA Security+ objective:

- **4.1** Compare and contrast identity and access management concepts

Identity and access management, like most CompTIA Security+ topics, bring a ton of concepts and specific jargon that serious students need to digest before implementing systems in the real world. This module explores identification and AAA (authentication, authorization, and accounting), then looks at concepts of trust, such as authentication structures and federated authentication.

Identification and AAA

Identification, authentication, authorization, and accounting work together to manage assets securely. This section briefly reprises what you read about in the Introduction on core security concepts.

Imagine an asset, a shared resource, as a box. *Authentication* functions like a lock on that box. For a user to access the box, he must have some kind of key or *credentials* to get through the lock (Figure 3-4). The information in those credentials identifies the user in respect to that system. (That's the *identification* part.) In analogy terms, it's a pretty complicated lock that opens different portions of the box depending on the key used.

Authorization determines what the user can do with the contents of the box with the specific credentials he used. Authorization is nuanced, because of variables in what people can do. Consider a shared folder on a Windows system in a LAN that contains a single file. You can do a lot to that file. You can view the file, edit the file, or delete the file. (You can do much more than this, but this is enough for now.) Authorization defines what a user may do to that file. Think of authorization as a checklist (Figure 3-5).

Accounting means to keep a historical record of what users do to shared resources. Look at accounting as a sign-in sheet associated with the shared resource (Figure 3-6).

Figure 3-4
Authentication
as a lock

Figure 3-5
Authorization as
a checklist

Figure 3-6
Accounting as a
sign-in sheet

Identification and Authentication

The typical locked box and key analogy struggles when taken from physical access to electronic access. Granting access in the physical world, like a door lock on a real door, works fine because people don't generally hand out a key to someone they can't identify. In the electronic world, how do we identify individual users?

Back in the early days of PC networking—for example, early versions of Windows that predated NTFS—this problem was simply ignored. Resources such as shared folders had no associated user accounts. If you wanted to share a folder, you just gave that folder a single password, which in turn was passed out to everyone to whom you wanted to give access (Figure 3-7).

More commonly today, user accounts identify individual users. A user account is generally nothing more than a line in a table (remember the user names in password storage in the previous chapter?) that identifies an individual user by some value, such as a User Name, UserID, Social Security Number, and so on. Figure 3-8 shows one example of a user account in Windows Server.

A user account must include some authentication factor(s) to provide any kind of security. Identification is by itself insufficient for authentication. An authentication factor reveals some aspect of the identified user that is unique to that user. Passwords are very common, but just scratch the surface. Let's look at authentication factors in a lot more detail.

Figure 3-7
Old Windows
shared folder

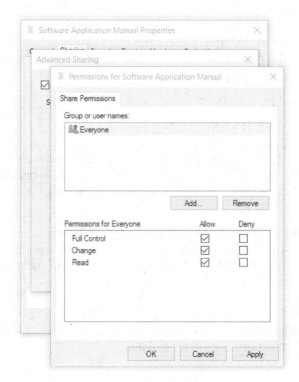

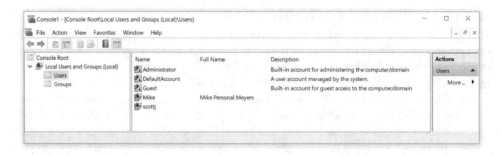

Figure 3-8 Windows Server user account

Authentication Factors

Authentication systems use different characteristics of identification to identify a user and validate her credentials. These different methods—or *factors*—depend upon the method of identification used. Several different factors can be used either separately or, preferably, together. *Single-factor* authentication uses only one factor. *Multifactor* authentication uses more than one factor. (You'll also see the term *two-factor* authentication to describe systems that use two factors.) Using more than one factor at a time provides more security and represents better authentication. There are five common authentication factors used in computing:

- Something you know
- Something you have
- Something you are
- Something you do
- Somewhere you are

EXAM TIP The CompTIA Security+ exam will test you on the difference between single-factor and multifactor authentication. Single-factor authentication uses only one factor; multifactor uses at least two factors.

Something You Know The *knowledge factor* relates to something you know, typically used when you identify yourself to a system with a user name and password combination. You know your user name and password, and use your memory to present them to the system (Figure 3-9).

Although you use two details for this credential, it is still considered a single-factor form of authentication because it involves only something you know. This single-factor form of authentication can be compromised easily if someone gains access to it—in this case, if they learn your user name and password. If you've written them down somewhere

Figure 3-9
Knowledge
factor

or told someone your user name or password, you have effectively transferred that factor to the other person, and it could be considered compromised.

Something You Have The *possession factor* relates to something you have. You physically possess an object to use as an authenticator. Scanning a gym membership card to gain access, for example, uses something you have. When used in this manner, the card alone is a single-factor form of authentication.

More often than not, however, these types of authenticators require some additional method of authentication. Typically, this could be something you know, such as a personal identification number (PIN) or password. When used in this manner, the card and PIN are a multifactor form of authentication. You use two different *types* of factors: the possession factor and the knowledge factor.

Smart cards and tokens are probably the most commonly used multifactor form of authentication that uses the possession factor. *Smart cards* are plastic cards with electronic chips in them that contain a limited amount of information related to the user, such as public and private keys. Smart cards enable users to access facilities, secure areas, and computer systems.

Physical tokens usually display a complex series of changing numbers. When a token is used to access a system, the user must also enter a PIN or password known only to her, in conjunction with the token and its own number. The system uses these two factors to validate the user. Figure 3-10 shows an example of a token.

Figure 3-10
Possession factor

Figure 3-11
Inherence factor

Something You Are   The *inherence factor* relates to something you are, relying on a person's unique physical characteristics that can be used as a form of identification, such as fingerprints, retinal eye patterns, iris patterns, handprints, and voiceprints (Figure 3-11). These are all unique characteristics of a person and difficult to replicate or fake.

Inherence factors can also be used in conjunction with an additional factor in a multifactor authentication system. Newer laptops and smartphones often arrive with a fingerprint scanner built into them, for example, and the user must scan his fingerprint and enter a PIN or password to access the system. Secure facilities may also require fingerprint or handprint factors in their authentication systems. It's also not unusual to see multiple inherence factors used for an even stronger authentication system.

Something You Do   The next factor is a bit less common—it doesn't have the fictional name, *action factor*—but is slowly coming into mainstream use as authentication technologies become more mature. This factor relates to something you do, meaning that when you present your credentials to the system, you must perform an action (Figure 3-12). The best example of this type of authentication factor is when you use a finger or hand gesture on a smartphone or tablet to log in. The pattern you create using your hand is the something you do. The user credentials database of the system you access stores that pattern. When the authentication system confirms that these patterns match, you gain access to the device or system.

Figure 3-12
Action factor

Figure 3-13
Location factor

Some forms of authentication that use this type of gesture are single-factor if that's the only thing you're required to do to access the system. Other authentication systems may also require an additional factor, such as entry of a PIN, making it a multifactor form of authentication.

Somewhere You Are   The *location factor* relates to your location when you authenticate. This factor could use either physical or logical locations and requires you to be in a certain location when you authenticate to the system (Figure 3-13). From a physical perspective, for example, in a highly secure facility, you may need to use a specific workstation, located in a certain room, to authenticate to the system before you can work on it from any other location. Because you would likely have to authenticate with other physical protections and controls to get into this room, this very secure form of authentication would allow only a limited number of people to access the system.

From a logical perspective, a location factor could be used as an authentication factor if you are required to authenticate from a certain device that has a specific digital certificate assigned to it, or from behind a certain network device, physical port, or even a subnet. This doesn't necessarily limit you by requiring authentication from a single physical location; rather, the logical location with respect to the network and the authentication system being used would be important. This might ensure that you do not attempt to authenticate from an untrusted network or device.

NOTE   An additional authentication factor that you won't see on the CompTIA Security+ exam is the *temporal factor*, relating to some*when* you are. Systems can set specific login times and restrict others, for example.

Authorization

Authentication gets you in the door of a shared resource; the key unlocks the box. Authorization defines what you can do once you authenticate. Users have rights or permissions to do certain things to shared resources. This presents some unique challenges because different resources often have wildly different permissions based on the type of resource.

To get an idea how resources can vary, let's consider two different types of resources: a printer and a Web page. Figure 3-14 shows permissions you can assign to a shared

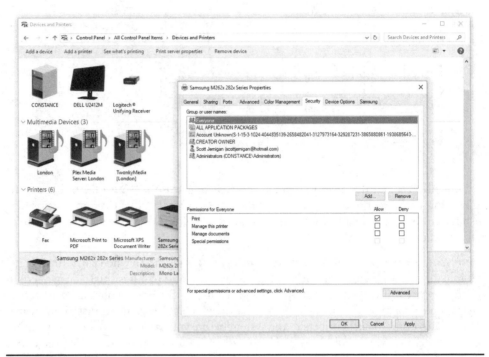

Figure 3-14   Printer permissions in Windows 10

printer in Windows. Note three permissions: Print, Manage this printer, and Manage documents. These permissions make sense as these are the actions we need to do to a printer.

Compare printer permissions to the permissions of a Web server program, shown in Figure 3-15. A simple HTTP server only has two permissions: allow access or deny access.

The downside to applying permissions to user accounts is that users and their permissions change over time. People quit, employees get promoted, customers leave, students graduate, and so on. Keeping up with the process of creating/deleting users and adding/changing permissions when people's situations change can be an administrative nightmare.

Groups streamline this process by organizing similar users into collections called groups. Applying permissions to groups lowers administrative work. When a user needs permission changes, you can assign the user to the group with the appropriate permissions. Almost every type of authorization uses the idea of groups. Figure 3-16 shows group settings for FileZilla, a popular FTP server program.

Authorization goes deeper than simply users, groups, and permissions, but this level of detail should suffice for now. We'll dive deeper into authorization throughout this chapter.

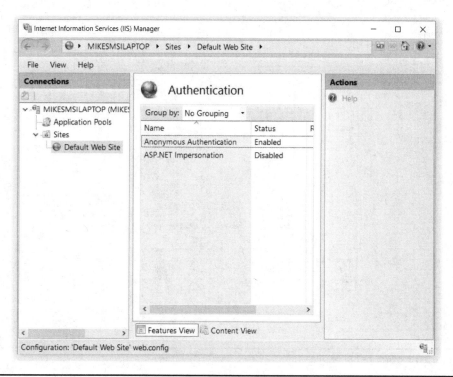

Figure 3-15 Web permissions in Internet Information Services

Accounting

Accounting or *auditing* enables security professionals to keep track of the accesses that take place on any given resource over time. Windows enables administrators to set audit policies on many aspects of the computer. Figure 3-17 shows the Local Security Policy snap-in on a standalone Windows 10 computer. Note the categories of audits in the background; the window on top shows auditing set to track failed logon attempts. Windows domain administrators would use the Group Policy Management Console (GPMC) to audit domain-level access to resources.

The technologies that support authentication, authorization, and accounting are known as AAA. We'll delve into these technologies in more detail in later chapters, but for now make sure you understand that accounting/auditing is very much a part of access management.

 EXAM TIP You can use Event Viewer in Windows to view logs of what you've set the computer or domain to audit. Pay attention to the wording of the question to know whether you're setting audit policy or viewing logs of audit events, then pick the right tool.

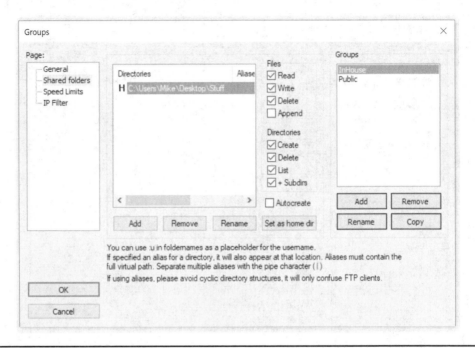

Figure 3-16 Groups in FileZilla

Trust

Access management builds on the concept of *trust* in a couple of ways. First, the system must trust that the user presenting credentials is in fact the user represented by those credentials. Second, the system must trust the integrity of the user credentials database, in that the data is current and correct and the system is functioning normally and returns the correct information so the user can be validated.

Organizations must trust their own authentication systems and, sometimes, those of another entity or organization. In this section, we'll discuss authentication across organizational boundaries, both from within and outside an organization. This authentication often involves trust relationships that must be established between hosts, systems, and other organizational entities.

Centralized and Decentralized Authentication

When an organization manages all its user accounts, credentials, and authentication systems as one unified system, this is said to be *centralized authentication*. In a centralized enterprise authentication system, credentials are stored in one database and user accounts have uniform security policies and requirements that apply across the entire organization. The authentication system performs authentication services for all systems, data, and resources across the enterprise. Often, you will hear the term *single sign-on (SSO)* in relation to a centralized system; this means that a single set of user credentials is used to

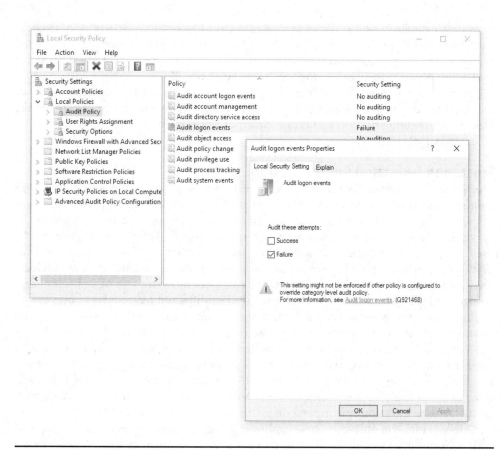

Figure 3-17 Local Security Policy snap-in

access resources across the enterprise. Whether a user is allowed or denied access to those resources depends on the authorization and access control policy in place, not the user's credentials in the authentication process. In a centralized model, all hosts and resources trust the central credentials database to take care of authenticating the user for them; after that, it's merely an issue of whether or not that user has the correct rights, privileges, and permissions to access a resource or perform an action.

A decentralized model is quite different. In this model, authentication occurs on a per-system, per-host, and even per-resource basis. No centralized authentication mechanism serves to validate the user's identity first; each system or resource makes an authentication decision based upon its own user credentials database or access control list.

In a small office setting, for example, each user may be an administrator for her own workstation and have the ability to create accounts on that workstation. If another user wants to access a shared folder on another user's workstation, he would need a separate user name and password—on that workstation—just for that resource. It usually won't be the same user name and password he uses for his own workstation; even if an effort is made to duplicate these across workstations, both accounts still reside in separate databases on each workstation and are therefore not technically the same. If a password in one set of credentials changes, for example, this doesn't guarantee that the other set of credentials on the other workstation will be updated as well.

Decentralized systems do not trust each other's credentials database or authentication mechanisms; they require a user to authenticate using his own systems and credentials. Decentralized authentication also means that user account and password policies will be different as well.

Trusts and Federated Authentication

Outside of organizational boundaries, users must often be authenticated to systems within another organization's infrastructure. Examples of this include business partner relationships, where employees need to access documents in the partner company's network, or university students who must access an affiliate university's shared library resources. In these examples, each organization may have its own centralized authentication system that trusts its own users and systems, but not users outside the organization's boundaries. Two ways of allowing outside users to access resources internal to an organization, and authenticating those users, are through trust relationships and federated systems.

Authentication systems can establish a *trust relationship*, enabling users from each system to authenticate to the other's resources. The authentication system in one company, for instance, may trust the authentication decisions (and vice versa) of a partner company, allowing its users to access sensitive resources such as shared folders and files. Trusts can be one-way or two-way (bidirectional); two entities may trust each other's authentication systems, but the relationship can also be such that entity A trusts entity B's authentication systems and decisions, but the reverse is not true.

One variation on this trust relationship is called a *transitive trust*. In this type of trust relationship, there are more than two entities; if Company A trusts Company B's authentication systems, and Company B trusts Company C, then Company A may also trust Company C's systems by default. More often than not, though, trust relationships between entities must be explicitly established, instead of defaulting to transitive trusts.

 EXAM TIP The CompTIA Security+ exam asks questions about how trust relationships work with authentication, such as how a transitive trust relationship works. A transitive trust usually means that the organization trusts another entity simply because they are trusted by someone else that the organization trusts.

A *federated* system involves the use of a common authentication system and credentials database that multiple entities use and share. This ensures that a user's credentials in Company A would be acceptable in Company B and Company C, and only access permissions would be the determining factor in accessing systems and data. Windows Active Directory is a good example of a federated system in practice; user credentials from different domains could be used in other domains if they are all part of the same Active Directory forest.

EXAM TIP The CompTIA Security+ objectives refer to use of federated systems as *federation*.

Module 3-2: Access Management Controls

This module covers the following CompTIA Security+ objective:

- **4.3** Given a scenario, implement identity and access management controls

Protecting resources using authentication and authorization requires application of security controls. Security controls used for accessing resources are known generically as *access management controls* or *access controls*.

NOTE The NIST organizes all access controls into a security control family called *AC* in the influential NIST Special Publication 800-53 (revision 4).

A good *access control model* defines how to organize access and provides a framework for providing access to resources. To help understand how a security control compares to an access control model, let's compare an example of each.

Here's a typical security control:

"All passwords will be a minimum of eight characters and include uppercase, lowercase, and numerals."

Here's a very similar access control (model):

"The owner of the data will define the access others have to a piece of data."

This module discusses the most common forms of access control models. After discussing the different models, we'll switch from controls to the more practical access control mechanisms. Access control mechanisms are the tools used to implement access control models.

Access Control Models

The introduction of electronically stored data in the early days of computing compelled the IT world to start thinking about ways to organize access to ensure good security. A number of attempts at developing access control models were developed, but it wasn't until the U.S. Department of Defense *Trusted Computer System Evaluation Criteria (TCSEC)* "Orange" book (Figure 3-18) that a robust model emerged.

The TCSEC quantified several well-known access control models; over time, more have been added. There are arguably about ten access control models used in the industry, but the CompTIA Security+ exam objectives only lists five: mandatory access control, discretionary access control, role-based access control, rule-based access control, and attribute-based access control.

Figure 3-18
TCSEC cover

Mandatory Access Control

A *mandatory access control (MAC)* model applies to highly secure environments, such as defense or financial systems. With mandatory access control, a user is granted access to a system or data based upon his security clearance level. Data is assigned different labels that designate its sensitivity and the security clearance required to access it. Administrators grant users, who also have security clearances assigned to their accounts, access to specific systems or data, based upon their need-to-know requirements. Even on the same system, users who have the requisite security clearances don't always get access to all of the data at the same clearance level. Each user's job requirements must also indicate a valid need to access the data. MAC models are typically either confidentiality or integrity models. A *confidentiality model* emphasizes protection against unauthorized access, and an *integrity model* emphasizes the need to protect all data from unauthorized modification.

Discretionary Access Control

Discretionary access control (DAC) is what most users encounter on a normal basis. Microsoft Windows, as well as macOS and Linux systems, typically use DAC in both standalone and network environments. With DAC, the user who has created or owns an object, such as a file or folder, has the discretion to assign permissions to that object as she sees fit. Administrator-level access isn't required to assign permissions; any user who creates or owns the resource can do so. Discretionary access control is a very flexible model, and users can assign rights, permissions, and privileges both to individuals and groups of users, which can be logically created in the system based upon different functional or security needs.

 EXAM TIP The discretionary access control model is the only model that allows normal users to dictate who has permissions to objects such as files, folders, or other resources.

Role-Based Access Control

Role-based access control, on the surface, sounds like access control using groups, but this isn't necessarily the case. Although DAC models can be used to assign permissions, rights, and privileges to traditional groups, role-based access controls almost exclusively use predefined roles, rather than groups or users. These predefined roles must already exist in the system, and users must be assigned to these roles to have the access levels granted to the roles.

A role-based access control model is *not* discretionary. The creator or owner of a resource cannot necessarily assign a user to a particular role simply to give him access. Normally an administrative-level user must assign a user to a role. Roles might include supervisory roles, administrative roles, management roles, or data change roles that have an increased level of access to systems, data, or other objects.

Rule-Based Access Control

Rule-based access control is a model that is rarely seen as a standalone type of access control model. It's typically integrated with other access control models, such as discretionary or mandatory access control. In rule-based access control, all accesses granted in the system are based upon predefined rules, which might include restrictions on when, how, where, and under what circumstances a user may access a system or resource. A rule, for example, may state that between the business hours of 8 A.M. and 11 A.M., only the accounting department may have write access to a particular database; but between 1 P.M. and 4 P.M., users in accounting, marketing, and production may have read and write access to the database.

Rules may apply to users or groups of users, and they may even specify the workstations that must be used, the type of permissions that apply to the resource, and so on. An example of rule-based access control is that used in more advanced firewalls, which lists a series of rules that users, network devices, hosts, and network traffic must meet in order to access other hosts and resources on the network.

Attribute-Based Access Control

All of the previous access control models share a user-centric attitude towards access. Users are important, but limiting. In the last few years a number of more granular, more powerful access control models have been adopted. The *attribute-based access control (ABAC)* model replaces users with attributes. While an attribute may be any form of identifying information, it's commonly divided into functional groups, such as subject attributes (name, clearance, department) or object attributes (data type, classification, color). We then connect policies to the access control. When someone wants to access data, ABAC uses preset rules that considers attributes and policies to make a decision about access.

Access Control Mechanisms

Access control models help organize access, but like any concept, any framework, they are useless by themselves. Organizations need real-world methods, real-world mechanisms to authenticate, identify, and authorize. The tools used to take advantage of the authentication factors (something you know, something you have, etc.) you learned back in Module 3-1.

NOTE There are arguably thousands of access control mechanisms, but the CompTIA Security+ objectives only cover a few of the most important and common ones. In addition, the exam goes into great detail on some of these mechanisms, while barely touching others. To make sure we cover the exam objectives, some of the mechanisms listed in this module (user name/ password is a great example) get quite a bit more coverage later in the book.

Keep in mind that these mechanisms are only parts of a larger access management system. Let's make a point to see how these implementations work. Later chapters revisit these to see how they work in the real world.

User Name/Password

The user name/password combination has been around from the earliest days of access control. You'd be hard pressed to find an application or operating system that doesn't use user name/password as the primary access control mechanism, from logging into a Linux system to connecting to a game server (Figure 3-19).

Operating systems rely on user accounts, secured by user name and password, for basic *file system security*. The permissions associated with a user account say what that user can do with data stored on the system, such as adding, deleting, or taking ownership. User accounts are a fundamental access control mechanism for every operating system.

Many applications likewise rely on user names and passwords to control access. You can set up database programs, for example, to require an additional login before a user can access or manipulate data. Such fundamental *database security* begins with a user name and password.

User accounts, user names, and passwords are so important, both to the real world and to the CompTIA Security+ exam, that Module 3-3, "Account Management," is dedicated to user accounts, groups, permissions, and the many aspects of user name/password used for access control.

There's a good reason that just about everything turns to user name/password for access control. User name/password is fast, it takes little storage on systems, it leans

Figure 3-19   Author's Steam account login

completely on the something you know authentication factor (so nothing to lose or accidently drop in a toilet), and possibly most importantly, people are used to entering user names/passwords for just about anything.

Today, though, multifactor authentication is more and more popular, especially when higher security is needed. That's where additional access control mechanisms are important. Let's move beyond user name/password and consider other ways to do access control.

One-Time Passwords/Tokens

In any form of authentication, the best type of password is one that's used one time then never again. A *one-time password (OTP)* is generated and used only once, and it is never repeated. But how can two separate parties somehow magically know the same password if it's only to be used once and then thrown away? The trick to using an OTP is there must be some type of independent, third-party, separate-from-the-two-sides-of-a-secure-communication tool that generates these passwords/keys in such a way that both sides of a communication trust the third party. This third-party password generator is known generically as a *token*. Hardware tokens are physical devices (refer back to Figure 3-10) and software tokens are … software that generates these OTPs. Figure 3-20 shows a software token used for a *World of Warcraft* account.

Hardware and software tokens are great examples of one-time passwords in action. The OTP provided by a token is used in conjunction with another mechanism, such as a regular password, to provide better security in a multifactor environment.

Figure 3-20
WoW software
token

Another example of one-time password use is during a secure communications session, where the secure protocols automatically generate a session key that is used only during that particular session. The session key could be considered a one-time password. Diffie-Hellman ephemeral keys are a great example of OTPs.

TOTP   A one-time password, like any password, is going to work whether you use it instantly or later, so it's important to give a time limit to any OTP you generate. Also, given that no date and time is ever the same, time is a great factor to help generate totally unique OTPs. A *time-based one-time password (TOTP)* uses time as a factor to assist in generating the OTP. In the previous example regarding a token, the TOTP changes very often, sometimes after only a few seconds. Therefore, it must keep its time synchronization exactly with the authentication database. If the user is even one or two seconds off from using the correct TOTP displayed on the token, authentication fails.

Normally, the user has a set number of seconds to input the correct password before it changes and another one must be used. This has many advantages, including the prevention of replay attacks. Another advantage is that it can be very difficult to predict TOTPs, based upon the time factor that is input into the algorithm used to create them. This can make it very difficult for an attacker to guess what TOTPs might be used.

Tokens are not the only devices that can use TOTPs. Google, using strong authentication practices for example, may send a TOTP to a personal device, such as a smartphone, that you would be required to have in your possession during authentication. Your Google

Figure 3-21
TOTP codes from
a smartphone

account may require you to input this TOTP within a certain amount of time, and after you receive a text message with the TOTP, you would input this password, usually a set of digits, into the corresponding field on the screen. You would then be authenticated and allowed to access your Google account. Figure 3-21 shows TOTP codes for different applications on a smartphone.

EXAM TIP   The CompTIA Security+ exam may ask about using one-time passwords. OTPs typically are generated by tokens or mobile devices to facilitate multifactor authentication.

HOTP   One algorithm used to generate OTPs is the *HMAC-based one-time password (HOTP)* algorithm. If you recall from Chapter 2, the Hash-based Message Authentication Code (HMAC) provides for message authentication and data integrity. HMAC can use either MD5 or the SHA series of hashing algorithms and various key sizes. In the case of HOTP use, the user is authenticated against the centralized authentication database, and the HMAC value is calculated by the authentication server and sent to the user via an authentication device such as a token. Several popular authentication mechanisms that use mobile devices, such as smartphones, make use of HOTP.

Biometric Access Controls

Biometric access controls use a person's physical characteristics (something you are) to provide strong user identification. The *biometric factors* listed in the CompTIA Security+ exam objectives are fingerprints, retina and iris patterns, voice patterns, and faces. These physical characteristics are unique to every individual and are very difficult to mimic or fake. This makes biometric authentication an extremely secure form of authentication in theory, although sometimes the methods used to implement it are not as secure and can be circumvented. You should understand some terms and concepts in biometric authentication for the exam and as a security professional.

Fingerprints   Fingerprints were one of the first technologies adopted as a biometric access control. *Fingerprint scanners,* like the one shown in Figure 3-22, are common in many keyboards, laptops, and mobile devices.

Retina/Iris Patterns   The human retina and iris have unique patterns that lend themselves to identification. *Retinal scanners* for access controls date back to the early 1990s, but their cost relegated them to extremely secure environments. They've made a huge impression in popular culture (Figure 3-23).

Improvements in camera resolution, computing power, and hardware pricing brought iris scanners into the forefront. *Iris scanners* are far more common than retinal scanners, while providing almost the same amount of accuracy (Figure 3-24).

Figure 3-22
Android
fingerprint
scanner

Figure 3-23
Retinal scanner
in *Half-Life* game

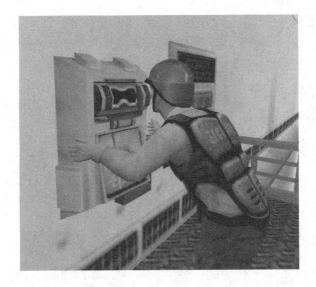

Voice Recognition   *Voice recognition* for speech to text holds a strong niche for dictation. Most mobile devices—like smartphones—and personal assistant hardware use voice recognition tools such as Google Assistant, Microsoft Cortana, and Apple Siri. But voice recognition as an access control hasn't gained any real acceptance due to its low accuracy compared to other biometric technologies.

    NOTE   It's a lot easier to fake a person's voice than a person's iris pattern.

Facial Recognition   Facial recognition has become a popular and powerful access control for several applications. The Windows Hello API, built into every version of Windows 10, is a *facial recognition* tool (Figure 3-25). Most facial recognition tools require extra functionality, especially cameras that include infrared so the camera knows it a real face and not a photo.

Figure 3-24
Iris scanner

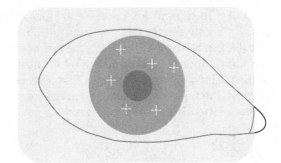

Figure 3-25   Windows Hello

Biometric systems are not foolproof, and several levels of errors, with specific terms, are associated with these errors. First is *false rejection rate*, or *FRR* (also known as a type I error). This relates to the error caused from rejecting someone who is in fact an authorized user and should be authenticated. Second is the *false acceptance rate*, or *FAR* (also known as a type II error). FAR indicates the level of errors that the system may generate indicating that unauthorized users are identified and authenticated as valid users in a biometric system. Both error rates can be dealt with by tuning the relative sensitivity of the biometric system in question; however, tuning it too much to reduce one type of error usually results in increasing the other type, so a trade-off is involved. This trade-off is usually tuned to the level of the *crossover error rate (CER)*, which is the point at which one error rate is reduced to the smallest point that does not result in an increase in the other error rate. Figure 3-26 illustrates this concept.

EXAM TIP   The CompTIA Security+ exam may ask questions about the difference between the false rejection rate (FRR) and the false acceptance rate (FAR) in biometrics. The FRR is the rate of errors from incorrectly rejecting authorized users. The FAR is the rate of errors from incorrectly authenticating unauthorized users. The crossover error rate (CER) is the point at which the system must be tuned to reduce both types of errors effectively without increasing either one of them.

Figure 3-26
The crossover
error rate

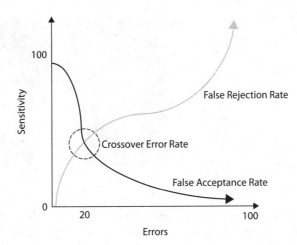

Figure 3-26
The crossover
error rate

Certificate-Based Access Control

Asymmetric encryption, using the exchange of public keys, is a powerful access control tool. The exchange of public keys, especially in the form of robust PKI certificates, makes a level of identification that's hard to beat (Figure 3-27).

The challenge to using tools like certificates is that they are tricky to carry around for individuals. Since a certificate is nothing more than binary data, there needs to be a method for individuals to carry their certificates. Smart cards, PIV cards, and common access cards ride to the rescue for *certificate-based authentication*.

Smart Cards   Adding a storage chip to a standard credit card–sized plastic card creates a way for an individual to store personal information, a *smart card*. The term "smart card" isn't a standard by itself, although a number of standards for data organization, physical dimensions, contact versus contactless, voltage, and so on, fit under the term. Figure 3-28 shows a few examples of smart card–enabled credit cards. Note the slightly different contact types.

Figure 3-27
Certificate as an
identity tool

Figure 3-28
Smart card
contacts

Smart cards can store any binary data, not just certificates. Some applications use smart cards that store symmetric keys, digital signatures, PINs, or personally identifiable information (PII). There is no law of physics or law of man that says how you use a smart card or what is stored on that card. Two NIST documents—Special Publication 800-78 and FIPS PUB 201-2—provide frameworks for the adoption, organization, and administration for smart cards.

NOTE The most common symmetric key type used on smart cards is 3DES; the most common asymmetric key type is RSA.

Personal Identification Verification Card Smart cards for access control certainly predate the NIST's involvement, but there were no well-received standards. Almost anyone using smart cards up until the early 2000s used vendor-specific systems and, as you might imagine, there was little to no interoperability. The framework provided by Special Publication 800-78 and FIPS 201-2 and the subsequent adoption of that framework by civilian departments in the U.S. federal government spurred the industry to create a single method to use smart cards for access control.

The result of these publications is the *personal identification verification (PIV)* card. If you're a civilian and you work for or directly with the U.S. federal government, you almost certainly are issued a PIV card (Figure 3-29).

PIV card standards provide a wide range of interoperability, ease of administration, tremendous flexibility, and rock-solid access control. The PIV standard gives individual agencies quite a bit of leeway as to exactly what is stored on a PIV, but it gives very strict rules on how that data is stored if you choose to use it. This includes physical as well as electronic data. PIV cards must be constructed and printed to strict rules. Specific areas of the card are reserved for a head shot photo, expiration date, smart chip, and so forth (Figure 3-30).

Common Access Card The U.S. Department of Defense has its own version of PIV card called the *common access card (CAC)*. CAC builds on the PIV standard, adding different versions for active military, civilian employees, contractors, and so on.

Figure 3-29

PIV card

SAMPLE CARD

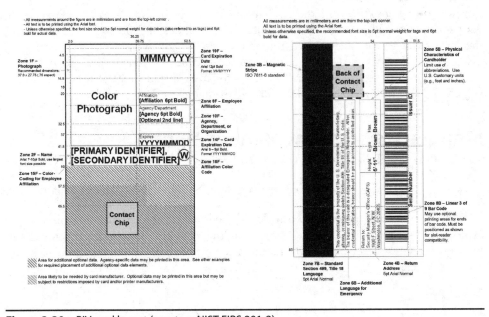

Figure 3-30   PIV card layout (courtesy NIST FIPS 201-2)

Figure 3-31 Key fob

Physical Access Control

Physical access control describes the mechanisms for admitting and denying user access to your space. This applies to doors, door locks, and facilities in general. More specifically, the term refers to the objects used to enable users to gain secure access. Smart cards, discussed previously, can function as physical access control mechanisms. *Proximity cards* rely on a different frequency, but function similarly. Another typical tool is a *key fob* (Figure 3-31). These are used at places like gyms that allow 24/7 access.

Module 3-3: Account Management

This module covers the following CompTIA Security+ objective:

- **4.4** Given a scenario, differentiate common account management practices

User accounts and passwords provide the bedrock of access control. This module explores user account types, issues with mingling accounts on a single machine, and managing permissions. We'll also analyze account administration best practices and account policies.

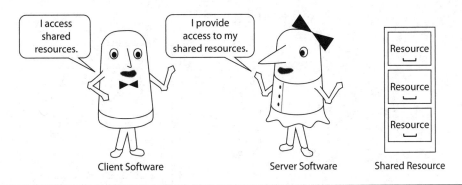

Figure 3-32 Client, server, and resource

User Accounts

User accounts provide a method to authenticate and authorize individual users to a resource. In general, you have some type of server software offering a resource and some type of client software trying to access that resource. (See Figure 3-32.)

NOTE Server software is not necessarily running on the same physical computer as the resource it shares, although it often does.

User accounts are data structures, usually stored on the serving system that store two discrete features: a unique identifier (a user name) that identifies the user, and a shared secret (a password) used to handle the authentication (Figure 3-33).

Assuming a successful login, the client authenticates and can access any resource the server allows. The server issues the client software some form of access token. The server software uses the access token to handle the authorization, defining the permissions the user has to the shared resources via some form of access control list. Figure 3-34 shows an access control list as attributes assigned to each resource.

Figure 3-33 Authenticating to a server

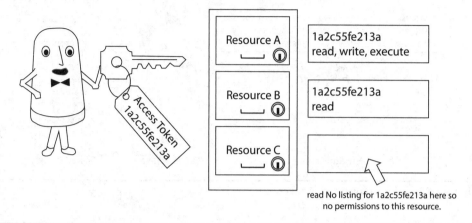

Figure 3-34   An access token handles authorization.

 NOTE   In Windows, the access token is known as a *security identifier (SID)*.

We need to add one more issue here. When you run a server offering shared resources, sometimes there are housekeeping or security issues—issues that have nothing to do with the resources themselves, but rather the server as a whole that we must deal with in order to support good authentication and authorization. For example, what if the server cares about the user's password length? We call these *rights* or *privileges* and we'll see more of these shortly.

Account Types

Serving systems that employ user accounts organize their accounts into different types to help categorize their use. You should know these user account types: user, administrator/ root, privileged, service, and guest.

User

The *user account* is created for and allocated to the people needing access to shared re-sources. In a perfect world, every individual needing access to resources has his or her own user account, although sometimes there are exceptions.

Administrator/Root

Every serving system, in particular every operating system, has an account that has com-plete power over the resource as well as the complete serving system. This super account is often automatically created when the OS is installed. In Windows this account is called *administrator* (often shortened to *admin*); in macOS and Linux/UNIX, this account is called *root*.

The admin/root account is powerful. It has complete and total access to all resources on the serving system. It has access to all permissions to the system. In general, avoid using these powerful accounts unless you are performing a job that requires them.

Privileged

A *privileged account* sits between a user account and an admin/root account. We generally create privileged accounts to delegate some aspect of system or account management. For example, an admin might assign the right to update software to a user account, making it privileged.

Service

In some cases individual processes, not actual people, need rights and/or permissions to a serving system. A backup program, for example, might need read access to any file on a computer to make a proper backup. In these cases we create (or the operating system automatically creates) *service accounts*.

 NOTE Service accounts usually aren't held to password complexity or password changing controls, making them a vulnerability to protect.

Guest

Guest accounts have minimal rights and privileges, often used for temporary access to resources. In most cases guest accounts are premade by operating systems, and in almost every case they are disabled by default. Note the down arrow on the guest account in Figure 3-35 showing it is disabled.

Mingling Accounts

Sometimes it's impossible or impractical to assign a single user account to every individual in your organization. Two important considerations in managing accounts are the use of multiple accounts, usually by one individual, and the use of shared accounts, which may be used by multiple individuals. In some circumstances, the use of multiple user accounts, or even shared accounts, may be required. In these cases, we have to balance this functionality with security.

Multiple Accounts

Normal user accounts are allowed to perform typical user actions, such as editing documents, checking e-mail, and performing daily work. Higher-level account privileges on the host or network may be required by administrative-level or privileged users because of their duty or job position requirements. But if we assign the normal user account higher-level privileges, it increases the potential for bad things to happen. First, the user could routinely abuse his privileges. Second, if a malicious entity obtains the user's account and password, she could perform harmful actions using those elevated privileges. Finally, if the user is logged into the system with that privileged account, any malware or

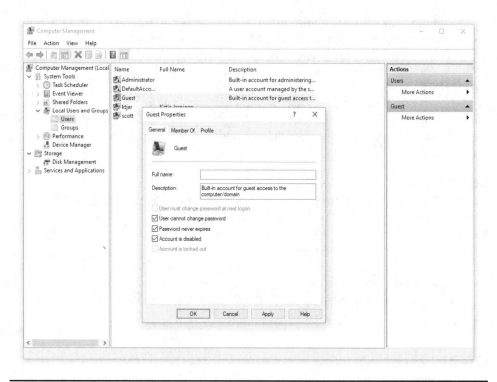

Figure 3-35 Disabled guest account on Windows 10 Professional

software that requires elevated user privileges can take advantage of that account, potentially taking harmful and sometimes unknown actions on the system.

The answer to this problem is through the controlled use of *multiple accounts*—in other words, a user would have a normal user account with lower-level privileges, plus a second user account with very specific higher-level privileges. The user would use her lower-level account to perform routine duties—actions such as accessing e-mail and files, editing documents, and other actions that require no special privileges. When the user needs to use higher-level privileges, such as creating accounts, installing devices, and updating software, she could authenticate to the privileged account and log out of the account when the action is complete. This way, the user restricts her use of the privileged account only to the times when it is needed, and she is not constantly authenticated as a privileged user. This reduces the attack surface on the system or network and the possibility of those privileges being abused. It also makes it easier to hold the user accountable for any actions performed using those higher-level privileges by auditing those accounts.

Some general rules for maintaining multiple accounts include the following:

- Using different login names, different passwords, and different permissions and privileges for both accounts.

- Different group assignments should be made for those accounts, plus a higher degree of auditing of their use.

- Users should not stay logged into the system using privileged accounts; they should be allowed to log into them only when they need them.

- Users should have to follow a process of logging in and authenticating to the system with those accounts before they are allowed to use them.

- Users should be allowed to perform only certain actions while they are logged into those accounts and should be required to log out when they're done.

- Multiple accounts, particularly privileged ones, should be documented and reviewed periodically to determine whether they are still needed and to ensure that they are being used properly.

Shared Accounts

In a *shared account,* several users can log in using the same user name and password for the account—in other words, several people can access the same account. You can quickly see how sharing accounts could cause issues with accountability and non-repudiation. If someone used that account to change file permissions, delete data, or even create another user account with elevated permissions, who would you trace the action to? The abuser could be anyone who has access to the account and knows its user name and password. Even strictly auditing the account would not tell you who used it (Figure 3-36).

In general, the use of shared accounts/credentials (also sometimes referred to as *generic* or *group accounts/credentials*) should be avoided at all cost; however, sometimes you must make exceptions because of critical functionality requirements. For example, shared accounts can be used for a resource or system that does not allow the use of multiple accounts to access and use it—perhaps only one account can be used to access it. Usually these are older systems, and users must all use the same account to use the resource. Another example is a system that must be available constantly, such as a military weapons system or another system that requires that any user be able to access the console or desktop of the system immediately. Suppose, for example, that the operator of a military weapons system

Figure 3-36
We are all User22!

steps away from the system desktop and locks it. If an enemy were to attack suddenly, the situation might call for another operator to access the system immediately to initiate defensive actions. If the system is locked and the second user can't access it or must wait for the other user to return, the response would be delayed, potentially costing lives. Very particular circumstances can require the use of shared accounts.

Although they should be avoided whenever possible, shared accounts should be carefully controlled if they are used. Anyone who has access to the shared account should be documented and briefed on its care and use. Some systems may allow a user to be logged in as a normal user and then authenticate to the shared account. In this case, the system may audit the use of the shared account, the time it is used, the actions performed with it, and the authenticating user, thus ensuring accountability. If the system does not have this capability, users should have to log their use of a shared account manually, as well as what actions they took while using it. These manual and system logs should be scrutinized carefully and often to make sure that people are using the account for its intended purpose, and securely.

 EXAM TIP Shared or generic accounts/credentials should be used as minimally as possible. When their use is absolutely required, shared accounts must be documented, audited, and carefully controlled.

Managing Permissions and Rights with User Accounts

Permissions and rights are generally assigned on an individual basis to user accounts or to logical groups that have been created for common functional and security needs. We'll look at both methods and discuss the need to review and monitor privileges periodically to ensure that they're being used appropriately.

The principle of *least privilege* guides decisions about user permissions and rights, meaning that administrators never give a user account more rights and permissions—the least amount of privilege—than is needed for the user to do his or her job. A great example of least privilege is *time-of-day restrictions* to make sure that users have access to their systems only during the times they should be at their machines. There's no reason for Penny in Accounting to have access to her system at 2 A.M. on a Sunday morning (unless Penny works strange hours)!

User-Assigned Access Control

One of the reasons to create individual user accounts is that it enables administrators to assign the accounts specific rights and permissions. User accounts allow users to identify and authenticate themselves to the system, access and interact with resources, and perform their daily jobs. Set up properly, these accounts also enable administrators to trace the actions performed by the user account to the physical user. When a user requires access to a system or resource, administrators assign specific privileges to her user account. When a user requires access to yet another resource, we assign her even more privileges. At some point, users may no longer require access to certain resources or privileges to perform actions on the system. When that happens, administrators can also reduce the user's privileges or revoke certain permissions.

These types of actions occur daily with most user accounts in large organizations. You'll find, however, that many user accounts have common functional needs and security requirements. Managing permissions on an individual user account basis can be inefficient and difficult. Although certain user account permissions need to be administered on an individual basis, the preferred way of managing permissions is by assigning them to groups, discussed next.

Group-Based Access Control

On a system, a *group* is a logical collection of user accounts that have common functions, access, and/or security needs. The most efficient way to assign user rights and permissions is to assign them to groups. This allows the appropriate privileges to be assigned to the entire group of users only once, rather than assigning privileges to individual user accounts each time new users require the same privileges (Figure 3-37).

User accounts can be placed in and removed from groups easily. You can assign user accounts to multiple groups to reflect different functional and security needs.

One disadvantage to group-based privileges is that a user account may be placed in a group and eventually forgotten about. Later, if the organization does not want a user to have certain privileges, an admin examining the individual user account wouldn't see the group privileges there. Another disadvantage is that group privileges are often cumulative. For example, if a user is assigned to the administrators group, he usually has elevated privileges. If he is assigned to a functional group as well, such as accounting or marketing, he may use his administrative-level privileges to affect certain transactions that are not authorized.

Group membership should be examined closely, as well as cumulative permissions and the continuing need to have them. Reviewing privilege requirements and continuously monitoring them is important, as we'll discuss next.

 NOTE Use groups to assign user rights and permissions to resources whenever possible. This makes the process much more efficient and secure.

Figure 3-37
Groups assign permissions to users with common functions.

All of us sales folks are in the SALES group.

Figure 3-38
Administration is
more than fixing
passwords.

> I forgot my password!

> Kill me.

Account Administration

The typical network administrator has common repetitive tasks that affect company security (Figure 3-38). Let's look at onboarding/offboarding, user audits and reviews, and continuous monitoring.

Onboarding/Offboarding

The most important time for any user account is during the onboarding and offboarding of personnel. During the onboarding process, a new employee should have a new account created, using some form of *standard naming convention* to enable ease of use by everyone.

NOTE Failure to use a standard naming convention is the bane of small businesses that start to grow. Even tiny companies should always pick a standard naming convention for all user names and stick to it.

Offboarding is even more tricky. When an employee separates, administrators do not typically delete the user account. Instead, they reset the user account with a new password used only by the administrator and the account is disabled for a set amount of time. This makes data recovery easy.

User Audits and Review

Network administrators should periodically audit access to systems and resources for several reasons. First, compliance with any organizational access control policy may require periodic review. Second, users often are transferred within an organization, they may be hired or terminated, or they may be promoted or demoted. In all of those cases, users likely don't require the same access to systems and data. Unfortunately, if access is not reviewed on a periodic basis, users may move around within the organization and retain privileges even when they no longer need them. This is a problem commonly called *privilege creep*, and it violates the principle of least privilege.

The best way to perform these audits is by looking at two very specific areas: permission auditing and review and usage auditing and review. What permissions does the user have across all shared resources? What resources is he actually using (usage audit)? Is he using all he has? Does he have too many permissions due to privilege creep? Here is where the administrator makes changes to rights and permissions to stick with least privilege. This audit process is an essential part of *account maintenance*, the collective procedures to make sure users have access to what they need over time, with changing projects and responsibilities, and nothing else.

Some highly sensitive systems or data require periodic access reviews called *recertification* to ensure that unauthorized users have not been inadvertently given inappropriate permissions to sensitive data. Access reviews involve reviewing audit logs, object permissions, access control lists, and policies that specifically direct who should have access to systems and data and under what circumstances. That's another reason it's a good idea to document exactly who has access to sensitive systems and data and when that access will expire; it makes access reviews a great deal easier.

Continuous Monitoring

Continuous monitoring is a form of auditing that involves examining audit trails, such as logs and other documentation, to ensure accountability for actions any user performs. With continuous monitoring, administrators can continuously check to ensure that systems and data are being accessed properly and by authorized personnel. Monitoring may involve automated means or manual review of logs or documentation. In any event, administrators look for signs of improper access by unauthorized persons or unauthorized actions authorized people may take, such as unauthorized use of account privileges; use of accounts by unauthorized users; unauthorized creation, deletion, or modification of data; and so on.

Continuous monitoring enables administrators to be sure that users are performing only the authorized actions they are allowed to perform on the network. This supports the security concepts of authorization and non-repudiation, as well as accountability. Figure 3-39 shows the different options available for auditing in Windows, a necessary part of reviewing user access and continuous privilege monitoring.

 EXAM TIP The organization should review the need for higher-level privileges on a frequent basis and continually monitor the use of those privileges. This ensures accountability and prevents security incidents from occurring.

Account Policies

Account policies are an organization's means of ensuring that accounts are created and maintained in a uniform fashion across the organization. Although there certainly should be a written account policy for the organization, technical policy settings should be in place to implement these policies within the system. For example, Windows has several account policy settings that you can use to enforce certain restrictions on user accounts. In the following sections, we will look at different aspects of *account policy enforcement*, including managing user accounts and credentials, password policies, and circumstances that may require user accounts to be locked out or disabled. Figure 3-40 shows some of the technical policy settings in Windows that are used to manage accounts.

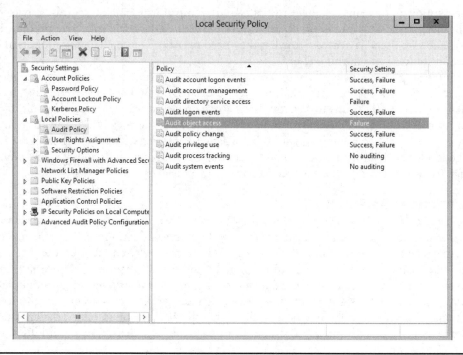

Figure 3-39   Audit Policy settings in Windows

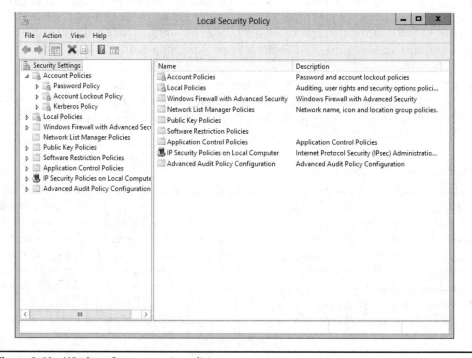

Figure 3-40   Windows Server security policies

Credential Management

Credentials are used to identify and authenticate users and include authenticators such as user accounts and passwords, smart cards, and biometrics. *Credential management* is the overall management process used to control credentials and ensure that they are created and used properly. There are two primary ways of managing credentials: centralized and decentralized management.

Central account management involves the use of an overall enterprise accounts database, typically integrated into various systems in the network. Microsoft Windows Active Directory is an example of a centralized accounts and credentials database. Credentials are stored within this database and managed by one authority within the organization. Under centralized credential management, all accounts are managed using a uniform set of policy requirements. For example, a central account policy may require that all organizational user accounts consist of a last name and first initial. It may also require that passwords meet certain requirements. Normally, centralized credential management is preferred, since it makes it much more efficient to handle user account and access issues.

Decentralized credential management may be used in smaller organizations or in organizations that are either functionally or geographically separated. In a decentralized scheme, the accounting department, for example, may manage all of its own user accounts, separately from the organization. Other departments may perform this function the same way; there may be separate user account databases for engineering, marketing, and production. Each department would be responsible for its own unique account policy requirements.

One problem with decentralized management is the lack of interoperability of accounts between departments. If a user requires access to a resource in the accounting department, for example, but her user account resides in the marketing department, then she might have to have two separate user accounts, one in each department. She would also likely have different account and password requirements to meet.

Examples of decentralized accounts databases would include those that are unique to a single Windows system, a Windows workgroup environment, or a standalone Linux system. Each of these accounts databases resides only on the system or host; the databases are not distributed across the entire enterprise network. Decentralized credential management also can create problems with account synchronization when accounts are trusted across different security domains.

 NOTE Credentials can be managed on either a centralized or decentralized basis.

Group Policy

The concept of group policy can often be confusing, because it can mean two different things. In Microsoft Windows, *group policy* describes how different system and environmental settings are pushed down to different users and computers. Even though it's called *group* policy, it doesn't necessarily use groups as its logical policy unit. Group policy settings can be pushed down to individual users, individual computers, groups of users, entire domains, or even geographically separated sites. These policy settings might include limitations on user rights, software settings, network settings, and so on. Figure 3-41 demonstrates how group policies are managed in Windows Active Directory.

The other meaning of *group policy* is that, whenever possible, users should be managed in defined logical groups, by functional, geographical, or security requirements. In other words, users in the accounting department can be placed in a logical accounting group, which would be used to manage all of their resource needs and security requirements. Managing users by groups enables administrators to assign users to resources and grant privileges and permissions more efficiently. For example, the users group, where normal users without special privileges reside, is different than the administrators group, where users requiring administrative-level privileges might be placed.

 NOTE   Logical groups should be used to manage common user functions and security requirements whenever possible.

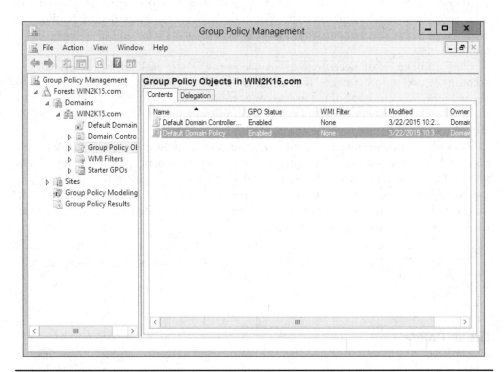

Figure 3-41   Managing Windows' Group Policy

Password Length and Complexity

We've all been told about the necessity to have strong passwords. But what makes up a strong password? In the early days of computers and the Internet, people used their dog's and children's names, birthdays, and other common, easy-to-remember things as passwords. Passwords were usually very short, five or six letters at best, and normally made up of letters of the alphabet. As malicious hackers came on the scene, however, they quickly learned that passwords could be defeated and guessed by simple mathematics (since short passwords did not yield a lot of different combinations to try) or by guessing the users' passwords by learning different characteristics about them and their personal lives.

Today, we are trying to get away from simple user names and passwords as means of identification and authentication, but we're still a long way from that. Although businesses and government agencies use multifactor methods such as smart cards, PINs, and biometrics, the average user still uses user name and password combinations in many of their applications, including users in the business world. So we still have to account for the possibility that passwords will be stolen and cracked by malicious entities. To make it harder for hackers to steal and crack passwords, we have created password construction rules that make password guessing and brute-forcing more difficult.

A password consists of several linear characters. In the early days, the *character space* of the password—the number of possible characters—made them easy to guess, because passwords were usually no more than four or five characters long. If, for example, the password was constructed of only numbers, then a four-character password would have only 10,000 possible combinations. This might seem difficult for a human to guess, but a computer could crack this password in seconds. Even if you added one more character, the password would have 100,000 possibilities—still very easy for a computer to figure out. Today, the general rule is that the longer the password the better, because the different combinations of password possibilities is far more difficult to crack. These days, most organizations recommend, and sometimes require, a password length of at least 14 to 20 characters. Even a password this long, however, if it uses only numbers or letters, could be easily broken by a computer in a matter of minutes. That's where complexity comes in.

Password *complexity* takes into account the numbers of character sets that can be used to construct a password. In a four-character password that used only numbers, for each possible character, there would be only 10 possibilities (digits 0–9). If you added another character set, such as all lowercase letters of the alphabet, the number of potential characters would increase to 36 possibilities per character (digits 0–9, and lowercase alphabetic letters a–z). Obviously, this would increase the character space and the complexity of the password. A four-character password would increase from 10,000 possible combinations to 1,679,616. Again, this sounds like an awful lot of combinations, and it would be very difficult for a human to crack this password in a reasonable amount of time. Computers can attempt thousands of combinations per second, however, so it wouldn't take long to crack a four-character password, even with this many combinations.

Although it goes a long way toward increasing the character space of a password, adding more character sets, as you can see, also increases the number of password combinations.

Rather than using only numbers and lowercase letters, most organizations also require the use of uppercase letters and special characters. Adding those two character sets increases the character set even more. Ideally, we want users to construct passwords that are not only longer in length, but that use at least one of each of those four character sets, preferably at least two of each.

The more complex a password, the more likely the user won't be able to remember it, and that means he'll probably write it down; this is something to consider when requiring complex passwords. Users must be trained on how to develop secure passwords that they can remember without compromising them by writing them down. Many users find that constructing a password from an easily remembered phrase a viable solution to this problem. I'm a military aviation fan, so one of my old passwords was Mikelikesthef14tomcatsapg-71radar. (Yes, I'm a serious nerd.)

Watch out for *keyboard walks*, the process of making a password by just moving up or down the keys on the keyboard. The password Mju7Nhy6Bgt% looks like a really complex password, for example, but watch the keyboard while you type it. It's a keyboard walk and every password cracker knows it.

 EXAM TIP   Password complexity consists of increased length and character sets. Both contribute to the character space (number of possible combinations) and a password's security.

Password Reuse and History

Two essential elements of your account policy are restricting password reuse and maintaining a password history. It does no good to require users to change their password periodically, if they are only going to change it to the same password they have been using for years. A password reuse setting in your account policy would prevent users from reusing the same password they have used for a certain number of passwords. For example, setting your password reuse policy to 10 would prevent users from using their last 10 passwords. That way, they are forced to use an entirely new and different password.

This is made possible by the password history, which stores the user account's passwords for a certain number of password change cycles. If the password policy history is set to 10, for example, the system would store the user's last 10 passwords. Beyond this setting, the user can, of course, reuse a password, but setting stringent password aging requirements would prevent the user from reusing passwords for a particular period of time. If, for example, passwords are required to be changed every 90 days, and the password history is set to 10, then the soonest a user could reuse a password would be 900 days. By that time, the user probably won't even remember the old passwords, so odds are an old password won't be reused. Figure 3-42 shows a Windows Server password policy management console, which includes password history settings and complexity requirements.

 EXAM TIP   Password reuse should be limited so that users cannot continually reuse old passwords.

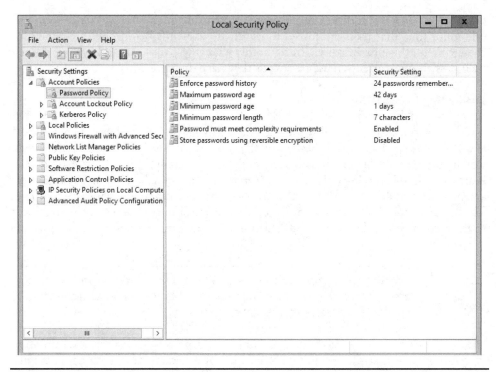

Figure 3-42 Managing password policies in Windows Server

Account and Password Expiration

Accounts and passwords shouldn't be set to last forever; in most cases, they should be at least manually reviewed to see if they are still required. Some accounts and passwords, however, should be set to expire. Accounts for temporary workers, for example, could be set to expire after a predetermined period of time, such as 90 days. These accounts could be reviewed shortly before the time period expires to see if they are still needed. Passwords, on the other hand, should be set to expire for everyone in the organization, to include administrators and even senior executives, because, over time, passwords could become cracked by malicious hackers, lost, or otherwise compromised. Password expiration shortens the amount of time that an attacker may have to crack a password and use it. Depending on password length and complexity, it can take an inordinate amount of time to crack. The idea is to make sure the passwords expire before they are cracked.

When the password is set to expire, the system should notify users a certain number of days (set by the system's account or password policy) ahead of time so that they have ample opportunity to change to a new password. If a user does not change her password within the allowed amount of time, her account should be locked, so that she cannot use the account again until the password is changed. This forces the user to change her password, and when she again creates a new password, the expiration time for that password is reset. In addition to password expiration times, some systems even set a minimum time that users are forced to use their passwords before they are allowed to change them; this prevents users from rapidly changing passwords and cycling through their password histories to reuse passwords they have used previously.

Disabling Accounts

Accounts may be temporarily disabled for various reasons. The organization may not want to revoke, retire, or delete the account permanently, since the user may need it at a later date. Perhaps a user has repeatedly input an incorrect password—the system would automatically disable the account to prevent its compromise, in case an attacker is attempting to brute-force the account. Or an account may be temporarily disabled if a user is on vacation—or if he is under investigation for a crime involving the computer. The user may not be allowed to use the account during either of these two circumstances, so the account would be manually disabled until management determines that it can be re-enabled.

 EXAM TIP The CompTIA Security+ objectives use the term *disablement* to describe the process of disabling user accounts. It's all part of account policy enforcement, an essential aspect of IT security.

For whatever reason, disabling an account should prevent its use for a set duration. It should require that the account be re-enabled by a separate user with administrative privileges, and include a documented reason as to why the account has been both disabled and re-enabled. It may be organizational policy to disable an account for a predetermined amount of time after a user has left the organization; in those cases, policies should also set a time after which the account will be permanently deleted.

 EXAM TIP Accounts should be disabled temporarily whenever a user does not need access to the system. They should not be permanently deleted until you determine that a user will never need access to the system again.

Account Lockout

Account lockout is a part of an account policy that is used to protect user accounts from being compromised. Many accounts are disabled after a number of incorrect password attempts. The account can be locked for a predetermined period, such as an hour or two, or until an administrator manually re-enables the account. This prevents brute-force password attacks. Account lockouts also normally show up in audit logs and could alert the administrator to a potential attack—or, at minimum, a user who is having issues with his account or password. Most account lockout thresholds are set to a small number, usually between three and ten, which is enough to prevent a brute-force attack but forgiving of a user who may have simply forgotten or mistyped his password. Figure 3-43 illustrates the default lockout policy settings in Windows.

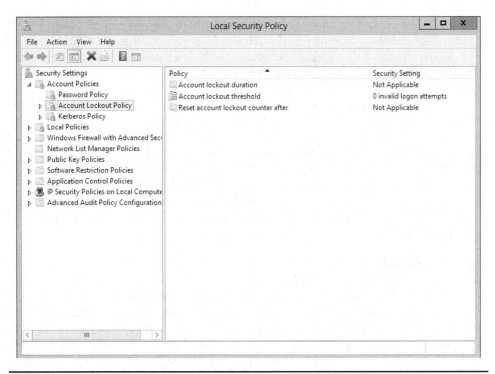

Figure 3-43   Default lockout policy settings in Windows

 EXAM TIP   You should always set account lockout as part of your organization's account policy. If account lockout is not set, a malicious user could use brute-force techniques to guess a password and access an account.

Account and Password Recovery

Account and password recovery should be considered when you're developing account policies and procedures. In Windows, the account identifier is known as the *security identifier*, or *SID*. In UNIX- and Linux-based systems, account identifiers are known as *user identifiers*, or *UIDs*.

If an account is simply disabled, it can easily be re-enabled whenever management or policy dictates. If the account has been deleted, accidentally or intentionally, recovering it may be more difficult. Simply re-creating an account isn't the same thing as re-enabling it. Even if you were to re-create the account with the same user name, the identifier that the system uses for it will be different. The system uses identifiers to assign privileges and allow access to different areas of the system. Re-creating an account means that you've created a different account, so the user rights and privileges used on the original account would not apply to the new account—you must completely reassign them from scratch.

You can also recover an account by restoring part of the accounts database from a backup. This isn't always the preferred method, however, because it is difficult to restore only discrete pieces of the database pertaining to the user account. Typically, the entire database might have to be restored, which would also undo any other changes that were made since the account was lost or deleted.

Password recovery typically occurs only if the password has been stored somewhere offline, such as in a secure file or container. Often, organizations will record highly sensitive passwords for system services or critical personnel and store them in secured and encrypted files or in a secure container, such as a safe, for example. If passwords have not been stored offline, recovery could be difficult if a system goes down. Some older systems might store passwords in plaintext, which is highly undesirable, but it might make passwords easier to recover. The best way to "restore" a password is simply to create a new one. This is especially true if the password has been lost and may have been compromised.

Location-Based Policy

The prevalence of accessing e-mail on smartphones has led to security policies based on location of devices, what CompTIA calls *location-based policy*. If an employee loses a company smartphone that's set up to receive and send e-mail messages, this presents a clear danger. Smartphones know where they are, for the most part, because of interaction with cell towers. Companies can implement policies that restrict features of smartphones, like e-mail, when the user goes outside a given geographic area. Or the policies can be set up to provide an automated notification about an unsafe location, such as when travelling abroad.

Module 3-4: Point-to-Point Authentication

This module covers the following CompTIA Security+ objective:

- **4.2**   Given a scenario, install and configure identity and access services

Now that this chapter has covered most of the critical concepts of access management, it's time to move from the theoretical into the practical. This module looks at the protocols and methods that enable a client to access a server securely.

The best place to start this is at the beginning of the Internet; a time when cable modems, cellular WANs, and fiber to the premises weren't considered; a time when computers sat in your house, unconnected to any network. If you wanted to connect to the Internet, you had to make a remote connection from your computer to a remote server of an Internet Service Provider (ISP) that in turn connected to the Internet.

Back in the early 1990s, just about everyone had a physical telephone line. Using an analog modem and a telephone number, we could dial in to a system that was connected to the Internet, and then we were connected as well (Figure 3-44).

The protocol that made all this work was the *Point-to-Point Protocol (PPP)*. In essence, PPP turned a modem into a network interface card (NIC). The PPP client dialed up the remote PPP server and made a virtual Ethernet connection, just as if your computer at

Figure 3-44
Ancient
connection
options

home was connected to the switch at the remote server's location. From here the PPP server would send out DHCP requests just like a modern system does.

NOTE Point-to-point in this context means taking a single computer and making a single, one-to-one connection to a remote network. Don't confuse these remote connections with modern technologies such as VPN. VPN requires a system *already* on the Internet to make a private connection. A point-to-point connection means your client is not on any network.

The problem with PPP was that it was remote. A PPP server had a phone number that anyone could call and PPP servers weren't cheap, so PPP came with a number of authentication protocols. Three of these protocols—PAP, CHAP, and MS-CHAP—dominated and continue to dominate point-to-point authentication.

PAP

The *Password Authentication Protocol (PAP)* is the oldest authentication protocol used to pass user names and passwords to a central authentication server. PAP was usually seen with older dial-up remote connection methods and actually predates Point-to-Point Protocol (PPP). Unfortunately, PAP does not pass user names and passwords securely during authentication by default; this information is generally sent over the network in clear text, making it easily intercepted by someone using a network sniffer.

EXAM TIP The ancient and non-secure PAP has been deprecated. You should always use an authentication protocol that hashes or encrypts user credentials that travel across a network connection.

CHAP/MS-CHAP

The *Challenge-Handshake Authentication Protocol (CHAP)* is an Internet standard method (described in RFC 1994) of authenticating users or a host to a centralized authentication server. CHAP is an older protocol that replaced sending user name and password information over clear text, as non-secure implementations of PAP did. CHAP was primarily used over PPP connections, and it was the first of several different versions of challenge-response authentication protocols. In CHAP, the authentication server sends

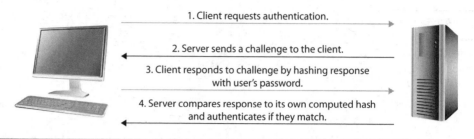

1. Client requests authentication.

2. Server sends a challenge to the client.

3. Client responds to challenge by hashing response with user's password.

4. Server compares response to its own computed hash and authenticates if they match.

Figure 3-45   The CHAP authentication process

a challenge message to the user or host. The user inputs his password, and the system hashes the combination of the password and challenge together, using a one-way hash function. The host then sends this hashed response back to the authentication server. The authentication server, which knows the user's password, repeats the hashing process with the password and challenge, and produces its own hash value. If the hash values match, then the authentication server knows that the user input the correct password and the user can be authenticated. If the hash values do not match, authentication fails. Figure 3-45 illustrates how this process works.

CHAP periodically reauthenticates clients during a session; this process uses a three-way handshake. CHAP can prevent replay attacks and also enables the user to authenticate without directly sending his password over non-secure network connections. Microsoft developed its own version of the CHAP protocol, MS-CHAP, and later MS-CHAP v2, which was used in earlier versions of Microsoft Windows. It is been all but deprecated on all recent versions of Windows in favor of more secure authentication mechanisms such as Kerberos.

 EXAM TIP   CHAP relies on challenge and response messages and hashed passwords, as do other modern protocols. This ensures that passwords or other user credentials are never sent over the network in clear text.

Remote Access Connection and Authentication Services

The next sections explore various remote authentication services and protocols that enable external authorized users and hosts to authenticate into an internal network. These methods are normally used for older dial-up and Integrated Services Digital Network (ISDN) connections, but we'll also look at the two primary tunneling protocols that can provide remote access services for VPN connections—the subject of later modules, so we won't go much in depth here.

Authentication, authorization, and accounting (AAA) apply to functions performed by authentication services, such as remote authentication services. In this context, *authentication* and *authorization* mean the same thing, although there might be intermediary devices that provide certain related services rather than having a host authenticate directly with a centralized authentication server or database.

The accounting function, when used in the context of remote access, describes the process of accounting for connection time and billing functions, another throwback to the older days of dial-up, when users paid for their connection to an ISP by the minute or hour. These days, users typically connect via a broadband method that is "always on," such as DSL or cable modem. Although users are still charged for their service, it's typically on a flat-rate basis and not by the minute or hour. Still, the accounting function of remote access takes care of this aspect of the connection, including time of connection, the traffic that was used over the connection, and which hosts connected at which times to make use of the connection.

RADIUS

The *Remote Authentication Dial-In User Service (RADIUS)* protocol was originally developed to provide for remote connections through older dial-in services. RADIUS provides AAA services to clients and providers. It is a standardized Internet specification and falls under several different RFCs, including RFC 2058, RFC 2059, and others. A basic client/server protocol, RADIUS uses User Datagram Protocol (UDP) as its transport protocol on ports 1812 (for authentication and authorization) and 1813 (for accounting functions).

RADIUS has a few interesting terms you need to know. A *RADIUS client* is not the host attempting to connect; it is the network access server itself, which remote hosts connect to. This server is an intermediary that processes the connection request and passes it onto other servers, called *RADIUS servers*, which provide authentication services and can be either Windows or UNIX-based servers. Active Directory, in fact, can provide for authentication services to RADIUS clients, acting as a RADIUS server, through the Microsoft remote access and VPN services. In terms of security, though, RADIUS is a bit lacking. Although the communications between the RADIUS client and the RADIUS server are encrypted, communications between the RADIUS client and the remote host are not. Unfortunately, user name and password information could be intercepted between the remote host and the RADIUS client. RADIUS can support a variety of authentication methods, including some of the older ones, including PPP, PAP, and CHAP.

 EXAM TIP A RADIUS client is the network server that receives the connection request from the remote host and communicates with the RADIUS server. It is not the remote host itself.

Diameter

Diameter is an AAA protocol proposed to replace RADIUS. Its name is actually a pun and doesn't really stand for anything. It makes sport of the fact that the diameter of a circle is twice the radius. Diameter supports a wider variety of authentication protocols, including the Extensible Authentication Protocol (EAP). It uses TCP port 3868 instead of the UDP that RADIUS uses. It also can handle more advanced security using IPsec and Transport Layer Security (TLS).

TACACS, XTACACS, and TACACS+

The *Terminal Access Controller Access Control System (TACACS)* supplanted RADIUS and allows a remote user to connect and authenticate to a network via an intermediary TACACS server. It works pretty much the same way as RADIUS, with a few exceptions. XTACACS, which stands for Extended TACACS, provides additional functionality for the TACACS protocol. It also separates the authentication, authorization, and accounting functions out into separate processes, even allowing them to be handled by separate servers and technologies. TACACS+ is a Cisco-designed version of the older TACACS protocol that enables newer, more secure authentication protocols to be used over it, such as Kerberos and EAP. It also permits two-factor authentication. It has become an open standard. Unlike the issues that plague RADIUS with encryption between the remote host and the RADIUS client, TACACS+ encrypts all traffic between all connection points, to include user names and passwords. Unfortunately, TACACS+ is not backward-compatible with the earlier versions of the protocol. TACACS uses TCP port 49 by default.

Module 3-5: Network Authentication

This module covers the following CompTIA Security+ objective:

- **4.2** Given a scenario, install and configure identity and access services

The point-to-point authentication methods described in the previous module are powerful tools for solutions to situations where a single client needs to authenticate to a single server acting as a gatekeeper to a larger network. Yet what do we do when we have many systems already connected on a single LAN? Unlike point-to-point, a client computer wanting to authenticate connects to many computers at all times (Figure 3-46).

Authentication on a LAN has serious issues that methods such as MS-CHAP or RADIUS simply do not or cannot address. Let's look at issues a LAN brings to access management and then look at the authentication methods and protocols used in most LANs to provide network authentication.

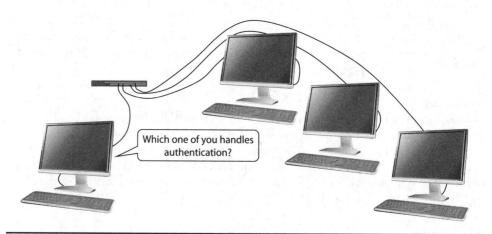

Which one of you handles authentication?

Figure 3-46 Network authentication is a different animal.

The Challenge of LAN Access Management

LANs change the concept of access management in a number of ways. First, LANs are much more permanent compared to most point-to-point connections. The desktop computer in your office, connected by a Gigabit Ethernet connection to your main switch, is probably going to spend a few years connected to your LAN. This means that the system needs some form of initial authentication to identify that computer to the network. Plus, we also need some method to authenticate *any* user who sits down in front of that computer to access network resources. Second, LANs are very fast compared to most point-to-point connections. If we are going to authenticate, we need fast protocols that allow systems to authenticate quickly. Third, most anything done on LANs is broadcast to every other computer on the broadcast domain, requiring authentication methods that allow for many systems to authenticate and authorize each other (Figure 3-47).

The permanency of LANs is motivation for a feature you don't see in point-to-point connections. With a LAN, the systems tend to be relatively fixed and permanent, but users tend to move around. This means that a good LAN network access solution has the flexibility to enable any user to sit at any computer and authenticate themselves to the network as a whole.

The last and possibly biggest issue is the concept that any single system may offer shared resources to properly authenticated and authorized users on any system. This creates an issue in that every system on the network has its own authentication database, almost always user accounts/passwords. Unless something else is done, a user must authenticate to every system on the LAN individually (Figure 3-48).

The interesting thing to consider about the presence of many computers on a LAN is that they all have operating systems. Therefore, all modern operating systems come with some form of networking tools that include naming of systems, sharing of resources, and some form of authentication method to support all of this. The networking authentication built into Microsoft Windows has become the predominant network authentication method for all networks. Apple computers use Windows File Sharing and Linux/UNIX systems use a protocol called Samba (Figure 3-49). If you want to understand network authentication, you need to learn about Microsoft networking and Microsoft authentication methods.

Figure 3-47
Network access control must be flexible.

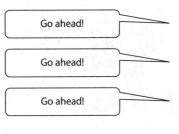

Figure 3-48 In a LAN each system is an island.

Microsoft Networking

Microsoft networking has been around for a very long time and has gone through an incredible number of changes and iterations, but we can make a few straightforward breakdowns. First, all Windows systems are organized in one of two ways: workgroups or domains. In a workgroup, every Windows system stores local user names and passwords and controls access to its own resources. In a domain, all computers authenticate to a single authentication server known as a domain controller (Figure 3-50). A modern Windows domain stores far more than just user names and passwords. This more advanced, very powerful domain type is known commonly as Active Directory (AD).

Every Windows computer on earth is either a member of a workgroup or a domain. Using workgroups is the default network organization and is very common in homes and small offices. In a workgroup, a user must have an account on every system from which they wish to access shared resources. I often get around this issue by making the same account with the same password on every system. Domains require a system running

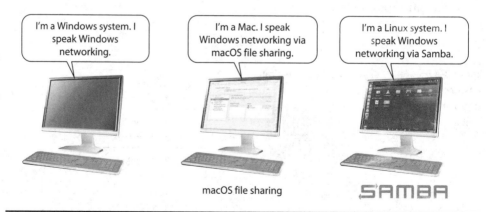

Figure 3-49 Everybody speaks Windows!

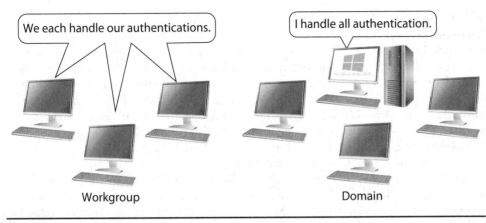

Figure 3-50 Workgroup vs. domain

special, powerful, and expensive Windows Server operating systems (Figure 3-51). Every computer on the network then goes through a special process of joining the domain. Once a computer joins the domain, it authenticates to the domain controller. A user can log onto any system in the domain and log onto the domain—the perfect example of single sign-on in action.

 NOTE Windows' domain single sign-on function is so popular that other operating systems will use Samba to enable individual systems to log onto a Windows domain controller even if they have no interest in sharing folders.

Workgroups and domains are very important in that Windows uses very different authentication methods depending on whether there is a workgroup or a domain. In a workgroup, Windows uses the very old, slightly vulnerable but easy to implement and backward-compatible NT LAN Manager (NTLM). Windows domain controllers use the powerful and robust Kerberos authentication protocol.

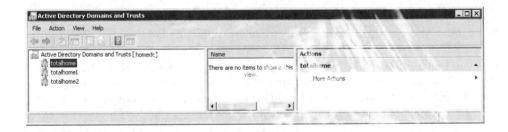

Figure 3-51 Windows Server domains

NTLM

Microsoft developed a series of proprietary authentication protocols early on during Windows development, and for the most part, they have been deprecated and are no longer included in new versions of the Windows operating system. You should be aware of them for the exam, however, and you may actually run into some of these from time to time in your professional career. The *LAN Manager (LANMAN)* protocol was developed and included in Microsoft Windows NT. Like any first attempt, it had weaknesses. For example, its hash-stored passwords are easily broken if they are obtained by an attacker. LANMAN was disabled by default starting in Windows Vista and shouldn't be used unless you're running legacy clients that require it.

NT LAN Manager (NTLM) was created by Microsoft to replace LANMAN and is backward-compatible with the older protocol. It's also a very non-secure protocol, and it was quickly replaced by NTLM version 2. Both versions are challenge-response authentication protocols and work similarly to CHAP. Version 2 is used in modern iterations of Windows, but only for workgroup authentication. Kerberos is the default authentication protocol for Windows domains (see next section), but there are still times when NTLM v2 is used, even in domains. These instances include authenticating to a server using only an IP address, authenticating to a different AD network that has a legacy trust enabled, or authenticating a host to a non-AD domain. In these instances, Windows will default to using NTLM v2.

 EXAM TIP   Understand the situations in which Windows will default to using NTLM v2 instead of Kerberos for its authentication protocol. Usually this occurs where there is no AD environment and the host is communicating in a workgroup setup.

Kerberos

The *Kerberos* network authentication protocol is used in modern Active Directory implementations. It began as a project of the Massachusetts Institute of Technology (MIT) and has been implemented as a centralized, single sign-on authentication mechanism. It is an open standard, supported officially as an Internet standard by RFC 4120. As of this writing, the most current version of Kerberos widely in use is version 5.

Kerberos uses a system based on authentication tickets and timestamps that are issued out to the authenticated user. Timestamps help prevent replay attacks because the tickets expire after a short time and must be refreshed, requiring that the user be reauthenticated and the ticket reissued. Kerberos's timestamps rely heavily on authoritative time sources throughout the network architecture, so many implementations also provide for a network time server.

Time synchronization is critical in Kerberos. A classic usage case is the "I can't log into my domain" problem. If clients are outside a certain tolerance for time difference with the Kerberos server, the users logging into those clients will not be authenticated. The default tolerance for time differences is 5 minutes in an Active Directory network, although this can be changed. Windows systems lean heavily on time synchronization and constantly keep their time synchronized with their domain controller.

Kerberos uses several components, which you should be familiar with for the exam. First is the *Kerberos Key Distribution Center (KDC)*, which is responsible for authenticating users and issuing out session keys and tickets. In Active Directory implementations, the domain controller serves as the KDC. There is also an *Authentication Service (AS)* and a *Ticket-Granting Service (TGS)*. Although they are not required to be on the same host, these services frequently are, for simplicity and efficiency's sake, on AD domain controllers in a Windows environment and are part of the KDC implementation.

When a user logs into the system, the AS verifies her identity using the credentials stored in AD. The user is then issued a *Ticket-Granting Ticket (TGT)* by the AS, which can be used to access resources throughout the domain. The TGT expires after a certain amount of time, so it must be periodically reissued. When a user wants to access a resource in the domain, the TGT is presented to the TGS for authentication and the TGS generates a session key for the communications session between the user and the resource server. This is known as a *service ticket* and is used for the duration of the access to the resource. When a user later needs access to the same or a different resource, the older ticket is not reused and a new service ticket is generated.

Note that the process we've described is specific to Windows AD implementations of Kerberos, but the principles are the same regardless of what operating system and LDAP-based implementation is in use. A network that uses Kerberos as its authentication protocol is called a *Kerberos realm*. Kerberos uses both TCP and UDP ports 88, and it uses symmetric key cryptography. Figure 3-52 illustrates the Kerberos process in Windows AD.

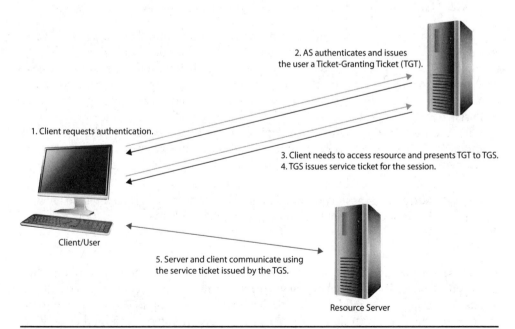

Figure 3-52 Kerberos process in Windows environments

LDAP and Secure LDAP

The power of modern Active Directory networks requires a language that allows different domain controllers to query each other's ADs. This is where LDAP comes into play. The *Lightweight Directory Access Protocol (LDAP)* isn't an authentication protocol; it's used to assist in allowing already authenticated users to browse and locate objects in a distributed network database (like a Windows Active Directory spread out among two or more domain controllers). It's also used to facilitate authentication and authorization for these objects. LDAP is a modern replacement for older X.500 directory services protocols. Although the most popular iteration of LDAP (its current version is version 3) can be found in AD, other platforms use LDAP as well, including the popular OpenLDAP. LDAP uses both TCP and UDP ports 389. There is a secure version of LDAP that uses TCP port 636. It's primarily LDAP over SSL (LDAPS), and it has been deprecated with LDAP version 2.

NOTE   Keep in mind that LDAP is not an authentication protocol, but it does facilitate authentication and resource access.

Module 3-6: Identity Management Systems

This module covers the following CompTIA Security+ objective:

- **4.2**   Given a scenario, install and configure identity and access services

Single sign-on (SSO) for network authentication has been around for a long time. We've already covered single sign-on in a LAN with Microsoft Windows domains as probably the best single example. As powerful as single sign-on is for LANs, it traditionally has never been used on the Internet. Anyone who has spent any amount of time bouncing from one secure Web site to another appreciates the hassle of remembering user names and passwords for every site.

With the proliferation of Internet services comes *password fatigue*, the user-based syndrome of "I have to set up yet another user account and password to remember for [insert name of new, must-have Web site] service too? Not again!" (Figure 3-53).

NOTE   In fairness, Windows domain single sign-on can span multiple LANs, but it's not commonly used to secure public Web sites.

The idea of one user name and password to rule them all has merits, certainly, but also opens a huge discussion about how to keep that identity secure. Plus, it requires understanding how to establish trusts such that a user can sign on to one site and in some way then transfer that authentication to other sites in a secure fashion. This module explores

Figure 3-53
Many passwords
to memorize

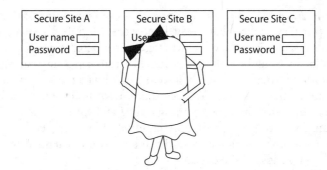

identity management systems (IMSs), tools used to simplify secure access to multiple Internet-based services via single sign-on. We'll start with the physical, with security tokens, then look at shared authentication schemes. The module finishes with single sign-on options.

Trust

One of the great powers of a Windows domain SSO is the fact that there is always a domain controller (and maybe a few secondary domain controllers) that stores a single repository of users and their associated passwords. When you log onto a Windows domain, you log onto a domain controller. Once your user account authenticates, the different servers provide authorization to their resources via your Windows security identifier. Every computer on the domain trusts the domain controller.

Web sites have no domain controller to handle authentication. To make some form of IMS work for the most distributed of all networks, the Internet, requires trust. Every IMS begins by giving any Web site that wants to use it some way to trust someone big like Google, Facebook, or Twitter. The Web site treats the sign-in you use with a trusted big platform as an option or a replacement for your signing in at the Web site itself. The individual sites, however, still handle their own authorization (Figure 3-54).

Figure 3-54
This site has a lot
of trust.

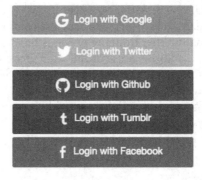

In general, an IMS provides a connection to log into one of these big platforms and, in turn, provides a token that the little sites use. Module 3-2 touched on the concepts of tokens, physical objects that enable access to restricted areas or content. A *security token* in an online IMS can be a physical thing, like a smartphone, that contains authentication or password information. It might also be a bit of data that stores some form of descriptor for the authentication used. You see this sort of token manifest in game systems, for example, where you change something online and a message is sent to your smartphone. The change will go through only by entering the security code sent to the phone. The stored security information in security tokens is often hashed to prevent access in the event of theft or loss of the device.

EXAM TIP The CompTIA Security+ exam objectives refer to a security token as a *secure token*.

Shared Authentication Schemes

Shared authentication schemes use various protocols, languages, and mechanisms to provide easier access to online resources for people. The two most prominent schemes are SAML and OpenID Connect.

The *Security Assertion Markup Language (SAML)* provides a format for a client and server to exchange authentication and authorization data securely. SAML defines three roles for making this happen: principle, identity provider, and service provider. The client or user is often the *principle*. The principle wants something from the *service provider (SP)*, the latter often a Web service of some kind. The *identity provider (IdP)* contains information that can assure the SP that the principle is legitimately who he says he is. Systems using SAML can use any number of methods for authentication, including passwords and user names.

Many companies—big ones, like Facebook, Google, and Microsoft—use *OpenID Connect* as an alternative to SAML, enabling users to log into other services using their respective credentials. Figure 3-55 shows a typical use of OpenID Connect. The user accesses a new (to him) Web-based service and can log in using his Facebook or Google account.

OpenID Connect handles the authentication part of the identification process, but relies on *OAuth* for authorization. OAuth enables things like users granting information to Web sites without revealing their passwords.

Many SSO standards rely on SAML for secure communication between principles and SPs. The SSO standards differ from the previous standards (such as OpenID Connect) in that the latter require additional use of the same user credentials. SSO standards do not.

The *Shibboleth* SSO system, for example, uses SAML (versions 1.3 and 2.0) to authenticate to various federations of organizations. As discussed in Module 3-1, federations enable content providers to provide content without retaining any personal information about clients or principles. This applies to Web-based systems as well as LAN- and domain-based systems.

Figure 3-55
Sign in with
Google!

Questions

1. Which of the following terms describes the process of allowing access to different resources?

   A. Authorization

   B. Authentication

   C. Accountability

   D. Identification

2. Which of the following states that users should be given only the level of access needed to perform their duties?

   A. Separation of duties

   B. Accountability

   C. Principle of least privilege

   D. Authorization

3. Which of the following access control models allows object creators and owners to assign permissions to users?

   A. Rule-based access control

   B. Discretionary access control

   C. Mandatory access control

   D. Role-based access control

4. An administrator wants to restrict access to a particular database based upon a stringent set of requirements. The organization is using a discretionary access control model. The database cannot be written to during a specified period when transactions are being reconciled. What type of restriction might the administrator impose on access to the database?

   A. Access restricted by the database owner

   B. Access based upon membership in a logical group

   C. Access from a particular workstation

   D. Time-of-day and object permission restrictions

5. Which of the following allows a user to use one set of credentials throughout an enterprise?

   A. TACACS

   B. RADIUS

   C. Single sign-on

   D. TACACS+

6. Which of the following is used to prevent the reuse of passwords?

   A. Disabling accounts

   B. Account lockout

   C. Password complexity

   D. Password history

7. Which of the following are the best ways to ensure that user accounts are being used appropriately and securely? (Choose two.)

   A. Periodically review assigned privileges.

   B. Allow users to maintain their privileges indefinitely, even during promotion or transfer.

   C. Continuously monitor accounts, through auditing, to ensure accountability and security.

   D. Ensure that users permissions stay cumulative, regardless of which group or job role they occupy.

8. Which of the following authentication factors would require that you input a piece of information from memory in addition to using a smart card?

   A. Possession

   B. Knowledge

   C. Inherence

   D. Temporal

9. You are implementing an authentication system for a new company. This is a small company, and the owner has requested that all users be able to create accounts on their own individual workstations. You would like to explain to the owner that centralized authentication might be better to use. Which of the following are advantages of centralized authentication? (Choose two.)

   A. Centralized security policies and account requirements.

   B. Ability of individuals to set their own security requirements.

   C. Ability to use single sign-on capabilities within the entire organization.

   D. Requirements have different user names and passwords for each workstation and resource.

10. Under which of the following circumstances would a Windows host use Kerberos instead of NTLM v2 to authenticate users?

    A. Authenticating to a server using only an IP address

    B. Authenticating to a modern Windows Active Directory domain

    C. Authenticating to a different Active Directory forest with legacy trusts enabled

    D. Authenticating to a server in a Windows workgroup

Answers

1. **A.** Authorization describes the process of allowing access to different resources.

2. **C.** The principle of least privilege states that users should be given only the level of access needed to perform their duties.

3. **B.** The discretionary access control model allows object creators and owners to assign permissions to users.

4. **D.** The administrator would want to impose both a time-of-day and object permission restriction on users to prevent them from writing to the database during a specified time period.

5. **C.** Single sign-on allows a user to use one set of credentials throughout an enterprise to access various resources without having to reauthenticate with a different set of credentials.

6. D. The password history setting in the account policy is used to prevent the reuse of older passwords.

7. A, C. Periodic reviews and continuous monitoring are two ways to ensure that accounts and privileges are used in accordance with organizational policy and in a secure manner.

8. B. The knowledge factor would require that you input a piece of information, such as a password or PIN, from memory in addition to using a smart card.

9. A, C. Centralized system security policies as well as the ability to use single sign-on throughout the organization are two advantages of centralized authentication.

10. B. When authenticating to a modern Windows Active Directory domain, Windows uses Kerberos as its authentication protocol by default.

4

Tools of the Trade

IT security professionals use a lot of tools to keep networks secure. These tools range from go-to utilities that run from the command-line interface of just about every operating system to more complex tools for scanning network activity. A phenomenal amount of a security professional's time is spent setting up and monitoring logs of system activities so that when that bad actor steps in or some odd action occurs, they're ready to save the day.

This chapter explores essential IT security tools in four modules:

- Operating System Utilities
- Network Scanners
- Protocol Analyzers
- Monitoring Networks

Module 4-1: Operating System Utilities
This module covers the following CompTIA Security+ objective:

- **2.2** Given a scenario, use appropriate software tools to assess the security posture of an organization

It always gives me a chuckle when newbie security techs ask, "Could you provide me a list of all the tools and utilities you use to support IT security?" It's not that I don't have advanced tools; it's just that most of the time the utilities built into every operating system are all I need to handle a host of issues.

This module covers many of the utilities included in Windows and UNIX/Linux systems. These utilities are listed in the CompTIA Security+ objectives and, more importantly, every good tech should recognize all of these as well as know where and when to use them (Figure 4-1).

Let's look at a dozen or so tools:

- ping
- ipconfig
- ifconfig
- ip
- arp
- netstat
- netcat
- tracert
- nslookup
- dig

Figure 4-1
We love utilities!

ping

If you want to know that two TCP/IP systems share the same network, the go-to tool is *ping*. The ping utility takes advantage of the fact that by design all TCP/IP hosts respond to ICMP requests. When one system successfully pings another host, you automatically know that the other system is connected and is properly IP addressed. Figure 4-2 shows a successful ping running in a Windows terminal.

In Windows, ping runs four times and stops automatically. In Linux, ping runs continuously until you press CTRL-C. To get ping to run continuously in Windows, use the –t switch.

The ping utility has uses beyond simply verifying connectivity. Running ping using a DNS name, for example, is a great way to verify you have a good DNS server. Look at Figure 4-3. Note that the ping is unsuccessful, but the ping successfully resolves the DNS name to an IP address.

```
Command Prompt                                          —   □   ×

C:\Users\scott>ping 192.168.0.1

Pinging 192.168.0.1 with 32 bytes of data:
Reply from 192.168.0.1: bytes=32 time=1ms TTL=64
Reply from 192.168.0.1: bytes=32 time<1ms TTL=64
Reply from 192.168.0.1: bytes=32 time=3ms TTL=64
Reply from 192.168.0.1: bytes=32 time=2ms TTL=64

Ping statistics for 192.168.0.1:
    Packets: Sent = 4, Received = 4, Lost = 0 (0% loss),
Approximate round trip times in milli-seconds:
    Minimum = 0ms, Maximum = 3ms, Average = 1ms

C:\Users\scott>_
```

Figure 4-2   ping in Windows

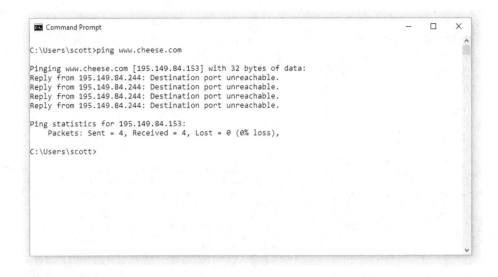

Figure 4-3 ping resolving an IP address

The ping utility offers many more features that IT security professionals use all the time. Here's a list of some of the more useful switches:

- **–a** Resolve addresses to hostnames
- **–f** Set Don't Fragment flag in packet (IPv4 only)
- **–4** Force using IPv4
- **–6** Force using IPv6

ipconfig

The *ipconfig* command is the Windows-only reporting utility that shows the current status of the network settings for a host system. Figure 4-4 shows a sample output from ipconfig in Windows 10.

Typing **ipconfig** by itself gives some basic, but important, information. ipconfig has the following six switches that are particularly useful. Typing **ipconfig /all**, for example, lists virtually every IP and Ethernet setting on the system.

- **/all** Exhaustive listing of virtually every IP and Ethernet setting
- **/release** Releases the DHCP IP address lease (see "About DHCP" later in this module)
- **/renew** Renews the DHCP IP address lease
- **/flushdns** Clears the host's DNS cache
- **/displaydns** Displays the host's DNS cache

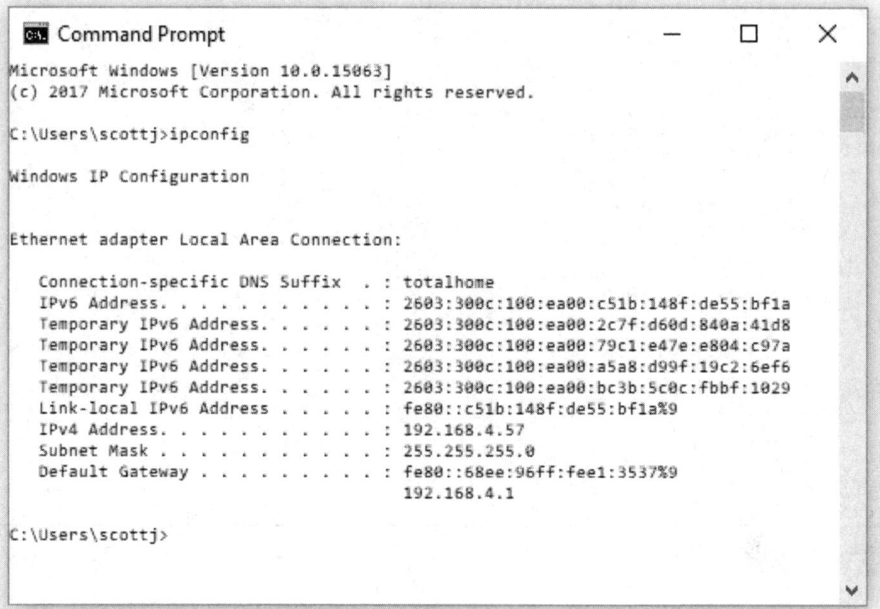

Figure 4-4 Results from running ipconfig

ifconfig

The *ifconfig* command is the functional equivalent to ipconfig for UNIX/Linux operating systems. Figure 4-5 shows ifconfig running in Ubuntu Linux. Unlike ipconfig, ifconfig goes beyond basic reporting, enabling you to configure a system. The following example sets the IP address and the subnet mask for the Ethernet NIC eth0:

```
sudo ifconfig eth0 192.168.0.1 netmask 255.255.255.0
```

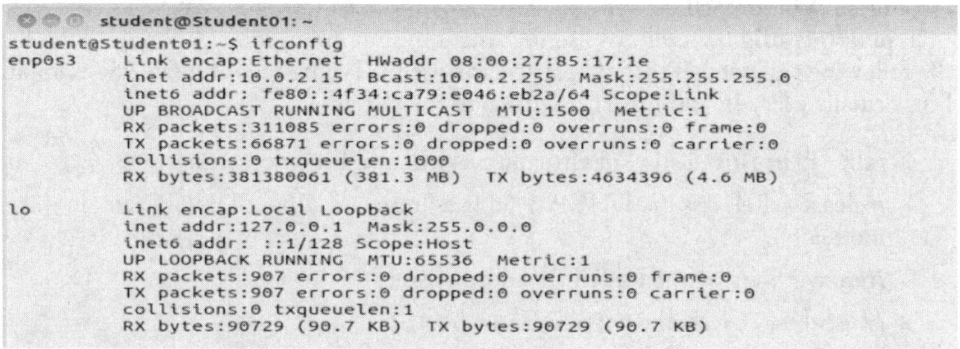

Figure 4-5 ifconfig in Ubuntu

NOTE Linux systems also have the *iwconfig* command exclusively for wireless connections.

ip

If you're looking to do anything serious in terms of IP and Ethernet information on a Linux system, the cool kid is the *ip* command. The ip command replaces ifconfig, doing many of the same tasks, such as viewing IP information on a system, checking status of network connections, managing routing, and starting or stopping an Ethernet interface.

The syntax differs from ipconfig and ifconfig, dropping a lot of the extra non-alphanumeric characters and shortening switch names. To see all the Ethernet and IP information for a system, for example, just type this:

```
ip a
```

arp

Every host on a network keeps a cache of mapped IP-to-Ethernet addresses for the local network. The *arp* command enables you to observe and administer this cache. Interestingly, both the Windows version and the Linux version use the almost same switches. If you want to see the current cache, type the command as follows (Windows version):

```
C:\>arp -a
Interface: 192.168.1.75 --- 0x2
  Internet Address        Physical Address      Type
  192.168.1.1             14-dd-a9-9b-03-90     dynamic
  192.168.1.58            88-de-a9-57-8c-f7     dynamic
  192.168.1.128           30-cd-a7-b6-ff-d0     dynamic
  192.168.1.255           ff-ff-ff-ff-ff-ff     static
  224.0.0.2               01-00-5e-00-00-02     static
  224.0.0.22              01-00-5e-00-00-16     static
  224.0.0.251             01-00-5e-00-00-fb     static
```

(Several output lines have been removed for brevity.)

The dynamic type shows a listing under control of DHCP. Static types are fixed (the multicast addresses that start with 224 never change) or are for statically assigned IP addresses.

NOTE arp is only for IPv4 addresses. IPv6 uses the Neighbor Discovery protocol.

The arp command enables detection of *ARP spoofing*, when a separate system uses the arp command to broadcast another host's IP address. Look carefully at this arp command's output and note that two systems have the same IP address:

```
C:\>arp -a
Interface: 192.168.1.75 --- 0x2
  Internet Address      Physical Address    Type
  192.168.1.1           14-dd-a9-9b-03-90   dynamic
  192.168.1.58          88-de-a9-57-8c-f7   dynamic
  192.168.1.58          23-1d-77-43-2c-9b   dynamic
```

Given that most operating systems return an error when this happens, you might think using arp isn't helpful. But arp at least provides the MAC address for the spoofing system, which might help you determine the offending system.

 NOTE The arp command (lowercase) displays information on aspects of the system that use the Address Resolution Protocol (ARP). The mapped cache of IP-to-Ethernet addresses, for example, is the ARP cache. arp and other command-line utilities listed here are lowercase to reflect the case-sensitivity of UNIX/Linux systems.

netstat

The *netstat* command is the go-to tool in Windows and Linux to get any information you might need on the host system's TCP and UDP connections, status of all open and listening ports, and a few other items such as the host's routing table.

Typing **netstat** by itself shows all active connections between a host and other hosts:

```
C:\Users\Mike>netstat
Active Connections
  Proto  Local Address          Foreign Address         State
  TCP    127.0.0.1:5432         MiKESLAPTOP:50165       ESTABLISHED
  TCP    127.0.0.1:5432         MiKESLAPTOP:50168       ESTABLISHED
  TCP    127.0.0.1:5432         MiKESLAPTOP:50175       ESTABLISHED
```

You can see that the first few lines of any netstat show a number of active connections with the loopback address (the 127.*x.x.x*). These are used by Microsoft for several different information exchanges such as the Cortana voice recognition utility. Other connections show up as more varied IP addresses:

```
  TCP    192.168.1.75:57552     167.125.3.3:https            CLOSE_WAIT
  TCP    192.168.1.75:58620     msnbot-25-52-108-191:https   ESTABLISHED
  TCP    192.168.1.75:60435     61.55.223.14:33033           ESTABLISHED
  TCP    192.168.1.75:60444     92.190.216.63:12350          ESTABLISHED
  TCP    192.168.1.75:60457     42.122.162.208:https         ESTABLISHED
  TCP    192.168.1.75:60461     62.52.108.74:https           ESTABLISHED
  TCP    192.168.1.75:60466     a14-112-155-235:https        CLOSE_WAIT
  TCP    192.168.1.75:60537     65.55.223.12:40027           CLOSE_WAIT
```

```
mike@VirtualUbuntu:~$ sudo netstat
Active Internet connections (w/o servers)
Proto Recv-Q Send-Q Local Address          Foreign Address        State
tcp        0      0 10.0.2.15:39822        atl14s77-in-f4.1e:https ESTABLISHED
tcp        0      0 10.0.2.15:35096        avocado.canonical.:http ESTABLISHED
tcp        0      0 10.0.2.15:46080        dfw25s27-in-f14.1:https TIME_WAIT
tcp        0      0 10.0.2.15:34910        dfw28s02-in-f3.1e:https ESTABLISHED
tcp        0      0 10.0.2.15:47550        13.32.188.5:https       ESTABLISHED
tcp        0      0 10.0.2.15:38942        ec2-52-33-209-128:https ESTABLISHED
tcp        0      0 10.0.2.15:45932        dfw25s27-in-f14.1e:http ESTABLISHED
tcp        0      0 10.0.2.15:60528        dfw25s27-in-f3.1e:https ESTABLISHED
tcp        0      0 10.0.2.15:39332        ec2-52-31-101-251:https ESTABLISHED
tcp        0      0 10.0.2.15:47408        ec2-52-36-207-192:https ESTABLISHED
tcp        0      0 10.0.2.15:41358        atl14s77-in-f4.1e1:http ESTABLISHED
tcp        0      0 10.0.2.15:46082        dfw25s27-in-f14.1:https ESTABLISHED
tcp        0      0 10.0.2.15:50714        dfw25s12-in-f46.1:https ESTABLISHED
tcp        0      0 10.0.2.15:45204        ec2-52-34-28-127.:https ESTABLISHED
tcp        0      0 10.0.2.15:53268        13.32.188.161:https     ESTABLISHED
tcp        0      0 10.0.2.15:35900        72.21.91.29:http        ESTABLISHED
tcp        0      0 10.0.2.15:45664        server-54-230-204:https ESTABLISHED
Active UNIX domain sockets (w/o servers)
Proto RefCnt Flags      Type       State         I-Node   Path
unix  2      [ ]        DGRAM                    18094    /run/user/1000/systemd/notify
unix  17     [ ]        DGRAM                    10886    /run/systemd/journal/dev-log
unix  2      [ ]        DGRAM                    10887    /run/systemd/journal/syslog
unix  7      [ ]        DGRAM                    10899    /run/systemd/journal/socket
```

Figure 4-6 netstat in Linux

The preceding netstat output shows the open connections on this system, mainly HTTPS connections for Web pages. In the State column on the right, ESTABLISHED identifies active connections and CLOSE_WAIT indicates connections that are closing.

Typing **netstat** in Linux gives the same information, but in a slightly different format. At the very bottom are the associated UNIX sockets. A socket is an endpoint for connections. This data is very long and not very useful. Figure 4-6 shows just the first few lines.

Typing **netstat –a** in Windows or Linux shows the same information as netstat alone, but adds listening ports. This is a very powerful tool for finding hidden servers or malware on a host. Look carefully at the following command. Notice that HTTP port 80 and HTTPS port 443 are listening. This instantly tells you that the host is an HTTP/HTTPS server. You must then answer the question: "Should this system be running a Web server?"

```
C:\Users\Mike>netstat -a
Active Connections
  Proto   Local Address        Foreign Address        State
  TCP     0.0.0.0:135          MiKESLAPTOP:0          LISTENING
  TCP     0.0.0.0:445          MiKESLAPTOP:0          LISTENING
  TCP     0.0.0.0:3780         MiKESLAPTOP:0          LISTENING
  TCP     127.0.0.1:9990       MiKESLAPTOP:0          LISTENING
  TCP     127.0.0.1:17600      MiKESLAPTOP:0          LISTENING
  TCP     192.168.1.75:80      MiKESLAPTOP:0          LISTENING
  TCP     192.168.1.75:443     MiKESLAPTOP:0          LISTENING
  TCP     192.168.1.75:6698    MiKESLAPTOP:0          LISTENING
  TCP     192.168.1.75:13958   MiKESLAPTOP:0          LISTENING
```

(Lines removed for brevity.)

Running netstat with the –b option displays the executable file making the connection. Here's netstat running in Windows PowerShell using both the –b and –a options (with many lines removed for brevity):

```
PS C:\WINDOWS\system32> netstat -a -b
Active Connections
   Proto  Local Address           Foreign Address          State
   TCP    0.0.0.0:135             MiKESLAPTOP:0            LISTENING
 [svchost.exe]
   TCP    0.0.0.0:80              MiKESLAPTOP:0            LISTENING
 [svchost.exe]
   TCP    0.0.0.0:17500           MiKESLAPTOP:0            LISTENING
 [Dropbox.exe]
   TCP    0.0.0.0:47984           MiKESLAPTOP:0            LISTENING
 [NvStreamNetworkService.exe]
   TCP    192.168.1.75:6698       MiKESLAPTOP:0            LISTENING
 [SkypeHost.exe]
   TCP    192.168.1.75:58620      msnbot-65-52-108-191:https  ESTABLISHED
 [Explorer.EXE]
   TCP    192.168.1.75:62789      msnbot-65-52-108-205:https  ESTABLISHED
 [OneDrive.exe]
```

Researching open ports and processes in netstat is nerve wracking. What are these programs? Why are they listening? A quick Web search of the filename often gives you excellent guidance as to which programs are good, which are evil, and which you simply don't need.

 NOTE   The netstat command works perfectly well with IPv6.

Netstat is an incredibly powerful tool and this short description barely touched its capabilities. For the CompTIA Security+ exam, you should experiment with netstat both in Linux and in Windows.

netcat

netcat (or *nc*) is a terminal program for Linux that enables you to make any type of connection and see the results from a command line. With nc, you can connect to anything on any port number or you can make your system listen on a port number. Figure 4-7 shows nc connecting to a Web page.

```
mike@VirtualUbuntu:~$ nc -v www.google.com 80
Connection to www.google.com 80 port [tcp/http] succeeded!
```

Figure 4-7   Connecting to www.google.com with nc

```
mike@VirtualUbuntu:~$ nc -v www.google.com 80
Connection to www.google.com 80 port [tcp/http] succeeded!
GET / HTTP/1.1

HTTP/1.1 200 OK
Date: Tue, 06 Jun 2017 01:50:18 GMT
Expires: -1
Cache-Control: private, max-age=0
Content-Type: text/html; charset=ISO-8859-1
```

Figure 4-8   Successful connection to www.google.com with nc

The nc command is a primitive tool. To get any good information from the connection, the user must know the protocol well enough to type in properly formed input data. Since this is a Web page, type **get index.html HTTP/1.1**, as this is what the Web server is expecting. Figure 4-8 shows the result.

The challenge and the power of nc come from the fact that it's a tool for people who know how to type in the right commands, making it great for penetration testing or, if you're evil, hacking. Imagine making a connection to a server and typing in anything you want to try to fool the server into doing something it's not supposed to do!

The nc command even works as a handy scanning command. Find a server, guess on a port number, and try connecting! The nc command works perfectly with scripts. It's relatively easy to write a script that tries 1024 port numbers one after the other, automating the scanning process.

NOTE   Windows lacks an equivalent to netcat, but Ncat from https://nmap.org/ncat/ has very similar functionality.

tracert

If you want to know how packets get from a host to another endpoint, the best tool is the Windows *tracert* command. Linux uses the almost identical command called *traceroute*. Run tracert as follows:

```
C:\>tracert www.robotmonkeybutler.com
Tracing route to www.robotmonkeybutler.com [64.98.145.30]
over a maximum of 30 hops:

  1     5 ms     9 ms     5 ms   192.168.4.1
  2     5 ms    18 ms    10 ms   10.120.17.101
  3    15 ms    14 ms    19 ms   ae201-sur04.airport.tx.houston.comcast.net
[68.85.253.229]
  4    14 ms    10 ms    17 ms   ae-0-sur03.airport.tx.houston.comcast.net
[68.85.247.29]
```

(Hops 5 through 12 removed for brevity.)

```
13    71 ms    66 ms    179 ms  xe-0-10-0-3-5.r05.asbnva02.us.ce.gin.ntt.net
[130.94.195.234]
14    63 ms    60 ms     69 ms  iar02-p3.ash.tucows.net [64.98.2.10]
15    65 ms    68 ms     70 ms  csr-p6.ash.tucows.net [64.98.128.14]
16    59 ms    58 ms     67 ms  url.hover.com [64.98.145.30]

Trace complete.
```

The power of tracert comes by running it before there are any problems. If you look at the previous example, you see the first two hops use a private IP address. This is correct, because this network has two routers between the host and the ISP—in this case, Comcast. Let's say we run this command again and get this result:

```
C:\>tracert www.robotmonkeybutler.com
Tracing route to www.robotmonkeybutler.com [64.98.145.30]
over a maximum of 30 hops:

1     5 ms     9 ms      5 ms  192.168.4.1
2     5 ms    18 ms     10 ms  10.120.17.101
3    [10.120.17.101] reports: Destination host unreachable
```

The tracert successfully made it through both internal routers, but couldn't make it to the ISP. In this case we know there's something wrong between the gateway and the ISP.

Going Graphical

Need something a little more graphical in your life? There are many interesting graphical tools that enable you to access these commands graphically. Graphical tools often provide easier-to-grasp information that the command-line tools lack. Try TCPView from Windows Sysinternals instead of netstat. Or maybe replace boring old ping/traceroute with PingPlotter from Pingman Tools (Figure 4-9). There are a ton of great tools out there. Take your time, do some research, and find the ones you enjoy.

 NOTE tracert is often a great way to determine the ISP just by looking at the router names.

About DHCP

Dynamic Host Configuration Protocol (DHCP) is the standard protocol used for automatically allocating network addresses within a single broadcast domain. Every broadcast domain that uses DHCP must have a DHCP server that allocates IP addresses based on a preconfigured DHCP pool configured on the DHCP server. When a DHCP client boots up, it broadcasts for a DHCP server to give it the needed IP information, including (but not limited to) IP address, subnet mask, default gateway, and DNS server. When a DHCP client logs off, it usually releases its lease, opening an IP address for use to any other DHCP client that might request a lease.

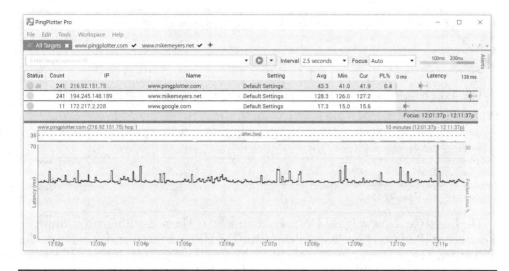

Figure 4-9 PingPlotter in action

There are no DHCP-only utilities common in any operating system. Windows users can perform an ipconfig /release to release a lease or ipconfig /renew to renew a lease. The biggest issue with DHCP and a common use case is when a DHCP server is not present on a broadcast domain. In this case, use a quick run of ipconfig to see if your system is running an Automatic IP Address (APIPA). APIPA addresses always start with 169.254 and are a surefire way to diagnose a DHCP problem.

DNS Tools

DNS security issues can create huge problems for IT security professionals. Techniques such as spoofing or replacing a host's DNS server settings give an attacker tremendous insight as to whom the host is communicating. There are two tools used to diagnose DNS issues: nslookup and dig.

nslookup

The *nslookup* tool, built into both Windows and Linux, has one function: if you give nslookup a DNS server name or a DNS server's IP address, nslookup will query that DNS server and (assuming the DNS server is configured to respond) return incredibly detailed information about any DNS domain. For example, you can run nslookup to ask a DNS server for all the NS (name server) records for any domain.

This power of nslookup has been used for evil purposes. For that reason, no public DNS server supports nslookup anymore for anything but the simplest queries. But there are still good reasons to use nslookup.

NOTE nslookup works similarly in both Linux and Windows.

The most basic way to run nslookup is to type the command followed by a domain. For example:

```
C:\WINDOWS\system32>nslookup www.totalsem.com
Server:   cdns01.comcast.net
Address:  2001:558:feed::1
Non-authoritative answer:
Name:     www.totalsem.com
Address:  75.126.29.106
```

The first server is an assigned DNS server for a host. The non-authoritative answer is the returned IP address for www.totalsem.com. The URL www.totalsem.com is a public Web server. The totalsem.com domain has a private file server, however, named server1 .totalsem.com. If that URL is queried by nslookup the following happens:

```
C:\WINDOWS\system32>nslookup server1.totalsem.com
Server:   cdns01.comcast.net
Address:  2001:558:feed::1
*** cdns01.comcast.net can't find server1.totalsem.com: Non-existent domain
```

This is good. The authoritative DNS server is configured to protect this private server and therefore not respond to an nslookup query.

While almost all the features of nslookup no longer work, one feature stands out in that nslookup can tell you if an IP address is a functioning DNS server. Run nslookup interactively by typing **nslookup** to get a prompt:

```
C:\WINDOWS\system32>nslookup
Default Server:  cdns01.comcast.net
Address:  2001:558:feed::1
>
```

Then type in the IP address of the DNS server you want to check:

```
> server 8.8.8.8
Default Server:  google-public-dns-a.google.com
Address:  8.8.8.8
>
```

Note that it returns a DNS name. This means there is a reverse DNS zone; a very good sign, but still not proof. Let's make it resolve a known-good DNS name:

```
> www.totalsem.com
Server:  google-public-dns-a.google.com
Address:  8.8.8.8

Non-authoritative answer:
Name:     www.totalsem.com
Address:  75.126.29.106
>
```

If instead we got this response:

```
DNS request timed out.
    timeout was 2 seconds.
*** Request to [4.7.3.4] timed-out
>
```

we instantly know that the server IP address is not a functional DNS server.

dig

The *dig* command is a Linux-based DNS querying tool that offers many advantages over nslookup. dig works with the host's DNS settings, as opposed to nslookup, which ignores the host DNS settings and makes queries based on the variables entered at the command line. dig also works well with scripting tools. The dig tool is unique to Linux, although you can find third-party Windows dig-like tools. dig is simple to use and provides excellent information with an easy-to-use interface. Figure 4-10 shows a basic dig query.

dig has some interesting features that are much easier to use than the same functions in nslookup. For example, if you want to know all the mail server (MX) servers for a domain, just add the MX switch, as shown in Figure 4-11.

 NOTE The Linux *host* command isn't listed on the CompTIA Security+ objectives, but is a great tool and one of my favorites. Know nslookup and dig for the exam, but check out the host command too!

```
mike@VirtualUbuntu:~$ dig totalsem.com

; <<>> DiG 9.10.3-P4-Ubuntu <<>> totalsem.com
;; global options: +cmd
;; Got answer:
;; ->>HEADER<<- opcode: QUERY, status: NOERROR, id: 11252
;; flags: qr rd ra; QUERY: 1, ANSWER: 1, AUTHORITY: 0, ADDITIONAL: 1

;; OPT PSEUDOSECTION:
; EDNS: version: 0, flags:; udp: 1280
;; QUESTION SECTION:
;totalsem.com.                  IN      A

;; ANSWER SECTION:
totalsem.com.          1799     IN      A       75.126.29.106

;; Query time: 27 msec
;; SERVER: 127.0.1.1#53(127.0.1.1)
;; WHEN: Wed Jun 07 12:17:22 CDT 2017
;; MSG SIZE  rcvd: 57
```

Figure 4-10   Simple dig query

```
mike@VirtualUbuntu:~$ dig robotmonkeybutler.com MX

; <<>> DiG 9.10.3-P4-Ubuntu <<>> robotmonkeybutler.com MX
;; global options: +cmd
;; Got answer:
;; ->>HEADER<<- opcode: QUERY, status: NOERROR, id: 46722
;; flags: qr rd ra; QUERY: 1, ANSWER: 5, AUTHORITY: 0, ADDITIONAL: 9

;; OPT PSEUDOSECTION:
; EDNS: version: 0, flags:; udp: 1280
;; QUESTION SECTION:
;robotmonkeybutler.com.          IN      MX

;; ANSWER SECTION:
robotmonkeybutler.com.   900    IN      MX      10 ALT4.ASPMX.L.GOOGLE.com.
robotmonkeybutler.com.   900    IN      MX      1 ASPMX.L.GOOGLE.com.
robotmonkeybutler.com.   900    IN      MX      5 ALT1.ASPMX.L.GOOGLE.com.
robotmonkeybutler.com.   900    IN      MX      5 ALT2.ASPMX.L.GOOGLE.com.
robotmonkeybutler.com.   900    IN      MX      10 ALT3.ASPMX.L.GOOGLE.com.
```

Figure 4-11   Querying for MX records (output reduced for brevity)

Module 4-2: Network Scanners

This module covers the following CompTIA Security+ objectives:

- **2.2**   Given a scenario, use appropriate software tools to assess the security posture of an organization

- **2.3**   Given a scenario, troubleshoot common security issues

What is on my network? This is one of the most important questions a good IT security professional must answer. Several software and hardware tools, known collectively as *network scanners*, help answer this question.

Network scanners use protocols on a network, almost always a LAN, to determine as much information about the LAN as possible. In essence, a scanner is an inventory tool. There's no single standard or type of network scanner. Different network scanners use a variety of protocols, standards, and methods to query the hosts on the LAN. Given that virtually every network in existence uses the TCP/IP protocol stack, it might be more accurate to use the term *TCP/IP network scanner* when describing these tools.

Scanning Methods

Every scanner scans differently, but they try to find certain common data. Here's a short list of some of the more important items every network scanner will inventory:

- Topology
- MAC addresses
- IP addresses
- Open ports

- Protocol information on open ports
- Operating systems

A good network scanner compiles this information and presents it in a way that enables security people to understand what's going on in the network. A network scanner enables *network mapping* on many levels.

The one area that IP scanners do not usually cover are protocols underneath TCP/IP. For example, a TCP/IP scanner isn't commonly going to verify the Ethernet speed/type. There are network scanners that do inventory lower protocol information, but they tend to be more specialized. With that in mind, let's dive into network IP scanners. In general, we turn to this information for two reasons: baselining and monitoring.

Scanning Targets

Think of a *baseline* as a verification of the network assets. Security professionals run baselines to make sure of exactly what is on the network. This a great time to build an "official" inventory that defines and details every computer, server, printer, router, switch, and WAP in the network infrastructure.

Once you know what's on a network, you can then occasionally reapply a network scan to verify that there are no surprises on the network. Compare recent scans to the baseline and look for differences. Any sort of *baseline deviation*—things that have changed—can help secure the network. In such a scenario, monitoring enables *rogue system detection*, such as finding rogue WAPs, unauthorized servers, and other such security breaches.

Network scanners are everywhere. If you go into Network and Sharing Center in Windows (assuming your firewall settings aren't too restrictive), you'll see a perfectly functional, although very simple, network scanner (Figure 4-12).

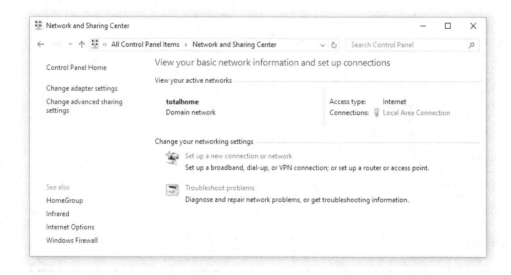

Figure 4-12 Windows network information

Scanner Types

Network scanners tend to fit into one of two categories: simple or powerful. Simple scanners make quick, basic scans. They require little or no actual skill and only provide essential information. Powerful network scanners use many protocols to drill deeply into a network and return an outrageous amount of information.

Simple Network Scanners

Simple scanners are easy to use and invariably have pretty graphical user interfaces (GUIs) to improve usability. The free and surprisingly powerful *Angry IP Scanner* from Anton Keks (http://angryip.org) does a good job using simple protocols, mainly ping, to query a single IP address or an address range. If you just want to count the systems in a simple LAN and you have confidence that your internal network isn't blocking ICMP messages, Angry IP Scanner is a great tool (Figure 4-13). Angry IP Scanner is good for a single network ID and it does some basic port scanning, but that's about it.

 NOTE Angry IP Scanner and, in fact, most scanning tools will set off your anti-malware tools. In most cases you'll need to shut off the anti-malware; or better yet, go through whatever process is needed to make these scanners exempt from the anti-malware software.

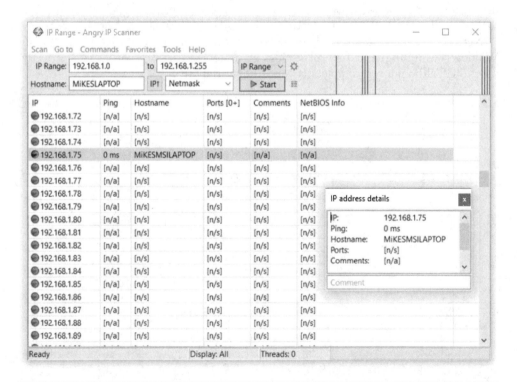

Figure 4-13   Angry IP Scanner

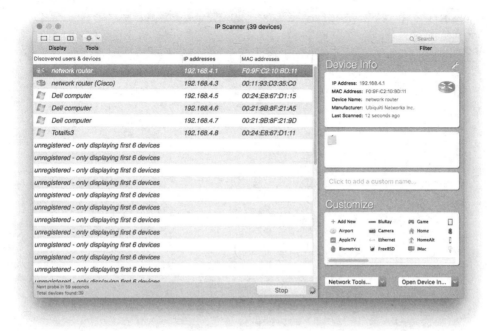

Figure 4-14   IP Scanner

Simple scanners aren't limited to Windows. macOS users have similar tools. One of the more common and popular is *IP Scanner* by 10base-t Interactive (http://10base-t .com). Like Angry IP Scanner, this tool uses only the simplest protocols to query a local network. Compare Figure 4-14 to Figure 4-13 and see how they share a somewhat similar interface.

There are also several excellent simple network scanners for smart devices running Android and iOS operating systems. Given that these devices all have dedicated 802.11 connections, almost all of these simple IP network scanners tend to give excellent wireless information. One of my favorite scanners is Fing (https://www.fing.io/). Note the screenshot of Fing in Figure 4-15.

Nmap: A Powerful Network Scanner

Simple scanners are wonderful tools if you're looking for quick scans that grab IP addresses, open ports, and maybe a Windows network name, but little else. But what if you're looking for more? What if you have multiple address ranges? What if you want to know the public key for that SSH you found on a system? What if you have a routed network and you want to install multiple sensors that all report back to a single system? In that case you'll need to turn to a powerful network scanner.

Among the many contenders in the network scanner market, the one that every security professional should know, and the one explicitly listed in the CompTIA Security+ exam

Figure 4-15
Fing scanner on
Android

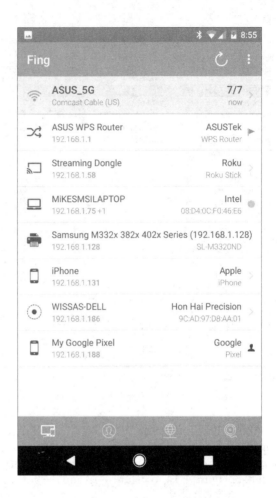

objectives, is Nmap (from www.nmap.org). Originally written back in the mid 1990s by Gordon Lyon, Nmap established itself as the gold standard for TCP/IP network scanners early on and has retained its prominence through ongoing updates from the Nmap community. Nmap is so popular that it shows up in popular media, such as the movies *The Matrix* (Figure 4-16) and *Judge Dredd*.

 NOTE Nmap runs on most OSes, but it runs best on Linux/UNIX systems.

Having said all these nice things about Nmap, be warned: Nmap is a command-line tool with a powerful and incredibly complex number of switches and options. Nmap is complicated to master; there are many thick books and long online Web page Nmap tutorials that do a great job showing you the power of Nmap. (Also, GUI overlays that

```
 Port          State         Service
 22/tcp        open          ssh

No exact OS matches for host

Nmap run completed -- 1 IP address (1 host up) scanneds
# sshnuke 10.2.2.2 -rootpw="Z10N0101"
Connecting to 10.2.2.2:ssh ... successful.
Attempting to exploit SSHv1 CRC32 ... successful.
Reseting root password to "Z10N0101".
System open: Access Level <9>
# ssh 10.2.2.2 -l ro█
```

Figure 4-16   Nmap used in *The Matrix*

run on top of Nmap are available, such as Zenmap, discussed shortly.) It is impossible to give you any more than the lightest of touches on Nmap in this module. Fortunately, the CompTIA Security+ exam will not test you intensely on this tool, but it will expect you to have a good understanding of its capabilities and some of the basic syntax, and that we can do here.

Do yourself a favor, download Nmap and try it.

Nmap Basics   In its simplest form, Nmap is run from a command line. I can run a very simple Nmap command, as shown in Figure 4-17, against my home router. Nmap scans the 1000 most common port numbers by default. In this case it located four open ports: 53 (my router is a DNS forwarder), 80 (the router's Web interface), and 515 and 9100 (I have a printer plugged into the network).

```
mike@VirtualUbuntu:~$ nmap 192.168.1.1

Starting Nmap 7.01 ( https://nmap.org ) at 2017-06-08 23:05 CDT
Nmap scan report for router.asus.com (192.168.1.1)
Host is up (0.0061s latency).
Not shown: 996 closed ports
PORT      STATE SERVICE
53/tcp    open  domain
80/tcp    open  http
515/tcp   open  printer
9100/tcp  open  jetdirect

Nmap done: 1 IP address (1 host up) scanned in 0.16 seconds
mike@VirtualUbuntu:~$
```

Figure 4-17   Basic Nmap command

```
Scanning scanme.nmap.org (45.33.32.156) [1000 ports]
Discovered open port 22/tcp on 45.33.32.156
Discovered open port 80/tcp on 45.33.32.156
Increasing send delay for 45.33.32.156 from 0 to 5 due to 11 out of 36 dropped probes since last inc
rease.
Discovered open port 9929/tcp on 45.33.32.156
Discovered open port 31337/tcp on 45.33.32.156
Completed Connect Scan at 23:53, 7.65s elapsed (1000 total ports)
Initiating Service scan at 23:53
Scanning 4 services on scanme.nmap.org (45.33.32.156)
Completed Service scan at 23:53, 6.14s elapsed (4 services on 1 host)
NSE: Script scanning 45.33.32.156.
Initiating NSE at 23:53
Completed NSE at 23:53, 5.45s elapsed
Initiating NSE at 23:53
Completed NSE at 23:53, 0.00s elapsed
Nmap scan report for scanme.nmap.org (45.33.32.156)
Host is up (0.061s latency).
Other addresses for scanme.nmap.org (not scanned): 2600:3c01::f03c:91ff:fe18:bb2f
Not shown: 992 closed ports
PORT      STATE    SERVICE      VERSION
22/tcp    open     ssh          OpenSSH 6.6.1p1 Ubuntu 2ubuntu2.8 (Ubuntu Linux; protocol 2.0)
| ssh-hostkey:
|   1024 ac:00:a0:1a:82:ff:cc:55:99:dc:67:2b:34:97:6b:75 (DSA)
|   2048 20:3d:2d:44:62:2a:b0:5a:9d:b5:b3:05:14:c2:a6:b2 (RSA)
|_  256 96:02:bb:5e:57:54:1c:4e:45:2f:56:4c:4a:24:b2:57 (ECDSA)
25/tcp    filtered smtp
80/tcp    open     http         Apache httpd 2.4.7 ((Ubuntu))
|_http-favicon: Unknown favicon MD5: 156515DA3C0F7DC6B2493BD5CE43F795
| http-methods:
|_  Supported Methods: GET HEAD POST OPTIONS
|_http-server-header: Apache/2.4.7 (Ubuntu)
|_http-title: Go ahead and ScanMe!
135/tcp   filtered msrpc
139/tcp   filtered netbios-ssn
445/tcp   filtered microsoft-ds
9929/tcp  open     nping-echo   Nping echo
31337/tcp open     tcpwrapped
Service Info: OS: Linux; CPE: cpe:/o:linux:linux_kernel
```

Figure 4-18   Part of a more aggressive Nmap scan

Nmap can just as easily scan an entire network ID. For example, this Nmap command will run the same command except generate a very long output to the terminal:

```
nmap 192.168.1.*
```

By adding a few extra switches, –A to tell Nmap to query for OS version and –v to increase the "verbocity"—in essence telling Nmap to grab more information—you can get a lot more information. Nmap also works perfectly fine for any public-facing server. Figure 4-18 shows part of the Nmap scan against Nmap.org's purpose-built public server scanme.nmap.org.

Note that not only does Nmap detect open ports, it pulls detailed information about each port, including the RSA key for the SSH server, HTTP server version, and the title to the index page as well as NetBIOS ports.

Zenmap   Nmap outputs can be massive, so in many cases we don't use this interactive mode of terminal screen output and instead direct our output to XML files that we can then use other tools to analyze, including graphical tools. Nmap provides a wonderful GUI called Zenmap that enables you to enter Nmap commands and then provides some handy analysis tools. Figure 4-19 shows the topology screen from Zenmap, showing a complete network.

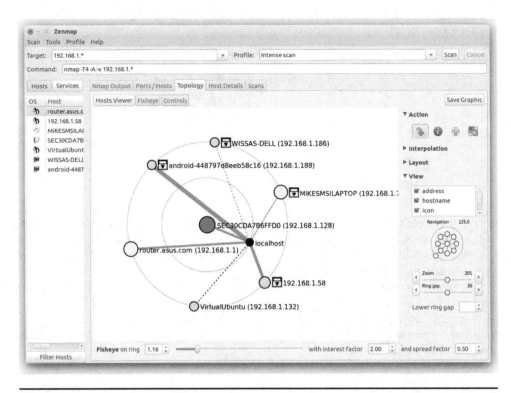

Figure 4-19   Zenmap

As previously mentioned, this is just the lightest of tastes of the powerful Nmap scanner. Nmap is a critical part of many Linux security packages, including the powerful Metasploit framework.

Module 4-3: Protocol Analyzers

This module covers the following CompTIA Security+ objective:

- **2.2**   Given a scenario, use appropriate software tools to assess the security posture of an organization

If network scanners collect and inventory the hosts on a network, then it's the job of *protocol analyzers* to collect and inventory the network traffic on a network. The CompTIA Security+ exam uses the term *protocol analyzer*, but that's a fairly broad term. The IT industry defines protocol analyzers as any type of hardware or software that analyzes any form of communication. In IP networks, all data transmits via Ethernet frames or IP packets contained in those frames, so the better term is *packet analyzer* (Figure 4-20).

Figure 4-20
I'm a protocol analyzer.

If something is going to analyze packets, it is first going to need, well, packets! It needs some program that can put a NIC into promiscuous mode so that the NIC grabs every packet it sees. This frame/packet grabber program needs to monitor or sniff the wired or wireless network and start grabbing the frames/packets. So, a packet analyzer is really two totally separate functions: a packet sniffer that grabs the frames/packets, and the packet analyzer that looks at all the collected packets and analyzes them (Figure 4-21).

This combination of sniffer and analyzer leads to a funny name issue. Any of the following terms are perfectly interchangeable: packet analyzer, network sniffer, network analyzer, and packet sniffer.

 NOTE Different network technologies need different sniffers. If you want to analyze a wired network, you need a wired sniffer. If you want to sniff a wireless network, you need a wireless sniffer.

Figure 4-21
Sniffers and analyzers

Networks generate a huge number of packets. Even in a small home network, moving a few files and watching a few videos generates hundreds of thousands of packets. A good analyzer needs two features. First, it must provide some type of interface that allows the security professional a way to inspect packets. Second, it must provide powerful sorting and filtering tools to let you look at the packets that interest you while eliminating the ones you do not want to see.

Why Protocol Analyze?

Collecting and analyzing data via a protocol analyzer enables you to perform wildly detailed analyses. Here are six examples of the types of questions a protocol analyzer can answer, providing huge benefits to the security of your network:

- Count all the packets coming through over a certain time period to get a strong idea as to your network utilization.
- Inspect the packets for single protocols to verify they are working properly (of course, this means you must know how these protocols work in detail).
- Monitor communication between a client and a server to look for problems in the communication.
- Look for servers that aren't authorized on the network.
- Find systems broadcasting bad data.
- Find problems in authentication by watching each step of the process in detail.

 NOTE Protocol analyzers require skilled operators with a firm grasp of TCP/IP protocols. The more a tech understands protocols, the more useful a protocol analyzer will be.

You can find quite a few protocol analyzers today, but the CompTIA Security+ exam focuses on two very good protocol analyzers: Wireshark and tcpdump. Both tools are powerful and complicated. Unlike network scanners, there have no simple versions. You can get some great work done without detailed knowledge of the tool, however, but in the hands of a skilled professional who understands both the tool and TCP/IP, a protocol analyzer can answer almost any question that arises in any network.

The CompTIA Security+ exam isn't going to ask detailed questions about protocol analyzers, so we'll only cover a few of the more basic aspects of these tools. But, like Nmap from the previous module, it would behoove you to make an investment in learning and using one or the other of these amazing tools.

Wireshark

Wireshark is the Grand Old Man of packet analyzers, originally developed in 1998 by Gerald Combs as Ethereal. In 2006, Ethereal was forked from the original development team and renamed Wireshark. Wireshark may be old, but it has an amazing development team that keeps this venerable tool sharp with a huge number of updates.

Wireshark is not only powerful but completely free and works on all major operating systems (and quite a few not so common ones as well). Its default GUI is so common that even a few competing protocol analyzers copy it for theirs.

Let's start with that interface, as shown in Figure 4-22. The interface has three main panes. At the top is a list of all the frames currently captured. (Wireshark shows each Ethernet frame, a feature that few other protocol analyzers provide.) In the middle are the gritty details of the frame currently selected in the top frame. At the bottom is the raw frame data in hexadecimal.

Wireshark is just the protocol analyzer; it requires a sniffer for packet capture. Capturing is handled by *libpcap* in Linux or *WinPcap* on Windows systems. Wireshark will install the proper sniffer during the installation of Wireshark itself. Wireshark will also start up the sniffer when you start Wireshark.

You begin the process of using Wireshark by starting a capture. As shown in Figure 4-23, Wireshark locates your network interfaces and gives you the opportunity to select which interface you want to start capturing.

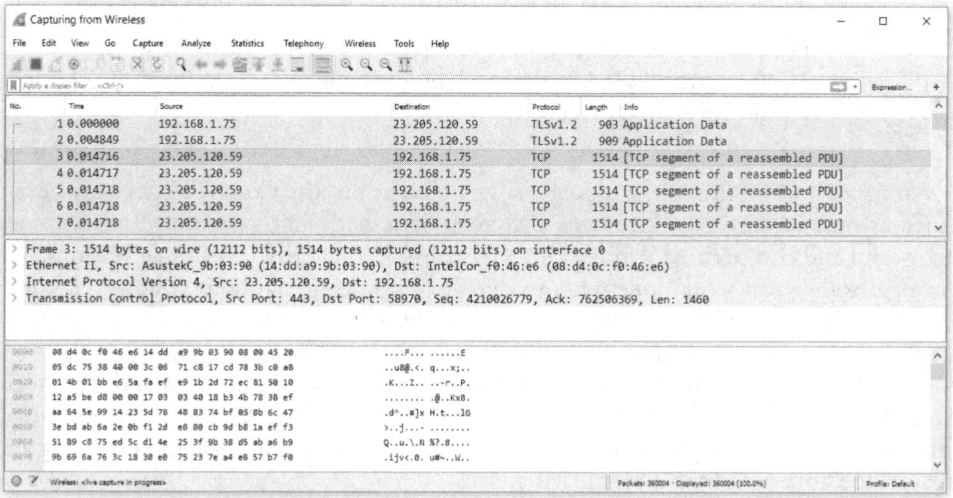

Figure 4-22   Wireshark main screen

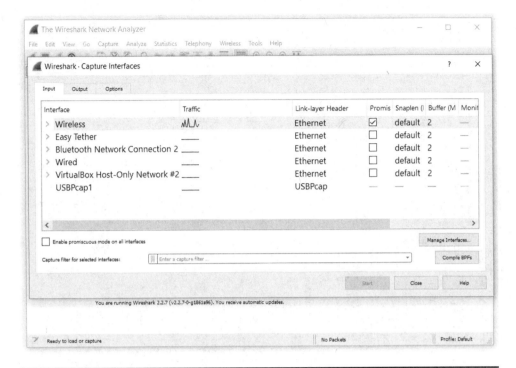

Figure 4-23   Selecting network interface

Once you start a capture, at some point you then stop the capture. From there you can filter and sort the capture by source or destination IP address, source or destination port number, protocol, or hundreds of other criteria. Wireshark has an expression builder to help you with complex filters. In Figure 4-24 the expression builder is creating a filter for a DHCP server response that is passing out the IP address 192.168.1.23.

NOTE   You can use a filter on the incoming packets or you can just sniff everything and filter afterward.

Wireshark by default captures and analyzes packets in real-time, so you can analyze as things happen. Sometimes, on the other hand, you need to record data over a period of time and then run tools for analysis for baselining or historical reference. Imagine a

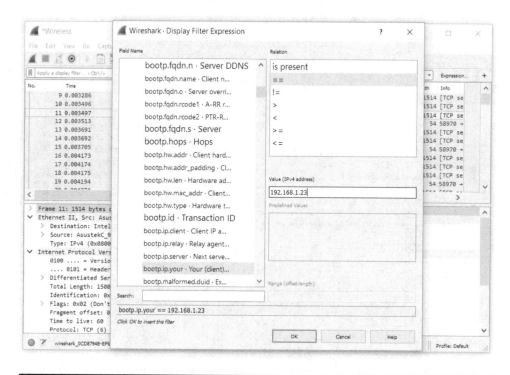

Figure 4-24 Expression builder

situation in which a tech wants to capture all HTTP traffic between 12 A.M. and 4 A.M. on a specific server. In this case, instead of running Wireshark all night, he or she will turn to a capture-only tool such as TShark. TShark is a command-line tool that works well with scripting and scheduling tools (Figure 4-25). TShark saves the capture in a format called pcap that a tech can load into Wireshark the next day for analysis.

```
PS C:\Program Files\Wireshark> .\tshark -D
1. \Device\NPF_{7AAB8953-B1FF-4C05-B7B4-8FE73B9F1C5D} (Local Area Connection* 10)
2. \Device\NPF_{0FF11516-8476-439D-A881-7D602CF86E0E} (Local Area Connection* 9)
3. \Device\NPF_{D6CC7E27-6AB2-44D2-80D4-1B26B031652A} (Npcap Loopback Adapter)
4. \Device\NPF_{1DA7160C-F255-46FD-BB35-C017BD637DA1} (Bluetooth Network Connection)
5. \Device\NPF_{174CD92A-32DA-4E7D-8F55-14A27F0BFAF7} (Local Area Connection 11)
6. \Device\NPF_{597E72A6-E268-484A-8348-90535E77B6B9} (VirtualBox Host-Only Network)
7. \Device\NPF_{07B2D520-E047-4A6E-9E02-9F924A6E7927} (Local Area Connection)
8. \Device\NPF_{E3AB0328-FA73-4C9D-A173-6EF6AA130632} (Ethernet)
PS C:\Program Files\Wireshark> .\tshark -i8
Capturing on 'Ethernet'
    1   0.000000 192.168.44.2 → 192.168.4.8   NBSS 55 NBSS Continuation Message
    2   0.187179 192.168.4.8 → 192.168.44.2 TCP 94 445-51072 [ACK] Seq=1 Ack=2 Win=260 Len=0
    3   1.886295 192.168.44.2 → 192.168.4.12 DNS 78 Standard query 0x8207 A beacon.dropbox.com
    4   1.911807 192.168.44.2 → 192.168.4.12 DNS 78 Standard query 0x8207 A beacon.dropbox.com
    5   2.146493 192.168.4.12 → 192.168.44.2 DNS 220 Standard query response 0x8207 A beacon.dropbox.com CNAME beacon.v.dro
pbox.com A 162.125.34.129
    6   2.147157 192.168.44.2 → 192.168.4.12 DNS 78 Standard query 0xad09 A beacon.dropbox.com
    7   2.171178 192.168.44.2 → 192.168.4.12 DNS 78 Standard query 0xad09 A beacon.dropbox.com
    8   2.171253 192.168.4.12 → 192.168.44.2 DNS 220 Standard query response 0xad09 A beacon.dropbox.com CNAME beacon.v.dro
pbox.com A 162.125.34.129
    9   2.198842 192.168.4.12 → 192.168.44.2 DNS 220 Standard query response 0xad09 A beacon.dropbox.com CNAME beacon.v.dro
pbox.com A 162.125.34.129
```

Figure 4-25 TShark in action

```
student@Student01:~$ sudo tcpdump
tcpdump: verbose output suppressed, use -v or -vv for full protocol decode
listening on enp0s3, link-type EN10MB (Ethernet), capture size 262144 bytes
21:47:03.901138 IP 10.13.212.153.netbios-ns > 10.13.212.255.netbios-ns: NBT UDP
PACKET(137): QUERY; REQUEST; BROADCAST
21:47:03.963882 IP 10.13.212.205.16290 > 10.13.212.1.domain: 6713+ PTR? 255.212.
13.10.in-addr.arpa. (44)
21:47:03.987695 IP 10.13.212.1.domain > 10.13.212.205.16290: 6713 NXDomain 0/0/0
 (44)
21:47:03.987890 IP 10.13.212.205.46128 > 10.13.212.1.domain: 29782+ PTR? 153.212
.13.10.in-addr.arpa. (44)
21:47:04.011270 IP 10.13.212.1.domain > 10.13.212.205.46128: 29782 NXDomain 0/0/
0 (44)
21:47:04.011517 IP 10.13.212.205.19145 > 10.13.212.1.domain: 18048+ PTR? 1.212.1
3.10.in-addr.arpa. (42)
21:47:04.035326 IP 10.13.212.1.domain > 10.13.212.205.19145: 18048 NXDomain 0/0/
0 (42)
21:47:04.035526 IP 10.13.212.205.26167 > 10.13.212.1.domain: 54489+ PTR? 205.212
.13.10.in-addr.arpa. (44)
21:47:04.646279 IP 10.13.212.153.netbios-ns > 10.13.212.255.netbios-ns: NBT UDP
PACKET(137): QUERY; REQUEST; BROADCAST
21:47:05.398838 IP 10.13.212.153.netbios-ns > 10.13.212.255.netbios-ns: NBT UDP
PACKET(137): QUERY; REQUEST; BROADCAST
```

Figure 4-26   tcpdump

tcpdump

As popular as Wireshark is, especially in Windows, many Linux/UNIX techs swear by *tcpdump*. tcpdump predates Wireshark by almost a decade and was the only real protocol analyzer option for Linux/UNIX until Wireshark was ported over in the very late 1990s (Figure 4-26).

tcpdump is amazing at sniffing packets, but is very difficult to use as a protocol analyzer, relying on complex command-line switches for sorting and filtering. No worries! Plenty of graphical protocol analyzers, even Wireshark, run on Linux (Figure 4-27).

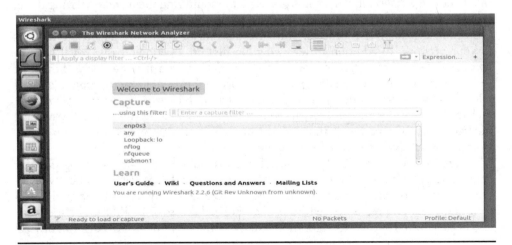

Figure 4-27   Wireshark in Linux

Module 4-4: Monitoring Networks

This module covers the following CompTIA Security+ objectives:

- **2.2** Given a scenario, use appropriate software tools to assess the security posture of an organization
- **2.3** Given a scenario, troubleshoot common security issues

Every organization with proper security includes continuous network monitoring to recognize and address performance and security events. This monitoring manifests as the collection of data from a wide variety of sources, one being the standard device and system logs inherent to every operating system. Another source is data from devices running protocols designed specifically for network monitoring, such as the Simple Network Management Protocol (SNMP). SNMP data collected for network monitoring includes intrusion detection/prevention system alerts, firewall alerts and logs, and real-time network monitoring. Real-time network monitoring involves protocol and traffic monitoring (also known as *sniffing*) using a protocol analyzer, so that the data may be collected and stored for later analysis.

Let's start with log file management and real-time monitoring, then finish with continuous monitoring in detail.

Log File Management

Device and system logs are basically the files, or audit trails, that exist on the device and are generated through a logging service or facility on the host. These logs can contain a wide variety of information, including performance and security information, of course, but also may include a much deeper, detailed level of information on applications, OS operations, and other types of information that may be useful in certain circumstances, but not necessarily on a daily or routine basis. It's surprising how much data builds up in log files on a device; if you are not proactive in monitoring them and reviewing them, they can lose their usefulness.

Log management is concerned with the logistics of managing all the device logs in your network. In addition to reviewing log files on a periodic basis, you'll need to consider a few other aspects of log management. First, you have to decide how long to keep log files, since they take up a lot of space and may not exactly contain a lot of relevant information—unless you need to look at a specific event. Sometimes *governance*, including regulations and other legal requirements, may require you to keep system log files for a certain amount of time, so log management is also concerned with secure storage and retrieval of archived log files for a defined period of time.

Secure storage and retrieval of archived logs is required simply because log files can contain sensitive information about systems and networks, as well as other types of sensitive data. You must ensure that log files are accessible only to personnel authorized to review them and are protected from unauthorized access or modification. You must also be able to retrieve the log files from storage in the event of an investigation or legal action against your organization, as well as comply with audit requirements imposed by law. Log management is concerned with all of these things, and effective policy regarding managing the logs in the organization should address all these issues.

Because we are looking for particular types of information on a routine basis, we want to configure logging to give us only that pertinent information. This will help us easily find the relevant information we need and will eliminate the massive amounts of information we really don't need on a routine basis. For event-specific information, such as a major performance issue, an outage, or even a significant security event, a lot more information may be needed during those specific circumstances only, so we may go into the system and temporarily configure logging to give us far more detailed information when we really need it. Getting that level of detail on a routine basis, however, would likely make our logs unmanageable and limit their usefulness.

For example, let's say that you are monitoring a potential hacking attempt. You may change the audit level of your network devices or internal hosts to include more detailed information on processes, threads, and interactions with lower-level hardware. This level of detail can produce a vast amount of logs very quickly, which can fill up device storage and be very unwieldy to examine. Because of this, you'd want to enable this level of logging only for a short while, just long enough to get the information you need. After that, you'd want to reduce the logging level back to normal.

Decentralized vs. Centralized Log Management

Daily log management and analysis activities are essentially how security professionals handle security events throughout the network and on different systems. They simply review the log files that most operating systems and network devices generate. There are two common ways to achieve log management: decentralized or centralized.

In environments such as very small networks that don't have large infrastructures or in isolated network segments, *decentralized log management* is usually the norm. This means that administrators usually must visit every network host, collecting the logs manually and reviewing them either there at the host or by manually offloading them to a centralized storage area for later analysis.

Centralized log management means that the log files from different machines are automatically sent to a centralized logging facility or server, such as a syslog server, for example. This is more what enterprise-level log management is about. Most administrators review logs from a centralized logging facility on the network. Enterprise-level log management products are designed to collect logs from various sources and correlate them into one unified management interface, so the administrator can look for trends or events and timeline correlation.

Security Information and Event Management

The traditional way to manage logging and monitoring in a network was to sit down at a system and look at the log files generated by the system, reviewing them for the events of interest. This is not the most efficient way to manage network monitoring and analysis activities.

Many organizations use *Security Information and Event Management (SIEM)*, an enterprise-level technology and infrastructure that collects data points from a network, including log files, traffic captures, SNMP messages, and so on, from every host on the network. SIEM can collect all this data into one centralized location and correlate it for analysis to look for security and performance issues, as well as negative trends, all in real time. SIEM infrastructures usually require a multitier setup consisting of servers designated as centralized log collectors, which pass log events onto other servers designated for mass log storage, which are accessed by devices focused purely on real-time correlation and analysis.

Note that although SIEM requires real-time monitoring technologies, just because you're using some of these real-time technologies doesn't necessarily mean you are using SIEM. SIEM unifies and correlates all the real-time events from a multitude of disparate sources, including network alerts, log files, physical security logs, and so on. You could still have real-time monitoring going on, but without combining and correlating all those different event sources. A true unified SIEM system is required to do that.

Log Types

Logs record events on systems. You'll most commonly hear them referenced as *event logs*, as in the case of Microsoft Windows operating systems. Linux systems refer to them as *syslogs*, or system logs.

Operating systems also store their log files in various locations and in various formats, some of which are compatible and some of which are not. In any event, security personnel often refer to these logs as *security* or *audit logs*, or sometimes as *audit trails*, because they provide information on events that are of a security interest. Security logs audit access to a particular resource or system. Audit logs can record very specific information about an event, to include user names, workstation or host names, IP addresses, MAC addresses, the resource that was accessed, and the type of action that occurred on the resource. This action could be something such as a file deletion or creation; it also could be use of elevated or administrative privileges.

Very often, security personnel may audit when users with administrative privileges are able to create additional user accounts, for example, or change host configurations. Figure 4-28 shows an example of a Linux audit log.

Access logs are resource-oriented and list all the different types of access that occur on a resource, such as a shared folder, file, or other object. Most systems can produce access logs for a specific resource, but often this must be configured on the resource itself to generate those logs. You can use access logs that are not system-generated. For example, you can have manually generated access logs for entrance into a facility or restricted area.

One of the biggest issues in network security and monitoring is keeping up with all the different log files available and using them in the most efficient and reasonable way possible. This can be a challenge when you may collect logs from thousands of devices, which record hundreds of thousands of network and security events per day. Being able to produce useful and accurate information from these log files, especially in an enterprise-level network, can be an impossible task if performed manually.

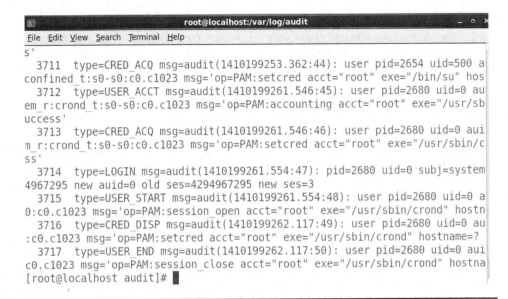

Figure 4-28   An example of a Linux audit log file

Log Analysis

Log analysis usually means reviewing logs and looking for specific information in the log files, such as security events; and then correlating those individual events with an overall problem or issue comprising a series of related events over a specific time frame. This can reveal information, both from logs and other sources, to determine the nature of a problem, how it occurred, how to deal with it, and how to prevent it from happening again in the future. Log analysis enables detection of trends on a network and devices that may affect long-term performance and security.

Security Events

Security events reveal potentially unauthorized activities or data access happening on the network, and they can take a wide variety of forms. In some cases, a security event may point to a particular instance of unauthorized access—called *access violations*—or network misuse; in other cases, you may have to collect a series of events from different logs across several devices, as well as other information from the infrastructure, to determine if a security event occurred. *Logs and events anomalies* can provide a wealth of information for the security professional; in such scenarios, you can fix many network flaws.

Examples of important security events include unauthorized access to resources, unauthorized users, and even actions by authorized personnel. Even in an unsuccessful event, such as failed login attempts by an external unauthorized user, you still may want to know so that you can proactively detect and prevent this type of incident in the future.

Network-specific events that you may monitor include detection of *rogue machines* (unauthorized machines that connect to your wireless or wired networks), interfaces that don't normally have hosts connected to them, or certain types of traffic passing over them. Other networking events that may warrant monitoring include the use of ports or protocols that aren't used by any of your applications on the network, and unusually large amounts of traffic targeted at a specific host or using an unusual protocol. These are, of course, not all-inclusive instances of the types of things you might want to monitor on the network, but they are common starting points.

Elements of security events recorded in log files that you need to investigate include information about the users or entities that access (or attempt access to) objects and resources, and the resources themselves. To collect all data regarding a security event, you must enable logging or auditing both within the system and on the object itself. An example of a Windows Server security event log is shown in Figure 4-29.

Continuous Monitoring

Continuous monitoring is a proactive way of ensuring that the network administrator receives all the different logs and other data points throughout the network from all network devices and all systems, on a constant basis. This data is continually fed into

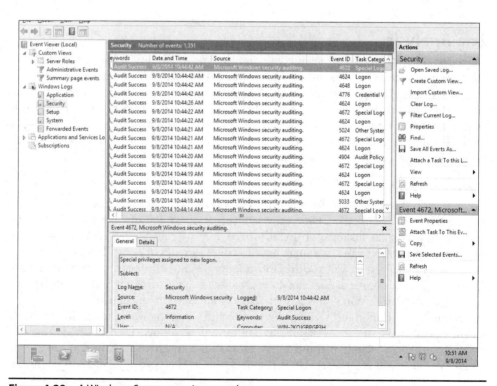

Figure 4-29   A Windows Server security event log

centralized monitoring consoles and applications, which provide the real-time ability to combine it with all the different other types of data received, so that the administrator can correlate it and look for performance or security issues happening on the network. Continuous monitoring also enables network and security personnel to perform trend analysis and detect possible issues that haven't occurred, but that may occur if events unfold without further prevention or mitigation.

This is as opposed to *manual, ad hoc* log management that is frequently seen in smaller or older networks, where an administrator may go to a dozen different hosts and manually review logs. Continuous monitoring can also ensure that security personnel receive alerts on different events when those events reach certain thresholds.

Auditing

Auditing is an important part of ensuring accountability on the network, and it serves several purposes. Auditing enables traceability between actions taken by the user on a particular resource and a user entity. This type of auditing is effective because you can examine logs and other data points to analyze certain events and construct a timeframe and event sequence surrounding an incident.

Auditing can confirm or verify that security policies are being followed and obeyed. It can also help determine that the technical security procedures and configuration rules implemented on the network fulfill and support security policies, ensuring compliance with the policies.

Auditing also consists of other activities, such as performing network sniffing traffic analysis; running password cracker software; and performing vulnerability assessments, penetration tests, compliance audits, and other types of security assessments. Auditing can reveal *weak security configurations* on various network devices that must be addressed. It can also reveal both *unauthorized software* in the enterprise and *license compliance violations*, such as using open-source software for commercial purposes.

 EXAM TIP License compliance violations not only can lead to hefty fines, but oppose two core security principles, availability and integrity.

Auditing is an important part of risk management simply because it provides a means to confirm that risk mitigations are in place and functioning.

Real-Time Monitoring

There are occasions when simply reviewing log files or receiving alerts from logs just isn't fast enough to detect or prevent security issues. The worst time to discover that a serious security issue has occurred is after it's over, since you can't stop an attack or prevent damage to systems and data after the fact. At that point, you're in reactive mode, and the best you can do is try to determine what exactly happened and prevent it from occurring again. Although damage control after an event is important, a better solution is to have real-time monitoring techniques and methods employed in addition to system and device logs. Real-time monitoring can take several forms, including traffic monitoring, as well as device health and status updates, which are continuously sent to a centralized console.

Real-time monitoring enables a network administrator to receive alerts or alarms as the event is happening, giving them the time and resources to stop an attack or security issue actively and prevent damage to systems and data. Real-time monitoring is a form of continuous monitoring and closely links to SIEM, discussed previously in this module.

SNMP

The *Simple Network Management Protocol (SNMP)* enables proactive monitoring of network hosts in real time. Devices that use SNMP have a small piece of software known as an *agent* installed on them, and this agent can report certain types of data back to a centralized monitoring server. This agent is configured with a *Management Information Base (MIB)*, which is a very specific set of configuration items tailored for the device. Using the MIB, the agent can relay very specific event information to a centralized console in real time. These events are known as *traps* and are essentially specific events configured with certain thresholds. If a configured threshold is reached for a particular event, the trap is triggered and the notification or alert is sent to the management console. These traps and messages can let an administrator know about the device status and health. In other words, the administrator could get information on when the device is up or down, whether its hardware is functioning properly or not, if its memory or CPU use is too high, and other interesting details about the device. In some cases, these trap messages could indicate an active attack against the device or some other type of unauthorized access or misuse.

Alarms and Alerts

A significant security or performance event that occurs on the network produces *alarms* and *alerts*. Ideally, alarms and alerts are sent from host and device monitoring systems in real time, so that they can be acted on quickly. They are usually set to notify an administrator if a certain type of occurrence or activity happens on the network. This could be a certain protocol or port being accessed, certain types of traffic coming into the network, or a particular resource being accessed by a certain individual, for instance. Alarms and alerts are usually configured in advance via rules set up on the network monitoring or intrusion detection systems so that if any of these preconfigured events occurs or exceeds a specified threshold, the systems will send an alarm or an alert to a centralized management console or to an administrator. For example, if network traffic exceeds a certain level for a certain protocol, or it is directed at a certain network host, then an alert can be triggered and the network administrator will be notified. Since most network alarms and alerts can be configured to send in real time, the administrator is better able to take timely action to eliminate the threat, reduce the risk, or prevent a negative event from doing damage to systems and data on the network.

Trend Analysis

Trend analysis enables a network administrator to correlate different data sources and data points from various places in the network, such as log files, intrusion detection system logs, wireless and wired sniffing, as well as other event sources, and seek to identify on-going trends in both performance and security. Trend analysis enables an administrator to look at seemingly unrelated events for *patterns*, which can indicate emerging issues or areas of concern. For example, if we see a user who unsuccessfully attempts to access a restricted file only one time, it's likely unintentional and may not be cause for alarm. However, if we look for patterns of usage from a certain user who continually attempts to access files to which he does not have access, we would see that a trend exists, showing that the user is attempting to access data that he shouldn't, and this may be an ongoing or long-term security risk. We could then notify the individual's supervisor for remedial security training or disciplinary action for attempting unauthorized access to sensitive data. Trend analysis is very important in being able to use network monitoring proactively, rather than simply reacting to every security event that occurs.

Reporting

Reporting is the portion of network monitoring at which the administrator receives reports from the different data points from different audit trails and logs, from network intrusion detection systems, and so on, and correlates this data in a report that shows different types of trends or activities occurring on the network. Reporting can be used to identify performance and security issues—in some cases well in advance of their actual occurrence, through trend analysis. Reports should be clear and concise, and should identify clearly what's happening on the network with regard to security. Reporting should happen not only at the event level, when certain alarms or alerts are triggered and the administrator is notified, but also on a larger, macro level, so security administrators and management are able to develop an idea of what kind of security trends are occurring on the network because of different network monitoring data points, such as user activities, network traffic, resource access, and so on. Most network monitoring devices and utilities provide different levels of reports that can be consolidated and produced for both event-level activities and emerging trends over time.

Questions

1. What does nslookup do?

   A. Retrieves the name space for the network

   B. Queries DNS for the IP address of the supplied host name

   C. Performs a reverse IP lookup

   D. Lists the current running network services on localhost

2. What is Wireshark?

   A. Protocol analyzer

   B. Packet sniffer

   C. Packet analyzer

   D. All of the above

3. One of your users calls you with a complaint that he can't reach the site www .google.com. You try and access the site and discover you can't connect either but you can ping the site with its IP address. What is the most probable culprit?

A. The workgroup switch is down.

B. Google is down.

C. The gateway is down.

D. The DNS server is down.

4. What command do you use to see the DNS cache on a Windows system?

A. ping /showdns

B. ipconfig /showdns

C. ipconfig /displaydns

D. ping /displaydns

5. Which of the following displays the correct syntax to eliminate the DNS cache?

A. ipconfig

B. ipconfig /all

C. ipconfig /dns

D. ipconfig /flushdns

6. Which tool enables you to query the functions of a DNS server?

A. ipconfig

B. nslookup

C. ping

D. xdns

7. The Windows tracert tool fails sometimes because many routers block _____ packets.

A. ping

B. TCP

C. UDP

D. ICMP

8. Which tools can you (and hackers) use to open ports on your network? (Choose three.)

A. Port scanner

B. Nmap

C. Angry IP Scanner

D. hostname

9. Which tools are used explicitly to monitor and diagnose problems with DNS?

    A. Nmap or Wireshark

    B. nslookup or dig

    C. ping or pathping

    D. tracert or pathping

10. Your manager wants you to institute log management and analysis on a small group of workstations and servers that are not connected to the larger enterprise network for data sensitivity reasons. Based upon the level of routine usage and logging, you decide not to implement a management console but intend to examine each log separately on the individual hosts. What type of log management are you using in this scenario?

    A. Centralized log management

    B. Enterprise-level log management

    C. Decentralized log management

    D. Workgroup-level log management

Answers

1. **B.** The nslookup command queries DNS and returns the IP address of the supplied host name.

2. **D.** Wireshark can sniff and analyze all the network traffic that enters the computer's NIC.

3. **D.** In this case, the DNS system is probably at fault. By pinging the site with its IP address, you have established that the site is up and your LAN and gateway are functioning properly.

4. **C.** To see the DNS cache on a Windows system, run the command ipconfig /displaydns at a command prompt.

5. **D.** The command ipconfig /flushdns eliminates the DNS cache.

6. **B.** The tool to use for querying DNS server functions is nslookup.

7. **D.** The Windows tracert tool fails because it relies on ICMP packets that routers commonly block.

8. **A, B, C.** The hostname command simply returns the host name of the local system. All other tools mentioned can scan ports to locate network vulnerabilities.

9. **B.** The nslookup tool and the more powerful dig tool are used to diagnose DNS problems.

10. **C.** In this scenario, you are using decentralized log management, since you are not using a centralized log management facility or console to collect all the applicable logs and review them in one place.

Securing Individual Systems

A typical security professional bandies about the term *attack surface*, meaning a cumulation of all the vulnerabilities for a specific infrastructure item. For a gateway router, for example, the attack surface refers to every option that an attacker might use to compromise that router, from misconfiguration to physical damage or theft (Figure 5-1).

This chapter explores the attack surface of one of the most vulnerable parts of networks, the individual systems. An *individual system* for the purposes of this chapter is a single computer running Windows, macOS, Linux/UNIX, or Chrome OS, in use every day. This includes desktops, laptops, servers, and workstations. It also includes mobile devices, but only to a lesser degree. We'll see more of those systems in later chapters.

The typical individual system on a network has hardware, software, connections, and applications, all of which are vulnerable to attack. The chapter first examines some of the more common attack methods, building on concepts that you learned in earlier chapters. The next modules explore different angles of individual system attack surfaces, from hardware to operating systems and applications. We're even going to cheat a bit and go beyond individual systems to discuss issues like firewalls and intrusion detection; these topics span both individual systems and networks (Figure 5-2).

Module 5-2 explores resiliency strategies that apply to systems, meaning both individual systems and the systems that make bigger entities function. Although the CompTIA Security+ exam focuses on individual systems for details about resiliency, it assumes security professionals know how the same principles apply on a larger scale.

 NOTE One attack surface variety this chapter does not cover is Internet applications—that is, Web apps. While these applications certainly run on individual server systems, local users on a LAN generally do not use those systems. These applications have their own class of problems that warrant their own chapter. We'll go into Internet application attacks—and how to stop them—in Chapter 8.

Figure 5-1
An attack surface

This chapter explores methods for securing individual systems in eight modules:

- Types of System Attacks
- System Resiliency
- Securing Hardware
- Securing Operating Systems
- Securing Peripherals
- Malware
- Securing Network Access
- System Recycling

Figure 5-2
We need to
protect systems.

Module 5-1: Types of System Attacks

This module covers the following CompTIA Security+ objective:

- **1.2** Compare and contrast types of attacks

Any network is nothing more than a series of systems connected via fiber, copper, or wireless connections. But a physical connection isn't enough. To function on a network, the system must possess the necessary hardware and software to connect to a LAN and communicate via IP, sending and receiving properly formatted TCP/UDP/ICMP packets. To perform this, a system consists of four independent features: network-aware applications, a network-aware operating system, a network stack to handle incoming and outgoing packets, and proper drivers for the network interface. Collectively, these features are the attack surface for an individual system.

To understand the types of attacks unleashed on systems, let's put all these features in order, as shown in Figure 5-3. We can then explore how bad actors can take advantage of vulnerabilities in each of these features to compromise our individual systems.

Attacking Applications

Applications are always the first line of attack surface for most attacks on individual systems. Given the tens if not hundreds of thousands of applications available to any operating system and the lack of any uniform patching and support methods for these many applications, it's easier for bad guys to explore the attack surface of the application and find some form of exploit. The most common form of attack against applications are man-in-the-middle attacks.

Man-in-the-middle attacks against applications either target the authentication process of the application or attempt to intercept the data from an already authenticated session. In either case, an attacker seeks any application that lacks authentication or has weak authentication, such as Telnet. Second to targeting non-authenticated applications, man-in-the-middle attacks look for applications that lack encryption or have poor encryption. This makes intercepting the data for an existing session easier.

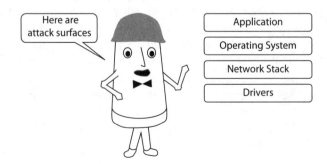

Figure 5-3
Individual
systems' attack
surfaces

NOTE An attack based on a previously unknown and unpatched vulnerability is known as a *zero-day attack*. A zero-day attack isn't unique to applications, but the CompTIA Security+ exam specifically mentions them in Objective 1.2, under Application/Service attacks.

Attacking the Operating System

Today's operating systems withstand most attacks well and are rarely the first best choice for an attack surface due to good patching from the operating systems' makers. Note that patches are only good if they're used. If users fail to perform good and timely patch management (and this is always a problem), operating systems can be an excellent attack surface. In general, successful operating system attacks exploit privilege escalation and services.

Privilege Escalation

Privilege escalation, the process of accessing a system at a lower authentication level and upgrading (escalating) authentication to a more privileged level, presents attack opportunities. All of the common operating systems require every user and every process accessing the system to go through some form of authentication/authorization procedure. If an attacker can access a system using a low-level access account such as public, everyone, or guest, he or she may find a bug that gets him or her to the highest access levels (root, administrator, etc.).

 NOTE A *service account*, unlike an account used by people (guest, user, root), is used by some process running on the system that needs access to resources. The nature of service accounts prevents typical authentication methods because they lack anyone to type in a password. This makes system accounts a prime target for attacks. Over the years hundreds of well-known exploits have used service account privilege escalation as an attack surface.

Operating systems are designed to prevent privilege escalation. Windows, for example, disables the guest account by default. Attackers need to find some type of bug, sometimes even through an application running on the operating system, that gives them higher privilege. Alternatively, attackers can find an alternative login that may not have a higher privilege but might give access to something that lets them do what they need to do. If an attacker wants to access a printer, he doesn't need root access, just some account that has access to that printer.

 NOTE Well-patched operating systems are extremely resilient to privilege escalation.

Services

The CompTIA Security+ exam objective mentions operating system services as an attack surface option. The challenge here is figuring out what CompTIA means by services. For a Windows-centric person, a *service* is any process that works without any interface to the Windows Desktop. You can access all running Windows services using the aptly named Services app (Figure 5-4).

Attacking a Windows service is pretty much the same as attacking an application. Attackers can use man-in-the middle attacks if possible, or they can use privilege escalation if they can find an exploit.

A more Internet-centric person would define *services* as processes that listen on a TCP/UDP port to provide some sort of (again aptly named) service. In Windows, you can see TCP/IP services, including the process providing that service, using netstat –a –b (Figure 5-5).

Linux users don't have this confusion. A Linux service is only a process listening on a TCP/UDP port. Linux does not separate processes that interface to the desktop from those that do not. There is no Linux equivalent to Windows' Services app.

Application/services attacks aren't limited to local assets, like a Windows Server or a specific program running on a LAN. In CompTIA Security+, these attacks apply right up the network stack. Let's go there now.

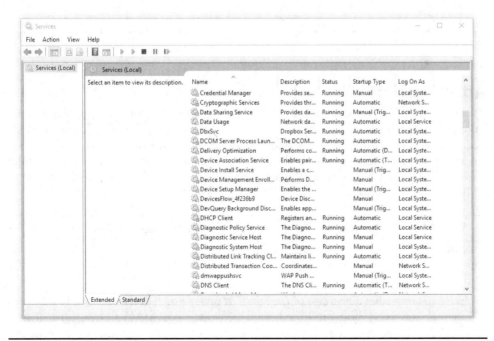

Figure 5-4 Services in Windows

```
Administrator: Windows PowerShell                                              —  □  ×
[Dropbox.exe]
 TCP    127.0.0.1:50702        MikesDesktop:50701      ESTABLISHED
[Dropbox.exe]
 TCP    127.0.0.1:55868        MikesDesktop:65001      ESTABLISHED
[nvcontainer.exe]
 TCP    127.0.0.1:65001        MikesDesktop:55868      ESTABLISHED
[nvcontainer.exe]
 TCP    192.168.4.47:49692     msnbot-65-52-108-200:https  ESTABLISHED
 WpnService
[svchost.exe]
 TCP    192.168.4.47:49866     162.125.6.3:https       CLOSE_WAIT
[Dropbox.exe]
 TCP    192.168.4.47:49926     msnbot-65-52-108-229:https  ESTABLISHED
[OneDrive.exe]
 TCP    192.168.4.47:51032     162.125.18.133:https    ESTABLISHED
[Dropbox.exe]
 TCP    192.168.4.47:51036     162.125.18.133:https    ESTABLISHED
[Dropbox.exe]
 TCP    192.168.4.47:51092     TOTALFSVID:microsoft-ds ESTABLISHED
Can not obtain ownership information
 TCP    192.168.4.47:51122     162.125.34.129:https    ESTABLISHED
[Dropbox.exe]
 TCP    192.168.4.47:51425     proxy-42:http           ESTABLISHED
[chrome.exe]
 TCP    192.168.4.47:51499     162.125.6.3:https       CLOSE_WAIT
[Dropbox.exe]
 TCP    192.168.4.47:51500     162.125.17.132:https    CLOSE_WAIT
[Dropbox.exe]
 TCP    192.168.4.47:51501     162.125.6.3:https       CLOSE_WAIT
[Dropbox.exe]
 TCP    192.168.4.47:51507     162.125.32.5:https      CLOSE_WAIT
[Dropbox.exe]
 TCP    192.168.4.47:51527     162.125.34.129:https    TIME_WAIT
 TCP    192.168.4.47:51530     162.125.34.129:https    TIME_WAIT
 TCP    192.168.4.47:51533     40.84.149.239:https     TIME_WAIT
 TCP    192.168.4.47:51538     162.125.6.3:https       TIME_WAIT
 TCP    192.168.4.47:51539     ec2-54-164-63-33:https  ESTABLISHED
[Dropbox.exe]
 TCP    192.168.4.47:51540     162.125.17.5:https      TIME_WAIT
 TCP    192.168.4.47:51542     162.125.34.129:https    ESTABLISHED
[Dropbox.exe]
 TCP    [2603:300c:100:ea00:9d08:3504:6442:2df3]:50330  [2600:1402:19:2a4::76a]:https  CLOSE_WAIT
[WinStore.App.exe]
 TCP    [2603:300c:100:ea00:9d08:3504:6442:2df3]:50331  [2600:1402:19:2a4::76a]:https  CLOSE_WAIT
[WinStore.App.exe]
 TCP    [2603:300c:100:ea00:9d08:3504:6442:2df3]:50332  [2600:1402:19:2a4::76a]:https  CLOSE_WAIT
[WinStore.App.exe]
 TCP    [2603:300c:100:ea00:9d08:3504:6442:2df3]:50333  [2001:559:10:186::57]:https  CLOSE_WAIT
[WinStore.App.exe]
 TCP    [2603:300c:100:ea00:9d08:3504:6442:2df3]:50334  [2400:cb00:2048:1::c629:d6bb]:http  CLOSE_WAIT
```

Figure 5-5   Internet services

Attacking Network Stacks

Attacking the TCP/IP stack on an individual system is second in popularity only to application attacks. If an attacker can in some way change an IP address or MAC address to fool the underlying stack, she has a perfect tool for man-in-the-middle attacks. An attack that replaces a legitimate IP address with another and fools the system to send data to that other IP address is *IP spoofing*. The same type of attack directed to MAC addresses is *MAC spoofing*.

NOTE   *Spoofing* means to replace a legitimate value with a fake one.

ARP poisoning takes advantage of the fact that pretty much every network in existence is Ethernet and every host on an Ethernet network has a MAC address burned into every NIC. For one computer to send an IP packet to another computer on an Ethernet network, the IP packets must sit inside an Ethernet frame. An Ethernet frame consists of both a destination MAC address and a source MAC address. So the sending system needs both the destination host's IP address and the destination host's MAC address.

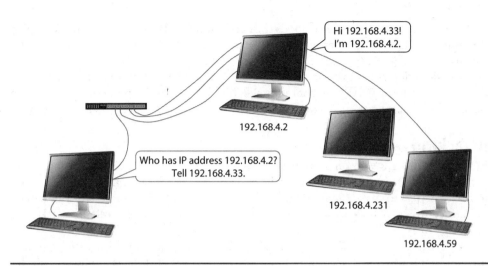

Figure 5-6 Typical ARP

But what if the sending system doesn't know the destination MAC address? In that case the sending system performs an Address Resolution Protocol (ARP) broadcast to determine the MAC address for that host.

Typically, when a system wants to send an IP packet, it broadcasts an ARP that looks something like Figure 5-6.

The system then caches the ARP discovery for a minute or two. With the right software, however, it's fairly easy to ARP poison a network by having an attacking system send MAC spoofing information on the network, as shown in Figure 5-7.

Figure 5-7 ARP poison in action

A good ARP poisoning utility floods the network with ARP responses, always keeping the legitimate target from getting the upper hand and filling every other system with spoofed ARP data in their caches. The only real weakness to *ARP spoofing* is that a good network detection system will see the huge number of ARP responses and recognize this distinctive feature of an ARP poisoning attack. It can in turn block the system sending out the many ARP responses or, at the very least, set off an alarm for network administrators.

Attacking Drivers

Every piece of hardware on a computer (with the exception of RAM) communicates with the operating system via device drivers. Attackers either can send communications to device drivers to make them do things they were never supposed to do, or can replace the device drivers with corrupted device drivers to gain privilege escalation or launch spoofing attacks.

There are two attack surfaces to manipulate device drivers to do malicious things, driver refactoring and driver shimming. Neither attack surface is unique to device drivers—both are present in any type of code —but they are the two best ways to attack an individual system via its device drivers.

Refactoring

Programming is all about inputs and outputs. A piece of code takes input and, based on that input, does some type of output. For software developers, *refactoring* means to rewrite the internals of a piece of code without changing the way it reacts to input or how it performs output.

The many device drivers that talk to system hardware are certainly code. Hardware manufacturers always want to make their drivers faster and smaller, so refactoring is a common feature with device drivers.

Refactoring can have a slightly different, malevolent definition. *Refactoring* in an alternate definition can mean to reprogram a device driver's internals so that the device driver responds to all of the normal inputs and generates all the regular outputs, but also generates malicious output. A refactored printer driver that works perfectly but also sends all print jobs to an evil remote server is an example of this other type of refactoring.

Shimming

Refactoring was a very common attack for many years, but today all operating systems use *driver signing* that confirms the exact driver files used. The operating system detects any changes and deals with them in one way or another, so replacing a device driver's files isn't as easy as it used to be. To get around this issue as an attacker, instead of replacing a signed file (or files), why not just throw another file or two (with the extra evil code) into the system?

A *shim* is a library that responds to inputs that the original device driver isn't designed to handle. Inserting an unauthorized shim, called *shimming* or a *shim attack*, is more common than refactoring because it does not require replacing an actual file—it merely relies on listening for inputs that the original device driver isn't written to hear.

EXAM TIP Every operating system provides a method of driver signing that is designed to prevent refactoring attacks on our device drivers.

Denial of Service

A *denial of service (DoS)* attack tries through any number of means to shut down an application, an operating system, or network server. DoS attacks range from simple continuous ping packets (an early, primitive DoS attack) to sophisticated purpose-designed DoS applications. More commonly today you see a *distributed denial of service (DDoS)* attack, a DoS attack that uses many systems to greatly enhance the effectiveness of attacks on a target.

Module 5-2: System Resiliency

This module covers the following CompTIA Security+ objective:

- **3.8** Explain how resiliency and automation strategies reduce risk

What if you could design a system such that even if it were successfully attacked, the system could in some way quickly (as in a matter of seconds) rebuild itself or, even better, weather an attack without the attack being able to do any real damage? That's the idea behind *system resiliency*: adding technologies and processes that don't stop attacks, but enable the system to recover easily (Figure 5-8).

EXAM TIP Resilient systems don't eliminate risk. That's impossible! Resilient systems fight off attacks more readily than systems with less resilience. They handle risks better, in other words. The principles here apply to individual systems and to larger "systems," such as an enterprise network.

Figure 5-8
I rebuff your pathetic attempts!

There are many ways to make systems more resilient, but it helps to organize these methods into three main categories: non-persistence, redundancy, and automation. *Non-persistence* simply means to possess a non-persistent method to bring a system back quickly to its pre-attack state. *Redundancy* means to have more than one of some functioning feature of a system or even another complete system. *Automation* refers to the programming and sensing tools that enable compromised systems to use their non-persistence and redundancy to recover themselves with little or no human intervention.

Non-persistence

A typical individual system is *persistent* in that it has a fixed set of hardware, a fixed operating system, and a fixed configuration. If you were to go up to a system, turn it off, and turn it back on again, you would have the same hardware, the same operating system, and the same configuration. It is persistent.

The downside to a persistent system is that if an attack takes place, that attack will in some way change some aspect of that persistent state. The attack might wipe a hard drive. It might inject evil device drivers. It might create privileged users you don't want on the OS. If any attack takes place, there's a good chance you'll have to go through some painful recovery process. This might include reinstalling an operating system, or rebuilding from backups. These are time-consuming processes and ones to avoid by using less persistent systems.

Achieving this means pursuing one of three options:

- Virtualization/snapshots
- Revert/rollback tools
- Live boot

Virtualization/Snapshots

There are many reasons virtualization has taken over the world of serving systems these days. One reason is the ease of recovery by simply shutting down a virtual machine (VM) and then restarting it without affecting any of the underlying hardware. But another feature, and the one that very much fits under the idea of non-persistence, is the snapshot. A *snapshot* is the stored difference between the files in one version of a VM and the files in another version. While the snapshot procedure varies from one virtualization platform to another, imagine a perfectly functional VM where you change a single device driver, only to discover over time that the device driver is buggy and keeps causing your VM to crash every two minutes or so. If this were a classic persistent system, you'd have to reinstall the device driver (on a system that's crashing every two minutes…what fun!). If you made a snapshot of the system before you installed the device driver, however, you could simply revert to the earlier snapshot and bring the system back to its original function (Figure 5-9).

Snapshots are a critical non-persistence tool for VMs. Every time you change a driver, update an application or service, patch a client OS, or take any other action that makes any significant change to your VM, run a snapshot.

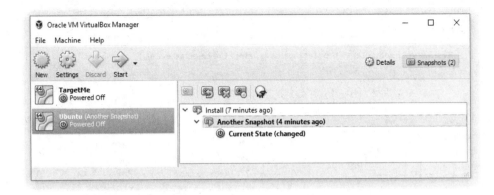

Figure 5-9 Snapshots in VirtualBox

Revert/Rollback

Every technician has made some change to an operating system, only to find that the change he or she made is flawed in some way. A bad driver, a poorly distributed patch, or an OS update that fails to perform the way the tech thought and causes problems can make the tech want to go back to the way things were before the change was made. If you have a virtual system, you can easily erase such changes via a snapshot. On a fixed traditional system, it's not that easy. Every major OS has some form of revert/rollback method to bring a system back to a previous state. All revert/rollback methods work by making the OS aware of changes and then storing files or settings in such a way that techs can look up previous states and tell the OS to go back to one of those states.

EXAM TIP In general, use the word *revert* when talking about returning an OS to a previous state. CompTIA uses the term *revert to known state*. Use *rollback* when you mean to uninstall new device drivers. CompTIA calls this *rollback to known configuration*.

Microsoft Windows enables you to create *restore points*—a capture of the overall operating system and drivers at that moment in time—that enable you to revert the operating system to an earlier configuration (Figure 5-10). Windows restore points aren't perfect. They don't save user information or installed applications; but other than those two issues, restore points are very powerful.

Device drivers, especially video card drivers, often have unforeseen problems that motivate us to return to a previous driver version. Equally, a refactored device driver might wreak havoc on an otherwise perfectly good system. Again, Windows has an elegant solution in the Roll Back Driver feature, as shown in Figure 5-11.

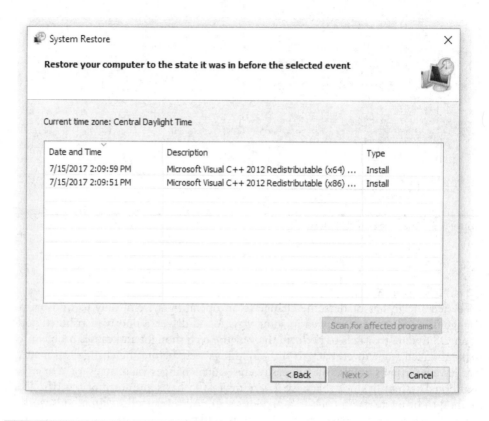

Figure 5-10 Restore points in Windows

Apple macOS machines rely on *Time Machine*, a program that records snapshots of the state of the computer over time to an external drive (Figure 5-12). If you support Macs, establish Time Machine for every system.

Apple macOS doesn't have a roll back driver feature similar to that in Windows for two reasons. First, Apple checks all drivers much more aggressively than Microsoft; so bad, refactored, or shimmed drivers almost never happen. Secondly, Time Machine supports drivers as well, making a separate rollback feature unnecessary.

VMs and Automation

Many modern networks use virtualization technologies to provide both rollouts and rollbacks of many systems all at once. With a *master image*—the desktop environment for users of very specific hardware and configurations—a central server can push that image to every local computer. Automation/scripting can make rollouts regular, such as after patch Tuesday—and configuration validation (i.e., it works!)—so users always have up-to-date builds. This kind of automated course of action helps keep systems current.

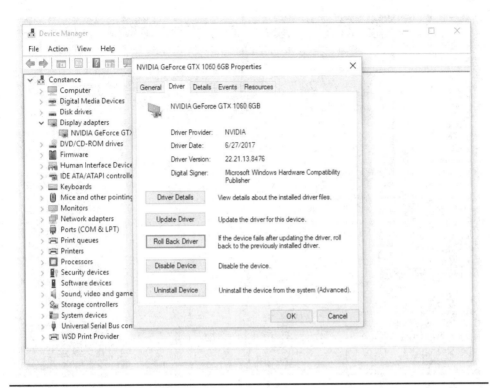

Figure 5-11   Roll Back Driver in Windows

Plus, master images enable network administrators to respond very quickly to problems. With continuous monitoring, as you'll recall from Chapter 4, network administrators keep up with the reporting from network monitoring and managing tools. If a recent rollout hits snags, the network techs can fix the master image and, with a manual rollout, essentially "roll back" the problematic build. Similarly, if a new bug or attack causes problems, a fixed and validated master image can be quickly deployed.

EXAM TIP   Virtual machine developers, like VMware, enable you to create a *template* of a completed VM that you can use to create identical versions of the VM. Templates provide excellent flexibility and rapid deployment of additional servers as needed.

Live Boot Media

If you want the ultimate in non-persistence on a non-VM system, you can always use some kind of live boot media. *Live boot media* are complete, installed operating systems that exist on bootable media. The names change to match the media. On optical media,

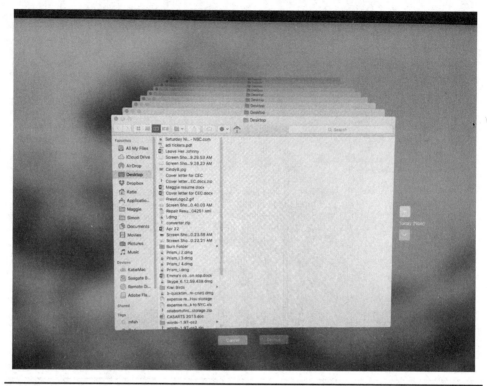

Figure 5-12 Time Machine in macOS

for example, they're called live CDs; for consistency, bootable flash-media drives should be called *live sticks* (they're not), but they're usually just called *bootable USB flash drives*. You boot a system to the live boot media and use the OS as configured. Your system doesn't even need a hard drive. Live boot media are very popular in Linux environments, giving you an opportunity to try a Linux distro without installing it on your hard drive (Figure 5-13).

Live boot media go way beyond test-driving Linux. You can easily install a carefully configured system, say a DNS server, to a live boot and run the entire server in that fashion. As long as the serving system doesn't need to store any persistent data (like a database that changes), you can run almost any OS/application combination from a live boot media. One of the most popular live boots is Kali Linux, the go-to Linux distro, stuffed full of many IT security tools (Figure 5-14).

Redundancy

Non-persistence provides excellent resiliency in most cases, but falls short in data storage. Snapshots/reverts are wonderful for subtle changes in operating systems, such as a security patch or a driver update, as they don't require much mass storage space. They simply

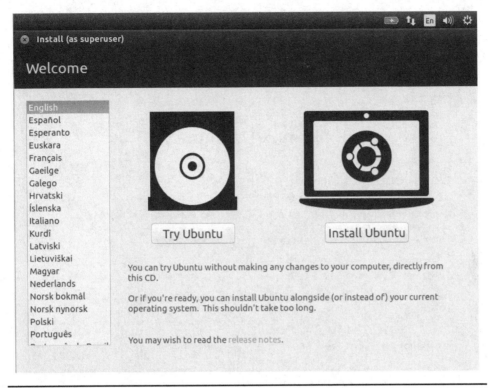

Figure 5-13 Live CD installation option in Linux

aren't designed to deal with big changes to data, such as customer databases, inventories, users' file storage, and other such data that requires a lot of hard drive space. Traditionally, this type of data is backed up daily; in this situation, turn to redundancy to provide the system resiliency needed.

But where to apply redundancy? There are several options. You can create redundant mass storage, redundant systems (including their mass storage), even redundant networks (including all the systems and all their mass storage). You can create more than one copy of non-OS critical data so that if one copy dies, another copy is ready to go to keep the systems up and running. Redundancy is everywhere!

The Benefits of Redundancy

At first glance, it's easy to look at redundancy as nothing more than a backup of storage, systems, or even networks, but true redundancy is far more powerful. First is *fault tolerance*. With fault tolerance, the secondary storage, the system, and the network are online and ready to go. If something goes wrong, the data on the storage or the services provided by the system can have a minimal amount of disruption. Second, redundancy provides *high availability*. High availably means using redundancy in such a way as to ensure that certain levels of operational performance are balanced against risk. Third, you can work

Figure 5-14 Kali Linux downloads

on one of your services offline with minimal impact to your customers, whether that's adding capacity or repairing a component. Let's look at the redundancy technologies that provide both fault tolerance and high availability.

Storage Redundancy

Redundant array of independent disks (RAID) is a fault tolerance technology that spans data across multiple hard drives within a server or workstation. This level of fault tolerance specifically addresses hard drive failure and balances the need for data redundancy with speed and performance. RAID uses multiple physical hard drives to create logical drives, usually making it transparent to users. Data is spanned across the different physical drives, along with metadata (usually parity information), so that if any one drive fails, the other drives in the RAID set can continue to provide data while the single drive is replaced.

Figure 5-15

Examples of RAID configurations

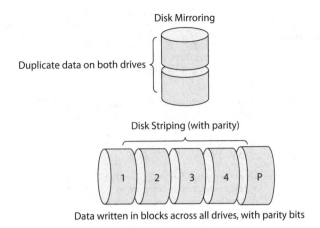

There are several different RAID levels; which one you should use for a system depends upon different factors, including the number of available disks and the balance of total available space for storage, as well as the levels of speed and performance the system requires. RAID levels can be implemented in several ways. *Striping* typically means writing pieces of data equally across two physical disks. *Mirroring*, in contrast, completely duplicates data on each disk. Using more disks, you can include *parity* information, which enables data to be restored in the event of a single disk failure. You'll find combinations of all these. Figure 5-15 illustrates examples of different RAID levels using these techniques.

There are trade-offs for each of these different methods, which include total amount of storage space, speed, performance, and the number of disks required in the RAID array. Table 5-1 summarizes some of the different RAID levels and their details.

System Redundancy

RAID is certainly the go-to technology to provide fault tolerance for mass storage, but what about systems? What happens if the Web site sits only on one Web server and that server fails? Server redundant technologies such as load balancing, clustering, and virtualization provide both fault tolerance and high availability.

Load Balancing   *Load balancing* is a high-availability technology that disperses the requests for a service to multiple servers in a balanced way so that the servers share the load. The load-balancing method may be *round-robin*, where each server takes a turn responding to requests, or it might involve a front-end gateway router that disperses requests to servers based on their current load (Figure 5-16).

In many cases we want to keep a thick client or Web browser attached to a specific Web server via a load balancer. This allows the user session to maintain consistency with that Web server; otherwise, the client could be directed to a server that does not have the details on the session in progress. Most load balancers handle this by using a browser cookie to identify the session details. This is called *session affinity* or *sticky session*.

RAID Level	Details	Minimum Number of Physical Drives Required
RAID 0	Disk striping; does not use mirroring or parity; provides for performance only with no redundancy.	2
RAID 1	Disk mirroring; all data is completely duplicated on both disks; uses no striping or parity but provides for full redundancy at the expense of the loss of half the total available disk space for duplication.	2
RAID 5	Disk striping with parity; parity information is spread across all disks evenly; 1/n of the total disk space available is used for parity.	3 to n
RAID 6	Disk striping with double distributed parity; this allows for failure of up to two drives.	4
RAID 1+0 (or sometimes seen as RAID 10)	Disk mirroring with striping; combines both RAID levels 0 and 1 for performance and redundancy; a stripe of two mirrored arrays.	4
RAID 0+1	Disk striping with mirroring; combines both RAID levels 0 and 1 for performance and redundancy; a mirror of two striped arrays.	4

Table 5-1 Summary of RAID Levels

 EXAM TIP Sticky session is the common industry phrase for using browser cookies to identify session details. The CompTIA Security+ exam will use affinity—not even session affinity—for the same meaning.

Figure 5-16
Load balancing

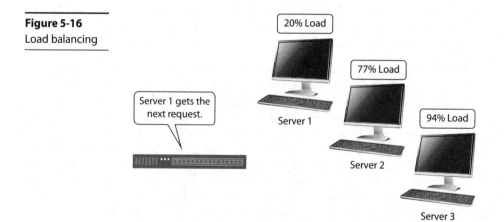

Clustering   Clustering is a technology that allows you to have several identically configured servers running at one time, which appear as one logical server. This enables fault tolerance, because if one server fails for any reason, the others continue to perform without the users being aware of the failure. Clustering requires specialized software, but is a must in environments that require enterprise levels of high availability.

Two types of clusters are usually found in high-availability environments. The first is called an *active/active* configuration, where all servers in the cluster are up and running constantly, load balancing, and responding to all requests. If any server in the cluster fails, the others are already up and running and providing those services. The other type of cluster is called an *active/passive* configuration. In this setup, only one server is actively responding to requests, with other servers in the cluster in a standby mode. If the server providing services fails, the standby server becomes the active cluster member and responds to requests after a brief transition time. Active/active configurations provide immediate availability, since they are already up and running; active/passive configurations may incur some latency or delay while the standby server becomes active.

EXAM TIP   The CompTIA Security+ exam might ask about *distributive allocation*, which in this context refers to spreading of resources— processing, storage, and so forth—among multiple servers. Other uses of the term refer to military or industrial uses, where cyber assets—such as processing units, networking gear, sensors, and so on—are positioned to make them harder to target than if they were in a single location. Most likely, CompTIA prefers the first definition.

Virtualization Services   Nothing beats virtualization for giving you all the benefits of redundancy, especially high availability, without outrageous cost and time. First, virtualization solutions are incredibly scalable. Let's say you develop a new Web app and launch it on a single Amazon S3 server, and suddenly your product is a huge hit (and the single server is swamped). Virtualization services like Amazon S3 make it easy to spin up more copies of your server (although you can do this locally—on *prem*, as they say—as well). Add as many as you want and need!

Virtualization also enables *geographic scalability*. Is your new Web site big in Japan? Just tell Amazon to spin up some new servers over in Japan so your customers in Tokyo get the same speed and response as your U.S. users (Figure 5-17).

The other amazing high-availability power of virtualization comes from elasticity. Going back to the Web app idea, some Web apps have cycles of high and low demand (tickets sales, sports broadcasts, etc.). These cases require scalability both in terms of expanding and contracting on an as-needed basis, better known as *elasticity*. All virtualization providers have simple features to add or remove server instances automatically based on predetermined load values.

NOTE   Industry uses the term *template* to describe a server purchase. For example, you might order a certain tier of stuff. "I want a medium cluster with a blue level of security and redundancy." That's the template. Once you get it, you take a snapshot of it and can rebuild it at any time. So sweet!

Figure 5-17 Virtualization makes geographic scalability easy.

Module 5-3: Securing Hardware

This module covers the following CompTIA Security+ objectives:

- **2.1** Install and configure network components, both hardware- and software-based, to support organizational security
- **3.3** Given a scenario, implement secure systems design

Many years ago, an overly cocky security tech friend presented a challenge to me. He said that he had secured a server system so perfectly that no unauthorized person could access the data, and he challenged me to try. Accepting the challenge, I didn't waste a moment trying to attack the system remotely. Instead, I simply put on some work clothes to look like a maintenance man, went to the location, and used my social engineering skills to gain entry. Once inside, I found the server and yanked out every hard drive. With plenty of time and completely nonsecure hardware, it was just a matter of cracking a Windows login and ... success!

There's a strong lesson here for any security person. Physical possession of mass storage—or complete systems that hold the mass storage devices—is every attacker's dream. Granted, getting to the data might be a challenge, but every pawn shop, every classified advertising medium, and every law enforcement office in the USA is filled with stolen systems. If an attacker can get to the physical system, no firewall, no network login, no wireless access point is going to prevent him from eventually getting to the precious data.

Secure hardware presents the last line of defense for these types of attacks. Virtually every piece of hardware that runs an Intel- or ARM-based CPU comes prepackaged with powerful tools to lock down a system to secure individual computers from physical attacks.

This module starts with a discussion of a few of the nasty types of interference that might attack a system. The module then covers many of the technologies used to protect systems from attacks, both intentional and unintentional.

Avoiding Interference

The world is filled with all kinds of kinetic energy sources that bombard individual systems with radio, magnetic, and electrical jolts that at best cause headaches, and at worse cause massive destruction. Let's look at EMI, RFI, and EMP.

EMI

Every piece of matter that holds either an electric or a magnetic charge emanates an electromagnetic field around it. These electromagnetic fields are good. Without them, electric motors and many other critical technologies wouldn't work. They become problems, however, when one item's electromagnetic field interferes with the operation of another device by creating *electromagnetic interference (EMI)*.

The term electromagnetism covers every form of energy that travels through space. This includes microwaves, radios waves (see "RFI" next), visible light, infrared waves, and X-rays. When one source of EMI gets too close to a piece of equipment that is susceptible to the form of electromagnetism, problems happen. One example might be an electric motor that generates a field that prevents a CAT6a UTP cable from transmitting data. Another example might be a nearby 802.11 WAP that transmits on the same channel as another WAP.

In general, EMI doesn't destroy hardware, but it prevents communication by interfering with signals passing through media. To prevent EMI, you must either remove the device generating the EMI, create distance between the device generating the EMI, or shield the emanating device or your media. Figure 5-18 shows one of many EMI solutions, shielded twisted pair (STP) cable.

If you run into situations with slow data transmission, especially at a specific time (when the AC is turned on, or when the 3-gigawatt hydroelectric generator in the windmill farm above your house is spinning), assume EMI. Move the source, provide shielding, or, if you live under a windmill farm, move.

RFI

Radio frequency interference (RFI) is EMI that transmits in the radio frequency range. As the name implies, an RFI source generally only interferes with another radio source, although if strong enough it might also interfere with speakers and copper transmission lines.

The most common RFI source is with the 802.11 and cellular WAN radio bands. If you're having trouble with phone calls or a wireless LAN, you might want to consider RFI problems.

 NOTE Both 802.11 and cellular WANs almost always have automatic channel-hopping features that automatically tune devices to the least congested channel.

Figure 5-18
STP cable

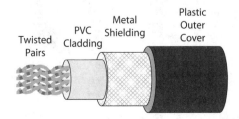

Figure 5-19
EMP

EMP

Electromagnetic pulse (EMP) is the discharge of an electrical current through the air, arcing from a point of a relative positive charge to a point of a relative negative charge (Figure 5-19). While EMI is often a hassle and prevents good communication, EMP is a far more serious issue that easily leads to the physical destruction of equipment.

EMP comes in two common forms: *electrostatic discharge (ESD)* and *lightning*. ESD is that classic shock you get from grabbing a doorknob while you're petting a cat in your silk pajamas as you drag your stocking feet along some carpeting. ESD might be a mildly shocking inconvenience to humans, but it can destroy unprotected circuits, especially the integrated circuits used in computer equipment.

Protect equipment by shielding it in protective cases; only use properly grounded power supplies. When working on very sensitive equipment, such as CPUs and RAM, always use anti-ESD wrist straps like the one shown in Figure 5-20.

Figure 5-20
Anti-ESD wrist
strap

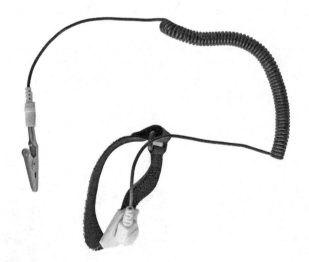

ESD is bad, but if you want to see the power of EMP, there's nothing like a little lightning to ruin your equipment and your day. All homes and smaller office buildings are well protected against nearby lightning strikes with good grounding plus anti-surge devices on all important electrical equipment. For protection against direct strikes, large office buildings are usually equipped with lighting rods that direct strikes away from the interior of the building through thick conducting cables.

NOTE There is another type of EMP that comes from nuclear detonations. If you encounter that form of EMP, you're not going to be worrying about your computers!

Securing the Boot Process

IT professionals need to plan for many contingencies so that users have secure computers with which to work. At the system level, for example, they must assure the security of individual system components by securing the supply chain. Second, they must implement technologies that will protect data in the event of theft or unauthorized physical access to systems. This section explores four aspects of physical security:

- Securing the supply chain
- Using TCG technologies
- Using TPM for security
- Incorporating HSMs

NOTE The title of this section, "Securing the Boot Process," is a pun for computer hardware geeks. The boot process for CompTIA A+ techs refers to the stages or steps a computer goes through from the moment you press the power button to the time you see the login screen. This section should more accurately be titled "Securing the Tools Users Need to Get Computing Done," but that seemed a bit much.

Securing the Supply Chain

Securing the supply chain for computing needs accomplishes a couple of very important things. First and most obvious, your users have tools to do computing work. Second, and more to the point here, securing the supply chain means getting gear you can trust not to be compromised in some way.

Hardware manufacturers have several standards and best practices to support your hardware. One of the more recognized standards is the *Open Trusted Technology Provider Standard (O-TTPS)*. O-TTPS is a standard created by the Open Group that has been adopted by the International Organization for Standardization/International Electrotechnical Commission (ISO/IEC JTC 1) as ISO/IEC 20243. This standard provides a framework that give organizations the tools to create best practices for supply chain security, using *commercial off-the-shelf (COTS)* technology as wells as *information and communication technology (ICT)* products.

Figure 5-21
Trusted
Computing
Group

Using TCG Technologies

The IT industry knew back in the mid-1990s that putting together all this technology was going to take a lot of big companies working together, so AMD, Hewlett-Packard, IBM, Intel, and Microsoft got together and formed an organization now called the *Trusted Computing Group (TCG)*. Over the years, TCG has included roughly 100 of the most important hardware and operating system manufacturers (Figure 5-21).

TCG is solely responsible for all the most popular technologies that, when used collectively, make your system very secure. Let's look at those technologies and see how they work.

Using TPM for Security

Most modern computers ship with a chip called a *Trusted Platform Module (TPM)* (see Figure 5-22) that works with system firmware—UEFI in current PCs, for example—to provide a baseline level of security and trust. The operating system relies on this *hardware root of trust* to check for low-level changes at boot up. These changes can happen from malware, for example. Depending on the system, any tampering could lead to automatic loading of a last known good system or a system stop.

 EXAM TIP Modern personal computers rely on unified extensible firmware interface (UEFI) for firmware, as you'll recall from your CompTIA A+ studies. For some reason, the CompTIA Security+ objectives also mention the older style firmware, basic input/output system, or BIOS, in the same discussion. If you see BIOS and not UEFI and the answer is definitely firmware, go with BIOS.

Figure 5-22
TPM chip

This boot-level security, called generically *secure boot*, can also work with more centrally controlled systems. During the boot process, the TPM and UEFI generate reports about the process and can send those reports to a remote system, like a central authentication server. This process is called *remote attestation*.

EXAM TIP   Windows 8 and later enables a feature called Secure Boot that takes advantage of TPM and UEFI to provide precisely that option. Also, the CompTIA Security+ objectives refer to remote attestation as simply "attestation."

Disk Encryption   Disk encryption has been around in one shape or another for a long time and certainly predates TPM chips, but the presence of TPM provides a powerful tool for encrypting drives. Every operating system supports *full disk encryption (FDE)*. The FDE tool that comes with Windows Pro versions is called *BitLocker*. To encrypt a drive with BitLocker, you must have a motherboard with a TPM chip and you must have TPM enabled in UEFI (Figure 5-23).

You can go even more secure with disk encryption with a *self-encrypting drive (SED)*. A SED has onboard circuitry that automatically encrypts and decrypts all data on the drive. From the outside, a SED looks exactly like any other drive. It works on both traditional hard disk drives (HDDs) and solid state drives (SSDs). A SED often comes with extra features, such as instantaneous drive wiping, that high-security folks really enjoy.

Incorporating Hardware Security Modules (HSMs)

The many processes that take advantage of asymmetric key storage, authentication, encryption/decryption, and other functions can often swamp general-purpose CPUs

Figure 5-23   BitLocker in Windows

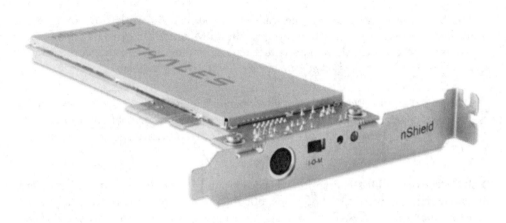

Figure 5-24   HSM PCIe card

and operating systems. For Web servers, ATMs, or other applications that perform an unusually high amount of key handling, it's usually a good idea to offload this work to other hardware. A *hardware security module (HSM)* is any type of hardware that's designed to do this work. An HSM might look like a network appliance, supporting one or more servers; it might be a USB device; or like Figure 5-24, it might look like a PCIe card you install on a system. When cryptography is slowing down a server's response time, an HSM, with its optimized processors designed to handle cryptographic functions hundreds of times faster than an equivalent general-purpose CPU, will speed up key handling dramatically. HSMs are expensive, but when time is of the essence, HSMs are the way to go.

Module 5-4: Securing Operating Systems

This module covers the following CompTIA Security+ objective:

- **3.3**   Given a scenario, implement secure systems design

The previous module discussed several tools to secure hardware and made more than one reference to securing operating systems and applications. This module carries the story forward, first focusing on selecting the right operating system for the job; and second, applying well-known security controls to design the right security for different operating systems and situations.

Operating System Types

Computing is everywhere, from powerful servers passing out virtual machines to thousands of users to tablets used by toddlers to play simple games. As a security tech, you'll run into plenty of situations where you'll need to make sure you're getting the right type of operating system for the job at hand. There are over 15 different versions of Microsoft Windows alone. Which one do you need for your job?

To help you, the CompTIA Security+ objectives clearly list an assortment of operating system types you'll need to know for the exam. Let's go through each of these types—server, workstation, mobile, appliance, and kiosk—and define a few OSes out there that fit each.

EXAM TIP The CompTIA Security+ objectives list "network" as a type of operating system. Traditionally, a network operating system (NOS) functioned primarily to provide sharing among networked systems. All modern operating systems include such sharing features and functions, so the concept of a standalone NOS is obsolete.

You'll also see specialized operating systems in network hardware, such as routers, referred to as network operating systems. See the upcoming "Hardening Operating Systems" section for more information on securing network devices.

Server

Server operating systems have several features to support multiple types of server applications. In the Microsoft Windows world, there are separate Windows Server versions. Windows Server comes preinstalled with powerful networking applications such as DNS and DHCP servers. Windows Server has much stronger hardware support features such as support for more than two physical CPUs and more RAM. Windows Server supports a huge number of connections, whereas all other Windows versions support a maximum of 20 connections. Last, Windows Server contains Microsoft's proprietary but powerful Active Directory, the cornerstone of Windows single sign-on (Figure 5-25).

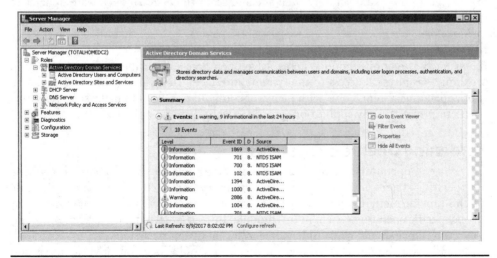

Figure 5-25   Active Directory Server Manager

Most Linux distros have server versions as well, but Linux doesn't limit CPUs or connections. For the most part, a Linux server distro concentrates on preinstalling features such as DNS and DHCP servers. Additionally, most Linux server distros guarantee longer support.

> **NOTE** As we go through this list you should chant the phrase *least functionality* as you consider each type. Never use more operating system than you need.

Workstation

A *workstation* operating system is normally the main version, the most common version used by consumers. In Windows that means Windows 10. For Apple that means macOS. These are the OSes running on most desktop systems and laptops.

Mobile

Who doesn't know the two primary *mobile* operating systems, iOS from Apple and Android from Google? A *mobile OS* provides specific support for a limited amount of hardware and is always preinstalled and preconfigured (for the most part).

Appliance

An *appliance* operating system refers to the firmware powering the thousands of different types of devices designed to perform a specific function, from 802.11 WAPs, to thermostats, home routers, network-attached storage, and so on. An appliance will have a very customized operating system, often a custom Linux distro, burned into firmware. There are two points to these operating systems. First, take your time to learn the interface. You probably won't interact with it very often, because a good appliance often just works. Second, go to the manufacturer's Web site and see if there are any firmware updates to make sure the appliance is patched.

Kiosk

Kiosks, such as demonstration systems, have open access. That means that everyone in proximity has physical access to the system's interface. Kiosks need to be locked down. Kiosk operating systems come with plenty of configuration tools to make sure users can't open a terminal, run any applications you don't want them to, or increase their privileges.

Hardening Operating Systems

Hardening an operating system means several things, but mostly it's about configuring the operating system and setting security options appropriately. Although all operating systems provide methods and interfaces for *secure configurations*, we're not going to focus on one specific operating system in this module. Instead, we'll focus on several configuration settings that should be considered regardless of operating system.

Regardless of the operating system in use, you should focus on privilege levels and groups (administrative users and regular user accounts); access to storage media, shared

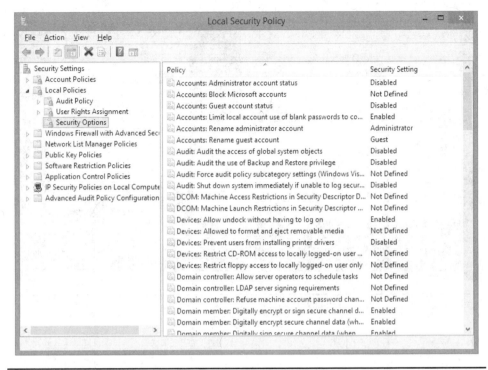

Figure 5-26   Security options in Windows 8

files, and folders; and rights to change system settings. Additional settings you should evaluate include encryption and authentication settings, account settings such as lockout and login configuration, and password settings that control strength and complexity, password usage, and expiration time. You also should consider other system settings that directly affect security, including user rights and the ability to affect certain aspects of the system itself, such as network communication. These configuration settings contribute to the overall hardening of the operating system.

Figure 5-26 shows a sample of some of the different options that you can configure for security in Windows. Figure 5-27 shows other options that you can configure in a Linux operating system.

Trusted Operating System

A *trusted OS* is a specialized version of an operating system, created and configured for high-security environments. It may require very specific hardware to run on. Trusted operating systems are also evaluated by a strict set of criteria and are usually used in environments such as the U.S. Department of Defense and other government agencies, where multilevel security requirements are in place. An example of the criteria that a trusted OS must meet is the *Common Criteria*, a set of standards that operating systems

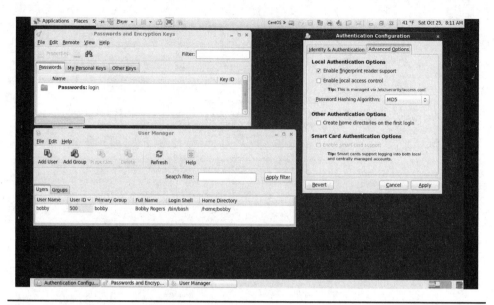

Figure 5-27 Security options in Linux

and other technologies are evaluated against for security. Trusted operating systems have very restrictive configuration settings and are hardened beyond the level needed for normal business operations in typical security environments. Examples of trusted operating systems include Trusted Solaris, SE Linux, and Trusted AIX. Some operating systems, such as Windows 10 and Windows Server, have been certified as trusted operating systems, with certain configuration changes.

Host-Based Firewalls and Intrusion Detection

In addition to setting up security configurations on a host, you need to protect the host from a variety of network-based threats. Obviously, network-based firewalls and network-based intrusion detection systems (NIDSs) work to protect the entire network from malicious traffic. Host-based versions of these devices are usually software-based, installed on the host as an application. Their purpose is to filter traffic coming into the host from the network, based upon rules that inspect the traffic and make decisions about whether to allow or deny it into the host in accordance with those rules. Host-based intrusion detection systems (HIDSs) serve to detect patterns of malicious traffic, such as those that may target certain protocols or services that appear to cause excessive amounts of traffic, or other types of intrusion.

Host-based firewalls and HIDSs may be included in the operating system, but they can also be independent applications installed on the host. Like their network counterparts, you should carefully configure them to allow into the host only the traffic necessary for the host to perform its function. You should also baseline them to the normal types of

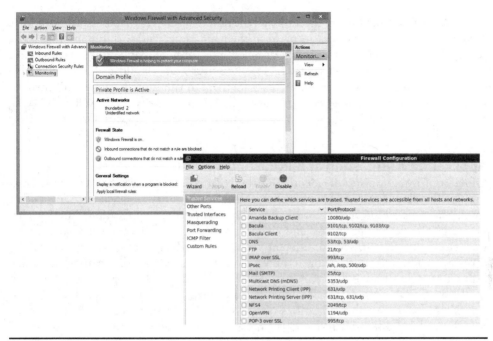

Figure 5-28 Comparison of Windows and Linux firewalls

network traffic that the host may experience. Also like their network counterparts, you should update host-based firewalls and HIDSs with new attack signatures as needed and tune them occasionally as the network environment changes to ensure that they are fulfilling their role in protecting the host from malicious traffic, while permitting traffic the users need to do their jobs. Figure 5-28 shows a side-by-side example of Windows and Linux firewalls.

Disabling Unnecessary Ports and Services

Almost every host runs services that it doesn't need. In addition to wasting processing power and resources, a host that is running unnecessary services is also a security concern. Services can be vulnerable to attacks for a variety of reasons, including unchecked privilege use, accessing sensitive resources, and so on. Adding unnecessary services to a host increases the vulnerabilities present on that host, widening the attack surface someone might use to launch an attack on the host. One of the basic host hardening principles in security is to disable any unnecessary services. For example, if you have a public-facing Web server, it shouldn't be running any services that could be avenues of attack into the host, or worse, into the internal network. For example, a public-facing Web server shouldn't be running e-mail, DHCP, DNS, and so on. Internal hosts have the same issues; workstations don't need to be running FTP servers or any other service that the user doesn't explicitly need to perform his or her job functions.

You should take the time to inventory all the different services that users, workstations, servers, and other devices need to perform their functions, and turn off any that aren't required. Often, when a device is first installed, it is running many unnecessary services by default; often these do not get disabled. Administrators should take care to disable or uninstall those services, or at least configure them to run more securely. This involves restricting any unnecessary access to resources on the host or network, as well as following the principle of least privilege and configuring those services to run with limited-privilege accounts.

Application Whitelisting or Blacklisting

Often, security administrators identify software that is harmful to computers or the organization for various reasons. In some cases, software may contain malicious code; in other cases, the organization may want to allow the use of certain applications, such as chat programs, file sharing programs, and video games (Figure 5-29). You can restrict access to these applications in several different ways, one of which is blacklisting. *Blacklisting* involves an administrator adding an undesirable piece of software or an application to a list on a content filtering device, in Active Directory group policy, or on another type of mechanism, so that users are not allowed to download, install, or execute these applications. This keeps certain applications off the host. Applications may be blacklisted by default until an administrator has decided on whether to allow them to be used on the host or the network.

Whitelisting works similarly to blacklisting, except that a whitelist contains applications that are allowed on the network or that are okay to install and use on hosts. A whitelist would be useful in an environment where, by default, applications are not allowed unless approved by an administrator. This ensures that only certain applications can be installed and executed on the host. It also may help ensure that applications are denied by default until they are checked for malicious code or other undesirable characteristics before they are added to the whitelist.

Figure 5-29
But I need to play
CounterStrike!

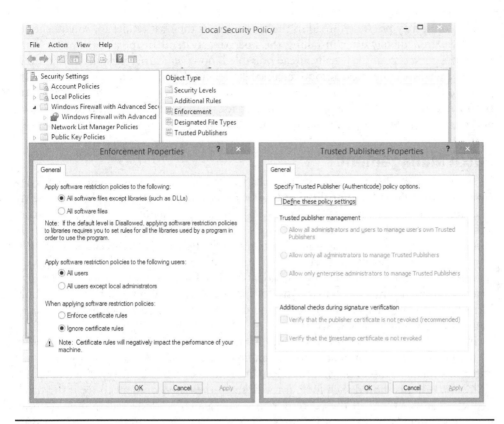

Figure 5-30   Application control in Windows 8

Applications and software can be restricted using several different criteria. You could restrict software based upon its publisher, whether you trust that publisher, or by file executable. You could also further restrict software by controlling whether certain file types can be executed or used on the host. You could use these criteria in a whitelist or a blacklist.

Figure 5-30 shows an example of how Windows can do very basic whitelisting and blacklisting using different criteria in the security settings on the local machine. When using blacklisting in a larger infrastructure—using Active Directory, for example—you have many more options to choose from.

Disable Default Accounts/Passwords

Out-of-the-box, operating systems often include default accounts with passwords that are either blank or don't meet the organization's password complexity requirements. Some of these default accounts may not even be necessary for the normal day-to-day operation of the host. A good example of such an account is the Windows default guest account.

This account may not be required in the environment the host resides in, so you should disable it immediately after installing the operating system. In most versions of Windows, the guest account is usually already disabled; however, earlier versions of Windows were installed with the guest account enabled by default. Linux operating systems are also prone to this issue. A default Linux installation includes many accounts, all of which you should examine to see if they are really needed for the day-to-day operation of the host, and then disable or delete any that aren't necessary.

Patch Management

It's not unusual for issues to arise occasionally with operating systems, where bugs are discovered in the OS, or functionality needs to be fixed or improved—and, of course, newly discovered vulnerabilities must be addressed. Operating system vendors release patches and security updates to address these issues. For the most part, operating systems are configured to seek out and download patches from their manufacturers automatically, although in some cases this must be done manually. This process is called *patch management*. In a home environment, it's probably okay for hosts to download and install patches automatically on a regular basis. In an enterprise environment, however, a more formalized patch management process should be in place that is closely related to configuration and change management.

In a patch management process, administrators review patches for their applicability in the enterprise environment before installing them. Admins should research a new patch or update to discover what functionality it fixes or what security vulnerabilities it addresses. Admins should then look at the hosts in their environment to see if the patch applies to any of them. If they determine that the patch is needed, they should install it on test systems first to see if it causes issues with security or functionality. If it does cause significant issues, the organization may have to determine whether it will accept the risk of breaking functionality or security by installing the new patch, or will accept the risk incurred by not installing the patch and correcting any problems or issues the patch is intended for. If there are no significant issues, then the admins should follow the organization's formal procedure or process for installing the patch on the systems within the environment. Typically, this is done automatically through centralized *patch management tools* (software), but in some cases, manual intervention may be required and the admins may have to install the patch individually on each host in the enterprise.

 EXAM TIP Look for a question about the output of patch management tools on the CompTIA Security+ exam. This output can be simple, such as an application or OS prompting for updates. Or it can be more nuanced, especially with customized software from vendors.

In addition, admins should run a vulnerability scanner on the host both before and after installing the patch to ensure that it addresses the problem as intended. They also should document patches installed on production systems, so that if there is a problem that they don't notice immediately, they can check the patch installation process to determine if the patch was a factor in the issue.

Module 5-5: Securing Peripherals

This module covers the following CompTIA Security+ objectives:

- **1.2** Compare and contrast types of attacks
- **2.4** Given a scenario, analyze and interpret output from security technologies
- **3.3** Given a scenario, implement secure systems design
- **3.5** Explain the security implications of embedded systems
- **3.9** Explain the importance of physical security controls

Peripherals are a problem. They're not very secure. As an IT security tech, you need to understand how bad actors take advantage of keyboards, USB flash drives, printers, monitors, and other peripherals to compromise the security of individual systems.

This module explores peripherals, the technologies and their weaknesses, the ways bad actors attack using peripherals, and what you can do to secure the peripherals or, in some cases, how you can secure the ports on systems to protect from nonsecure peripherals. The module closes with a discussion on physical security.

Locating Vulnerabilities

Peripherals provide two areas of vulnerability. First, anything not directly connected to your system is a risk. Wireless keyboards can be used as a vulnerability to get into a system. A networked printer can capture data and even print it out for the bad actor. Someone sneaking in a keystroke recorder between a user and her keyboard is a common problem. Second, the ports on your system are a huge problem. Figure 5-31 shows one of my favorite tools, a Hak5 USB Rubber Ducky. I just plug it into any USB port and it starts sending preconfigured commands, such as capturing keystrokes and delivering a payload to compromise the system.

Wireless Peripherals

Wireless peripherals such as wireless keyboards and wireless mice are common and convenient, freeing us from messy cables and allowing more freedom of configuration. The problem with wireless peripherals is that they typically use Bluetooth as the wireless connection. Although Bluetooth is a mature and secure technology, an improperly configured Bluetooth peripheral is easy to hack. Let's take a moment and talk about the two old but still valid Bluetooth attacks, bluejacking and bluesnarfing.

Bluejacking

Although becoming rarer these days, Bluetooth attacks happen. In the early days of Bluetooth, protocols did not have adequate security measures built in, and devices by default allowed themselves to connect with any Bluetooth device that requested it. This enabled attackers to connect their Bluetooth device surreptitiously with an unsuspecting person's device and steal information from it, such as contacts and other personal information. These attacks are becoming rare because the Bluetooth protocol has evolved over time,

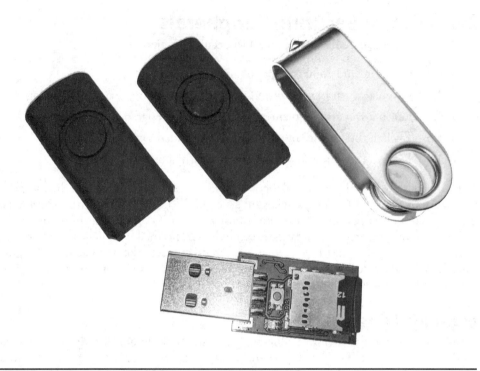

Figure 5-31   USB Rubber Ducky

and now more security measures are built into the protocol by default. Additionally, most Bluetooth devices have to undergo a type of authentication with each other, called *pairing*, which makes intercepting traffic between them more difficult. Another factor contributing to the rarity of these types of attacks is that Bluetooth has a very limited range: an attacker would have to be within around 35 feet of the victim to conduct the attack successfully.

However, legacy devices are still in use, as well as new devices that are not configured securely, that are susceptible to Bluetooth attacks. One of the major attacks on Bluetooth is called *bluejacking*. Bluejacking involves sending data to a target device, such as a smartphone, usually in the form of unsolicited text messages. Although mostly harmless, bluejacking can be annoying at best and constitutes harassment at worst. Bluejacking does not involve removing data from the device, however.

Bluesnarfing

Bluesnarfing is yet another Bluetooth attack, in which the attacker steals data from the target device by connecting to an unsuspecting user's device. Bluesnarfing can be used to get contacts, e-mails, text messages, pictures, videos, and other sensitive data. Once again, this type of attack is very rare these days, since most vendors have fixed vulnerabilities in their device operating systems, and because of upgrades to the protocol itself.

You can stop both bluejacking and bluesnarfing attacks easily by making sure you don't leave your device in discoverable mode, to prevent anyone from pairing to your device.

802.11

802.11 isn't nearly as popular for connecting peripherals directly to a system, but many peripherals can connect to an 802.11 network as a host. Printers and multifunction devices (MFDs) are very commonly connected with 802.11. This book dedicates an entire module to 802.11 security; this module discusses only 802.11 vulnerabilities for peripherals, especially printers and MFDs.

Bad actors love a good 802.11 printer to use as a pathway to your network. Wireless devices don't change IP addresses very often, so it's easy to spoof an attacking device to look like a printer. Make sure you're using WPA2 PSK encryption at a minimum. If you have a printer that guests need to access, consider setting up a second SSID with minimum permissions. Almost all but the most basic WAPs can generate two or more SSIDs (Figure 5-32).

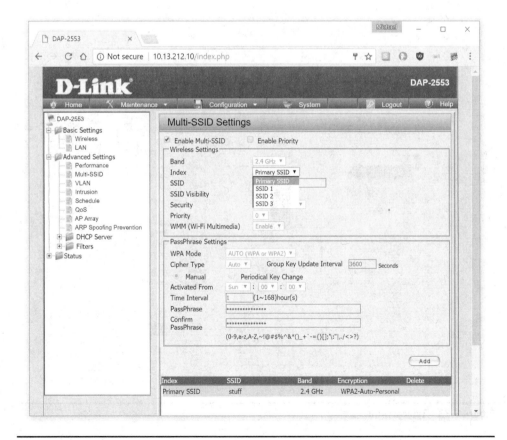

Figure 5-32 Multiple SSID settings

Many peripherals, but especially printers and MFDs, use utilities and services that are persistent on one or more systems. These utilities can be handy, although I think the main reason they exist is to sell printer cartridges to you (Figure 5-33). If you use any of these, make sure you run the latest version. Also note which ports it opens on your system. If possible, try to use nonstandard port numbers to keep the bad actors guessing.

 NOTE MAC filtering can be useful for wireless peripherals or wireless servers.

The last 802.11 issue that shows up in peripherals is *surprise wireless*. 802.11 chipsets are so small that you can embed them into USB thumb drives or microSD cards. Make sure you know your peripherals and disable any wireless radios you don't need, such as those on Wi-Fi–enabled microSD cards.

Figure 5-33 Typical printer utility

Embedded Systems

An embedded system is a complete system embedded in some type of device. An embedded system has a CPU, RAM, mass storage, and an operating system. Many peripherals, certainly most printers and MFDs, but others such as digital cameras, are often embedded systems. Generally, a peripheral has an embedded system if there's some kind of configuration screen like the one shown in Figure 5-34.

There's nothing wrong with peripherals with embedded systems other than you need to think of that peripheral as being more like a system than a peripheral. Check with the manufacturer from time to time for any firmware updates and keep peripherals updated. Also consider the fact that the peripheral may have interesting ports that a bad actor might use. Turn off or block any unused ports on the peripheral to prevent unauthorized access.

USB Ports

Any unused USB port on a system is a huge vulnerability. A bad actor can easily plug in a Bluetooth adapter and instantly use his or her own Bluetooth keyboard. They can insert a Rubber Ducky like discussed earlier and hack your system. I recommend disabling every unused USB port, usually leaving only one open in front of the system, thus easily observed.

USB ports are everywhere! Many monitors/displays have handy USB ports. Most printers and MSDs have USB ports. Even many home routers have USB ports. Those are the most important ones to turn off because you rarely observe them.

Figure 5-34   A configuration screen is a sure sign of an embedded system.

EXAM TIP Look for an exam question on removable media control. The question is about disabling USB ports or, more specifically, not allowing access to USB ports to malicious actors.

External Storage

External storage devices, often HDDs or SSDs in enclosures, are very common and handy peripherals for backups, temporary storage, and data transfer. The downside to external storage is—you guessed it—security. These drives can be stolen, which makes the data on these drives easy picking for bad actors.

NOTE Self-encrypting hard drives are a natural option for external storage.

If you're using external drives, at the very least consider an FDE solution like BitLocker if you have a TPM chip. If you don't have a TPM chip, consider a third-party FDE tool like CipherShed (www.ciphershed.org). CipherShed is free, open source, and works with all operating systems.

Physical Security

You can stop theft with some good physical security. First, almost all desktop and server system cases come with anti-intrusion alarms. If anyone opens the case, the system sets of an audible alarm.

Second, get a cable lock, particularly if you place a laptop in a tempting location for thieves. All laptops come with a reinforced cable lock port. You should consider Kensington Computer Products Group (www.kensington.com) for a variety of excellent cable locking systems.

Finally, don't forget a screen filter. Screen filters are excellent tools to narrow the field of vision. This prevents shoulder surfers from observing the content of your screen.

Module 5-6: Malware

This module covers the following CompTIA Security+ objective:

- **1.1** Given a scenario, analyze indicators of compromise and determine the type of malware

No matter how many anti-malware tools, no matter how much training given to users, every week the news of some attack shoots across the screen and fills security people with terror.

The CompTIA Security+ exam will challenge you with scenario questions that expect you to recognize the symptoms of certain types of malware. Let's go through the following 12 types and make sure you're aware of the differences:

- Virus
- Crypto-malware/ransomware
- Worm
- Trojan horse
- Rootkit
- Keylogger
- Adware
- Spyware
- Bots/botnet
- Logic bomb
- Backdoor
- RAT

Virus

A *virus* is a piece of malicious software that must be propagated through a definite user action. In other words, it normally cannot spread by itself. It requires a user to initiate, in some way, the execution of the virus. Sometimes this action is very subtle, and the unsuspecting user may not even know that his actions are executing a virus. For example, he may open an infected file or executable, spawning the virus. Normally, viruses are propagated via download from malicious Internet sites, through removable storage media (USB sticks, for example) passed along from person to person, or through the transmission of infected files from computer to computer via e-mail or file sharing.

Viruses have a variety of effects on computers and applications. These effects range from affecting performance by slowing down the system, filling up storage space, and slowing down the host's network connections, to more serious impacts, such as recording passwords and other sensitive information, and rendering the host completely unusable or even unbootable. Some viruses infect files, while others, usually more serious ones, infect the boot sector of media. These boot-sector viruses automatically execute in the computer's memory when the host boots up; at that moment, there is no OS-based antivirus software loaded to detect or eradicate it, so it has already done its damage by the time the OS loads. Usually, the only way to get rid of a boot-sector virus is to boot the host off of a known good (meaning clean and free of malware) media, such as a new hard drive, bootable CD/DVD disc, or a USB stick. The boot media should also have specialized antivirus software loaded on it to detect and clean the infection.

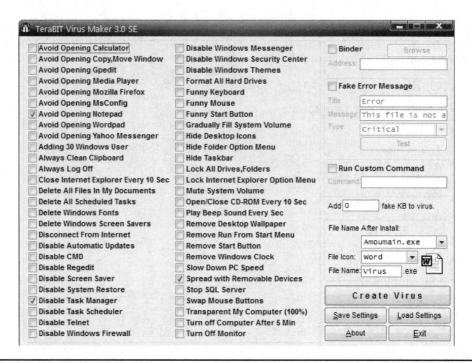

Figure 5-35 TeraBIT Virus Maker, a virus creation program

You might have wondered why it seems so easy for hackers to create viruses that can do so much damage; in fact, there are many programs on the Internet that help hackers create viruses easily. Some require extensive programming skills, and others are simple graphical programs that require almost no knowledge at all. Figure 5-35 gives an example of one such program, TeraBIT Virus Maker, but there are hundreds more out there.

- **Symptoms:** System slowdown; some action against your system.
- **Action:** Use an anti-malware program from a live boot to clean the virus.

Crypto-malware/Ransomware

Crypto-malware uses some form of encryption to lock a user out of a system. Once the crypto-malware encrypts the computer, usually encrypting the boot drive, in most cases the malware then forces the user to pay money to get the system decrypted, as shown in Figure 5-36. When any form of malware makes you pay to get the malware to go away, we call that malware *ransomware*. If a crypto-malware uses a ransom, we commonly call it *crypto-ransomware*.

Figure 5-36 CryptoWall, an infamous crypto-ransomware

Crypto-ransomware is one of the most troublesome malwares today, first appearing around 2012 and still going strong. Zero-day variations of crypto-malware, with names such as CryptoWall or WannaCry, are often impossible to clean.

- **Symptoms:** System lockout; ransom screen with payment instructions.
- **Action:** Use anti-malware software from a live boot to clean the crypto-malware.

NOTE Most crypto-malware propagates via a Trojan horse. See the upcoming "Trojan Horse" section for more information.

Worm

A *worm* is much like a virus, in that it can cause disruptions to the host, slow down systems, and cause other problems. However, a worm is spread very differently from a virus. A worm is usually able to self-replicate and spread all over a network, often through methods such as instant messaging, e-mail, and other types of network-based connections. The big difference between a virus and a worm is that a virus can't spread itself; in other words, a virus requires a user action to replicate and spread. A worm doesn't have this problem and can automatically replicate over an entire network with very little user intervention. This unfortunate characteristic of a worm is what causes it to be a significant problem in large networks. Examples of famous worm infections include MyDoom, Blaster, and the Win32Conficker worm.

- **Symptoms:** System slowdown; unauthorized network activity; some action against your system.
- **Action:** Use an anti-malware program from a live boot to clean the worm.

Trojan Horse

A *Trojan horse* isn't really a type of malware; it's more a method by which malware propagates. Named after the Greek Trojan Horse of mythological fame, a Trojan horse is a piece of software that seems to be of value to the user. It could be in the form of a game, utility, or other piece of useful software. It is malware, however, and serves a specific function. Usually a Trojan horse has the goal of collecting personal information from a user, including user credentials, financial information, and so on. It can also be used as a generic container used to spread viruses and worms. (Note that symptoms and actions will follow the payload type, so will vary a lot.)

 EXAM TIP The CompTIA Security+ exam oddly refers to Trojan horse malware as simply "Trojans."

Rootkit

A *rootkit* is a piece of malware that attempts to infect critical operating system files on the host. Often, antivirus software cannot easily detect rootkits, so they can reside on the system for quite a while before detection. Additionally, they can thwart antivirus software because they can send false system information to it, preventing it from detecting and eradicating not only itself but other viruses as well.

- **Symptoms:** Often no symptoms at all. System slowdown; unauthorized network activity.
- **Action:** Depends on the rootkit. Use rootkit-aware anti-malware software from a live boot to quarantine the rootkit; or possibly manually remove the rootkit.

Keylogger

A *keylogger* is a piece of malware that records keystrokes. Most keyloggers store a certain number of keystrokes and then send the stored keystrokes as a file to the bad actor. Recorded keystrokes are one of the best ways to collect passwords, filenames, and other highly personalized types of information. Keyloggers are not all evil. They are a very common feature for parental control software. Figure 5-37 shows one example, Spyrix Free Keylogger.

NOTE Keyloggers also manifest as malicious hardware dongles that sit between your keyboard and your system.

- **Symptoms:** Often no symptoms at all. System slowdown; unauthorized network activity.
- **Action:** Use anti-malware software from a live boot to remove the keylogger.

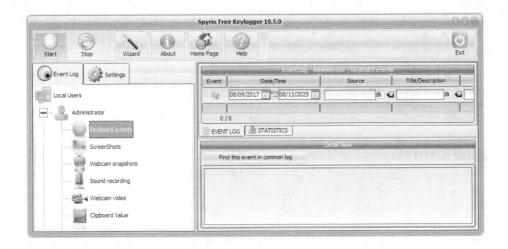

Figure 5-37 Keylogger interface

Adware

Adware is the name given to often annoying advertisements that come in the form of pop-up messages in a user's browser or on a user's screen outside of a browser session. These messages usually want the user to visit a site, buy a product, or click the ad itself. At best, these messages can be irritating, interrupting a user's activities with the pop-up message, but sometimes they are a real hindrance to productivity, often redirecting the user's home pages in the browser or spawning several (sometimes dozens to hundreds) of pop-ups or Web sites at once.

Computers get adware infections pretty much the same way they get other types of malware. The user may click a Web link or download something that changes browser or other configuration settings on the host, resulting in the continuous stream of pop-ups. Adware can even be included with purposefully downloaded, seemingly unrelated applications. Sometimes the user is asked to allow the installation of an add-in or browser helper object (BHO) to view a certain file type or run a piece of browser-based software. Most of the time, unsuspecting users will allow the installation by default, opening the door to pop-ups, automatically spawned programs, and browser redirection.

- **Symptoms:** Unauthorized Web browser redirection; pop-up ads.
- **Action:** Use an anti-malware program from a live boot to clean the adware.

Spyware

Spyware isn't a type of malware; it's more of a goal for some types of malware. Spyware is a virus or Trojan horse in form, but we tend to classify spyware by its function rather than type. Spyware is used for the specific purpose of surreptitiously observing a user's actions and recording them, as well as stealing sensitive data, such as passwords, credit card information, and so forth. Spyware can send data back to the attacker, quietly of course, so that the user can't easily detect it. Spyware can also dump data into a file so an attacker can later retrieve it directly from the system if she has physical access. Spyware can affect hosts through various means, in usually the same way that other malware does.

 NOTE The spyware aspect of a malware can take many forms. Look to the specific payload type for all the malware symptoms and the actions you should take to combat it.

Bots/Botnet

A *botnet* is a distributed type of malware attack that uses remotely controlled malware that has infected several different computers. The idea is to create a large robot-like network used to wage large-scale attacks on systems and networks. Once the malware is installed on the host, the attacker can control hosts remotely and send malicious commands to them to be carried out. The hosts are called *bots*, or *zombies*, because they obey only the orders of the attacker once the attack begins. Most botnet attacks are in the form of distributed denial-of-service (DDoS) attacks. Among the different attack methods that botnets can use is sending massive amounts of malware to different computers, sending large volumes of network traffic, and performing other methods designed to slow down or completely disable hosts and networks. Botnet attacks can spread rapidly once activated and can be very difficult to counter. In fact, one of the attack methods used during an attack is to infect other hosts and have them join the botnet.

- **Symptoms:** Usually undetectable until activated. System slowdown in some cases.
- **Action:** Use an anti-malware program from a live boot to clean the bot.

Logic Bomb

A *logic bomb* is often a script set to execute at a time or if certain events or circumstances take place on the system. It is designed to take malicious actions when it executes. An example of a logic bomb is a script that has been written to begin erasing file shares or disk storage at a certain time or date. Most logic bombs are timed to execute by including them as a scheduled event using the operating system's event scheduling facility, such as the AT command in Windows or the cron utility in Linux-based systems. A logic bomb is *not* necessarily a form of malware—at least it's not the kind that can easily be detected by anti-malware software.

Logic bombs are usually the result of a malicious insider or a disgruntled administrator; most of the logic bomb attacks recently sensationalized in the news media involved a rogue administrator dissatisfied with employers for whatever reason. Detecting a logic bomb can be troublesome; it usually requires examining any files, utilities, and scheduled jobs the malicious user had access to, as well as auditing the user's actions and reviewing the access logs that recorded any use of his privileges.

- **Symptoms:** Usually undetectable until activated. System damage, data loss.
- **Action:** Restore system from backups.

Backdoor

A *backdoor* is an entry method into a piece of software (application or operating system) that wasn't intended to be used by normal users. Most backdoors are created as a maintenance entry point during software development, usually by the programmers creating the software. These maintenance backdoors should be closed prior to software release, but often they are either forgotten about or left open intentionally to bypass security mechanisms later after the software is released, either by the programmer or a malicious entity.

 NOTE A few smartphones and other mobile devices manufactured in China have been found to have backdoors.

Backdoors can also be created by hackers during an intrusion into a system; often their goal is to have a way back into the system if their primary entry point is taken away or secured. Again, backdoors usually bypass security mechanisms that normally require identification and authorization, so this is a serious security issue. Vulnerability testing can often detect these unauthorized entry points into a system, but sometimes more in-depth testing methods, such as penetration testing or application fuzzing, may be required to find them.

 NOTE Like Trojan horses, a backdoor is a method of entry into a system, not a malware type. Look for the specific payload type to determine symptoms and actions you should take to protect or remediate.

RAT

RAT stands for one of two things. First, RAT stands for *remote administration tool*, which is some form of software that gives remote access for administrators and IT support. RAT also means *remote access Trojan*, which is a remote administration tool maliciously installed as a Trojan horse to give a remote user some level of control of the infected system. This can be as simple as just opening a Telnet server on the infected system to full-blown, graphical remote desktops. RATs are often an important part of a botnet.

- **Symptoms:** Usually undetectable until activated. System damage, data loss.
- **Action:** Restore system from backups.

Module 5-7: Securing Network Access

This module covers the following CompTIA Security+ objectives:

- **2.1**   Install and configure network components, both hardware- and software-based, to support organizational security
- **2.4**   Given a scenario, analyze and interpret output from security technologies

Security professionals rely on various tools to enable users to accomplish a fundamental task: secure access to a TCP/IP network. This module explores the following tools:

- Anti-malware programs
- Data execution prevention
- File integrity check
- Data loss prevention
- Application whitelisting
- Firewalls
- Intrusion detection

Anti-malware

Anti-malware has come a long way from the early antivirus programs we used back in the 1990s. These first tools were drive scanners, using signatures to look for known viruses and doing their best to clean them out of systems. As time progressed, more features came online such as e-mail scanners, HTTP scanners, and RAM scanners. It wasn't uncommon for a single anti-malware tool to possess five or six different scanning types.

 EXAM TIP Look for exam questions specifically addressing the output from *antivirus* software. Just substitute anti-malware software and you'll see the obvious answer.

Today's anti-malware tools include *point scanners*—often called real-time scanners—that provide real-time scanning of all incoming data, looking for malware signatures. Point scanners don't care about the type of data. They look for malware signatures in e-mail and Web browsers. Whatever application you use, a good point scanner will find and stop the malware before it infects your system (Figure 5-38).

 EXAM TIP Almost all anti-malware tools include a point scanner and a mass storage scanner. Look for an exam question about advanced anti-malware tools; this is it.

Data Execution Prevention

In the early 2000s, a series of malware worms attacked the Internet, infecting memory areas with buffer overflows and propagating themselves by attempting to contact random IP addresses. These worms were relatively easy to detect, but their ability to execute code in areas of memory normally used only for data storage proved to be a bit of a problem. To stop these types of attacks, Intel and AMD forwarded a new feature, now in all CPUs, called the No eXecute (NX) bit. All operating systems were updated to support the NX bit. In Microsoft Windows, NX bit support is called Data Execution Prevention (DEP). The generic term for this is *executable space protection*. I'll use DEP in this explanation for ease of use (and what you'll see on the CompTIA Security+ exam).

DEP is almost always on by default on every Windows operating system. Be aware that you can disable it in the system setup utility. Assuming DEP is enabled in firmware, there's always a place to check it in your operating system. Figure 5-39 shows DEP in Windows 10.

 NOTE DEP should always be on, quietly protecting systems from buffer overflows. The need to turn off DEP is rare.

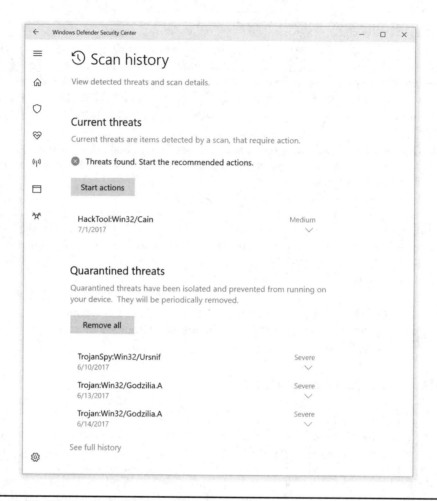

Figure 5-38   Windows Defender detecting malware

File Integrity Check

If malware is to be persistent, it must find a place to hide in your mass storage. One popular strategy of malware is to create its own place to hide by replacing otherwise perfectly good files, both executable and data files, with refactored versions (Figure 5-40).

To defeat these bad actors, we can use a file integrity check as part of our anti-malware routine. As the name implies, a file integrity check makes sure the right files are in the right place. Most file integrity checks start with a hash of the file itself, but may also add

- File date/Time
- Version number (if executable)

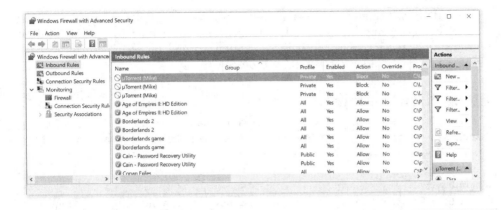

Figure 5-39   DEP settings in Windows 10

- Digital signature
- Meta data (Modify Date)

By recording these values at installation of the operating system or application, a file integrity checker can verify without a doubt that the files being checked are the right ones.

Data Loss Prevention

If your data is precious, you might want to add some data loss prevention (DLP) tools to the individual servers storing that data. Most DLP solutions are designed not only to keep your data's integrity at 100 percent, but also to do several other jobs. Some DLP packages verify backups exist and are in good order. Some DLP packages monitor if data is being moved or copied (they call this data-in-motion). Some DLP packages provide removable media control—called *USB blocking*—to prevent local copies being created. DLP works in all sorts of appliances, from enterprise routers to cloud-based services.

Figure 5-40
Which is the real one?

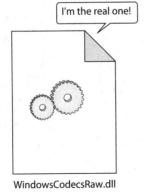
WindowsCodecsRaw.dll

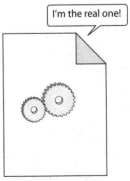
WindowsCodecsRaw.dll

You'll find DLP employed in mail gateways, protecting e-mail messages and delivery. The mail gateway might employ DLP along with a spam filter to proactively delete known unsolicited messages and with encryption features for secure e-mail. (See also Chapter 8 for more discussion on secure protocols.)

Application Whitelisting

File integrity checks are a great tool to verify the operating system and the applications installed on a system is correct, but users can throw spanners into the works. iTunes, Google Play, and Windows Store make it easy for users to install applications on their systems (Figure 5-41)? We need a method to control what users install on their issued machines.

We need to create a security control that defines all the applications a user may install on their issued systems. Alternatively, we can make a whitelist that defines the programs they can *run* on their systems. That way they can install programs all day long, but they won't be able to run them. Every operating system has a method to perform *application whitelisting*, which you read about earlier in Module 5-4. I won't repeat the details here. In Windows, you can create a security policy that either prevents installation or prevents running any application except the ones listed using Group Policy Editor (Figure 5-42).

Firewalls

When most people think of a firewall, they think of some expensive box sitting on a rack that protects their network from Internet bad actors. That is certainly true. Those are network firewalls, and we will discuss those types of firewall in detail in the next chapter. But you know about another type of firewall from Module 5-4, host-based firewalls. No system that accesses the Internet in any way should go without one. Let's reprise the details.

A firewall is a device or software that inspects IP packets and filters them based on preselected criteria. In general, a network firewall faces out, acting as a shield from naughty things trying to get into your network.

Figure 5-41
That app isn't useful.

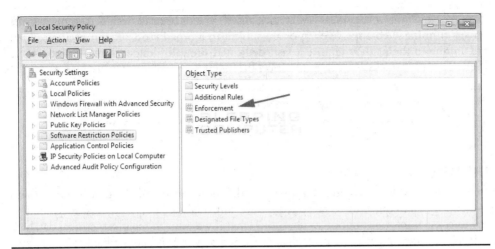

Figure 5-42   Whitelisting an application in Group Policy Editor

A host-based firewall works on the premise that you already have a network firewall, so the host-based firewall instead watches what traffic goes in and out of your system, preventing unauthorized executables from accessing your network (and the Internet) without your permission.

Windows Firewall is a great example of a host-based firewall. It will block or allow connections based on the application/process names (Figure 5-43), something that no network firewall can do as network firewalls have no idea what applications are running the connections.

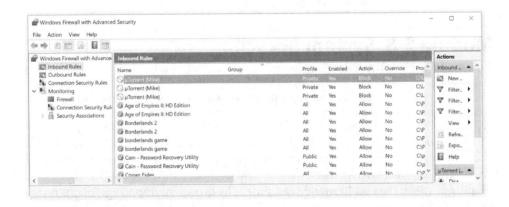

Figure 5-43   Windows Firewall at work

A *Web application firewall* is a very specialized type of firewall designed to protect the servers running Web apps. Web apps are subject to a broad cross section of attacks that are unique to them; they require a fast, dedicated firewall, designed only to stop these Web app–only attacks. A Web application firewall is an excellent security feature.

NOTE   Web application firewalls often manifest as a separate appliance, acting as a proxy between your Web app server and the Internet.

Intrusion Detection

In a perfect world, we would instantly know the moment some bad actor is trying to do something evil to our individual systems. Sure, anti-malware guards against malware trying to come into or out of our systems, but what if we want to see if our critical database is being accessed in a way we don't like? What if a new user is being added to our system without our approval? What if the boot order is being changed? There's a lot of intrusive stuff that can happen to our systems that is outside the realm of malware (or our anti-malware missed something and we want a second line of defense).

This is where *host-based intrusion detection system (HIDS)* and *host-based intrusion prevention system (HIPS)* tools come into play. A HIDS detects intrusions and reports them. A HIPS actively works to stop an intrusion by doing something about it. Network-based intrusion detection systems (NIDS) and network-based intrusion prevention systems (NIPS) protect an entire network, whereas host-based intrusion detection and protection are for individual systems.

EXAM TIP   Look for questions that require you to differentiate between HIDS and HIPS, especially in terms of output. The former detects and reports; the latter actively works to stop an intrusion. The output of reporting tools will reflect these different goals.

Module 5-8: System Recycling

This module covers the following CompTIA Security+ objective:

- **2.2**   Given a scenario, use appropriate software tools to assess the security posture of an organization

There comes a time when hard-working individual systems must say farewell. Technology becomes dated, upgrading is impossible or not cost effective, feature sets are lacking, or a massive hardware failure (like a smoked motherboard) makes a repair simply not worth the cost in money and time. The process of disposing systems is called *system recycling*.

There are two different ways to recycle. First, take a complete system to a scrapper that shreds the system—plastic, metal, everything—and recycles the core materials (Figure 5-44).

Figure 5-44
Shredded
computers

Alternatively, system recycling means to give the computer to someone else who needs it. Charitable organizations, schools, and private individuals badly need computers and will gratefully accept even somewhat dated systems.

In either case, the great issue for IT professionals is to ensure that none of the data on the soon-to-be-recycled mass storage devices survives. This process, called *data sanitation*, takes on several forms and steps, but once again the NIST provides a handy publication (SP 800-88 Revision 1, *Guidelines for Media Sanitization*, Figure 5-45) to help.

NIST SP 800-88 Revision 1 breaks data sanitation into three main methods: clear, purge, and destroy. Each of these methods ensures the data on mass storage won't leave the infrastructure, but the methods vary in terms of security, convenience, and cost.

NOTE   Data destruction is only one part of system recycling, but it's the only one CompTIA Security+ covers.

Clear

Clear means to tell the device through user commands inherent to the mass storage device to sanitize the data. One example of a clear would be to send commands to a hard drive to erase data. However, clearing isn't just a simple erase. It must eliminate data from the mass storage device in such a way as to ensure the data cannot be read again, even if forensic tools are used to try to recover the data.

The biggest question marks when it comes to clearing mass storage are HDDs and SSDs. The built-in erase/delete, format, and partition commands from any operating system generally do not remove data. True removal requires disk wiping utilities that overwrite the data on the entire drive. Figure 5-46 shows the interface of a highly regarded clearing/wiping tool, Parted Magic (www.partedmagic.com).

NIST Special Publication 800-88
Revision 1

Guidelines for Media Sanitization

Richard Kissel
Andrew Regenscheid
Matthew Scholl
Kevin Stine

This publication is available free of charge from:
http://dx.doi.org/10.6028/NIST.SP.800-88r1

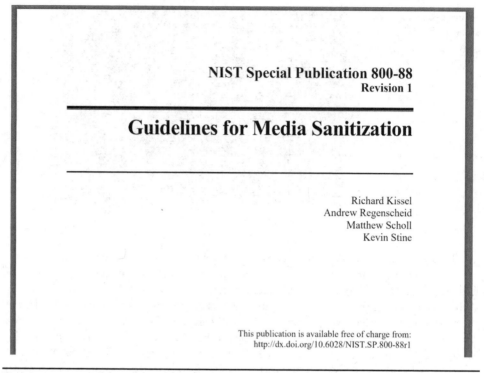

Figure 5-45 NIST SP 800-88, Revision 1

There's an old wives' tale that claims (depending on who you hear this story from) that you must overwrite data six or seven or nine times before the underlying data cannot be recovered forensically. In response to this, SP 800-88 Revision 1 says:

For storage devices containing *magnetic* media, a single overwrite pass with a fixed pattern such as binary zeros typically hinders recovery of data even if state of the art laboratory techniques are applied to attempt to retrieve the data.

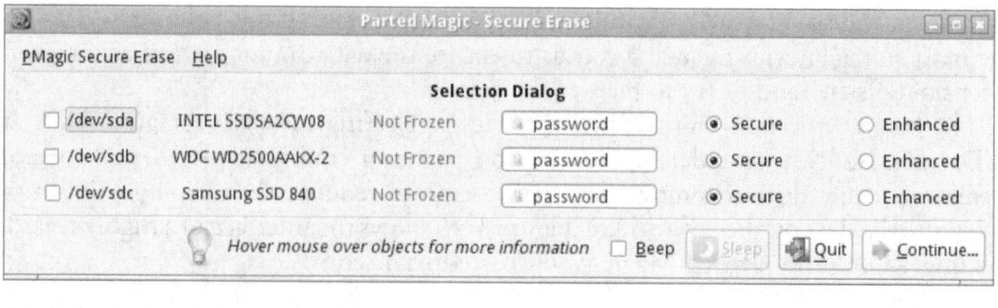

Figure 5-46 Parted Magic

For the overly paranoid, or for those whose employers require you to be so, however, the U.S. Department of Defense wiping standard, DoD 5220.22-M, performs many overwrites. It should be noted that even the U.S. DoD no longer requires this standard for data sanitation.

NOTE A general rule on clear: if the device is an appliance (a router, a smartphone, a multipurpose printer), a factory reset will often sufficiently clear the device. This isn't a guarantee and it's always a good idea to refer to the manufacturer directly.

Purge

Purging means to use anything other than an internal command to sanitize the data on the media. Probably the best example of purging is *degaussing* magnetic media. Degaussing means to expose the media to very powerful magnetic fields. Degaussing is 100 percent effective on HDDs, but is useless with SDDs as they do not store data magnetically. There are companies that will degauss for you, but organizations that need to do a lot of degaussing can buy their own degaussing machine.

Unfortunately, degaussing also destroys the media. Once an HDD is degaussed, the drive is destroyed. But not all purging is destructive. One potential alternative that might be available is *cryptographic erase (CE)*. If by chance you have something on mass storage that is encrypted with an asymmetric key, you can render the data undecipherable by eliminating the key pair, or at least the public key.

Destroy

Last, and certainly the most fun way to achieve data sanitation, is to physically *destroy* the media. Data destruction methods depend on the media, but generally if it burns, you can incinerate it, and if it doesn't burn, you can crush it or shred it. Plenty of companies offer services to destroy media, and there are also drive destroyers that will destroy hard drives.

Questions

1. Rick logs into a public system as Guest and guesses correctly on a simple password to gain administrative access to the machine. What sort of attack surface does this represent?

   A. Man-in-the-middle

   B. Privilege escalation

   C. Service vector

   D. Zero-day

2. John receives a driver-signing error for a specific DLL file in his Windows system. This a classic symptom of what sort of attack?

A. ARP poisoning

B. MAC spoofing

C. Refactoring

D. Shimming

3. Samantha recommended new systems for a group of developers at remote locations. Each system is identical, with high-end processing components. For storage, she needs a solution that provides storage redundancy and performance. She goes with RAID for each system, selecting four drives. Each user can lose up to two drives and not lose data. What RAID did she select?

A. RAID 0

B. RAID 1

C. RAID 5

D. RAID 6

4. Jason gets a tech call from Jill in accounting. Her system works fine most of the time, but every once in a while it loses connection to the wireless network. An inspection of Jill's workstation shows that it's right next to the employee break room. The break room has the typical appliances, such as refrigerator and microwave. Further questioning determines that the network drops most frequently at lunch, though sometimes during the typical afternoon break time. What could the problem be?

A. EMI

B. EMP

C. ESD

D. RFI

5. The Trusted Computing Group introduced the idea of the _____, an integrated circuit chip that enables secure computing.

A. TCP

B. TPM

C. EMP

D. EMI

6. John's home system has automatic updates from Microsoft, yet at his office, his organization has a more formal method of updating systems called

_____.

   A. Automatic updates

   B. Patch management

   C. TOS

   D. Whitelisting

7. Which of the following best describes a Bluetooth attack that attempts to steal data from another device?

   A. Bluejacking

   B. Bluesnarfing

   C. Man-in-the-middle

   D. Pairing override

8. What sort of malware requires the user to pay to remove the malware?

   A. Trojan horse

   B. Keylogger

   C. Adware

   D. Ransomware

9. Marisol notices a small dongle between her USB keyboard and her system. Which of the following is most likely?

   A. She is using an inline encryption device.

   B. She has a TPM module.

   C. Someone has installed a keylogger.

   D. Someone has installed a logic bomb.

10. Degaussing is associated with which form of data sanitation?

   A. Clear

   B. Purge

   C. Destroy

   D. Recycle

Answers

1. **B.** Privilege escalation scenarios have the bad guy increasing the scope of what he can do once authenticated to a system.

2. **C.** A refactoring attack tries to replace a device driver with a file that will add some sort of malicious payload.

3. **D.** A RAID 6 array requires at least four drives, but can lose up to two drives and still not lose data.

4. **A.** Get rid of that microwave oven! Electromagnetic interference can cause all sorts of problems, especially with wireless networks.

5. **B.** Trusted Platform Module (TPM) chips store a unique 2048-bit RSA key pair for security purposes.

6. **B.** Patch management describes the process used to keep systems updated in the enterprise.

7. **B.** Bluesnarfing attacks seek to gain data from a Bluetooth-connected device.

8. **D.** Ransomware demands payment to restore files.

9. **C.** A random USB dongle can be a malicious device, such as a keylogger.

10. **B.** Although a degausser essentially renders a hard drive unusable, it falls into the category of purge.

The Basic LAN

Now that we've discussed hosts, it's time to turn our attention to networks. We've touched on several aspects of network security, including secure protocols, network-based attacks, and so on. We've just scratched the surface, and we have even more to cover in terms of securing the network portion of an infrastructure. This chapter discusses network security at a greater depth, focusing on all the different elements of the network that are connected to provide secure communications for networks ranging from the smallest home LANs to a complete enterprise-level network. The chapter is presented in four modules:

- Organizing LANs
- Securing LANs
- Virtual Private Networks
- Network-Based Intrusion Detection/Prevention

Module 6-1: Organizing LANs

This module covers the following CompTIA Security+ objectives:

- **2.1** Install and configure network components, both hardware- and software-based, to support organizational security
- **3.2** Given a scenario, implement secure network architecture concepts

This module reviews local area network (LAN) technologies, including devices, architectures, and secure networking principles. Although we've already briefly discussed secure network protocols, we'll take an in-depth look at network security, discussing network devices and how to configure them securely, the design elements that go into a secure network, and different security methods and technologies that help make up secure network administration.

Network security is an extremely important part of security in general, so reach back into your mind for all the knowledge and experience you've gained from CompTIA Network+ studies, as well as real-life experience. Also understand that this module is not a CompTIA Network+ exam review, although it discusses many topics that may serve as a reminder of those studies. This module focuses on the security aspects of networking (Figure 6-1).

Figure 6-1
This is more
than a CompTIA
Network+ review.

I can haz
netwerking?

Goodness, no! We're going
way beyond CompTIA
Network+ here!

Many network devices have critical security functions that you should know and understand how to configure. Let's look at switches, routers, network firewalls, and a bunch of other devices that make up the LAN.

NOTE The CompTIA Security+ exam uses the term "topology" very differently than the CompTIA Network+ exam!

It All Begins with Topology

Consider a typical network you might see in a small business. This network has servers and workstations, wireless networks, and at least one Internet connection, as well as all the switches, routers, firewalls, VPNs, and other equipment that makes a network hum.

Any successful network infrastructure starts by organizing the network into specific zones or topologies to verify network functions in the most efficient and secure way possible.

A person with any amount of network experience will find confusing the CompTIA Security+ exam's use of the words *topology* and, to a lesser extent, *zone*. Topology traditionally means the path by which frames propagate around a network. Terms like mesh, ring, and star-bus have been used for decades in this context. In CompTIA Security+, a zone or topology is a functional subgroup of a network. Terms like LAN, DMZ, and extranet are used (Figure 6-2).

To ensure your comfort level with this unorthodox term use, let's talk about the boxes used to connect systems and how CompTIA defines these terms.

Switches

A *switch* connects individual hosts into a broadcast domain. A single broadcast domain is the most basic form of LAN. From a network perspective, a switch does this job very well. Figure 6-3 describes a LAN.

The simplest LAN only requires a single switch, but as networks become more complex, it's common to see multiple switches working together. Figure 6-4 shows a LAN that spans three floors; each floor has its own switch, connecting all the hosts

Figure 6-2
A whole new
world of terms!

on that floor. In the basement, there is an *aggregation switch*, sometimes also called a backbone switch that creates a convenient point to plug in a router to connect the LAN to the Internet.

Normally, switches physically segment LANs into different pieces, but a better switch can also logically separate hosts into entirely different LANs, called *virtual LANs (VLANs)*. We'll discuss VLANs a bit later in this module. For now, you should know that VLANs enable network administrators to separate sensitive hosts from other hosts based upon a logical VLAN assignment.

Routers

Routers are network devices that filter and forward IP traffic from one LAN to another. When you interconnect two or more LANs with a router, you create the most basic version of a *wide area network (WAN)*. WANs may be much more complex. A single network with many broadcast domains all interconnected by routers is still a single WAN (Figure 6-5).

Figure 6-3   A LAN

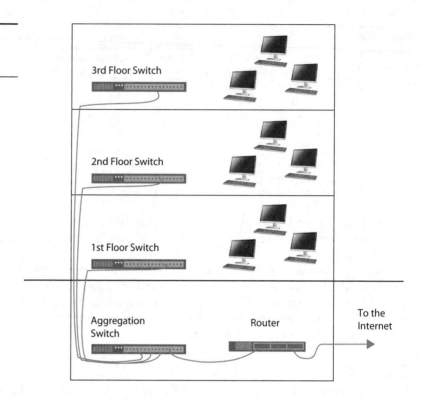

Figure 6-4
Aggregation switch

Routers not only interconnect LANs, they separate them. First, routers block all broadcasts. Second, security professionals use a router's separation of LANs as chokepoints to inspect and block some of the packets going back and forth. To do so requires an extra layer of function via a network firewall.

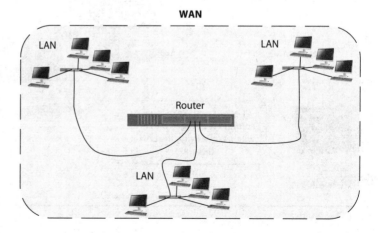

Figure 6-5
A WAN

Network Firewalls

A network firewall, like the host-based firewall discussed in the previous chapter, filters IP traffic based on rulesets known generically as *access control lists (ACLs)*. A network firewall may manifest as a specialized hardware device or as software that runs on a computer using a traditional operating system. A router works by inspecting the traffic based upon preconfigured rules (the ACL), determining whether the traffic should be allowed into or out of a network.

 NOTE Given that routers interconnect LANs, adding firewall features to a router is a natural combination.

Network-based firewalls typically protect entire network segments. Traditionally, firewalls were thought of in terms of separating only public networks from private networks; but modern security theory also emphasizes the use of firewalls in an internal network to separate sensitive network segments from other internal networks. Firewalls can filter traffic based upon a wide variety of criteria, including port, protocol, network service, time of day, source or destination host, and even users or entire domains. More advanced firewalls can also do deep-level traffic inspection, so even traffic that meets rules allowing it to pass through the firewall could be denied due to the content of its traffic.

The 'Nets

Let's get some more terms out of the way. A private WAN that uses the TCP/IP protocol is an *intranet*. A private TCP/IP network that provides external entities (customers, vendors, etc.) access to their intranet is called an *extranet*. The biggest TCP/IP network of all, the one we all know and love, is called the *Internet*.

DMZ

The best way to connect a LAN to the Internet is to use a firewall-capable router to act as the interconnect between the LAN and an internet service provider (ISP). While simple LANs handle this nicely, a network that includes public servers must have a more complex topology that protects Internet systems but still enables public servers less-protected access. To do this, create a *demilitarized zone (DMZ)*. A DMZ is nothing more than a LAN, separate from the internal LANs that contain workstations and private servers. The DMZ connects to the Internet via a lightly firewalled router, and an internal network connects to the DMZ via a much more aggressively firewalled router (Figure 6-6).

NAT

The IT industry developed *network address translation (NAT)* when it became apparent that the IP version 4 (IPv4) address space had rapidly approaching limits. More and more organizations had larger numbers of hosts but were unable to obtain the numbers of public IP addresses to support those hosts. To slow down the inevitable exhaustion of

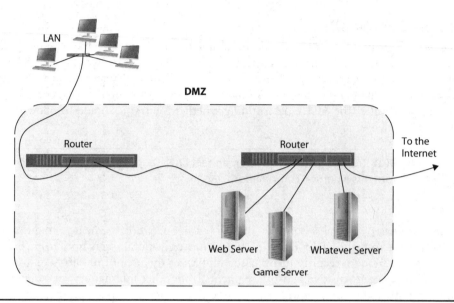

Figure 6-6 A DMZ

IPv4 addresses and provide a way for larger organizations to use very limited numbers of public IP addresses, NAT was used, along with the private IP address space mentioned earlier. This enabled internal hosts to have their own non-routable IP address ranges that could comfortably accommodate even large numbers of hosts.

NAT requires a network device capable of handling public-to-private IP address mappings, such as a router or security device. NAT works like this: An organization can have only one pubic IP address or just a few public IP addresses. It can have many more internal hosts than the number of available public IP addresses, because it can use NAT to map the public IP addresses dynamically to internal private IP addresses during communications sessions.

There are a few ways to do this. First, you can map one public IP address temporarily to a single private IP address, or to a pool of private IP addresses. In *port address translation (PAT)*, the internal client's source port is kept in a table and used in the translation process, so that when external communications are returned for that client, the device handling NAT knows which client the traffic is intended for. You can also use a pool of public IP addresses, if you have more than one, in the same manner. You can also use *static NAT*, which creates a persistent mapping of a public IP address to a private one. This is typically used only when an internal host needs to receive traffic constantly from external clients, such as a Web server. Static NAT, however, should be used minimally whenever possible.

From a security perspective, NAT enables the organization to hide its internal IP address range from external networks and clients. This can help prevent attacks on specific hosts, since external clients won't know the internal IP address of any hosts. NAT can also help prevent certain types of attacks that require spoofing of a victim's IP address. If an attacker doesn't know the victim's IP address, or can't send traffic into the internal network because the firewall or security device blocks inbound traffic from its internal address space, then the attacker can't easily spoof addresses or initiate certain types of network attacks. Until recently, NAT caused certain types of security protocols, namely IPsec, not to function properly; however, this issue was resolved with later versions of the protocol.

Wireless

You can add wireless as a topology to a network in a couple of ways. A common way is to create an *infrastructure* wireless network. This is done by using *wireless access points (WAPs)* to make interconnects between the wireless network clients and the wired network (Figure 6-7).

An alternative is a wireless *ad hoc* network. An ad hoc wireless network doesn't use a WAP. Instead, one client establishes a wireless network and others join. The ad hoc network method was designed for quick and easy wireless networks and was designed with wired network connections in mind. Ad hoc networks, while rare, are fully supported by every wireless client.

Segregation

A good, secure network architecture organizes components into physical or logical groupings. This practice, which can be achieved through segmentation, segregation, or isolation, enhances security and, in some cases, improves network performance.

- *Network segregation* means to create and enforce an ACL that controls which hosts may communicate with which other hosts and what information they may transfer. Segregation helps security.

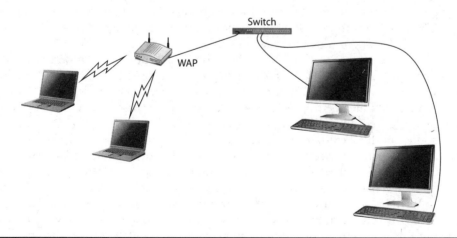

Figure 6-7 A WAP providing an infrastructure network

- *Network segmentation* means to partition a single network into two or more, usually smaller, networks. Segmentation improves efficiency by reducing the size of the broadcast domain, but has little to do with security.

- *Network isolation* means to separate one network from another. This protects one network from another, but prevents direct communication.

Separating network components into groups can happen in multiple ways. An *air gap*, for example, creates a *physical* separation between the trusted and secure network servers and hosts, and the less-secure machines available to visitors and other external users. Secure government facilities typically offer such separation, for example. The proliferation of Wi-Fi networking in modern networks has created a need to create a two-tiered network isolation. One group enables access to the Internet wireless to everyone, the *Guest zone*. The other Wi-Fi access enables authenticated Wi-Fi devices to get to the company's secure resources.

An air gap can manifest as a logical separation of networks, rather than a physical one. The most typical use of logical segregation or isolation is through virtual LAN (VLAN) switch technology. Let's go there now.

 EXAM TIP The use of virtualization—with virtual servers and systems—requires the same diligence with security as do physical machines and networks. The concepts and implementations of segregation, segmentation, and isolation apply to virtualized networks just as much as to physical networks.

VLANs

You know that the defining characteristics of a LAN are that hosts are on the same subnet; that they communicate with each other without the need to be routed; and that they use hardware (MAC) addresses to identify each other during communications. A VLAN doesn't depend upon the physical layout of the network; it doesn't matter if the hosts are physically sitting next to each other or are located several buildings apart. A VLAN creates a logical network in which to assign hosts.

Once a host is assigned to a VLAN, it follows LAN conventions, as if it were physically a part of a LAN. You create VLANs on switches by configuring the switches to establish and recognize VLANs with certain characteristics. These characteristics include an IP subnet and VLAN membership. VLAN membership can be based upon the switch port the host is plugged into (called a port-based VLAN); it can also be based upon the MAC address of the client (a MAC-based VLAN). You could also have a protocol-based VLAN, which would ensure that any client with an IP address on a subnet would be assigned to a VLAN by default. You can assign different hosts to different VLANs, even if they plug into the same switch and sit right next to each other.

Since VLANs operate with the same characteristics as normal LANs, broadcasts are not passed between them. In fact, it's necessary to route traffic between VLANs. You could use a traditional router for this, or, more often, you could configure the switch to route between VLANs (called *inter-VLAN routing*). If VLANs need to access networks

Figure 6-8
VLANs on a
switch

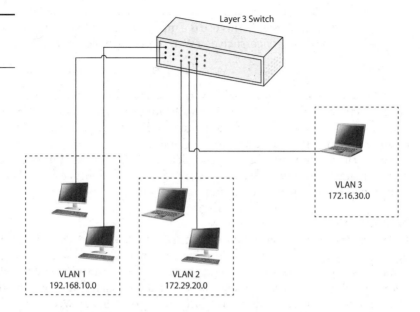

that aren't controlled by the switch, the traffic must pass through a traditional router. Figure 6-8 illustrates an example VLAN setup.

VLANs contribute to security because they enable administrators to separate hosts from each other, usually based upon sensitivity. In other words, you can assign sensitive hosts to a VLAN and control which other hosts access them through the VLAN. Since VLANs are logical (and software-based), you can control other aspects of them from a security perspective. You can control what types of traffic can enter or exit the VLAN, and you can restrict access to hosts on that VLAN via a single policy. You can also provide for increased network performance by using VLANs to eliminate broadcast domains, the same as you would with a traditional router.

Load Balancers

A *load balancer* is a network device used to provide efficient and seamless workload sharing between network devices (such as routers or firewalls) or hosts, typically Web or file servers or storage devices. Placed strategically between devices, a load balancer enhances security and efficiency. You can also purchase network devices with native load balancing capability allowing the same functionality with a paired device, but the implementation is more complicated.

High-Availability Clusters

A load balancer contributes to security by providing for high availability. If a server goes down, the load balancer can transparently and immediately provide for availability by transferring network and resource requests to an identically configured backup server. An *active-passive* high-availability cluster like this has one server active and the second passive, acting as a failover or backup.

NOTE   A cluster in this use is a group of servers that work together to provide a service, such as a Web site, Web service, or database.

In an *active-active* high-availability cluster, the load-balanced services perform the same functions at the same time, but with different transactions. As an example, two load-balanced Web servers would respond to different users' browser requests. The load balancer manages the traffic and requests going to each of the members of the service or device cluster for which it is responsible. This helps provide for efficiency, eliminates delays or latency, and provides for system and data availability if a member of the cluster is unable to fulfill requests or requires maintenance.

Scheduling

Load balancers may use several different criteria to determine scheduling—that is, which device gets a particular request. A load balancer may base its decisions on network traffic conditions, for example, or it may use a turn-based system (otherwise known as a *round-robin* type of system), or it can send traffic based on available resources on the target systems in more advanced products. It is important to note that Web sites and applications need to maintain session affinity across load-balanced resources. For example, if there are two Web servers behind a load balancer and a user's initial session is sent to Web server A, the affinity between that user and the application thread active on Web server A must be maintained. Otherwise, the user's experience on a Web site would not be consistent—Web server A would have some of the information and Web server B would have other parts, resulting in a useless session, broken shopping cart, and so on.

A load balancer receives traffic for other devices or services via a virtual IP address. In a simple application, one Web server would receive and process all user sessions. In the preceding Web site example, both Web servers have individual IP addresses and both need to receive and process network traffic. To enable this, all the traffic is sent to a virtual IP address that is hosted on the load balancer, which forwards the relevant traffic to each resource behind it. This address is labeled "virtual" because it only exists for the purpose of routing traffic and it is assigned to a device that already has a hardware-relevant IP address. A load balancer in an enterprise environment could host hundreds of virtual IP addresses for different applications.

NAC

Network Access Control (NAC) provides network protection and security by prohibiting hosts from connecting to the organization's infrastructure unless they meet certain criteria. A NAC device is used as an entry point or gateway into the network, typically for remote or mobile clients. This device checks the health and security settings of the client—a *host health check*—against a specified set of criteria before allowing it to access the network. For example, a NAC device could check the client for the latest antivirus signatures, the latest security updates, and other security configuration items. If the client does not meet these requirements, the NAC device does not allow the client to connect to the network. Additionally, the NAC device might be able to update the client dynamically or reconfigure certain options so that the client could proceed with authentication and connection to the infrastructure. NAC could also be used to authenticate devices, allowing only authorized devices to connect. Normally, a NAC device would be placed on a secure segment within a DMZ network.

NAC supports devices using agents or runs agentless. *Agent-based NAC* tracks many features of potentially inbound devices, such as software versions, and so on. The agent-based approach enables very fine control over allowing a device to connect to the network. The criteria used for an agent-based approach can be *permanent* or *dissolvable*. The former means the device that wants access to the network must have some software loaded—that software stays loaded. A dissolvable agent system runs something once on the device and admits or denies access; the software is then deleted.

Agentless NAC (such as one based on Windows Active Directory) would apply group policy rule to enforce the controls that an agent-based NAC device would do directly.

Module 6-2: Securing LANs

This module covers the following CompTIA Security+ objectives:

- **2.1** Install and configure network components, both hardware- and software-based, to support organizational security

- **2.2** Given a scenario, use appropriate software tools to assess the security posture of an organization

- **3.2** Given a scenario, implement secure network architecture concepts

With a solid LAN topology, you now have the foundation to populate your LAN with a cross section of boxes: switches, routers, and other equipment that add functionality and security to keep a LAN secure. This module tours a simple, Internet-connected LAN, with a typical SOHO-style topology, to explore the security features covered by the CompTIA Security+ exam.

To help organize the tour, let's break a SOHO LAN into three pieces: the LAN, the Internet connection, and the public-facing server that resides inside our DMZs. Figure 6-9 shows the three pieces.

 NOTE Wireless networks also need security and are an important part of just about every network out there. Wireless security gets its own discussion in Chapter 7.

Securing the LAN

To have a LAN you must have at least one switch. A perfectly functional LAN consists of nothing more than a single host and a single dumb switch, although in all but the smallest LANs you'll usually see two or more managed switches, creating the broadcast

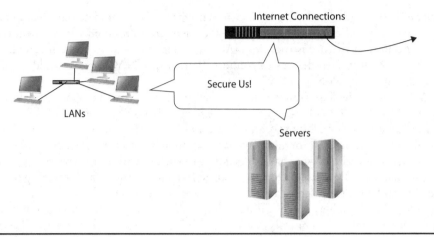

Figure 6-9   The three pieces of the LAN

domain that defines a LAN. Most installations use rack-mounted switches with professionally installed structured cabling (Figure 6-10).

Traditionally, a switch filters and forwards Ethernet frames, memorizing the MAC addresses of all the connected hosts and then creating point-to-point connections for all unicast traffic while at the same time remaining completely capable of supporting broadcasts.

Figure 6-10
Switches in a rack

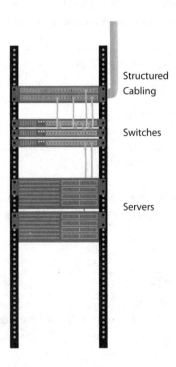

OSI Layers

The term *Layer 2 switch* comes from the Open Systems Interconnect (OSI) seven-layer model (Figure 6-11). Switches filter and forward Ethernet frames by inspecting their MAC addresses; that means that switches work at the Data Link layer (Layer 2).

Starting around 2005, manufacturers released more advanced switches, called Layer 3 switches that added Layer 3 functions atop the traditional switch capabilities. These switches look like any other switch, and they still do Layer 2 switching quite well, but they use powerful application-specific integrated circuit (ASIC) chips that give them the capability to do anything a router can do with much lower latency than a traditional router. For decades, a router was basically a computer with two or more built-in NICs, running its own operating system and handling all the filtering and forwarding in software.

The easiest way to separate a Layer 3 switch from a router is to understand where each is used. Layer 3 switches are incredibly handy for any network that uses VLANs. Remember, a single VLAN is still a LAN, so we normally need a way to connect our VLANs via routers. All Layer 3 switches not only act as routers but, because they are also Layer 2 switches, make all the VLANs on your network and provide easy interconnections between those VLANs via inter-VLAN routing.

 EXAM TIP You'll need to understand the differences between Layer 2 and Layer 3 switches. Traditional Layer 2 switches only handle Ethernet frames; Layer 3 switches can function at the packet level.

Routers have many features that make them better for interconnection of non-VLAN networks. For example, a router might have one or more dedicated WAN ports with features that Layer 3 switches lack, such as the ability to connect to a non-Ethernet network like DOCSIS (cable modems). We will discuss routers a bit more later in this module; for now let's return to switch security.

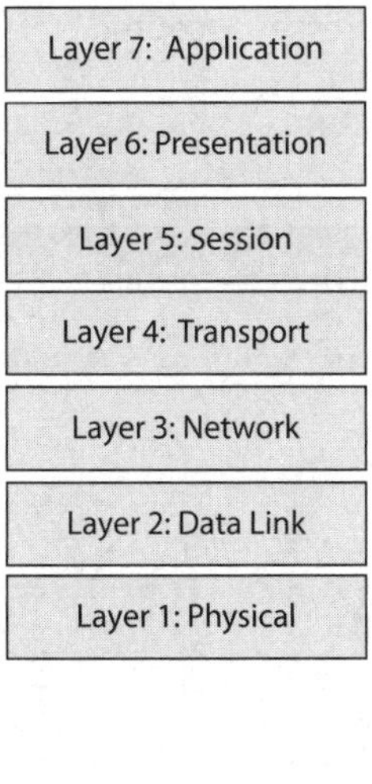

Figure 6-11
The OSI seven-layer model

Layer 7: Application
Layer 6: Presentation
Layer 5: Session
Layer 4: Transport
Layer 3: Network
Layer 2: Data Link
Layer 1: Physical

NOTE Most enterprise environments contain multiple Layer 3 switches.

Port Security

Bad actors love access to a network's switch. Access to a switch opens vulnerabilities to attacks. ARP spoofers steal the MAC addresses of legitimate systems, enabling man-in-the-middle attacks. Denial-of-service attacks can flood a switch with confusing MAC information. An attacker can plug in a rogue DHCP server, knocking systems off the network. They can start sending out IPv6 neighbor discovery packets, telling the hosts that the attacking system is their gateway and redirecting traffic (Figure 6-12).

Switch ports require security to protect against these attacks. Flood guards and loop prevention are a few of the features you'll see in all better switches. Keep in mind that port security is applied to individual ports.

Flood Guards Although flooding and water damage are definitely a threat to computing resources and people, in this context we aren't talking about the types of floods associated with natural disasters. We're talking about flooding from excessive or malformed traffic that enters a network. A network can encounter several different types of floods, based on various protocols, such as ICMP floods, UDP floods, and MAC floods.

Attackers use traffic floods primarily to conduct denial-of-service attacks on networks and hosts, since many hosts and network devices don't always react very favorably to excessive amounts of traffic or malformed traffic. Because flooding is a routine tactic of attackers, most modern network devices (and even some hosts) have flood protection built into their operating systems. These *flood guards* work by detecting excessive traffic (by volume, as well as by rate of speed) and take steps to block the traffic or drop it, so that the host doesn't have to process it. Most security devices, such as intrusion detection systems, firewalls, and robust network devices like better switches, have flood guards built in.

NOTE Flood guards protect against DoS attack by limiting the number of new MAC addresses accepted.

Figure 6-12
Just give me one
port, just one…

I'm one plug away from totally nailing your network. Sweet!

Figure 6-13 Trusted DHCP server

Another common feature on better switches is called persistent MAC or sticky MAC addressing. In many networks, a host is plugged into a port and it stays there for years. We can configure the switch port to only accept frames from that MAC address, preventing bad actors from unplugging the host and plugging in their evil system.

Some switches give you the ability to only accept DHCP or IPv6 data from anything but certain MAC addresses. If a bad guy manages to insert a new DHCP server on your LAN, your switch will ignore any DHCP (or IPv6 or ICMP) traffic from that device, because it's not on the list of trusted devices (Figure 6-13).

Loop Prevention Switches are amazing tools. Let's say you have a single switch and, due to LAN growth, you managed to fill all the ports. With switches, you can just connect another switch, automatically increasing the size of your broadcast domain. If necessary, you can connect many switches together; there is no real limit, as long as you never create a loop (Figure 6-14).

Loops wreak havoc on unprotected switches, almost instantly causing the entire LAN to spin out of control in what we call a *bridge loop*. Virtually all managed switches today come from the factory with Spanning Tree Protocol (STP) for *loop prevention*. STP gives switches the capability to talk to each other automatically as they learn about all the other switches in the LAN. With STP enabled, switches work together; if a bridge loop suddenly appears, they will block one of the ports along the loop to protect the network (Figure 6-15).

Figure 6-14
Loops are bad.

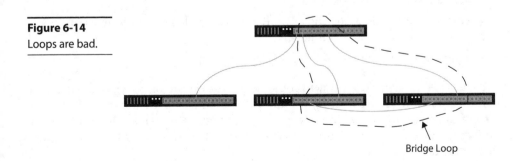

Figure 6-15
STP to the rescue!

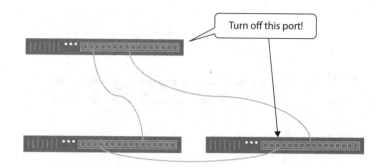

Internet Connection

LANs access the Internet through a router called the *default gateway*. The default gateway connects directly (or indirectly through in-house routers) to an Internet service provider (ISP), which in turn connects to a router higher up on the Internet.

Given the position of the default gateway at the edge of the network, it is a natural location to place a firewall to protect the local network. Network firewalls manifest in many ways, but the most common is at the default gateway, which includes a bevy of firewall features (Figure 6-16).

The primary function of any firewall is to inspect incoming IP packets and block the packets that could potentially hurt the hosts on the LAN. To do this, today's firewalls have three very different methods: stateless, stateful, and application-based.

Stateless Firewalls

A *stateless* firewall looks at every incoming packet individually without considering anything else that might be taking place (ergo *stateless*). Stateless firewalls, also called packet filters, are the oldest type of firewall. If you're going to have a firewall inspecting every packet, you must have some form of checklist that the firewall uses to determine whether a packet should be blocked. This is the router's access control list (ACL). The ACL for an Internet gateway firewall is a unique tool that defines what makes a packet good or bad.

A stateless firewall's ACL can only define aspects of an IP packet to filter. A typical ACL would include these aspects:

- **IP address**   Block specific incoming/outgoing, destination/source IP addresses or complete network IDs
- **Port number**   Block specific incoming/outgoing, destination/source port numbers or ranges of port numbers
- **Time/date**   Block based on time of day, day of week

A stateless firewall makes it easy to combine filters to create surprisingly sophisticated ACL rules. You can set up a basic home firewall, for example, to keep your child's desktop system from accessing any Web pages (ports 80 and 443) between the hours of 10 P.M. and 6 A.M. on school nights. Figure 6-17 shows the ACL interface for a home router with a built-in firewall.

Figure 6-16   Typical gateway

One feature of all ACLs is the idea of *implicit deny*. Implicit deny means that by default there is no access unless the ACL specifically allows it. For example, every firewall's ACL denies all incoming IP packets unless a particular packet is a response from a request initiated by one of the hosts on your LAN.

Stateless firewalls are simple and work well in many situations but fail miserably in the face of many situations where inspecting and blocking without consideration of the state isn't helpful. Consider a simple FTP session, run in the classic active mode:

1. A host inside the LAN (1.2.3.4) initiates a connection to an outside FTP server (2.3.4.5) using destination port 21 and, for this example, a source port of 12,345.

2. The firewall notes that an internal host has initiated an outgoing connection on port 21.

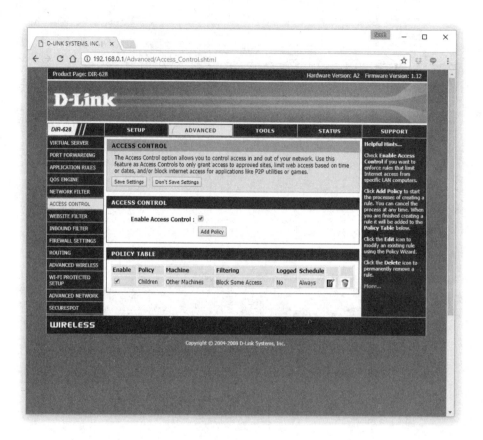

Figure 6-17   Firewall ACL interface

3. The FTP server responds to 1.2.3.4, port 12,345 with source IP address 2.3.4.5 and source port 21. The firewall recognizes this incoming connection as a response and does not block it.

4. The FTP server initiates a data connection to 1.2.3.4, port 12,345 with source address IP 2.3.4.5 and source port 20.

5. The firewall does not recognize this incoming connection and, because of implicit deny, blocks the connection.

Stateless firewalls were such a problem for FTP that the FTP protocol was redesigned to use a second, passive mode. Passive mode only uses port 21.

Just as you can harden a switch against bad actors spoofing a legitimate system's MAC addresses, you can protect against IP address spoofing with a firewall. Helping to prevent IP address spoofing on our networks is one area where stateless firewalls still do a great job.

Routers can use several *antispoofing* techniques. A very popular one is to have a router query its DHCP server for legitimate systems on the network. Every initial packet going out is cross-checked against the DHCP server's IP address list.

Stateful Firewalls

A *stateful* firewall understands the procedures and processes of different Internet protocols and filters any form of communication that is outside of proper procedures. A stateful firewall understands several functions expected in normal TCP and UDP communication and uses that intelligence to inspect the state of that connection. Stateful firewalls collect several packets in a connection and look at them as a state to determine if the communication meets correct protocol steps. One great example is how a stateful firewall can monitor a TCP connection. Every TCP connection starts with three messages, known as TCP's three-way handshake:

1. The initiating system sends a SYN message, requesting a TCP connection.

2. The responding system sends a SYN/ACK message, informing the initiating system it is ready to start a connection.

3. The initiating system sends an ACK message, acknowledging the responding system.

Figure 6-18 shows a Wireshark capture of a three-way handshake.

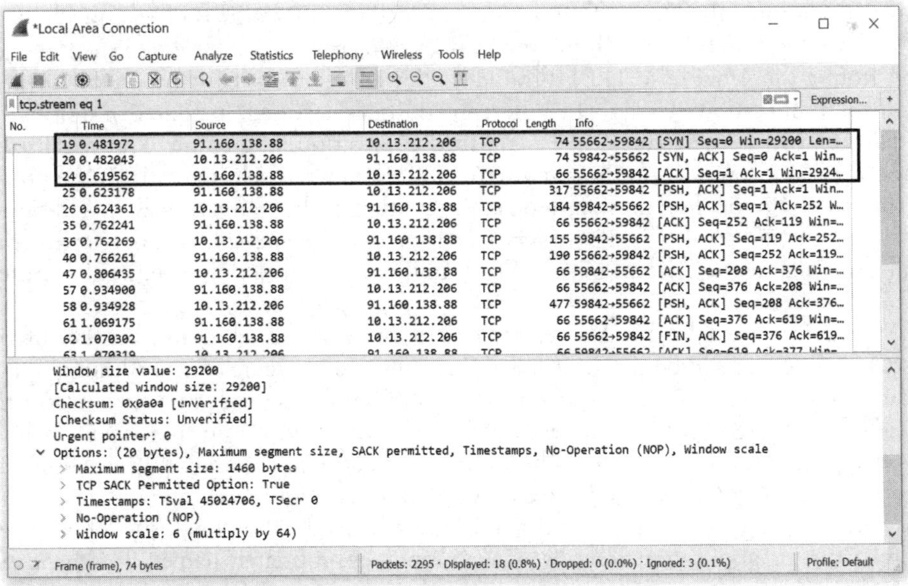

Figure 6-18   TCP three-way handshake

Let's say we have a stateful firewall protecting a Web server. It allows the incoming SYN connection from an unknown Web browser (a firewall protecting a public-facing server must allow incoming connections), but it stores a copy of the incoming packet in a table. It also allows the outgoing SYN/ACK packet from its server, and keeps a copy of that as well. When the Web browser responds with a proper ACK message, the firewall sees this as a good connection and continues to keep the connection open. If the Web browser does anything that makes the stateful firewall think the connection is outside of the protocol, on the other hand, it will block the connection for a certain amount of time.

Stateful firewalls don't have ACLs. They come from the manufacturer with all the state-smarts they're ever going to have. For most stateless firewalls, it's simply a matter of turning them on or off to enable or disable firewall duties.

 NOTE Very advanced stateless firewalls (from companies like Cisco or Juniper) may have a few *filters* (don't call them ACLs) for their stateless firewalls, but those are outside the scope of the CompTIA Security+ exam.

Application Firewall

An *application* firewall has deep understanding of both the stateful and stateless aspects of a specific application (HTTP is by far the most common type of application firewall) and can filter any traffic for that application that could threaten it. Application firewalls can be thought of in two different contexts. In the first, an application firewall is an appliance or network device that works at all seven layers of the OSI model and can inspect data within protocols. Think of a situation in which HTTP traffic is filtered in a firewall. In an ordinary stateful firewall, the traffic is filtered based upon an established connection from an internal host. HTTP traffic is allowed in or out based upon whether the protocol itself is allowed, over which port the traffic is destined, its source or destination IP address, if it is the result of an established connection, and so on. This means that filtering is done based upon the *characteristics* of the traffic itself, rather than the *content* of the traffic. Application firewalls look at the content of the traffic as well, in addition to its characteristics. So, if HTTP is otherwise allowed into the network, an application firewall also looks at the content of the HTTP traffic, often detecting whether the content itself is allowed.

Application firewalls can be network-based or host-based; in the context of our discussions for this module, host-based firewalls are more relevant. Although most industrial static hosts do not use application firewalls specifically on their platforms, some of the more modern hosts, especially consumer devices, do have them. A host-based application firewall controls the applications and services on that device only, and it secures their connections to the network and interfaces with each other.

Given the huge number of Web applications living in the cloud, just about every manufacturer of application firewalls for Web apps—appropriately named *Web application firewalls (WAFs)*—also provides cloud-based virtual appliances (Figure 6-19).

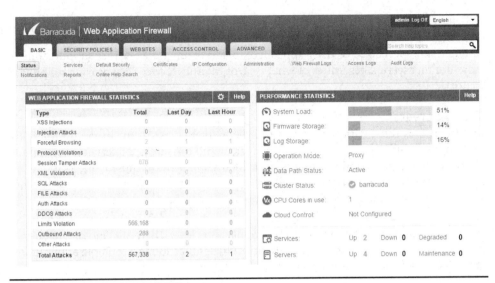

Figure 6-19 Barracuda cloud WAF settings

NOTE Application firewalls are often referred to as Layer 7 firewalls because OSI Layer 7 is also known as the Application layer.

In a way, we can separate application firewalls from stateless and stateful firewalls in terms of their primary job. Application firewalls are designed to protect public-facing servers providing specific applications, so we can call them *application-based firewalls*. Stateless and stateful firewalls mainly protect LANs from the many evils that come from the Internet, so we can call them *network-based firewalls*. If you don't have a public Web application server or an e-mail server (or a few other applications), you have no need for this type of firewall.

EXAM TIP If the CompTIA Security+ exam asks you to identify the difference between application-based firewalls and network-based firewalls, remember the purpose of each type. Application-based firewalls protect public-facing servers running applications; network-based firewalls protect LANs from external threats.

Servers

Anyone providing a server that offers any service to the public Internet has a big security job ahead of them, and the CompTIA Security+ exam objectives reflect the importance of this effort with many security topics covering what it takes to protect servers. In fact, the entire Chapter 8 goes into detail on what's needed for different Internet services, such as Web and e-mail.

Before we start lighting up Web or e-mail servers, there's a lot we can do to place them in a safe place in which they can operate quickly and safely. We can choose from among many specialized security appliances to add to any network that supports one or more Internet servers, regardless of what type of Internet service they provide, to provide security.

Proxy Servers

The Internet is filled with servers and the clients that access them. In many situations, we find it helpful to put a box between the client and the server for certain applications. These boxes accept incoming requests from clients and forward those requests to servers. Equally, these boxes accept responses from servers and then forward them to the clients. These boxes are known as *proxy servers* or often just *proxies*.

EXAM TIP Proxies work at the application level. There are Web proxies, e-mail proxies, FTP proxies, and so forth. Proxies that support multiple applications are known as *application/multipurpose proxies*.

Proxies come in one of two forms: forward or reverse. A *forward proxy* is known to the client system, often in the same LAN, taking the requests from the client, maybe doing something with the request, and then forwarding the request to the server just like any other client (Figure 6-20).

Forward proxies are popular in organizations such as schools where the network administrators need to apply security controls to Internet access. A forward Web proxy almost always includes a strong firewall to check outgoing requests for blocked URLs, time-of-day restrictions, and anything else that needs be monitored to support the security policies of the organization.

A *reverse proxy* is used to protect servers. Reverse proxies are usually inside the same LAN as the servers. They always contain an application firewall to check the incoming requests for attack vectors and then pass the good requests to the server (Figure 6-21).

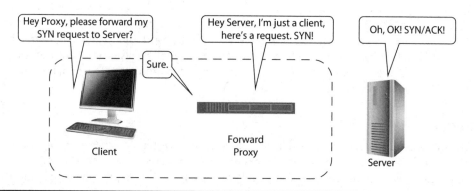

Figure 6-20 Forward proxy

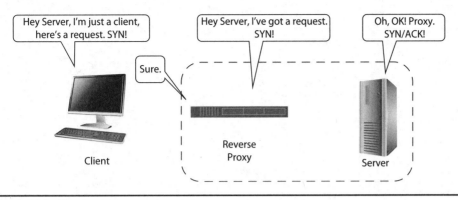

Figure 6-21   Reverse proxy

Proxies work at the application level, so traditionally a system's application must be configured to use a proxy. If a client is to use a forward Web proxy, then every Web browser on every client is configured to use it. Figure 6-22 shows the proxy settings in a Web browser.

All this configuration is a pain, especially if you have a thousand users all using different Web browsers. So why not let your router simply inspect all the data going out on the application's port numbers and simply redirect those packets to your proxy? That's the idea behind a *transparent proxy*. Most forward proxies support a transparent mode to do just this.

Honeypots/Honeynets

A *honeypot* is a host designed to be compromised, so it has multiple vulnerabilities. A honeypot is placed on the network to attract the attention of malicious hackers, hopefully drawing them away from being interested in other, more sensitive hosts. If an attacker victimizes a honeypot, you can study his methods and techniques to help you better protect the actual network against those same methods and techniques.

Honeypots can be boxes that are misconfigured or intentionally not patched, or they can be prebuilt virtual machines. There's even software out there that can emulate dozens or hundreds of hosts at the same time, spanning several different operating systems, including different versions of Windows, Linux, macOS, UNIX, and so on. A *honeynet*, as you might guess, is an entire network of honeypots on their own network segment, used to get a hacker bogged down in a decoy network while the administrator locks down and secures the sensitive network and records and tracks the actions of the hacker.

EXAM TIP   The CompTIA Security+ exam might ask about tools for assessing the security posture of an organization. Analyzing the actions and attacks on a honeypot can help with those assessments.

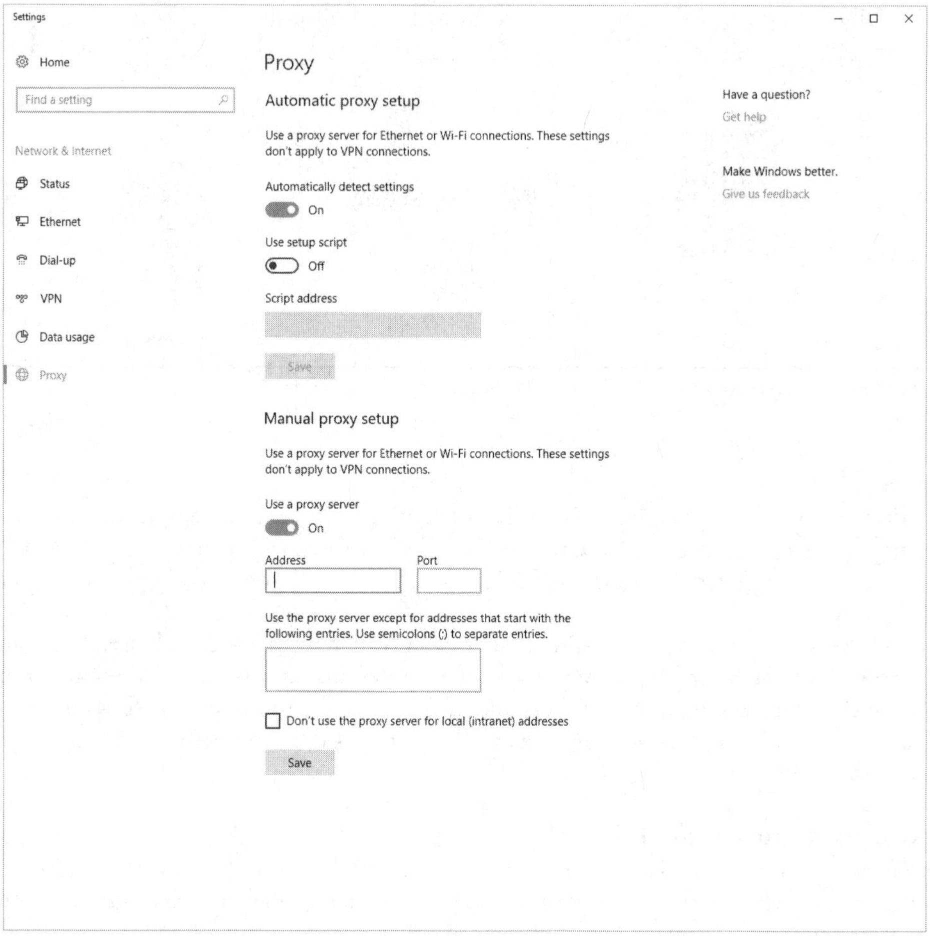

Figure 6-22   Web proxy settings

DDoS Mitigators

Distributed denial-of-service (DDoS) attacks can create huge problems for organizations, and IT professionals must implement protections that prevent DDoS attacks, or at least lessen the effects of such attacks. CompTIA calls these *DDoS mitigators*. Dealing with an active DDoS attack requires a level of hardware that can eliminate enough of the attack to keep your site up and running for your customers. DDoS mitigators are more like a service than just an appliance. A good DDoS mitigator combines onsite appliances (designed to do nothing but filter out DDoS attacks at outrageously high speeds); geographical DDoS elimination (even more boxes, placed around the globe, stopping the actors from ever getting anywhere near your servers); and instant recognition of zero-day attacks to keep your site running.

Module 6-3: Virtual Private Networks

This module covers the following CompTIA Security+ objectives:

- **2.1** Install and configure network components, both hardware- and software-based, to support organizational security
- **3.2** Given a scenario, implement secure network architecture concepts

A *virtual private network (VPN)* uses the public Internet as a direct connection between a single computer and a faraway LAN or two faraway LANs. This is not a remote desktop connection, or a terminal or a Web page connection. A VPN puts a single system or a separate LAN on the same broadcast domain, the same Layer 2 connection just as if the faraway system were plugged directly into the LAN's switch.

A successful VPN connection gives your remote system an IP address on your LAN. You can print from the remote system to your LAN's printers. You can see all the shared folders on other computers on the LAN. You are there. Well, at least your Ethernet frames are there.

VPNs are incredibly powerful for remote single users or remote networks that need to get to a LAN's internal servers. VPNs are a well-established technology and are easy to implement. Most enterprise environments have VPN access for employees and, in some cases, vendors. SOHO environments can use VPNs as well. My home network, for example, is configured to let me access my home network from anywhere on the Internet.

Given the popularity of VPNs and given the fact that they enable people to move potentially sensitive data across the wide-open Internet, VPNs are a very attractive target for the CompTIA Security+ exam. This module dives into VPNs, first describing how they work, and then looking at the many protocol choices available for setting up a VPN.

How VPNs Work

To make a faraway computer manifest as a local computer on your LAN, you need to do several actions. First, you need to connect to the other network over the Internet. That means you need a system with a public IP address that accepts VPN connections. Second, you need to create a second network connection that uses the Internet connection you've established to allow you to send LAN traffic over the Internet. Third, it would probably be a good idea to encode your data to keep private whatever files, print jobs, or other information you're sending to the faraway LAN.

VPNs work in one of two different ways. You can connect a single system to an existing LAN in what is called *remote access*, or you can connect two complete LANs in what CompTIA calls *site-to-site*. Figure 6-23 shows the two options.

To make a connection, at least one system must have a VPN server, more commonly called a *VPN concentrator*, that's designed to accept remote connections from either a single system (for remote access) or another VPN concentrator (for site-to-site). A VPN concentrator is often special VPN software installed on edge routers, or it may be VPN server software installed on a system inside your network. In either case, one system connects to the VPN server and makes a connection (Figure 6-24).

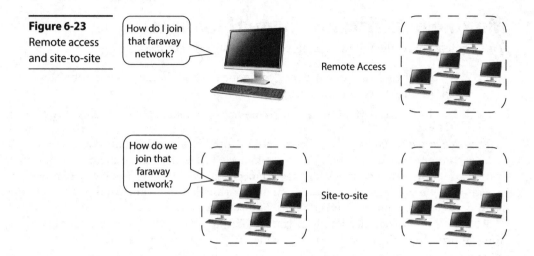

Figure 6-23
Remote access
and site-to-site

VPN connections require tunneling or embedding of IP traffic inside other packets. The VPN to VPN connection gets made, in other words, and then the true traffic happens inside the secure connection. The VPN concentrators continually insert the local traffic in Internet packets and send them through the tunnel; or they receive incoming Internet packets, strip away the outer IP information and send the remaining frame to the local network (Figure 6-25).

NOTE Site-to-site VPN concentrators generally never disconnect. We call these *always-on VPNs*.

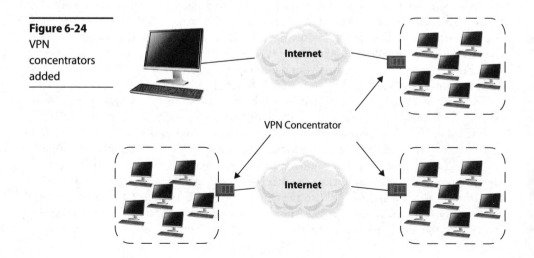

Figure 6-24
VPN
concentrators
added

Figure 6-25
VPN tunnel on
one endpoint

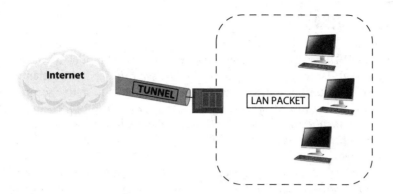

One early problem with VPNs was that once you connected to a LAN, that was your only connection. Your IP address and default gateway were on that LAN; you used that LAN's DHCP and DNS servers. That meant if your computer was connected to a VPN and opened a Web browser, your computer went through the VPN connection and then went back out and used the Internet connection on your LAN. This is called a *full tunnel* and is a terrible way to get to the Internet. Current VPN technologies enable you to configure a VPN connection to send only LAN traffic through the tunnel. All other traffic ignores the tunnel. This is a *split tunnel* and is the most common type of tunnel.

 EXAM TIP The CompTIA Security+ exam will most likely ask you to differentiate between full-tunnel and split-tunnel VPN connections.

Early VPNs

The first VPNs used one of two competing protocols. The *Point-to-Point Tunneling Protocol (PPTP)* was developed by Microsoft to include VPN connection technologies within Microsoft operating systems. PPTP enables a client to send data in it, much as you would a letter in an envelope. The PPTP packet contains the destination IP address of the network you are attempting to connect to. Inside this PPTP envelope is the traffic that will pass through the external VPN connection device intended for the destination network. This traffic would not be secure using PPTP alone; Microsoft uses its proprietary Microsoft Point-to-Point Encryption (MPPE) protocol to secure traffic traveling over PPTP. PPTP uses TCP port 1723. It's rarely seen over VPN connections these days, as most modern VPNs use some form of IPsec or SSL/TLS VPNs, described later.

Layer 2 Tunneling Protocol (L2TP) was developed jointly by Microsoft and Cisco, but it has become an Internet standard. Microsoft contributed aspects of its PPTP, while Cisco used its proprietary Layer 2 Forwarding (L2F) protocol. Like PPTP, L2TP is only an encapsulation protocol, simply providing transport services and protecting data through untrusted networks (such as the Internet) to get it to a destination network. L2TP still sees some adoption but is also fading to IPsec and SSL/TLS VPNs.

IPsec VPNs

Internet Protocol Security (IPsec) is a security protocol that works at the Internet layer of the TCP/IP model (or the Network layer of the OSI model, if you are inclined to view it that way). IPsec was developed to provide security services (authentication and encryption) for IP traffic, since IP does not have any built-in native security protections. IPsec is more of a family of security protocols; three major protocols make up IPsec. The first is the *Authentication Header (AH)* protocol, which provides authentication and integrity services for IP traffic. AH can be used on the entire IP packet, including the header and data payload.

The second protocol takes care of encryption services, and it's called the *Encapsulating Security Payload (ESP)* protocol. ESP can provide protection for the entire IP packet as well, depending upon which mode IPsec is used in. Obviously, encrypting the IP header can cause problems if routers and other devices can't read the header information, including the source and destination IP addresses. Between hosts on a network, the header information isn't usually required to be encrypted, so ESP doesn't have to be used. This is called IPsec's *transport mode*. In transport mode, header information is not encrypted so that hosts and network devices can read it. The data, on the other hand, can be encrypted to protect it, even within a LAN. The other mode that IPsec is associated with is called *tunnel mode*. Tunnel mode is used when IP traffic is encapsulated and sent outside of a LAN, across WAN links to other networks. This is what happens in VPN implementations that use IPsec. In tunnel mode, since the IP packet is encapsulated in a tunneling protocol (such as L2TP), all the information in the packet, including headers and data payload, can be encrypted. So, ESP is typically used only in tunnel mode.

The third IPsec protocol—*Internet Security Association and Key Management Protocol (ISAKMP)*—is used to negotiate a mutually acceptable level of authentication and encryption methods between two hosts. This acceptable level of security is called the *security association (SA)*. An SA between two hosts defines the encryption type and method, algorithms used, types of cryptographic keys and key strengths, and so on. The Internet Key Exchange (IKE) protocol is used in ISAKMP to negotiate the SA between hosts. IKE uses UDP port 500 to accomplish this.

While IPsec is usually seen in VPN implementations, paired up with L2TP as its tunneling protocol, IPsec can be very effective in securing traffic within a LAN, particularly sensitive traffic between hosts that an organization wouldn't want to be intercepted and examined. IPsec offers a wide variety of choices for encryption algorithms and strengths and is very flexible in its configuration. You can choose to protect all traffic between certain hosts or protect only certain aspects of traffic, such as certain protocols or traffic that travels between certain ports.

TLS VPNs

The only serious competitor to IPsec VPNs are VPNs using the SSL/TLS protocol. This is the same SSL/TLS protocol used in secure Web pages. SSL/TLS VPN connections don't require special client software installed on the system that wants to connect to the remote network. That system uses only a Web browser and SSL/TLS security to make the VPN connection.

Module 6-4: Network-Based Intrusion Detection/Prevention

This module covers the following CompTIA Security+ objectives:

- **2.1** Install and configure network components, both hardware- and software-based, to support organizational security
- **3.2** Given a scenario, implement secure network architecture concepts

Network intrusion detection systems (NIDSs) and *network intrusion prevention systems (NIPSs)* look at attacks coming into the network at large instead of into a host. Attacks could be in the form of malformed network traffic or excessive amounts of traffic that would easily exceed a host's threshold to handle effectively. An attack could also manifest as malicious content embedded in traffic, or other forms of malware. Network intrusion handling also might look at massive DDoS conditions, such as those caused by botnet attacks.

Detection vs. Prevention

One point of interest is the difference between a NIDS and a NIPS. A NIDS is a *passive* device and focuses on detection alone, making it a *detection control*. It detects network traffic issues and alerts an administrator to these issues, also logging the events in the process. A NIPS, in contrast, is an *active* (CompTIA Security+ uses the term *inline*) device and focuses not only on detecting network attacks, but on preventing them.

 EXAM TIP The CompTIA Security+ exam will most likely ask you to contrast inline versus passive network intrusion systems: NIPS are inline; NIDS are passive.

In addition to performing the same functions as a NIDS, a NIPS also tries to prevent or stop attacks by taking a series of preconfigured actions, based upon the characteristics of the attack. A NIPS may dynamically block traffic from a certain source address or domain, for example, or block a certain port or protocol if it detects issues with it. A NIPS can take other actions as well, such as shunting traffic to other interfaces, initiating other security actions, tracing the attack back to its origin, and performing some analysis on the attack, but these are all dependent upon the feature set of the NIPS.

Detecting Attacks

Whether your goal is to detect and prevent attacks or solely to detect them, network intrusion tools need some method to detect attacks. In general, NIDS/NIPS solutions act very much like firewalls in that they inspect packets. Detection falls into four types: behavioral, signature, rule, and heuristic.

NOTE Many NIDS/NIPS vendors' detection solutions perform combinations of these four types of detection.

Behavioral/Anomaly

A *behavioral-* or *anomaly-based* system detects attacks after comparing traffic with a baseline of patterns considered normal for the network. For this to work, the intrusion detection system must be installed and then given the opportunity to "learn" how the normal flow of traffic behaves over the network. This can take time, but once the NIDS/NIPS establishes a good baseline of normal network traffic, the system will detect any unusual or anomalous traffic patterns that don't fit into the normal network traffic patterns and issue alerts on them as potential attacks.

NOTE Anomaly-based systems rely on rules and heuristic methods to determine when behavior on the network differs from normal. See the upcoming "Rule" and "Heuristic" sections for more details.

Signature

A *signature-based* system, on the other hand, uses preconfigured signature files (similarly to how anti-malware applications work), which are stored in the NIPS/NIDS database. These signatures define certain attack patterns based upon known traffic characteristics. Like an anti-malware solution, a signature-based NIDS/NIPS must also have its signatures database updated frequently, since new attack patterns are recorded by the security community often. These updates will usually come through a subscription-based service from the NIDS/NIPS vendor, although some community or open-source signatures may be available as well.

Rule

Another type of intrusion detection system is a rule-based system. It uses preconfigured rules in a ruleset, much like a firewall, to detect possible attacks. For example, if the system detected an excessive (beyond a set number or threshold) number of ICMP packets directed at a destination IP address on the network, the system would activate a rule, send an alert to administrators, and, in the case of a NIPS, stop the attack. Obviously, an administrator could configure unique rules for the organization based upon its network environment and historical attack experiences, but these types of systems are also usually included as part of either a signature- or behavioral-based system.

NOTE Rule-based is more a strategy used with the other three than a detection type—but who are we to argue with CompTIA Security+?

Heuristic

Finally, a heuristic system combines the best of both anomaly-based and signature-based systems. It starts out with a database of attack signatures and adapts them to network traffic patterns. It learns how different attacks manifest themselves on the network in which it is installed and adjusts its detection algorithms to fit the combination of network traffic behavior and signatures.

Which Is Best?

There's no way to answer that question, and in fact, detection systems are evolving so quickly that even these four types, while sufficient for purposes of the CompTIA Security+ exam, are arguably too simple when applied to the most modern NIDS/NIPS solutions. Although there are advantages and disadvantages to both anomaly-based and signature-based systems, often, modern NIDS/NIPS are hybrid systems and may use both techniques.

NOTE Host-based IDS/IPS solutions are almost always signature-based products.

The big measurement for the quality of a NIDS/NIPS boils down to the solution's detection *analytics*, as in how accurately they parse data. The goal of a NIDS/NIPS is to detect attacks and, in the case of the NIPS, do something about them. The great issues are false positive and false negative rates. Too many false positives will give you heartburn as you continually jump up and down from alarms that mean nothing. A false negative is even worse, as that means your NIDS/NIPS fails to catch actual attacks. The secret is to adjust the sensitivity of the NIDS/NIPS to create the best balance possible.

EXAM TIP Look for an exam question about advanced persistent threats (APTs), such as a terrorist organization trying to hack into a government agency, and the tools used to stop these attacks. Better security appliances implement unified threat management (UTM), marrying traditional firewalls with other security services, such as NIPS, load balancing, and more.

Configuring Network IDS/IPS

In general, an NIDS/NIPS consists of many components. The core component of any IDS/IPS is the sensor, the device that monitors the packets, searching for problems. Given the nature of detection versus prevention, a NIPS sensor must be installed in-band to your network traffic, while a NIDS sensor, being passive, is normally installed out-of-band. In-band means the sensor processes all the traffic flowing through the network in real time. An out-of-band sensor processes traffic, but not in real time. Figure 6-26 shows two sensors installed in a DMZ as examples of *in-band versus out-of-band* installation.

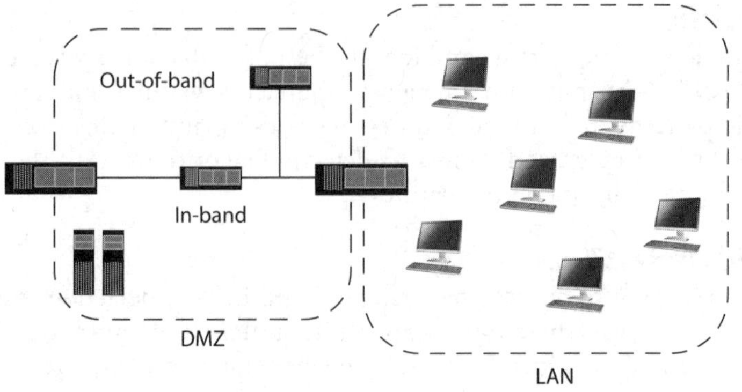

Figure 6-26
In-band and
out-of-band
installations

Out-of-band

In-band

DMZ

LAN

All packets must go through in-band sensor devices. Out-of-band sensor devices need some form of network connection that enables them to see all the traffic. Just plugging it into a switch only allows the sensor to see traffic to and from the switch plus broadcast traffic. If you want an out-of-band device to grab packets, you need a network tap or a port mirror.

Network Tap

A *network tap* is a device that you can insert anywhere along a run to grab packets. The network tap in Figure 6-27 works for 10/100/1000 BaseT Ethernet runs. You place this in the run (you'll need to run a few patches cables for in/outs) and then add an out-of-band sensor to the right-hand side.

Port Mirror

A *port mirror* (also called a Switch Port Analyzer, or SPAN in Cisco devices) is a special port on a managed switch configured to listen for all data going in and out of the switch. Unlike a network tap, port mirroring is convenient and easily changed to reflect any changes in your NIDS/NIPS monitoring strategy.

Figure 6-27 Garland Technology Network Tap P1GCCB (Photo courtesy of Garland Technology, www.garlandtechnology.com)

NOTE Port mirror solutions are very handy when you want to monitor more than one VLAN at a time.

Many vendors sell single-box solutions to handle routing, firewalling, proxy, anti-malware, and NIPS. These Unified Threat Management (UTM) boxes are excellent for several situations (especially when you have a single Internet access and no public-facing server). One area in which UTM thrives is monitoring: with only a single appliance to query, it's easy to get the information you need. Yet if you have a more complex NIDS/NIPS setup, monitoring the NIDS/NIPS gets a bit more complex.

Monitoring NIDS/NIPS

A newly installed NIDS/NIPS is only as good as the organization around it that handles the monitoring. Even the most automated NIPS needs a surprisingly high degree of monitoring, making sure humans react to attacks and remediate as needed. When you find yourself in a situation where this much monitoring takes place, you'll find Security Information and Event Management (SIEM). We've already discussed SIEM broadly back in Chapter 4, but now that we have a specific job to do, let's revisit SIEM. This time we'll plug in a few parts of a typical SIEM installation for aggregation and correlation.

Collecting Data

When it comes to SIEM, it's all about *aggregation*: collecting data from disparate sources and organizing the data into a single format. Any device within a SIEM system that collects data is called a *collector* or an *aggregator*. In a simpler NIPS setup with three sensors, it's common to have a single server that acts as a collector, querying the sensors for data in real time.

Correlation

The next part of SIEM that fits nicely into NIDS/NIPS is correlation. *Correlation* is the logic that looks at data from disparate sources and can make determinations about events taking place on your network. (Note that a correlation engine could be in-band or out-of-band, depending on the placement of the NIDS/NIPS.)

In its most simple form, a correlation engine might query a log, see that the same event is logged from three different sources, and eliminate duplicates (*event deduplication*). A correlation engine uses the event of time constantly, so it's critical that all devices have *time synchronization* for correlation engines. A well-correlated log will have common fields for which we can configure the NIPS system for *automated alerts and triggers*. Finally, it's critical that all logs are archived.

EXAM TIP The CompTIA Security+ exam might ask about rather serious log archival practices, such as writing all log files to write once, read many (WORM) drives. WORM media offers tamper-proof data. CD-R and DVD-R discs have been used for WORM storage. Several vendors offer magnetic media drives that lock out any changes at the hardware level.

Questions

1. Which one of the following types of filtering is used to control traffic *entering* a network?

   A. Egress filtering

   B. Ingress filtering

   C. Implicit deny

   D. Explicit deny

2. Which network device is used to send traffic to different physical networks, based upon logical addressing?

   A. Router

   B. Switch

   C. Load balancer

   D. Firewall

3. Which type of device is used to provide network protection and security by preventing hosts from connecting to the organization's infrastructure unless they meet certain criteria?

   A. Switch

   B. NAT device

   C. Firewall

   D. NAC device

4. All the following characteristics describe VLANs, *except*:

   A. VLANs require routing between them.

   B. VLANs separate hosts into logical networks.

   C. VLANs can be used to apply security policies and filtering to different segments.

   D. VLANs allow any host plugged into the switch to become a member of the virtual segment.

5. Which of the following would be needed to block excessive traffic from a particular protocol?

   A. Flood guard

   B. Loop protection

   C. ACL

   D. 802.1X

6. Which of the following describes a network device that intercepts user or host requests and then makes those requests to other hosts or networks on behalf of the user?

   A. Proxy

   B. Firewall

   C. NIDS

   D. NIPS

7. Which of the following types of connections does a VPN concentrator control? (Choose two.)

   A. Device VPN

   B. Client VPN

   C. User VPN

   D. Site-to-site VPN

8. A NIPS is considered a _____ type of control.

   A. detective

   B. preventative

   C. network

   D. host

9. Which of the following terms refers to combination of multifunction security devices?

   A. NIDS/NIPS

   B. Application firewall

   C. Web security gateway

   D. Unified Threat Management

10. Which of the following does an application firewall focus on for traffic filtering?

   A. Traffic content

   B. Protocol and port

   C. Source or destination IP address

   D. Domain name

Answers

1. B. Ingress filtering is used to control traffic entering a network.

2. A. A router is used to send traffic to different physical networks, based upon logical addressing.

3. **D.** A Network Access Control (NAC) device is used to provide network protection and security by preventing hosts from connecting to the organization's infrastructure unless they meet certain criteria.

4. **D.** VLANs do not allow any hosts plugged into the switch to automatically become a member of the virtual segment; membership is based upon switch port, MAC address, or IP address.

5. **A.** A flood guard is used to block excessive traffic from a particular protocol.

6. **A.** A proxy is a network device that intercepts user or host requests and then makes those requests to other hosts or networks on behalf of the user.

7. **B, D.** A VPN concentrator manages connections for both client and site-to-site VPN connections.

8. **B.** A network intrusion prevention system (NIPS) is considered a preventative type of control.

9. **D.** Unified Threat Management refers to a combination of multifunction security devices.

10. **A.** An application firewall focuses on traffic content for filtering, rather than on traffic characteristics.

Beyond the Basic LAN

It's rare to run into any size of enterprise, from a home office to a campus enterprise, that doesn't have a wired LAN (or two) that acts as the core of the enterprise network. The Internet connects to that LAN, and the servers have nice Gigabit Ethernet cards plugged into the powerful switches. The enterprise might even have a DMZ with an Internet server, but all have this core, wired network.

It's time to expand from this core LAN and start adding the other technologies that are so common in modern networks. We'll start with the most common of all, 802.11 wireless, making sure you're comfortable with the core protocols that collectively make 802.11 work. We'll then move to observing the many attacks, old and new, that bad actors use to take advantage of 802.11 vulnerabilities. Then it's time to see how we can harden 802.11 networks to make them less susceptible to attack.

Once we're done with 802.11, the rest of the chapter goes through a potpourri of subjects. Next is virtualization and cloud security. This two-part module looks at virtualization and then leads to virtualization's cousin, cloud computing. Be prepared to see a lot of terms you saw in Chapter 6 repeated here, just with the term "virtual" added.

After virtualization and cloud computing we'll cover mobile devices. From smartphones to tablets and Bring Your Own Device, you'll see why the CompTIA Security+ exam has several objectives covering this topic (and you may find yourself doing some rather interesting stuff with your phone).

Next is embedded systems. This module is short, but interesting, and for security-conscious people, a little bit terrifying.

Last is physical security, a module that explores fences, security guards, and fire extinguishers—because as any person who's experienced with CompTIA will tell you, it's not a CompTIA exam without talking about fire extinguishers.

Module 7-1: Networking with 802.11

This module covers the following CompTIA Security+ objectives:

- **4.3** Given a scenario, implement identity and access management controls
- **6.3** Given a scenario, install and configure wireless security settings

A reader posed this question: "If you could pick one attack surface to try first to penetrate a network, what would it be?" Perhaps not surprisingly at this point in the book, my answer was "Go for the Wi-Fi!" From the day 802.11 first rolled out in the very late 1990s, the 802.11 standard has shown several vulnerabilities, from the well-documented WEP and WPS exploits to more sophisticated attacks such as the TLS handshake. An astute security professional, capable of properly configuring good-quality wireless access points (WAPs), should have no problem making an 802.11 network relatively secure. Unfortunately, very few people have that capability, and that's why wireless provides a good first attack surface (Figure 7-1).

It is impossible to understand how to attack 802.11 or how to secure it without a solid understanding of 802.11. For that reason, this module explores two threads. We'll start with an overview of 802.11 security protocols (and some non-802.11 protocols that 802.11 uses). We'll then tour 802.11 authentication methods, including advanced authentications that only the most secure wireless networks implement.

 NOTE I'm assuming that you know the essentials about 802.11 networks from studying CompTIA A+ or Network+ (or equivalent wireless network training) before tackling CompTIA Security+. If that's not the case, check out one of my *All-in-One* or *Passport* books on the subject.

Wireless Cryptographic Protocols

When wireless networking was first adopted in the consumer and business markets, no secure wireless protocols were available to prevent eavesdropping and traffic interception. As people became more security conscious, they realized that they needed encryption and authentication protection on wireless networks, as they had on wired networks. Even though the wireless medium is different, security was still a necessity. This resulted in the development of several *cryptographic protocols*—protocols meant to ensure security via encryption and cryptography, with varying degrees of effectiveness, which have been slowly implemented in wireless networks over the years. As technologies have improved, these wireless cryptographic protocols have improved as well, including newer and more

Figure 7-1
Wireless systems
provide a
tempting attack
surface.

secure methods of authenticating devices and encrypting traffic. In the next few sections, we'll discuss the different wireless security protocols, their advantages and disadvantages, and how you should implement them in your wireless network.

The Legacy of WEP

Wired Equivalent Privacy (WEP), the first security iteration of 802.11, used a shared password encryption scheme that within a few years was discovered to be mathematically crackable. The primary reason for this weakness came from poor key usage with the RC4 encryption. Today's WEP cracking tools will extract a WEP key in just a few minutes.

You'd think that, knowing WEP is so easily cracked for so long, no one would use WEP, correct? Wrong. According to Wigle.net, the popular 802.11 database, around 9 percent of all 802.11 networks use WEP encryption, although the number is slowly dropping (Figure 7-2).

RC4

RC4 was built into WEP as its encryption protocol and was very efficient because, as a streaming protocol, it rapidly encrypts 1 bit (rather than entire blocks) of plaintext at a time. It uses a wide range of key sizes, from 40-bit to 2048-bit keys.

RC4 alone is not necessarily a weak protocol and is found in other secure protocol implementations beyond WEP. However, WEP poorly implemented the RC4 protocol, adding to the already numerous security flaws found in its design. For this reason, as well as the issues involved with small initialization vectors, small key size, and static key repetition, WEP is not suitable for use in modern wireless networks and should be avoided whenever possible.

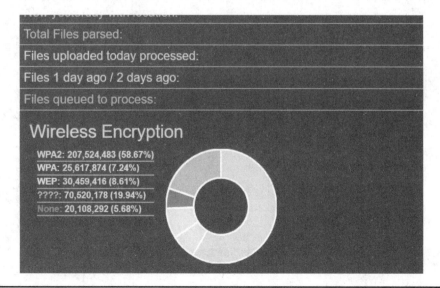

Figure 7-2   WEP is still out there (source: https://wigle.net/stats).

WPA

When the wireless industry (specifically, the Wi-Fi Alliance) recognized the inherent security flaws in WEP, they realized they needed to do something very quickly to stem the growing problem of unsecured wireless networks using WEP. Simultaneously, the Institute of Electrical and Electronics Engineers (IEEE) began developing a new security protocol standard for wireless networks, known as 802.11i, but the standard was delayed for various reasons. The Wi-Fi Alliance implemented what was really a stopgap measure in the interim to replace WEP. The result was *Wi-Fi Protected Access (WPA)*, introduced in 2003.

WPA has several advantages over WEP, including the use of dynamic keys and larger key sizes. WPA, also unlike WEP, requires either no authentication, authentication to a RADIUS server (Enterprise Mode – WPA-ENT), or the use of a pre-shared key. Originally conceived for personal or small business infrastructure networks, this setup is called *WPA-Personal* (sometimes referred to as WPA-PSK, for Pre-shared Key), and can be used to authenticate wireless client devices and wireless access points mutually. *WPA-Enterprise*, robust but complex and hard to use, was developed for larger infrastructures and requires the use of the 802.1X authentication protocol, which we will cover a bit later in the module. Figure 7-3 lists the different protocol options found on wireless routers.

TKIP

WPA uses *Temporal Key Integrity Protocol (TKIP)* for generating encryption keys. TKIP makes it possible to use dynamic keys, which are generated on a per-packet basis. This means the keys are not repeated for different transmissions, but require a different encryption key on each individual packet. TKIP, combined with an improved implementation of the same RC4 stream cipher that WEP uses, provides WPA encryption. TKIP

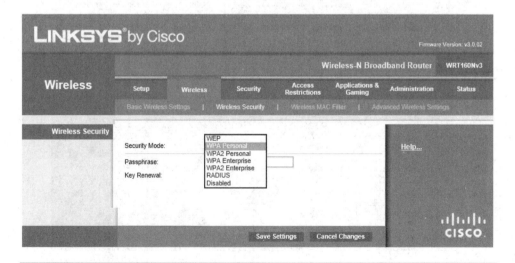

Figure 7-3   Wireless protocol choices on a wireless network

enables backward-compatibility with legacy WEP, uses 128-bit keys, and uses a 48-bit initialization vector.

WPA2

Wi-Fi Protected Access, version 2, is the name of the final official implementation of the 802.11i wireless security protocol standard developed by the IEEE. It offers several improvements over the original WPA, but is backward-compatible due to its inclusion of TKIP in its protocol suite. Like WPA, WPA2 also has two different implementations: *WPA2-Personal* (using a pre-shared key) and *WPA2-Enterprise*, which work the same way as they do in WPA.

A WPA/WPA2 passphrase can be from 8 to 63 case-sensitive ASCII characters, or 64 hexadecimal characters. Now, this passphrase is not the actual WPA/WPA2 key; the passphrase is used to generate the 256-bit pre-shared key that must be entered into all wireless devices on the same wireless network. Note that this is different from the way WEP implements its passwords; the WPA/WPA2 passphrase is not the key itself.

EXAM TIP   Remember that WPA uses TKIP; WPA2 uses AES.

AES

The *Advanced Encryption Standard* is used by a wide variety of encryption applications. It was adopted as the official encryption standard for the United States by the National Institute of Standards and Technology (NIST), after an open competition with several different competing algorithms. AES uses the Rijndael encryption algorithm and is considered much stronger than previous symmetric algorithms used in wireless networking, such as RC4.

AES is the encryption algorithm used in WPA2 and uses a particular process, or *mode*, within WPA2 to encrypt traffic. This mode is called the *Counter-mode (CTR) Cipher Block Chaining Message Authentication Code Protocol (CMC-MAC)* or, adding it all together, CCMP. CCMP uses a 128-bit key and 128-bit block size (since it is a *block* symmetric cipher, as opposed to the *streaming* RC4 symmetric cipher used in WEP and WPA), as well as 48-bit initialization vectors (IVs). The larger IV sizes help prevent replay attacks from being conducted against WPA2 (see "Replay Attacks," later in the chapter).

NOTE   Wireless devices often have an encryption setting that lets you choose between AES, TKIP, and mixed mode. In *mixed mode*, both AES and TKIP are supported. It is not recommended.

WPS

You can fairly easily join to a wireless network any system that has a screen and input method (keyboard, mouse, or touch screen). Joining a system, such as a printer, that lacks a screen and input device is much harder. In many cases they require separate setup programs or painfully complex configurations through tiny text screens and pressing up and down buttons through entire alphanumeric strings to type in passwords.

Figure 7-4
Typical WPS
button on home
router

Recognizing the popularity of wireless devices in non-enterprise networks, the Wi-Fi Alliance introduced *Wi-Fi Protected Setup (WPS)* in 2006. The goal of WPS is to enable anyone to join a WPS-capable device to a WPS-enabled wireless network just by pressing two buttons. Press the button on the WAP (Figure 7-4), then press the button on the device you want to join to the network; your device connects to the SSID and takes on the WAP's WPA2 encryption. Neat!

Alternatively, every WPS-enabled WAP comes with a fixed eight-digit pin code to allow devices without a WPS button (like a laptop) to connect to the WAP. You pressed the button on the router and then entered the router's pin code as the SSID's password.

Unfortunately, the eight-digit code has two problems. First, only seven of the eight digits are used (the eighth digit was only a checksum). Additionally, the seven digits are confirmed in two groups: the first three values, then the last four. This means it only takes about 11,000 guesses to crack a WPA pin code. Yipe!

So What Do We Use?

If you install an 802.11 network, the Wi-Fi Alliance states that you must use either WPA2-ENT or WPA2-PSK with a robust password. On all my PSK networks I make a point to use a 15- to 20-character length password. Here's one of my favorites (please don't hack me): *ioncelivedinsedalia*.

EXAM TIP   The CompTIA Security+ exam may ask about the appropriate methods to use to secure wireless networks, by which it means which cryptographic protocol should be used in different types of networks. A typical question will describe a scenario and then prompt on using PSK versus Enterprise versus Open cryptographic protocols. You might need to compare WPS with other methods. Also, see "Captive Portals" in Module 7-3 for one more comparative method for connecting securely.

Wireless Authentication Protocols

We've spent some time discussing wireless encryption, as well as wireless authentication, between a simple wireless client and its access point. Most of the discussion has been very general and could apply to small home wireless networks, small business networks, and even, to a degree, large enterprise-level wireless networks. Now let's take a moment to talk about the enterprise side of wireless networking, which usually involves more complex authentication methods and may involve using a wireless network to connect into a larger corporate wired network. We'll talk about different authentication methods and protocols that are primarily used in enterprise infrastructures, particularly when using the more advanced features of WPA and WPA2.

 EXAM TIP Authentication protocols, as the name suggests, authenticate users to a network. Cryptographic protocols provide security mechanisms, such as encryption. Secure networks, wireless as well as wired, require use of both types of protocols.

802.1X

802.1X is an IEEE standard, just like the 802.3 Ethernet standards and 802.11 wireless networking standards. The great thing is that, while 802.1X is probably most seen on corporate wireless networks as the preferred form of authentication and *access management control*, it is not a wireless standard at all and can be used in wired networks as well. This actually makes it easier for wireless and wired networks to interoperate, since they can use the same authentication methods and can connect to each other quite easily. 802.1X is called a *port-based* access control method and can use a wide variety of different security protocols. In that respect, it's more of a security authentication framework than a protocol itself, since it allows various protocols to be used for authentication.

802.1X uses some interesting terms you may need to be familiar with for the exam. First, a wireless client device is known as a *supplicant* in an 802.1X environment. A wireless access point that uses 802.1X authentication methods is called the *authenticator*, and the source providing the authentication services to the wireless network is called the *authentication server*. 802.1X is interoperable with a number of remote access services and protocols, such as RADIUS and TACACS+, as well as centralized authentication databases such as Active Directory. This enables wireless clients to authenticate to traditional infrastructures using these different types of services.

 EXAM TIP The built-in wireless client in Windows usually lacks the features to connect to 802.1X wireless networks. Third-party clients are often required.

802.1X can use several different types of authentication protocols, such as EAP, EAP-TLS, EAP-TTLS, PEAP, LEAP, and EAP-FAST. Let's check out this string of all cap acronyms now.

EAP

Like the 802.1X authentication protocol, the *Extensible Authentication Protocol (EAP)* isn't so much a protocol as a security framework that provides for varied authentication methods. Many different protocols fit into the EAP framework, and that's really why it was devised in the first place. EAP recognizes that there are several different authentication methods, including certificate-based authentication and other multifactor authentication methods, such as smart cards and so on. EAP can still allow the traditional user name/ password combination of authentication as well. EAP also allows for mutual authentication between devices as well as directory-based authentication services. There are several different variations of EAP, some older, and some more suitable for use than others. These include EAP-TLS, EAP-TTLS, Protected EAP (PEAP), EAP-MD5, and even the old MS-CHAPv2 used in older Microsoft clients, now known as EAP MS-CHAPv2. Let's cover the EAP versions mentioned in the CompTIA Security+ exam objective.

EAP-TLS

EAP Transport Layer Security (EAP-TLS) was for years the primary EAP variation used on high-security wireless networks. As the name implies, EAP-TLS uses the same TLS protocol used on secure Web pages. EAP-TLS requires both a server-side certificate and a client-side certificate (client-side certificates are rarely used on Web pages, but the TLS protocol certainly supports their use).

Client-side certificates are an administrative headache because every laptop, smartphone, tablet, or printer on the network must have a unique certificate. Losing a device requires disassociating the missing device's certificate to ensure security. If you want the ultimate in 802.11 authentication security, however, EAP-TLS is the way to go.

EAP-TTLS

EAP Tunneled Transport Layer Security (EAP-TTLS) may share a similar-sounding acronym to EAP-TLS, but it is a completely different EAP variation (Figure 7-5). EAP-TTLS goes beyond the TLS protocol, adding a tunnel to provide better security. EAP-TTLS only requires a server-side certificate. EAP-TTLS is considered to be functionally equivalent to PEAP (see next).

PEAP

Protected EAP (PEAP) is a version of EAP that uses Transport Layer Security (TLS). It was originally invented to correct problems with EAP and was developed as an open protocol by different vendors, such as Microsoft, RSA, and Cisco. PEAP is similar to EAP-TLS and requires a digital certificate on the server side of a connection to create a secure TLS tunnel. There are different versions of PEAP, depending upon the implementation and operating system, but all typically use digital certificates or smart cards for authentication.

LEAP and EAP-FAST

Lightweight Extensible Authentication Protocol (LEAP) is a proprietary protocol developed by Cisco and used in their wireless LAN devices for authentication. LEAP uses dynamic WEP keys and provides for mutual authentication between wireless clients and a

Figure 7-5
Configuring
802.1X on
a Windows
wireless client

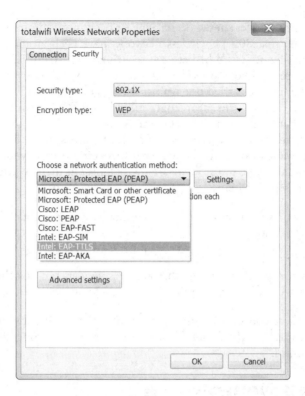

centralized RADIUS server. LEAP requires wireless clients to reauthenticate periodically, and when they do, they must use a new WEP key.

Cisco has replaced LEAP with *EAP-FAST* (for *Flexible Authentication via Secure Tunneling*), which addresses LEAP's security issues. EAP-FAST is lightweight but uses TLS tunnels to add security during authentication.

 EXAM TIP The CompTIA Security+ objectives refer to a *RADIUS federation* authentication protocol, which mashes two terms you explored back in Chapter 3. A *federated* system involves the use of a common authentication system and credentials database that multiple entities use and share. A RADIUS federation could connect those systems wirelessly using RADIUS servers.

Module 7-2: Attacking 802.11

This module covers the following CompTIA Security+ objectives:

- **1.2** Compare and contrast types of attacks
- **6.3** Given a scenario, install and configure wireless security settings

Attacks on wireless networks have never been more common than they are today, but why? Given that 802.11 wireless networks have been around for more than 15 years, you'd think by now we'd be better at securing them. Truth is, we are better, but the bad guys have gotten better as well. In this module, we'll discuss various wireless threats and attacks that can be carried out against wireless networks and unsecure wireless protocols (such as the famous and surprisingly still relevant WEPCrack). This module will discuss the attacks at length, so that by the next module, you'll be ready to learn the various ways you can harden wireless access points and networks against these types of attacks.

If you want to do some attacking (of the ethical variety, of course!), the first thing you'll need are some tools. There are many tools out there to attack, but in general you'll need three separate items:

- A good survey/stumbler tool to locate wireless networks and obtain detailed information
- Some kind of tool to start grabbing wireless packets
- Some type of attack tool that analyzes the data you've collected and grabs the passwords, keys, credentials, or whatever you want to grab

With those concepts in mind, let's turn to the specific toys in the attacker's toolbox. You'll see these on the CompTIA Security+ exam and, hopefully, use them for good in the real world.

Wireless Survey/Stumbler

To attack a wireless network, you first need to find one to attack. To do this, you use wireless survey/stumbler utilities. There are many such tools. Even the wireless client built into your operating system easily locates the wireless networks and will tell you the channel and encryption type. That's OK for users, but if you want to attack you need a more serious survey tool. You need a survey tool that not only sees the wireless network, but also grabs critical information such as GPS location, WAP MAC address, detailed encryption type, WPS enabled, and so on. Figure 7-6 shows an Android Wi-Fi analyzer I use.

Packet Grabber

Once you've found a target, you then need to start grabbing packets. To do this, you'll need some form of packet-capture tool that grabs wireless packets and gives you some control as to what packets you want to grab. Again, you have choices, but Airodump-ng—one of the many powerful tools that are part of the Aircrack-ng wireless suite, is very common and well supported (Figure 7-7).

Attack Tools

The entire goal of attacking wireless networks is to gather information. Every attack requires some type of utility that helps you do whatever you want to do. Do you want to crack WPS? There's a tool for that. Want to crack WEP? There's a tool for that. Want to intercept credentials? There's yet another tool for that.

Figure 7-6
Wi-Fi analyzer on
Android

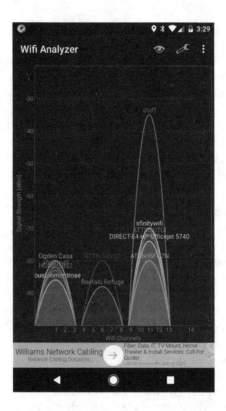

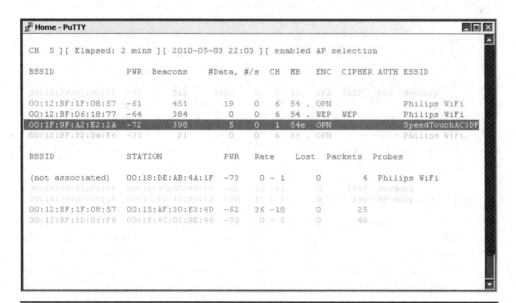

Figure 7-7   Selecting a specific WAP with Airodump-ng

The problem with any attack tool is that none of them are easy to use. None of these utilities have slick, well-tested GUIs. There is no such thing as a tool where you click one button and it does the attack for you. You must understand the attack. You must understand the vulnerability. You must understand the underlying protocol. You must understand the nuances of the tool. You must mentally prepare yourself for a thousand failures before you finally get the options, the switches, the driver versions, the updates, and whatever else comes along before you can get to your goal of a successful attack.

With that understanding in mind, there are some pretty great tools out there for wireless attacks. As a starting point, check out Aircrack-ng, a suite of tools that handles several popular attacks, concentrating on WEP and WPA cracking.

Rogue Access Points

Rogue access points are a form of attack that involves setting up a false or fake AP to attract unsuspecting people to connect to it, so that a malicious person can then monitor all of the victims' network traffic. Hackers use several techniques to set up rogue APs. In a basic attack, the attacker uses an AP configured for very weak or nonexistent authentication. This makes the victim think that it's an open, or free, Internet AP. Often a rogue AP will broadcast a very strong signal so that users think it's the best free Internet access point compared to several others. Rogue APs work very well where there are several APs already transmitting, such as areas within range of businesses or establishments that offer free wireless access to their customers.

Another variation of this attack is called the *evil twin* attack. In this attack, a hacker could set up a rogue AP that is broadcasting the same (or very similar) Service Set Identifier (SSID), which appears as the wireless network's name to ordinary users. Often, however, these evil twins do not use the same security levels as the legitimate AP, making it easy to connect to them. Unsuspecting users connect to this AP, thinking that it's one that they normally should connect to. Once connected, the attacker can intercept the user's network traffic through the evil twin, including user names, passwords, and any other traffic passed over the AP. The evil twin attacker can gain user credentials that may also be used on other wireless networks, allowing the attacker to connect to the legitimate APs and begin an attack on those networks. The hacker may even further connect this rogue AP to the Internet, so the user never suspects that she is connected to the rogue AP. Figure 7-8 shows an example of how an evil twin wireless network also appears with a legitimate one. Notice that the two are named similarly but are not configured the same in terms of required security.

Jamming and Interference

Occasionally, a wireless network can experience interference from another wireless device, which can occur, for example, when two wireless access points are using adjacent frequencies or channels. Interference can interrupt and interfere with wireless network transmission and reception. For the most part, this interference is unintentional. *Jamming* is a form of intentional interference on wireless networks, designed as a denial-of-service (DoS) attack. This type of attack is perpetrated by overpowering the signals of a

Figure 7-8
An evil twin rogue wireless access point is named similarly to a legitimate network AP.

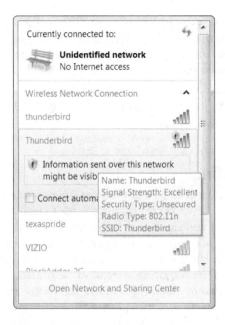

legitimate wireless access point, typically using a rogue AP with its transmit power set to very high levels. However, other electronic devices can also be used to create interference, or jamming, in wireless networks, including specialized devices that can be acquired from the Internet or put together by hobbyists.

Jammers are also commonly used to help evil twin attacks. By jamming a legitimate WAP's channel, all clients will automatically try to go to the evil twin (Figure 7-9). Even if your legitimate WAP tries to switch to another channel, a good jammer tracks the channel changes and continues to jam.

Figure 7-9
Jammer working with an evil twin

Jam channel 6 with
Wi-Fi jammer

Legit WAP on channel 6
SSID: Thunderbird

Evil Twin WAP on channel 1
SSID: Thunderbird

The only way to prevent jamming and interference is to look proactively for sources of wireless signals that are not coming from the corporate wireless network. The sources are usually in the same frequency range and may come from malicious wireless clients or rogue wireless access points.

NOTE   Jamming is universally illegal. In many countries even owning a jammer is illegal.

Packet Sniffing

Just as wired networks can be sniffed for unencrypted data that can be captured and analyzed, wireless networks are also susceptible to traffic sniffing. Sniffing traffic on wireless networks, however, can be a little bit more difficult. Usually, an attacker has to have a special wireless network card that can intercept packets and inject traffic on to the network. The attacker usually also must have a special driver for the network card, if he is using the Windows operating system, or he must be able to put a network card into what's called *monitor* or *promiscuous* mode in Linux. Once the attacker has his equipment set up, it's simply a matter of using the sniffing software of choice, such as Wireshark, for example. Figure 7-10 shows a Wireshark capture of a packet sniffing session conducted on a wireless network.

NOTE   All wireless sniffer tools require a special wireless NIC driver.

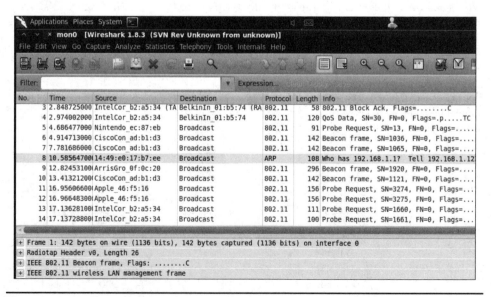

Figure 7-10   Packet sniffing a wireless network

Deauthentication Attack

If the wireless network traffic is encrypted, then the only traffic the attacker is usually going to get are beacon frames and other types of wireless management traffic, in addition to a lot of encrypted traffic he can't read. The attacker must already have the wireless key or conduct attacks against the wireless network to get the key. Covering the various attacks that a hacker can launch against a wireless network is beyond the scope of this book, but some of them involve disconnecting (also called *deauthenticating*) a wireless host from the WAP, so that the victim is forced to reconnect and exchange the wireless key, allowing the attacker to intercept the key and crack it. There are different methods for conducting this type of attack, and if it is successful, an attacker can either join or intercept traffic from the wireless network. Figure 7-11 shows an example of a deauthentication attack, conducted using the `aireplay-ng` command in the Aircrack-ng tool suite. This tool is popularly found on Linux-based systems, particularly security distributions.

 EXAM TIP You'll hear the term *disassociation attack* as a form of deauthentication attack.

Near Field Communication

Near field communication (NFC) enables devices to send very low-power radio signals to each other by using a special chip implanted in the device. NFC requires that the devices be extremely close to, or even touching, each other. NFC can be used for a wide variety of consumer and business applications, including quick payments with NFC-enabled smartphones and cash registers, parking meters, and other really cool and convenient transactions. NFC uses radio-frequency identification (RFID) technologies and unfortunately is vulnerable to several types of attacks. These attacks include eavesdropping by another NFC device, man-in-the-middle attacks, and relay attacks (relaying modified information back and forth from the victim's device, pretending to be the victim). Many Wi-Fi Protected Setup–enabled devices (see "WPS Attacks" later in this module) also use NFC, making wireless hacking of WPS-enabled networks easy.

```
root@bt:~# aireplay-ng -0 10 -a $AP -c $CLIENT mon0
20:08:52  Waiting for beacon frame (BSSID: 00:23:69:C1:E8:95) on channel 3
20:08:53  Sending 64 directed DeAuth. STMAC: [00:22:43:80:45:FB] [ 0|64 ACKs]
20:08:54  Sending 64 directed DeAuth. STMAC: [00:22:43:80:45:FB] [ 0|63 ACKs]
20:08:54  Sending 64 directed DeAuth. STMAC: [00:22:43:80:45:FB] [ 0|63 ACKs]
20:08:55  Sending 64 directed DeAuth. STMAC: [00:22:43:80:45:FB] [ 0|64 ACKs]
20:08:55  Sending 64 directed DeAuth. STMAC: [00:22:43:80:45:FB] [ 0|63 ACKs]
20:08:56  Sending 64 directed DeAuth. STMAC: [00:22:43:80:45:FB] [ 0|64 ACKs]
20:08:57  Sending 64 directed DeAuth. STMAC: [00:22:43:80:45:FB] [ 0|64 ACKs]
20:08:57  Sending 64 directed DeAuth. STMAC: [00:22:43:80:45:FB] [ 0|61 ACKs]
20:08:58  Sending 64 directed DeAuth. STMAC: [00:22:43:80:45:FB] [ 0|64 ACKs]
20:08:59  Sending 64 directed DeAuth. STMAC: [00:22:43:80:45:FB] [ 0|62 ACKs]
20:08:59  Sending 64 directed DeAuth. STMAC: [00:22:43:80:45:FB] [ 0|61 ACKs]
root@bt:~#
```

Figure 7-11   Conducting a deauthentication attack against a wireless client and its AP

Replay Attacks

In a *replay attack*, data, particularly credentials such as user names and passwords, is intercepted and replayed back on the network to an unsuspecting host. The goal of the replay attack is to retransmit those credentials back to a host, effectively allowing the attacker to impersonate the victim. Credentials or other data passed in clear text is most vulnerable to replay attack, although certain versions of weak encryption algorithms can also be vulnerable to these types of attacks. Even if the attacker can't read the victim's credentials due to encryption, weak authentication methods may allow retransmitted credentials to be used to authenticate to a host. Note that this type of attack isn't unique to wireless networks; wired networks also suffer from replay attacks (Figure 7-12).

Strong encryption methods are one defense against this type of attack. Another defense against this attack is through the use of *timestamping*, which limits the use of the credentials to a very narrow time period. The use of the Kerberos authentication protocol in Windows Active Directory networks, which makes heavy use of timestamps, counters the problem of replay attacks. Still another way of defending against this type of attack is for the originating host to digitally sign the traffic it sends. This assures the receiving host that the credentials or other data it receives are authentic.

 EXAM TIP The CompTIA Security+ objectives categorize a replay attack as a type of *application/service attack*. Others that fall into this category are denial-of-service (DoS) and privilege escalation attacks, which you learned about in Chapter 5. You'll see many more in Chapter 8.

WEP/WPA Attacks

Like any streaming encryption, RC4 needs initialization vectors (IVs) to seed its encryption methods for protecting wireless traffic. Unfortunately, the IVs in WEP are considered weak, in that they are only 24 bits in length. This short length guarantees that WEP must repeat the IVs frequently, meaning that after sniffing a few million packets, an attacker can crack the WEP key mathematically (an *IV attack*). Today a number of off-the-shelf tools (such as the freeware Aircrack-ng) make cracking any WEP-encrypted SSID easy.

Figure 7-12 Replay starts with a man-in-the-middle.

WPA has its weaknesses. It uses RC4 encryption, and cracking methods were developed to crack WPA—although it is much harder to crack WPA than WEP.

Although both WPA and WPA2 are very strong wireless security protocols, if your SSID uses Pre-Shared Key with a weak passphrase, they are both easily cracked, since the four-way handshakes they use to negotiate a connection between devices contain the WPA/WPA2 encryption key. This four-way handshake can be intercepted after a deauthentication attack forces a wireless client and AP to reestablish their connection and reauthenticate with each other. Once intercepted, a weak key can be cracked using standard dictionary or brute-force attacks, again using tools such as Aircrack-ng.

WPS Attacks

A WPS-enabled wireless router can connect to another WPS device (wireless printers are the most common) through a number of different methods. These methods all use a WPS personal identification number (PIN), which is enabled simply by pushing a button on the wireless router and the device. This PIN is used as the network's secure WPA key. This WPS PIN is susceptible to brute-force attacks.

 EXAM TIP The CompTIA Security+ exam might query you about an attack used in older Microsoft networks. A *pass the hash* attack takes advantage of weak points in the NT LAN Manager (NTLM) and LANMAN protocols, which you learned about back in Chapter 3. If the attacker has the hash of a user's password, the attacker can skip any kind of brute-force attack and use the hashed password to access the network. Modern Windows systems mitigate against this sort of attack, though the best defense is to not allow network administrators to log in to suspect systems and thus expose their passwords.

Module 7-3: Securing 802.11

This module covers the following CompTIA Security+ objectives:

- **2.1** Install and configure network components, both hardware- and software-based, to support organizational security

- **2.2** Given a scenario, use appropriate software tools to assess the security posture of an organization

Despite what you might think after reading the many scary stories from the previous module, it's not difficult to create a robust and secure 802.11 wireless network. In this module we'll discuss a number of design considerations, security features, and administration tools to make your Wi-Fi network as secure as possible.

Designing Wi-Fi

Network design that incorporates wireless connectivity offers choices these days in the type of access points to use and other design considerations. Let's start with installing access points.

Fat vs. Thin Access Points

An organization's choice of which technology to employ to provide wireless connectivity depends on several factors, including the location and complexity of its primary office network and the design philosophy and needs of individual enterprise offices. The CompTIA Security+ exam objectives list "fat vs. thin" as a standalone comparison, but the choice boils down to where you want to manage the security on the network.

A *fat AP* has all the bells and whistles, including a management console where you can configure typical security controls, such as access control lists (ACLs), white and black lists, encryption, and so on. A fat or *thick* AP is also called a *controller-based AP*. You manage each fat AP individually or, in the case of some vendors, manage all APs by sending them instructions from a global console to enact locally. A *thin AP* typically just acts as a repeater, taking the wireless signal and pushing it to a managed access control (AC) switch that handles encryption and other security. A thin AP is referred to as a *standalone AP*.

Here's an example of how design philosophy, location, and complexity dictate which technology to employ. A standalone satellite office in Brazil might need a fat AP to handle the wireless needs of the ten users and provide connectivity back to the home office. A building with multiple floors and hundreds of users might rely on one awesome switch (plus a redundant backup) to control dozens of thin access points.

 EXAM TIP Expect a question or two on the exam that compare or contrast controller-based APs versus standalone APs.

Antenna Types

Standard 802.11 wireless implementations use various antenna types that offer different performance and security considerations. You may see several types and shapes of antennas; the way they are constructed can help determine the antenna's gain and directional capabilities. *Gain* increases wireless signals but also increases RF noise and interference proportionally, so there's a trade-off between signal strength and noise.

Although you can use antennas that transmit or receive in one or two different directions, most 802.11 wireless antennas are *omnidirectional* and transmit in all horizontal directions to multiple receivers; this keeps in line with the point-to-multipoint architecture that wireless networks use. Uni- or semi-directional antennas may help from either a security or performance standpoint, since they can be directed toward a specific access point or direction and will send and receive signals in that direction only.

Antennas are also designed and made based upon the intended frequency band; earlier antennas were specific to either the 2.4 GHz (802.11b/g/n standards) or the 5 GHz (for the 802.11a/n/ac wireless networks) frequency bands. Some antennas can also transmit a stronger signal based upon how they are constructed. Figure 7-13 shows examples of typical wireless antennas. More modern antennas, however, are included inside wireless access points and clients, rather than as cumbersome extensions that are easily broken, and Figure 7-14 displays the difference between a newer access point with internal antennas and an older one with external antennas.

Figure 7-13
Examples
of wireless
antennas

 EXAM TIP Expect questions on the CompTIA Security+ exam about setting up a wireless network. Specifically, you should see questions on signal strength, band selection, and bandwidth. Such questions require you to know about types of antennas and when to use 2.4 GHz or 5 GHz frequencies depending on location specifics.

Site Surveys

The site survey is a technical assessment of the area in which a wireless network will be installed and operating. Usually, a site survey is performed before the wireless network is even installed, although sometimes it might be performed periodically when looking at network performance or before expanding the wireless network to accommodate new access points or additional capacity. Site surveys help technical personnel understand the different issues that may be present in an area where the wireless network will be operational. These issues may affect considerations such as area coverage, network growth, access point and antenna placement, required power levels, and even network capacity (level of usage of the wireless network). Some of these issues include proximity to potential interference sources (such as other wireless networks), environmental and physical

Figure 7-14
Internal and
external
antennas

considerations (physical obstacles that may limit wireless signals, such as buildings, for example), and, of course, potential security issues (public areas where wardriving may happen, for instance). Figure 7-15 illustrates some of the data collected during a survey when using a wireless or RF survey tool.

When conducting a site survey, a technician usually measures potential coverage distances, identifies obstacles that may block wireless signals, and performs various tests to see where antenna and access point placement will be optimal. The technician will usually map out the area and identify potential sources of interference, such as power cabling, cell towers, or other RFI-producing sources. Technicians also should plan for capacity, meaning that they need to know how many users will be connecting to the wireless network at any given time, and what types of data or applications they will be using over the wireless network.

Although this might not seem like a security consideration, remember that availability of data is directly tied to security (remember the CIA triad: confidentiality, accountability, integrity). Once the site survey has been accomplished, the technician usually provides recommendations to managers and the team that will be installing or expanding the wireless network, so they can configure it optimally for both performance and security.

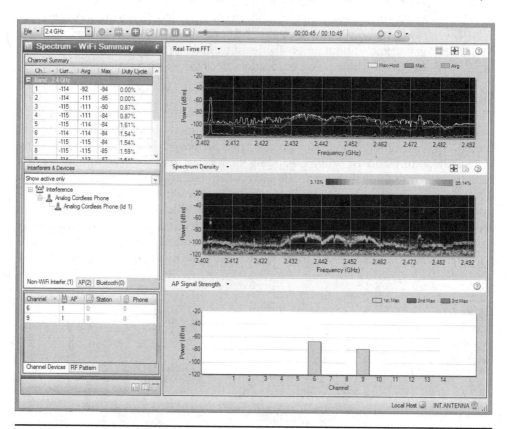

Figure 7-15   Viewing the Wi-Fi spectrum when performing a site survey

Finally, note how many WAPs a site will need. Clearly mark any longer areas that could use a *wireless bridge*—a device that connects WAPs more readily.

Antenna Placement

Antenna placement is important not only in making sure that people are able to get a strong enough signal to access the wireless network, but also for security reasons. An antenna located too close to an outer wall of a facility makes the wireless signal easier to pick up outside the facility, which makes it easier for wardrivers and others to pick up your wireless signal and attempt to hack your network. Ideally, both for performance and security reasons, antenna placement within a facility should be centralized; in other words, antennas should be centrally located throughout different areas of the facility so that they can adequately span all areas of coverage within a facility, without being too close to exterior walls or the roof whenever possible.

Wireless Configuration

A good layout of enterprise-level WAPs, properly placed and using the right antennas, is a great start for any wireless network. Now it's time to take advantage of the many 802.11 features to protect your network.

SSID Broadcasting

The SSID is the wireless network name. This name is usually broadcast out to let wireless clients know that it exists. Nontechnical users rely on SSID broadcasting to locate and connect to networks. Early in the wireless revolution, standard security practices held that to secure a wireless network, you should keep the SSID from broadcasting; this was a practice called *SSID hiding* or *cloaking*. This practice prevented casual wireless snooping and was meant to keep unauthorized people from connecting to a wireless network. The theory was that if they couldn't see the network name, they couldn't connect to it. These days, most wireless network clients can pick up all the nearby wireless networks, even if they have cloaked SSIDs. And you can easily install software on a wireless client that can tell you what the wireless SSID is, simply because wireless clients can also broadcast SSID information out. Even if people can't see the network name, they will see that an unknown wireless network does exist. Then a determined hacker can connect to it.

In addition to cloaking SSIDs, some security administrators also recommend renaming the SSIDs from the default wireless access point name that is usually broadcast when you first install an access point. This may be a good idea to help users connect to the correct network, but from a security perspective it isn't effective and may actually confuse users, causing them not to be able to connect to a wireless network.

MAC Filtering

Remember that the MAC address is burned into every single network card manufactured, including wireless network cards, and these addresses are used the same way. Remember that the MAC address is a 12-digit hexadecimal number that identifies the manufacturer of the card and the individual card itself. Because it can identify the individual network card, and by extension the client, some administrators filter wireless network access by the MAC address of the client. Most wireless access points have the ability to do MAC filtering, either allowing or denying a particular MAC address (and the host that has the MAC address) on the network.

MAC filtering is frequently used as a security measure, since it can deny access to wireless network cards that are listed in a table on the access point. However, you should know that it's quite simple to spoof a MAC address, so, like SSID cloaking, this isn't a very effective security measure and should not be used by itself to protect a wireless network.

The other part about MAC filtering is that if you are going to use it as a security measure (in conjunction with other more secure measures, hopefully), you should configure MAC filtering to *allow* certain MAC addresses only, rather than attempt to *deny* certain MAC addresses. This is simply because you can deny only what you know about; of course, it's difficult to deny a MAC address that you don't know exists. So MAC address filtering should be used on a default deny basis (deny all), with only a few addresses as exceptions. Figure 7-16 shows my home WAP's MAC filtering settings.

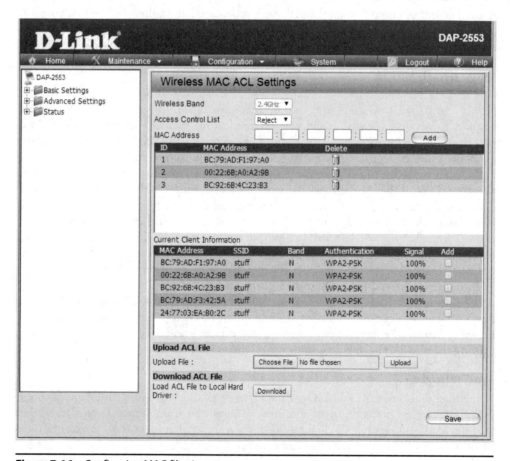

Figure 7-16 Configuring MAC filtering

Power Level Controls

You may be tempted to think that boosting the power on your wireless access point gives you better performance and enables your clients to connect to your network with a stronger signal. You'd be right about that, except for a couple of things. The first thing is that raising the power levels on your WAP beyond a specified level may be illegal in certain areas. Most WAPs have preset power levels, usually a balance between what's legally acceptable in its intended region and performance requirements. However, it isn't too difficult to download nonstandard firmware or software that allows you to change those power levels, sometimes beyond the legal limit allowed in your area. The second thing is that the higher power levels on your WAPs can adversely affect the security on your network. This is because the more powerful your signal, the farther out that signal is going to be transmitted. So, in addition to all of your authorized clients being able to see the wireless network, get a really good signal, and connect to it, unauthorized people (read: hackers or people looking for free Internet connectivity) will also be able to do the same thing.

In addition to limiting antenna placement to centralized areas within your facility, you should reduce antenna power levels to the lowest acceptable point at which users can still receive a strong signal from the network. This prevents the signal from leaving your facility as much as possible. You may even have to lower the power levels and simply provide more access points throughout the facility to keep the signals confined to the immediate area, as a sort of trade-off. It's probably not realistic to think that you're going to be able to limit stray signals fully, but limiting them to as short a distance as possible outside your facility can help your security posture, since any would-be hacker may have to get unacceptably close to your building to hack into or connect to your network.

Captive Portals

Captive portals (Figure 7-17) are usually seen on enterprise wireless networks, rather than small office-home office (SOHO) networks. You also may see captive portals in hotels or other businesses that provide wireless network access to customers. Captive portals provide a secure method for authenticating a wireless client in a couple of ways. First, it may be impractical to share a pre-shared key or device certificate with everyone who is authorized to use the wireless network (think airport customers or hotel guests, for example), but the wireless network may still require some sort of authentication. A captive portal setup allows a wireless client to connect to the wireless network and reach only a single Web site, where the users must authenticate to the wireless network before they can use it any further. A business may provide wireless access for its external partners or customers rather than allowing them to use its interior corporate wireless network. The captive portal would help serve such a function in this case. It allows for authentication and can assist in accounting for wireless network access that has been paid for by a customer. For authorized employees connecting to a corporate network, a captive portal can also serve as a type of network access control, since an otherwise authorized wireless device may have to use certain protocols or have certain requirements present to connect to the network (patches, antivirus signatures, and so on).

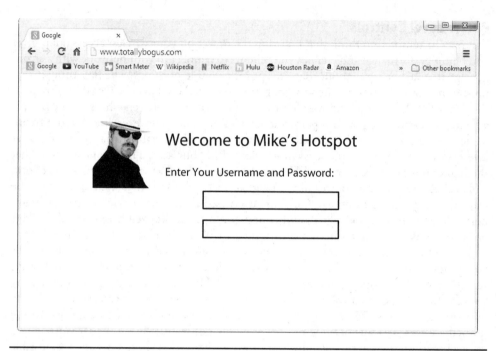

Figure 7-17   Mike's captive portal

VPN over Wireless

People in your organization may have occasion to travel, especially if they are members of the sales force or managers who have to attend meetings in offsite locations. Very often they will find themselves in hotels or working at customer or partner sites that do not have secure wireless connections. This may be due to resources, legacy equipment, or lack of trained security or networking personnel on site. In any case, your employees may need to connect securely to your organization's network to perform their job functions while working remotely. Obviously, you don't want them to send sensitive data over unsecure wireless networks, where the data may be intercepted and compromised. One solution to this problem is to use virtual private networking (VPN) technologies to secure wireless connections from your mobile employees back to the corporate infrastructure.

Remember from the discussions on VPNs earlier in the book that you can use different protocols and technologies to implement a VPN. As a quick refresher, a site-to-site VPN involves two different VPN concentrators at both the main and the remote sites that connect the two locations together. Clients on either side of the VPN concentrator connect to each other just as they would if they were in the same building over a wired network; however, they are simply going through the VPN concentrator in their own office, which sends encrypted traffic to the other VPN concentrator at the other location. Most of the time, this type of VPN will use either wired or leased lines from the local telecom provider or ISP to provide the Internet connection that the VPN will use.

It's usually the mobile clients (client VPN connections) that may use wireless networks, and those are the ones you really have to worry about.

You should set up a VPN concentrator on the perimeter of your corporate network infrastructure specifically for these mobile clients. It should require both authentication and encryption for all traffic it receives from the mobile clients. On the client side, you may have to set up VPN client software (in the case of VPN connections secured with L2TP and IPsec), and configure the correct settings in the software. Secure Sockets Layer (SSL) VPN connections and Transport Layer Security (TLS) VPN connections don't really require much configuration on the client side, other than possibly installing client-side digital certificates, making it so they can easily connect to the corporate VPN via a secure Web browsing session. SSL/TLS VPN portals are more limited in functionality than when VPN client software is used; the mobile users are limited to what functions they can perform on the secure portal, instead of their computer becoming a virtual member of the corporate network, as is the case when using client VPN software. In either case, however, the connection is much more secure than it would be if the user is forced to use an unsecure wireless network.

Security Posture Assessment

Part of a network professional's job is to use tools to assess the security posture of a network. With wireless networks, that means to run assessment tools to probe the network, looking for any errors in implementation or any weaknesses.

The cool part for you is that you already know the assessment tools—you used them to attack wireless networks in Module 7-2! Use Aircrack-ng, Wireshark, and any number of *wireless scanners/crackers* to probe wireless networks.

Module 7-4: Virtualization Security

This module covers the following CompTIA Security+ objectives:

- **3.2**   Given a scenario, implement secure network architecture concepts
- **3.7**   Summarize cloud and virtualization concepts

Virtualization dominates today's computing world. If you're accessing a Web app on the Internet, you are almost certainly accessing a virtual machine. If you use iCloud, Dropbox, or Google Drive, your files, photos, and songs are stored on virtual machines. Even within most LANs our Windows and Linux servers are commonly virtualized.

This module covers virtualization and the many security issues involved with virtualization. One issue to keep in mind as you go through this module is the close relation between virtualization and the cloud, which we'll cover in the next module. After you learn about virtualization, you'll see many of these concept in the next module—you'll be surprised how many security features span between both virtualization and the cloud (Figure 7-18).

Figure 7-18
Cloud and
virtualization are
closely related.

EXAM TIP The CompTIA Security+ exam might ask you to compare various virtualization and cloud services, noting the location of these services. Pay attention in this module and the next to the differences between on-premise versus hosted versus cloud services, primarily about who's responsible for maintenance and service. (On-premise means you have to do the work; hosted services have techs who don't work directly for you; cloud abstracts the whole thing away and you just don't worry about it.)

You probably have an idea of what virtualization involves. However, you may have learned about only part of it, or perhaps you have been peripherally involved in setting up a virtual environment. Maybe you've put together a test lab on a single PC and run a few virtual machines on it, or perhaps you've designed and architected an entire virtualized environment for a large organization. In any case, you'll need to be familiar with several important concepts for the exam, so we're going to cover them here. These concepts include the basics of how virtualization works, the different types of hypervisors that can be used, and virtualization architecture. We'll get into some of the things that virtualization can do for us as networking and security administrators. We'll also talk about the security considerations of virtual environments, to include risks and security controls that we may want to implement with those environments.

Virtualization Architecture

In the basic sense, *virtualization* means that we usually run an entire instance of an operating system on a host physical machine. The *virtual machine (VM)*, or *guest* as it is sometimes known, exists as a file in an application. Applications known as *hypervisors* (or virtual machine monitors) create and use these files to initiate a guest machine. When the machine is turned on, the hypervisor acts as a mediator between the host operating system and the guest operating system, providing access to both physical and logical resources. These resources could include sound cards, network connections, hard drives, USB drives, and any other peripherals that a physical machine could use.

As far as the virtual machine is concerned, it doesn't "know" that it is not a physical machine; it functions as if it were a completely solid physical device. That means that it behaves as a physical device and can run applications, service user requests, make network connections, and so on. Virtual machines can be used as file servers, user workstations,

DNS servers, Web servers, and almost anything else that a physical machine is used for. Unfortunately, this also means VMs have the same weaknesses as physical devices, and they must be secured and hardened against attack.

Virtual machines can be almost any operating system—Windows, Linux, UNIX, BSD, and (to a lesser extent) macOS operating systems can all be virtualized. Even the Android operating systems used in mobile devices can be run as a virtual machine. The host machine, on the other hand, can also run various operating systems, including Windows, Linux, or macOS. The real requirement is that a compatible application must create and run virtual machines on a particular host operating system. That brings us to the discussion of hypervisors.

A *hypervisor* can be an application that creates and runs virtual machines. There are two types of hypervisors: Type 1 and Type 2 (Figure 7-19). A Type 1 hypervisor is a limited-function, stripped-down operating system in its own right. It runs the host machine and serves to provide the single functionality of managing the virtual machines installed on it. These types of hypervisors are usually called *bare-metal* (or sometimes *native*) hypervisors, because they provide a very limited functionality and only boot up the physical machine and handle resource access from the virtual machines. Several popular Type 1 hypervisors are available; some of them are even free to use. Microsoft has a Windows-based hypervisor (Hyper-V); the Linux community has a lot, such as Kernel-based Virtual Machine (KVM). Commercial hypervisors are also available, such as those developed by VMware.

EXAM TIP The CompTIA Security+ objectives use Roman numerals for the hypervisor types, so Type I and Type II.

For the most part, Type 1 hypervisors are usually installed and then run in "headless" mode, meaning that they don't require a user to sit down at a keyboard console or monitor. They are usually managed remotely through client software on a workstation after their network connectivity has been set up. Figure 7-20 shows an example of how VMware's ESX server, a popular bare-metal hypervisor, is accessed and managed remotely via the vSphere client. Rarely, an administrator might have to sit at a console at the host server to perform configuration tasks that can't be done remotely.

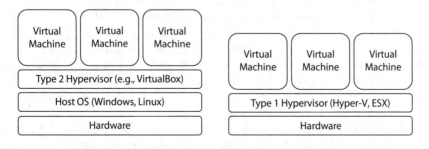

Figure 7-19 Type 1 and Type 2 hypervisors

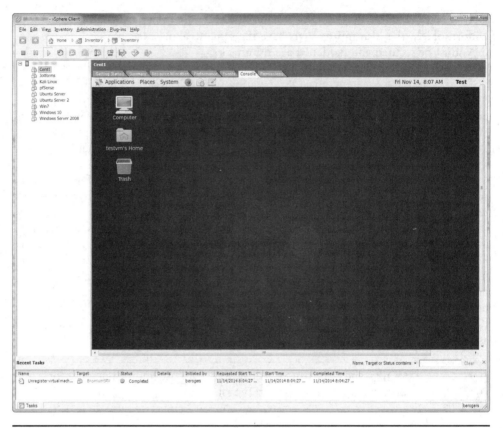

Figure 7-20   Accessing an ESX server through the VMware vSphere client

You might be more familiar with a Type 2 hypervisor if you have ever set up a small virtual environment. This type of hypervisor is an application that runs on top of a host operating system. You may have used a hypervisor product such as VMware Workstation, Oracle VirtualBox, or Parallels for macOS. These are Type 2 hypervisors that can be used to create and manage a limited number of virtual machines. Usually these types of hypervisors are used in small environments to create and test different aspects of virtualization. For larger production environments used in businesses, Type 1 hypervisors are normally used and are typically installed on very powerful, robust physical hardware. Figure 7-21 shows the user interface of VirtualBox, a popular free hypervisor application produced by Oracle.

Virtual machines can also have unique network architectures. They can use multiple network configuration options, depending upon the type of host system they are installed on. You can configure a network connection that is directly connected to the outside network through the host machine's network interface card, and the VM receives its IP addressing information from the outside network. This is called *bridging*. A VM could also receive its IP addressing information directly from the hypervisor installed on the host. In this regard, the hypervisor acts as a Dynamic Host Configuration Protocol

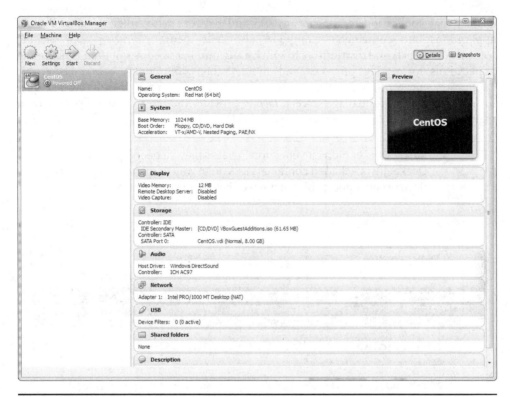

Figure 7-21 The VirtualBox Type 2 hypervisor

(DHCP) server and provides private IP addressing (through network address translation, or NAT) to the virtual hosts. The host would then act as the default network gateway for any VMs installed on it. It's also possible, if you so desire, to set up a virtualized network within the host so that only virtual hosts can communicate with it and each other. In other words, they can't contact the outside world through the virtual network unless the host is configured to allow it. You can configure the network portion of the virtual environment in several different ways, based upon how you want virtual machines to communicate with the outside network, the host, and each other.

Application Cells/Containers

VMs are great. VMs enable you to use the wildly powerful hardware of modern computers to create full operating system environments that you enable or disable at will. The OSes run applications. They network. They are, for all intents and purposes, unique computing machines. A VM requires an operating system, a license for that OS, configuration, security, and so on. But what if your network needs are simpler?

Containers offer a related experience to a VM, except that they include only the essentials of a network application—what you might think of as a server, plus programming that enables that application to run on any OS and network with other systems. Putting applications into containers—CompTIA also calls them *application cells*—enables software developers and distributors to spin up any number of copies of their functioning applications for testing purposes and more. When done right, containers enable application spin-up to happen almost instantly, and makes it much easier and simpler for network admins to manage servers. *Docker* provides the most common platform, or management system, for containers (Figure 7-22).

 NOTE Docker didn't invent containers, as they've been around for decades. Docker just packaged containers as a great way to manage application development and deployment in a clever and easy-to-use way.

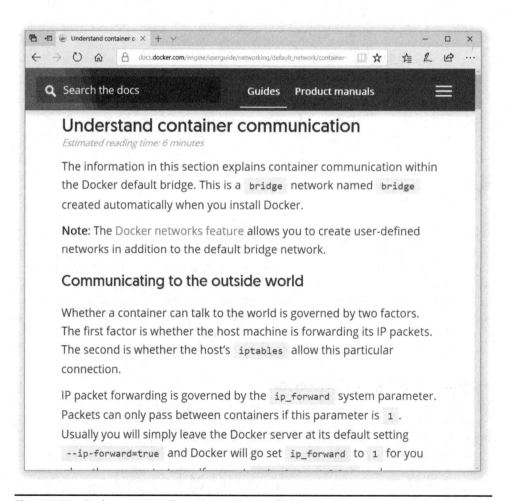

Figure 7-22   Docker container discussion

Virtualization Risks

Of course, even beneficial technologies like virtualization have inherent risks. Virtualization is the solution to many problems, such as scalability, hardware production, and even security in some respects, but it also has risks. For example, with virtualization, single points of failure for host machines are risks, because if the host machine becomes unavailable, loses connectivity, or encounters a serious hardware error, all the virtual machines that reside on it are also lost. In addition, because multiple virtual machines may be running on a host, and some may have several services running on them, this adds to the attack surface of the host. All the services that the virtual machines run communicate with the outside world and the network, so they all represent different attack vectors as well. These represent a threat not only to each virtual machine, but also overall to the host.

Yet another risk involves redundancy and availability. Although virtualization helps in ensuring redundancy and availability, failure on the part of administrators to take advantage of these features could result in the loss of critical data if a virtual machine fails and it has not been backed up or otherwise preserved. Security could also be considered at risk with virtual machines because complacent administrators often mistakenly think that securing the host machine is enough, and sometimes they forget to secure the guest machines as well. So don't be surprised when you encounter a fairly secure host machine that has guest machines running on it that have blank passwords or default security configurations. Remember that almost any risk that a physical machine can incur can also be incurred on a virtual machine. You should take the same security measures on VMs that you take on a physical machine.

VM Sprawl

Once you have a hypervisor up and running, authorized users can easily whip up new VMs anytime they wish; that creates a problem called VM sprawl. *VM sprawl* is the out-of-control creation of VMs outside your security control. Your marketing department spins up a new Web server for a job fair; the engineering department makes a VM to test some new software they're thinking about buying; the IT department adds extra servers to run, as they say, stuff.

VM sprawl is a huge problem without a simple answer other than good monitoring. Network administrators need to implement policies or practices for *VM sprawl avoidance*. Every hypervisor has authentication tools to limit who can make VMs. Use those tools. Make clear policies that prohibit users from building their own hypervisors or, even worse, buying their own cloud VMs! Other than that, your job is to maintain good inventory of all existing VMs and ongoing monitoring to look for new VMs that shouldn't be there.

VM Escape

VM escape takes place when a user inside a VM finds a way to break out (escape) the VM and somehow get into the underlying hypervisor/host operating system. Network security people need to know the problem and implement, as much as possible, *VM escape protection*.

On the good side, VM escape exploits terrify the IT world and, once detected, are very quickly patched. On the downside, there is no anti-VM escape tool. Hopefully, you'll have intrusion detection or intrusion prevention tools to mitigate the attack, like any other attack. As mentioned earlier, VMs need all the same security tools used on real systems.

Hardening Virtual Machines

Locking down and securing virtual machines is not much different from doing the same to physical hosts. All the security considerations for physical hosts also apply to virtual machines. They require frequent patching and updating; they require locking down configuration settings; they need secure account settings; and when setting up users, you should follow the principle of least privilege. One nice thing about a virtual machine is that once you have hardened the configuration as needed, you can always use it as a baseline and replicate it multiple times, so that each virtual machine you create starts out with that hardened baseline and requires only recent patches or configuration changes. This makes it much easier to deploy machines on a large-scale basis.

VMs require network connectivity to ensure that patches get updated in a timely manner. You also need to make sure that you install anti-malware on the VMs, since, like all networked hosts, they are susceptible to malware from Web sites, malicious files, and so forth. They should all also have host-based firewalls or multipurpose packages that take care of firewall, anti-malware, and intrusion detection software.

In addition to the normal things that you would do to secure physical hosts, virtual machines lend themselves to some other security measures. When not active, they are simply files located in storage, and as such they can be protected through permissions, encryption, and separation, the same as you would protect any other types of sensitive data files. They can also be copied and stored securely on secure media. Also like physical machines, they should be backed up periodically to ensure availability; we'll talk about backing up virtual machines next.

Snapshots and Backups

Like physical machines, virtual machines also need to be backed up from time to time. Virtual machines also have some advantages, however, in that they are native files located on a file system of some sort, so you can treat them like files for backup purposes as well. You could perform file backups to network-based or offline storage, and you could also encrypt these files when they're backed up. You can also restore these files at will if a virtual machine fails or becomes inaccessible. And you can use them to create additional duplicate virtual machines for redundancy purposes.

You can also perform snapshots on VMs. A *snapshot* is a point-in-time backup of the current system state of the VM. This means the VM would back up and preserve any applications in use, user data, or other configuration details specific to that system's state at that moment. You could take a snapshot of a virtual machine before installing a new application or a critical patch, for example, and save the snapshot so that if the patch or software caused a functionality or security issue, the snapshot could be restored, enabling you to revert to the state the virtual machine was in before the installation. You can use incremental sets of snapshots or combine them with traditional backup methods to maintain highly focused, comprehensive system state backups for availability.

Using Virtualization for Security

Virtual environments can provide stable, segregated environments in which to test applications, software, and even malicious code. Virtualization can also contribute to system and data availability by maintaining multiple redundant copies of identical virtual machines. In the next few sections, we'll go into a bit more detail on how virtualization contributes to the overall security posture in the organization.

Patch Compatibility

You already know that you should test patches before applying them to production environments. This is because sometimes patches have unforeseen negative effects on production hosts, which can quickly take down critical operations. One thing that a virtual environment can give you is a complete test environment that mirrors the production environment. You can copy a physical machine and create an identically configured virtual machine out of it. You can use this to your advantage by creating an almost exact replica of your physical environment in the virtual world, and test your patches, configuration changes, and updates in this test environment before you apply them to the physical machine. This helps avoid unintentional issues when you apply patches to production machines. It also provides you an opportunity to see where issues may exist and determine ways to correct them before the patch goes into production.

Host Availability and Elasticity

Virtual environments offer organizations real flexibility in the use of their infrastructure for both availability and elasticity. Virtualization supports *availability* in that you can almost instantly duplicate production hosts (whether physical or virtual) in a virtual environment, adding redundant capabilities for availability purposes or assets for use when existing hosts aren't enough. You can copy physical machines and convert them to virtual machines and, because virtual machines are merely files, you can copy and reinstantiate them as new additional virtual machines (with a few basic configuration changes, of course).

Virtualization provides *elasticity*, meaning you can expand, duplicate, reconfigure, repurpose, and reuse resources in the environment (in this case, virtual hosts) on the fly, as the need for them arises or shrinks. This provides an organization flexibility in its use of resources, saving physical machines and reallocating, activating, and deactivating hosts as needed in dynamic-use situations. Virtual machines can be provisioned, configured, and stored in advance for just such instances.

Virtualization applies to networking components as well, enabling rapid scalability and adaptability of networks of virtual machines. *Software defined networking (SDN)* enables centralization of portions of the routing and switching (such as creation and maintaining of routing tables), that can then be rapidly pushed to routers and switches that only handle the packets and frames. Current SDN boxes employ security features that can rapidly respond, automatically, to attacks such as distributed denial-of-service (DDoS) attacks.

Security Control Testing

Virtualization enables security professionals to test various security controls on virtual hosts, either before implementing them in production or as changes to the production environment occur. You can configure different controls to test effectiveness and functionality, to ensure that the appropriate control is implemented correctly for the environment. This can help confirm whether a new security patch will break an application; whether a configuration change is effective in reducing a vulnerability; whether a change to an operating system's function or configuration breaks its security baseline; and whether a target host is configured as securely as you need it to be for vulnerability and penetration-testing purposes.

Sandboxing

Sandboxing provides an enclosed environment in which to run potentially dangerous applications, or even malware, to determine the effect they would have on the environment. Often, security professionals need to see the effects of an application or software on a host to determine how it interacts with the system and the network. This can help them identify potential issues with untrusted software, such as executables and scripts. Sandboxing allows you to test potentially harmful software in a controlled, isolated environment, without the possibility of affecting other hosts or allowing unwanted communication to the network. Virtualization provides sandboxing capabilities by giving you the option of running an isolated virtual host for that purpose.

Module 7-5: Cloud Security

This module covers the following CompTIA Security+ objective:

- **3.7** Summarize cloud and virtualization concepts

We're used to seeing computers in offices, work centers, data centers, and at home. *Cloud computing* simply means to move those computers, or at least some aspect of those local computers, to a location only identified with an IP address or a DNS name. It enables you not only to look for data on the World Wide Web, but to store it there, so it's accessible from anywhere. And it goes even a step beyond that, processing the data in the World Wide Web/Internet/cloud. You can think of cloud computing just as you would any other service or utility you pay for—such as water, electricity, cable, phone, Internet, and so on—except that now you're paying for computing as a utility.

 NOTE Cloud computing isn't just for the public Internet. You'll see private clouds as well later in this module.

Cloud computing got its name from the many network architectural diagrams, such as the one shown in Figure 7-23, where the Internet is portrayed as a cartoonish cloud figure, meaning it's abstracted from the rest of your network beyond your perimeter and Internet service delivery point.

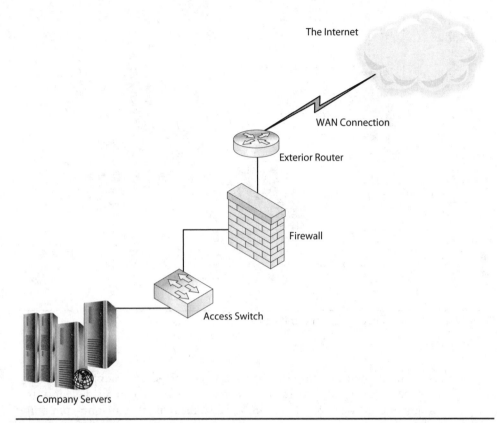

Figure 7-23   The cloud

Cloud computing offers many advantages, because it removes all the responsibility and overhead for maintaining data storage and processing in your computer or even on your premises, and hands it over to what is known as a *cloud provider*. A cloud provider essentially is a third party that owns a huge data center full of physical and virtual servers, with multiple, extremely fast connections to the Internet. The provider installs different types of operating systems and applications on its servers to be able to provide different services to its customers via the Internet.

As you'll see in the next several sections of this module, all types of services can be offered via a cloud provider. We'll discuss those next, and then we'll get to the real point of this module: the risks associated with cloud services. We'll also talk about the security controls to consider when you're outsourcing data and services to a cloud provider.

Cloud Deployment Models

There's not really a one-size-fits-all *cloud deployment model*—online services that people can rent or buy. The next few sections explore several types of cloud services offered

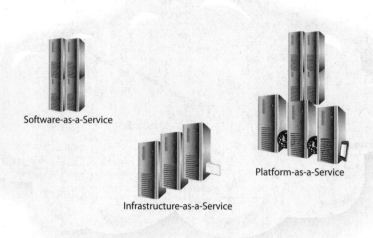

Figure 7-24 A notional cloud service architecture

by providers. Some of these are simplistic, such as data storage, for example, but others are very complex and can supplement or even replace parts of enterprise-wide infrastructures. Many of these types of services are scalable, meaning that anyone from home users, to small businesses, to large corporations can make use of them. We'll discuss these from a business perspective, of course, but similar principles apply, whether a business is a small-office/home-office type of setup or large corporate enterprise that spans several geographical locations. In Figure 7-24, you can see an example of how cloud services might be organized.

Software-as-a-Service

With *Software-as-a-Service (SaaS)*, customers run software that's stored in the cloud (almost always on a virtualized server) and used via a Web URL or, in some cases, a client program stored on a local system. SaaS is wildly popular today. Voice over IP (VoIP) services such as Skype and Google Voice provide voice/video communication. *Cloud storage* solutions such as Dropbox and Microsoft OneDrive provide terabytes of storage for files; by definition, that storage resides outside the physical network. Even traditional office applications are now available via SaaS. Microsoft offers Office as an SaaS solution via Microsoft Office 365 (Figure 7-25).

SaaS offer several advantages to businesses. First, the licensing cost of software is often less expensive when it is used via the cloud. The software licensing may be subscription-based, so an organization may purchase licenses based upon numbers of users or concurrent connections. Second, the organization is spared the legal ramifications of

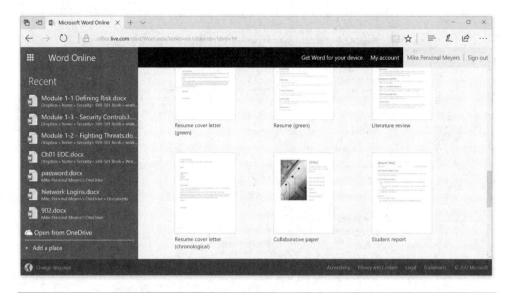

Figure 7-25   I wrote this textbook entirely with Office 365.

software piracy, since an application on the cloud can't be easily copied and transferred from computer to computer or taken home by employees. In fact, the organization doesn't have to store or manage any media at all, because the software is stored and used in the cloud, with the exception of occasional small components that may be downloaded to a user's workstation.

Security-as-a-Service (SECaaS) is a subset of SaaS that focuses only on bundling security solutions. As you might imagine, the security solutions offered run the gamut of every security solution you would implement on premises, such as security assessments, vulnerability scanning, and so on.

Infrastructure-as-a-Service

Infrastructure-as-a-Service (IaaS) goes beyond posting simple software applications in the cloud. IaaS provides entire machines, such as Windows or Linux hosts, for example, for remote connection and use. Of course, these aren't physical machines; they are virtual machines hosted by a cloud provider's infrastructure. Users simply connect to them via the Remote Desktop Protocol (RDP) or another secure remote connection protocol and use them as they would any other computer. Users can run applications installed on the virtual machine, create content, process data, and perform any other typical tasks they would perform on a physical machine. Figure 7-26 shows the interface for Amazon Web Services EC2 IaaS creating a new VM (AWS calls them *instances*).

Usually, however, IaaS implementations provide servers rather than workstations; server virtual machines are usually what most businesses need out of an IaaS provider. The advantage of having virtual servers through an IaaS provider is that the business

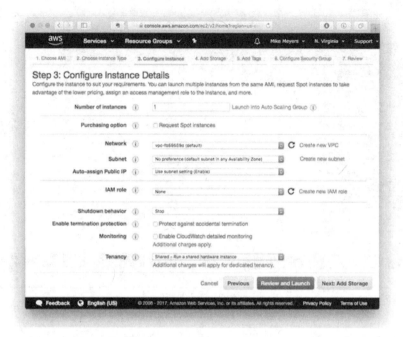

Figure 7-26 Interface for AWS

doesn't have to provision, manage, or maintain huge server farms or data centers—all that's done for them by the provider. The provider is responsible for patches, updates, configuration, and so on. Additionally, licensing for servers provided through an IaaS contract is usually far more streamlined, and cheaper.

Platform-as-a-Service

The next type of cloud service is *Platform-as-a-Service (PaaS)*. PaaS offers a business a computing platform—such as a Web application server or database server, for example—that it can use to provide services both internally and to customers on the Internet. Many online storefronts use this model to conduct business, rather than hosting on their own premises the physical servers, Web sites, databases, and applications. Again, the advantages of using this type of service are cost savings, no requirement to build and maintain the infrastructure on site, and the guarantee of around-the-clock availability—plus, someone else takes care of the patching and configuration work.

Although the types of services we've mentioned are the main ones listed in the exam objectives, they are also the three primary types of services you'll see in the cloud provider world. There are many other types of "something-as-a-service" that cloud providers offer. One of the more interesting is *Desktop-as-a-Service (DaaS)*, which literally provides your users with their own desktops. Their actual machines don't really matter: they can be full desktops, thin clients, tablets, or smartphones. No matter where your users are located or what they have in their hand, they have instant access to their desktop. DaaS competes directly with more traditional *Virtual Desktop Infrastructure (VDI)*, where an enterprise sets up a central server to provide desktop interfaces for users. Just like with other virtualization and cloud-based services, DaaS takes the managing of hardware and software out of the hands of local IT, freeing them up for other tasks.

 EXAM TIP The CompTIA Security+ objectives list *Virtual Desktop Environment (VDE)* as a synonym for VDI. VDI is a tool developed by Citrix for creating desktop environments, certainly, but VDE are not common replacement initials for VDI. VDE usually stands for *Virtual Distributed Ethernet*, a networking virtualization technology used in Linux.

Cloud Architecture Models

Although I stated that cloud environments are operated primarily by large companies with huge data centers, this isn't always the case. In fact, an increasing number of clouds are popping up that follow a few different architecture models. These include private clouds, public clouds, and a few other models we'll briefly go over. Any of these various cloud architectures may be used, depending on the organization's specific needs and its reliance on third-party providers or its requirements to keep computing resources in house.

Private Cloud

In a private cloud, as you'd expect, the cloud environment—the infrastructure, network devices, connections, and servers—is for the exclusive use of one party, such as a business. Now, just because it is a private cloud, it doesn't necessarily mean that the infrastructure also resides physically within the business's own data center on its physical premises. It could certainly be that way (military organizations and very large corporations often host their own private cloud, for example), but a private cloud can also be hosted by a third-party provider as a contracted service. Regardless of where the environment is hosted, a private cloud is for the use of the business that's paying for it—it's not for public or shared use. It can still host the same types of services I've described. A private cloud may cost the organization a bit more if it's hosted within a data center it owns and operates, but this cost is usually absorbed by the cost of operating the data center itself. An organization can save a bit of money if a third-party provider operates it for them, however. Another advantage of a private cloud, other than exclusive use, is that the organization may be able to exert more control over data security and availability levels.

Public Cloud

A public cloud is pretty much the opposite of a private one. A public cloud is usually operated by a third-party provider that sells or rents "pieces" of the cloud to different entities, such as small businesses or large corporations, to use as they need. These services and the "size" of the piece of cloud an organization gets may be scalable, based on the customer's needs. Customers usually don't get direct connections to the provider, as they might in a private cloud model; the connections are typically made over the existing customer's

Internet connections. Several business models are used for these types of clouds, including subscription models, pay-per-use, and so on. Unlike a private cloud, the security and availability levels are pretty much standardized by the provider and offered as part of the contract; organizations purchasing those services may not have any control over those terms. Examples of public cloud providers include offerings from Amazon Web Services (AWS), Google Cloud Storage, and the Microsoft Cloud.

Community Cloud

A community cloud is made up of infrastructures from several different entities, which may be cloud providers, business partners, and so on. In this structure, common services are offered to all participants in the community cloud, to one degree or another. An example of a community cloud is one that is shared among universities or educational institutions. Each institution provides a piece of infrastructure, and the cloud may include third-party providers as well, to form a cloud shared by all.

Hybrid Cloud

A hybrid cloud is, as you would probably guess, any combination of the cloud models described previously. You could have public/private hybrids, private/community hybrids, and so on. A hybrid might be used because all parties need common cloud services (common application or Web platforms, for instance, on linked or connected Web sites), while maintaining their own private or community clouds for other purposes. Hybrid clouds could be constructed in many different ways, using third-party providers, private or shared data centers, and so on, as well as different types of connections (direct, Internet-only, and so on). Figure 7-27 sums up the relationships between the different cloud types.

Cloud Computing Risks and Virtualization

Now that we've discussed exactly what cloud computing is, how it works, and the different services that you can access from the cloud, let's talk about some of the risks that are incurred with cloud computing. We'll also discuss the risks that are inherent to virtualization, because virtualization is one of the core technologies that make cloud computing work the way it does. Cloud computing depends on virtualization because these cloud-based services, such as platforms, infrastructure, and software, don't all run on physical computers; virtual computers are provisioned to provide these services to a particular customer or business, so they have their own distinct infrastructures that can be changed as needed. Remember that virtualization basically means that a computer can host multiple instances of operating system environments, so a single powerful server can potentially host dozens or even hundreds of virtual machines dedicated to different customers and services. Data centers belonging to cloud services providers contain sometimes hundreds of servers that can host literally thousands of virtual computers for their customers.

Of course, even powerful, redundant technologies like cloud computing and virtualization have security risks. No infrastructure is without risk completely, so you have to take into account the risks that are inherent to cloud computing and virtualization when managing risk within your organization. Although these services are outsourced to third-party providers, the organization still incurs a degree of risk, as well as the business

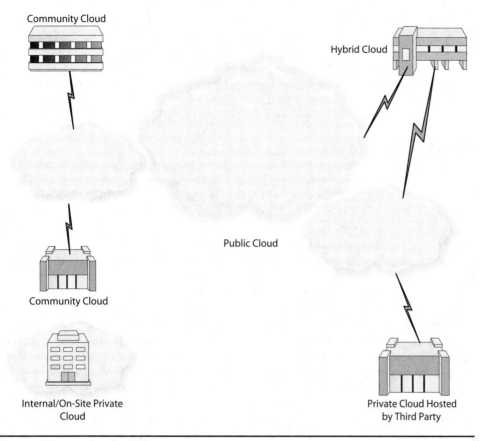

Community Cloud

Hybrid Cloud

Public Cloud

Community Cloud

Internal/On-Site Private
Cloud

Private Cloud Hosted
by Third Party

Figure 7-27   Interface for AWS

and legal responsibility for maintaining services and data. In the next two sections, we'll talk about some of the risks involved with virtualization and cloud computing.

Virtualization Risks

As mentioned earlier, some risks are inherent to virtualization. Depending upon how the third party has structured the virtual environments it manages, virtual machines suffer the same risks as physical computers. For example, just as a physical computer could be vulnerable to a data loss, a virtual machine could also be vulnerable to virtual drive crashes, data corruption, and so on. These virtual machines could be single points of failures if they are not backed up regularly, or if there are no redundant systems to take their place if they go down. These two risks, however, are easily mitigated by providers that design and build robust virtualization environments in data centers. Virtual machines are very easy to back up and replicate, simply by taking snapshots and regular full backups of their data on a periodic basis. In the event a virtual machine goes down, an exact copy of it could almost immediately take its place with very little loss of processing time.

Other, more practical, risks of virtualization include risks to the entire data center, or even the physical server the virtual machines reside on. This could include power loss, environmental disasters, and hardware or operating system issues with the physical machine. These risks can also be mitigated with proper backup and redundant systems. Probably a more realistic risk is that of improper access by employees or other unauthorized parties to data that resides on a virtual machine. Just like physical machines, virtual machines can be hacked or compromised if appropriate security controls are not in place.

Cloud Computing Risks

Risks to cloud computing are really variations on a recurring theme; we've discussed the risks of allowing third parties to store, handle, and process an organization's data. Cloud computing falls into that category and incurs the same types of risks. Lack of control is probably the biggest risk to the organization, in that the business has to depend on someone else to secure its data. Risks include all of those that may affect data confidentiality and unauthorized disclosure, data and system availability to authorized users and customers, and data integrity through unauthorized modification of data the business entrusts to cloud providers.

Because data is placed in the hands of a third party for safekeeping, the organization doesn't often have the control or visibility into the security measures taken by cloud providers to protect its information. The business must rely on the cloud provider's due care and diligence in protecting data the same way it would be protected if it resided within the confines of the business's infrastructure. One particular risk involves cloud storage services, which use the cloud to store critical and sensitive data belonging to the business. In addition to being a possible single point of failure for data loss through potential infrastructure issues, cloud storage is also a possible leaking point for data to unauthorized persons. Although the company may have contracted cloud storage services for all employees to use, there's still the possibility that certain persons, even within the organization, can access data they should not be able to when it is stored in the cloud. There's also a possibility that employees have their own personal cloud storage services to which they may transfer organizational data, resulting in data loss or unauthorized access.

EXAM TIP *Cloud access security broker (CASB)* refers to a layer of software between a cloud application and an enterprise or organization, designed to provide security. Most commonly, the major cloud organizations, like Google, Amazon, Microsoft, and so on, have invested heavily in automated controls implemented through application programming interface (API) modules. You can rely on these companies for proper security.

A second type of CASB is called proxy-based. These rely on a third party's software in between the cloud service provider and an organization or enterprise that uses those services. As of this writing, proxy-based services inject more security problems rather than reduce security risks. The proxy-based services seem to have briefly appeared, but flamed out. If you get asked about CASBs on the exam, focus on the API-based models.

Appropriate Controls to Ensure Data Security

Although we like to say that cloud computing is unique and different from services that are hosted on premises within a business, both the risks and the security controls are very similar to what you would encounter when storing data locally on business-owned servers. There are a few differences, of course, but the major risks of data loss and compromise, as well as data unavailability, are the same in both cloud-based and in-house models. Likewise, the controls used to protect data are also similar. The next two sections discuss some of the controls that organizations should consider with regard to cloud services, emphasizing the controls that are somewhat different from in-house models where needed.

Contract Agreements and Security Policy

One major difference between controls used in cloud models versus controls used in in-house data storage and processing is the use of contract agreements. Although different divisions within the same business may have memorandums of understanding between them, these aren't the same thing as the contracts that you usually find between a business and a cloud service provider. Such a contract is extremely important, because it sets the tone for the expectations of data security, system availability, and the responsibilities both parties have to live up to in protecting data. The contract between the parties sets the minimum security and privacy expectations; legal and regulatory governance may also provide protections for the type of data the cloud provider is responsible for protecting.

We discussed (way back in Chapter 1) the different types of contract documents a business can establish with third-party providers, as well as the importance of outlining all of the security requirements in those documents. The contract should specify, either in its content or as an attachment, security requirements and controls that the third-party provider must adhere to. The contract should also specify details regarding access controls, availability levels, disclosure, and other security issues.

Although both organizations have their own internal security policies, these policies are often incompatible with each other and usually apply only to data that's processed internally to an organization. The contract agreement should set up a joint security policy that both the business and the provider have to adhere to, with regard to system interfaces, data protection, and so on. Some of these things can be negotiated between the parties; often, however, some businesses find that cloud providers are fairly rigid in how they will conduct security and privacy within their infrastructures, even with regard to protecting data that belongs to the business. All of this should be carefully considered and negotiated up front, whenever possible.

Security Controls

Beyond the controls specified in the contract agreements, organizations need to consider practical security controls when outsourcing services to cloud-based providers. Tight authentication and authorization controls should be in place, so that only authorized users in the business can access data stored and processed in the cloud. These controls could include multifactor authentication technologies, restrictive permissions, limited application access to data, and so on. Data and system availability controls must also be in place; these include the typical controls such as redundant systems, regularly scheduled backups, redundant communication lines, and so forth. Data should also be protected while at rest (in storage) and in transit (during transmission) through encryption whenever possible.

In addition to the technical controls designed to protect data and systems, organizations need to put security programs in place that cover disaster recovery and incident response. The business may be relying on the cloud provider to provide those services to the organization itself, so these guarantees must be in place; however, the cloud service provider also needs to implement their own programs and procedures in the event a disaster or incident affects their own data center or infrastructures or the ability to provide services. Cloud providers should have processes in place to respond to disasters that directly affect them and the services they provide to their customers, as well as to respond to incidents that may affect unauthorized disclosure of data, denial-of-service conditions, and so on. In addition, the business should be allowed to audit or review the cloud provider's security controls to ensure that the provider is following the terms of the agreement. All of this should be spelled out in the contract.

Module 7-6: Embedded System Security

This module covers the following CompTIA Security+ objective:

- **3.5** Explain the security implications of embedded systems

From the watch on your wrist monitoring your heartbeat and tracking your steps, to the interface screen in your car, to the heating and air conditioning systems that heat and cool our offices, embedded systems fill our world. There's a good reason for these systems proliferating our lives: they add levels of functionality to almost every technology in existence.

Static host is a term describing some of the newer types of nontraditional devices we are seeing more of in this age of the *Internet of Things (IoT)*. This means that any type of device, from a handheld gaming system, to a *wearable technology* device (like a fitness-tracking watch), to a television, to the heating and air conditioning controls that make your home comfortable (*home automation* devices), can be connected to the global information grid—the Internet. These hosts more likely have chip- or firmware-based operating systems (called embedded operating systems) than traditional operating systems. They may be *general purpose* devices (think iPads and other tablets), or they may be *special purpose* devices (such as a set-top box that streams Netflix, Hulu, and Pandora into your television). We even have static hosts in our automobiles, in the form of cellular- and Bluetooth-enabled entertainment systems that also receive GPS signals.

Static hosts aren't immune from requiring security; in fact, since they permeate our lives so much and actually have access to our most sensitive information (credit card info, physical address, e-mail, location data, and so on), securing them requires taking a much deeper look. Although traditional security methods help, some of these devices and environments require that we pay special attention to security using other methods. This module looks at securing static hosts and the environments in which the hosts operate.

But like any IT technology, embedded systems have significant security issues, and in a few cases utterly terrifying security issues. To help you understand these issues, this module has three main goals. First is to clearly define the term embedded system. Second is to tour the large number of devices specifically defined in the CompTIA Security+ objectives as embedded systems. Third is to consider security issues involved with embedded systems.

Embedded Systems

An *embedded system* is a complete computer system—CPU, RAM, storage, operating system, drivers, etc.—whose only job is to perform a specific function either by itself or as part of a larger system. While that is all that's required to be an embedded system, there are a number of traits that are common to the vast majority of embedded systems:

- Embedded systems tend to be much smaller than a typical general-purpose PC.

- Embedded systems are almost always headless and require some form of remote connection to configure them.

- Embedded systems tend to run a *real-time operating system (RTOS)* such as Windows Embedded Compact (Figure 7-28). An RTOS is designed to respond in real time to inputs. RTOS is critical for anti-lock brakes, safety stops, and so forth.

- Embedded systems generally run advanced integrated circuits such as a *system on a chip (SoC)*, which combines a complete computer with I/O features such as 802.11, graphics/display output, Bluetooth, and potentially many more items depending on the need.

Figure 7-28
Windows
Embedded
Compact

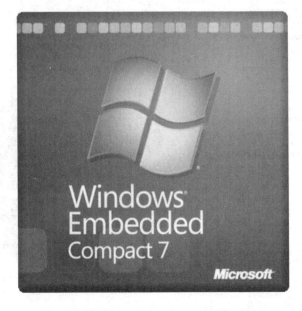

NOTE   There are hundreds of SoCs, customizable to tens of thousands of unique configurations, available today.

Embedded systems are at the heart of static hosts. An embedded system typically is a network-connected functional computer system that is integrated as part of a larger device or system. Embedded systems are usually very specific in functionality and aren't used as fully functional computer systems. Examples of embedded consumer-based systems include *smart devices*, computing devices that connect to the Internet for more information and access to resources. These are TVs, photo printers and multifunction devices (MFDs), entertainment devices, game consoles, and so on. Certain industrial computer systems are also embedded devices; these systems are used to control utility and production facilities and equipment, and we'll discuss them a bit later in the module. Figure 7-29 shows an example of a smart home automation device.

SCADA/ICS

Supervisory control and data acquisition (SCADA) is a newer buzzword in the security industry, although it's actually been around for a number of years. SCADA systems are used in industrial applications, such as utilities (electric plants, sewage treatment centers, nuclear power plants), production facilities (for control of manufacturing systems, for example), and other specialized applications. Heating, ventilation, and air conditioning (HVAC) controls also fall into this category and are often automated and connected to

Figure 7-29

A smart home automation device

the Internet or other networks to monitor and control environmental elements such as temperature and humidity in a facility. You'll often hear the term *industrial control system (ICS)* associated with SCADA.

Although SCADA systems have been around for a very long time, only in recent years have they become an important issue in the information security world. This is because we have only recently discovered that these systems are more and more often being connected to the Internet, and often in an unprotected state. They run TCP/IP protocols and often use embedded versions of some of the popular consumer operating systems, such as Windows or Linux. This makes them prime targets for hackers, who attack SCADA systems to damage critical infrastructure, launch denial-of-service attacks, and generally create mischief and outright harm. Since SCADA systems often connect to very critical systems, it's not too hard to imagine a hacker attacking and gaining control of these systems and seriously affecting power, water, and other utilities and services on a massive scale. There have even been reported instances of hackers compromising SCADA systems and launching attacks on an organization's traditional internal network infrastructure through them.

Methods of mitigating these types of attacks include the traditional ones, such as encryption, authentication, and patch management. In the case of many of these systems, infrastructure controls, such as intrusion detection systems (IDSs) and firewall devices, should also be implemented. One other method that should be examined is the complete separation of these networks and their devices from public networks, such as the Internet.

In-Vehicle Computing Systems

Cars are now computerized; that's a fact of life. The consumer market now demands cars with built-in systems that provide navigational functions, entertainment functions, and even, in some cases, access to the Internet. Obviously, car manufacturers want to cater to consumers by including all of these great features, as well as the ability to access vehicle health information via network connections. These network connections may include Bluetooth, Wi-Fi, or even, in some cases, cellular connectivity. So if computers are now being built into cars, or added in as aftermarket devices, what are the security ramifications? And how do you secure in-vehicle computer systems? Will it become necessary to install a firewall in your car?

And it's not just cars that have computing systems. Aircraft of all sorts, both manned and unmanned, have increasingly sophisticated computing systems, many connected to extended networks and the Internet. Your next *unmanned aerial vehicle (UAV)*—that's a drone, for all you normal folks—guaranteed will have multiple *embedded camera systems*, high-end wireless networking capabilities, and an SoC to run them all.

From a security perspective, in-vehicle computing systems have some of the same common vulnerabilities that other systems have, which may include network security issues, such as the vulnerabilities that are already inherent to Bluetooth, Wi-Fi, and cellular technologies. There are also issues involving firmware and patch updates to the systems. Many of these systems have USB or SD card ports, for example, to upload firmware updates or play media content on the devices. Perhaps someday someone will develop a virus or other type of malware that could be injected into these types of systems via a removable media device.

Other security issues may be only the speculative fantasies of geeks, such as a hacker taking over your car and driving it while you're going down the road or conducting a denial-of-service attack on your engine or transmission, resulting in the car coming to a complete halt on the freeway. However remote these possibilities may be, they may not be too far down the road (pun intended). In short, vehicular computing systems are a new frontier, for both security professionals and hackers. Although traditional security methods and controls will probably work to a large degree, other methods will have to be developed to ensure that these types of static hosts are well protected from malicious users and attacks.

Securing Embedded Systems

Now that we've discussed a few of the many possible variations of static hosts you may encounter in your travels, we can discuss the different methods for securing these hosts. Obviously, since these hosts still have some things in common with traditional devices, such as IP connectivity, we can employ traditional methods to help secure them, such as firewalls, patching, and so on. We'll cover those methods next, but we'll also go over methods that may be unique to these types of devices.

Security Layers

Defense-in-depth means you should use multiple layers and multiple security techniques to protect your network and hosts. You shouldn't rely on only one security control or defense. If you rely only on a single security control, and that control is compromised, then you have nothing left to protect your network. Here's an example.

Many people who are uneducated on security matters think that a firewall is the be-all, end-all for security. They think that a firewall installed secures a network. We know, as security professionals, that this isn't so. If that single firewall is compromised, an attacker gains an open gateway into a protected network.

Defense-in-depth says we layer defenses with multiple security methods. Certainly, we have firewalls, but we also have border routers on our perimeter. We also use other means, such as encryption and authentication, to secure data and systems. We use anti-malware software to combat viruses, Trojan horses, and the like. These different layers contribute to the overall security of the network and hosts; without any one of them, we would be more vulnerable.

In terms of static hosts, you should use multiple different security layers to ensure the security of the host and environment in which it resides. A few of these layers include not only network protection, such as the use of firewalls and network segmentation, but also traditional host-based security methods, such as operating system patches, anti-malware, and so on. Also, don't overlook the benefits of device encryption to protect data at rest, as well as transmission encryption using protocols such as TLS/SSL and SSH, for example. And, of course, whenever possible, use strong authentication methods with static devices. Many of these devices don't have particularly strong authentication methods; tablets, for example, may be able to use certificate-based authentication, or strong passwords. Other types of devices, such as smartphones or the navigation system in your automobile, may use only a four-digit PIN, for example. Regardless of the device's ability to use different authentication methods, you should use the strongest available methods that the device can support.

Control redundancy and diversity are also aspects of a layered security model that you should implement for both static and traditional hosts. Control redundancy refers to having multiple controls in place to perform a similar function. This ensures that if one of these controls is unavailable or is disabled, the other controls will continue to perform that function, so there will be no loss of protection. For example, having multiple firewalls in the DMZ is an example of control redundancy. If one becomes unavailable or is compromised, the others still fill that protection need. Control diversity, on the other hand, means that you will have multiple controls, but they will not be the same identical control, and an attacker would have to circumvent or disable them in different ways. For instance, with multiple firewalls in the DMZ, if they all come from the same vendor and are all the same model, they are more likely to incur the same vulnerabilities. Having a diversity of models and vendors for your firewall architecture would ensure that if a new zero-day vulnerability for one particular firewall is released, it would probably not affect any of the others. This principle applies not only to firewalls, of course, but to other security controls as well. This principle also has to be balanced with the need for standardization and interoperability within the network architecture. Figure 7-30 sums up our discussion on security layers, control redundancy, and control diversity.

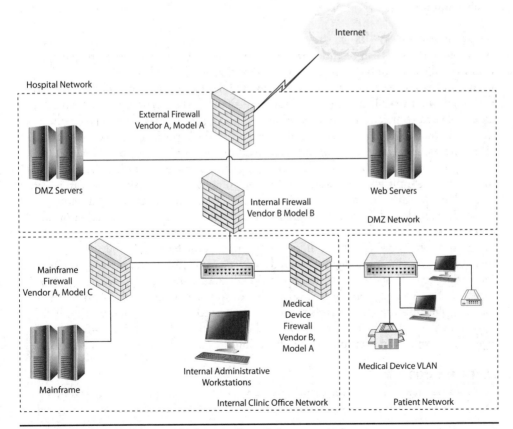

Figure 7-30   Security layers, multiple controls, and diverse controls

Network Segmentation

Static hosts should often be separated from other traditional hosts for various reasons, through network segmentation. Let's take an interesting type of unconventional host, for example: *medical devices*. These *special purpose devices* definitely fit the definition of static hosts; they often run embedded or specialized versions of operating systems (Linux or even Windows, for example), they fill a highly specialized need, and they are very often connected to an IP network. If you keep up with the current state of medical devices, then you know that they, too, can be accessed through traditional hacking methods over the network that disrupt their function. Can you imagine the consequences of someone hacking into a network of these devices and interfering with one that monitors the health of a critically ill patient, or one that functions as an insulin pump?

That's why these devices are afforded special care in a hospital network; they are very often segmented physically away from the network and may also be segmented logically as well, through the use of virtual LANs (discussed in depth in Chapter 6) and separate IP address ranges, in addition to being protected by internal firewalls and other security devices. Wireless medical devices pose an even bigger risk, since wireless networks and hosts are easily accessed by malicious persons. Network segmentation offers just one layer of defense; other layers should also be used to ensure that these specialized devices are not easily compromised.

Application Firewalls

Application firewalls can be thought of in two different contexts. In the first, an application firewall is an appliance or network device that works at all seven layers of the OSI model and can inspect data within protocols. Think of a situation in which HTTP traffic is filtered in a firewall. In an ordinary stateful firewall, the traffic is filtered based upon an established connection from an internal host. HTTP traffic is allowed in or out based upon whether the protocol itself is allowed, over which port, its source or destination IP addresses, if it is the result of an established connection, and so on. This means that filtering is done based upon the *characteristics* of the traffic itself, rather than the *content* of the traffic. Application firewalls look at the content of the traffic as well, in addition to its characteristics. So if HTTP is otherwise allowed into the network, an application firewall also looks at the content of the HTTP traffic, often detecting whether or not the content itself is allowed.

Application firewalls can be network-based or host-based; in the context of our discussions for this module, host-based firewalls are more relevant. Although most industrial static hosts do not use application firewalls specifically on their platforms, some of the more modern hosts, especially consumer devices, do have them. A host-based application firewall controls the applications and services on that particular device only, and it secures their connections to the network and interfaces with each other. Figure 7-31 shows an example of an application firewall specific to Android devices.

Manual Updates

Nontraditional hosts often don't lend themselves to automatic updates. This could be the case for several different reasons. First, some of these hosts are not always connected to

Figure 7-31
An Android
firewall

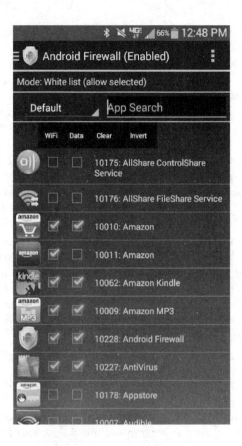

the Internet. In the case of SCADA systems, or medical devices, for example, there may be no way to connect them to the Internet without incurring a security risk. Second, the vendor may not have included an automated update process with the device. Some devices may require the download of a patch, an image, or a piece of firmware that has to be manually installed on the device using a very specific process, often resulting in rebooting the device into a special maintenance mode. A third reason might be that the data sensitivity of the systems in question might be so high that the organization can't perform automatic updates or connect them to the Internet for classification reasons. For example, some U.S. government systems, particularly those of a classified nature, cannot be connected to the Internet.

For these reasons, manual updates may be required for some static hosts. If you have the ability to automate device updates, then obviously you should use that method as much as possible, since it ensures that updates are applied in the most efficient way possible. On the other hand, manual updates can give you the opportunity to test patches and other software updates before applying them to a production system. Often updates are downloaded manually first, tested in a test environment that mirrors the production systems, and then applied to the production systems only when you can be sure that they will cause no ill effects. You should also record manual updates, so that you can trace any issues that arise from them back to a particular patch or update.

Firmware Version Control

Many of these types of devices frequently get firmware updates. Remember that firmware is typically applied as updates to programming in the chips on the hardware portion of the system, rather than as patches to the operating system or application software. Firmware updates can fix issues with both the operating system and hardware on a device, as well as provide for security patches. They can also add new features to a device. For personal devices, firmware version control may not be a big issue; often if the user experiences any issues with the device after the firmware has been updated, the user can reverse the update process and regress to an earlier version rather easily. In an enterprise environment, however, it's extremely important to maintain version control on firmware updates, because a firmware update may cause issues with production software or devices that the organization needs to fulfill its business purposes. As I mentioned previously when discussing manual updates, you should first test firmware updates in an appropriate environment, and then apply them to production devices only after you have confirmed that they cause no ill effects. You also should record firmware versions in a central database. Also check any firmware updates that are necessary to see if there are any known issues with any versions of software or hardware that the organization is using on the device.

Wrappers

Wrappers are used in different ways in the computing world. At its core, a wrapper is nothing more than a programming interface for different services that exist on the host, which are then translated to be compatible with other services on other hosts, via networking protocols. Wrappers are used to expose interfaces to different services on a host to other services in a controlled and consistent manner, usually via the network. In a security context, you've probably heard of the TCP Wrappers service, which is used to "wrap" networking protocols securely, providing a filtered software interface to hosts. TCP Wrappers function more like access control lists, allowing only certain network hosts to access those protocols on the device. TCP Wrappers, implemented as a service and commonly found on UNIX and Linux systems, serve as a rudimentary form of firewall service for network protocols on the host.

For static hosts, programmers may implement wrappers in different ways, since embedded and other specialized operating systems may require translation for their services and protocols to other hosts and the network. Discussions on implementation of any of these wrappers for any particular device is beyond the scope of this book, but from a security perspective, programmers should ensure that wrappers provide only the minimum functionality necessary to communicate with the device. They should also take encryption and authentication into account when designing wrappers for embedded devices, ensuring that there is some level of control over protecting data that transfers over these interfaces, and allowing some level of control over external host and user access to them. Additionally, programmers should configure wrappers to allow minimum access possible from external interfaces, devices, and protocols. From a user perspective, most users won't ever need to access wrapper interfaces with embedded devices. From an administrator or security perspective, however, you may occasionally need to access these interfaces through different configuration methods for the static or embedded hosts you're working with.

NOTE Wrappers and their cousins, packers and crypters, can have less-than-benign uses. In other words, some software can hide from anti-malware software—by pretending to be a typical wrapper—and then run malicious code once into the network or system.

Module 7-7: Mobile Devices

This module covers the following CompTIA Security+ objective:

- **2.5** Given a scenario, deploy mobile devices securely

A study conducted on a certain popular Web site asked tens of thousands of users to enumerate the five most precious items in their lives. Almost 90 percent of the respondents listed their smartphone, and of that 90 percent, almost half listed their smartphone as the number one most important item in their lives! Even more interesting, roughly 20 percent of respondents listed not only their phone but a second mobile device (second phone or tablet) as well!

Mobile devices are here to stay, and it's our job to keep these devices secure. This module starts with connecting mobile devices to networks. From there we'll break mobile security into two distinct but slightly overlapping issues: mobile device management and the challenges of bring your own device (BYOD).

Mobile Connections

The power of mobile devices comes from their connectivity. Without some form of connection to a host computer, a network, or the Internet, your mobile device can't sync contacts, update apps, or copy your pictures. The Security+ objectives specifically enumerate a number of connection methods used in mobile devices that we need to cover. Although many of these connections are well known, a few of them, while fairly common, are not familiar to many users.

Cellular

Direct sniffing of cellular voice and data isn't easy, assuming you're using a late-generation 4G/LTE GSM phone. Built-in voice encryption requires a bad actor to emulate a cell tower, an expensive and tricky process with serious legal ramifications. The biggest issue to cellular involves the devices that automatically switch from cellular to Wi-Fi, when available, to save data rates.

Figure 7-32
Author's Xfinity
hotspot

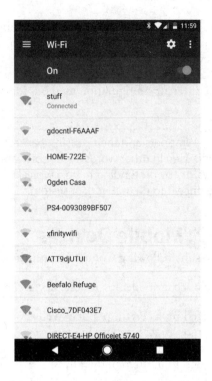

Wi-Fi/Bluetooth

Earlier modules cover Wi-Fi in detail and Bluetooth a bit more lightly. Every wireless security aspect covered previously applies to mobile devices but they add a few more problems. One of the most challenging issues in Wi-Fi comes from stored profiles. Mobile devices can grab standardized hotspot SSIDs pushed out by ISPs such as "xfinitywifi" or "attwifi" and some will in turn become mobile hotspots that seem very similar to the initial hotspot (Figure 7-32).

Near Field Communication

Many mobile devices use NFC, just like you read about in Module 7-2, for quick payments and such. All the security issues for NFC apply to its use in mobile devices.

 NOTE Android embraces NFC heavily. Apple typically uses NFC only for the Apple Pay app, although Apple is slowly opening iOS to more NFC options.

USB

If you want security, the only real option is USB. As a wired, direct connection to a host system, USB communications are difficult to compromise. All mobile operating systems support USB syncing of contacts, calendaring, photos, and so forth, although none of

Figure 7-33
Third-party USB
sync

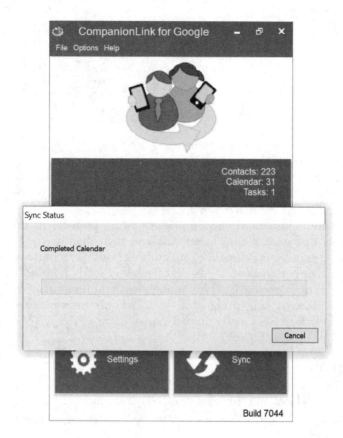

them make it easy, often forcing users to use third-party tools (Figure 7-33). USB is also quite limiting, as updates only take place when you're actually connected, making real-time updates impossible.

Infrared

Your author loves his Android phones if for no other reason than only Androids (and not all of them) come with an infrared (IR) transmitter known generically as an infrared blaster. IR blasters can emulate any IR remote control, turning any Android into a universal remote. Since these devices only transmit simple remote-control commands, there is no risk to your mobile device. The risk is that any IR blaster can quickly take complete control of any device designed to receive those commands, making the Android the bad actor. The only real defense is to block the IR receivers.

ANT

Adaptive Network Technology (ANT) is a low-speed, low-power networking technology. Wi-Fi and Bluetooth are powerful wireless tools, but both of these technologies require

Figure 7-34
ANT USB dongle

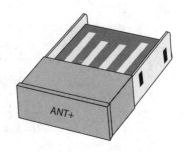

rather chatty, relatively power-hungry devices. Bluetooth isn't nearly as power hungry or as fast as Wi-Fi, but when you have very small devices such as heart rate monitors, even Bluetooth uses too much power.

Garmin introduced the proprietary ANT protocol around 2007 for low-power sensors that don't send a lot of data and that often go for extended periods of time without transferring data (like your author's heart rate monitor that's used at most once a week). The latest version of ANT is called ANT+. ANT/ANT+ is a superb protocol that's incredibly low powered and has enough bandwidth for many devices. ANT is encrypted with AES, so hacking isn't an issue (yet). The only downside to ANT/ANT+ is that Apple devices lack an ANT radio. In that case we need an ANT/ANT+ USB dongle to talk to our ANT device (Figure 7-34).

SATCOM

Satellite communication (SATCOM) has progressed a long way from the first generation of satellites over 20 years ago. Today's satellite providers offer both voice and data, although at extremely slow and expensive rates compared to terrestrial Wi-Fi and cellular.

Mobile Devices in the Business World

When so-called "smart" devices entered the consumer market, they were all the rage because, beyond traditional voice communications, they enabled users to communicate with friends, family, and associates nearly simultaneously in several new ways, by using social media sites, sharing photos and videos, using text and chat messages, and so on. They also became the ubiquitous computing platform, replacing traditional desktops and laptops to a large degree, enabling users to play games, manage their finances, dictate short documents, and perform other tasks. The problem was, however, that users expected to see the same cool, wide-ranging functions on their work computers as well, but the business world hadn't caught up with the mobile device app explosion. As a result, many users started bringing their devices to work, most of the time without management approval, and doing company work on them. Figure 7-35 shows examples of some of the personal mobile devices that tend to wander into the office from time to time.

That's all changed now, of course, as businesses are rapidly adopting mobile devices into their infrastructures. Businesses now issue smartphones and tablets to employees, provide for their communications links and Internet services, and allow employees to use these devices to perform work functions—and, in some cases, even do some of their personal stuff on them.

Figure 7-35 Personal mobile devices that tend to show up at work (photo courtesy of Sarah McNeill Photography, used with permission)

Unfortunately, any new technology or change in the business infrastructure introduces new security issues. Sometimes organizations are in such a hurry to implement new technology that they overlook security issues, and their main focus is on how much stuff the technology or device can do. In other words, the focus is on the functionality of the device or technology rather than on security. With the infiltration of mobile devices into the business world, however, developers and engineers, business managers, and even users to a certain degree have worked to make mobile devices use more secure.

The next few sections explore some of the security features that mobile devices offer, and how to integrate them into the corporate infrastructure and networks. We'll also examine prevalent issues to consider when integrating an employee's personal device with the business network.

Mobile Device Management

Mobile device management (MDM) is a relatively new process in the business infrastructure, in which the company can bring mobile devices under the umbrella of their existing end-user device management, just as they would for traditional desktops and laptops. The goal of MDM is to enable a company to centrally manage all the devices that connect to the company's network—not just the devices that are tied to a desk and don't walk out of the office in someone's pocket. Many considerations go into MDM, including the wide variety of vendors, platforms, operating systems, applications, features, and even telecom providers for these devices. Unless the business standardizes on one vendor or platform, it may find that managing all of these different devices can be a challenge.

Essentially, through MDM, a business can manage a mobile device using the same technologies and methods used for traditional desktops and get the same level of control. Figure 7-36 shows an example of a basic MDM software user interface.

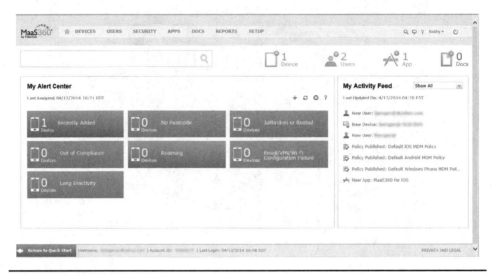

Figure 7-36 Basic MDM software

Deployment Models

The *deployment model* with mobile devices specifies how employees get a mobile device in their hands. The model defines issues such as whether the corporation provides devices to employees or employees bring their own devices. The deployment model defines aspects of mobile device management.

Corporate-Owned, Business Only (COBO)   A COBO deployment model means that the organization issues the employee a mobile device and holds ownership of the device, the maintenance of the device, and the applications and the data on the device.

Bring Your Own Device (BYOD)   Everyone already has a smartphone, and BYOD deployment means to have employees bring their own devices and use them for the organization. This brings up a number of security issues, as BYOD compels employees to offer some amount of control of their personal systems to the organization.

Choose Your Own Device (CYOD)   With CYOD the organization offers a selection of mobile devices from which employees can choose. Employees either buy the phone outright or the organization owns the device and offers them an attractive rental for the duration of their employment. In either case, the organization has complete control over the mobile device (although employees may install personal apps).

Corporate-Owned, Personally Enabled (COPE)   Similar to COBO, with COPE the organization issues a mobile device, but unlike COBO, employees are allowed to install a specific number of preapproved (white-listed) apps for their personal use.

Containerization   BYOD, CYOD, and COPE all share a common problem: how can we separate the organization's applications and data from the employee's applications and

Figure 7-37
Containerization
on an Android

data on the same device? Every mobile operating system supports containers to address this issue. A *container* is nothing more than a virtual operating system just as a virtual machine is virtual hardware. Using containerization enables the organization to create a separate operating system on the mobile device, completely separating the employee's applications and data from the organization's.

Figure 7-37 shows one example of containerization offered on an Android system. Note that there are two Contacts, two Calendars, and two Play Store apps. Using containerization enables this feature.

Containerization normally relies on *storage segmentation*, the practice of partitioning off storage areas in the device, usually to provide separate areas for company or sensitive data and personal data. Through storage segmentation, it's possible to impose different access controls on specific types of data. Figure 7-38 describes the concepts of sandboxing (that you read about in Module 7-4) and containerization. Storage segmentation can be imposed on the device's built-in storage area or on removable media as well.

Virtual Desktop Infrastructure (VDI)   If an organization wants to avoid the issue of device ownership altogether, it can get around the problem completely by offering a Virtual Desktop Infrastructure (discussed back in Module 7-5). With a VDI, every employee has a virtual machine running on a server owned by the organization. The employee may access this machine via any device running any operating system and is presented a virtual desktop with the applications the employee needs.

Figure 7-38
Containerization used to separate apps and data from each other

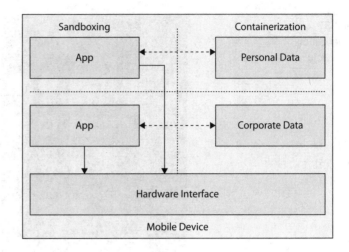

Inventory Control and Asset Tracking

One of the great things about using mobile devices in the business is that they can be used anywhere. Unfortunately, however, that means that the devices don't always reside on the company property. They walk off with the user, so the company often doesn't know exactly where they are and what they're being used for, or even who's using them. As with traditional desktops, inventory control is important with mobile devices, perhaps more important, since they are portable. Several technologies make it easier to manage mobile devices, even when they are off the company campus.

We will discuss many of these technologies later when we get into device-specific security methods, but for now understand that we can't implement any of them well unless they are part of an overall MDM infrastructure. MDM allows for the centralized control of devices, including inventory control, so not only do you always know where the device is, but in many cases, you know which authorized users have control over it. Since mobile devices tend to talk to the MDM infrastructure often, you can have an almost 100 percent real-time inventory of your mobile devices at your fingertips via the MDM software. Of course, the traditional method of having a user bring the device to you or going to the office to scan it with a barcode reader can also make sure that you know the device is safely checked in or out.

Along with inventory control, asset tracking is important. Asset tracking means knowing where your devices are at all times, who has them, and what they are being used for. Asset tracking can be provided through the MDM infrastructure as well as via the device—such as GPS and other location-based services, as well as software agents that can be placed on the devices when they come under management control. Combined with strong security policies applied to mobile devices through MDM, asset tracking can provide visibility into what's happening with these devices at all times. Figure 7-39 illustrates how location services can show you the exact location of a device.

Figure 7-39 Location services make it easier to track mobile device assets.

Device Access Control   Yet another management goal of business when integrating mobile devices into its networks is to control what data, systems, and resources the mobile devices connect to and access. As with any other device or user, the goal is to make sure that people using mobile devices can access only the data and systems they need to do their job, and no more. Your organization can and should definitely use traditional access controls, which include restrictive rights, permissions, and privileges. You can implement these controls at the resource level, such as assigning permissions to a folder or file, but you can also implement them at the network level. For example, modern mobile devices can use strong authentication mechanisms, such as certificate-based authentication, which you can integrate with your network's directory services, such as Active Directory. This can prevent an unauthorized user from stealing a mobile device and attempting to connect to your network and access your resources. Other traditional methods of access control that you can use in conjunction with mobile devices include firewalls, network access control devices, and so on.

On the flip side of device access control, in addition to the desire to control access to network resources within the business perimeter, most administrators also want to control what a device can access and do when it leaves the company network. This can be harder to control, of course, since the device is no longer under the physical or logical control of the company. It may connect to unsecure home or hotel networks, for example, or to unsecure free Wi-Fi networks that have no required authentication or encryption. These are challenges when trying to control devices remotely and control what they can access off site. Fortunately, administrators can apply MDM security policies to devices to control access to certain content (content management), applications, as well as Internet sites. These policies prevent users from doing things or accessing content that's prohibited by the company. Figure 7-40 illustrates how this works.

Figure 7-40
MDM can
push security
configuration
and policies to all
mobile devices in
the enterprise.

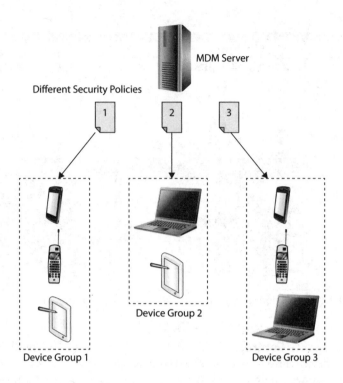

Geotagging Geotagging is the process of including in a file, such as a picture or video file, metadata that contains the location information of the device when the file was created or processed. For example, people often take pictures and geotag them with location information, which might include the GPS coordinates, time and date stamps, and other types of information, to include a description of an event. Geotagging is useful from several perspectives in the corporate environment. A forensics analysis of a device, for example, could include looking at geotag information in the file metadata so the investigator might determine patterns of where the device has been and how it has been used. Geotagging also may serve a purpose in verifying the time, date, and location of an employee who performs a certain action, which may be required for compliance or policy reasons.

 NOTE The CompTIA Security+ exam objectives use the term *GPS Tagging* for Geotagging. These terms are synonymous.

The use of geotagging in tracking employees and their activities must be carefully considered, however, in environments where users are allowed to process corporate data on their own personal devices. As with all personal data, geotagging can give away information that an employee might not want the company to have, especially if it involves information of a personal nature. We'll discuss that environment later in the module. As with all the other issues discussed here, geotagging should be addressed in policy documents.

Remote Management   Remote management is the key to protecting data in the corporate infrastructure. As mentioned, once the device leaves company property, it's difficult to control it—that is, unless the company has installed and configured remote management capabilities. This requires admins to configure the MDM software properly, as well as the settings on the device itself. Remote management enables a business to reach out and touch the device virtually to monitor its location and use, as well as to protect data in the event the device is lost or stolen. You need to be aware of a few different remote management functions for the Security+ exam, as well as for use on the job.

Geolocation uses the GPS feature of the mobile device to locate it. Figure 7-41 shows the Google device manager (called Find My Device) locating the author's phone as he watches the Houston Astros instead of working on this book.

Remote wiping (or *remote wipe*) is a capability you should use in the event a device is lost or stolen and is not likely to be recovered. In this scenario, the MDM software would enable you to send commands to the device that will completely wipe its storage areas, erasing sensitive data, configuration, and so on. Wiping the device could effectively render it useless, or at least reset it back to factory conditions.

Remote control is another security feature that you can enable on the device through MDM software. You can use this feature to take over the device if a user can't figure out how to do something, of course, but a more useful security feature might be to take control of the device to prevent its misuse or to extract data from it before it's wiped.

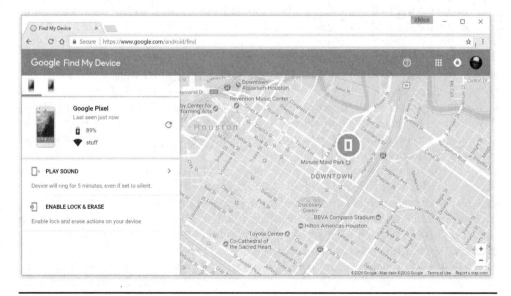

Figure 7-41   Google device manager

You can also remotely unlock a device using this feature if the user has forgotten a passcode and doesn't want to keep typing it in and risk wiping the device after several incorrect entries.

Onboarding/Offboarding   Managing mobile devices starts with the processes the organization uses in onboarding and offboarding mobile devices. *Onboarding* encompasses all of the processes used to introduce a new mobile device into the network and assign it to the user. This includes *provisioning* the device to ensure that the device has the right settings to access the mobile service provider or telecom provider, as well as installing all of the company-approved applications on the device. Provisioning also entails making sure the right user permissions and accesses are installed on the device, such as user names and passwords, digital certificates, and so on. The point of onboarding and provisioning a device is to make sure that the device is fully functional so that a user can use it to process company data.

Offboarding, as you might guess, is almost the exact opposite of onboarding and provisioning. During *offboarding*, the device is collected from the user, and access to the network with this device is taken away. In an orderly offboarding process, user data is removed from the device and, if applicable, returned to the user. Corporate data is also removed from the device and stored or disposed of as appropriate. The device might be decommissioned completely, removing it from inventory and disposing of it, in the case of legacy devices or devices that no longer function properly. If the device is not disposed of, it might be reused within the enterprise and issued to another user; in that event it would go through the onboarding and provisioning process again (although it may not require as much in terms of device activation, and so on). If the device has been collected from the user based upon a violation of policy or the law, the device might also be subject to forensics analysis and examination, as well as retention of any personal and corporate data on the device. In any event, a process should be established within the organization for both onboarding and offboarding mobile devices securely.

Application Management and Security

Application management means that the organization determines what applications can be installed and used on the mobile device, as well as where it gets those applications from. The organization can impose technical policies on devices that prohibit them from downloading applications from certain app stores, for example, and restrict them to downloading applications only from the internal company app repository or a specific vendor or platform app store.

Application management also means exercising control over what apps can do on the device, as well as what data they can access. For example, an organization can use certain methods to prevent a user's personal app from accessing any corporate data stored on the device. These methods may include restricting copy and paste operations, restricting a user's personal e-mail app from accessing the corporate e-mail's contacts list, and other controls. Application control can be imposed on the device using different technical policies, as well as tight control over user rights and privileges on the device. Other methods, such as sandboxing and containerization (discussed earlier in this module) can be used to separate applications and data from each other so that no interaction is possible between them.

Application Security The organization should exert some sort of control over the security of the applications themselves, simply because there may be security and interoperability issues with all the different apps on mobile devices. Some of these applications may not exactly work well with company-approved enterprise applications, and some of these apps may not store, process, or transmit sensitive data securely. The organization may want to control which types of apps can be installed and used on mobile devices, using either MDM or *mobile application management (MAM)* technologies. The company may also want to set up its own app store, rather than allowing users to download apps from a vendor's app store. An admin can push notification services to devices, defining what apps are included.

Application Whitelisting In application whitelisting, the organization allows only certain trusted applications to be installed on mobile devices. The organization may exclude certain applications due to security, interoperability, or even licensing issues. Applications that are acceptable in the organization might include secure e-mail applications, file transfer applications, and productivity applications. Whitelisting allows the organization to include accepted applications in policy configuration files that are sent to and maintained on the mobile device. These policies may prevent a user from downloading and using unapproved apps or from using certain vendor app stores. Often, secure configuration files for these apps are also included for an app when the device is provisioned.

Encryption and Authentication

Using encryption on mobile devices can protect data while it is stored on the device, or during transmission from the device back to the corporate network through untrusted networks, such as the Internet. Mobile devices can make use of encryption in various ways, including encrypting both internal and removable storage, and providing encryption for secure data exchange during file transfer and e-mail, for example. The key point about encryption is that, although most mobile devices support current encryption standards, the different levels of encryption, including algorithm and strength, as well as encryption negotiation methods, must be configured identically on both the device and the end point, such as a server or network device. If the two devices don't have compatible encryption methods configured, neither will be able to send or receive information securely. In some cases, using different encryption methods may prevent them from communicating at all.

Authentication You'll remember from earlier discussions that the first step in the authentication process is for the user to identify herself, either through a user name and password combination or through some other form of multifactor authentication means, such as a smart card and pin, biometric thumbprint, and so on. Once the user has identified herself, the authentication process verifies and validates the user against a database of credentials. The user is authenticated only when the system can confirm that she is, in fact, the user who presented the identification to the system, and no one else.

Mobile devices use the same types of authentication systems and technologies that traditional desktops and server systems use. The catch is that they must be compatible with existing authentication systems, such as user name and passwords (including length and complexity requirements), PIN codes, biometric methods, and digital certificates. MDM concepts and principles require a password or PIN or both. Regardless of the authentication method used, mobile devices must support the different standards and protocols used in an enterprise authentication system. Supporting the authentication process is the process of managing a user's credentials, including user name, password, and even the cryptographic keys associated with digital identities. These topics are covered next.

Credential and Key Management   *Credential management* involves all of the processes and technologies involved with provisioning and maintaining user accounts and credentials. This usually includes account provisioning, creating secure passwords for users, and ensuring that passwords are managed throughout their lifecycle (including password changes, compromise, and so on). Credential management also may involve issuing and managing digital identities, which are commonly associated with digital certificates and cryptographic keys.

Key management refers to the ability of the organization to manage cryptographic keys—the digital certificates and keys that people use to authenticate to corporate systems. The organization could use these digital certificates for e-mail authentication, digital signatures, and encryption, and to ensure data integrity within the organization. Key management involves managing the lifecycle of cryptographic keys from their creation through their destruction, and all of the use that occurs with them in between. An organization must issue digital identities securely to users by confirming their identities, setting them up for the proper usage, installing them on mobile devices, and troubleshooting any issues with them. Between the events of key creation and destruction, cryptographic keys may also be subject to reissue, suspension, revocation, and renewal. All of these processes require that the organization have a stable certificate management process installed, even before the introduction of mobile devices into the business environment. The organization may install digital identities on mobile devices to enable secure access of corporate e-mail and other sensitive resources. Because of the mobile nature of these devices, and the possibility of device loss or theft, it's also very important for the organization to have the processes in place to suspend or revoke cryptographic keys quickly and their associated digital identities if needed.

Context-Aware Authentication   User names, passwords, certificates, and other authentication schemes require tremendous overhead to maintain these security frameworks. But there's a new idea, just recently coming into fruition: context-aware authentication. Context-aware authentication is extra power added to the authenticating tool that enables it to look at the context of the entity authentication. The context may include the user name, the MAC address of the device they're using to connect, what resources they are attempting to access, time of day, even their location. Context-aware authentication software holds the promise of making authentication with mobile devices much easier and more secure.

Enforcement and Monitoring for Device Security

Now that we've talked about a few of the main security goals from a corporate perspective, let's talk about some of the methods for enforcement and monitoring of device-specific security measures that can help ensure that sensitive data is protected. Some of these measures are already included on the device and can be quite effective when used by themselves, and others are effective only when integrated into the corporate MDM infrastructure. All measures are used to protect the device and its data from unauthorized access and loss.

Rooting/Jailbreaking   Every mobile device comes from the factory with root access protected from the user. This is an important aspect of all mobile operating systems, as reserving root access enables the creator of the OS to update software, provide containerization, and impede a number of security vulnerabilities that giving root access would allow. When a user roots an Android system or jailbreaks an iOS system, they are taking root access. Any good MDM software can detect this during onboarding or during ongoing monitoring to let the organization know if this takes place.

One of the main reasons people root/jailbreak their mobile device is to grab applications from third-party app stores that will not work as desired without root access (plenty of third-party apps run on non-rooted or non-jailbroken phones as well). Whether you root/jailbreak or not, third-party app stores are outside the control of Apple and Google and do not provide any security. Figure 7-42 shows one third-party store for Android apps, F-Droid.

Sideloading   The standard Android installation file type is the APK file. Normally, APK files are downloaded automatically from Web stores and installed. However, it is possible to copy an APK file from a thumb drive, an SSD drive, or even across the network or Bluetooth and install the APK file without any interference from a Web store. This is called *sideloading* (Figure 7-43). Sideloading is risky because there are no safeties on the installation media. Aside from agreements with employees not to sideload, there's no foolproof current mechanism to enforce or monitor a prohibition.

Firmware   Every mobile device stores the core operating system on firmware. Like any firmware these days, it is possible to update that firmware, to install *custom firmware*. Normally, we only update firmware when the OS maker has carefully tested the update and then automatically performs the update. However, usually you should not perform firmware updates unless the mobile device has plenty of charge and is connected via USB or Wi-Fi. You should disable the capability to update via cellular, called an *over the air (OTA) update* or *firmware OTA update*. This is usually a simple setting on the device or an MDM policy setting.

It's very common to install custom firmware—called ROM, for read-only memory—on an Android device, especially if it's an older phone that is no longer updated. These custom ROMs are handy but will void warranties and wreak havoc with any installed apps, and thus should never be installed unless there's a very specific reason.

Carrier Unlocking   A carrier may lock a phone so that the phone will only accept SIM chips from that carrier. An unlocked phone can accept a SIM chip from any carrier. For years, unlocking was nearly impossible to accomplish, but today in most countries

Figure 7-42
F-Droid

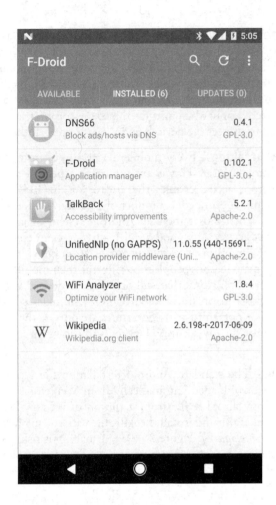

carriers are required by law to unlock a phone when requested. That's great for private users, but an organization may not want users to unlock their phones and perhaps install apps that break corporate security.

Texting/Voice Monitoring   Texting via SMS or MMS is ubiquitous for everyone who uses a phone, but an organization may want to monitor texting to ensure users aren't blowing through their plan limits.

USB OTG   All smart devices connect directly or indirectly to USB. Normally, the device acts as a USB client, enabling a system to connect to a desktop, for example, to transfer a file. Almost all Android phones also have *USB On-the-Go (OTG)*. USB OTG–capable devices automatically turn into hosts when plugged into USB client devices like thumb drives or even mice. You can turn off USB OTG to prevent users from copying data off their system just by plugging in a thumb drive (Figure 7-44).

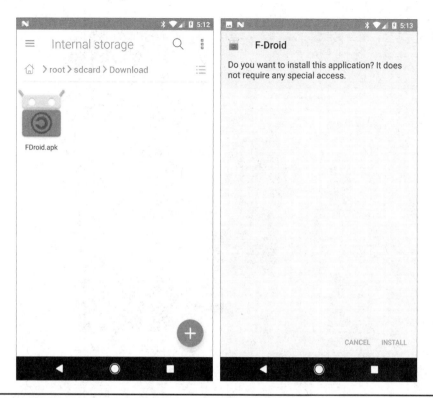

Figure 7-43   Two screens from sideloading F-Droid app

Wi-Fi Direct/Ad Hoc   In most cases, mobile devices use Wi-Fi by connecting to a WAP broadcasting an SSID, just like a portable computer. This is known as *infrastructure mode*; all the traffic goes through the WAP, even if your device communicates to another device on the same SSID. With *Wi-Fi Direct*, enabled devices can connect directly to each other if in range, much like Bluetooth devices can pair. There's generally a PIN code to share and the devices automatically negotiate to see which one will be the soft access point, or soft AP. Wi-Fi Direct is available on most Android devices, but not Apple products as of this writing.

Another traditional method for connecting wireless devices is *ad hoc mode*, where devices connect in a mesh network as a group of peers. There's no WAP involved.

Finally, *mobile ad hoc networks (MANETs)* are a form of wireless ad hoc mode, used for on-the-fly communication. Every mobile device becomes a router, moving traffic to other stations near by. You can find MANETs in use in many applications, such as mobile military communications, vehicular networks, and more, where there is need for connection that requires no radio or cellular tower. MANETs are just off the CompTIA radar for the current Security+ exam, but expect to interact with them a lot in an IT security career going forward.

Figure 7-44
USB OTG

Tethering/Mobile Hotspot All mobile operating system have the tethering feature. *Tethering* means to have a mobile device sharing its cellular connection with another system via USB. *Mobile hotspot* is the ability for a mobile device to share its cellular connection as a WAP via Wi-Fi. There are handy features, but they can be expensive to use and expose a system to bad actors. Turning off these features is a common security control.

Payment Methods Digital wallet payment systems continue to gain adoption. As of late 2017/early 2018, there are several well-funded digital wallet offerings, including Android Pay, Apple Pay, and PayPal. If an organization authorizes a specific payment method, the organization should obviously monitor usage of that service.

Screen Lock and Device Lockout A screen lock enables a user to lock access manually to the device from anyone, unless the person inputs the correct passcode or pin. While the screen lock is engaged, the device may have only very limited functions, including the ability to make an emergency phone call or advance tracks if some sort of media file is playing on the device. In any event, more advanced operations and data access are prevented while the screen lock is engaged. In addition to being manually engaged by the user, screens can be configured to be locked after a certain amount of inactivity on the device—3 minutes, for example. This prevents unauthorized access to the device if the user lays it down or someone grabs it while the user is still logged in.

Device lockout occurs when the device prevents someone from accessing it because the person has incorrectly entered the password or pin too many times. If this is a valid user, and he has simply forgotten his passcode, lockout features can take different actions. First, the user might simply be locked out of the device for a specified period of time, giving him enough time to contact the company and either obtain the correct passcode or have an administrator remotely unlock the device. Lockouts can also be more drastic, such as wiping the device after a certain amount of incorrect passcode entries. More advanced features may include having a device remotely contact the administrator if it has been locked out.

Full Device Encryption Full device encryption protects all the data on a mobile device. With this security feature, the storage device itself, such as the device's internal hard drive, is fully encrypted and can't be used unless it's decrypted when the device is powered up. In some cases, you could set full device encryption to require a passcode or passphrase on startup, before the user even logs on. In other cases, you could also make sure that the device storage can't be accessed periodically, even while it's on, without the user reauthenticating occasionally.

GPS Services All mobile devices have certain built-in technologies and functions to help determine their precise location and provide location-based services to the users. The most common technology is GPS. Today, GPS receivers are built into almost every mobile device. In addition to typical user services, such as finding the nearest restaurant or gas station, location-based services using GPS can assist network administrators in managing mobile devices in the enterprise in several different ways. First, they can use GPS to help maintain an accurate location fix on the device. This might be necessary if the organization wants to ensure that devices are used only in certain areas or tracked by location. These same services can also be used to help the network administrator maintain a fix on the device if it gets lost or stolen. Another use of GPS and location-based services is to ensure that the device remains on company property, a practice called *geofencing*. Geofencing ensures that a mobile device stays within a preset perimeter established by the administrator, using MDM software. If the device leaves the company property or gets beyond this perimeter, it will send an alert to the administrator. In addition to GPS, mobile devices can also use Wi-Fi networks to ascertain their location information, although this isn't as accurate.

External Media Most mobile devices made today can accept different types of removable media, such as Secure Digital (SD) cards or their smaller counterparts, mini- and micro-SD cards. These external media cards are used to store additional data to help prevent using up all of the device's primary storage. In the enterprise, removable storage media can be used in different ways. First, through MDM policy, removable storage media could be used to store all of the user's personal data, versus corporate data. This way, when the device is returned to the network administrator, all she has to do is remove the SD card that contains the personal data. A business can also do the exact opposite and allow only corporate data to be stored on the removable media. That way, when the device leaves the company property, the removable media could be stored on site, reducing the risk of data loss when the device is out of the company's physical control. In either situation, data could be encrypted on the removable media, so that if it's removed from the device, it can't be accessed.

Disabling Unused Features   From your experience in securing user desktops in the organization, you probably already know that one of the best security practices you can use is to disable any unused features, services, ports, protocols, and so on, because doing so reduces the computer's attack surface. For example, if the user is only typing e-mails, surfing the Web, and so forth, he probably has no need for applications or services on the box that might allow him to perform administrative actions on the network. Likewise, the server running the company's Web page probably doesn't need to have e-mail services running on it. In any case, the same is true with mobile devices.

Depending largely on what the business's security policy states, users may not need to have certain services running on their mobile devices. They also may not need to use some of the native apps that come on some mobile devices, such as smartphones. This might include third-party or free e-mail programs, chat programs, games, and so on. Through MDM policy, as well as MAM, you can limit what applications and services a user can access and use on a mobile device. Of course, this may not make you very popular with the employees in the company, but it will go a long way toward helping to secure mobile devices that connect to your network.

Onboard Camera and Video Concerns   The use of onboard cameras and video is another interesting security issue in the corporate environment. Since almost all mobile devices have some sort of built-in camera or video recorder, this can be an issue in the corporate environment with regard to using the device in sensitive areas or processing sensitive corporate information on the device. It can also be a privacy issue, in that people have the right to choose whether to be photographed or filmed in certain settings. With smartphone video capabilities being fairly ubiquitous, many employees, especially in sensitive areas, would not want to find that they are now the subject of a viral YouTube video, for example! Obviously, the company would probably not want this as well. In some highly sensitive data processing areas, companies prohibit cameras of any type, meaning that smartphones, tablets, or other items the user might normally use to process company data on would have to be excluded from the areas in question.

The use of cameras and video recorders of any type, including those on mobile devices, should be addressed in security policies, to set rules on where and how they may be used, or even banning their use in certain areas and situations. The policy may simply require that they be turned off within the company property or certain secure areas, or it may prohibit mobile devices with cameras from being brought into certain areas at all. Policy may also further state that any employee taking unauthorized pictures or videos of any persons or areas may be subject to having their device confiscated and their video or pictures deleted from the device.

Audio Recordings   Mobile devices have *recording microphones* as well as video options, so enforcement and monitoring options must take these into consideration as well. A device in a pocket or pack can capture conversations that could do damage to an organization.

Module 7-8: Physical Security

This module covers the following CompTIA Security+ objective:

- **3.9**   Explain the importance of physical security controls

Perimeter and physical security is not normally a concern of IT security professionals. If it doesn't involve bits and bytes, packets, and encryption, then we don't usually have much to do with it. Physical security is important, because it not only helps protect our data, systems, and networks, but it also provides for personnel safety. As an information security professional, you need to be aware of how perimeter and physical controls are used to protect your systems and people. In this module, we'll look at perimeter and physical controls from both the safety and protection standpoints. First, though, we're going to look at the different types of security controls in general and discuss the control types and their functionalities, so you can get a better idea of how controls work.

Classifying Controls

You probably already know that a security control is a measure or mitigation put in place to prevent something bad from happening or to increase security in a system or facility. If you go back and look at earlier modules in the book that discuss risk and terms associated with threats and vulnerabilities, you will remember that controls are essentially put into place to minimize risk and to reduce the likelihood of a threat exploiting a vulnerability or the impact to a system if it does occur. It's important that you understand how security controls are categorized. Security controls can be sliced and diced in several different ways, and for the exam, you need to know how to classify controls in terms of types as well as their functions. In the next two sections, we'll examine the different control types as well as what functions these controls serve.

Control Types

Different books and security professionals refer to the basic control types using different terms. You need to be aware of three basic control types, how they are classified, and the various names used to refer to them. *Administrative controls* are also frequently called *managerial controls*. These controls are associated with the paperwork and program management aspects of security, such as policies and procedures, personnel policies, acceptable use policies, and so on. Administrative (managerial) controls form the basis of the other types of controls, because policies drive everything we do in security.

The second type of control is the *technical* or *logical control*. You'll hear either term used in different texts and by different security professionals. Technical or logical controls are basically the computer-based measures that you might encounter in everyday hands-on security, such as firewalls, encryption technologies, access control lists on routers, secure protocols, and so on.

The third type of control is known as either *physical* or *operational controls*. You'll see some distinction between these actual controls, however, in that physical controls are typically lumped with environmental controls, and operational controls may be sometimes lumped in with administrative controls. Physical controls are associated with safety, environmental factors such as temperature and humidity, gates, guards, firearms, security cameras, and so on. Operational controls can be thought of as the actual operational procedures used for particular physical security processes. For example, requiring a visitor to sign in before entering a restricted area such as a data center may be considered an operational control. Again, you'll hear these two terms used interchangeably.

Figure 7-45 illustrates the differences between administrative, technical, and physical control types.

Control Functions

Control functions focus on a certain aspect of security, such as deterrence, detection, and so on. It would be nice if the different control types (administrative, technical, and physical) all fell neatly into these different control functions, but, unfortunately, they don't. Some administrative controls, for example, might be considered deterrent controls (an acceptable use policy, for example), while others might be considered preventative controls (think background checks on employees).

If that weren't bad enough, it's also possible that the different individual controls may be considered to fill more than one function. For instance, the acceptable use policy could be a deterrent, in that it deters people from performing actions that are prohibited by the organization. Of course, it won't deter everyone; some people will still violate this policy. However, part of this acceptable use policy should also state what the consequences are if the policy is violated. This part of the policy might be considered corrective in nature.

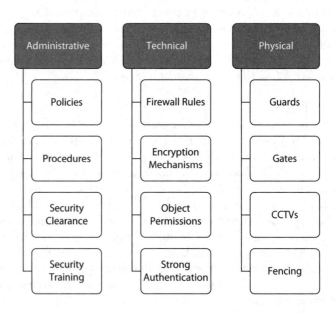

Figure 7-45
Administrative, technical, and physical control types

Administrative	Technical	Physical
Policies	Firewall Rules	Guards
Procedures	Encryption Mechanisms	Gates
Security Clearance	Object Permissions	CCTVs
Security Training	Strong Authentication	Fencing

So it can be confusing, and a little bit difficult, to classify controls precisely in terms of one distinct function or another. Adding to the confusion is that this is all very subjective. What one security professional may consider a preventative control, another may consider corrective, detective, or compensating. It really depends upon the context of how the control is used. In any case, let's briefly discuss each of the different control functions you are likely to see on the exam and in the real world.

Deterrent   A *deterrent control* tries to deter people from committing security violations or from performing actions that are inherently not secure. An example of a deterrent control is the acceptable use policy or closed-circuit television (CCTV) cameras placed conspicuously in different areas of facility. These controls would deter someone from committing a security violation or a prohibited act, simply because they may be afraid of getting caught or suffering the consequences of those acts. Deterrent controls are usually effective because the users *know* they exist; if users have no idea that a control exists, and that there are consequences for violating it, then it doesn't do much to deter them. That's actually the distinguishing factor between a deterrent control and a preventative control.

Preventative   A *preventative control* doesn't have to be visible or known to the user in order to prevent a security issue from happening. Although the value of a deterrent control is that users are aware of it and know there will be consequences if they violate it, a preventative control does its job regardless of whether the users know about it or not. For example, a preventative control might be a rule in the firewall designed to filter out the port and protocol that a certain type of malware uses. It prevents this malware from coming into the network, but users don't necessarily have to be aware of it for it to be effective. Another example, this time using a physical control, may be an electronic locking system at the entrance to a secure area. It prevents unauthorized users from entering the area; they don't have to be aware of it for it to be effective.

Detective   A *detective control* tries to detect and alert security personnel if a violation has occurred or if a non-secure condition exists. For example, a detective control can be an intrusion detection system (IDS) alert that notifies an administrator if the network starts to receive massive amounts of malformed packets from the Internet. The IDS will detect this condition and alert the administrator, and it could also take preventative or corrective actions. In this case, the technical control in use could be considered a detective control, a preventative control, and even a corrective control, all at the same time. Another detective control might be the security event logs on a Windows server that record all security-relevant events that occur on the host. While reviewing these event logs might be a manual task, if a security incident is uncovered during the review, this makes it a detective control. Physical security controls can also be detective in nature; a motion sensor that alerts when someone unauthorized enters a restricted area is a detective control.

Compensating   Compensating controls can be difficult to understand, simply because most controls could be compensating in some way or another for different weaknesses. A *compensating control* is really a control you might use to make up for a *temporary* shortfall or weakness in the system or facility, in case another control you already have in place fails or is temporarily not working properly. The temporary nature of a compensating control is what classifies it as a compensating control and not one of the other control functionalities. If the control will be replaced or made permanent, then it's simply reclassified as one of the other control functionalities. As an example, suppose someone cut a large hole in a perimeter fence while trying to break into a facility. Until the fence can be repaired, there's a gaping hole there that someone could still try to use for unauthorized entry. Until it's repaired, you might deploy extra guards to that area or put up some other type of barrier to prevent someone from going through the hole in the fence. The damaged portion of the fence will eventually be repaired, and that might be the more permanent control action. In the meantime, however, the extra guard or temporary barrier would be considered compensating controls.

Corrective   A *corrective control* is also difficult to understand, simply because this type of control is normally considered one of the other control functionalities (that is, deterrent, detective, and so on). In the example with the IDS, after detecting an anomalous bit of network traffic and alerting an administrator, the IDS might automatically block traffic coming from a particular source IP address or domain, or even drop traffic matching a particular protocol to stop the attack. This would be considered a corrective control, simply because it corrects a security issue that was otherwise not being mitigated at the time. If a rule is later entered into the IDS to make this corrective action permanent, then it might not be considered a corrective control any longer; it might be classified as a preventative control.

Recovery   A *recovery control* is used to recover from an incident or security issue. What distinguishes this from a corrective or compensating control is that it's used to restore operations back to a normal state. For example, suppose the hard drive in a server fails and it must be restored from backup data. Restoring the backup will be the recovery control implemented to bring the server back to an operational state. As with all the other control functionalities mentioned, controls could be classified as recovery, preventative, or other control functionalities at the same time as well. The same backup can also be viewed as a preventative control in different circumstances, since it prevented data from being lost.

Now that I've thoroughly confused you with a discussion of control types and functionalities, and how they overlap a great deal, understand that for the exam you will likely be able to tell by context what type of control a question is asking about, as well as a particular functionality. Keep in mind, however, that the classification of control types and their control functions can be quite subjective. Table 7-1 lists the different control functionalities and some possible controls that may fall into the category.

Physical Controls

Physical controls complement administrative and technical controls by controlling physical access to information systems and areas, and to protect the people who work in the facility housing the systems in those areas. Physical access controls help protect systems and people from threats such as theft, intruders, and unauthorized access. Physical controls have both security and safety considerations.

Control Functionality	Examples	Control Type(s)
Deterrent	Fences, guards, CCTVs, system warning banners	Physical, technical
Preventative	Firewall rules, IPS, file permissions	Technical
Detective	Audit logs, IDS, recorded video, alarm systems	Technical, physical
Compensating	Extra guards	Physical
Corrective	Network traffic shunting, personnel suspension or termination	Technical, administrative
Recovery	Data backups, spare equipment, alternate processing facility	Technical, physical

Table 7-1   Control Functionalities with Examples

Perimeter and Safety Controls

Perimeter controls surround a facility or a sensitive area to prevent unauthorized personnel from entering those areas. They also protect the authorized people who are allowed to enter those areas. Perimeter controls have both a security value and a safety value, and in the next few sections, we'll discuss both of those aspects.

Perimeter controls are the first line of defense at a facility. They protect the facility, its personnel, and its equipment from a variety of threats, such as theft, physical harm, natural disasters, or even terrorist attacks. Perimeter controls usually include the standard gates, guards, and other physical security measures. You might wonder whether a particular control should be classified as a physical perimeter control or a safety control; the classification depends on whether the control is used primarily to ensure the safety of personnel or to provide for protection against security problems or threats that may target asset vulnerabilities. The answer is subjective, because some controls may fall under both categories.

Fencing   *Fencing* is the first big physical deterrent most facilities use to keep unwanted and unauthorized visitors out. Fencing is often used at facilities that require higher security than a simple lock on the door. Fencing can be intimidating to would-be trespassers or attackers, particularly tall fencing with barbed wire strung across the top. Fencing can be very expensive, but it serves several purposes.

First, fencing establishes specific entry and exit points around the facility. It establishes an area between outer entry and inner entry points, creating a buffer zone of sorts, to provide distance between the facility entrance and the public area. A well-lit buffer zone makes it more difficult for a trespasser or thief to get from the fence to the facility without being seen. Second, a fence can artificially create those entry points in specific areas around the facility. In other words, someone can't simply walk up to the side of the building and try to enter through a window; they first must pass through a central entry gate to get in. When the fence is built, the entry gate can be placed wherever it makes sense for more easily controlled access; it doesn't necessarily have to be at the front door of the building.

Figure 7-46
A high-security
fence

When planning facility security, you should consider several characteristics of fencing. The first is height. Depending upon the desired security level, a short fence (about 4 feet) might be okay to keep out the general public and curious trespassers. Higher fencing, possibly 7 or 8 feet high, is used to deter even very athletic and determined people from getting in. Barbed wire strung across the top of the fence provides a little extra incentive for people to decide that breaking into your facility is not worth the trouble. Fencing should be in good repair, not rusty, firmly in place in the ground to prevent someone from digging under it, and secured with concrete whenever possible.

Another consideration is the fence's wire gauge. The gauge of the wires that make chain-link fence, for example, is important to fence strength. Fences come in various wire gauges, but a good gauge for secure fencing is 11, 9, or 6 gauge. Six gauge is the thickest fencing wire and provides the strongest fence. Gauge size directly affects how easily an intruder may cut through the fence. Mesh size is also a characteristic to consider. Mesh size refers to the size of the holes between the wire mesh. Smaller mesh sizes are much better for security than larger mesh sizes, because the smaller holes make it more difficult to climb the fence. Figure 7-46 shows an example of a high-security fence.

Signage   *Signage* is very important as a deterrent mechanism in and around the facility. Signage can also contribute to the safety of personnel. *Signs* can warn intruders away from restricted areas and instruct authorized personnel to the proper security and safety procedures. Signs can direct personnel during an evacuation to the correct exit points, warn personnel about potential safety hazards in the facility, or help them find proper safety or fire suppression equipment. In short, the value of signs cannot be understated, because they may be required to help deter unauthorized activities or intruders but

Figure 7-47
Signage that
protects people
and equipment

can also help protect the safety of the people who work in the facility. In some cases, signage throughout a facility may be required by laws or safety regulations to prevent the organization from being involved in liability issues.

Signs should follow national and international standards for symbols and colors, especially those that mark hazardous conditions. New employees should be briefed regarding the signs, as periodically all employees should be updated. Signs should be placed in well-lit areas and not obstructed by large objects. Figure 7-47 shows how a well-placed sign can help protect both personnel and equipment from unauthorized access and harm.

Lighting   *Lighting* is another critical aspect of perimeter security. During evening or dark hours, lighting can help ensure that trespassers, attackers, and thieves are deterred from venturing out into open areas when trying to approach a facility or harm its personnel. Lighting can be placed at various points along the perimeter fence, at least at distances that allow the outer edges of the areas of light projected from poles to overlap with each other (usually no more than about 20 or 25 feet for tall poles, or about 8 to 10 feet for smaller ones). Lighting should also be placed at gates, door entrances, along sidewalks, and in foyers or entryways. Emergency lighting should be in place throughout a facility in the event of a power outage.

Some lights may be controlled differently than others, depending upon their location and security needs. For example, fence perimeter lighting may be programmed with a timer to come on at certain hours only, such as from dusk till dawn. Such fencing is naturally lit by daylight during daytime hours, and fencing is usually placed in easy-to-see areas. Other types of lighting make use of motion sensors that turn lights on only when someone approaches an area. Still other types of lighting may be lit when an alarm or IDS is triggered.

Locks   *Locks* are physical security controls that can help keep unauthorized persons from entering doorways, secure areas, and perimeters. Depending on where the locks are placed and what other security measures are in place, locks can be simple and inexpensive or very complex. Although most locks can keep casual intruders out, they really serve only to delay a determined intruder for a certain amount of time and rely on multiple other physical controls to assist in keeping an intruder out. Delay factor is sometimes a consideration in choosing a lock for a particular use.

Among the different *lock types* are hardware (or mechanical) locks and electronic locks. Most hardware locks use ordinary keys and can be purchased from a hardware store. Combination locks, which require a numerical combination or pin code to unlock them, and locks built into the door or other type of entrance (such as a gate, vault, or *safe*) are also popular hardware locks. Each has advantages and disadvantages, depending on the level of security you require. Each also has different variations. Ordinary padlocks, referred to as *warded locks*, may appear to be strong, but they can easily be cut or picked. Physical locks, called *device locks*, are used to lock down items that are easily stolen, such as laptops. Some mobile devices have a special slot to facilitate this type of lock.

Electronic locks are more sophisticated and may use various protection mechanisms. Usually, an electronic lock uses a PIN code and may be known as a *cipher lock*. Electronic locks usually have their mechanisms protected by metal containers or embedded into walls. They may be programmable, offering configurable options, such as the ability to program in separate PINs for different people, a lockout threshold for the number of incorrect PIN entries, a lockout delay, and so on. They also may be tied to other security measures, such as smart card and biometric mechanisms.

Security Guards   *Security guards* are the quintessential picture of physical security controls. Most facilities that have any type of physical security have guards, and despite all of the new advances in technologies that might one day eliminate them, human guards will likely be a cornerstone of facility security for years to come. Guards offer several advantages over electronic physical controls. First, guards are human beings and can make the split-second decisions that are sometimes needed in fast-moving security, safety, or emergency events. Second, a well-trained guard force can provide vast, intelligent coverage of all physical security areas within a facility. If guards have solid, comprehensive security procedures they execute on a timely basis, they can help eliminate the huge majority of physical security problems. Guards are required to be conscientious, observant, well-trained, and even a little bit suspicious and paranoid to do their jobs well.

The disadvantages of using guards don't outweigh the advantages, but you should be aware of them all the same. First, guards require resources, such as specialized equipment, training, and even monetary resources (whether contracted out or as part of the organization's own internal security force). Maintaining a guard force can be quite expensive and has challenges that are typical to maintaining human resources, such as pay, benefits, disciplinary problems, promotions, and so forth. Guards are human beings, like any other employee, and some have the same weaknesses that any other employee would have, regardless of specialized security training. Human beings miss things sometimes, they aren't always as observant as you would like, and sometimes they can fail to follow security procedures to the level you need. They can also be subject to social engineering attacks (discussed in a later module). All-in-all, however, guards provide an effective set of security controls that are considered deterrent, preventative, detective, corrective, compensating, and recovery, all at the same time. They can also be assisted by other types of physical security controls, including alarms, surveillance devices, and other IDSs.

Video Surveillance and CCTVs   *Closed-circuit television systems (CCTVs)* can be placed throughout a facility. CCTVs use cameras to record surveillance video and transmit it to a central monitoring station, which enables guards to extend their view of the facility. CCTV systems detect and watch intruders in areas where guards can't be all the time. Some considerations with CCTV devices include whether the device will be used indoors or outdoors. Outdoor environmental factors such as temperature, wind, rain, and so on can affect how well certain CCTV devices work outside. The size of the area under CCTV surveillance is also a consideration, in that the field of view (how large an area the camera can "see") for different CCTV systems varies. The amount of light in an area is also a consideration when you install CCTVs in an area, since more light provides a better picture of the area. Some CCTV systems are specifically designed for use in poorly lit or dark areas.

CCTV systems should be integrated with other physical security systems, such as alarms, motion detectors, and so on, and should be directly integrated with the central monitoring console used by the physical security personnel. They should also allow you not only to view areas in real-time, but to record events to media for later review. Systems should also date and timestamp those recordings so that a realistic timeframe of events can be reconstructed if needed.

There is some speculation as to which is better—a human guard or a video surveillance system. Human guards can make quick decisions and perform a wide variety of security functions, but they can't be everywhere at once and they can miss things. Additionally, a guard's memory may or may not be reliable when trying to determine exactly what happened during an incident. Video surveillance systems, on the other hand, can be placed wherever you need them, can provide real-time surveillance of areas, and can record video for later playback and review. Any speculation over which to use isn't really worthwhile, though; a good layered physical security system should use both guards and video surveillance systems to provide comprehensive coverage of a facility. Video surveillance systems can be used to extend the eyes and ears of guards into places where they can't be all the time. Guards can quickly be dispatched to any areas that video surveillance picks up any potential security issues and can effectively mitigate those issues. Guards and video surveillance systems complement each other and should be used together. Facilities security managers shouldn't need to make the choice between guards or video surveillance because of budget or resource restrictions; they should simply use both.

Mantraps   *Mantraps* guide and control individuals physically as they enter or exit a facility. A mantrap is a small room or compartment, with two doors that are individually locked, usually electronically. One individual at a time enters the mantrap, and the entry door is locked. There's usually some type of authentication station in the room, or even a one-way glass window so that a guard can observe the individual and confirm his or her identity, or ensure that the visitor doesn't possess any unauthorized weapons or items. The individual may have to use biometrics or a smart card and PIN to authenticate themselves at the station. If the individual is properly authenticated,

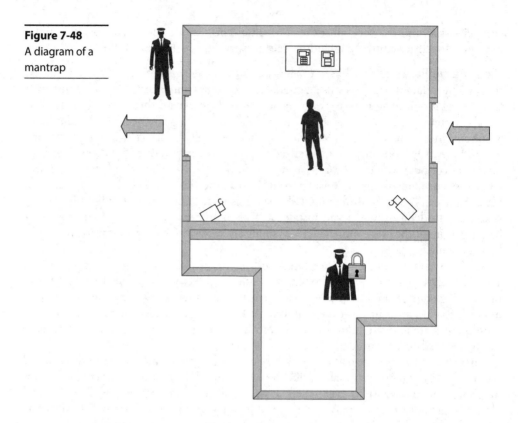

Figure 7-48
A diagram of a mantrap

the exit doors open and allow the person to enter into the secure area. If the individual is not authenticated, or the guard suspects an issue with the person, he or she can be detained in the mantrap until the proper authorities or security personnel can be summoned to help secure the person. Mantraps are normally used in highly secure facilities when positive authentication of personnel is of critical importance. Mantraps also are used to control tailgating and piggybacking, making them virtually impossible. Mantraps may also use additional security features, such as video cameras, body scanners, metal detectors, and even scales to compare weights when a person enters and exits a facility. This last measure might be employed to ensure that individuals are not stealing items from the facility on exit. Figure 7-48 shows a diagram of a mantrap.

Access List   You've already read that access lists can be used to determine who has access to a particular piece of data, information system, or shared resource on a network. An access list can also be used in the physical security world to determine who can access a particular sensitive area, whether they require an escort or not, and if they are allowed to escort others into an area. An access list can be a typewritten list posted at the entrance door to a sensitive area, showing a list of names of people who are authorized to enter the area, or it can be an electronic access list integrated into a facility's physical security system. If a person's name is entered into the system, their access badge will allow them to enter the sensitive area. If it's not entered into the system, they might be denied access or a guard or a manager may be alerted that an individual who is not on the list is trying to enter a secure area.

Biometrics We've already discussed biometrics extensively throughout the book, but more from a technical or logical control perspective than from a physical security perspective. Biometrics can also be used to control physical access to facilities in secure areas. In addition to smart cards and PINs, biometrics can be used to provide for multifactor authentication that may be required for entrance into a secure area. Examples of biometric methods used for secure entry into a facility include thumbprint scans, palm scans, retinal or iris scans, and voiceprint recognition. Since each of these methods uniquely identifies an individual, combined with another factor, such as a passphrase or PIN, they can provide for secure access and entry into sensitive areas.

Proximity Readers A *proximity reader* device is used to help authenticate personnel entering or exiting a facility. The person places a smart card or other access device near the sensor so it can be read via RFID or another passive wireless technology. The reader receives information from the card regarding the individual's identity. The individual may further authenticate by using a PIN or biometric methods, such as a thumbprint scan, retinal scan, or voiceprint. In addition to proximity readers, full contact readers are also available for a facility to use. These readers require that a smart card or other device actually touch the reader or be swiped into the reader a certain way so that it can read a barcode or other type of coding on the card. Full contact readers normally don't require any kind of passive wireless radio signals. For more efficient and economic use, the same smart cards used to authenticate people physically can also be used to authenticate individuals to information systems, enabling a sort of one-stop physical single sign-on capability. Figure 7-49 shows an example of a proximity badge reader.

Barricades *Barricades* are physical security devices that can block unauthorized personnel from entering an area. Barricades are often used in the area surrounding a

Figure 7-49
A proximity
badge reader

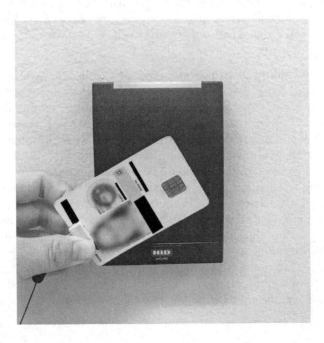

Figure 7-50
Common
bollards

facility to keep vehicles from getting too close to a building, for example. They can also be used inside a facility to control the flow of people through secure areas.

Barricades can be made out of various materials, including concrete and metal. They are usually constructed to delay a determined intruder long enough for security and other response personnel to neutralize any threats posed by the intruder. *Bollards* are examples of barricades that might be placed outside of a facility around drive-through areas, parking lots, and even sidewalks. Figure 7-50 shows an example of bollards.

Lock Down A lot of data centers use physical security devices around servers and other computing equipment. Some have *cages* that enclose the server area and require *keys*, *tokens*, or *cards* to access the area. Others use *secure cabinets* or *enclosures* to protect servers from physical access. These devices stop malicious—or clueless—people from disrupting important systems.

Protected Cabling Distribution Physical security also involves protecting equipment and systems, but it wouldn't be very effective if the cables that connected the systems were damaged or cut. The systems wouldn't be able to communicate, rendering them as ineffective as if someone had destroyed or damaged them. Protecting physical cabling is as much about facility design as anything else. The facility should be designed so that physical cabling is run outside of normal traffic areas, through ducts in the walls or ceiling. Their end connection points should be physically protected from unauthorized access, by placing termination points such as switches in locked closets, and protecting end-user device connection points in offices and other rooms from unauthorized access. In addition to physical security design, protecting cabling involves other possible measures, including using shielded cabling to prevent eavesdropping (or using fiber cable); configuring systems to send alarms when a connection is lost, possibly indicating a cut or damaged cable; and even using technical or logical controls that prevent unauthorized devices from connecting to end-user cable connection points, such as network outlets, by controlling port access.

Alarms and Intrusion Detection Systems   Physical *alarm systems* and *intrusion detection systems* are a must in any physical security program. Alarm systems can be loud and obnoxious, such as fire or tornado alarms, but they can also be silent alarms that sound or activate only at a guard station. Silent alarms alert security personnel without alerting an intruder that he or she has been discovered, giving security personnel time to reach and subdue the intruder. Alarm systems can be activated by any number of factors, including manually by personnel, by opening alarmed doors, and even by motion sensors in an area.

Motion detection involves sensing the presence of a person in an area using different types of sensors. Motion sensors might use invisible light beams that are emitted from photoelectric sensors in a room; breaking the light beams would trigger the alarm. The beams could be lasers or *infrared detection* devices. Or the sensor could monitor environmental factors such as temperature, humidity, and air pressure, so that an individual entering that area would change those factors and cause the temperature to rise a few degrees or the air pressure or flow to change slightly. These almost imperceptible changes to the environment might indicate unauthorized personnel in the area and trigger an alarm. Yet another type of motion sensor are plates in the floor that detect weights or pressure on the plates; individuals stepping on one of these plates would trigger an alarm. Keep in mind that motion sensors and some other advanced types of physical intrusion detection systems are typically used only in highly secure areas, although commercial and private grade motion sensors can be used in small businesses and homes.

Escape Plans and Routes   *Escape plans* directly affect personnel safety. In addition to the standard plans that are required for fire evacuation and other disasters, escape plans should also be provided in the event of human-based threats, such as terrorist attacks, active shooters, thieves, or other types of intruders. All escape plans basically include the same requirements: they should show all the possible exits from a facility, provide for facility-wide notification in the event of an emergency that requires evacuation, and provide for orderly exit of all personnel, including accounting for everyone in the facility so that no one accidentally gets left behind. Escape plans should be written with personnel safety as the top priority; they should not normally include provisions for shutting down equipment, backing up data, and so forth. Although those areas are important in the event of a disaster, saving human life and preventing injury must come first, before worrying about data or equipment. The time to worry about backing up data occurs well before a disaster strikes.

Escape routes are of critical importance during an emergency or other disaster, simply because all the personnel working in the facility need to know how to get out in the event of a fire or another type of incident. If this hasn't been planned for in advance, confusion and mayhem may result in someone getting hurt or not being able to get out of the facility safely. Most local laws and regulations stipulate that escape routes be established, briefed to personnel, and posted throughout a facility so they can be referenced in the event of an emergency. Escape routes should provide for the safest, quickest, and most efficient way out of the building, and they should never be blocked by any obstacle or be made difficult to access. Building alarms and electronic locks should be configured to trigger in the event of a disaster so that alarms sound loudly to alert people to an incident, and so that electronic locks do not fail open so that people can use otherwise secured doors to get out of a building. Figure 7-51 shows a posted escape route for a facility.

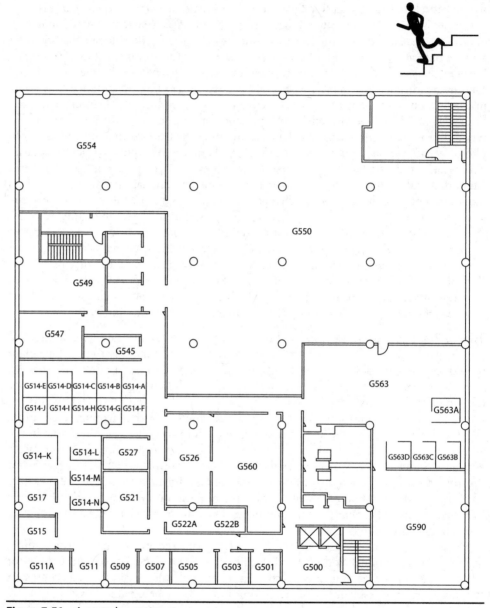

Figure 7-51 A posted escape route

Testing Controls and Drills   Security personnel should test perimeter controls periodically to ensure their effectiveness. Testing involves exercises and drills that are conducted on a frequent basis to make sure that the controls work properly. It does no good to have a secure entryway if you're not sure it'll work in the event someone actually tries to break into it. Physical security testing should be conducted against the facility by authorized personnel who are trained on those types of tests. Guards should be tested for following their procedures and being able to react quickly and efficiently to physical security threats. Security personnel should also test automated and electronic alarms and physical security systems to make sure they work properly and will actually detect and alert a real threat. While some tests should be preplanned and scheduled regularly, some of these tests should be conducted on a no-notice basis, so that people have to remember what to do and react quickly in the event of a physical security threat. Although tests can be inconvenient and sometimes disrupt operations, they're a necessary evil to make sure that physical security controls work the way they're supposed to.

Drills are a form of testing in which incident and disaster response procedures are tested to ensure that everyone knows what to do and that the procedures function effectively. A drill can be a fire drill, a tornado drill, or even an active shooter drill where everyone practices what to do in the event a disgruntled employee or someone from outside a facility intrudes with the intent of perpetrating acts of violence on people or facilities. Drills should be carefully planned out and executed frequently, sometimes with no notice, so that facility managers are able to determine if everyone knows what to do when unexpected emergencies occur. Like other types of disaster response testing, drills should be monitored for compliance with procedures, as well as for those instances where procedures don't work the way they should. Drills can tell you whether the right procedures are in place, whether everyone knows what to do, and whether the right supplies and equipment are in place to evacuate everyone from the facility quickly and efficiently. They can point to training deficiencies and help you improve your emergency procedures.

Module 7-9: Environmental Controls

This module covers the following CompTIA Security+ objective:

- **3.9**   Explain the importance of physical security controls

Environmental security is not one of those things that IT professionals typically think about; it's one of those things that the facility folks usually take care of, right? Au contraire! As a security professional, the environment that your systems are housed in affects their security in at least one very important way: availability. Remember earlier in the book where we discussed the CIA triad, which consists of confidentiality, integrity, and availability? Availability is one of the key concerns for security professionals, and both environmental security and physical security directly affect system availability for your users.

This module explores modifying and managing interference, fire suppression, HVAC controls (including temperature and humidity), hot and cold aisles, as well as environmental monitoring. You need to know how these things affect the availability of systems, both for the exam and, more importantly, as an IT security professional.

EMI and RFI Shielding

Electromagnetic interference (EMI) and *radio-frequency interference (RFI)* are two types of electrical interference that can cause issues with the electrical power that flows into your systems. Either can result from power entering your facility or supplying your systems that is not considered "clean" power. In other words, it's incoming power that has electrical interference and voltage fluctuations (sometimes referred to as *line noise*). These two types of interference can cause issues with power that could affect your systems, causing them occasionally to freeze, reboot arbitrarily, or do other weird things.

EMI can be created by all kinds of sources, including lightning, electrical motors or generators, and even fluorescent lighting that's been installed too close to power or data cables. An organization that is planning to move into a new or renovated building can address some of these issues in advance with good facility design, but you don't always get that luxury if you've moved into an existing facility that has these problems. And even if you can spend a lot of money, you can't always tear apart walls or ceilings and rip out and rerun cabling, any more than you can control the type of power the power company supplies to your facility. However, there are some things you can do to help prevent and minimize EMI.

The first preventative measure is to use specially shielded Ethernet cable (Figure 7-52) that can prevent outside interference from causing line noise. This type of cable reduces the amount of EMI in both data and power cabling. It can allow cleaner data transmissions, as well as cleaner power, to get to your systems. The second thing you can do is to use power conditioners, uninterruptible power supplies (UPSs), and other devices that clean up power before it gets to your systems, ensuring that a consistent and constant source of clean power is delivered to your computer equipment. These special devices are also known as *voltage regulators* or *line conditioners*. Most modern data centers have this type of equipment, as well as robust power cabling and construction, so that they can deliver clean power to equipment.

Figure 7-52
Shielded
Ethernet cable

EXAM TIP   Better data centers offer *Faraday cages* for sensitive equipment, which are devices that prevent RFI, EMI, or EMP from damaging contents stored. Faraday cages are named for the English scientist—Michael Faraday—who created them way back in the 19th century.

Fire Suppression

Fire is a serious issue that can affect the safety of personnel as well as that of equipment and facilities. To protect against fires, you first should know how to prevent them, then how to detect them, and finally how to suppress them when they do occur. Prevention is your best insurance policy against fire damage; make sure that the work space is free of combustible materials and that all hazards that could cause a fire are minimized as much as possible. Prevention also means educating people on the different causes of fires and how *they* can help prevent them.

Absent prevention, detecting a fire is also important. Quick detection means that you can save lives and prevent damage to facilities and equipment. Detection methods include heat, smoke, light, and gas detection. Obviously, simple smoke detectors located throughout the facility will help, but you also may need more advanced detection systems in large operations or data centers. Some detectors are smoke activated, others are heat activated. You also may need to install temperature sensors throughout areas that are hard to see or reach, where there may be a lot of equipment that heats up easily, or where there are major power outlets or connections. Photoelectric devices detect changes in light intensity, so they can detect smoke or intense light from flames. Other types of fire detection equipment include devices that can detect hazardous fumes or gases that may result from fires burning plastics and other noxious materials.

There are four basic classes of fire, and each has its own preferred method of suppression. Because fire reacts differently to different materials, there are some suppression methods you would not want to use with certain fires. For example, you would not want to spray water on an electrical fire because of electrical shock hazards. You also would not want to spray water on a flammable liquid fire, because it can cause a fire to spread uncontrollably.

Although some data centers have sprinkler or sophisticated water suppression systems (wet and dry pipe, and deluge systems) to put out large fires, water can pose several disadvantages. First, as mentioned in the case with electrical fires or flammable liquids, this can actually cause the fire to be worse or can cause other hazards. Second, even if water can put out the fire, it's likely going to damage electrical equipment, furniture, and facilities, especially if it's a large amount of water dumped onto a huge fire. Earlier data centers also used Halon gas, which was shown to be extremely dangerous to humans (it removes all of the oxygen out of the room, not only putting out the fire, but also potentially suffocating any of the survivors), as well as harmful to the ozone layer in the atmosphere. Halon was banned in 1987, however, and it hasn't even been manufactured in several decades.

NOTE For those of you who are CompTIA A+ or Network+ certified: Do these fire extinguisher examples sound familiar? They should, because they are on all three exams.

Most modern data centers these days, instead of having some type of water or Halon fire suppression systems, have foam fire suppression systems, such as FM-200 or another approved chemical foam. This type of system not only is very effective for putting out large fires, but is also typically safe for humans and equipment. It may be a real pain to clean up the mess afterward, though! Fortunately, if the fire is caught early enough, it can be extinguished with ordinary hand-held fire extinguishers that should be located throughout the facility (by law). It's best to use the type of fire extinguishers that are appropriate for the type of fire you have. Table 7-2 lists the different classes of fires, their characteristics, and the different materials that are in the appropriate fire extinguishers for those types.

HVAC

Heating, ventilation, and air conditioning (HVAC) systems ensure that the environments that humans work in, and that equipment functions in, are kept comfortable, at the right temperature and well ventilated, and that the air quality in them is at a consistently good level. These systems are an important part of any business, to be sure, but they are that much more important in an operations or data center that has a lot of hot equipment and requires controlled temperature and humidity levels. Most large data centers may even have their own dedicated HVAC systems that are separate from the rest of the facility, since computing equipment tends to draw a lot of power and requires very sensitive, specialized equipment to keep it within an acceptable range. Most HVAC controls are automated and can be controlled from a centralized facility, such as a physical plant or operator console.

Temperature and Humidity Controls

As part of the HVAC system within a facility, temperature and humidity controls are of critical importance in a data center. Most people find that data centers are cooler than they find comfortable, so it's not unusual to see people dressed in sweaters or light jackets inside of a data center, even on a hot August day in Alabama or Texas. This is because equipment tends to heat up a great deal during its normal operation, and when you have a great deal of equipment crammed into what may be a small room, the temperature can rapidly increase. To that end, temperature controls are designed to keep room

Table 7-2	Class	Type	Contains
Types of Fires and Appropriate Fire Extinguishers	A	Combustibles (wood, paper)	Foam, water
	B	Liquids (gasoline, oil)	CO_2, foam, powder
	C	Electrical (electronic equipment)	CO_2
	D	Combustible metals (sodium, magnesium)	Powder

temperatures cool. In addition to breaking down and simply not operating properly, overheated equipment can also be permanently damaged and can occasionally start fires.

Humidity, the amount of moisture in the air, is also an issue in data centers, regardless of the season. If the weather or climate is dry, the air contains less moisture, and this can cause a lot of static electricity. Static electricity in a data center is a bad thing, because if two components touch, or even if a person touches a piece of sensitive electronic equipment, static electricity can damage that equipment. On the other hand, in high humidity areas or seasons, there's more moisture in the air, which of course can adversely affect electrical equipment. Moisture can cause condensation, which means that water can drip into electrical components, damaging them or causing them to short out and possibly start a fire. Either way, too much humidity or not enough humidity is a bad thing for computing equipment.

Devices that monitor humidity in a data center are called *hygrometers*, or sometimes, if the device can measure both temperature and humidity at the same time, *hygrothermographs*. Like automated temperature controls and other HVAC equipment, these devices can be centrally monitored through a remote console and alert operators whenever the temperature or humidity changes from certain levels. HVAC controls can be automatically or remotely adjusted based upon information received from these monitors.

Hot and Cold Aisles

Hot and cold aisles are a concept that relates to designing the layout of data centers intelligently and efficiently. In this type of setup, aisles of equipment racks are set up such that there are alternating hot and cold aisles, enabling cooler air to be blown into equipment as hotter air is pulled away from them. This involves not only arranging equipment in certain ways by aisle (usually with the different pieces of equipment in the different aisles facing each other), but also using ventilation and air ducts appropriately within these hot and cold aisles, both in the floors and ceiling. Figure 7-53 illustrates how hot and cold aisles work.

Figure 7-53
An example of
hot and cold
aisles

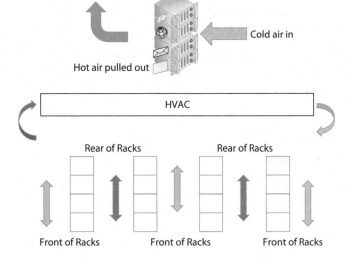

Environmental Monitoring

Even if all of the controls we've discussed so far in this module are installed and working, monitoring the environmental controls is still very important, because things can occasionally happen—equipment can break, power cabling can go bad, HVAC systems can break down, humans can fiddle with temperature and humidity controls, and so on. *Environmental monitoring* ensures that systems maintain a constant state of ideal temperature, humidity, and power. Environmental monitoring is also used to detect smoke and heat that would indicate the early stages of a fire, and it is a very effective preventative control in this aspect.

Environmental monitoring can be part of your networking facility monitoring systems; you can place environmental sensors throughout a facility that automatically report their status to operator consoles on the same systems that help you monitor other aspects of the network, such as device status, throughput, bandwidth, network traffic, and so on.

Questions

1. Which of the following would be considered static hosts? (Choose all that apply.)

   A. HVAC systems controlled by remote access over an IP network

   B. Game consoles with Internet access

   C. A user workstation in an office

   D. A pumping mechanism in a sewage treatment plant that uses an embedded Linux operating system

2. Which of the following terms describes the use of several different manufacturers and models of Web proxy devices in a layered security architecture?

   A. Control compensation

   B. Control redundancy

   C. Control diversity

   D. Defense-in-depth

3. Which of the following refers to a programming or software-based interface used to manage connections and traffic access to and from a host?

   A. Firewall

   B. Wrapper

   C. Firmware

   D. Embedded OS

4. All of the following are characteristics of fencing you should consider when deploying it around your facility, *except*:

   A. Gauge

   B. Height

   C. Mesh

   D. Fire rating

5. Your manager wants you to deploy signage around your facility that expressly warns potential intruders that the facility is alarmed and that intruders will be met with armed response. In this situation, what kind of control functionality is the signage fulfilling?

   A. Preventative

   B. Deterrent

   C. Compensating

   D. Corrective

6. Which of the following can happen if an attacker sets the power levels on a rogue access point to overpower the wireless transmissions of a legitimate access point?

   A. Jamming

   B. Beaconing

   C. Deauthentication

   D. Spoofing

7. Computer-based measures that you might encounter in everyday hands-on security, such as firewalls, encryption technologies, access control lists on routers, and secure protocols are what type of control?

   A. Administrative

   B. Deterrent

   C. Physical

   D. Technical

8. Which of the following technologies requires that two devices be touching each other in order to communicate?

   A. 802.11i

   B. WPA

   C. Bluetooth

   D. NFC

9. Your manager wants you to make sure that enough fire extinguishers are available in the data center to take care of possible electrical fires. Which class of fire extinguishers should be used in the data center?

   A. Class A

   B. Class B

   C. Class C

   D. Class D

10. Heating, ventilation, and air conditioning (HVAC) systems control all of the following environmental factors in a data center, *except*:

    A. Power

    B. Temperature

    C. Humidity

    D. Air filtration

Answers

1. **A, B, D.** User workstations in an office would not be considered as static or specialized hosts.

2. **C.** Control diversity is a concept that describes the use of several different manufacturers and models of Web proxy devices in layered security architectures.

3. **B.** A wrapper is a programming or software-based interface used to manage connections and traffic access to and from a host.

4. **D.** Fire rating is not a consideration when deploying fencing, since fences are not designed to prevent or suppress the spread of fires.

5. **B.** In this situation the signage is acting as a deterrent control, since it relies on potential intruders knowing about what it says and understanding the consequences in order for it to be effective.

6. **A.** Jamming can occur if an attacker sets the power levels on a rogue access point to overpower the wireless transmissions of a legitimate access point.

7. **D.** Technical, or logical, controls—such as firewalls, encryption technologies, access control lists on routers, and secure protocols—are the typical computer-based measures that you might encounter in everyday hands-on security.

8. **D.** NFC requires that two devices be touching each other in order to communicate.

9. **C.** Class C fire extinguishers are the appropriate type used in electrical fires.

10. **A.** Power is not controlled by HVAC systems.

Secure Protocols

To get two hosts to communicate securely requires addressing numerous factors. What authentication should they use? What encryption? How do they initiate the secure communication? How is it terminated? What happens if something doesn't work as expected? Any competent programmer can write her own secure methods to deal with these questions, but that's a silly waste of time. Secure, standardized, well-tested, and well-known protocols implemented provide better answers to these questions and better solutions as well.

Secure protocols give huge benefits. First, with a standardized secure protocol, programmers may write code that's guaranteed to work with other systems using the same protocol. Second, a secure protocol is well-tested by thousands of third parties, giving everyone involved with that protocol confidence in its security. Third, a well-known protocol is constantly under review and being improved, ensuring that the protocol continues to stay secure.

This chapter examines the many secure protocols used in TCP/IP networks. It begins with the core protocols like DNS. From there, the chapter launches into security for both the Web and e-mail. The rest of the chapter explores Web apps, covering both their attack vectors and the tools used to develop secure Web applications.

Module 8-1: Secure Internet Protocols

This module covers the following CompTIA Security+ objective:

- **2.6** Given a scenario, implement secure protocols

The Fathers of the Internet (any *The IT Crowd* fans out there?) never designed the TCP/IP stack for security. No one thought to add security to the TCP or UDP applications that ran on the Internet. Why should they? Back then most people assumed the Internet would never get beyond a few thousand computers and no one thought that the Internet would one day be a platform for e-commerce or contain personal/private information. Over time security was added, but almost every application initially came out with a completely non-secure version, requiring a later redesign to add security.

EXAM TIP One of the most common TCP/IP protocols, DHCP, appears only obliquely on the secure protocols list on the exam. Cisco implements a feature in IOS called DHCP Secure IP Address Assignment. This combats DHCP spoofing attacks and its best use case is in network address allocation attack scenarios. You first ran into these types of attacks way back in Chapter 5, on MAC spoofing. You won't be tested on the specific IOS feature, but should know that these tools exist.

The problem is that all of these non-secure protocols still work perfectly, albeit not securely. Security professionals must recognize situations where they need to replace non-secure protocols with their secure equivalents. This module tours six secure versions of Internet applications that initially came out as non-secure: DNSSEC, SNMP, SSH, FTPS, SFTP, and SRTP. The CompTIA Security+ exam doesn't expect you to have expertise in these secure protocols, but it does expect you to have a basic understanding of them, their general use, their port numbers, and situations where they are appropriate.

 EXAM TIP One of the non-secure protocols without a secure counterpoint is the Network Time Protocol (NTP). NTP *doesn't* figure on the CompTIA Security+ exam objectives directly, but it certainly does indirectly. A use case scenario where NTP figures is in *time synchronization*. In an attack or accident that causes NTP to fail or hiccup so that time in a network is out of sync, the most common result is the inability for users to log into the network.

DNSSEC

The *Domain Name System (DNS)* resolves Internet names to IP addresses. So, for example, when you type in www.google.com, DNS resolves the Internet name to the IP address that your computer and other networking devices along the way need to connect you to that site. DNS consists of clients (hosts that need to get name resolution services) and servers (used to provide name translation services).

Without going too far back into CompTIA Network+ territory, remember that DNS uses *authoritative* servers that host DNS *zones*, which are the domain namespaces of the organization and its subdomains and hosts. Authoritative servers for a DNS domain can be primary or secondary servers. Primary servers host the writable copy of the zone file and replicate it to the secondary servers. A *zone file* is a mapping of host names to IP addresses and is used to make the name-to-IP address translation.

Hosts make DNS queries to servers, and responses can come from authoritative servers or caching servers. Caching servers retain in their own memory caches the name resolution responses they have received to queries they have previously made to other DNS servers. Caching servers may not necessarily host DNS zones of their own; they may merely make requests on behalf of hosts and cache the responses they receive for future requests. DNS as a protocol uses TCP port 53, as well as UDP port 53, and is an Application layer protocol. TCP is used for zone transfers between primary and secondary servers, while UDP is used for queries and responses between hosts and servers.

Figure 8-1
A spoofed DNS address

DNS Server

DNS cache poisoning is the most common attack against DNS servers. If an attacker can target a DNS server to query an evil DNS server instead of the correct one, the evil server can in turn tell the target DNS server spoofed DNS information (Figure 8-1). The DNS server will cache that spoofed information, spreading it to hosts and possibly other DNS servers.

EXAM TIP The CompTIA Security+ exam objectives refer to DNS cache poisoning as simply *DNS poisoning*. Expect to see the shortened term on the exam.

To prevent cache poisoning, the typical use case scenario is to switch to *Domain Name System Security Extensions (DNSSEC)* for domain name resolution. DNSSEC takes advantage of DNS's tree-like structure to digitally sign every zone file for (eventually) every domain in the DNS hierarchy. The DNS root as well as all top-level domains (.COM, .EDU, etc.) and hundreds of thousands of other DNS servers now use DNSSEC.

EXAM TIP DNSSEC does not change port numbers, but uses port 53 just like regular DNS.

SNMP

Simple Network Monitoring Protocol (SNMP), mentioned back in Chapter 4, is the basis for many network monitoring tools. SNMP uses *SNMP agents*, installed by default on most network devices, that respond to queries (*gets*) from SNMP manager programs. Agents can also be configured to send *traps*, asynchronous communication from agents to managers (Figure 8-2).

SNMPv1 and SNMPv2 lacked any form of security beyond a password transmitted in the clear. Anyone who could intercept the conversation between agent and managers could read critical data information. SNMPv3 is identical to SNMPv2 but adds robust and flexible encryption. The modern use case scenario for securely monitoring routing and switching is to use SNMPv3.

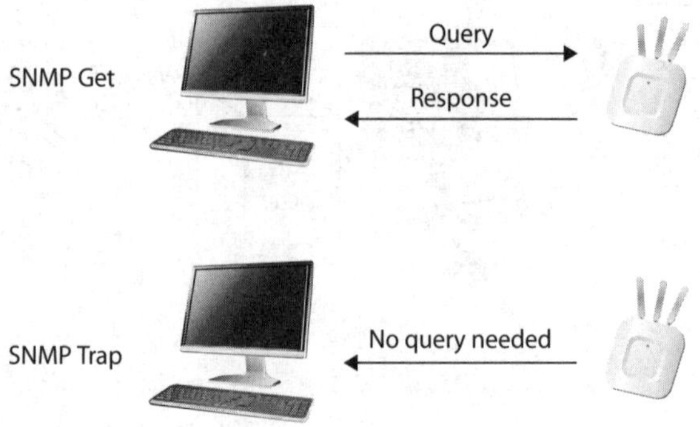

Figure 8-2
SNMP gets and traps

SNMP Get   Query →
             ← Response

SNMP Trap   ← No query needed

EXAM TIP   All versions of SNMP use UDP ports 161 and 162.

SNMP support is very common on all enterprise network devices. In any user case where you want direct monitoring of routers, switches, wireless access points, or individual computers, SNMP is the protocol you need.

SSH

Telnet enables local control over a remote system, an essential tool since the beginning of the Internet. One of the most important goals of the Internet was to create a remote terminal connection to far-flung systems. Unfortunately, Telnet has no security other than a simple user name and password transmitted in the clear. A series of attacks on networks in the late 1980s and early 1990s—not only on Telnet, but equally on unsecured FTP sites (see "FTP," next)—showed the need for secure protocols. The *Secure Shell (SHH)* protocol was invented as a direct replacement for Telnet and other non-secure remote terminal programs. Plus, in a bit of foresight that over time has proven to be utterly amazing, SSH was designed to run in a tunneling mode, enabling any other application to run within an encrypted SSH tunnel. Best use case scenario for secure remote access is to use SSH rather than telnet.

EXAM TIP   SSH uses TCP port 22.

FTP

The *File Transfer Protocol (FTP)* enables users to upload and download files to and from an FTP server, which contains a repository of files set up by an organization for its users or customers. FTP is inherently a non-secure protocol, simply because it does not encrypt any data sent or received. All traffic is unencrypted, so it is subject to interception by a malicious entity with the use of networks sniffers. FTP has no built-in security mechanisms; it does have a form of weak authentication that can be used, but again, even the authentication traffic is not encrypted or otherwise protected, so credentials are subject to sniffing as well. FTP is an Application layer protocol and uses two TCP ports to function, ports 20 and 21. These ports are for data and control commands, respectively.

Modern systems require much more security, so a typical use case scenario about file transfer means substituting FTP for one of its more secure relatives. These protocols are FTPS and SFTP.

FTPS

FTP over SSL (FTPS) is a secure version of FTP that can be used over a Secure Sockets Layer (SSL) or Transport Layer Security (TLS) secure session connection. (See "SSL" and "TLS" in Module 8-2 for details on the protocols.) Adding SSL or TLS enables users to perform FTP file transfers securely, using built-in encryption and authentication mechanisms (usually involving public and private keys). Unlike other applications that use SSL or TLS, FTPS uses TCP port 990.

 EXAM TIP Network people use a lot of phrases to spell out the initials FTPS, such as FTP over SSL as defined here, or *FTP Secure*. As of this writing, the CompTIA Security+ Acronyms list oddly defines FTPS as *Secured File Transfer Protocol*. That's an error that hopefully you won't see on the exam.

SFTP

The SSH protocol suite includes several security utilities. One of these, SCP, is used to copy files back and forth during an SSH session with a single host. These file transfers are usually ad hoc and limited to that SSH session only. There are times when users require a more permanent secure file transfer solution beyond that of a single session. The organization could set up an FTP site for just such an instance, but you already know that FTP is not secure. For a more permanent, secure file transfer solution, SFTP is a good choice. SFTP (also known as SSH-FTP) uses SSH, so it protects data through encryption and authentication services. It functions similarly to normal FTP, but all data is encrypted, so it can't be easily intercepted or read.

 EXAM TIP The CompTIA Security+ Acronyms list describes SFTP as *Secured File Transfer Protocol*, a common phrase that implies the purpose of the protocol.

SFTP is *not* the same thing as regular FTP or FTPS, so don't confuse them. SFTP does not use SSL at all. Additionally, there is yet another way you could use SSH: like other non-secure protocols, such as Telnet and HTTP, you could send regular non-secure FTP through an SSH tunnel. Note that when used in this manner, it is not the same thing as SFTP.

Confused yet? Table 8-1 helps to clarify it for you by breaking down the different file copy and transfer protocols.

Protocol	Security Method	Notes
FTP	None	Ordinary file transfer with no security built-in. Uses TCP ports 20 and 21.
FTPS	FTP over SSL	Uses SSL's built-in encryption and authentication methods. Uses TCP port 990.
SCP	Secure file copy utility included in SSH suite	Ideal for copying files during individual SSH sessions. Uses TCP port 22.
SFTP	Secure file transfer utility included in SSH suite	Ideal for transferring files on a more permanent basis. Uses SSH and TCP port 22.
FTP tunneled over SSH	Regular FTP tunneled through SSH	Not normally used, and not a built-in utility. Works the same as FTP over SSL.

Table 8-1 Various Ways to Copy and Transfer Files Securely and Non-securely

SRTP

Real Time Protocol (RTP) is a critical component of almost every form of telephony over IP, such as Voice over IP (VoIP). Like so many protocols before it, RTP has no real security, making interception of voice calls easy and forcing many VoIP application vendors (Skype is a great example) to create their own proprietary encryptions.

Unlike the time frame between so many unsecure protocols and their secure versions, just a few years later the industry adopted Secure RTP (SRTP). SRTP is more of an extension to RTP than its own unique protocol, using the same port as RTP (by default UDP 5004, although this is easily and often changed). SRTP adds a few headers to support encryption and message integrity.

The massive growth of video and audio across the Internet and the need to secure them creates a number of use cases where existing voice and video solutions using RTP need to switch to SRTP. While the exact switching method varies from solution to solution, in many cases little more than a patch and a few updates are all that's needed to make non-secure voice and video well secured.

 EXAM TIP Look for a question on the CompTIA Security+ exam about media gateway appliances, devices designed to help companies transition from the ancient PBX telephone systems to modern IP-based voice systems. The Cisco MGX 8880 was a typical device that handled these duties.

Module 8-2: Secure Web and E-mail

This module covers the following CompTIA Security+ objectives:

- **2.1** Install and configure network components, both hardware- and software-based, to support organizational security
- **2.6** Given a scenario, implement secure protocols
- **3.2** Given a scenario, implement secure network architecture concepts

Web applications have displaced many of the more traditional TCP/IP applications. In the past if you wanted to transfer a file to another person, for example, you would probably use FTP. FTP is still popular, but for many file transfer scenarios, cloud-storage Web apps such as Google Drive, iCloud, or Dropbox are very popular.

Yet for all this moving to Web apps, e-mail, perhaps the most traditional of traditional TCP/IP applications, still eludes Web app domination, at least for the enterprise. Most users no longer use e-mail applications for personal e-mail, instead using Gmail, Yahoo!, or other Web-based e-mail services. In the enterprise, however, standalone e-mail apps are quite common. Both Windows and macOS come by default with an e-mail app, and Microsoft Office's productivity apps almost always include a copy of the venerable Outlook.

There's no doubt the predominance of the Web motivates the industry to ensure good security for HTTP. There are also plenty of powerful protocols to secure e-mail from prying eyes. This module looks at the tools used to secure both Web and e-mail applications. It examines in more detail terms bandied about since almost the beginning of this book, such as TLS, to clarify how these secure protocols help keep Web pages, Web apps, and e-mail secure.

HTTP

The *Hypertext Transfer Protocol (HTTP)* enables users to access Web resources on the Internet. Hosts can use HTTP requests to send and receive Hypertext Markup Language (HTML) documents as well as other Internet content from Web applications.

HTTP is not a secure protocol by itself. All content sent over an HTTP request and response is unencrypted—that is, it is sent in plaintext, which can be easily intercepted and read by anyone, including malicious hackers. Sending sensitive data over ordinary HTTP can be very non-secure. One solution to this issue was developed by sending HTTP traffic over more secure protocols, in particular TLS (see the upcoming "TLS" section).

HTTPS

HTTP over SSL (HTTPS) sends normal HTTP traffic over an encrypted SSL or TLS connection. SSL and TLS can be used to send almost any protocol, though, providing security services for that traffic. A typical use case scenario for substituting HTTPS for HTTP is when a client wants a Web store that can handle secure monetary transactions. HTTPS is essential for e-commerce. Another use case scenario is with subscription services, such as Microsoft Office 365. All the big Software-as-a-Service (SaaS) providers use HTTPS by default to secure authentication. HTTP uses TCP port 80, and HTTPS uses TCP port 443, the port used by SSL and TLS.

 NOTE Both HTTP and HTTPS reside at the Application layer in the OSI model.

SSL

The *Secure Sockets Layer (SSL)* protocol provides both encryption and authentication services between hosts during data transmission. For encryption services, it encrypts the entire session between two hosts in an SSL tunnel. Any traffic that is sent between the hosts during that session is encrypted and protected from unauthorized interception. For authentication, SSL normally uses digital certificates to authenticate a server to a client. However, SSL also supports mutual authentication where both the host and client exchange certificates.

TLS

SSL has been vulnerable to an increasing number of attacks due mainly to vulnerabilities to downgrade attacks, allowing attackers to take advantage of weaker algorithms. Because of the weaknesses in cryptographic algorithms used in various versions of SSL, the *Transport Layer Security (TLS)* protocol was developed to replace SSL a while back, and has now all but completely replaced SSL. Currently, all modern operating systems, browsers, and Web-based applications support TLS.

From a functional standpoint, SSL and TLS are very similar. In fact, while TLS has supplanted SSL, it's very common to see references to SSL/TLS, especially when discussing aspects where the two protocols are virtually identical. SSL/TLS uses TCP port 443 for backward compatibility with SSL-based technologies.

TLS secures sensitive data transferred during Web sessions. In addition to providing secure session services for Web traffic, TLS is used to protect other protocols that require secure sessions such as SFTP.

 EXAM TIP The increased use of SSL throughout modern networks can produce a security risk if not managed properly. The big intrusion detection system (IDS) device developers, like Cisco, produce appliances CompTIA calls *SSL decryptors* that can decrypt SSL traffic and inspect it on the fly. Use of such appliances will add a serious layer of protection to a network.

SSL/TLS Handshake

TLS connections require a back and forth interaction between client and server—called the *SSL/TLS handshake*—to establish identity and authentication. If a client wants to create a secure HTTPS connection with a server, the client first creates an HTTP connection. It then begins the SSL/TLS handshake to establish that connection. Here's a somewhat simplified overview of the steps:

1. Client hello
2. Server hello
3. Key exchange
4. Finish

Client Hello The client, already connected to the server via HTTP, initiates the HTTPS connection with an SSL/TLS *hello* message. This message informs the server that the client wants to connect via HTTPS, and describes the types of key exchange the client supports. Figure 8-3 shows part of the client hello captured in Wireshark.

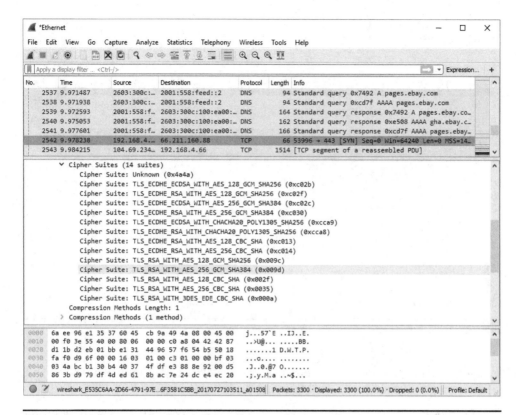

Figure 8-3 Cipher suites in client hello message

Every cipher suite defines everything needed in the key exchange on a single line. Inspecting one of these suites in detail, the following line informs the server of a single cipher suite the client can perform:

```
Cipher Suite: TLS_ECDHE_ECDSA_WITH_AES_128_GCM_SHA256 (0xc02b)
```

A single cipher suite contains very specific combinations of authentication/key exchange, encryption, and integrity protocols.

The preceding line indicates that the client can perform the following:

- **TLS_ECDHE_ECDSA**   This is the authentication method, Elliptic-curve Diffie-Hellman Ephemeral key exchange using the Elliptic-curve Digital Signature Algorithm.

- **AES_128_GCM**   This is the encryption, AES-128 as the block cipher using GCM mode.

- **SHA256**   This is the integrity protocol, SHA-256 HMAC for the authentication hash.

Server Hello   The server reads the client hello, choosing a cipher suite from the list. It then responds with the cipher suite it chose plus any information to begin the key

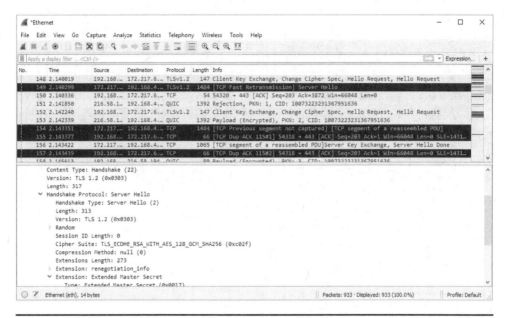

Figure 8-4 Selected cipher suite in server hello message

exchange. Figure 8-4 shows part of the server hello message captured in Wireshark, declaring the cipher suite and also beginning the key exchange.

Key Exchange   From this point, there are several message options depending on the cipher suite. Two common commands are key exchange and change cipher spec. *Key exchange* handles any part of the key exchange process and *change cipher spec* handles any adjustments to the exchange process. TLS can pack multiple TLS commands into a single TLS packet to speed things up. It's not uncommon to see a single TLS packet as shown in Figure 8-5.

Finish   Once the client and the server are satisfied that the key exchange has worked, the SSL/TLS tunnel is now established. Both sides signify setup is complete with finish messages. Figure 8-6 shows a server sending a *finish* command (Wireshark calls them Hello Done). Also notice the encrypted packets below the finish command.

EXAM TIP   The SSL/TLS handshake is one of the more computational demanding aspects of implementing this level of security. Device manufacturers have developed hardware appliances—called *SSL/TLS accelerators*—that take the handshake burden off the systems.

E-mail

Whether you use a Web client or a more traditional client, e-mail is an important Internet application. E-mail uses specific protocols, and you must understand how they work (and of course know the port numbers).

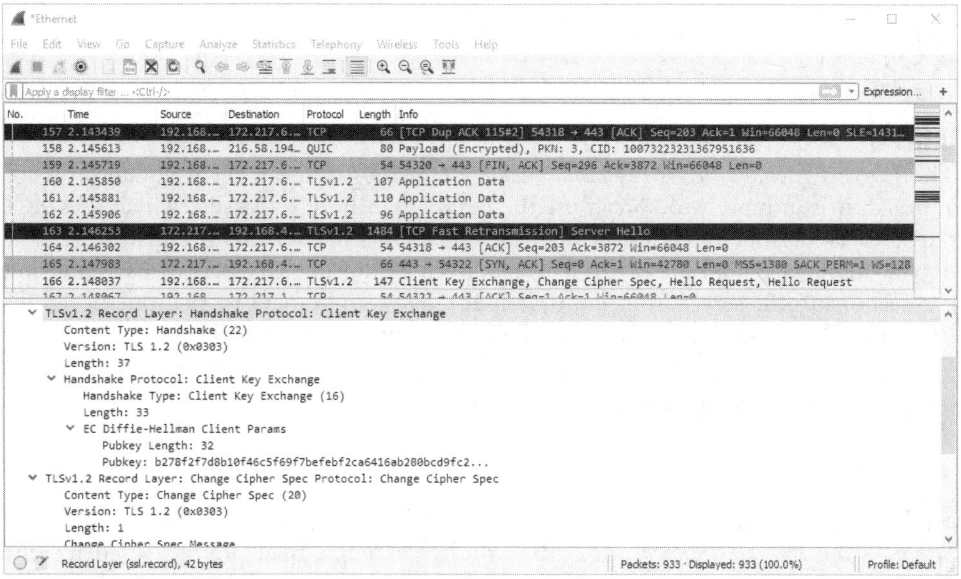

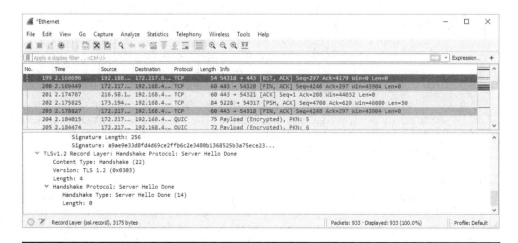

Figure 8-5 Key exchange (in this case, Diffie-Hellman) and change cipher spec in a single TLS packet

POP3

The *Post Office Protocol version 3 (POP3)* is an e-mail client protocol used to receive e-mail through client applications. Client applications that use POP3 access the user's mailbox and download all the e-mail in the inbox, and then delete the mail from the server. This can confuse some users, especially when they log in to their e-mail account from different clients and find that their e-mail has "disappeared." POP3 allows only one connection at a time to the user's inbox.

Figure 8-6 Finish command (Hello Done) followed by encrypted packets

EXAM TIP POP3 uses TCP port 110.

IMAP4

The *Internet Message Access Protocol version 4 (IMAP4)* is also a client e-mail protocol, although it is in more widespread use these days than POP3. IMAP4, which uses TCP port 143 by default, can connect to an organizational or Web-based e-mail server and download client e-mail messages. It differs from POP3 in that you can have multiple connections to the server from multiple user clients, and e-mail isn't automatically deleted from the server. Like POP3, IMAP4 is also a non-secure protocol.

EXAM TIP IMAP4 uses TCP port 142.

SMTP

Simple Mail Transfer Protocol (SMTP) is the server-side e-mail protocol used to send e-mail messages from an organization's e-mail server. SMTP is an Application layer protocol that uses TCP port 25. Like some of the older protocols discussed in this module, SMTP has no built-in security mechanisms. It provides no authentication between hosts or for users, and it relies on external authentication mechanisms such as Lightweight Directory Access Protocol (LDAP)-based directory systems for authentication.

Besides being a non-secure protocol, SMTP is also vulnerable to various attacks. SMTP is vulnerable to an *SMTP relay attack*, where a malicious person can connect to the SMTP server and send e-mail from it, spoofing the organization's users and e-mail addresses. This attack can be prevented by configuring the SMTP server not to allow unauthenticated connections and by disallowing SMTP relay.

EXAM TIP You'll recall LDAP from way back in Chapter 3 as the protocol used to assist in allowing already authenticated users to browse and locate objects in a distributed network database. The CompTIA Security+ objectives mention *LDAP over SSL (LDAPS)* as one of the secure protocols. While this is technically true, LDAPS was deprecated right along with LDAPv2 way back in 2003. LDAPv3 uses extensions that make use of secure protocols such as TLS to provide security today.

You might see an exam question that posits a use case scenario about directory services that would substitute LDAP for LDAPS; choose that answer if it seems obvious. In reality today, current versions of LDAP provide secure extensions.

Securing E-mail

For decades, none of the big three e-mail protocols—POP, IMAP, or SMTP—had any form of encryption. Everything you did, including sending your user name and password, was in the clear. To give encryption to these protocols, the Internet folks added SSL/TLS and let your e-mail run through the encrypted tunnel, just as HTTP runs through an SSL/TLS tunnel.

Three secure versions of the previously non-secure mail protocols go by a few names, but the CompTIA Security+ exam objectives call them *Secure POP*, *Secure IMAP*, and *Secure SMTP*. Let's stick with those. Each of these secure e-mail protocols uses a unique port number as follows:

- Secure POP uses port 995.
- Secure IMAP uses port 993.
- Secure SMTP uses port 465.

All e-mail servers support secure e-mail protocols. In typical use case scenarios, you configure a secure e-mail protocol simply by adding a certificate to the e-mail server and setting up the secure ports. On the client side, you need to configure each e-mail account to use secure e-mail protocols. Figure 8-7 shows my e-mail account settings in Office 365.

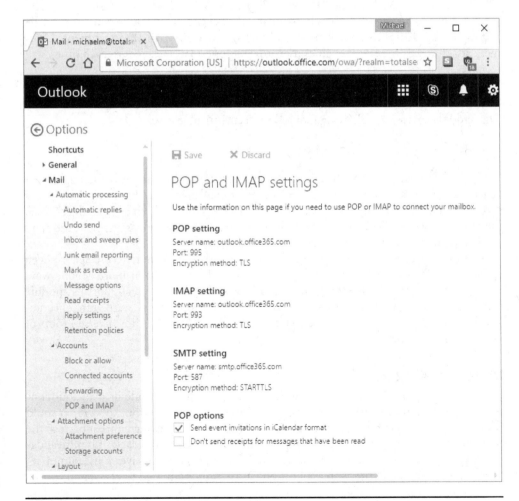

Figure 8-7   Secure e-mail settings in Office 365

Wait a minute! Note that the SMTP server uses port 587 instead of 465. This is an older version of secure SMTP called STARTTLS. STARTTLS is functionally equivalent to secure SMTP, but uses port 587 instead of port 465.

MIME, S/MIME

Multipurpose Internet Mail Extensions (MIME) is the protocol built into every e-mail client that enables users to make e-mail attachments. MIME works by converting the attached file to text, using headers so that the receiving e-mail client can then convert the text files back into the original file type. MIME's ability to attach files created an opportunity for users to use their own e-mail security protocols, even if their e-mail servers didn't use secure POP, IMAP, or SMTP. Secure e-mail protocols only work if you have an e-mail server configured to support them. In most cases, users have no control over their servers and must use e-mail servers that still use insecure POP/IMAP/SMTP. In these cases, user can take control of their e-mail security using Secure Multipurpose Internet Mail Extensions (S/MIME). S/MIME was developed from MIME, but took the concept a step further, as S/MIME enables individual e-mail clients to attach personal certificates and digital signatures to e-mail messages just like any other MIME attachment. Using these attachments, S/MIME enables users to encrypt e-mail messages to each other.

Module 8-3: Web Application Attacks

This module covers the following CompTIA Security+ objective:

- **1.2** Compare and contrast types of attacks

Given the popularity of Web apps on the Internet today, they are easily the single most generic target for all kinds of attacks. The biggest challenge to Web application attacks is the public nature of the Web. As an Internet-facing server, a Web app is subject to all the types of attacks already discussed in the book (plus a few more); as an application, it's subject to attacks unique to applications.

This module covers the many types of attacks that bad actors tend to use against Web applications. We've previously covered a number of these attacks in more generic ways (attacking the network, attacking individual hosts, attacking servers), so this module concentrates on how these attacks affect Web applications. We'll start with injection attacks, then discuss hijacking and related attacks, and finish with a diverse group of other types of attacks.

Injection Attacks

In its basic form, an *injection attack* inserts—*injects*—additional code or malicious content into a site, typically using an opening provided through user input. *User input* could come from a field on a form or via one of several methods for posting content back to the Web server. Injecting data into a user input field works because of a lack of input validation. *Input validation* should occur when the Web application receives a user input request, and it means that the Web application has been programmed to check and restrict user input to a valid range of responses. For instance, input validation would check for, and prevent, a user entering alphabetic text data into a field that requires numerical values. Lack of input validation allows a malicious user to circumvent the expected data in the field and add or embed data that might be used to get a different response from the application or server.

Several different types of content can be injected into a Web application, including SQL statements, operating system commands, LDAP commands, and XML. Each of these types of injectable content takes certain actions to cause specific reactions from the Web application and server. Attackers can use these injection attacks to gain unauthorized access to data, execute commands on the Web server itself, and set up the server for further attacks. We'll cover some of these injection attacks in the next few sections.

Command Injection

Command injection is a technique with which a malicious user could append or embed commands into a user input request and cause either retrieval of information from the system or command execution on the host itself. The malicious user could include application-specific commands, such as database commands, operating system commands, and even commands that can affect the network, such as those needed to connect to a shared network resource. Most command injection attacks are tailored to the operating system or application used on the server, but some generic commands, especially those embedded in URLs, can affect a variety of systems in different ways.

For example, let's say you have a URL that looks like this:

```
http://confidential/cgi-bin/appscript.pl?doc=secret.txt
```

You could alter that URL by appending a pipe symbol on the end, along with a command, like so:

```
http://confidential/cgi-bin/appscript.pl?doc=/bin/ls|
```

On a Linux-based system, this embedded command would execute a directory listing on the target computer. The PERL script that executes on the server as part of the normal application (appscript.pl) would allow a command to be executed on the host also, since it can pipe the command to the shell.

SQL Injection

Database programmers use *Structured Query Language (SQL)* to create and manipulate database structures as well as the data that resides in those structures. Most relational databases use some variation of SQL to manage their data structures (such as tables, views, and so on). With the wide availability of databases residing as part of a back-end tier for Internet-facing Web applications, attacks on those databases and their structures are commonplace.

Many of these attacks use the SQL language to attack a database, through vulnerabilities in the Web application, usually in user input fields. For example, if you had an application that asked for a user name and e-mail address on a form, an attacker could attempt to manipulate this user input to include SQL commands as part of the input.

Figure 8-8

An SQL injection attack

> Welcome {Unregistered User} - Cart contains 0 items at $0.00 　　　　　View Cart
>
> ## Login to Your Account or Register for a New Account
>
> **Login to Your Account**
>
> Email Address: `'mary`
>
> Password: [　　　　]
>
> [Login]

This is called *SQL injection*, because it sends SQL input (normally in the form of SQL database manipulation commands) to the database. The results returned to the user could be responses to those commands, including responses that give up important data to the user.

Figures 8-8 and 8-9 show examples of a simple SQL injection used in a Web login form and the resulting response from the credentials file, which shows data the user isn't authorized to see.

LDAP Injection

LDAP is used in distributed directory service structures that contain network, user, and computer information. LDAP is used to query the directory services database in order to locate network-based resources. The most popular examples of distributed directory service are Microsoft Active Directory, OpenLDAP, and NetIQ eDirectory. They are all based on the X.500 Directory Services standard and use LDAP to provide standard communication services between directory-based objects.

LDAP injection can be performed on any directory services database that has not been secured; its purpose, like other forms of injection, is to get data from the directory database that a user would otherwise be unauthorized to obtain. Some Web applications use directory services databases to perform their intended functions (service authentication or data lookups, for example). LDAP injection involves embedding LDAP query commands into routine Web application requests and getting data back in response. For instance, a malicious user could embed LDAP commands into an input request and retrieve a list of all the user names in the directory database.

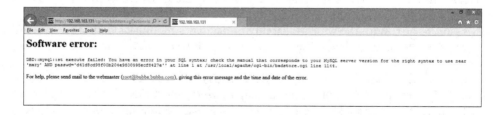

Figure 8-9   The result of the SQL injection

XML Injection

The eXtensible Markup Language (XML) is similar to HTML and other markup languages. It provides a standards-based way to encode documents for consistent, unified presentation and formatting. It is often used to format data elements from database applications that are viewed through Web applications. *XML injection*, similar to the other types of injection attacks discussed here, sends malicious XML content to a Web application, taking advantage of any lack of input validation and XML parsing.

The challenge to XML injections is that they literally fit into any type of attack. One possible example would be an attacker injecting a large dollar value into a known XML field called credit balance. It is important to harden Web pages against these types of attacks.

Hijacking and Related Attacks

Any Web session has control tokens used to track the status of the session at any given moment. A token might be a cookie tracking the contents of a shopping cart, for example, or it might be some JavaScript variable tracking your character's location in a Web-based game. Whatever and wherever your session tokens might live, any form of attack that attempts to manipulate these tokens in a way that attacks the mechanism of your Web site is known generically as a *session hijacking attack*.

Cross-Site Scripting

Cross-site scripting (XSS) attacks can affect both hosts and Web applications. It comes in the form of malicious script content injected into a vulnerable Web site, usually one that the client browser trusts. Because content from a trusted site often has elevated access to a browser or its components, the malicious content could be sent to a client and have these elevated privileges as well. From there, it can access sensitive information on the client, including content and session cookie information. This information could contain user credentials as well as financial information (in the form of credit card or bank account numbers), for example.

XSS attacks are very common; in fact, these types of attacks are estimated to be a large majority of Web-based attacks today, surpassing even buffer overflows in frequency (see "Buffer Overflow," later in the chapter). Many Web sites are vulnerable to XSS attacks, usually through malformed HTML requests or via active content and scripting languages such as Java, JavaScript, ActiveX, Visual Basic Script (VBScript), Flash, and others. Although there are many variations of XSS attacks, Figure 8-10 illustrates one way that a simple XSS attack could work.

Cross-Site Request Forgery

Cross-site request forgery (XSRF) attacks attempt to steal authentication information from session cookies during a user's current browsing session. The user is normally tricked into visiting a malicious Web site through redirection or phishing, and the malicious Web site executes code that attempts to steal the authentication information and impersonate the user. Note that this attack requires that the user already be authenticated to the secure site, so that their session credentials are stored in the browser.

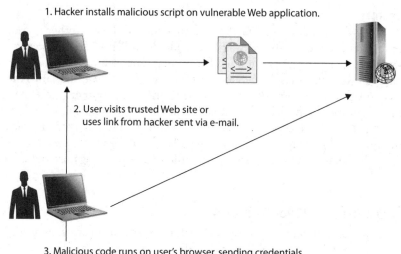

1. Hacker installs malicious script on vulnerable Web application.

2. User visits trusted Web site or
   uses link from hacker sent via e-mail.

3. Malicious code runs on user's browser, sending credentials
   to hacker via Web site or allowing hacker to log into Web site using user's credentials.

Figure 8-10   A simple XSS attack

Cookies

Cookies are small text files stored on a browser that contain information about the Web sites you visit. In some cases, cookies are used to retain user preferences for the site, but cookies can contain sensitive information, such as user credentials or financial data (credit card information, for example) as well. These last types of cookies are *session cookies*, since they are (supposedly) not persistent and expire for each session and must be renewed for subsequent sessions. Cookies are stored as text files, and although they are not easily human readable, they are not encrypted.

Web sites that use the Adobe Flash player for certain content offer a different type of cookie called a *local shared object* or *flash cookie*. Flash cookies store user information and can be a security concern due to privacy issues.

Attacks that take advantage of cookies usually come in the form of stealing session cookies from a user's Web browser and using the session information contained therein to authenticate as the user. Cookies can be collected via a Web-based script or intercepted during a traffic capture using a sniffer. Protecting against cookie-based attacks involves using techniques such as enforcing new session authentication periodically from a Web site, cookie expiration, and control of cookie use through the browser security settings. Figure 8-11 shows an example of a basic cookie text file.

NOTE   A *zombie cookie* is a particularly nefarious type of cookie that re-creates itself from an external source outside the cookie storage area.

Figure 8-11 Example of a cookie file

Man-in-the-Browser

Man-in-the-middle attacks are common and popular attack vectors for Web applications. One popular variant called *man-in-the-browser* is a client-side attack, initiated by the user inadvertently running a Trojan horse on his or her system. This Trojan horse in turn grabs communication between the client and the server, silently sending whatever data the attacker wants to a third location while still seemingly working perfectly to the user.

Clickjacking

Clickjacking is an older form of attack where a malicious/compromised Web site places invisible controls on a page, giving users the impression they are clicking some safe item that actually is an active control for something malicious.

One of the more common forms of clickjacking comes from an HTML data structure called an iFrame. An *iFrame* is basically a Web page within a Web page, complete with its own controls and applications.

Header Manipulation

As part of normal communications with Web applications, the Web application and the browser exchange request and response messages so the client can access content in the Web application. These HTTP requests and responses have headers that contain information such as commands, directives, and so on. A *header manipulation* attack modifies these headers so they contain malicious information, such as harmful commands and scripts. When the client receives these manipulated headers, the client often executes these commands, resulting in malicious actions occurring on the client. Beyond executing simple commands, manipulating HTTP headers can allow an attacker to carry out other attacks, such as cross-site scripting, session hijacking, cookie stealing, and injection attacks. A mitigation for this type of attack is to configure Web application servers to ignore client-side headers, since they are usually the source of header manipulation.

Other Web Application Attacks

Other attacks can be executed against a server hosting a Web application. These don't necessarily require injection, although often they are carried out through an injection attack. Some of these attacks might yield only information about the system that a hacker could use to formulate an attack, such as Web server version or directory structure, but other attacks can result in direct unauthorized access to sensitive data. Some attacks can even allow the attacker to run privileged commands or arbitrary code on a host. We'll discuss some of these attacks in this section, including DNS attacks, directory traversal, overflow attacks, add-ons, and zero-day attacks.

DNS Attacks

One of the best ways to wreak havoc on a Web application is to mess with its associated DNS. Users rely on DNS to get to specific Web apps. By attacking DNS, bad actors can prevent users from even getting to the Web app itself. Let's consider some forms of DNS attack.

Domain Hijacking   *Domain hijacking* means to take control of a legitimate domain registration in some way that the actual owner does not desire. DNS registration procedures today are quite robust, making domain hijacking tricky in most cases. However, in some cases hijacking still takes place. Organizations generally have a domain registrar such as GoDaddy (www.godaddy.com). If the user is attacked by some form of man-in-the-middle attack, the user might send the password to that account to a bad actor. Often a DNS domain comes with an e-mail account that allows a bad actor to access the registration. Domain hijacking is correctable, but sometimes takes days if not weeks, which is plenty of time for a Web app to lose its customer base.

DNS Amplification   *DNS amplification* is a form of distributed denial-of-service (DDoS) attack that attacks a Web application's DNS server instead of the Web app itself. DNS amplification attacks work in various ways, but the goal is to confuse legitimate DNS servers by sending spoofed/malformed DNS queries in some way to amplify what's normally a simple, single DNS query into hundreds of queries.

Typosquatting/URL Hijacking   Most Internet users have made a typo while entering a URL and suddenly discovered themselves on a completely different Web site than the one they intended. Con artists and scammers have bought up many domains that differ just slightly from a legitimate site, preferably with a spelling that people commonly mistake. That's called *typosquatting*. A user might type www.aamazon.com and think he or she is headed to the commercial giant, Amazon, but then end up at some sleazy or dangerous site. The big companies buy up the typo-prone domain names, but smaller sites are vulnerable.

Another method of typosquatting—also called *URL hijacking*—involves registering the same domain name as a legitimate company, but with a different top-level domain. For example, rather than legitcompany.com, the hijacker might register legitcompany.biz. The alternate Web site might mimic the legitimate site in the hopes of getting personal or financial information from unsuspecting users.

Directory Traversal

Directory traversal is an attack in which the entire directory of a Web site and its server are examined with the intent of locating files of interest to the attacker. These could include nonpublic files that contain sensitive information; or configuration or content files that an attacker may alter to gain information to launch further attacks on the system or network. Directory traversal attacks are conducted by entering different directory levels into a URL or user input field, causing the Web application to change directories and sometimes display the contents of a directory. You can prevent this attack through user input validation, as well as restricting the URL from displaying directory names in the Web application. Additionally, at the operating system level, you can secure files and directories with the proper access permissions to prevent unauthorized users from being able to read files or list directory contents.

Buffer Overflow

A *buffer overflow* is a condition by which an attacker, through malicious input or an automated exploit, sends unexpected input into a program, usually into its memory registers or buffers. The unexpected input could be a different data type than expected or an abnormally large amount of data that crashes a buffer when it can hold only a finite amount of data. A buffer overflow condition exceeds the limits of the application and is used to cause error conditions that may result in denial-of-service for the application or server, unexpected access to sensitive data, ability to run administrative commands or utilities on the host, or even the ability of the attacker to execute arbitrary code on the host. You can prevent buffer overflows through secure coding practices, including input validation, data type and length restrictions, error-handling routines, and bounds checking for memory allocation.

Arbitrary Code Execution or Remote Code Execution

Malicious hackers can execute commands, scripts, applets, and other types of programs on a host that enable them to run whatever type of code they wish. They can perpetrate these *arbitrary code execution* attacks through injection, malware, or any number of other attack vectors. *Remote code execution* is a variation of this type of attack that can often be run after an attacker gains a remote shell to a host. The effectiveness of both of these types of attacks is enhanced if the attacker has gained elevated privileges on the host.

Zero-Day Attacks

Very often, hackers (and security professionals) discover previously unknown vulnerabilities for operating systems, applications, and other software or code. Occasionally, not even the vendor knows that the software includes an exploitable vulnerability, so they may not have a patch or fix for it immediately. A *zero-day attack* exploits those vulnerabilities.

Since there are no known patches or mitigations for the attack, the hackers are free to exploit these vulnerabilities without fear of having them mitigated or, in some cases, even discovered. Zero-day vulnerabilities usually have some sort of available mitigation or fix within a few days or weeks; but that's more than enough time for a hacker to take advantage of any associated vulnerabilities.

Module 8-4: Secure Applications

This module covers the following CompTIA Security+ objectives:

- **3.1** Explain use cases and purpose for frameworks, best practices and secure configuration guides
- **3.4** Explain the importance of secure staging deployment concepts
- **3.6** Summarize secure application development and deployment concepts

In the earlier days of security, most of the focus was on securing networks. As time passed, the focus turned to securing operating systems. Eventually, as more vulnerabilities were discovered in applications (both traditional client/server and Web applications), more of an emphasis was placed on application security. *Application security* not only means hardening an application, much like you would a network device, operating system, or host, but also means considering security throughout the software design and development processes.

Application security begins with the process of developing well-hardened applications written from the ground up to resist attacks. But it doesn't end there. The developers of a great Web app understand that changes will take place, that performance, feature, and security goals are continually defined and redefined, making security a part of the ongoing evolution of the life of a Web application.

This module explores the lifecycle of a Web application and the security involved at each step. The software creation *environment* follows four distinct points:

1. **Development:** creating the new code

2. **Test:** verifying the code works as specified

3. **Staging:** positioning the final code in as close to the real world as possible

4. **Production:** running the code in the real world

NOTE The CompTIA Security+ exam doesn't test on programming skills, merely the aspects of applications that relate to IT security.

Development

Developing any but the simplest Web applications requires a vast amount of organization and planning. Any Web app starts with a vision, but to bring that vision to fruition, developers must define a huge number of very specific requirements and goals and then fulfill them on a timely basis. The result of these requirements and goals often manifest as a *baseline*, a minimum set of performance values that define a certain aspect of what the application must do.

Resource vs. Security Constraints

A big part of applying security to application development is the ongoing battle of resources versus security constraints. Developers must constantly assess their resources against the burden of adding security, all the while trying to find the best balance between the two. More security adds hardware, bandwidth, and maintenance costs.

Security Baseline

While any application may have hundreds of baselines, a *secure baseline* defines the core of what the developers must do to make the application secure. In a way, you could look at the security baselines more like the application's security controls.

Benchmarks/Secure Configuration Guides

An application is only as secure as the hardware, operating system, and network infrastructure devices on which it resides. Earlier chapters stressed the need for good benchmarks and configurations, but it's always a good idea to double check everything your application needs. Verify security at this point before an application is working. Keep in mind that there are plenty of *platform/vendor-specific guides* to help. Always start with a good *general-purpose guide* (this book is a great resource), but also realize every Web server software, every operating system, every application server, and certainly every network infrastructure device has clear secure configuration guides to help administrators harden every part of the platform your applications need. Use them.

Offloading Encryption

It's standard to run Web applications on top of HTTPS for good security. The Web server that the Web application runs on has all it needs to support HTTPS, but that is on top of any and all processing of the Web app itself. If the Web application has a large adoption, it's easy to overwhelm a single Web server.

There's plenty a developer can do to reduce workload. Adding more servers and load balancing, as described back in Chapter 6, for example, is very common. Another job that's easily taken off a server's plate is handing encryption/decryption by implementing *crypto service providers* or *crypto modules*. Crypto service providers and crypto modules do the same job: handling all forms of encryption requested by one or more systems. They can be software built into the system or hardware software modules connected to the system.

The only real difference between crypto service providers and crypto modules are where they are implemented. Crypto service providers are more Windows centric, while crypto modules are more open source. Both can handle virtually any cryptographic algorithm, so an important part of the implementation of these devices is *algorithm selection*. Given that Web servers lean heavily on TLS, it's important to select a crypto device that supports PKI exchange (Diffie-Hellman, RSA, and Elliptic-curve algorithms) as well as AES for symmetric encryption.

Platform

Understanding how applications function presents two challenges. First, what type of code is the application running and where does this code exist? Second, two systems are involved, a server and a client. Since the application is code, it must be running on one of those two systems, but which one? It's not necessarily clear where the application runs. Answering these two questions defines what is called the application's *platform*.

Executable or Runtime?   The classic application is an executable file that runs on a local computer. A programmer writes the executable file in some form of programming language such as C++ within some form of integrated development environment (IDE) like the one shown in Figure 8-12. When complete, the programmer runs the code through a compiler to create the executable file.

Executable code works well on a standalone system, and a local computer's executable programs easily access a remote computer's data, but standardized application protocols

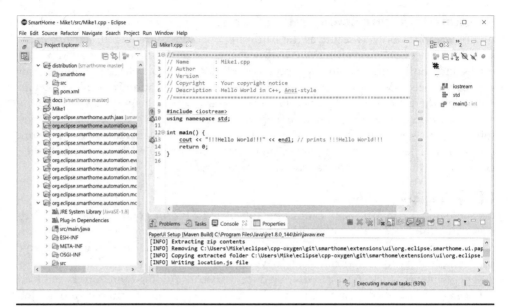

Figure 8-12 Eclipse IDE

like HTTP add complexities that make executable files fall short. When a program is compiled, the resulting executable file is for a specific operating system. When you send an HTML file from a server to a client's Web browser, however, there are too many variables: What Web browser is the client running? What operating system? What is the client's screen resolution?

This problem is avoided by running applications using *runtime* or *interpreted code*, specifically designed to work with Web browsers. There are many languages used; today Python and JavaScript are the most common.

Unlike executable code, interpreted code isn't compiled. Interpreted code isn't designed for a specific operating system. Interpreted code is never as fast as compiled code, but it's flexible, and on the Web that's a huge benefit over executable code.

 EXAM TIP Look for a question on the exam that contrasts compiled versus runtime code. Follow the comparison we've just presented and you'll have no problem.

Server or Client Side?

Server or Client Side? So where does the interpreted code run? You have two choices here. In one case you run the code on the server, building a new Web page for the client and then sending that page to the client. The client then sends traditional HTTP commands back to the server, which reads that data and creates another Web page. The alternative is to run the code on the client. In this case the browser must know how to download the script and then run it. The Web server in most cases acts like little more than a database.

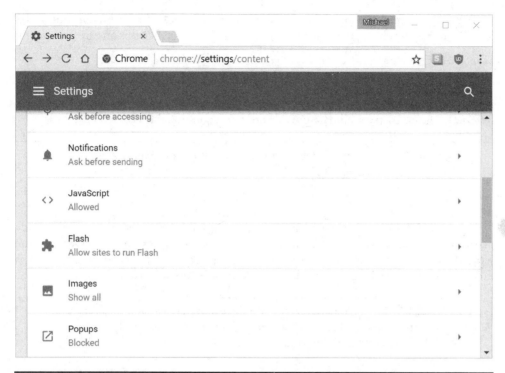

Figure 8-13   Enable/disable options for JavaScript and Flash in Chrome browser

JavaScript is the dominant server-side interpreted language. All browsers run JavaScript by default. All browsers can turn off running scripts, although turning off JavaScript will make most Web sites functionless (Figure 8-13).

 NOTE   In general, a server-side platform is more secure than a client-side platform, but client-side is generally faster.

Secure Coding Techniques

Whether the platform is client side or server side, good development practices require thinking about security from the moment the application is first considered. The Comp-TIA Security+ exam objectives mention several specific coding techniques, all of which are well known and commonly used on all Web applications.

Input Validation   The previous module described injection attacks that use manipulated inputs to do malicious things to Web applications as well as the system running the Web apps. Common types of these attacks include command insertion, cross-site scripting, buffer overflows, and SQL injection.

Proper input validation helps prevent these types of attack. If a Web application asks for a last name, the chances that someone has a crazy last name like this one are pretty slim:

```
\esc format C: /y
```

If the characters \, :, or / appear in the last name input, a Web app with proper input validation will reject that data. Alternatively, the Web app can sanitize the input. *Sanitizing* means to allow all data but strip out any questionable characters.

 NOTE Do yourself a favor and look up this famous Web comic: https://xkcd.com/327/.

Input validation varies dramatically when comparing server-side versus client-side platforms. In classic server-side applications, the code executes on the server and the server handles most if not all validation. As you might guess, client-side applications execute code on the client and the client has to handle the validation.

 EXAM TIP Look for a question on the exam that asks about server-side versus client-side execution and validation. This essentially asks which machine is doing the work.

Error Handling Despite all the testing done to prevent bugs, every application has bugs that cause errors. All Web servers or database backends have default error screens that give bad actors a lot of information to help them crack a Web application. Figure 8-14 shows an example of a default error screen from Microsoft IIS Web server. Note the great information (for attackers) placed on the screen.

Proper error handling isn't going to stop all errors, but it will prevent errors from appearing on the user interface for easy viewing by attackers. Figure 8-15 shows an example of a better error-handling page.

 NOTE There are well-established procedures to perform good error handling. One great resource is the Web Application Security Project (OWASP). Check it out at www.owasp.org.

Server Error in '/database/users.table' Application.

lastname.customer.preview attempted divide by zero.

Description: An unhandled exception occurred during the execution of the current user request. Please review the state table for more information about this error.

Exception Details: SystemDivideByZeroException: Attempted to divide by zero

Source Error:

Figure 8-14 Web server default error screen

Figure 8-15
Good error-
handling
example. (Yes,
that's me,
dressed up like
Henry VIII.)

Oooops!

Looks like there's an error with the database. Please retry now.
If the error persists contact support: mike@notarealdomain.com

Normalization   *Normalization* is a database term meaning to store and organize data so that it exists in one form only. For example, a user database has the three tables shown in Figure 8-16.

Notice how the StudentID and CourseID fields are used for indexing (think of an index field as a sorting tool). That's great, but also notice how the CourseName and Instructor fields are repeated in two tables. This is unnecessary and not good normalization.

In this simple example, only a few fields are repeated in a database. Now imagine a Web app that takes data from thousands of users in multiple tables, all with their own complex fields. Failure to normalize exposes databases to excess size, potential logic errors, and overall inefficiency.

Stored Procedures   Most Web apps count on some form of database backend to handle the storage and manipulation of whatever data the apps need. These databases come in standardized formats that usually respond to Structured Query Language (SQL) queries. SQL is a powerful language, and bad actors who know SQL well can wreak havoc on an ill-prepared database.

Stored procedures harden Web apps. A stored procedure is a piece of code, custom written by the developers of the app and stored in the database. These stored procedures only respond to a specific query format defined by the developer. Stored procedures make it much harder for bad actors to use common SQL queries to access a database.

Data Exposure/Encryption   Any Web app is going to have data moving between the server and the client. Additionally, in some cases a Web app might need to store some data locally on the client for certain amounts of time (like an online Security+ practice

Figure 8-16
Poor
normalization in
a database

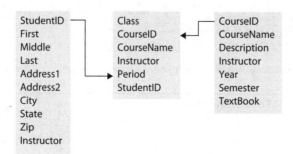

suite at https://hub.totalsem.com). Every Web app should take advantage of HTTPS to protect the data-in-motion, but HTTPS is useless once the data gets to the client or the server. In these cases, exposed data that needs hiding—maybe a database, maybe a simple temporary data structure, or in some cases even the local code itself—must be encrypted.

All the popular interpreted programming languages provide access to different encryption tools, based on well-understood and strong cryptographic algorithms, such as AES. Trying to write homemade encryption is never a good idea.

The nature of interpreted code is that the system must read it as quickly as possible, making encryption a less-than-attractive option. There are ways to *obfuscate* or *camouflage* code, on the other hand, so that it's extremely difficult to read. Figure 8-17 shows a form of obfuscation used with JavaScript called *minifying*. Minified code is stripped of everything but the core code itself.

Figure 8-17 Minified JavaScript

Code Reuse The phrase *don't reinvent the wheel* is a popular mantra in application development. Every language is filled with prewritten subroutines, objects, and tools, all generally packaged into *software libraries* to handle almost anything a new Web app might need. These software libraries might be free to use, or they might cost 20 percent (or some other percentage) of the entire budget for the application. In every case, though, reusing someone else's code—*code reuse*—adds security, saves money, and reduces development time.

NOTE Code reuse isn't limited to software libraries used by the Web app. It might be pieces of code used by the underlying Web server, the operating system, or even firmware/machine language in the hardware.

The downside to code reuse is that bad actors know that Web apps rely on it. These libraries must run in memory to work for the app. Bad actors know they're running and try to get access to this code, and can cause lots of trouble if they do get access. Over the years, attacks have appeared that exploit the reused code, exposing previously unknown vulnerabilities. The IT industry's response to these attacks varies from the no-execute (NX) bit, built into every CPU, to specialized tools designed to hide, disable, or scramble the reused code.

Third-Party Libraries and SDKs When a programmer uses third-party libraries or software development kits (SDKs), he or she assumes responsibility for any security risks introduced by their use. Does the library have a known vulnerability? What should the programmer do if a new attack appears against that SDK?

The answer here is vigilance. If an organization decides to use a third-party tool, research is key. Stay on top of any announcements. This usually isn't too hard; most third-party tool developers provide e-mail announcements for any breaking news.

One gotcha are *dependencies*, standard programs that many apps use for subroutines. A third-party library might not have any vulnerabilities, but it might use other third-party tools! Organizations like OWASP provide dependency checkers that programmers can run to see if both a third-party tool and any other tools upon which the third-party depends are also safe.

Dead Code *Dead code* is programming that's part of the finished application but doesn't do anything. Dead code is to programming as typos are to writing: writers try to avoid them, but they hippen. On the surface, there's no real security risk to dead code. Dead code adds compilation/interpretation time, makes the code bigger than it needs to be, and might confuse the next programmer reading the code, but none of these will get your system hacked. Use static analyzers to eliminate dead code. (See the upcoming section "Static Code Analyzers" for the details.)

Memory Management Web apps are programs, and programs must run in either the server's or the client's memory. Many attacks—buffer overflow and code reuse, for example—work by accessing a system's memory in some unauthorized fashion. Therefore, talking about memory as an attack vector isn't useful as much as talking about the more detailed attacks. The CompTIA Security+ exam objectives mention *memory management* as a secure coding technique, but it's part of the discussion of specific attacks.

Code Quality and Testing

Once an application has been written, or at least a functional part of the application is complete, it's time to move out of development and into *testing*, also often called *debugging*. At this stage, the application is tested for *code quality*—proper logic, efficiency, and response time. Testing is also the perfect place to verify security. There are many tools available for the programming team to use for debugging, and the CompTIA Security+ exam objectives specifically name a few of them.

This testing should not be confused with the real-time tools provided by most programming languages. Most languages provide a programming tool known as an *integrated development environment (IDE)*. An IDE supports code writing through real-time features that continually check the source code, as the programmer is writing the code, for items such as proper syntax. These features, while handy, can't check source code for logic errors or security problems. Instead, either a static or a dynamic analysis must be used.

Static Code Analyzers

A *static code analyzer* is a debugging tool that reads the source code but does not run the code. All applications use some form of static code analyzer, and most IDEs have one built in to the IDE itself. But programmers aren't limited to just the one in the IDE. Dozens of great static code analyzers are available; they tend to specialize in specific languages and packages. They are self-standing—they are plug-ins to IDEs. Pretty much, there are always three or four static analyzers that are appropriate for any one situation.

 NOTE Most programmers agree that it's good practice to run more than one static code analyzer on a single project.

Static analyzers are important, but they don't run the code; they're limited to looking solely at the static code. If you want to put the code through the wringer, you need to move to dynamic analysis.

Dynamic Analysis

Dynamic analysis is the process of checking an application, or at least a piece of an application, by running the code and observing the logic, inputs, interface, and memory management. Unlike static analysis, a proper dynamic analysis is far more manual; most, if not all, the application's functionality is tested. Dynamic analysis tools tend to work with tools such as memory trackers that give the testers a real-time vision of what the application is doing in memory to detect buffer overflow and code reuse weaknesses.

Input testing, or *fuzzing*, is one of the most important tests done dynamically. Fuzzing means to enter unexpected data into the Web app's input fields to see how the app reacts. Fuzzing can use simple random data (sometimes called *monkey fuzzing*) or it can use intentionally dangerous injection commands, such as entering \[drop table]:user into a last name field.

Model Verification

In programming, the term *model* defines how the developers expect some feature of the final code to perform. Is the monster supposed to explode in a blue flame when the user shoots it? Does an application's Enter Your Personal Information screen force the user into HTTPS? Does the CompTIA practice test application bring up a help screen if the user requests it? Models help programmers (and programmers' bosses) know what to expect of some aspect of the final product.

Model verification is the process of answering the question: "Is this aspect of the application, as it currently exists, matching up to the model of this aspect?" Model verification is often one of the most frustrating aspects to writing quality code, mainly because so much of model verification for software is subjective.

Staging

Staging moves the code from the developers' computers onto servers, which enables stress testing the application. *Stress testing* is aggressive testing of issues such as multiple user simultaneous inputs, multiple server data syncing, and other functions that just can't be emulated at the development stage.

Staging is *not* a real-world environment. Most staging functions take advantage of sandboxing. *Sandboxing* means to use test systems, almost always virtual machines (VMs), that enable developers to run the application aggressively, yet also keep the application safe and separate from anything but itself to protect the rest of the network from unexpected problems.

Production

There's a point where the testing is done and it's time to pull the trigger and get that Web application online and running. This is an exciting time for the developers of the Web application, because their product is finally exposed to the public Internet. This is where all the security issues discussed in this book come into play, such as firewalls, DMZs, load balancing, and intrusion detection/prevention.

The process of moving an application from the development environment to the production environment is called *provisioning*. The process of removing an application from the production environment is called *deprovisioning*.

One important part of the provisioning process, and almost always the last step before the application is uploaded to a server, is code signing. *Code signing* means to sign an individual executable/interpreted code digitally so that users have confidence the code they run is the actual code from the developer. Figure 8-18 shows an example of a warning sign from a Windows 10 system, notifying the user that the executable code is not known to Windows as an approved developer.

Getting Organized

Using the four-step application lifespan defined by the CompTIA Security+ objectives is convenient, but it's also an outrageous oversimplification, making application

development look like a linear process. The reality is that any Web application, even a simple in-house application, is a complex process that's never linear. Let's look at four *development lifecycle models*: waterfall, DevOps, Secure DevOps, and Agile.

Waterfall Model

Starting as far back as the mid-1970s, software development used a linear process known as the *waterfall* model. Like a waterfall, each step of software development had a start and an end, which then led down to the next step. Figure 8-19 shows the CompTIA Security+ steps placed in a waterfall pattern. I've added an important first step inexplicably left out by the CompTIA Security+ objectives: requirements. The *requirements* step formalizes the description of the application, defining what it is supposed to do and how it goes about doing its job. Requirements is always the first step in any waterfall development process.

DevOps

The waterfall model neglects the reality of application development and lifespan in the real world. The reason an application exists is to do some type of job, to be operational. The correct goal of development is to work closely with operations to ensure the application is effective, efficient, secure, up to date, and available. *DevOps*, a grammatically poor but fun-sounding combination of the words "development" and "operations," defines steps that show how the lifespan of an application is more cyclical than linear. A popular way to describe DevOps is the DevOps toolchain, as shown in Figure 8-20.

Figure 8-19
CompTIA
Security+
waterfall model
(with author
addition)

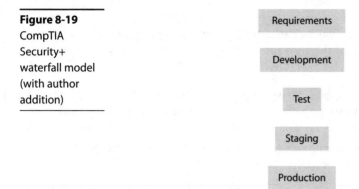

Requirements

Development

Test

Staging

Production

The CompTIA Security+ exam is not going to test on these steps. These steps are well known and understood throughout the industry, so you should know them too.

- **Plan**   What is needed? Requirements.
- **Create**   Develop the code.
- **Verify**   Test the code.
- **Package**   Get approvals, define how the product is released.
- **Release**   Provisioning software, schedules.
- **Configure**   Application storage, application configuration.
- **Monitor**   Monitor performance, security, end user experience.

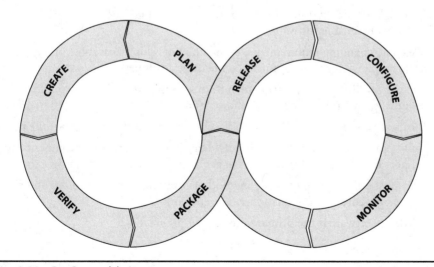

Figure 8-20   DevOps toolchain

Secure DevOps

Secure DevOps means to integrate security tightly into the DevOps toolchain. Security fits into almost every point of the DevOps cycle in what is known as *continuous integration*, but a few important areas are as follows:

- Run *security automation tools* to speed up security testing and eliminate human error. Automation is very popular for many aspects of security testing, such as fuzzing.

- Add strict *change management and version controls* to ensure faults aren't introduced into the application.

- Introduce *security concerns and requirements* at the planning stage to ensure strong security integration.

- *Integrity measurement* shows honesty, morality, and quality of the application.

- *Baselining* defines security objectives that the application must meet.

- *Immutable systems* are systems that once deployed are never upgraded, changed, or patched. They are simply replaced. This is easy to do in a VM environment.

- *Infrastructure as Code (IaC)* means to use preset definition files as opposed to manual configurations to set up servers. IaC prevents accidental vulnerabilities due to flawed server configurations.

Agile

From the moment the waterfall model was first formalized, a number of alternate models were forwarded, all with limited success. Years ago, representatives from these alternative models came together and generated the "Manifesto for Agile Software Development," which espouses the following 12 principles (http://agilemanifesto.org/principles.html):

1. Our highest priority is to satisfy the customer through early and continuous delivery of valuable software.

2. Welcome changing requirements, even late in development. Agile processes harness change for the customer's competitive advantage.

3. Deliver working software frequently, from a couple of weeks to a couple of months, with a preference to the shorter timescale.

4. Business people and developers must work together daily throughout the project.

5. Build projects around motivated individuals. Give them the environment and support they need, and trust them to get the job done.

6. The most efficient and effective method of conveying information to and within a development team is face-to-face conversation.

7. Working software is the primary measure of progress.

8. Agile processes promote sustainable development. The sponsors, developers, and users should be able to maintain a constant pace indefinitely.

9. Continuous attention to technical excellence and good design enhances agility.

10. Simplicity—the art of maximizing the amount of work not done—is essential.

11. The best architectures, requirements, and designs emerge from self-organizing teams.

12. At regular intervals, the team reflects on how to become more effective, then tunes and adjusts its behavior accordingly.

This manifesto didn't define a development model as much as it did a philosophy that stands on these 12 principles.

From this manifesto, a number of different development frameworks have been developed. A complete coverage of even one of the Agile frameworks is far outside the scope of CompTIA Security+, but let's take a moment to consider one framework called Scrum.

NOTE The word Scrum comes from the rugby scrum.

A *Scrum* is a process framework, a series of actions members of a development team need to do to keep software development moving as quickly and efficiently as possible. For example, every day every developer participates in a roughly 15-minute daily Scrum Meeting. In this meeting, every member of the team tells the other members several things:

- What they've done since the last daily Scrum Meeting.

- What they plan to have done by the next daily Scrum meeting.

- Any issues or problems that need to be resolved to keep them moving forward.

Many development teams manifest Agile in their organizations using Scrum principles. Scrum has a proven track record and a rich, complex methodology as well as its own set of certifications. But for the Security+ exam, just make sure you understand the idea of Agile as a philosophy and Scrum as one of the process frameworks designed to bring that philosophy to life.

EXAM TIP Expect a question or two on the CompTIA Security+ exam that asks you to contrast the waterfall versus agile development lifecycle models. Think linear for waterfall and non-linear for development.

Module 8-5: Certificates in Security

This module covers the following CompTIA Security+ objectives:

- **2.3** Given a scenario, troubleshoot common security issues
- **6.4** Given a scenario, implement public key infrastructure

Application security using public key infrastructure (PKI)-based digital certificates is a common tool used in many applications. While digital certificates using PKI was discussed way back in Chapter 2, the practical process of implementing certificates in a production environment creates an opportunity for interesting scenarios that address the steps (and missteps) that take place with certificates.

This module breaks the process of implementing a certificate into several sections. First, the module reviews the concepts and components of certificates, then moves into a discussion of PKI infrastructure as presented in Chapter 2, along with a few additional components. The next sections explore online and offline certificate issues and works on a PKI scenario. The last two sections detail all the major types of certificates and covers certificate formats; that is, how certificates manifest on systems.

Certificate Concepts and Components

Asymmetric encryption works through the orderly exchange of public keys. Sending a public key from one host to another is fraught with security issues. Digital certificates combat these security issues. A digital certificate is a preset data format that contains, at an absolute minimum, a public key plus a digital signature generated by the sending body.

The *X.509 standard* defines specific items that must be part of any certificate for use on the Internet. The X.509 standard requires that these data items are identified using X.509 standard *object identifiers (OIDs)*, strings of numbers separated by periods. Figure 8-21 shows some examples of OIDs: Code Signing and Windows Hardware Driver Verification. Other settings in Figure 8-21 seem to lack OIDs. They're there, but the Windows certificate viewer doesn't show them.

 NOTE OIDs are used in places other than certificates. Check out www.oid-info.com for exhaustive discussions on the uses of OID in technology.

PKI Concepts

For a certificate to provide the necessary security it must contain a digital signature from a third party. A certificate that lacks a third-party signature is called a *self-signed certificate*. So where does this third-party signature come from? Well, it must come from an organization that has its own certificate that can apply a signature to a certificate trusted by both the sender of the certificate as well as the receiver (Figure 8-22).

Figure 8-21
OIDs in a
certificate

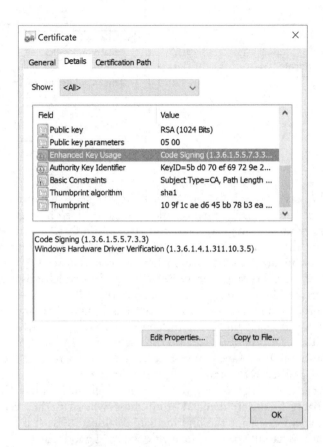

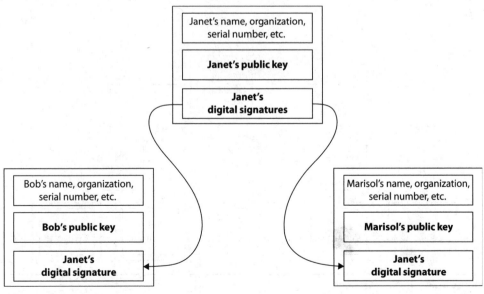

Figure 8-22 Bob and Marisol trust Janet's signature

Figure 8-23
Janet's self-
signed certificate

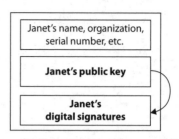

In this case, both Bob and Marisol trust Janet's signature, but who signs Janet's certificate? Janet signs her own certificate, creating a *self-signed certificate* (Figure 8-23).

As more users come into play, this structure grows. In this example, Julie stays at the top of the trust tree, but more people join directly to Julie; others may trust Bob or Marisol (Figure 8-24), creating what's known as a tree-shaped chain-of-trust model. Janet at the top becomes the *root certificate*. Bob and Marisol are called *intermediate certificates* and the rest are individual *user certificates*.

The process of getting a certificate isn't a user making her own and then somehow the third party fills in a blank line of the certificate. The person who a user trusts must make the certificate. A user generates a *certificate signing request (CSR)* and sends the CSR as part of an application for a new certificate. The third party uses the CSR to make a digital certificate and sends the new certificate to the user.

So what does Janet as the root get out of all this? Unless Janet makes some form of (probably financial) demand from those who trust her certificate, nothing! The same problem exists for the intermediate certificates. Trust is valuable and people and organizations happily pay for the confidence of a good trust.

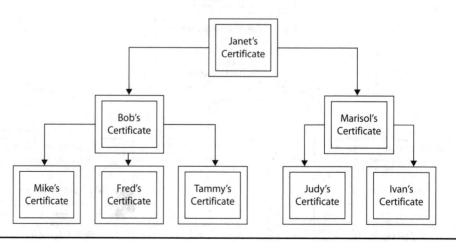

Figure 8-24   Tree trust model

NOTE For a single certificate, there is a specific path of trusts from a user certificate up to the root certificate. This is called a *certificate chain* and, as you might imagine, the process is called *certificate chaining*.

This trust model is the cornerstone of PKI, the primary method certificates are trusted on the Internet. PKI consists primarily of the following entities.

- **Certificate authority (CA)** Any organization that issues digital certificates and that also has a self-signed root certificate (also called a *trust anchor*) accessible on the public Internet (although there's an issue with this as you'll see shortly).

- **Intermediate CA** Subordinate organizations or entities to which CAs delegate the day-to-day issuance of certificates on behalf of the CA. They also issue intermediate certificates that handle the day-to-day security of the trust chain.

- **End certificates** The certificates issued by CAs or intermediate CAs used by secure servers to initiate secure sessions.

The PKI model used by the Internet consists of several certificate authorities, each creating their own separate tree trust model, as shown in Figure 8-25.

Online vs. Offline CA

The root certificate for a CA is an incredibly important certificate. Nevertheless, the nature of PKI means that the root certificate must be online, visible on the public Internet. Should this certificate be compromised in any way, the CA's entire PKI becomes useless. Many CAs take their trust anchor offline, using only their intermediate CAs for the day-to-day work. They bring the root certificates online only to issue new intermediate CAs, then take the root back offline.

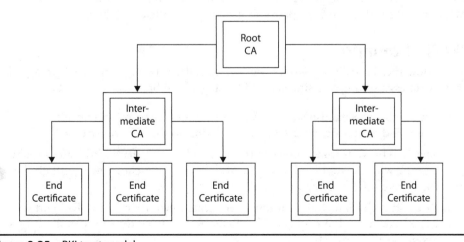

Figure 8-25 PKI trust model

Figure 8-26
Certificate chain
(a.k.a. the *path*)
in Windows

It's easy to see the PKI certificate chain in action by looking at the certificate store on any host. Figure 8-26 shows Windows certificate store, displaying the certificate chain (Windows calls it the certificate path) on its own tab in the dialog box.

PKI TLS Scenario

To see how these certificates work together, consider a basic scenario where a person wants to access a secure Web site using TLS using a Web browser.

1. During the TLS handshake, the Web server sends a copy of its entire certificate chain (end certificate, intermediates, and root) to the Web browser.

2. The Web browser stores copies of the root and intermediate certificates locally. Starting with the root certificate, the Web browser marches down through the chain, carefully checking each certificate.

3. Part of this check includes running Certificate Revocation List (CRL) and Online Certificate Status Protocol (OCSP). Refer back to Chapter 2 for details on these two important protocols.

4. Many Web servers speed up the OCSP process by using OCSP stapling. *Stapling* means to send a premade OCSP response automatically with every certificate in the chain. Web browsers designed to use OCSP stapling will use this premade response.

5. Assuming the certificate chain is correct, the Web browser accepts the certificates and the TLS handshake continues. If there's a problem—a *certificate issue*—the browser stops the handshake and gives an error, displaying some form of information to give the user a clue as to the problem (Figure 8-27).

Types of Certificates

It's common for those interested in X.509 certificates to explore HTTPS using TLS as the first exposure to certificates, but it's equally important to know that many applications beyond HTTPS use X.509 certificates. You'll even find variations among HTTPS certificates.

HTTPS Certificate Types

With a new entity, such as an individual who wants to set up his or her own secure Web server, the issuing CA must trust that entity. So how does a CA learn to trust that entity?

Figure 8-27
Certificate error
in Chrome on
Android

When PKI was first established, there was no ruleset that defined how a CA should trust a new potential entity to give them a certificate. Over time, a few extensions were added to certificates that defined different levels of trust. The CompTIA Security+ exam covers DV and EV.

DV Certificates   *Domain validation (DV)* certificates are the lowest level of SSL certificates. CAs issue DV certificates to the domain admin contact in the public record associated with a domain name. DV certificates are cheap (or even free) and the process is automatic, making for very quickly issued certificates.

The problem with DV certificates is that they are susceptible to phishing and man-in-the-middle attacks. There's no verification check that the DNS name matches the organization, nor is the organization itself checked.

EV Certificates   An *extended validation (EV)* certificate differs from a DV certificate, requiring a more rigorous process of verifying the applicant. The CA/Browser Forum (www.cabforum.org), a voluntary group of CAs and browser developers, maintains clear guidelines for their members to use to verify entities for EV certificates.

The steps for obtaining an EV certificate vary by organization type, but for a private organization to get an EV certificate, the following must happen:

1. Verify the organization is properly formed (incorporated, private).

2. Verify some form of registration of the organization (such as its Dun & Bradstreet rating).

3. Verify the organization's formal legal name against the name used on the EV application.

4. Verify the name and address of the organization or the name and address of a registered agent for the applying entity.

CAs have the right to add to this list of requirements.

EV certificates aren't required, but as the public continues to be aware of the extra trust involved with sites using EV certificates, any e-commerce site or other sensitive data services should move to EV for the extra security and trust.

The Green ... Something   One of the big sales pitches CAs employ to get people to recognize a site using an EV certificate versus a DV certificate is to use some form of interface change on the address bar—always green—that reveals the EV *siteness*. Which green thing shows up on the address bar depends on the individual Web browser; it can vary by browser version as well. Figure 8-28 shows two addresses on Google Chrome version 60.0.3112.113. The top uses a DV certificate; the bottom uses an EV certificate. Note the DV only says the word "Secure," while the EV shows the full name of the organization.

Wildcard Certificates

HTTP certificates typically are issued to specific URLs. For example, my company has one certificate for the www.totalsem.com Web site and a second certificate for our portal,

Figure 8-28 DV (top) and EV (bottom) address bars in Chrome

hub.totalsem.com. We purchased the two certificates at different times and from different CAs (Figure 8-29).

Wildcard certificates apply to a whole domain, rather than a specific URL. If we purchased a wildcard certificate for totalsem.com, every subdomain we create will use that certificate. This sounds great, right? We would need to purchase a single certificate to secure www.totalsem.com and hub.totalsem.com, two subdomains of totalsem.com.

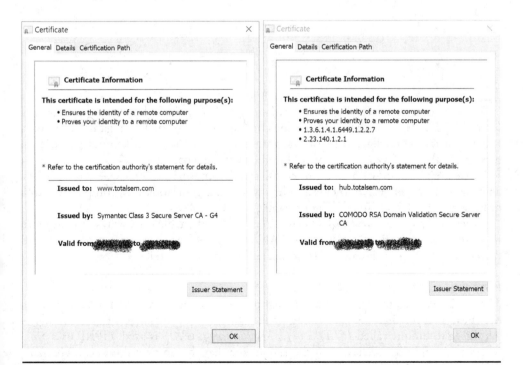

Figure 8-29 Two certificates for two different URLs on the same domain

Figure 8-30
Google is big
enough to
use wildcards
publicly.

The danger comes from rogue servers. Janet (my fictional employee) creates a custom server for some purpose that's outside the company purview, such as a game server or a torrent mirror. The wildcard certificate would apply to counterstrike.totalsem.com or torrents.totalsem.com just like it would to the legitimate company URLs.

There are places to use a wildcard certificate. An internal network where trust is less an issue is one example. Another example is when an organization is in complete control of its own CA, such as Google (Figure 8-30).

Subject Alternative Name (SAN) extensions to X.509 enable certificates that support more than one specific domain name. SAN certificates—as they're marketed—list the domains they support. Figure 8-31 shows a SAN certificate detail.

Pinning

There are scenarios where a bad actor might try to take over a CA and quickly update the entire PKI for that CA, generating perfectly legal (chain-wise) certificates. To combat this, a technique called *HTTP Public Key Pinning (HPKP)* is used. HPKP uses *pins*, which are simply stored hashes of the public key that the host machines can compare against to verify that the public key inside the certificate is the same as anticipated.

Figure 8-31
SAN certificate
that includes
wildcards

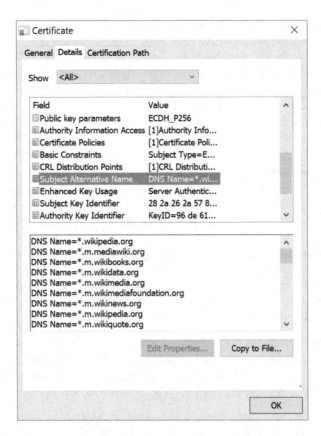

Other Certificates

X.509 digital certificates were designed from the beginning to support any application that needed a safe, trustable model for public key exchange. Granted, SSL/TLS handshakes are certainly the most popular single use of them, but there are plenty more. Here's a list of other popular formats for certificate use:

- E-mail
- Code signing
- Machine/computer
- User

E-mail Traditional e-mail has no encryption, making all e-mail easily read by man-in-the-middle attacks. E-mail certificates aren't used for authentication as in HTTP, but are used with S/MIME to generate encrypted e-mail. To use S/MIME, discussed earlier in this chapter, each e-mail account needs its own key pair. To encrypt e-mail messages, two e-mail users must first exchange public keys. The public keys are exchanged via e-mail certificates.

S/MIME e-mail certificates have lost a lot of popularity due to the growing popularity of secure SNMP/POP/IMAP protocols. In these cases, SSL/TLS certificates are installed on e-mail servers just as SSL/TLS certificates are installed on Web servers.

The one benefit to S/MIME is that individual users have complete control over their e-mail encryption. Modern versions do not provide point-to-point encryption as e-mail is only encrypted from server to server.

Web-based e-mail services (such as Gmail) provide end-to-end encryption. They use HTTPS exclusively.

NOTE Be ready for scenarios that challenge administrators for certain e-mail situations. Normally, e-mail uses unencrypted credentials/clear text for exchanging messages. A user that needs encrypted, secure e-mail communication must use S/MIME.

Code Signing *Code signing* verifies that an executable file is in good order via digital signatures. Application developers create key pairs, sign the code by encrypting a hash with the private key, and then distribute the code. Assuming users have the certificate from the developer, they can use the public key to verify the digital signature. Like e-mail, code signing uses PKI extensively (Figure 8-32).

Machine/Computer Assigning a certificate to individual computers isn't too common, but there are places where this is used. Very high security, enterprise-level 802.11 wireless networks using TTLS security can assign a *machine* certificate to every system. Figure 8-33 shows the configuration of TTLS on a Windows system.

User *User* certificates are used in unique circumstances where some application needs good security applied to individual users. On Windows systems that support Encrypting File System (EFS), each user on an individual host receives a certificate when the user activates EFS.

Certificate Formats

Certificates contain quite a bit of data that needs organization in terms of storage. A certificate sitting on a hard drive manifests as a file. Over the years a number of file formats have been developed. In general, these many formats can be organized by certain criteria. First, is the data encoded in binary format or in Base64 text? Second, what's being stored in the single file? Does the file format store just a single certificate, a completed certificate chain, or a full key pair?

There is no benefit of one format versus another. It's simply a matter of what type of certificate information is needed, what type of encryption is needed, and what a platform requires.

NOTE There are tools to convert most certificate formats into other formats.

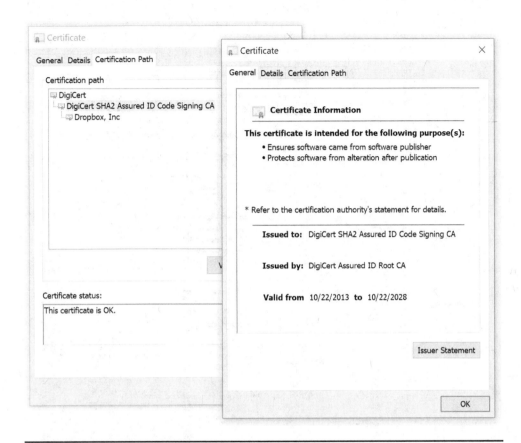

Figure 8-32 Code signing certificate

DER

Distinguished Encoding Rules (DER) is an early and complex binary format for storing pretty much anything desired in terms of certificates. DER is binary, storing single certificates, certificate chains, or private keys. A DER format uses either a .der or .cer extension. This type of format is often used with Java applications.

PEM

Named after a failed e-mail project, *Privacy Enhanced Mail (PEM)* format is a DER file encoded using Base64 instead of binary. Like DER format, it may contain single certificates, certificate chains, or private keys. PEM files come in a number of different file extensions: .pem, .crt, .cer, and .key.

 NOTE Apache Web servers need PEM files to store their certificates.

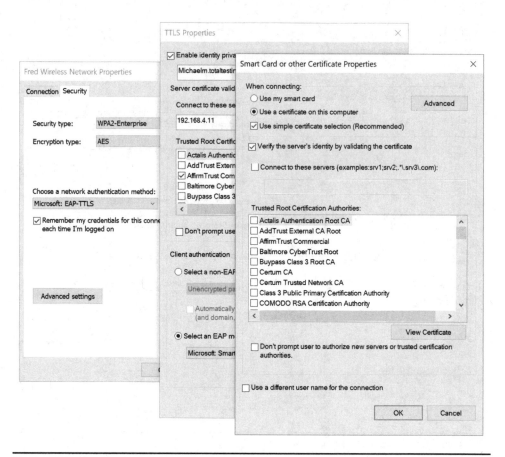

Figure 8-33 Configuring TTLS on a wireless network

PFX/PKCS#12

Leaving a certificate in the form of a file opens the file itself to risk from theft. *Personal Information Exchange (PFX)* files fully encrypt all the data in the file and require a password to open them. A PFX file may contain single certificates, certificate chains, or private keys, although in most cases it is used to store public/private key pairs. PFX is a binary file and is heavily used by Microsoft products. PFX files are also known as *PKCS#12*. These files use the extension .pfx or .p12.

P7B

Of all the format types, a *P7B* file only contains certificates or certificate chains. P7B will never contain a private key. P7B files use Base64 encoding and almost always have the extension .p7b. P7B files are also known as *PKCS#7*.

Key Escrow

Private keys tend to be forgotten in certificate discussions, but without a private key a certificate is useless. Any protocol that uses the idea of a server handing out public keys also means that the server in question must carefully and securely store a private key as well.

Loss of a private key can be disastrous, yet it happens more than one might think. There are plenty of scenarios where a hard drive fails, wiping out or corrupting a private key, rendering a server useless.

Key escrow is the process of an organization storing a copy of a server (or servers) key pairs for safety in a place where a third party might have access to them in case of a serious mishap.

Questions

1. Cache poisoning is directed against which of the following servers?

    A. DHCP

    B. Web

    C. Domain controller

    D. DNS

2. Which two of the following are secure FTP protocols?

    A. SSL

    B. FTPS

    C. SFTP

    D. TFTP

    E. SSH

3. The four-step process that initiates an SSL/TLS session is called a(n) _____.

    A. initialization

    B. authentication

    C. handshake

    D. connection

4. Encrypted IMAP uses which TCP port number?

    A. 995

    B. 993

    C. 465

    D. 587

5. Scott receives an e-mail from Mike with a digital signature attachment. Mike is probably using which of the following protocols?

   A. Secure SMTP

   B. SFTP

   C. TFTP

   D. S/MIME

6. Inserting unexpected text into a URL is what form of attack?

   A. Command injection

   B. SQL injection

   C. LDAP injection

   D. XML injection

7. What kind of attack manipulates a token on an established Web session?

   A. Buffer overflow

   B. LDAP injection

   C. Cross-site scripting

   D. Clickjacking

8. A new attack that is previously unknown to the security world is called a _____ attack.

   A. birthday

   B. header manipulation

   C. proto-malware

   D. zero-day

9. Which of the following is a minimum set of performance values that define a certain aspect of what the application must do?

   A. Requirements

   B. Agile

   C. Model

   D. Baseline

10. Scrum is a _____ based on the Agile philosophy.

   A. timing system

   B. DevOps cycle

   C. process framework

   D. manifesto

Answers

1. **D.** Cache poisoning attacks DNS servers.

2. **B, C.** The two secure FTP protocols are FTP over SSL and SSH FTP.

3. **C.** The four-step process that initiates an SSL/TLS session is called a handshake.

4. **B.** Encrypted IMAP uses TCP port number 993.

5. **D.** E-mail attachments of all sorts use MIME; the secure version is S/MIME.

6. **A.** A command injection attack inserts unexpected text into a URL.

7. **C.** A cross-site scripting attack manipulates a token on an established Web session.

8. **D.** A zero-day attack pounces on a previously unknown vulnerability in software or operating systems.

9. **D.** A baseline documents a minimum set of performance values that define aspects of an application.

10. **C.** A Scrum is a process framework based on the Agile program development philosophy.

Testing Your Infrastructure

Any infrastructure has vulnerabilities, whether in software flaws, network configuration choices, or employee foibles. Good, security-conscious organizations not only need to understand the ways attackers can gain access to their infrastructure, but also need to test infrastructure thoroughly for any weakness.

This chapter explores these themes in three modules:

- Vulnerability Impact
- Social Engineering
- Security Assessment

Module 9-1: Vulnerability Impact

This module covers the following CompTIA Security+ objectives:

- **1.6** Explain the impact associated with types of vulnerabilities
- **2.3** Given a scenario, troubleshoot common security issues

Testing infrastructure is a broad concept that involves just about every topic previously covered in this book. A big part of testing infrastructure involves understanding the impact of many common vulnerabilities. This module covers these vulnerabilities and discusses the impact of an attack against them.

I've grouped these vulnerabilities into four types: Device/Hardware, Configuration, Application, and Management/Design. As you read, keep in mind that while these four headings are not on the CompTIA Security+ exam, the individual vulnerabilities most certainly are.

 NOTE For some reason the CompTIA objectives list a few items, such as zero day, as vulnerabilities even though they are clearly threats. In the spirit of completeness, I've included them here.

Device/Hardware Vulnerabilities

As you've seen throughout the book, the individual boxes/things—home automation, switches, routers, smartphones, desktops, and so forth—have many vulnerabilities. Here are the ones specifically mentioned on the CompTIA Security+ exam objectives:

- Embedded systems
- End-of-life systems
- Lack of vendor support
- System sprawl/undocumented assets

Embedded Systems

Embedded systems—which we covered way back in Chapter 7—suffer from some specific vulnerabilities. The main goals of attacks against embedded systems are to take over the systems, prevent the systems from operating, or steal the data coming in and out of the embedded systems. The impact of unsecured vulnerabilities is potentially massive, from complete loss of resources relying on the system, to sensitive data loss. The ICS/SCADA industries, heavy users of embedded systems, understand the impact of an attack that could literally take down manufacturing systems or, possibly the worst-case scenario, cause the shutdown or destruction of rail systems and power grids.

End-of-Life Systems

End-of-life systems—like the essential Windows XP computer that had one critical function—have one serious vulnerability in that they may store sensitive data that bad actors might access. Data sanitization processes prevent the impact of these vulnerabilities by eliminating the data before the system passes out of the organization's hands and into recycling.

Lack of Vendor Support

All systems need some amount of vendor support. Vendors provide repair/replacement. Vendors provide firmware/software patches. Vendors usually provide some online user forums to give end users a place to discuss configuration and security. *Lack of vendor support* denies users the capability to address these important issues, creating serious vulnerabilities. The impact of these vulnerabilities is vast but includes potential system takeovers and data theft due to unpatched systems. When Microsoft stopped supporting and patching Windows XP, for example, the security flaws in the OS didn't go away. People who continued to use Windows XP became increasingly vulnerable to hacking. Lack of vendor support is almost always a motivation to stop using equipment and move to another vendor.

System Sprawl/Undocumented Assets

When an organization acquires any form of system, physical or virtual, in an unordered, uncontrolled, or unprotected fashion, that system will not benefit from the protection that organized IT security provides to the infrastructure as a whole. The acquisition of undocumented assets is called *system sprawl*, which either sounds quaint or like a bad 1980s horror flick. The impact of these types of systems can be devastating to an organization, enabling bad actors to take control of those systems, and potentially to control the entire infrastructure. Some of the most horrifying incidents in the history of IT security—such as an organization having every server in its internal network wiped clean—came from a vulnerable system, outside the control or even knowledge of the security group that's attacked by bad actors (not the 1980s kind).

Configuration Vulnerabilities

Every device that uses an IP address needs some amount of configuration. Almost every chapter thus far has discussed configuration, from routers to WAPs to IoT, but the CompTIA Security+ exam will test you on the impact of common vulnerabilities. A few of these vulnerabilities should ring familiar to you, but again, this module is all about the impact:

- Default configuration
- Misconfiguration/weak configuration
- Improperly configured accounts
- Improper certificate and key management

Default Configuration

If a device comes with firmware, it will have a default configuration. Default configurations are nice in that they often enable a device to work well for unsophisticated users. Classic factory defaults include user name/passwords, SSIDs, IP addresses, and DHCP servers. The downside to default configurations is that pretty much anyone with even basic knowledge of your devices may gain instant control. Entire Web sites are dedicated to default user names and passwords (Figure 9-1).

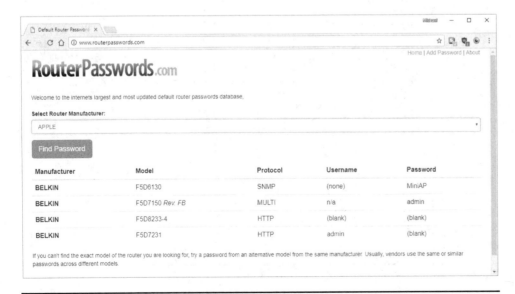

Figure 9-1 Typical user name/password site

The impact of such vulnerabilities varies depending on the type of device. Taking control of a home router may give a bad actor access to your personal data. Taking control of a WAP might give a bad actor access to anyone's data who accesses that WAP's SSID. Internet access might be stopped, although most attackers will prefer to not be so obvious.

Misconfiguration/Weak Configuration

Default settings might be unique to firmware-based devices, but misconfiguration or weak configurations cover just about every type of hardware and software in existence. *Misconfigurations* include enabling services or functions that leave a system vulnerable to an attack, such as leaving on FTP support for a Web server (Figure 9-2). Note that most devices have services and functions enabled by default. You need to disable anything unneeded.

Weak configurations, as the name implies, fail to take advantage of the full strength offered by a system or software. Two great examples here are weak passwords and weak encryptions. Once again using a Web server as an example, it's far too easy to provide support for older, weaker encryptions such as SSL when TLS is the way to go these days.

Improperly Configured Accounts

Almost everything has some form of account, and there are plenty of ways to configure accounts improperly. Default user names and passwords are typical examples, but this can go much deeper. Leaving guest or anonymous accounts active on server applications gives bad actors an easy entrée into a system, with the resulting impact being whatever evil they decide to do. Improperly configured operating system or file system accounts potentially could impact the system by giving unintentionally elevated privileges to otherwise normal users, exposing sensitive data to those who otherwise would not have access.

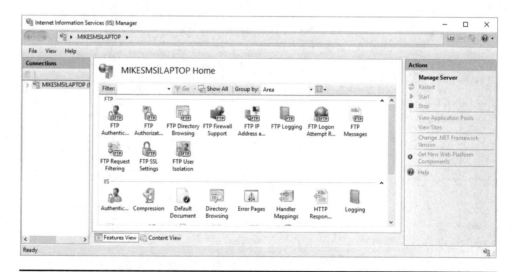

Figure 9-2   Do you really want FTP on this Web site?

EXAM TIP Look for a question on the CompTIA Security+ exam that talks about permission issues as a common security issue to troubleshoot. These happen when an admin grants permissions improperly or unwisely to a user account. You can troubleshoot such issues by reviewing groups periodically to ensure users are in only the proper groups.

Improper Certificate and Key Management

The most important aspect of certificate and key management is protection of your private keys. Giving a bad actor access to a private key stops the power of asymmetric encryption, leaving the application open to the impact of spoofing and data theft. Every operating system does a great job protecting certificates, so it's usually up to the admins and users to make silly mistakes. One of the most classic mistakes is exporting copies of certificates or keys outside the protected data store, as shown in Figure 9-3.

Application Vulnerabilities

Applications contain their own unique set of vulnerabilities, but the impact of the vulnerabilities often remains the same as seen with devices: taking control of the application, shutting down the application, and accessing data from the application. While many of these vulnerabilities were covered in Chapter 8 (along with full coverage of the hardening necessary), this section looks at several more:

- Race conditions
- Improper input handling
- Improper error handling

Figure 9-3
Exported certificate sitting on a Windows Desktop. Not smart!

- Memory/buffer vulnerability
- Pointer deference
- Resource exhaustion
- Weak cipher suites and implementations
- DLL injection

Race Conditions

Most applications take advantage of multitasking to run multiple processes/functions at the same time. Sometimes the effect of two or more simultaneous transactions can result in undesired results called a race condition. *Race conditions* manifest as counters, totals, and other usually integer values that simply don't add up correctly. The impact of race conditions varies from incorrect values in Web carts to system stops.

Improper Input Handling

Input is a classic area for attack vectors. Without proper input validation and data sanitization, as discussed in Chapter 8, attackers can use these injection attacks to gain unauthorized access to data, execute commands on the Web server itself, and set up the server for further attacks.

Improper Error Handling

No code is perfect, so it's important that coders do a good job dealing with the occasional error through good error handling. While the concept of error handling is well covered in Chapter 8, the impact of poor error-handling vulnerability manifests as downed servers and, in some cases, elevating an attacker's privilege.

Memory/Buffer Vulnerability

All code uses memory to handle the active operation of that code. RAM may be cheap these days, but applications must be programmed properly to be aware of the amount of memory they're using. The CompTIA Security+ objectives include three vulnerabilities that are so closely related that it makes sense to treat them as a single issue:

- Memory leak
- Integer overflow
- Buffer overflow

All three of these vulnerabilities describe some part of memory being filled beyond the programmed capacity. A *memory leak* is a general issue where a single process begins to ask for more and more memory from the system without ever releasing memory. Eventually, the system reaches a memory full state and stops working. *Integer overflows* are when a value greater than an integer variable causes the application to stop working. A buffer is a temporary storage area in memory to hold data, such as the results of a form input. Buffers are fixed in size. If too much data gets into the buffer, causing unpredictable results, that's a *buffer overflow*.

The impact of all these situations is similar in that the system will at best kick out an error (that hopefully is well handled) and at worst cause a system lockup.

Pointer Dereference

A pointer is an object used in most programming languages that "points to" another value in memory. Unlike a variable, a pointer references a memory location. When a pointer accesses the stored value, this is known as *pointer dereference*. If a bad actor can get a pointer to point incorrectly, a dereference can cause havoc to the code. For example, a null pointer dereference is a common way to try to force a buffer overflow. The impact of this vulnerability is the same as previously mentioned.

Resource Exhaustion

Resource exhaustion isn't a vulnerability, it is an attack that takes advantage of one or more of the memory-specific vulnerabilities previously described to bring down the system to create a denial-of-service type of attack. The impact is the denial of the use of that system.

Weak Cipher Suites and Implementations

The security industry does a very good job of keeping the IT world aware of the most secure forms of encryption. This is especially true of the cipher suites used with TLS. Chapter 8 shows how a TLS client will negotiate with a TLS server during the hand-shakes for certain cipher suites. If a bad actor can negotiate a weaker cipher suite, this makes their attack much easier. The impact of a successful attack is data loss through man-in-the-middle attacks and possibly privilege escalation to the server itself.

DLL Injection

A dynamic-link library (DLL) is a file used in Windows systems that provides support code to executable files. Every Windows system has hundreds of DLLs, most commonly stored in the \Windows\System32 folder (Figure 9-4). Most applications provide their own DLLs as well. DLLs help reduce code size and speed up processing.

DLL injection is a technique used by bad actors to get users to run malicious code. The code runs in the address space of another process and loads a malicious DLL. Once the DLL runs, all the usual impacts come into play: system control is one of the most common, used to zombify systems for distributed denial-of-service attacks.

Management/Design Vulnerabilities

Some vulnerabilities aren't as technical as the ones mentioned thus far. These are what I call management/design vulnerabilities. The following four specifically listed vulnerabilities cover broader issues—one might be tempted to call these all the rest:

- Untrained users
- Vulnerable business processes
- Architecture/design weaknesses
- New threats/zero day

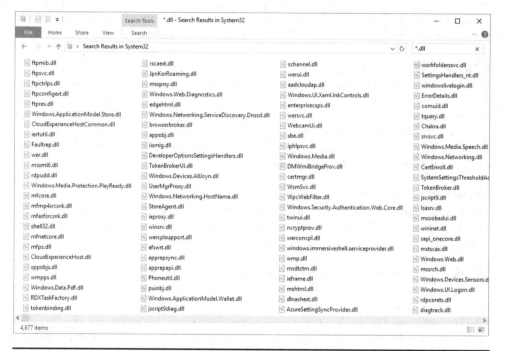

Figure 9-4   Just a few of the DLLs on Mike's laptop

Untrained Users

There are few issues that scare a security professional more than untrained users. Without proper training, users will unwittingly wreak havoc on your infrastructure from the inside. Every IT person has plenty of stories of users unintentionally:

- Installing their own home routers in the organization
- Wiping out entire hard drives with one command
- Shutting down gateway routers
- Giving away user names and passwords over the phone
- Copying sensitive data to thumb drives
- Making Facebook posts of their system information

The impact of untrained users spans the gamut of nightmares: data loss, data theft, loss of reputation, business opportunity, even legal issues. Failure to train users properly is simply not an acceptable situation for any organization.

Vulnerable Business Processes

Almost hand in hand with untrained users are vulnerable business processes. Back in Chapter 1, you learned that the concept of business impact analysis includes the recognition of critical business processes. Failure to secure vulnerable business processes impacts the bottom line of the organization, preventing the organization from doing its job. This would include financial loss and loss of reputation.

Architecture/Design Weaknesses

Any IT infrastructure has some amount of complexity. As the organization grows, that complexity increases exponentially. It's easy to insert design weaknesses inadvertently into your organization IT and security architecture. The impact of those weaknesses is they open unanticipated vulnerabilities to bad actors. The best way to avoid these weaknesses is solid initial design, good change management, plenty of ongoing vulnerability assessments, and occasional penetration testing.

New Threats/Zero Day

For some reason CompTIA calls *zero day* a vulnerability (in Objective 1.6) even though this is a threat and an attack (as noted in Objective 1.2). The impact of a zero day varies by the type of vulnerability the attack exposes. Good patching, good layered defense, and staying on top of the happenings in the security world are your only defense against a previously unknown attack.

Module 9-2: Social Engineering

This module covers the following CompTIA Security+ objectives:

- **1.2** Compare and contrast types of attacks
- **2.3** Given a scenario, troubleshoot common security issues

You've learned about the technical aspects of security, and you've seen how you can use technical measures, such as firewalls, encryption, strong authentication, and so forth, to secure data and systems. But what about the people who use and interact with the systems and data within the organization? What technical measures can you use to secure the system from human security issues? Is there a patch for being human? This module shifts gears and discusses the human element, focusing on human beings as a security weakness. In this module, we'll look at the types of attacks that can take place when an attacker finds and exploits vulnerabilities in the "wetware"—the human being. We'll also examine why these types of attacks are so effective.

Earlier in the book, we looked at some of the different types of technical attacks that can be perpetrated against a system or network. This module explores attacks against people. *Social engineering* essentially means that an attacker or malicious person can use weaknesses inherent in all people in general to try to gain information about a network, a system, or even an entire organization. In some cases, attackers can even get unsuspecting people to perform actions for them.

Human beings need to be social; we interact well as a species with each other, for the most part, and most human beings need that interaction. We want to be liked and to be helpful, we respect and fear authority, and so on. In some cases, our emotions, needs, desires, and opinions can be used against us by a malicious person who is adept at manipulating and influencing people. The next sections explore the targets and goals of an attacker when using social engineering attacks, and examines some of these attacks in depth and how they are executed.

Targets and Goals

As with any type of technical or physical attack on an organization, an attacker will use social engineering to further his goals in gaining information, harming systems, infiltrating a network, and so on. The attack methodologies used by attackers when launching social engineering attacks aren't much different from those used when launching technical attacks; the attacker simply must do some reconnaissance, find vulnerabilities, and exploit those vulnerabilities. In the case of social engineering attacks, the vulnerabilities usually come from people associated with the organization, network, or system, or even from other people peripherally involved with the organization.

Attackers use social engineering against people associated with the organization to gain access to stuff. That stuff can be passwords, network access, system access, and more. A target can be a system administrator, an executive, a maintenance person, an administrative assistant, or even a janitor. Even people who are loosely associated with the organization, such as occasional contractors, delivery personnel, and so on, can become targets of an attacker simply because they can offer an avenue of attack into the organization that may allow the attacker to connect with someone else who can get them deeper into the organization. Attackers don't always contact targets personally, although they may later in the relationship.

Common personnel issues provide targets. Attackers scope out and approach targets through social media, personal e-mail, social gatherings, and other venues. Policy violations, such as sharing login information, can present malicious actors unexpected attack routes.

Usually an attacker will try to gather information about a target first, finding out things about the person, such as hobbies, likes and dislikes, work and personal habits, relationships with other people, and so forth. The attacker tries to gather this information to establish a relationship with the target, or at the very least to take advantage of some weakness in the way the person interacts with the organization. In some cases, this approach can be a positive experience for the target, such as when the social engineer wants to establish a friendly relationship. In other cases, the relationship can be quite negative, such as when the attacker discovers some embarrassing or damaging information and wants to blackmail the victim into doing some misdeed. In any case, there's usually a reconnaissance phase before the attacker makes the actual approach and attack.

The attacker may have several goals, including getting past physical security in the organization, stealing information, getting physical access to a data center, and so on. An attacker will select a target that can get him closer to those goals. Often, the target of social engineering may just be a first or intermediate step in a series of attacks.

Types of Attacks

We'll look at several different types of social engineering attacks, including the basic types that you'll see on the Security+ exam. These attacks can range from the very simple to the very complex, and they may involve complicated scenarios or even multiple avenues of approach. You can probably use your imagination to come up with a dozen or more types of attacks or methods that a malicious social engineer would use to get what he wanted.

 EXAM TIP Many social engineering attacks involve *data exfiltration*, getting data off a computer without permission. An attacker can accomplish this in person, such as by gaining physical access to a system, inserting a thumb drive, and copying files. Data exfiltration can also happen through malware or social engineering, such as tricking an employee into providing confidential information to the "auditor." It's a catchy buzzword for theft.

Shoulder Surfing

Shoulder surfing, an attack that is often undetected by the victim, involves the attacker inconspicuously looking over the victim's shoulder at her computer screen to see what she is typing or viewing. This type of attack is usually one of opportunity; the attacker simply waits for the right moment to walk by the victim and look at what she is doing, or he invents a reason to engage the victim in conversation while he glances at the screen. Modern technology enables shoulder surfing with a smartphone camera from across a room. Proximity is a relative term.

The attacker can use shoulder surfing to steal user credentials, account numbers, and other sensitive information, although usually it's only in small amounts due to the brief and unpredictable nature of the attack. Users can thwart these attacks simply by being cautious with overly curious passers-by. Figure 9-5 shows how simple—and productive—shoulder surfing can be for an attacker.

Dumpster Diving

Often, organizations throw away papers, optical discs, and other types of materials they no longer need. These materials can contain sensitive information. A person with malicious intent can access that trash to try to gather information to use in an attack against the organization; an action with a cute name, dumpster diving.

Dumpster diving can help a social engineer gather all kinds of information about an organization from discarded company directories, organizational charts, server and operating system manuals, contract documents, financial records, and other items. For example, if the company throws away a bunch of user manuals on an older version of Microsoft SQL Server, an attacker might assume that the company recently upgraded to the newest version, and that might give him an idea about what vulnerabilities the new version could have. Company directories and organizational charts can give an attacker insight into who works where, how important he or she is, and who works for whom,

Figure 9-5
Shoulder surfing
yields good
results!

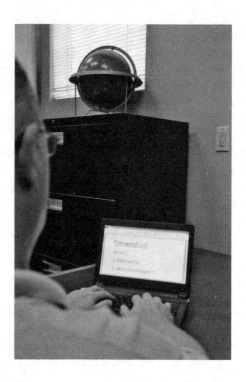

along with personal information, such as cell phone numbers and e-mail addresses. Attackers can use all this information to prepare and execute a social engineering attack on the organization's personnel.

Dumpster diving attacks are reasonably easy to prevent; the organization can simply screen its trash and make sure that it shreds or recycles sensitive documents and media. The organization must train employees to dispose of anything containing potentially sensitive information securely and not simply throw it into the dumpster. Additionally, the organization might want to install CCTVs or fences around its dumpsters and trash areas. In Figure 9-6, you can see an example of valuable information an attacker might find when dumpster diving.

Tailgating

In a typical *tailgating* social engineering attack, a bad actor follows an authorized person through a security checkpoint or door to gain access to unauthorized areas. Or it could involve a little bit of creativity: the intruder, with arms full, could ask for help opening a door to get in. Social engineers have also been known to ride in wheelchairs, walk on crutches, or otherwise appear to be disadvantaged and unable to open a door or get through a security checkpoint without assistance. To mitigate vulnerabilities associated with tailgating, an organization should require positive identification and authentication using access badges and accounting for every single individual who comes through a checkpoint.

Figure 9-6
Finding treasure
in a dumpster

Impersonation

An impersonator masquerades as a valid network user, perhaps someone with higher privileges or status in the organization than the victim. The social engineer impersonates a valid user over e-mail, telephone, or social media and convinces the victim that he works in the organization. This technique is effective only if the target doesn't personally know the user being impersonated. The victim may have heard of the impersonated user during business or may have seen his name on an organizational chart.

EXAM TIP Sometimes an intruder can actually be a valid network user. A disgruntled employee can do some serious damage to your network and systems. Troubleshooting insider threat scenarios requires careful monitoring of logs and reports, especially looking for patterns of company security policy violations.

Hoaxes

We've all probably received the e-mails stating that little Timmy is dying of a serious disease and wants his e-mail forwarded to 10,000 people, or that Bill Gates is giving away his fortune and you can receive a part of it if you forward the e-mail to 10 of your friends. You've probably also seen e-mails asking you to provide bank account information so that a deposed prince or forgotten relative can deposit millions of dollars into your bank account to save their fortune. These are, of course, hoax e-mails, and they usually merely waste the recipients' time, increase e-mail traffic in the organization, and cause a nuisance. A *hoax* is a lie or false story that leads one or more people to believe something is true that is very much not true.

Occasionally, hoaxes can be used to carry out serious, sophisticated attacks. For example, a chain e-mail hoax could also have a virus attached to it, and by forwarding it to 10 friends, you are, in fact, spreading the virus. A hoax could also be used to track who the recipient knows; some chain e-mails ask the receiver to forward the mail to several friends as well as the original sender. This would enable an attacker to gain information regarding the victim's associates, as well as their e-mail addresses.

Hoaxes aren't confined to e-mail; hoaxers can use fake Web sites, social media sites, and even telephone calls to perpetrate a hoax. Their goal may be to get donations, spread a fake story, or even simply to see how many people will fall for it. As with most other social engineering attacks, an organization's best defense against hoaxes is a good security education and training program for users.

Phishing

A *phishing* attack involves something that poses as a trusted source but attempts to deliver a malicious payload or gather personal or sensitive information from an individual, such as a Social Security number, driver's license number, credit card information, bank accounts, user names, and passwords. The attack typically involves an e-mail sent to a user claiming that the user needs to connect to or log on to a site (with the link provided, of course) to verify an account or other such pretext. The user clicks the link in the e-mail and is directed to a site that looks convincingly genuine, and may even mirror a real site. The phishing attack can take many forms at this point. The link might download malicious software that runs a ransomware attack, encrypting files or drives and then demanding money to decrypt the files. Alternatively, the unsuspecting user might input her credentials or information as the e-mail requests, not knowing that instead of passing on this information in a secure way to a legitimate site, she is simply handing it over to an attacker.

Phishing attacks have become increasingly sophisticated over the years; early phishing e-mails could be spotted as obvious frauds because they came from unknown or obfuscated domains, used broken wording or incorrect spelling and grammar in the message, and redirected the user to a site that was obviously not a legitimate business site. Nowadays, phishing attacks are executed with much more sophistication and precision; they often are very professional and convincing in their wording, use spoofed or similar-sounding domain names, and redirect users to professional-looking Web sites that may even provide some sort of fake functionality. Figure 9-7 shows an example of a phishing e-mail attack.

Note that phishing is different from *pharming*; in a phishing attack, the user is directed to a fake site through a link embedded in an e-mail. In a pharming attack, the user is redirected to a fake site through some other means, such as malware on the computer, host file poisoning, or redirection from a DNS server that has been compromised. The end results can be the same, however; if a user is redirected to a fake site through a pharming attack, the user's system may be attacked or the user enticed to input sensitive information into the site, which is then collected by the attacker.

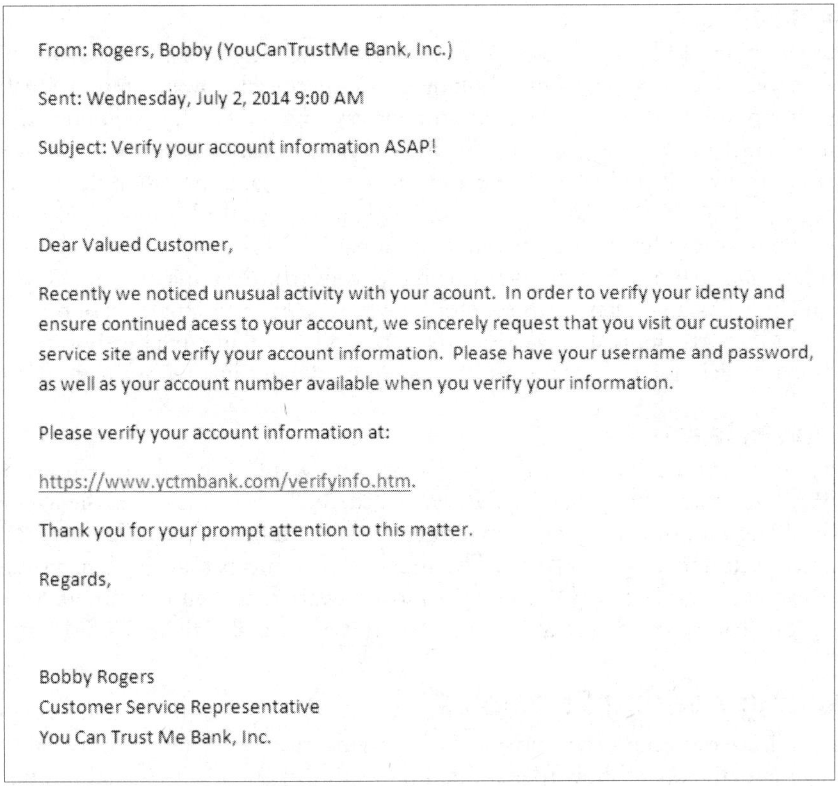

From: Rogers, Bobby (YouCanTrustMe Bank, Inc.)

Sent: Wednesday, July 2, 2014 9:00 AM

Subject: Verify your account information ASAP!

Dear Valued Customer,

Recently we noticed unusual activity with your acount. In order to verify your identy and ensure continued acess to your account, we sincerely request that you visit our custoimer service site and verify your account information. Please have your username and password, as well as your account number available when you verify your information.

Please verify your account information at:

https://www.yctmbank.com/verifyinfo.htm.

Thank you for your prompt attention to this matter.

Regards,

Bobby Rogers
Customer Service Representative
You Can Trust Me Bank, Inc.

Figure 9-7 A phishing e-mail

Whaling

Whaling is a variant of phishing, where the social engineer sends the phishing e-mail to a high-value target instead of the masses. Usually, whaling attacks target senior executives and others in important positions. These types of attacks involve much higher stakes, because senior personnel in the organization have information that may be considered more critical and of higher value to an attacker. Like phishing, whaling attacks can deliver a malicious payload or gather sensitive information.

Vishing

Vishing is yet another variant of phishing attacks that is often perpetrated over Voice over IP (VoIP) telephone networks. Vishing can be quite effective because it may use prerecorded messages and spoofed telephone numbers to convince a target that the message is legitimate. The attack may advise victims to go to a Web URL to correct or verify their information, or even to call a number, where the attacker will impersonate someone who has the authority to collect the information and "help" the victim.

Spear Phishing

The last variation of phishing attacks that we'll discuss is known as *spear phishing*. In this attack, the social engineer targets the phishing e-mail specifically toward an individual or associated group (think "the accounting department of company X"), instead of being generic enough to target many people at once. In the phishing e-mail, the attacker will often use information that can be linked to the victims, such as personal information the attacker has already gathered by some other means. Examples might include the last four digits of victims' credit card numbers or Social Security numbers, or partial date of birth. This lends credibility to the attack and makes it easier to persuade the victims that the e-mail is genuine. Another common spear phishing tactic is to spoof a known sender; for example, if Bob frequently receives PDF reports from Alice, a savvy attacker could spoof an e-mail to Bob from Alice containing a malicious attachment, and Bob would likely not think twice about opening it.

Watering Hole Attack

Attackers have another tool that targets groups who would normally ignore or resist a spear phishing attack. In a *watering hole attack*, the bad actor researches the Web-usage patterns of a group, such as a company or department, to find a Web site that the group commonly visits and evidently trusts. The attacker then infects that site. The group continues to access the infected Web site, blissfully unaware that their computers have been infected. The bad actor then steals information in typical malware-attack fashion.

Social Engineering Principles

Even though we train our users on what social engineering is, how it works, what to look for in such an attack, and how to avoid falling victim, these attacks are still quite effective. Why is that? Because it's very difficult to fight human nature; even when we know that something we're doing isn't quite right, that we're not following the proper procedures, or that we're breaking the rules, or that nagging little suspicious voice inside of us tells us that something's not quite right, we still fall for social engineering tricks. These attacks work because people are, well, human.

You should be aware of the social engineering *principles*—and their reasons for effectiveness—so that you can protect yourself and your users. An attacker can exploit almost all these principles as part of an elaborate lie, hoax, or other false pretense or context, to support the attacker's approach.

Authority

Attacks that use *authority* take advantage of two reactions most people have to authoritative sources, such as bosses, VIPs, and so on: fear and respect. People respect people in authority and sometimes even fear them, because interactions with them reveal that they are in a position of authority for a reason; they may have power over us, such as the power to fire us or give us raises, for instance. We also respect positions of authority because we're typically taught that tendency as we grow up, and we experience it when we enter the workforce. Because of our fear of and respect for authority, we sometimes bend over backward to do what we're being asked to do by an authority figure, regardless of how we feel about it. Sometimes we act out of fear of the authority figure, and sometimes we want to impress important people with our knowledge, helpfulness, the willingness to do our jobs, and so on. Attackers make use of these tendencies to convince us that we are *required* to take these actions by virtue of the position of authority they are exerting over us.

Intimidation

Intimidation can go hand-in-hand with the fear of authority. Of course, a target can feel intimidated by an authority figure he fears, but it doesn't necessarily have to be an authority figure. An attacker can pretend to be a loud, boisterous jerk who threatens the target with all manner of bad results if she doesn't get her way, for example. The attacker may pretend to be an irate customer who threatens to complain about the target's actions to his boss or another real authority figure. This kind of behavior typically intimidates people and can even cause them to want the attacker and their issues to "go away," so the victim is willing to do whatever it takes to satisfy the attacker's request as soon as possible. For example, consider a social engineer who calls the helpdesk and demands that her password be reset. She may yell and scream and threaten to talk to the helpdesk person's boss about his incompetence or lack of willingness to help if the helpdesk technician doesn't reset the password. A lot of new and inexperienced technicians fold to that type of intimidation; usually it's the better-trained and more experienced techs who know how to stay calm and handle difficult people and can thwart an attacker's use of intimidation as a social engineering technique.

Consensus/Social Proof

Other techniques used in social engineering are the *consensus* and *social proof* tactics. In these types of attack, the social engineer tends to be a little bit nicer, more understanding, and more sympathetic to the needs of the target. He attempts to find common ground with the target, such as a shared background, likes and dislikes, hobbies, or even opinions. He also may try to reason with a type of twisted common sense to get the target to agree that what he's asking for makes perfect sense, building a consensus with the victim and making the victim think his way, so to speak. Or, the social engineer will convince the target that everyone else is doing an action, so that action must be fine for the target to do too. Since people normally like to be agreed with, like to be accepted, and like to find common ground with people, they're more amenable to these types of attack. Additionally, everyone wants to think that they have "common sense," so they're more apt to break rules that don't seem to make sense if the attacker can simply get them to agree.

These types of attack may take a little bit more of an effort on the part of the attacker, simply because he has to do his homework and understand the target a bit better before he approaches and engages a target. The social proof aspect could involve the attacker dropping a few familiar names; this provides "proof" that the attacker is legitimate, since he knows someone who the target knows.

Here's an example: In a military setting, an attacker calls a helpdesk employee. The attacker presents the helpdesk technician with this scenario:

> I'm General Johnson's aide, Captain Smith. Can you believe this guy is asking *me* to have his password reset? It's incredible that he's so lazy he can't do it himself. What a guy.... But you know how it is to get an order from a general, right? You just do what you gotta do, even though it's against the rules, you know? Can you help me out?

This attack could be effective on many levels. First, the attacker is dropping names the technician may be familiar with, so the technician may be slightly intimidated. Second, the attacker is attempting to build rapport with the technician by pretending to be just an ordinary person trying to do his job. Third, the attacker willingly admits to the technician that he's asking the technician to break the rules, but he's hoping the technician will feel sorry for him and do so anyway because he's just following orders.

Scarcity

Scarcity is another tactic used in social engineering. Scarcity refers to offering the victim or target something that they really want, something that may be otherwise difficult to obtain. It may be something intangible, such as a promotion, a new position, or some other type of incentive. It also may be something very tangible, such as an object or something else the target wants. For example, the social engineer could offer the target courtside basketball tickets if the target will reset a password over the phone rather than requiring the "user" (the social engineer) to present identification in person. The scarce item may be something as simple as an exotic coffee, or sports tickets, or something the target may not think is important enough to question. The attacker may use the scarce item as a kind of a "thank you" for doing a favor, thus continuing to build a good relationship with the victim.

Urgency

An attacker may use *urgency* to get a victim to perform an action or provide information quickly, without being able to think about it clearly or confirm that the attacker really needs the information or is authorized to request the action. You may have heard of an attacker pretending to be an administrative assistant, calling on behalf of his boss, who is out of town and has locked her user account. The admin assistant urgently begs or otherwise pressures the target to unlock the account or change the password without confirmation from the user. There's usually some contrived story about how the user can't be contacted by phone or is currently on a plane and can't verify the request herself. The fake admin assistant may insist that he will get into trouble with the boss, or the boss has a critical meeting with a very important customer and needs immediate access to the account once she lands. All this false pretext conveys a sense of urgency designed to pressure the target into performing the desired action or even giving the attacker information. Combined with a person's natural desire to help someone in need, especially in an urgent or critical situation, this technique is often quite effective.

 EXAM TIP Urgency attacks work really well during penetration testing, where good guys probe a network on purpose to discover any vulnerabilities. See Module 9-3 for much more on pen testing.

Familiarity/Liking

People like to be liked. That's a simple fact of human existence. So, people respond positively to people who like them or take the time to get to know them. Developing a bond with a social engineering target can help the attacker better persuade and influence the target into giving him what he wants in terms of information or having the target perform certain actions for him. For example, let's say that the target works in a secure area that houses some cool technology or scientific experiments. The attacker establishes a familiar and friendly relationship with the victim and bolsters her ego, making her feel good about the relationship. The attacker then casually asks the victim to let him into the restricted area so he can see some of the cool stuff that goes on there. After a bit of pressure and cajoling, the target may give in and sneak the attacker into the restricted area when no one's looking, thinking that it won't hurt if they are there together, and it's only for a few minutes. It likely wouldn't take an attacker long to install a hardware keystroke logger, a listening device, a small hidden camera, or even a wireless sniffer unobtrusively, once the target gets him into the restricted area.

Trust

Trust is yet another factor in successful social engineering attacks. Humans have a propensity to trust, especially when they feel that trust has been earned, and when they feel trusted likewise. Social engineers know this and seek to establish different levels of trust between themselves and their victims, based upon the circumstances, their goals, and the level of rapport they can establish with the target. The attacker may need only a very low level of trust for some purposes, but may require a deep level of trust for others. The more an attacker needs from a target, the more trust they must establish with the victim. Often, these types of trust relationships can take weeks or even months to develop and involve using many of the techniques we've described previously to establish the relationship, develop a bond, and create trust between the attacker and the target. The attacker also may make the victim feel trusted as well, which can strengthen and hasten the trust relationship.

It's interesting to note that in most successful social engineering attacks, more than a single factor or technique is used; it's likely that none of these techniques would be very effective alone. Attackers can create complex situations involving multiple approaches to a target and use methods that establish trust, sway their victim's opinion and actions, and generally manipulate the victim. Of course, it really all depends upon the situation. Some social engineering attacks may involve only a brief interaction with a target that lasts only a few minutes and involves very simple attack methods. A simple attack, again, may be used to gain access to a more important person or put the attacker in a better situation to leverage a larger, more complex attack.

So, how do we prevent social engineering attacks? Training, which points you all the way back to Chapter 1.

Module 9-3: Security Assessment

This module covers the following CompTIA Security+ objectives:

- **1.4** Explain penetration testing concepts
- **1.5** Explain vulnerability scanning concepts

- **2.2** Given a scenario, use appropriate software tools to assess the security posture of an organization
- **2.3** Given a scenario, troubleshoot common security issues
- **5.3** Explain risk management processes and concepts

By this point, you've learned how to defend your systems and networks and the information that's processed on them. Assuming you've implemented all of the security methods you've learned about, you might be tempted to say that your systems and network are fairly secure. But suppose someone posed the question, "How do you know they're secure?" How can you measure the level of security you've implemented on your systems? Is it enough? You'll get answers to these questions by performing security assessments on your infrastructure. In this module, you'll learn a few things about assessing security as well as some security tools and techniques you can use to test security on your network.

You may have heard of the terms *security assessment*, *penetration test*, and *ethical hacker*. If you don't know what those terms mean, you'll learn a little bit about them in this module. When conducting a security assessment, you approach your system security from an aggressive or offensive perspective, rather than a defensive one. When you're working in defensive mode, you're implementing security controls that can help protect your systems, such as patching workstations and servers, encrypting traffic, creating firewall rules, and so on. Your focus in this capacity is on defending the network from attack and from data loss.

During a security assessment, you'll determine whether the security controls in place are adequate and will stand up to attacks or any other negative event that might cause a loss of data or systems. To do this, you have to take an offensive posture. This means using tools and techniques on your network that will help you see exactly how secure it really is. We'll talk about several different types of assessments, including risk assessments, vulnerability tests, and penetration testing. Understand that some of these assessments may involve using tools and techniques that are designed to circumvent security or at least determine how strong your security controls really are.

Before we get into the meat of this module, here's a word of caution: The tools and techniques we'll discuss are meant to be used for good purposes only. I'm not trying to train you to be malicious hackers or to compromise systems, but it's important that you understand how some of the same tools and techniques that hackers use can be used to test security on systems that you own and manage. In other words, use your Jedi powers for good, not evil!

Assessment Types

You can use several assessment types, each offering different tools and techniques, to achieve a variety of goals. Some assessments are meant to test security management practices, while others are meant to test the more technical aspects of systems. The types of assessments we'll discuss in the next few sections support the overall risk management process as well. We'll also talk about how to calculate the risk after you have performed some of these assessments to make your results more meaningful.

Threat Assessment

Use a *threat assessment* to determine what threats, both natural and man-made, exist that might negatively impact your systems and data. Remember that a threat is something that can do harm, so during a threat assessment you are trying to gather as much information as you can on what possible harm can befall your computing assets and data. This falls into the category of troubleshooting common security issues, such as asset management. Where do you get this information? There are several potential sources, and you should take advantage of as many of them as you can. Law enforcement and cybersecurity organizations can give you threat information particular to your market space, industry, and even geographical location that concerns the possible threats to your systems and data from a technical perspective. You can also get good information regarding threats from historical or statistical information that may apply to your particular industry or area. Often, larger organizations have their own threat assessment or intelligence units that can provide information on potential threats.

The key is to gather this information and see how it might apply to your particular situation. For example, if you work in the defense industry, then obviously intelligence sources can give you information on foreign intelligence threats, industrial espionage, and so on, from both a cybersecurity-specific view and a general view. You may be able to get information on the latest attack techniques and tools that an adversary may use to penetrate your network and steal data, for example. Another example might be if you work in the healthcare industry. There are specific cybersecurity threats out in the world that target both personal and protected health information; you could gather information concerning these threats from other similar institutions, government agencies, and so on. Your organization must use the expertise it has in order to determine to what level and how these threats would affect its infrastructure and data.

Vulnerability Assessment

A *vulnerability assessment* looks at systems, data, processes, procedures, and even the people element, to determine what weaknesses or vulnerabilities exist within those systems. All systems and processes have vulnerabilities somewhere; it's up to you to determine what they are, what threats could target them, and how to prevent threats from exploiting those vulnerabilities. A vulnerability assessment can be a very comprehensive effort across a large organization that looks at security management, procedures, policies, and so on. A vulnerability assessment can also look at the more technical areas as well, including patch management, secure configuration, protection of data in transit and at rest, and so forth. A vulnerability assessment should pick up any misconfigured devices, such as firewalls, content filters, and wireless access points, preferably *before* these devices go live.

You should look at vulnerabilities to the most detailed degree as possible. This means looking at individual systems, operating systems, applications, networks, processes, and so on. You would then match each of those vulnerabilities with a potential threat.

Risk Assessment

A *risk assessment* involves several elements, including the threat and vulnerability assessments we just discussed. A risk assessment determines whether the threats and vulnerabilities you've discovered are likely to be exercised against the particular vulnerability to produce an adverse effect (the impact). Impact is the level of harm to an organization if a particular capability, such as a server, process, or even data, were lost or diminished so that the organization could not fully utilize it. The likelihood is combined with the potential impact if the threat was to materialize against the vulnerability, and this is the risk to the system or data involved.

The risk assessment attempts to determine the level of risk to the system or organization. Risk can be expressed in qualitative terms such as high, medium, or low, or in quantitative terms expressed as numerical values, such as 1 to 10. The assessment is based on probability (likelihood), cost (impact), and other factors. Risk can be expressed in terms that apply to specific systems or data, in terms of program security management that apply to the business processes in the organization, and even as an overall cumulative risk to the organization itself. In the next few sections, we'll go a little bit more into calculating risk using some of the factors we just discussed.

Risk Calculations

Risk can be calculated following assessments, using factors such as threat, vulnerability, likelihood, and impact. Basic *risk calculations* are considered a must-know for the Security+ exam as well as more advanced security certifications, and this information is also useful in this place we like to call "real life." Let's take a few moments to go through how to calculate some of these factors that you study during a risk assessment.

Threats and Likelihood

To calculate risk, you must gather information regarding *threats* and vulnerabilities by performing a threat assessment for a system; then you can assign *likelihood* values for each threat. For example, if you determine that there is a significant threat of an insider stealing data from a particular system, you would assign a likelihood value to that threat. A *qualitative* value could be low, medium, or high, depending on how likely you think the threat is to materialize. A *quantitative* value might use a numerical value, such as a statistical probability (say, a 60 percent chance of occurrence), or a number on a scale of 1 to 10 (say, a 6), where 1 is *very unlikely* and 10 is *extremely likely*. You might be tempted to think that the use of a qualitative value (such as low, medium, or high) is very subjective and might not be as accurate as a quantitative. This, however, isn't always the case. Note that a qualitative or quantitative measurement doesn't necessarily mean that either is completely subjective or objective in nature; a qualitative measurement can be quite objective at times, and a quantitative measurement, even though it may use statistical values, can also be quite subjective. It really depends on *what* you are measuring and *how* you measure it.

Vulnerabilities and Impact

Vulnerabilities are also assigned values, in terms of impact. As mentioned, *impact* relates to how serious the damage would be to an asset or an organization if a threat were to materialize against a particular vulnerability. Impact values are also expressed in qualitative or quantitative terms. An impact may be rated very high if a server with company secrets were compromised by a hacker, for example. Impact is also often expressed in terms of cost to the organization in quantitative terms, such as dollars.

Note that threats and vulnerabilities aren't always easy to separate; if you can't determine a valid threat for a particular vulnerability, does the vulnerability really exist? That's more than just a philosophical question; from a practical perspective, you almost can't have a particular vulnerability if there is no matching threat, and vice versa, because there would be either nothing to defend or nothing to protect against. If a vulnerability exists, there must be a matching threat, and vice versa, in order for risk to exist.

Risk

Risk is a combination of likelihood and impact. As either increases, risk increases. In general, the higher the likelihood of a threat occurring, the greater the risk to the system or organization. And the greater the impact to the organization if the threat were actually exercised, the greater the risk is as well. You can calculate risk in several ways, beyond simply classifying it in terms of qualitative and quantitative. Some organizations use different "weights" for certain factors such as impact, or they develop complex formulas for calculating risk.

Remember that risk is also cumulative; several low-risk issues might amount to a higher risk when combined. At the same time, remember that risk tends to "roll up" as well. So the various risk levels you've calculated for many different subsystems in an organization roll up to a larger risk at the organizational level. Figure 9-8 shows a notional view from the National Institute of Standards and Technology (NIST) on how risk can be calculated qualitatively, based upon differing values of likelihood and impact.

Assessment Techniques

You'll need to know some basic assessment techniques for the exam and, probably more importantly, for your real-life work as a security professional. Several more advanced techniques are not covered here, but the following are some of the basic ones that will give you a solid foundation of knowledge.

Likelihood (Threat Event Occurs and Results in Adverse Impact)	Level of Impact				
	Very Low	Low	Moderate	High	Very High
Very High	Very Low	Low	Moderate	High	Very High
High	Very Low	Low	Moderate	High	Very High
Moderate	Very Low	Low	Moderate	Moderate	High
Low	Very Low	Low	Low	Low	Moderate
Very Low	Very Low	Very Low	Very Low	Low	Low

Figure 9-8 Example of risk determination using different values of likelihood and impact (from NIST SP 800-30, Rev. 1)

Baseline Reporting

Before you begin to look at assessing the vulnerabilities on a system or network, you should develop a *baseline*—an assessment of all the parts of the network, from software installed to ports and services open, to almost any configuration options on devices. Create documentation regarding the versions of operating systems on your boxes, their patch levels, configuration settings, ports and protocols used, and so forth. You should also use your first assessment as part of the baseline, so you have a starting point to compare any changes against. When you make changes to any of your systems based upon your security analysis, you should make these changes part of the new baseline after you have tested them and made sure they function properly and work as they should.

Code Review

Code review is a type of security assessment in which you actually examine as much of the source code of a system or application as possible to determine whether it has been written with security in mind. Of course, a full discussion on code review would be a book unto itself, so we'll describe it only in general terms here. During a code review, you're looking for common vulnerabilities such as input validation, bounds checking, memory allocation and usage, embedded passwords, weak encryption, use of static ports and protocols that may be unsecure, and so forth. The goal of a code review is to detect vulnerabilities before the application goes into production, but this isn't always possible, so you may have to conduct code reviews on applications and operating systems that are actually in use.

Review Architecture

Another way to assess security in a system is to *review its architecture*—how it's built and connects to other systems and interfaces. You also want to look at how it exchanges data with other systems. When reviewing the architecture, examine common security issues, such as security mechanisms built into a system to determine whether they are adequate in protecting data while it's in storage, during transmission, and processing. Some items you should review include authentication mechanisms, encryption mechanisms, secure exchange of data, backup utilities, and so on. Authentication issues and encryption issues fall under an architecture review. Again, this is one of those assessments that you hope to be able to perform before a system goes into production and implementation, so that you can mitigate any vulnerabilities before the system gets put in the use.

Review Designs

Another part of security engineering involves *reviewing the design* of the system. This is very much like looking at the architecture itself, but you are also looking at different products used in the system and what their vulnerabilities may be, how they have been configured for processing and exchanging data, and how their security mechanisms are supposed to work. In this case, you're looking for any security vulnerabilities introduced by the way the system was put together and connected to its own components and to any external systems.

Determine Attack Surface

You need to determine the attack surface to know in what ways the system is exposed to threats. A system with a large attack surface has many different vulnerabilities that are unprotected; it offers many different possible avenues of attack. Usually, these systems have unnecessary ports and protocols running on the box, unpatched operating systems and applications, configuration issues, possibly faulty authentication mechanisms, and weak encryption systems. A system with a small attack surface, on the other hand, has a locked-down configuration that has been patched as much as practicable, and it's running only the applications, ports, protocols, and services that are absolutely necessary for its function. The more the attack surface for a system or network has been reduced, the less likely it is to be attacked and the less effective an attack will be on it—in other words, it will be more secure.

Vulnerability Scanning

The purpose of *vulnerability scanning* is to identify vulnerabilities caused by lack of security controls, common misconfigurations, and so on. Vulnerability scanning *passively tests security controls*, because no actual exploits are attempted on potential vulnerabilities. In other words, a vulnerability scan will *identify vulnerability*, not what actually could be exploited. Vulnerability scans look for known weaknesses in a system, based upon operating system configuration, patch levels, software versions, running ports and services, and so on.

EXAM TIP Vulnerability scanning can identify vulnerability, identify lack of security controls, and identify common misconfigurations. IT professionals can then prioritize changes needed.

Vulnerability scanning software can be non-intrusive or intrusive, depending upon how it's configured. *Non-intrusive* scans are set to provide a cursory look at a system, preventing the scanner from affecting performance of the system being scanned. An *intrusive* scan, on the other hand, performs in-depth checking on potential vulnerabilities and in some cases can cause a system to crash or reboot, affecting availability for its users. In addition to configuring the level of intrusiveness for a scan, most scanning programs allow you to perform a credentialed scan versus a non-credentialed one. A *credentialed* scan gives you much more information, because you are able to access more information and configuration details about a system when logged in with valid privileged credentials than you would if you used a non-credentialed scan. A *non-credentialed* scan might be used in a black box or blind test (described next) when you have no knowledge of any system accounts.

NOTE See "Interpreting Security Assessment Tool Results" later in this module for discussion of *false positives* and *false negatives*. Sometimes vulnerability scanning—and penetration testing—return incorrect results. IT professionals need to look for those as well as accurate results.

Penetration Testing

Penetration testing (often shortened to *pen testing*), as opposed to vulnerability scanning, actually exploits weaknesses on a system. Although vulnerability scanning presents the possibilities regarding how a threat could be exploited, the results of a vulnerability scan are purely theoretical to a large degree. A vulnerability scanner doesn't tell you whether a threat could actually exploit any particular weakness, just that the possibility is there. Penetration testing, on the other hand, goes a step further. In addition to identifying vulnerabilities on the system, a penetration test can verify that a threat exists and that it actually could, in fact, exploit a given vulnerability.

 EXAM TIP When confronted with a question about pen testing versus vulnerability scanning on the CompTIA Security+ exam, keep in mind that pen testing exploits weaknesses, whereas vulnerability scanning only reveals possible weaknesses.

During a penetration test, *ethical hackers* (proud term for people who possess hacking knowledge and skills, but use their Jedi powers only for good) attempt to bypass security controls by actively testing them and exploiting any identified vulnerabilities. IT pros who do pen testing are commonly referred to as *pentesters*.

 EXAM TIP Penetration testing *requires permission* from the organization being tested and must occur during a time frame the organization approves. No permission means breaking the law and going to jail if caught! Ethical hackers obtain physical, written permission in the form of penetration testing documentation, such as a standardized authorization form from the Open Web Application Security Project (OWASP). OWASP provides (among other things) vendor-neutral forms in use throughout the IT industry for risk assessment to protect the companies that provide pen tests and other tests. The OWASP has vulnerability testing authorization documentation, for example, to provide cover for vulnerability testers.

The penetration testing process starts with information gathering, or what the pentest folks call reconnaissance. With *passive reconnaissance*, the *intent* is to keep the targeted company from detecting the information-gathering techniques. While almost nothing is *completely* undetectable, the pentester uses tools and techniques that make detection of activity difficult. The pentester gathers information such as IP address ranges used in the company network, dossiers on key personnel, and so on. Passive reconnaissance avoids the risk of discovery by the organization personnel.

With *active reconnaissance*, on the other hand, the pentester employs a broader range of tools, such as network mapping, port scanning, and more. Active reconnaissance puts the pentester at greater risk of discovery, but needs to happen as part of the testing process. (See "Banner Grabbing" later in this module for a good example of active reconnaissance techniques.)

The penetration tester performs attacks on the system to see if he or she can compromise the system, steal data, conduct denial-of-service attacks, and so on. Through penetration testing, a security professional can determine whether weaknesses can be exploited way before a malicious hacker tries.

You can use the results from penetration tests to determine how better to protect the system by mitigating the vulnerabilities that the tester was able to exploit. In some cases, you don't have to waste your time or resources mitigating vulnerabilities that actually might not be so easily exploitable in the real world. Of course, you shouldn't necessarily ignore these vulnerabilities, but you may be able to lower the risk incurred from them and spend your money and other resources on vulnerabilities that are actually exploitable and that may in fact be high-risk items.

You should be aware of a couple of different types of penetration tests. First, there's the *black box* test, in which an ethical hacker performs a penetration test on the system with no prior knowledge whatsoever about how the system is designed and architected, what defenses it may have, or any other characteristics about the system or network. The tester will have to perform footprinting and reconnaissance activities on the network to find out how it's connected and what its defenses are, as well as its weaknesses, just the same as a malicious hacker would do. Note that this type of testing is also referred to as *blind testing*.

The next type of penetration test is called a *gray box* test. In this type of test, the ethical hacker may have some limited knowledge of the network or systems, gained from the organization that wants the test. The ethical hacker may have an IP address range, for example, or a simple network diagram, or even a listing of the operating systems they will find on a network. Beyond this, though, they have no knowledge of any vulnerabilities in the system. A gray box test simulates an insider attack, someone who would have some knowledge of systems already. What sort of potential damage could an insider do? The gray box approach analyzes this aspect of network security.

At the other end of the spectrum is a *white box* test. In a white box test, the penetration tester has full knowledge of the network and access to network diagrams, detailed information about hosts and services on the network, and even previous vulnerability scans that may show weaknesses in systems.

Which type of penetration test the organization should choose depends on how much time (and money) it wants to spend on the tester getting information about the network versus actually trying to exploit the vulnerabilities. There may be value to having the tester start with no knowledge and trying to find out what they can, so that the organization can determine how much information a malicious hacker could actually get. On the flipside of that argument, the goal may be to exploit vulnerabilities versus trying to gain information about the system, so a full white box test can save time and money and enable the tester to focus on that important part of the assessment.

Two other characteristics of penetration testing aren't necessarily types of test, but they can affect how the test is performed. *Internal testing* approaches the test from the inside of the network; the test team plugs into the secured part of the network and attacks from within, testing internal security measures. *External testing* involves the test team hacking the perimeter of the organization first and working their way in; this allows the team to test the external defenses before testing the interior of the network.

Figure 9-9 The penetration testing process

As mentioned, in a blind (or black box) penetration test, the testers—the attackers, called the *red team*—have no prior knowledge of the network they are testing. In a *double-blind* type of test, the network defenders—called the *blue team*—also have no prior knowledge of the test and aren't aware of any attacks unless they can detect and defend against them. One of the goals of this type of test may be to see how the network defenders react and if they can even detect the hacking attempts on the system and the network.

Figure 9-9 shows the generic process of penetration testing.

 EXAM TIP Don't confuse the terms "black box," "white box," and "gray box" with other terms you may hear that describe the hacker. A *black hat* hacker, for example, is a malicious hacker who uses her knowledge and skills to compromise systems. A *gray hat* hacker is known to use her skills for both good and evil at times, and a *white hat* hacker is usually a penetration testing professional or *ethical hacker*.

Penetration testing can go very deep into an organization's systems. Post-reconnaissance, a pentester might start the attack by using social engineering techniques (posing as a trusted vendor) to get a user inside an organization to access a Web site for a security patch. The pentester controls that Web site and runs software that captures information about the system used to download the patch. After that *initial exploitation*, the pentester might install a backdoor entrance into the compromised system, to gain *persistence*—perpetual access to the company network.

As another option, the pentester could access the compromised system and, through *escalation of privilege*, run software tools that require administrator or root privilege. One such use of escalation of privilege is called a *pivot*, or *pivoting*, by which software tools discover previously hidden networks connected to the compromised system. Or, the pivot can happen along a new pathway, hidden or not. I can get to Bob's desktop, for example, and then pivot to a connected router. Armed with this new knowledge, the pentester can waltz deeper into the organization, exposing more and more weaknesses.

Organizations that are serious about the security of their systems hire penetration testing firms. If the ethical hackers can get in, then so can the bad guys. You need to assess the security of networks and systems for which you are responsible.

Tools

We've discussed various methods of conducting security assessments and penetration tests; now it's time to talk about some of the tools we can use to perform these assessments. Keep in mind that most of these tools are like a double-edged sword: They can be used for good purposes, by ethical security professionals, to maintain the security of their systems and networks. Or they can be used by malicious individuals to steal data, conduct denial-of-service attacks, hack into systems, and perform all sorts of other kinds of malicious mischief. It's up to you, of course, as a security professional, to use your newfound Jedi powers that you get from these tools for the good of your network and all humankind! Let's take a look at some of these tools now. Keep in mind that this is a sampling of the available tools that are out there; these are probably the simpler tools that every security professional should be familiar with, but far more sophisticated and advanced tools are available both to security professionals and, unfortunately, hackers.

Passive vs. Active Tools

Before we jump into the discussion of tools, we should discuss the difference between passive and active tools. You use a *passive* tool when you don't want to interfere with any hosts or networks. Passive tools primarily listen for network traffic or monitor the hosts they reside on. Hackers like to use passive tools because they're often difficult to detect, because they send out little to no data or evidence that they are attached to the network or host. Security professionals like to use passive tools because they don't interfere with the performance of the network. An example of a passive tool might be a passive sniffer (which we'll discuss in a moment).

An active tool, on the other hand, does in fact send out traffic or data to the network or host and actually interacts with systems. This is good from the perspective that you can usually gather more data and perform actions that can give you a better idea of the security of the systems you're working with. The bad part about an active tool is that it can cause performance problems or even interfere with network traffic and system operations if used improperly. Security professionals are usually very careful about using active tools, especially on a production network, because they don't want to interfere accidentally with the infrastructure or cause any damage to any systems. Hackers, on the other hand, use active tools to run exploits against vulnerable systems to compromise them. Fortunately, a drawback to active tools is that they usually are very easy to detect, making the job of a hacker that much harder. An example of an active tool would be a network scanner or vulnerability scanner, both of which we'll talk about as well.

Protocol Analyzer

A *protocol analyzer*, as you'll recall from way back in Chapter 4, processes data scanned by a packet sniffer. A sniffer collects network traffic, throughout the OSI levels, regardless of port, protocol, or service (provided it's one that the sniffer can understand). The protocol analyzer then processes the captured data. Wireshark analyzes data captured by *libpcap* in Linux or *WinPcap* on Windows systems, for example, either installed along with Wireshark.

The protocol analyzer examines the captured data to determine different characteristics about the traffic in order to troubleshoot network connectivity problems. You can also use it to intercept and collect traffic so that you can examine it for security issues. For example, you could intercept traffic on the network to see if any unauthorized FTP

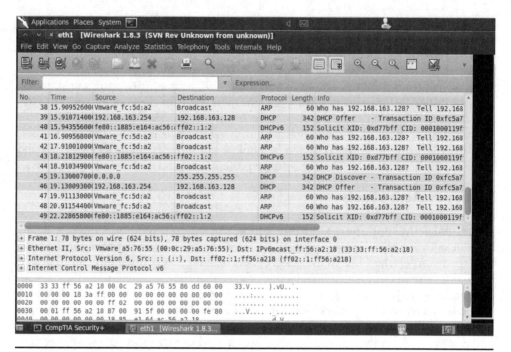

Figure 9-10 Wireshark, a popular network sniffer

servers are connected to the infrastructure. You could look for FTP traffic, determine the source IP address, and track down the unauthorized box and yank it from the network.

A malicious person, on the other hand, could use a sniffer to intercept traffic in hopes of capturing plaintext information, such as passwords, personal or confidential information, and so on. You can use encryption as one protection against a malicious person using a sniffer to gather information. Sniffers can still capture encrypted traffic, but since it can't easily be decrypted, the malicious hacker gets to see only garbage, unless he employs other, more sophisticated methods to decrypt the traffic.

You can use sniffers and protocol analyzers on either wired or wireless networks, provided the device has a supported wired or wireless network card that can be used to capture the traffic. Wireshark is probably the most popular protocol analyzer software among security professionals and hackers, because it works great and it's free. Wireshark is available for both Windows and Linux platforms. A screenshot of Wireshark in action is shown in Figure 9-10.

Network Scanner

A *network scanner* is a tool used to send specially constructed network traffic to the host to get it to reply in a specific manner. Because of the way the TCP/IP stack is implemented on various hosts, the replies that the host returns can indicate what the operating system is, what ports and services it is using, and whether it is susceptible to certain types

Figure 9-11

Results from the Nmap network scanner

```
Nmap scan report for 192.168.163.128
Host is up (0.00093s latency).
Not shown: 992 filtered ports
PORT      STATE SERVICE
135/tcp   open  msrpc
139/tcp   open  netbios-ssn
445/tcp   open  microsoft-ds
554/tcp   open  rtsp
2869/tcp  open  icslap
3306/tcp  open  mysql
5357/tcp  open  wsdapi
10243/tcp open  unknown
MAC Address: 00:0C:29:A5:76:55 (VMware)

Nmap scan report for 192.168.163.143
Host is up (0.00057s latency).
Not shown: 999 closed ports
PORT    STATE SERVICE
80/tcp open  http
```

of network-based attacks. As you'll recall from Chapter 4, Nmap is probably the most commonly used network scanner, and it is available for almost any OS you can imagine. Security folks use it to detect non-secure hosts on the network so they can fix them, while evil hackers use it to try to find attack vectors in vulnerable hosts. Nmap comes in both command-line and GUI flavors. Figure 9-11 shows output from the command-line version.

Vulnerability Scanner

A *vulnerability scanner* is software used to determine vulnerabilities on a host. The scanner can gather information about a computer, including what ports and services it is running, what software is on the box, the operating system and its version, what patches the box has installed on it, and even vulnerabilities that exist on the computer. A network-based vulnerability scanner, such as the popular Nessus scanner, can send specifically crafted network traffic to a host to elicit certain responses from that host. The responses from the computer can show vulnerabilities that might allow an attacker to compromise the host over the network, such as using unsecure protocols, weak encryption, open file shares, and so forth. A security professional can use a vulnerability scanner to discover weaknesses in the hosts on the network and fix those vulnerabilities, so hackers can't take advantage of them. A malicious person, on the other hand, can use a vulnerability scanner to determine how best to attack a host or network. Figure 9-12 shows an example of Nessus, one of the most popular vulnerability scanners.

Configuration Compliance Scanner

The flip side of a vulnerability scanner is a *configuration compliance scanner*, a tool that scans critical systems to see if they meet the compliance standards set by IT security professionals in an organization. A good scanner, like Nessus discussed earlier, can check for and report on systems out of compliance on any number of issues, such as password length minimums, permission issues, and much more. (Nessus is both a vulnerability scanner and a configuration compliance scanner.)

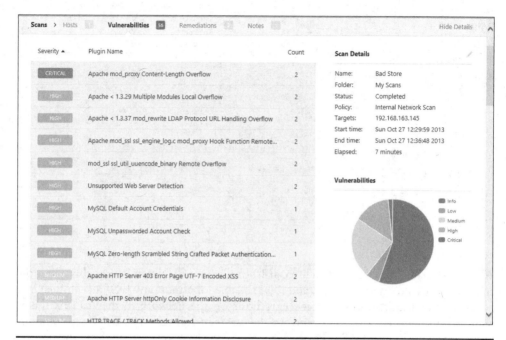

Figure 9-12   The Nessus vulnerability scanner

Checks are based on standard audit files for systems that IT security folks customize to fit the needs of their organization. If your company uses primarily Cisco systems for routers, switches, and other appliances, you could download the Cisco-specific Configuration Audit Policies file from www.tenable.com, add it to your Nessus scanner, and run it to check systems. (Tenable is the company that produces Nessus.) Tenable has literally hundreds of audit files tailored to specific systems that you can and should customize further.

Banner Grabbing

Banner grabbing is a technique that you can use to footprint a system and the services that run on it. For example, you could run the `telnet` command and connect to a certain Web server on TCP port 80, and in some cases, you might receive an error message that tells you the type of Web server software running on the box, its version, and other juicy information about it that might help you plan an attack against it. Banner grabbing is kind of a hit-or-miss technique, however, because a lot of modern network-based software by default is protected against giving up information about itself. Other software can be manually configured not to give up information, but oftentimes the administrator has not bothered to configure it this way. Other services, such as file shares, FTP servers, DNS and other network services, and even particular operating systems are vulnerable to different banner grabbing techniques. Figure 9-13 shows an example of banner grabbing.

Figure 9-13
Banner grabbing from a Web server

```
root@bt:~# telnet 192.168.163.130 80
Trying 192.168.163.130...
Connected to 192.168.163.130.
Escape character is '^]'.

?
<!DOCTYPE HTML PUBLIC "-//IETF//DTD HTML 2.0//EN">
<HTML><HEAD>
<TITLE>501 Method Not Implemented</TITLE>
</HEAD><BODY>
<H1>Method Not Implemented</H1>
? to /index.html not supported.<P>
Invalid method in request ?<P>
<HR>
<ADDRESS>Apache/1.3.28 Server at 192.168.163.130 Port 80</ADDRESS>
</BODY></HTML>
Connection closed by foreign host.
root@bt:~#
```

Penetration Testing with Metasploit

Imagine if a group of superbly skilled security experts got together, pooled their knowledge about every possible way to hack into systems and networks, and then *published that information on the Web*. Sounds scary and crazy, right? That's the team behind Metasploit, a platform for penetration testing by the good guys. As the Metasploit folks tell it, the bad guys already know this stuff. Legit companies need to know it too to arm themselves against the enemy.

NOTE   Metasploit today has free (community) and wildly expensive (pro) tools. The professional tools get into the realm of crazy good, but cost a lot. The best community front end right now is Armitage. (Google it!)

Metasploit can do pretty amazing things and is very much the go-to tool for pen testing today. The functions and features go well beyond the CompTIA Security+ exam, but you should explore this tool. Check it out here:

https://metasploit.com

EXAM TIP   The Metasploit Framework—CompTIA and a lot of other people call it an *exploitation framework*—gives companies a very programmable set of tools for creating exploits.

Interpreting Security Assessment Tool Results

Once you run all of your cool security tools against the system or network, you'll be tempted to plunge right in and start exploiting all the different vulnerabilities you find, or at least you'll want to begin to remediate them by changing configurations, installing patches, and throwing money and resources at the system. One word of caution about this, however: You can't always rely solely on the results of tool findings as a basis for your security and remediation strategy. Different tools interpret findings from different systems, well, differently. Some tools may find a vulnerability and indicate that it's a very high risk, while others may find the same vulnerability a low or medium risk. Some tools may not even find the vulnerabilities that other tools identified. For that reason alone, it's a good idea to use several different tools and look at the findings from a holistic approach.

Because of inconsistencies and tool findings, and because they don't give the entire picture of how your systems and networks are set up, you have to consider tool findings in addition to other factors when you analyze the results. For example, the tool may tell you that you have ports open on a system that may be high risk, but the tool doesn't know that you have an application or a valid business process that requires those ports to be open. You may have mitigated the risk of those open ports in a different way, such as by isolating the system on a restricted network, locking down application permissions, installing network security devices to protect the system, and so forth. So, even though a tool finding may indicate that the vulnerability is a high risk, you've mitigated that risk down to a lower level through other means, using other compensating security controls. This actually is part of your entire risk assessment, analysis, and mitigation strategy.

False Positives

When you're looking at tool findings and want a broader picture of how effective security controls are, be aware of false positives and false negatives. A *false positive* occurs when a tool finds a vulnerability that you know really isn't one. For example, I've seen a popular assessment tool find vulnerabilities associated with Microsoft's Internet Information Services (IIS) on a Linux box, which is pretty much ridiculous since IIS won't run on Linux! Of course, this is a fairly off-the-wall example of a false positive. Often, false positives are not so easy to detect and can be quite subtle. You may have to investigate the details of the findings to determine if it's an actual vulnerability. The good thing about a false positive is that it can be a relief to find that you really don't have a vulnerability even if the scanner detects one. The bad thing about a false positive is that you may expend resources, such as time and money, on correcting a vulnerability that doesn't really exist, before you determine it's a false positive. That's why it's a good idea to analyze each vulnerability and get confirmation from another tool or method before you assume that you actually have a vulnerability. False positives can create more work for you as a security person, which reduces your effectiveness in managing other, real vulnerabilities.

False Negatives

A false negative, on the other hand, can be a very serious thing. A *false negative* occurs when your tool doesn't detect a vulnerability, when in fact one exists. A false negative also occurs when a process or system allows unauthorized access, for example, where it should not. The potential for false negatives is another reason to use multiple tools when you perform security scanning on your systems. This is also a very good reason for performing in-depth penetration tests. A penetration test can locate vulnerabilities that ordinary vulnerability scanning may not detect, since experienced penetration testers know to try various tools and techniques on different types of systems that may allow them to compromise a system.

Questions

1. Which of the following vulnerabilities can be avoided with data sanitization?

   A. Embedded systems

   B. End-of-life systems

   C. Lack of vendor support

   D. System sprawl

2. Which of the following attacks is conducted by trying to get a view of sensitive information on a user's screen?

   A. Dumpster diving

   B. Tailgating

   C. Eavesdropping

   D. Shoulder surfing

3. You are a security administrator in a company, and a user has just forwarded a suspicious e-mail to you that directs the user to click a link to a banking Web site and enter their credentials to verify the account. What type of social engineering attack is being attempted?

   A. Phishing

   B. Vishing

   C. Man-in-the middle

   D. E-mail hoax

4. An attacker calls an administrative assistant and tells him that she is the new executive assistant for the company senior vice president. She claims the VP is traveling, and she needs access to certain sensitive files in a file share. The attacker tries to bully the admin assistant into giving her permissions to the file share by threatening to have him fired if he doesn't oblige. Which two characteristics of human behavior is the attacker trying to take advantage of in this attack? (Choose two.)

   A. Trust

   B. Fear of authority

   C. Social proof

   D. Respect of authority

5. A person calls and tells you that he has locked his account because he forgot his remote access password. He tells you that he doesn't have time to come down to your desk and positively identify himself because he is off-site at a customer facility and must present an important briefing to the customer within the next few minutes. He insists that he needs his remote access password changed immediately, but promises to come and see you after he returns to the office to verify his identity. What kind of social engineering tactic is being used in this attack?

   A. Authority

   B. Familiarity

   C. Intimidation

   D. Urgency

6. Your manager wants you to attempt to determine what security vulnerabilities may be present in an application before it goes into production. You're to take the application directly from the programmers and go through the program itself. Which of the following assessment techniques should you use first?

   A. Architecture review

   B. Design review

   C. Code review

   D. Port scan

7. Which of the following types of assessments actually exploits weaknesses found in a system?

   A. Code review

   B. Architecture review

   C. Vulnerability test

   D. Penetration test

8. You are performing a penetration test and are given only some basic information on the target system, including its IP address range and a basic network diagram. What type of penetration test is this considered to be?

   A. Gray box test

   B. Black box test

   C. White box test

   D. Double-blind test

9. A security testing tool that does not interfere with the operation of the system or network at all is considered:

   A. Active

   B. Passive

   C. Less accurate

   D. Easily detectable

10. Which of the following is considered a dangerous type of finding because it can actually mean that a potential security vulnerability goes undetected?

A. False positive

B. False negative

C. False flag

D. False scan

Answers

1. B. Eliminating data on end-of-life systems avoids vulnerabilities to sensitive data.

2. D. Shoulder surfing is an attack in which the perpetrator tries to view sensitive information on a user's screen.

3. A. A phishing attack is conducted by sending an e-mail to an unsuspecting user to get the user to click a link in the e-mail and enter sensitive information, such as credentials or other personal information, into the site.

4. B, D. The attacker is taking advantage of the human tendency to fear and respect authority figures.

5. D. The attacker is trying to use a tactic involving urgency of need to get the remote access password reset, without having his identity verified.

6. C. Code review is an appropriate assessment technique in this case to run first, since you are looking at the program itself before it goes into production. You would of course also run a network scanner and other tools against the box with the app loaded on it to test for security vulnerabilities.

7. D. A penetration test is designed to exploit any vulnerabilities found in a system.

8. A. A gray box test is one in which the tester is given only limited information on the target network.

9. B. A passive tool does not interfere with the operation or performance of the system or network.

10. B. A false negative can mean that an actual vulnerability goes undetected.

Dealing with Incidents

Bad things happen, even to the most security-conscious organizations. As an IT security professional, you need to know how to respond to negative events. This chapter explores responses to incidents ranging from the minor (like a system crash) to the major (natural disaster wiping out the company HQ) in three modules:

- Incident Response
- Forensics
- Continuity of Operations and Disaster Recovery

Module 10-1: Incident Response

This module covers the following CompTIA Security+ objective:

- **5.4** Given a scenario, follow incident response procedures

Most organizations can't afford to wonder *if* an incident will ever happen to them; they need to wonder *when*, because negative events or incidents will happen to every organization at some point. Incident response is not something that a business can simply ignore until an incident occurs. An incident response program requires careful planning in advance.

This module explores the basics of incident response, including planning, preparing, and executing a solid response. The module also discusses mitigation and recovery from incidents, and how to minimize the damage from a negative event by separating affected systems from unaffected systems.

Incident Response Concepts

Several critical concepts are involved with setting up and executing an *incident response plan*, a set of documents and procedures that specify policies and essential personnel roles to deal with an attack or system failure. Some of these concepts involve planning and management functions, such as developing policy, allocating resources, staffing an incident response team, using exercises and drills, and making sure that everyone is trained regarding their responsibilities. Other concepts involve putting the plan into motion and executing it when the incident occurs.

For purposes of our discussion of incident response, an *incident* is a negative event that adversely affects the organization, its data and systems, its people, and its overall ability to perform mission or business functions. An incident could be a malicious hacking attack from the outside. It could be an insider threat when someone steals proprietary data and sells it to a competitor; or it could be a natural disaster such as a fire or flood. This module focuses on incidents in general; Module 10-3 provides a more detailed discussion about business continuity and disaster recovery.

Risk Mitigation Strategies

This module and the two that follow emphasize what you have learned so far about risk management principles. Risk management balances cost against strategies to reduce threats and the impact of attacks. Incident management and response supports a risk management program by ensuring that the organization can address an incident quickly when it occurs, reducing the damage to the organization and systems. By having an active incident response program, you can control, investigate, and conclude a damaging event more quickly. This reduces risk and enables the organization to deal better with a variety of threats.

Incident Management

An incident response can seem like madness, but you should pay attention to a method for that madness. The National Institute of Standards and Technology (NIST) has provided a very good incident response methodology in its Special Publication (SP) 800-61, Rev. 2, "Computer Security Incident Handling Guide," which you can use in your organization. It covers the key areas of incident response, including preparation, detection and analysis, containment, and so on. The incident response lifecycle that NIST offers is illustrated in Figure 10-1. We'll discuss much of this methodology in this module.

Incident management is about having all the proper management buy-in, policies, and commitment of resources to the incident response program. This starts at the top of the organization, when senior managers and executives set the incident management response policy. The policy should direct the establishment of an incident response program, to include building an incident response team, establishing response time frames, defining different levels of incidents, and so on. The policy should also include the appointment of someone who has the overall responsibility for the program.

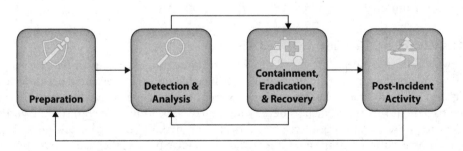

Figure 10-1   NIST's incident response lifecycle (from NIST SP 800-61, Rev. 2)

After senior leadership establishes the policy, the person with overall responsibility for the program selects staff for the incident response team, ensures they receive training, and purchases any equipment the team requires. The team then develops incident response procedures and prepares the organization to respond to the inevitable negative events that will eventually occur.

The *incident response plan*, which is more detailed than the policy itself, will outline the procedures involved with responding to the different types of incidents. The plan should contain information about the different levels and types of incidents, how to respond to them, who will be called, when an incident will be elevated to additional levels of management, and the general chain of events that must happen to contain the incident.

The security team should review all of the incident response policy and planning documentation on a periodic basis to ensure that it remains current and factors in any new changes to the operating or business environment. Many organizations review this documentation at least annually; in businesses where the operational environment and other factors frequently change, this review should occur more often.

An organization should also exercise its incident response plans occasionally to make sure that those folks who have responsibilities and duties related to a response know what to do. Testing these plans and running proper *exercises* can also help to ensure that all the right equipment is in place and that all the response processes work the way they should. Many of these items will be covered in the following sections.

Incident Response Procedures

All the planning to get an incident response plan in shape focuses around procedures that the organization will follow when an incident happens. A good set of well-written procedures will help the response go like clockwork; conversely, poor or nonexistent procedures will have everyone running around with their hair on fire wondering what to do and wasting valuable time. The incident response team can write procedures to a very detailed degree or very broadly, depending upon the activities that must occur when a response is initiated.

When writing the procedures, the team should seek input from the same people who will have to do the job during the actual response. For example, if the incident response plan dictates that a server be restored from a backup in case of a hacking attack, the people who must perform that task during an emergency should help write those procedures, to ensure that they can perform those tasks well. In any case, the organization should make sure that these procedures are well circulated to the right people and reviewed for accuracy and completeness. In the next few sections, we'll discuss procedures developed and used during preparation, as well as when the incident response plan is executed.

Preparation

Preparation is one of the most critical parts of incident response. If you are the person assigned overall responsibility for implementing the incident response program, you must make sure all the right equipment is in place, all the right people are assigned to critical positions, and all those people are trained on what to do, *before* the incident occurs.

You also need to have a good checklist of procedures that the team can use to respond quickly to and contain an incident. Good preparation also includes having a solid incident response plan that has been tested to make sure that an actual response flows as it should.

Staffing   Staffing the *incident response team* with qualified people is critical; if, during an incident, people don't have the training or the experience required to carry out the response, it will probably not go very well. Consider staffing the team with people who have experience in several different areas. Of course, you'll want technical people who have experience in networking, server administration, security, and so on. It helps if these people have worked in different areas during their careers so they can perform multiple tasks. You also need people who have expertise in areas such as incident response, business continuity, forensics, and disaster recovery, since your incidents may span different types of events and levels of response.

Outside of the technical team, you may choose to include representatives from a variety of areas within the organization, including HR, accounting, public relations, and so on. Management personnel will also need to be on the team, to coordinate the entire response. The same people who are responsible for planning the incident response strategy and providing input to the policy and procedures are likely going to be some of the same people who respond to an incident. It makes for a more effective response if this is the case, since those responders have the experience in developing the incident response program from the beginning and will be intimately familiar with how it is set up and how it should be executed.

In addition, the team will have to be trained on all their incident response tasks and responsibilities. Although some of these responsibilities may mirror their daily job activities, some of their response tasks may be outside of their daily routines. One other aspect of staffing your incident response team is that some of your team members, in the event of an actual incident, may come from outside of the organization and could include members of law enforcement, your Internet service provider, software and equipment vendors, and so on. You'll have to plan carefully how and when to integrate these outside participants into your team.

The U.S. federal government uses the term *Cyber Incident Response Team (CIRT)* to describe the IT security professionals who act first to implement an incident response plan in the event of a problem. This is also a term you'll see on the CompTIA Security+ exam. The generic term is the one used in this chapter, *incident response team*.

Developing a Response Strategy   A *response strategy* dictates how the organization will respond to different incidents. Some incidents, such as hacking attacks, require a level of response and possibly a unique response team. The sequence of response for incidents may also differ from those for other types of incidents, and the level of seriousness of an incident will factor into the response strategy. For example, if a piece of malware infects a single PC, it may be considered less serious and more easily contained than a worm that infects the entire network, so the level of response may be different.

The business's response strategy takes all of this into account. The strategy should define the various types of events that can occur, their levels of impact, and the measured responses that should be taken when they occur. The strategy should have *documented incident types* and *category definitions* that cover anything conceivable that could go wrong. The strategy should also indicate which *roles and responsibilities* are needed for each type of incident, and which skill sets will be needed for the incident response team members. The plan must outline procedures for *reporting requirements* and *escalation* when problems go beyond the capabilities of a team member.

If all of this sounds a lot like the risk assessment and analysis processes, it's because incident response, like many of the other things we will talk about over the next few modules, is part of the overall risk management strategy for the organization. Your incident response strategy can be defined as part of the policy document, or as a separate attachment that goes into more detail regarding how the organization will respond to the various incidents that will occur.

Putting It All Together   Once you have put together an incident response policy, staffed the team, and developed a strategy for responding to incidents, your organization must, of course, commit resources (time, money, equipment, facilities, and so on) to the program. This includes time for training the incident response team members as well as exercising the incident response plan. You'll need to acquire the appropriate equipment and supplies for the response, such as computers, forensics imagers, software, and so on. The organization should also set aside a workspace within the facility where the team can meet, organize, and manage the response. This can be a dedicated workspace or a space where they would normally work in the data center or on the operations floor. Either way, the organization needs to make provisions such that in the event of an incident, priority is given to the incident response team so that they can deal with the issue quickly and efficiently.

Exercising the incident response plan using various scenarios and methods is important to make sure the team members understand their responsibilities and how to perform the tasks they are given during the response effort. We'll talk more about the different methods of exercising response plans later in the chapter, but for now you should know that this exercise is a necessary evil you should plan to do at least annually, and possibly more often, and you should document it, for both recordkeeping purposes and continuous process improvement.

Incident Response Process

If you've ever been a bystander or an observer when an incident has occurred in an organization, you've probably seen a wide range of reactions when the event kicks off. In a well-organized *incident response process*, people quickly and efficiently perform their tasks without panicking, but with a sense of urgency. They have all the equipment and supplies they need to do their jobs, and the incident response process flows smoothly. At the other extreme, people run around with their hair on fire, wondering what to do, and not having a clear sense of direction. They may have to look for equipment to execute the response and may wind up taking production equipment offline to respond to an incident in another area of the business. Usually, however, an organization's response falls somewhere in the middle of the spectrum. As described in the previous section, *preparation* is important; it gives the organization a greater potential for success during an incident response.

EXAM TIP CompTIA Security+ includes preparation as part of the incident response process, though for many organizations that is a step prior to action. The incident response process on the exam has six steps— preparation, identification, containment, eradication, recovery, and lessons learned.

Most of what we've discussed up to this point involves the preparation phase of the NIST incident response lifecycle. Executing your incident response involves the next two phases of that same lifecycle: identification and analysis, as well as containment, eradication, and recovery. Detection involves understanding your infrastructure and environment and being able to discover indications that an incident has occurred. You can detect an incident in different ways, such as through automated intrusion detection systems, antivirus software, and logging alerts. Other incidents may be detected only through manual audits of different events, logs, and procedures.

Incident analysis involves looking at all the potential incidents that you discover to determine which are actual incidents and which are false positives. That can be a full-time job and may require dedicated staff. Because the organization is constantly generating computer and network logs and other data, it can be a challenge to stay ahead of the curve and examine the most recent data to determine whether the organization has suffered a negative incident such as a hacking attack. Some incidents are easy to detect, such as a serious malware attack, a Web defacement, or denial-of-service attack. Other incidents won't be so easy to see and may occur over long periods of time instead of during a workday or in a short time span. Event analysis and correlation is the subject of a much broader conversation than included in this module, but you should understand that analysis is the first step in determining whether you've experienced an incident.

The goal of incident analysis is to determine exactly what has happened. This includes answering such questions as these: Who is the victim? Who is the perpetrator? What systems or data does the incident affect? Where did the incident occur (on one machine, for example, or from the external network)? When did it occur? Exactly how did it occur? How does it impact the business? Some of these questions can be answered only through an in-depth forensics analysis, which is the subject of the next module. Analysis should tell you exactly what's happened and what you're facing, so you can respond appropriately in the next phase of the lifecycle, which is concerned with containing an incident.

The next phase (*containment*, *eradication*, and *recovery*, per NIST) involves stopping the incident, eradicating its effects, and recovering from the incident. For serious incidents, you can afford to spend only a short amount of time on analysis, and you may need to focus more on containing the incident to prevent further damage to the business and its infrastructure. During this phase, the incident response team is activated, and even if the cause of the incident and its details aren't known at the time, the team works to contain it and stop the damage.

If the incident is a network attack, for example, the team may need to take a drastic measure such as unplugging the organization from the Internet or shutting down certain services within the business. If it's a malware attack, the team should focus on containing the malware to the smallest number of systems possible and preventing its spread. If data is being extracted from the network, then containing it would mean stopping that data from leaving the network by shutting down a system or blocking traffic at the perimeter of the network, for example. In any case, the incident response strategy and procedures should dictate exactly how the organization should go about containing the incident and eradicating its effects.

Keep in mind that while this phase is going on, the organization should make every effort to preserve evidence of the incident for later analysis and action. This includes preserving log files, properly handling forensic evidence on systems, and so on. Preserving evidence is also a focus of Module 10-2.

Recovering from an incident involves getting the systems, data, and processes that depend on them back into operation. Depending on the nature of the incident, this may be easier said than done, since critical systems may be damaged or may need to be kept offline for the duration of the recovery, and these systems may be subject to evidence collection after an incident. Module 10-3 explores recovery processes after a disaster.

First Responder Procedures   *First response* is a critical phase of the incident response plan, simply because during the first few minutes or hours of an incident several things can happen that affect how well the organization is able to contain and recover from the event. First response is also critical in the preservation of evidence. We'll discuss first responder procedures from a general perspective, as they apply to most incidents and negative events. The first responder's overall duties should be to secure the scene (if necessary), determine the scope of the incident, try to determine the seriousness and impact of the incident, and start the notification process for the incident management and response team.

The first response may not be initially executed by members of the incident response team; an incident may be detected and responded to by the personnel or operators on duty at the time the incident occurs. If an incident is very serious, the response may not be able to wait until the response team is activated and called in. Because of this, all personnel should have some measure of training in responding to an incident, whether that training involves simply activating the team and notifying the appropriate personnel, or securing the scene, preserving evidence, stopping an attack, and so on. The level of response should allow the team to be notified and activated in time to prevent or minimize damage to the organization's infrastructure.

At the same time, however, the first responder should make every effort to preserve valuable evidence that investigators will need to analyze the incident. For example, if a workstation is being attacked over the network, the first responder may need to unplug that workstation from the network, but keep it up and running so that investigators can collect and analyze information regarding network connections, running processes, and so on. In some cases, it may even be desirable to allow the attack to continue so that investigators can collect data and use it to identify the attacker and how they got into the network in the first place. Management should discuss and make decisions regarding those actions in advance, before the incident occurs, and set forth criteria that dictates if and when certain actions will be executed by first responders, based upon the seriousness of the event. It's important that your procedures are detailed enough that these personnel who are less trained can execute the initial steps in an orderly fashion with a minimum of panic. Write down the procedures and make sure everyone knows where the procedures are located!

Incident Identification   A first response also involves *incident identification*, trying to determine the scope of the event, identify what kind of event it is, and determine what systems it affects. The scope of an incident would include, for example, whether the incident is confined to one workstation, involves only one group of users, or affects the entire network. The impact of the incident may be difficult to determine at first, so this may be the initial best guess on the part of the first responder. However, it may be better to overestimate the impact to the organization than to underestimate it to prevent serious damage to the infrastructure. The incident response team may find that a questionnaire or checklist is valuable in helping a first responder quickly determine the scope and impact of the incident.

Escalation and Notification   The other key piece of the first responder's actions is to notify management immediately so the incident response team can be activated and called in. The first responder should be prepared to provide as much information as possible to the incident response team lead so that this person can start the appropriate response measures as soon as he or she arrives. Documenting any actions taken along with any observations or events about the incident are other tasks for the first responder.

Once the team has been notified, the first incident response lead on the scene should determine whether the incident should be *escalated* to upper management, or even outside the organization, such as to the organization's Internet service provider or law enforcement. If outside expertise is required, the event may have to be escalated even further. The level of seriousness of the event, as well as the scope of the event, will determine how it's escalated. For example, if an incident such as a hacking attack affects the organization and its internal network, but could also spread to the Internet, another organization, or an upstream provider, the incident should be escalated as quickly as possible. Once again, the organization's incident management strategy and policy should dictate different levels of impact and how they are escalated based upon predetermined criteria.

Incident Isolation   The incident response team should also work on *containment*, to try to isolate the incident in impact and scope. For example, in the event of a malware attack, the team should try to isolate the workstations and servers that have been infected from the rest of the network to prevent the malware from spreading. In the event of a denial-of-service attack, the team could isolate the network segment under attack from the outside network, such as by quarantining the device or devices, removing it/them from the network, and even shutting it/them down completely.

Quarantining a device or system is designed to prevent an incident from spreading beyond that device or system to the rest of the infrastructure. It may mean unplugging the device from the network, or even dynamically switching it to an isolated network segment or virtual LAN. Reasons for quarantining a device include a malware attack, denial-of-service or other form of network attack, or even prohibited use by an insider. If a device is removed from the network, it may remain powered on so that valuable evidence can be collected from it, and then the device can be shut down and stored while the incident is being investigated. In any case, it should not be allowed back on the network until it has been sanitized and reimaged, to prevent recurrence of the attack or spread of any malicious software.

Data Breach These days, a data breach is one of the most commonly occurring security incidents you'll see plastered across the news. A *data breach* is the result of another security incident, whether it's an attack by hackers, a careless or malicious insider, or even an accident involving faulty processes or procedures. Regardless of the cause, data breaches should be responded to above and beyond the security incident that caused them. An organization will naturally respond to a hacking attack or malicious insider with routine response patterns that include intrusion detection systems, system hardening measures, and so on. The organization also must respond to the result of some of these incidents—the data breach itself—in unique ways.

A data breach normally involves data of a sensitive or protected nature, and most often involves data belonging to or concerning an entity outside the organizational business. If the breach is confined only to organizationally owned proprietary or sensitive data, then the organization takes the hit for the loss alone, in the form of lost business, revenue, or just sheer embarrassment. If the breach encompasses data concerning individuals or organizations outside the business, it's a much more serious issue and could involve not only loss of business revenue, but also legal sanctions and criminal punishment. Normally, the types of data involved in a serious breach include protected health data under the Health Information Portability and Accountability Act (HIPAA), personal financial information, and even personally identifiable information (PII) that could include names, dates of birth, addresses, Social Security numbers, and so on. A recent example of a breach that had multiple types of data was the Sony breach in late 2014. In addition to proprietary data (including actual movies), personal data regarding Sony employees was included in the breach. Along with potential fines and other liability issues, the company lost valuable intellectual property, as well as the confidence and goodwill of its stakeholders. In the long run, this may be more damaging than the sheer dollar value of the financial losses.

An organization's response to a data breach goes beyond the technical aspects of isolating network segments, removing malware, tightening down systems, and so on, although those technical measures are also included, of course. The organization may also have to respond to a data breach by informing the subjects of the data compromised, such as individuals or companies, as well as other entities, such as law enforcement. It may also have to inform regulatory organizations such as the U.S. Office for Civil Rights, in the event of a protected health information breach, or the Securities and Exchange Commission if financial data has been lost. Law enforcement agencies, such as the Federal Bureau of Investigation and other appropriate entities, may require notification about a data breach. Both state and federal laws dictate how an organization must respond to a data breach, what steps it must take to prevent further damage, and even how it must compensate the victims. Obviously, all this will involve not only upper management and the incident response team, but the organization's legal personnel and its public relations team, since the breach will likely be plastered all over the news. The organization should ensure that it has both a technical and a management incident response strategy in place to deal with data breaches.

Damage and Loss Control The damage from an incident is not always easy to determine. Damage includes technical damage to systems (such as malware infection), data loss, equipment damage or theft, and other direct impacts. Damage can also include costs related to containment of an incident, as well as costs of eradicating the cause and repairing damage to the infrastructure. These costs might be incurred in terms of labor dollars for response personnel, as well as equipment and software needed not only to clean up the incident, but also to mitigate its effects and prevent it from occurring again.

Damage can also include the intangible aspects of an incident, such as damage to public and consumer confidence in the organization and reputation in the marketplace. If proprietary or sensitive data is lost, the damage could include loss of business and revenue and the inability to compete in the marketplace. Additional damage can come in the form of legal or criminal proceedings against the organization that may result in heavy fines, imprisonment, or even shutting down the business.

Controlling and minimizing the damage and loss from an incident involves taking all the proactive security measures we've discussed throughout this book up until this point. These include all the administrative, technical, and operational measures used to secure an organization's infrastructure and data. Securing people, systems, and equipment are all key to controlling and minimizing damage and loss.

Post-Incident Activity

How an organization deals with an incident after it has been discovered, analyzed, investigated, contained, and eradicated is just as important as a response process. The organization must figure out how to learn from the event and use what it has learned not only to prevent the incident from occurring again, but also to determine how to deal with such events more effectively in the future. The organization should develop a post-incident strategy that includes collecting all the data regarding how the incident occurred, what steps it could have taken to prevent it, how effective the response was, and what it could have done better. All this information can be used to prevent and mitigate future negative events.

Mitigation Steps   Some of the mitigation steps that an organization should take include a proactive look at the threats and vulnerabilities on the network. This goes back to risk assessment and analysis and may mean that the initial assessment was either incomplete or too narrow in scope. The post-response to an incident should cause the organization to go back and examine its risk management process. Once it has examined threats and vulnerabilities, the organization should essentially beef up its risk management program by taking additional measures toward preventing and mitigating the types of incidents it just experienced. Management should look at putting additional resources toward controls that would have prevented the incident in the first place, as well as improving its incident response detection and response capabilities. This may mean spending additional money for equipment and supplies and providing additional training for incident response team members. In any event, the organization should look for deficiencies in its risk management processes and day-to-day business operations that could have contributed to the incident and the level of response.

Lessons Learned   Part of responding to an incident involves taking the *lessons learned* to heart and using them toward preventing future incidents and responding to them in a more effective way. The organization should examine the circumstances leading up to the incident in detail, making note of deficiencies and how to correct them, as well as the response to the incident, to improve the incident detection, analysis, containment, and eradication processes. These lessons learned should be documented as part of the overall final incident report, and incorporated into the organization's existing policies, processes, and procedures.

Reporting   There are several aspects of reporting during an incident response. During the response effort, the incident response team should report progress on the response and anything discovered about the nature of the incident to management, along with any outside agencies that require the information, such as law enforcement, for example. There should probably be at least a daily briefing for management (and law enforcement, if applicable) on the progress of the response, the damage to the infrastructure, and how the damage is being contained and eradicated.

After the response, the incident response team should submit a final report that details the entire incident from start to finish, the different activities performed as part of the response, the root causes of the incident and how it could have been prevented, any damage to the business or infrastructure, and recommendations for future actions. The report may include a cost breakdown of labor, equipment, and any other supplies needed to respond adequately to the incident. It may also include any deficiencies that were noted during the response, particularly in personnel, training, or other resources. In addition to the report that goes to management, compliance requirements may necessitate that a report be submitted to law enforcement, a regulatory agency, or even to other outside entities (particularly in the case of a data breach). This report may include some of the same information as the internal management report, as well as additional information that may be required for legal or compliance purposes. The organization should also make sure that anyone requiring copies of the incident response reports gets them, but it should also take measures to protect any sensitive or proprietary information contained in them.

Recovery/Reconstitution   Recovery operations, as well as getting the business processes back into operation, are covered more in depth in Module 10-3. However, it's important that after an incident the business processes and systems be brought back up to normal functionality as soon as possible to prevent further negative impact on the business. This may involve restoring data from backups, reinstalling servers or network devices, patching systems, and even installing new equipment. All the recovery operations will probably be focused on the damage that was done during the incident and involve recovering those systems and data damaged by the event.

Module 10-2: Forensics

This module covers the following CompTIA Security+ objectives:

- **5.5**   Summarize basic concepts of forensics
- **6.1**   Compare and contrast basic concepts of cryptography

Computer forensics was once a very small niche in the information security world. Over time, however, as computer-related crime and misuse have increased, it has become more important. Today, forensics is its own discipline within computer security. Computer forensics, like its medical and criminal counterparts, is a very exacting science. It requires strong skills and knowledge in a wide variety of areas, including operating systems, networking, information security, and even law. The procedures used in computer forensics must be very exacting and precise for the results to be useful and admissible in a court of law. Even in private or corporate investigations, the computer forensics investigator should always assume that the case may eventually go to court, so each case should be approached with a high level of investigative standards.

In this module, we'll discuss forensics concepts, procedures, and methods. We'll cover how to obtain and handle digital evidence as well as perform analysis on the evidence to be presented to law enforcement or corporate management. First, let's review some important computer forensics concepts.

Forensic Concepts

A computer forensics professional, like other security professionals, requires a variety of general and specific skills. The computer forensics investigator may see primarily Windows boxes in the course of her work, becoming adept at working on those operating systems. Likewise, Linux aficionados will be more comfortable working on those types of hosts. Networking gurus will also be more comfortable working with network forensics cases. Regardless of skills, expertise, and preferred areas in forensics, all investigators should be familiar with some fundamental concepts that apply to any type of case and any type of system. These concepts relate to collecting and handling evidence, as well as maintaining legal and ethical integrity of the investigation.

Impartiality and the Collection of Evidence

Many computer forensics investigators work for law enforcement or government agencies. Investigators also work for corporations, businesses, lawyers, and so on. Regardless of whom the investigator works for, the investigator's goal should always be to obtain, handle, and analyze evidence impartially. Even when working for law enforcement, the investigator should always seek to gather any evidence related to an incident or crime, even if that evidence is *exculpatory* in nature and may prove the innocence of a suspect. An investigator who only seeks to prove the guilt (looking for *inculpatory* evidence) of a suspect in an investigation cannot render a fair and impartial analysis of the evidence. All digital evidence, regardless of whether it points to innocence or guilt, must be treated with equal care when it is collected and analyzed.

Handling Evidence

The technical mechanics of handling evidence, such as use of the chain-of-custody, for example, will be discussed a bit later in the module, but for now you should know that handling evidence is a very critical aspect of conducting a forensics investigation. A forensics investigator is responsible for the following:

- Carefully controlling and monitoring evidence, including the circumstances under which it is collected, handled, stored, transferred, and disposed of

- Protecting electronic evidence such as system components—hard drives, workstations, media, and so on—by storing it in anti-static bags when possible

- Inventorying and labeling all evidence per the requirements of the investigating agency, with the investigator's name, date, item inventory number, and other pertinent information

- Photographing systems and evidence in their original, undisturbed state whenever possible before moving them or interacting with them

- Performing integrity checking mechanisms, such as hashing, on digital evidence whenever possible to ensure that it has not been tampered with or otherwise altered

- Establishing and maintaining the chain-of-custody throughout the life of the evidence and the investigation

Legal and Ethical Considerations

All computer forensics investigations should be approached from the perspective that they may ultimately end up in a court of law and be subject to legal rules for collecting, maintaining, analyzing, and introducing evidence into a court. In the United States, the Federal Rules of Evidence (FRE) prescribe the conditions under which computer-based evidence, such as files, logs, and so forth, may be entered into evidence for a criminal case. And the Federal Rules of Civil Procedure (FRCP) dictate how digital evidence may be presented in a noncriminal case. These two sources of rules should be reviewed and understood very well by computer forensics investigators.

In terms of evidence, several terms are used to describe it in terms of legality and admissibility. *Best evidence* is usually original evidence, such as *real evidence* (physical objects) and *direct evidence* (usually in the form of testimony regarding events that were personally witnessed by someone). *Circumstantial evidence* tends to support a conclusion but does not absolutely prove it. Evidence that attempts to reconstruct an event in question is known as *demonstrative evidence*, which can be in the form of charts, graphs, drawings, and so forth, used to help non-technical people, such as the members of a jury, understand an event. Evidence that directly supports or proves a definitive assertion could be considered *documentary evidence*.

Digital evidence is difficult to categorize in these terms, but is typically considered documentary evidence, since it could be documents, log files, images, and so forth. One key item about the admissibility of digital evidence is that it must be generated during normal business. In other words, log files can be considered admissible because the computer generates them as part of its normal operation. On the other hand, data created and entered into a computer by human beings is typically considered inadmissible, since it is subjective and not trustworthy.

Since 2006, the FRCP have required organizations to place all forms of relevant information, both electronic and physical, under *legal hold* if they reasonably anticipate litigation or government investigation in any form. That means that the company must stop typical cycling procedures that would result in the deletion of records, drives, or other sources that save electronic data.

Data Volatility

In terms of the technical aspect of data collection, the investigator should pay special attention to the *order of volatility*, because digital evidence is very fragile and can be easily altered or destroyed. The investigator should always approach the collection process with this in mind and should attempt to collect the most volatile data first, as the highest priority. The investigator will use different methods, tools, and techniques to collect different types of digital evidence, such as the contents of RAM, files from hard drives, log files from a firewall, and so on. A good computer forensics investigator will have a complete kit of tools and equipment necessary to collect evidence from a wide variety of sources. The key aspect, however, is collecting the most perishable data first.

Order of Volatility

Best practices offered in the computer forensics world, developed from law enforcement procedures, computer security practices, and other sources, dictate a certain order of collection of data by a computer forensics investigator. Obviously, the investigator should collect the most perishable data first, including data from a "live" collection involving a computer that is still powered on and may have data residing in memory or on the screen. As the order of volatility progresses, the investigator should collect data that is less and less volatile, such as that stored on a hard disk that isn't currently in use or powered on. The next few sections discuss the specific order of volatility and perishability of data, and how it is collected from each source.

RAM   System RAM is one of the most volatile locations of digital evidence you'll encounter as a digital forensics investigator. Because the contents of RAM are subject to change constantly, and because it can be wiped out whenever the computer's power is turned off, it is a high priority during evidence collection. You'll have to worry about collecting the contents of RAM if the system is powered on and running. This type of collection is called a *live response* and requires special tools and techniques to collect the contents while disturbing the data in RAM as little as possible. Digital evidence located in RAM includes running processes, network connections, active applications, active user data, and so on. It's also possible that encryption keys and passwords may exist in RAM in an unencrypted state, so they can be gathered as well during a live response.

Several tools can dump the entire contents of RAM into a file, and other tools can be used to gather information selectively on running processes and connections as well. These tools may dump this information into a text file or other type of database for further analysis. Both techniques should be used to collect as much perishable data as possible.

Hard Drives   Hard drives located within the machine are certainly the most valuable source of digital evidence, but they are lower down the list in order of volatility, since they do not lose their data when powered off or removed from the machine. A hard drive does not have to be examined using live response techniques; it should be removed from the computer after it has been powered down, and then analyzed later. We'll discuss the techniques used to gather information from hard drives and ensure its integrity later in the module.

Other Media and Sources of Digital Evidence   Most other types of media that offer a more permanent type of storage than system RAM can be examined after the machine has been powered down, inventoried, and taken to a laboratory. These types of media are also usually removable, such as optical discs, SD cards, and USB devices. This typically makes them the least volatile data, but no less important in the process of collection and analysis. As mentioned, you should go ahead and inventory them and start a chain-of-custody to protect their integrity.

Critical Forensic Practices

When discussing basic forensics concepts, certain practices are common to all investigations regardless of operating system in use, nature of the investigation, and so on. These practices are critical to an investigation, and although they are very basic in nature, they can make or break an investigation and may make the difference between the successful prosecution or dismissal of the case due to faulty forensics procedures. The next few items we will discuss are critical practices you need to know both for the exam and as a real-life forensics investigator.

First Response

First response to an investigation is a critical step in the process that affects the entire investigation and its outcome. It's one part of the process that can't be redone right the second time; it must be done correctly the first time, from the beginning. Most organizations don't employ a full-time qualified and trained forensics investigator; they might have qualified people who have other primary duties in the security or IT administration departments, and those personnel will act as first (and sometimes only) responders to an incident requiring forensic skills. At minimum, they should be trained on what to do—and what *not* to do—during the initial response to a forensics incident, including how to secure the scene, and how to approach and identify potential evidence, collect it, and secure it using chain-of-custody.

Securing the scene is the first task, and is certainly not least important; the first responder should make sure that only personnel necessary to the response and investigation be involved and have access to the scene. These may include representatives from the legal, HR, and security departments, as well as certain managers. You should be very careful, however, to make sure that the number of people aware of and involved in the response is kept to the absolute minimum. There will of, course, be people in the organization who sometimes overestimate their own importance and try to be involved in the investigation. This usually leads to difficulties in keeping the scene intact, investigating the case objectively, and being able to keep the investigation confidential.

    NOTE   Securing the scene sometimes takes subterfuge, such as using a ruse or note to get a suspected internal user away from his or her system and into a company breakroom. Investigators can swoop in quickly and secure the scene without interference.

During the initial response to an incident requiring a forensics investigation, the impulse is to begin immediately examining the system, plugging in disc imaging devices, and so on, but the first thing an investigator (or qualified responder) should do is photograph or take video of the scene. This is because the human memory is fallible and subjective, and it's often necessary to know exactly how a system was set up and running, to include its placement, devices plugged into it (and into which ports), and what was shown on the screen (if it's turned on) when the responder arrived.

 EXAM TIP The CompTIA Security+ exam refers to the action of photographing a screen as a *screenshot*, though that's technically a different thing. A forensics person wouldn't take a screenshot by pressing Print Screen in Windows, for example, because that would change the evidence. A photograph serves the same function.

After you have photographed the scene, you should begin to assess the situation. You'll need to determine in what state the computer is running. Is it powered off or on? Is a user logged in or logged out? What applications or processes are visible on the screen? Based upon this, as well as the nature of the incident (for example, hacking attack, computer misuse, criminal investigation, and so on), you must decide whether to do a "live" response by collecting evidence with the computer up and running or to collect data after the machine is powered off, if it isn't already. A live response can get valuable data that is in RAM, such as running processes, network connections, active sessions, and so on, but you also risk tainting the evidence by collecting it, since a live response can change data, files, and their access times. A discussion on data volatility and the order of collection is presented earlier in the module. In addition to deciding whether to perform a live response or not, you must also decide whether you should disconnect the system from the network. If the system is under attack, you must balance the desire to stop the attack and limit data loss with the possibility of gaining valuable information about the nature of the attack and the attacker. You'll make this decision based upon the critical nature of the data involved, the seriousness and impact of the attack, and the damage to the system and network.

 NOTE The first response certainly can differ if there's a law enforcement issue involved. In the latter case, an internal team wouldn't likely be touching any evidence at all.

A first response must also include a comprehensive inventory of all evidence collected and seized by the investigator. As a first responder, you should inventory systems, peripherals, and media, as well as any other device or item deemed relevant to the investigation. You should record the inventory on a form that allows you to enter the type of hardware device, make, model, and serial number of any item seized as evidence. You should also establish a chain-of-custody at this point, the details of which are discussed next.

Chain-of-Custody and Securely Handling Evidence

Evidence is any item that can be used to substantiate or support your case and the investigation. To be used in most legal proceedings, evidence items should be reliable and not subjected to the possibility of alteration or modification in any way. There should also be the assurance that the evidence has been under positive control and in secure storage at all times. This last part is accomplished through the chain-of-custody process. *Chain-of-custody* begins when the evidence is initially seized or collected, and establishes a continuous accounting of where the evidence is at all times, who has possessed it, what activities were performed on it, and the details of its storage, use, and transfer. This process helps to ensure the integrity of evidence and minimizes the possibility that it has been altered or tampered with. Chain-of-custody contributes to the admissibility and value of evidence in court.

In addition to the formal chain-of-custody process, evidence must be handled properly to make sure it does not get damaged, lost, tampered with, or stolen. Properly handling evidence includes storing it securely in locked cabinets or safes, storing it in a secure room that is restricted to certain personnel, conducting periodic inventories, documenting when evidence is removed or placed into storage, and documenting any analysis actions that take place with the evidence. Additionally, proper handling and storage requires taking into account considerations such as humidity, temperature, electrostatic discharge, and other environmental issues that inherently affect electronic devices and digital storage media.

The Importance of Time

Time is a critical element in a computer forensics investigation, in many ways. First, files on a computer are normally "stamped" by the operating system or file system with the system time and date to indicate when the file was modified, accessed, or created (referred to sometimes as the *MAC times*). Timestamping is an important consideration in a case, simply because it provides a record of when a suspect may have interacted with a file. Log files also use timestamping for events they record, such as login activity, file or folder access, use of privileges, and so forth. Even a forensics investigator's software used to collect and analyze evidence provides timestamps so that the activities the investigator performs can be tracked, verified, and used to provide confirmation of a sound analysis on the evidence.

The key to timestamping electronic data, such as files and logs, is time synchronization. On a network, hosts often get their time from a central source, such as a network time server or Internet-based time source running the Network Time Protocol (NTP) on UDP port 123. The hosts on the network, if set correctly, consider time zone differences between the local time zone and Universal Coordinated Time (UTC), which NTP normally uses. Still, it's a good idea to verify time zone settings and synchronization (as well as the use of NTP over manual time settings) when investigating, to ensure that a host is getting the correct time, or at least to account for time differences between file MAC times, log timestamps, and other events relevant to the investigation. A good investigation needs to record the *time offset*, the difference between the time stamp and the time zone, usually GMT.

It's worth mentioning here that the use of timestamps isn't limited to electronic files, data, and records. The investigator should also manually use timestamps on written or paper logs, forms, and so on to help enforce the accountability and validation of manual activities during the investigation. This is especially important on the chain-of-custody forms, as well as interview records and other manually created records pertaining to the investigation.

Preservation

Data integrity is a critical part of a digital forensics investigation. In addition to protecting physical evidence, such as removable media and hard drives, protecting the files on those types of media is just as important. Because digital evidence is subject to volatility and change, it's important to establish that the digital evidence collected remains unchanged throughout the course of the investigation, including the storage, analysis, and presentation of the evidence. Ensuring data integrity is called *preservation*. At the file level, this is achieved by a process called *hashing*. Hashing uses cryptographic algorithms (known as hashing algorithms), which offer a way to represent digital evidence (primarily files) as a numerical value (or *sum*) known as a *hash*. MD5 and the SHA series of hashing algorithms (such as SHA-1, SHA-2, SHA-512, and so on) are the hashing algorithms primarily used for this purpose.

The theory behind hashing is that if a hash (also called a message digest) is recorded for a file, any tiny change to the file will change the hash value. Even if one binary digit, or *bit* (a 1 or a 0), of a file changes, the measured hash value will change. This means that if a hash value is taken for a piece of digital evidence, and later a hash value is taken again for the same evidence, they should exactly match unless the evidence has been tampered with or changed. This process ensures digital evidence integrity and can be used against individual files, folders, or even complete images of an entire hard drive or other digital storage media. Figure 10-2 shows an MD5 sum generated for a file in the Linux operating system.

Track Man-Hours and Expense

The forensics investigator must be able to track all man-hours and expenses to ensure traceability and accountability for all actions taken and investigative materials purchased.

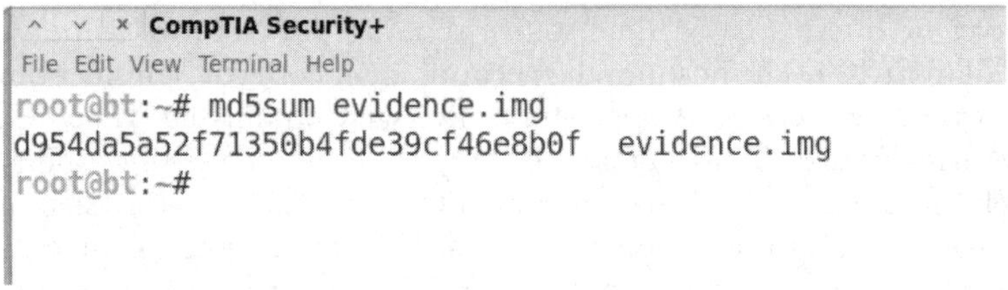

Figure 10-2

An MD5 hash generated for an evidence file in Linux

```
^  v  x  CompTIA Security+
File  Edit  View  Terminal  Help
root@bt:~# md5sum evidence.img
d954da5a52f71350b4fde39cf46e8b0f  evidence.img
root@bt:~#
```

EXAM TIP The CompTIA Security+ exam objectives use the term *Strategic intelligence/counterintelligence gathering (Active logging)*, presumably to mean actions a government investigator team can do to discover the perpetrators of incidents in the case of malicious actors. And, once discovered, to record faithfully all details about the attackers and what the government can do to attack the attackers, such as shut down Web sites, freeze accounts, and so on. Note that the incident response/forensics team *would not do* the counter-attacking.

Data Acquisition

Once evidence has been seized, the investigator must go through another process to capture the evidence, generically called *data acquisition*. Earlier we mentioned the process of gathering or capturing evidence in order of volatility, starting with system RAM and moving on to hard drives and other removable storage media. This process also includes evidence beyond a single workstation, such as network servers and any device that stores processes, transmits, or receives data in most forms. Some special-purpose devices will require more unique methods of capturing evidence, including dumping logs and configuration files from network devices, copying database structures, and so on. Any form of digital data, such as a file, an application, or a network capture, should be captured as needed. In the next couple of sections, we'll discuss a few aspects of capturing types of digital evidence.

Capture a System Image

A system image is usually a file or series of files that contains the entire contents of a hard drive or other digital storage media (as opposed to a photographic or graphic image). You could, of course, perform a routine copy of all files and folders on a hard drive to another media. This would get *some* of the digital evidence located on the drive, but it wouldn't get areas of the drive that contain deleted files, metadata structures, and so on. To get these crucial areas of the drive, you must go through a process known as *imaging* the drive. In the forensics imaging process, you're trying to get a bit-by-bit copy of the entire drive, to include hidden or system areas, slack space, file tables and other metadata, and so on, in addition to the files and directories that are normally visible to the user. Since routine copy processes don't typically capture all this data, you might use a forensic imaging program or even a special hardware device to capture an image from media. Once you've obtained the system image, you should perform a hash on the image files to establish their integrity. You should also make a backup copy of the system image and perform your forensics analysis on the backup, rather than on your original image.

EXAM TIP Capture a system image and take hashes using SHA-1 or MD5 to verify the acquired disk image. Do this again during the investigation to make sure nothing changed on the image.

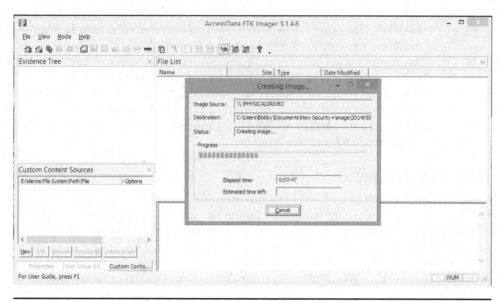

Figure 10-3 AccessData's FTK Imager capturing an image of a USB stick

Several forensics tools are available to capture system images, including commercial tools such as AccessData's Forensic Toolkit (FTK) and the EnCase commercial software suite. These commercial tools usually offer a full range of system image and digital evidence analysis functions as well. You can also use good old free Linux to obtain a system image, simply by knowing how to use the dd command. Additionally, there are hardware imaging devices specifically designed for forensics use; these can capture system images from different types of media and create their hash values at the same time. Figure 10-3 shows an example of AccessData's FTK Imager capturing an image of a USB stick.

 EXAM TIP The process in forensics for capturing every scrap of information, including hidden and deleted files, is called *recovery*.

Capture Video

Digital forensics investigations should try to *capture video evidence*. If the video is in the form of a file that comes off the workstation in question, you should treat it as you would any other file by establishing its integrity via hashing and analyzing it for its evidentiary value. Video that comes out of a surveillance camera is of equal value as evidence, but it may be stored as a digital file on a removable media or even in a central storage area of a workstation or server. Although rare these days, video could also be stored on a type of videotape, or it may come in a proprietary file format, depending upon the manufacture of the surveillance camera and system. In any case, the considerations for capturing video are like those of most other forms of evidence. It is seized the same way, accounted for, and handled using a chain-of-custody. If it's digital in nature or stored on tape or another type of media, it should be forensically copied and the analysis performed on the copy. If it's a digital format, it should also be hashed for integrity purposes. The analysis should be performed only on a copy of the original evidence, like all digital evidence, and may require conversion to a popular video format if its native format is proprietary in nature. Literally dozens of file viewers and analysis tools can be used to examine captured video.

Capture Individual Files

When you need only an individual file, take a moment to create a hash of the file and then copy the file and hash to a separate location, such as a thumb drive. Keep another copy of the hash in another, secure location.

Data acquisition for individual files is rare but useful in specific situations. One time, I found several images attached to an e-mail message. Suspecting that these images were using *steganography*—the science of hiding information in other data—I went through the secure data acquisition process and sent them to a forensics lab for analysis. Sure enough, the images contained text files.

 NOTE *Steganography tools* enable you to encrypt data within image, video, and sound files. These tools also enable decryption of those files.

Network Traffic and Logs

Network traffic and logs, as mentioned previously, are also viable forms of digital evidence as long as proof exists that the stored copies weren't manipulated. Logs can give insight as to the events that occurred on the network relating to network traffic that has occurred between hosts and servers, as well as between the internal network and the Internet. Most network devices log files in one of several common formats and store these files locally on the device or on a central storage device on the network. Log files are also used for event correlation. For instance, if you are tracking the actions of the user on a workstation who may have accessed prohibited content on the Internet, not only would you look at the files and logs on the workstation he used, but you'd also examine the logs on network devices, such as proxy servers and firewalls, to correlate the user's actions and times to establish a working timeline of the events.

Log files capture network traffic that has already occurred, but they don't capture information about active network traffic. This is where a network sniffer, sometimes called a *protocol analyzer* (the term used by CompTIA), is useful. You can use a sniffer, which could be either hardware or software in nature, to capture ongoing network traffic and save it to a file for later analysis. You can also examine the capture in real time, so that you can see what's currently going on in the network. This may be useful if you are investigating an ongoing attack, for example, and are trying to determine how the attacker is getting into the network or what type of data he is trying to steal or damage. This type of capture also may help you if you are investigating a user who is performing prohibited or criminal actions on the network, and you want to catch her in the act. You should store and treat network traffic capture files as any other type of digital evidence. You should analyze only copies of the files, taken after you have created hash values for them to establish integrity.

Witness Interviews

Part of data acquisition requires the forensics team to interview witnesses who may have information about the incident. The team records the witness interviews for later review. Seemingly unimportant details from one interview might mesh with details from other interviews to provide clues to solving the incident.

Analyzing Evidence

Acquiring and capturing evidence in a forensically sound manner, in accordance with established procedures that will hold up in court, is a huge part of the forensics investigation. Sometimes first responders who are not otherwise trained in forensics procedures are the people who collect digital evidence, and they may have no further involvement in its further analysis. At other times, the same people who collect it will also analyze it, and they must be trained with skills beyond those required by first responders. Analyzing digital evidence requires skills that include advanced knowledge of how hard drives and other storage media are constructed, file systems and bit-level construction of files and data, and so on. The forensics investigator also must know how encryption systems work and how a knowledgeable suspect may hide data in files. Forensics investigators can use tools to help with data analysis, which are used to reassemble pieces of data into usable evidence that communicate what a suspect was doing, how, and sometimes even why. In fact, forensics analysis is used to establish an indisputable chain of events and actions against a timeline, for the purposes of proving or disproving a suspect's innocence or guilt. A forensics analysis should answer six questions about actions and events that took place on the system or network: who, what, where, when, why, and how.

Common Analysis Tasks

Regardless of type of data or system examined, a forensics investigator must know how to perform some common tasks. Forensically sound data collection is one of those tasks, as well as knowing how to forensically copy or image digital storage media. A forensics investigator needs to know also analysis tasks, such as *analyze files and file systems*, *look for hidden files*, *recover deleted or corrupt files*, *decrypt data* that has been encrypted by a suspect, and *reconstruct a timeline of events* that occurred on the system or network. A forensics investigator may also have to be an expert in hacking attacks, so he can adequately analyze illegal penetrations into a system or network. Malware analysis is also a task a forensics investigator may occasionally perform, so being familiar with different types of malware and how they are constructed is also important.

Big Data Analysis

Traditionally, most forensics investigations involve single systems or are limited to a single network and its hosts. As more and more data is generated and distributed across the Internet, investigators are increasingly finding that they are investigating cases that involve *big data*, or very large and complex datasets. Some of these datasets are stored in huge data centers, or even in the cloud, and could be spread out across several geographical sites and systems. Performing data collection and analysis on big data is a huge task and will likely require teams of IT and forensics professionals if it involves large amounts of distributed data. The investigator will also collect and analyze smaller subsets of data related to the case at hand. One advantage to big data is that it usually isn't volatile; it is usually backed up quite extensively so there is no fear of data loss. The biggest challenge in an investigation involving big data is to locate data relevant to a case and extract that data using specialized tools (database query tools) and analyzing the smaller datasets. Otherwise, evidence obtained from big data should be treated as any other forensics evidence: data extracted from a large dataset should be copied, hashed, and analyzed using standard forensics tools. An extra effort on the part of the forensics investigator may be required to document carefully how data was extracted, under what circumstances, why it is relevant to the case, and how it was handled during analysis, for the benefit of the court.

Module 10-3: Continuity of Operations and Disaster Recovery

This module covers the following CompTIA Security+ objectives:

- **5.2** Summarize business impact analysis concepts
- **5.3** Explain risk management processes and concepts
- **5.6** Explain disaster recovery and continuity of operation concepts

Business continuity consists of the planning and processes that an organization undertakes to ensure that it survives and can function after a disaster or incident. This includes identifying critical processes, prioritizing systems and equipment, and determining the business impact if any of these processes or systems are unavailable to the organization for extended periods of time. Since this impact is closely related to risk analysis, the organization should perform this type of planning as part of, and in conjunction with, the organization's risk management processes.

Additionally, planning involves determining strategies to bring critical services, systems, and data back online after recovery so the organization can assume some level of operations. The organization must ensure that the preparation and logistics support is in place to bring these critical pieces back online. This module revisits the concepts of risk management covered in Chapter 1 and introduces business continuity planning concepts. The module will conclude with a discussion of the importance of exercising and testing the business continuity and disaster recovery plans.

Risk Management Best Practices

Risk management factors into business continuity. A business must plan for and mitigate risk, after all, to survive and thrive another day. Chapter 1 detailed risk management concepts, such as infrastructure, security controls, risk management frameworks, and industry-standard frameworks and reference architectures. This section provides a refresher on risk assessment and then goes into detail on change management.

EXAM TIP Pay attention to the nuances of risk management in the questions. Module 1-2 covered risk in terms of frameworks and best practices, for example. This module hits broadly on risk management concepts.

Risk Assessment

A *risk assessment* encompasses the activities that focus on the collection of information (threats, assets, vulnerabilities, and impacts) and analysis of that information to determine the degree of damage and impact to a system or business from threats. Risk management also seeks to quantify items such as cost, downtime, and so on, and to determine how those items can be mitigated or reduced. A risk assessment in terms of business continuity focuses on what relevant threats to business operations exist and how they impact the business's ability to function after a negative event.

Change Management

An IT infrastructure is an ever-changing thing. Applications are updated, operating systems change, server configurations adjust; change is a tricky part of managing an infrastructure. Change needs to happen, but not at the cost of losing security. The process of creating change in your infrastructure in an organized, controlled, safe way is called *change management.*

Change management usually begins with a *change management team.* This team, consisting of people from throughout your organization, is tasked with the job of investigating, testing, and authorizing all but the simplest changes to your network.

Changes tend to be initiated at two levels: strategic-level changes, typically initiated by management and major in scope (for example, we're going to switch all the servers from Windows to Linux); and infrastructure-level changes, typically initiated by a department by making a request to the change management team. Let's go over what to expect when dealing with change management.

Initiating the Change The first part of many change processes is a request from a part of the organization. Let's say you're in charge of IT security for an accounting department that includes dozens of accountants with dozens of PCs. A new version of their core accounting software has been released and the change management team needs to manage the upgrade securely.

Changes start with a *change request.* Depending on the organization, this can be a highly official document or, for a smaller organization, nothing more than a detailed e-mail message. Whatever the case, the initiating person or group needs to document the reason for this change. A good change request will include the following:

- **Type of change** Software and hardware changes are obviously part of this category, but this could also encompass issues like backup methods, work hours, network access, workflow changes, and so forth.

- **Configuration procedures**   What is it going to take to make this happen? Who will help? How long will it take?

- **Rollback process**   If this change in some way makes such a negative impact that going back to how things were before the change is needed, what will it take to roll back to the previous configuration?

- **Potential impact**   How will this change impact the organization? Will it save time? Save money? Increase efficiency? Will it affect the perception of the organization?

- **Notification**   What steps will be taken to notify the organization about this change?

Dealing with the Change Management Team   With the change request in hand, it's time to get the change approved. Most organizations rely on a well-written change request form to get the details. The *approval process* usually consists of considering the issues listed in the change request, but also management approval and funding.

Making the Change Happen   Once your change is approved, the real work starts. Equipment, software, tools, and so forth must be purchased. Configuration teams need to be trained. The change committee must provide an adequate *maintenance window*: the time it will take to implement and thoroughly test the coming changes. As part of that process, the committee must *authorize downtime* for systems, departments, and so on. Likewise, the committee provides *notification of the change* to those people who will be affected, if possible providing alternative workplaces or equipment.

Documenting the Change   The ongoing and last step of the change is *documentation*. All changes must be clearly documented, including but not limited to:

- Network configurations, such as server settings, router configurations, and so on

- Additions to the network, such as additional servers, switches, and so on

- Physical location changes, such as moved workstations, relocated switches, and so on

Business Continuity Concepts

An organization conducts *business continuity planning (BCP)* to ensure the continued function and operation of the organization in the event of a disaster or serious incident. BCP requires careful and deliberate planning on the part of organizational members, from executives all the way down to technicians. Business continuity planning involves a defined process, and it essentially starts by identifying the business assets (including equipment, people, systems, data, and processes) and determining how critical they are to the function of the business. BCP next examines these assets for degree of impact to the business in the event they are lost or nonfunctional during a disaster, and then prioritizes them for *order of restoration*. The impact on the business if critical assets and processes are lost could be financial or operational, or it could have other negative effects. In any case, BCP is designed to ensure that these assets are successfully and effectively recovered after a disaster so the business can continue operating. The next few sections outline some of the key processes and activities involved with BCP. You can find a more detailed discussion on business continuity and disaster recovery planning in the National Institute of Standards and Technology (NIST) Special Publication 800-34, Rev. 1, "Contingency Planning Guide for Federal Information Systems," which was written with government systems in mind but can be used by any business to aid in BCP efforts.

Business Impact Analysis

One of the first steps an organization must take in BCP is to conduct a *business impact analysis (BIA)* in which an organization identifies assets, determines their criticality to the organization and the impact if those assets are lost, and prioritizes them for restoration in the event of a disaster. If any of these steps sound familiar, it's because the BIA process closely mirrors parts of risk management.

The BIA is performed before other BCP steps, because the organization must know *what* it is protecting and how important those assets are to the business before it can plan on how to protect them. Once the organization has identified critical assets and their impacts, it can determine how best to protect them and how much resources it can afford to use to protect those assets, based upon differing threats and their likelihood of occurrence.

Identification of Critical Systems and Components

As part of the BIA process, the organization must identify critical systems and their components. Some of this depends upon the different points of view of the users and functional areas within the organization, so most functional areas in the organization should be represented when the BIA is performed. For example, both the human resources and accounting functions in the organization may each insist that their systems are more critical to the survival of the business than anyone else's. Likewise, the same might apply for engineering and production functions. This is one reason why top management should be involved in the BIA process, to provide objective decision-making capabilities as to which systems and components are critical, and in what priority they must be restored. Which systems and components are designated as critical may depend upon several factors, including the criticality of the processes they support. For example, if the business's primary mission is online order fulfillment for different products, the business will likely deem the systems and components directly involved in that process (such as Web servers, database servers, financial transaction systems, and so on) more critical than other support systems, such as human resources and accounting systems. The business deems those other support systems important, but it may not necessarily depend upon them for survival, at least in the short term, and to get back up and running again.

The organization should define exactly what constitutes a critical system or component. The organization may develop different categorizations of criticality, based upon the business process supported. For example, a priority one asset may be deemed as the most critical type, directly supporting the primary business mission. A priority two asset may support secondary business functions or even a support system. The organization could also define criticality in terms of system function. For example, it may designate all primary systems supporting the business mission as a priority one, and designate any backup or redundant systems as a priority two. Another such categorization may classify all Web servers as priority one, for instance. In any event, I can't overstate the importance of this part of the BIA process.

Removing Single Points of Failure

Without proper planning, or sometimes because of changes over time, an organization might discover it depends for critical function on a single specialized machine, person, or process, creating a *single point of failure*. If that essential entity fails, in other words, bad things happen. Smaller organizations can't necessarily avoid single points of failure, but organizations both small and large need to recognize those points and plan for the eventuality of failure. Let's look at a few examples.

Single points of failure include technologies and equipment such as a single server that processes a critical business function or a system that houses the only copy of a database. A single point of failure doesn't have to be technological, however. A person can also be a single point of failure. For example, suppose only one administrator has access to a piece of critical data or an encrypted file. If something happens to that administrator—she leaves the organization or becomes ill or dies—the organization will have lost access to that data or file. A process can also be a single point of failure. Without an alternative way of processing a financial transaction, for example, failure of the process involved means that the organization no longer has that capability.

During both the risk assessment and business impact analysis processes, an organization should identify single points of failure and eliminate them as efficiently as possible. The organization can accomplish this by purchasing more equipment (such as a backup server), appointing and training an alternate administrator to perform certain duties or have certain access in the event the primary administrator isn't available, and looking at processes critically for redundant capabilities. In eliminating single points of failure, redundancy is a key concept. Organization management may be reluctant to include redundant equipment, personnel, or processes, as this offers no immediate return on investment (ROI) and can be costly, but they will usually be glad they made the investment the first time a single point of failure fails. Redundancy is discussed a bit later in the module.

Business Continuity Planning

The purpose of business continuity planning is to produce a document, the business continuity and disaster recovery plan, which details disaster- and incident-related risks to critical systems, the impact if those systems are lost, and how best to preserve them. This document also specifies how to recover the organization after a disaster and continue business operations. The planning process that goes into producing the detailed plan involves personnel from the entire organization, at all management and technical levels. It involves technical personnel, human resources personnel, facilities and security personnel, and representatives from almost every part of the organization. A formal BCP team should be established and mandated with certain goals and tasks. Producing comprehensive continuity and recovery documentation should be one of those tasks, as well as establishing the concrete policies, procedures, and processes necessary to react to an incident, recover from it, and re-establish business operations.

Continuity of Operation Planning

Although they are parts of the same process, *continuity of operation planning (COOP)* and disaster recovery are two separate activities with distinct goals. *Continuity of operations (COO)* ensures that the business is functioning and operating again in its primary business mission, while disaster recovery is more of an intermediate step between the actual disaster event and bringing the business back to an operational state. *Disaster recovery planning (DRP)* is concerned with the reaction and response to a disaster and is focused on saving lives, preventing injury, and preserving equipment, data, and facilities. DRP will be discussed a bit later in the module. COOP ensures that the business has the appropriate systems, equipment, data, infrastructure, and, of course, people, to resume and maintain operations. This means that considerations such as backups, spare equipment, alternate processing sites, spare supplies, and so on, are equally important in keeping the business up and running. Figure 10-4 illustrates the relationship of business COO and disaster recovery processes and activities.

One fallacy in BCP is the assumption that COO means that the business will be back in a fully operational state equal to what it was before the disaster, but this usually isn't the case. In a serious disaster, most businesses will likely recover to an operational state that is somewhat diminished from normal function and operations. This is something that the organization should consider and prepare for during the planning process. The organization should determine the acceptable level for COO and how to achieve that target level. The organization may need to understand that assuming operations may be on a scaled or incremental basis, particularly in the event of a widespread disaster that affects other organizations, public infrastructures, and so on. Even a 50 percent

Figure 10-4

The relationship between continuity of operations and disaster recovery

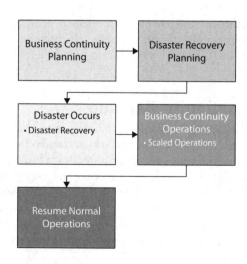

resumption of operations may be considerably better than none and may be even more than other businesses may be able to achieve in a widespread disaster. The organization should set a target COO level and plan on how to achieve that level.

Proper COOP should consider a lot of things aside from machines and locations. Such planning must include exercises for testing the plan; procedures for reporting—so called *after-action reports*; and failover systems that engage immediately in case of a sudden machine death. The COOP should detail alternate processing sites and alternate business practices. (These come up in detail later in the module.)

Disaster Recovery

DRP is really a subset of BCP. The major difference is that BCP is concerned with planning and getting everything in place such that the business functions can resume after a disaster, while DRP is mostly concerned with the practical and immediate activities following an event that include saving lives, preventing injury, salvaging equipment, relocating the physical business infrastructure to a recovery site, and so on. So, BCP is concerned with business-specific functions and operations, and DRP is more about the recovery operations. Both are important, but each focus on different parts of the same overall process.

IT Contingency Planning

IT contingency planning involves the planning, processes, and activities focused on maintaining a resilient, available infrastructure. This means ensuring that the organization has all the right IT equipment and systems that are performing their functions and contributing to the business processes of the organization. Contingency planning at first may sound like a short-term process, especially in the context of disaster recovery or business continuity, but it is an entire process that covers the lifecycle of the entire IT infrastructure in the organization. Equipment and systems become outdated, operating systems require upgrading, software requires patches, and new systems must be installed to handle increased use and provide increased capacity. Planning is required to manage these things, over both long and short terms. Contingency planning also means that the appropriate equipment and systems will be available in the event of an incident or disaster, and they will be able to process and transfer data even after the loss of infrastructure. This is possible only through the long-term planning process, by purchasing and installing redundant systems, planning on data backups, and using multiple redundant network paths. Not only does this type of planning lend resiliency to normal operations, but it also supports contingencies when there may be a loss of infrastructure.

Succession Planning

Redundancy applies to equipment and systems, naturally, and to people. In a disaster or incident, there are worst cases that can affect people, such as injury or death, but even in the best cases, critical personnel may not be able to get to the business location due to practical issues such as destroyed roads, massive power outages, weather, and other events that can occur in a disaster. *Succession planning* ensures that there are available personnel who can step up and lead or perform urgent activities necessary to help the organization recover from a disaster and continue its business operations. Succession planning applies to leadership positions, which are of course vital to business recovery and continuity operations, and to positions that must perform the hands-on work of disaster recovery and business continuity. For example, it's generally not a wise idea to have only one person who knows how to restore data backups to critical services. In the event of a disaster, that person is a single point of failure and would impede the organization's ability to restore operations if she can't make it to the business location to help restore those services. For that reason, every critical position identified during the planning process should also include alternate team members who can fill those roles in the event the primary responsible person is not available.

Likewise, succession planning should also include plans for a leadership chain-of-command and succession in the event key leaders are not available during a disaster. The organization should designate critical leadership positions with both primary personnel and alternates, in a line of succession, so that any leader who cannot respond to the incident has a backup person next in line who is able to take charge and lead the recovery efforts. The organization should document these plans, and all team members should know and understand the leadership succession plan, as well as how other critical positions will be filled by alternates in the event key personnel cannot be present. Training on the duties required by these critical positions is essential. All personnel identified for critical leadership and team member positions must be trained on the duties and responsibilities they will be expected to perform and fulfill in the event of a disaster.

High Availability

High availability is a term often used in relation to networked systems and equipment; it is the measure of the tolerance a business has for downtime with critical systems or processes. If an organization is primarily involved in e-commerce, for example, then a Web-based product ordering and processing system should be available 24 hours a day, seven days per week, since online orders can be taken at any time. Of course, high availability applies to critical services; the less critical a service or system is, the less availability it may require. Proper high availability in systems provides for *failover* measures—automatic switching to backup machines in the event a mission-critical server crash, for example.

 EXAM TIP   Assuring high availability requires *identification of critical systems*— that is, those with *mission-essential functions*—and taking steps to assure those systems stay up and have redundant systems in place if they fail.

High availability is measured in terms of what systems personnel refer to as "the nines." It's expressed as a percentage and decimal points of uptime. For example, you might see 99.99 percent availability, or even 99.999 percent availability (referred to as "5 nines" of availability). Obviously, the more decimal places, the higher availability required.

At first glance, there may not seem to be much of a difference between 99 percent availability and 99.999 percent availability. When you measure in terms of tolerable downtime, say, on an annual basis (365 days per year), then 99 percent availability is equivalent to an uptime of 361.35 days per year. That means that there will be a total downtime in that year of 3.65 days. For most organizations, especially in this modern

	Availability Percentage	Amount of Downtime per Year
Figure 10-5 Levels of high availability expressed as "the nines"	99%	3.65 days
	99.9%	8.76 hours
	99.99%	52.56 minutes
	99.999%	5.26 minutes

Internet age where customers expect to be able to order products and services instantly, at any time during the day or night, that amount of downtime would be unacceptable. Contrast that to five nines of availability, which is 99.999 percent availability, and is equivalent to slightly over 5 minutes of downtime per year (5.26 minutes). From a practical perspective, it's likely that all that downtime won't take place at once during the year, but during an incident or disaster, it could. This leads to discussion on how organizations can maintain a high availability percentage through system and process redundancy, and this is the topic of the next section. Figure 10-5 shows the different levels of high availability in terms of "the nines."

Redundancy

Redundancy is an important factor in maintaining the organization's ability to continue operations after a disaster. This means the organization must maintain redundant systems, equipment, data, and even personnel. It also may mean the organization maintains redundant facilities, such as alternate processing sites (see "Recovery Sites" later in the chapter for more details). Redundant processes are also important, since critical data or equipment (or even public infrastructure, such as power) may be unavailable, forcing the business to come up with *alternative business practices* for conducting its mission.

An organization can achieve redundancy in systems and data in several different ways, or usually in a combination of several ways at once. Redundancy is strongly related to the concept of fault tolerance, which is the ability of the system to continue to operate in the event of a failure of one of its components. Redundant systems, as well as the components they comprise, contribute to fault tolerance. Two ways to provide for both redundancy and fault tolerance include *clustering* and *load balancing*, terms that are usually associated with servers, data storage, and networking equipment (such as clustered firewalls or proxy servers), but that could be applied to a variety of assets and services. Data redundancy can also be provided by backups, which can be restored in the event of an emergency; this is discussed later in this module.

Clustering, in the traditional sense, means to have multiple pieces of equipment, such as servers, connected, which appear to the user and the network as one logical device, providing data and services to the organization. Clusters usually share high-speed networking connections as well as data stores and applications and are configured to provide redundancy if a single member of the cluster fails. The two simplest configurations involve either an active-active system or an active-passive system. In an *active-active* configuration, all servers or devices are online, and any one member of the cluster can service a data or application request at any given time (referred to as *load-balancing*). If any single member device fails, the other member devices in the cluster will service a request, and all will be transparent to the user. In an *active-passive* configuration, however, only designated members of the cluster can service requests, and in the event of their failure, another device must be designated as an active member. This configuration isn't always automatic and could require time and intervention on the part of an administrator.

Exercises and Testing

Even with the most extensive business continuity and disaster recovery plans, an organization may miss or fail to consider something. Its best-laid plans can come undone with unexpected events or contingencies. For these reasons, the organization should exercise and test its plans periodically to make sure they work as well as they should. It should exercise and test the plans whenever it makes significant changes to them or to the business environment, to ensure that the changes are considered in the plans. The organization should also exercise and test the plans periodically to refresh everyone's memory on what to do during an incident or disaster, and as part of regularly scheduled training. When you test business continuity and disaster plans, you can often discover things that were forgotten or weren't adequately considered. In this respect, testing your plans can help you improve them and consider any possible scenarios that could occur. Now let's discuss the different types of exercises and tests.

Documentation Reviews

The *documentation review* is the simplest form of test. In this type of test, the business continuity plan, disaster recovery plan, and associated documents are reviewed by relevant personnel, including managers, recovery team members, and anyone else who may have responsibilities directly affecting the plans. The team may review the plans in a group setting or by simply passing them along from team member to team member, who review them in turn. They should review the plans periodically, such as on an annual or semiannual basis, or at least when there are significant changes to the plans or the operating environment. During these reviews, they should check the plans for currency, effectiveness, resource allocation, and general common sense. They should document these formal reviews for historical record purposes and as part of compliance with governance (including corporate and legal requirements).

Tabletop Exercises

A *tabletop exercise* is a type of group review, sometimes literally conducted around the conference room table. In a tabletop exercise, there's a little bit more involvement compared to documentation review by the key players, including managers, team members, and other critical personnel who have business continuity and disaster recovery duties. During the exercise, the group may be presented with scenarios in which they will be directed to respond accordingly. The response can be verbal or written; typically, no actual recovery operations are conducted during a tabletop exercise. These types of exercises are useful in that they allow everyone involved to step through the business continuity and recovery processes and may help to point out deficiencies in the plans. They are also useful training tools and serve to help team members become more familiar with and accustomed to their roles within the plan.

Walkthrough Tests

A step above the tabletop exercise is the *walkthrough test*. In a walkthrough test, there's usually more involvement by relevant team members, and they may go through the motions of fulfilling their responsibilities and conducting the activities required during an actual incident or disaster. This test may be conducted partially in a conference room or entirely out in the actual operations areas of the business. Normally this test does not involve shutting down systems or performing actual recovery operations. Team members may simulate response activities as much as possible without conducting them. A walkthrough test can help point out logistical or practical issues not previously considered around a conference room table, such as the need to move heavy equipment (and maintain nearby the appropriate gear and tools to do so). This type of exercise is also useful as both a training tool and a way to ensure that the plan works as it should.

Full Tests and Disaster Recovery Exercises

At some point, the organization may conduct a full-scale test of its business continuity and disaster recovery plans. In these types of exercises, all personnel are usually involved and may conduct activities as they would during a real incident. A full test may involve shutting down systems to simulate their loss, recovering backup data to alternate systems, and activating alternate processing sites. It may also involve parallel processing using both production and backup systems. This type of exercise is the most involved and will likely take away some significant time from actual production activities. It should not, however, be permitted to impose unnecessary risk on the business by shutting down and recovering actual production systems during the exercise, as this may lead to an actual incident or real downtime. Since this type of test normally requires extensive resources, such as people, equipment, and so on, it is typically conducted infrequently.

Disaster Recovery

Now that you understand the business continuity planning process, let's look at another part of the process: disaster recovery. Up until this point, the discussion has centered on the planning piece. In this section, we'll look at some important concepts in executing that planning. Disaster recovery is concerned with all the activities that must happen after a disaster or incident has occurred, to protect lives and equipment and stabilize the environment within which the business operates. Internal factors, such as personnel, resources, training, and planning, all affect how well an organization responds to a disaster. External factors also affect disaster response, since the organization must depend upon utility companies, communications systems, emergency services, and other important aspects of the public infrastructure to respond to and recover from a disaster. This section discusses the importance of planning and how it affects the ability of an organization to recover from a disaster.

Disaster recovery planning should be a part of business continuity planning. There are subtle differences between these two processes, but essentially, DRP is a subset of the BCP an organization performs to ensure that it sustains its operations before, during, and after an incident or disaster. BCP is normally the first part of the process and usually involves a great deal of careful consideration. DRP is also performed during this process, but the disaster recovery operation occurs when a disaster or incident happens and the organization must react and recover. The DRP is typically a concrete, step-by-step procedure and process the organization executes to save lives, prevent injury, preserve data and systems, and return to an operational status.

Most information security texts and professionals break up threats and incidents into two main categories: environmental and manmade. This is because some of the reactions to the different kinds of threats, disasters, and incidents may be dependent on whether the disaster is an act of nature (unintentional, relying on environmental and physical security controls more than technical ones) or an act of man (hacking, data theft, insider threat, arson and so on, relying on more precise technical controls). Environmental disasters include weather (hurricanes, tornadoes, and flooding), earthquakes, lightning strikes, wind damage, and sometimes fires. Manmade disasters can also include fire (if set intentionally), accidents, theft, hacking, and so on. An organization needs to consider environmental and manmade threats as part of risk assessment and business continuity planning processes. A business located in Kansas may not necessarily have to do a lot of planning for hurricanes, for example, but it should consider tornadoes as a likely disaster that could occur and affect the business.

Disaster recovery plans should include considerations such as sounding alarms, notifying personnel, assembling the disaster recovery team, obtaining equipment and supplies, and the logistical planning necessary to move equipment physically and recover data when needed. These tasks should be done based upon system and data criticality and impact if lost, as determined during the BIA process. One important aspect of DRPs that you should remember for the exam (and in real life) is that *the top priority in disaster response and recovery is saving human lives and preventing injury whenever possible*. This is a higher priority than saving equipment, data, or facilities. DRPs should include personnel protection and safety measures as well. Of course, keep in mind that as IT security folks, it's not your sole responsibility to plan for things like safety; other, more appropriate people in the organization will plan those parts of the response. Nevertheless, in an actual emergency or disaster situation, everyone is responsible for safety.

Backup Plans and Policies

One of the key areas in preparing for a disaster is backing up data to prevent data loss in case the business loses a server or a disaster occurs and the business loses its entire data center. Because everything in security begins with policy, having a well-defined backup policy is an important start to being prepared for data loss in the event of a disaster. The overall backup strategy should specify the frequency and types of backups, of course, but, beyond that, it should specify what data is to be backed up and how. An organization can use several different methods to back up data, and these should be specified in the policy. Policy should also dictate which functional area is responsible for data backups, as well as how quickly data must be restored. The policy may also indicate whether data backups should be stored offsite, how they should be transported, if they should be encrypted, and so on, to protect organizational data further. The policy will also specify who is responsible for data backups, such as the IT department or server management team, for example. During a disaster, certain key positions may be designated as responsible for backups and restorations, if the disaster response team is not organized in the same way as the normal business operations are.

Supporting the backup policy should be the actual plans and procedures that will be used to perform backups. Policy gives direction on *what* must be done and *why*, but not necessarily *how*. For example, a policy would state that all information regarding customer credit card data must be recoverable within two days of a disaster to meet customer expectations and cannot be accessed by the third-party data storage vendor to remain in compliance with PCI regulations. This is where plans and procedures come in. The plans and procedures would then specify details such as how both the flat files and the database information are backed up and which encryption method to use. Backup plans and procedures should further define how backups are performed, the methods used, and regarding restoration. Management will normally write policy (based upon input from the appropriate technical folks), and the people implementing the policy will usually write the plans and procedures. These policies, plans, and procedures all support the overarching business continuity plan as well as any disaster recovery plans that must be implemented. Together, they ensure that the organization will be able to restore critical data in the event of a disaster or incident.

Backup Execution and Frequency

You can perform backups in several ways. There's no one right way; the methods you use depend upon several factors that the organization must consider. One of the most important factors is the criticality of data. In other words, how important is the data that must be backed up, and how quickly must it be restored to get the organization back up and running? Some backup methods can back up data more quickly than others but may restore data more slowly. Other methods back up data in certain increments based upon file archive bits. Any combination of these methods may be used for the optimum backup solution for the organization.

Backup frequency is another factor that the organization must determine. Data that rarely changes may need to be backed up monthly only. Daily transactional data, however, such as the type produced in financial or commercial transactions, may need to be backed up on a minute-by-minute basis, or even in near real-time, to ensure that the most current data is available and all-important transactions have processed. For example, if an earthquake suddenly hit and destroyed a company's primary e-commerce server, in a well-designed transactional backup system, the speed of recovery and failover is so lightning fast that a customer could click "Buy" and not even realize that the computer that registered the purchase was destroyed, because a new system came online 1000 miles away and recovered the customer's transaction without a visible slowdown. That is totally amazing!

Backup frequency is also related to criticality of data, as are the other backup considerations. If the organization has a low tolerance for losing data because of its criticality, it should increase the backup frequency. The tolerance for (and measurement of) the amount of data that an organization can afford to lose for any given time frame is discussed later in the module.

Backup Concepts/Types There are four basic types of backups: full backups, incremental backups, differential backups, and snapshots. Let's briefly discuss each.

In a *full backup*, regardless of whether you are backing up a shared folder, a single hard drive, a RAID array, or an entire server, everything is included in the backup set. At the basic file system level, a full backup also sets the archive bits on files to indicate that the files have been backed up. You can think of an archive bit as an on/off switch. If the archive bit is turned "on" (shown by a binary one in the file metadata), the file has been changed and requires a backup. If the archive bit is turned "off" (signified by a binary zero), the file has been backed up and the archive bit is said to have been "cleared." Full backups clear archive bits to show that the files have been backed up recently. Any changes to any of the files result in the archive bits being turned back on for those files. An organization may execute a full backup once weekly, for example, or even daily, as needed by the organization and depending upon the backup system it has available. Of course, the concept of archive bits applies only to files in the file system itself; it wouldn't necessarily apply to other types of data structures, such as database tables, for instance. However, other data structures may have similar metadata that indicates its backup or archive status.

The *incremental backup* typically backs up only files that have changed since the last full backup. In other words, when an incremental backup is run, it backs up only the files that have the archive bits turned on. After it backs up those files, it turns off the archive bits. If a full backup is run, and then files subsequently change, an incremental backup backs up only those files. Because data can change daily, incremental backups should run daily as well. If there is a data loss on the backup source itself, you can restore the data by first restoring the full backup and then all following incremental backups in the order they were run. Figure 10-6 shows conceptually how a backup scheme involving incremental backups might work.

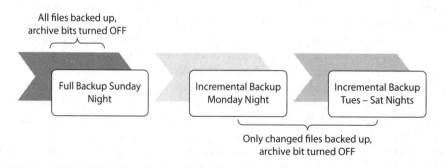

Figure 10-6 A backup scheme using full and incremental backups

The *differential backup* also gets only a subset of the total data and is also based upon the archive bit setting. However, the major difference between a differential backup and an incremental backup is that the differential backup does not clear the archive bit—it leaves it turned on. So, when you run a full backup, and then data changes, you can run a differential backup and it will back up the data files that have the archive bits turned on. Since a differential backup does not clear the archive bit, the next differential backup that you run will not only back up that same data, but will also add any additional files that have changed since the last differential (and full) backup. Differential backups, then, are cumulative. Normally, the first differential backup that you run after a full backup may not take very long to execute, but each subsequent differential backup that you run takes increasingly longer to execute because it is backing up more data than the previous differential backup. One advantage to differential backups, however, is that if you must restore data, you restore the full backup first, followed by only the last differential backup to be executed. No other differential backup is necessary for the restoration process, since the last backup contains all the accumulated changed data. Figure 10-7 illustrates the concept of using a combination of full and differential backups.

A *snapshot* stores a version of an operating system (including applications) at a given moment in time. These are common for individual system backups, such as System Recovery Snapshots in Windows and Time Machine backups in macOS. For servers and such, a snapshot as a backup refers to the powerful feature with virtual machines that enables you to save a version of a functional VM to restore very quickly if anything negative happens to the functional server. A company DNS server might run on a virtual machine, for example. If that server gets corrupted or compromised, rather than restoring it from backup, you could simply delete the image and load a clean snapshot.

To summarize, full backups must be run first and restored first. If incremental backups are used, then all incremental backups must be restored in the order they were executed. Incremental backups do not take very long to back up data, but because you must restore all of them, they can make restoration time a bit lengthy. Differential backups, on the other hand, initially back up data quickly, but slowly take longer and longer to back up. However, when a differential backup is restored, only the last backup needs to be restored after the full backup. A typical scenario might involve an organization executing a full

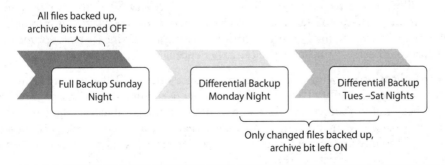

Figure 10-7   Using full and differential backups

backup on a weekly basis, followed by daily incremental or differential backups. It's also possible to mix and match these types of backups, but that is usually dependent on the type of backup software and system used. Finally, use a snapshot to load clean VMs to replace corrupted or compromised images.

Full, incremental, and differential backups, plus snapshots, are the most basic types but not the only types of backups. These four categories also tend to apply more to traditional backup sets (defined groups of files) than to arbitrary or loosely defined data. Think of financial transactions, for example, that come in many different formats, files, applications, and so on, and may be generated so fast that even a nightly backup would be too slow and inadequate to capture all the data needed to recover an operation if the data were lost. These types of datasets may be backed up on a near real-time basis using transaction or journaling methods, and the data may be backed up on a transaction or record basis instead of on a file-by-file basis. In addition to providing recovery during a disaster scenario, transaction-based backups and recovery can help you solve detailed problems and make it easier to correct certain transactions that failed, that were corrupted, or that were intentionally altered, instead of having to roll back a dataset to a certain point in time, destroying what could be perfectly intact, current data in the process.

Geographic Considerations

As companies move to integrate with and take advantage of cloud computing, they must consider a lot of issues, including off-site backups, distance and location selection, and legal implications such as data sovereignty.

Off-Site Backups   Storing backup drives at a location distant from your primary organization provides essential security in the event of a disaster. My company is in Houston, Texas, for example, the land of rodeos and hurricanes. Keeping a backup of our critical data—financial information, intellectual property, and so on—in some storage facility that's not going to be affected by Hurricane [name] next year is essential. [Shakes fist at memory of clean up after Hurricane Harvey!] The key for organizations is to determine how to keep that off-site backup as current as possible and secure as well. (See "Recovery Sites" later in this module for more details.)

Distance and Location Selection   Although cloud access can seem instant for many users, the distance between your primary location and online services and storage can make a difference in recovery from disasters. See "Recovery Sites" for some examples. The location of off-site backups and services matters because of law and international jurisdictions. Plus, as in my Houston+hurricanes example, picking a site not prone to the same sorts of disasters your home site can experience is very important.

Legal Implications   Who owns the data you save off-site? What laws apply to both content and searchability? The term *data sovereignty* encompasses many of these legal issues, specifically meaning that data stored in a country is subject to the laws of that country. What's legal in Pittsburgh might be legal in Paris, too, but wildly illegal in Istanbul. The location of your backup data and recovery sites can make a very big difference in how your data is treated.

Recovery Sites

Recovery sites are an important consideration in disaster recovery planning. Unfortunately, until they need it, your bosses may not understand the need for such a site. The reason for having a recovery site is to prepare for a disaster so that the business can operate if the primary site is compromised due to damage or destruction from a natural disaster, mass power outage, communications interruption, and so on. Even if your business primarily has an Internet storefront, it probably has a physical location that houses personnel, data, records, and business processes. Although the servers and infrastructure may be outsourced to a third party, the business's physical location may be rendered unusable during a disaster, and this alone may prevent the business from operating. Organizations should provide an alternate processing site.

You should know about three types of recovery sites to consider in disaster recovery planning. These are the three types you're likely to see on the CompTIA Security+ exam. The one you use depends upon a variety of factors, including cost and expense, the ability to provision a recovery site, and the need to recover the business either very quickly or to have the luxury of being able to wait a longer amount of time before recovering the business to an alternate location.

The three types of recovery sites that you need to know about, in order of increasing cost and required infrastructure, are the cold site, the warm site, and the hot site.

Cold Site   The cold site is attractive to a lot of organizations simply because it's probably the cheapest of the three. This is essentially empty floor space where you can set up business operations. The site may have no utilities connected and running at all, or it may have, at minimum, electricity and running water. It also may have heating and air conditioning, but will probably not have any communications connections, such as phone or Internet service. A cold site typically doesn't have any equipment or work areas set up—it's essentially just empty floor space waiting for the organization to move in if necessary. The best thing about a cold site is that it's cheap. The worst thing about a cold site is that it's so bare in terms of what it provides that it will likely take a long time to move the business into it and set up operations. The organization should decide which is more important, cost or recovery time, and decide on whether a cold site is appropriate. An organization that uses a cold site may have the luxury of a great deal of time before it has to recover the business to normal processing levels.

If you've never encountered a cold site, it may be because they are more rare than warm or hot sites. Organizations that use them either never expect to need them, also have backup warm or hot sites and the cold site is just a second backup, or use a similar concept in establishing alternate processing sites. For example, suppose a small grocery store chain has four grocery stores and outsources its IT processes. A single desktop computer in one store contains all employee data and graphics for newspaper ads for the stores. If that computer goes down, weekly full backups could be sent over to another store; if a disaster hits, they can simply buy a new desktop and keep it in one of the other stores. This is like having a "cold" capability, but at a "hot" site, if that makes sense.

Warm Site   As Goldilocks thought, a warm site may turn out to be just right for an organization. It's a little bit more expensive than a cold site, because it provides a little more than empty floor space. It will likely come with full utilities, including heat and air conditioning, electricity and running water, and perhaps even phone and Internet service already provided. A warm site could also come with some rudimentary workspace set up, such as tables and chairs. An organization that uses a warm site will typically also install some basic equipment that it would need for processing, such as workstations and some servers—probably not enough to run the full operations, but enough at least to get started while recovering the rest of the business to the recovery site. The organization may also install peripherals such as printers, scanners, and so on. Typically, this spare equipment likely wouldn't be updated with the latest operating systems, patches, applications, or even transactional data the business needs to get going again. But at least having all this equipment in place could cut down on the time it would take to recover the business to the recovery site and start processing again. A warm site may be a little bit more expensive than a cold site, but it may also provide a happy medium between cost and recovery time. An organization that uses a warm site usually has a need to recover operations reasonably fast, but it doesn't have to do it immediately.

Hot Site   As you might've guessed, the hot site is the most expensive recovery site. It offers a bigger bang for your buck, however, because a hot site has all the amenities—floor space, utilities, workspace, and fully mission-capable equipment—required to switch business processing from the primary site to the recovery site, with little interruption. This means that an organization can quickly resume operations after a disaster. All the equipment, applications, and data, including current backups and transaction data, are in place at the hot site, or at least they are readily available for restoration in the event of a disaster. This can be accomplished in several ways, including storing current backups at the recovery site, real-time transactional journaling, and sending live data to the recovery site frequently.

As mentioned, an organization must pay a heavy price in terms of cost and infrastructure for having a hot site available to the organization. But if the organization requires an almost immediate recovery back to full operations, the expense could be well justified. Many businesses would stand to lose a great deal of money by the hour or day if they could not restore processing quickly after a significant disaster. The bottom line is that the hot site can provide for almost immediate recovery, but at a greater cost.

One interesting note about hot (and even, to a degree, warm) sites is that because of big leaps in certain technologies, such as virtualization technologies, organizations are finding it much easier to establish and maintain these sites. Ten years ago, hardly anyone had a hot site, but they are much more common now because the equipment and space requirements for virtual machines (VMs) are so much less, and because it's so easy to keep the hot site VMs looking just like the live sites by just creating snapshots, cloning, or using other technology built into the VM software.

 EXAM TIP   An old trick to handling CompTIA recovery site questions is to remember the following: Hot sites are ready in hours, warm sites are ready in a day, and cold sites are ready in a week. This isn't exactly the case in the real world, but it will help on the exam.

So, how would an organization determine whether it needed a cold, warm, or hot site? Go back to the business impact analysis (BIA) that was conducted during your business continuity planning. The BIA process helps your organization to determine its assets, to prioritize those assets, and to determine how losing them would impact the organization in terms of cost, productivity, and so on. This analysis leads to determining two other critical pieces of information that can help your organization decide what type of alternate processing site it may need: *recovery time objective* and *recovery point objective*, discussed next.

Recovery Time and Recovery Point Objectives

As part of the business continuity and disaster recovery planning process, your organization will need to determine two important factors that influence how quickly it must recover operations, and how much data it can afford to lose during a disaster without preventing it from recovering. Normally, an organization would determine this during its business impact analysis. These factors are the recovery time objective (RTO) and the recovery point objective (RPO).

Recovery Time Objective   The RTO is the maximum amount of time an organization can be down due to a disaster or an incident. It could be hours or days, depending on the organization's tolerance for downtime. RTO can be calculated several ways, including averaging several RTOs for given processes and systems; or it could be standardized as the shortest amount of downtime allowable for the most critical business processes or systems. It could also be calculated as a cumulative result of the minimum time necessary it takes to restore several critical systems back into operation (using a process called *critical path analysis*).

Recovery Point Objective   The RPO is also measured in time, but in the context of data. It's the maximum amount of data that can be lost for the organization, after which the business cannot recover or would suffer significant loss. For example, in a near real-time transaction processing system, the RPO might be only a few minutes' worth of data that can afford to be lost. Another business may have a more tolerable level of data loss, and their RPO may be 24 hours' worth of data. RPO can be affected by several factors, including data criticality and the amount of data an organization creates or processes in a given timeframe. In the first example, the organization may have high volumes of data that must be processed quickly, such as financial or inventory data. The second example may indicate a business whose data throughput, in terms of creation or processing, is low or less frequent.

In bringing back the importance of our discussion earlier on transactional backups, let's say that an organization's RPO is very small and they can afford to lose only a few minutes of data. But let's also say that they have been the victim of a hacking attack that may have started a few days earlier. Obviously, they can't just wipe out the last few days' worth of data without a significant (and probably serious) impact to operations. How could they maintain their RPO, yet track down faulty or changed data? By using transaction-based recovery, and rolling back only certain records within the past few days of business, those that are suspect due to the hacking attack, that's how.

Questions

1. You are recommending personnel for incident response team lead positions. You have several candidates from which to choose and are recommending personnel based upon key characteristics. On which of the following characteristics should you base your recommendations? (Choose two.)

   A. Certifications

   B. Seniority

   C. Training

   D. Experience

2. Which of the following are considered part of executing an incident response? (Choose two.)

   A. Detection and analysis

   B. Preparation

   C. Containment and eradication

   D. Reporting

3. When you are collecting evidence at the scene of the crime, you should store electronic components in which type of containers?

   A. Plastic bags

   B. Paper bags

   C. Metal containers

   D. Anti-static bags

4. Which two United States evidence guidelines provide standards of submitting evidence into criminal and civil court cases? (Choose two.)

   A. Federal Rules of Evidence

   B. 4th Amendment of the U.S. Constitution

   C. Federal Rules of Civil Procedure

   D. Electronic Communications Privacy Act

5. You are the first responder in a company to a potential computer incident involving an employee's workstation. What is the first step you should take when you arrive at the scene?

   A. Unplug the workstation.

   B. Secure the scene.

   C. Capture the contents of RAM.

   D. Inventory the workstation and its peripherals.

6. Which of the following should be immediately established when collecting electronic components as evidence?

   A. Authority over the investigation

   B. Guilt of the suspect

   C. Chain-of-custody

   D. Sequence of events and timeline

7. Which two potential recovery and continuity issues are solved through succession planning? (Choose two.)

   A. Alternate business processes

   B. Lack of disaster recovery training

   C. Alternate leadership positions

   D. Critical disaster team member alternate positions

8. Which of the following clustering configurations involves a group of servers configured to service a request instantly and automatically if one of the members of the cluster fails?

   A. Passive-active

   B. Passive-passive

   C. Active-passive

   D. Active-active

9. Your business needs to be able to resume processing within 12 hours after a disaster. You are looking at recovery site options and decide that the site must have all utilities, redundant equipment, and daily data backups restored to the site. What type of recovery site have you decided to implement?

   A. Cold site

   B. Warm site

   C. Hot site

   D. Shared site

10. You are evaluating several possible solutions for alternate processing sites for your business. You decide that you can afford the expense of a warm site and balance it against the time it will take to set up and recover the business operations to the site. Which of the following are characteristics of a warm site? (Choose two.)

   A. Fully redundant equipment located at the site, loaded with the most current daily backups

   B. Some equipment located at the site to begin limited operations

   C. Heat, water, electricity, and communications in a standby mode

   D. No utilities

Answers

1. **C, D.** Training and experience are key characteristics to consider when recommending personnel for incident response team lead positions.

2. **A, C.** Detection, analysis, containment, and eradication are all steps performed when executing an incident response.

3. **D.** When collecting evidence at the scene of the crime, you should store electronic components in anti-static bags to prevent damage to them.

4. **A, C.** The Federal Rules of Evidence (FRE) and the Federal Rules of Civil Procedure (FRCP) are two standards that dictate how evidence should be introduced into criminal and civil courts, respectively.

5. **B.** Securing the scene is the first step a first responder should take in investigating a potential computer-related incident.

6. **C.** A chain-of-custody should be established immediately when collecting evidence from the scene of a crime.

7. **C, D.** Alternate leadership positions and critical disaster team member alternate positions are personnel issues that are resolved through effective succession planning as part of BCP.

8. **D.** An active-active cluster configuration will instantly and automatically service a request if one of the members of a server cluster fails.

9. **C.** Given the desired timeframe to recover the business operations, and the level of equipment and support at the site the business needs, this would be a hot site.

10. **B, C.** A warm site is characterized by having heat, water, electricity, and communications, often in a standby mode, as well as having some equipment located at the site to begin limited operations during a recovery.

Exam Objectives Map

Exam SY0-501

3.0 Architecture and Design

3.1 Explain use cases and purpose for frameworks, best practices and secure configuration guides.

About the CD-ROM

The CD-ROM included with this book comes complete with following features:

- Total Tester customizable practice exam software
- Secured PDF copy of the book for studying on the go
- Introduction videos from Mike Meyers
- Online video training from the author
- Online TotalSims simulations from the author
- Online Mike Meyers' Cool Tools

These features can be accessed by clicking the appropriate link in the CD-ROM interface.

If your computer's optical drive is configured to auto-run, the menu will automatically start upon inserting the CD-ROM. If the auto-run feature does not launch the CD-ROM, browse to the disc and double-click the Launch.exe icon.

System Requirements

The software requires Windows Vista or later and 30MB of hard disk space for full installation, in addition to a current or prior major release of Chrome, Firefox, Internet Explorer, or Safari. To run, the screen resolution must be set to 1024×768 or higher. The secured book PDF requires Adobe Acrobat, Adobe Reader, or Adobe Digital Editions to view.

Installing and Running Total Tester
Practice Exam Software

From the main screen you may install the Total Tester by clicking the Install Total Tester Practice Exams button. This will begin the installation process and place an icon on your desktop and in your Start menu. To run Total Tester, navigate to Start | (All) Programs | Total Seminars, or double-click the icon on your desktop.

To uninstall the Total Tester software, go to Start | Control Panel | Programs And Features, and then select the Total Tester program. Select Remove, and Windows will completely uninstall the software.

Total Tester Practice Exam Software

Total Tester provides you with a simulation of the CompTIA Security+ SY0-501 exam. Exams can be taken in Practice Mode, Exam Mode, or Custom Mode. Practice Mode provides an assistance window with hints, references to the book, explanations of the correct and incorrect answers, and the option to check your answer as you take the test. Exam Mode provides a simulation of the actual exam. The number of questions, the types of questions, and the time allowed are intended to be an accurate representation of the exam environment. Custom Mode allows you to create custom exams from selected domains or chapters, and you can further customize the number of questions and time allowed.

To take a test, launch the program and select MM Security+ 501 from the Installed Question Packs list. You can then select Practice Mode, Exam Mode, or Custom Mode. All exams provide an overall grade and a grade broken down by domain.

Secured Book PDF

The entire contents of the book are provided in secured PDF format on the CD-ROM. This file is viewable on your computer and many portable devices.

- **To view the PDF on a computer**, Adobe Acrobat, Adobe Reader, or Adobe Digital Editions is required. A link to Adobe's Web site, where you can download and install Adobe Reader, has been included on the CD-ROM.

 NOTE For more information on Adobe Reader and to check for the most recent version of the software, visit Adobe's Web site at www.adobe.com and search for the free Adobe Reader or look for Adobe Reader on the product page. Adobe Digital Editions can also be downloaded from the Adobe Web site.

- **To view the PDF on a portable device**, copy the PDF file to your computer from the CD-ROM, and then copy the file to your portable device using a USB or other connection. Adobe offers a mobile version of Adobe Reader, the Adobe Reader mobile app, which currently supports iOS and Android. For customers using Adobe Digital Editions and an iPad, you may have to download and install a separate reader program on your device. The Adobe Web site has a list of recommended applications, and McGraw-Hill Education recommends the Bluefire Reader.

Playing the Mike Meyers Introduction Videos

From the opening screen you can launch the video messages from Mike by clicking the Intro Videos & Cool Tools link, which will launch a submenu that includes links to the videos. Click the individual links to launch the video files using your system's default video player.

Mike Meyers CompTIA Security+ Video Training

Click the Mike Meyers' Video Training link on the main menu. The link will take you to the Total Seminars Training Hub. Select CompTIA Security+ Videos (SY0-501). Online video clips from Mike Meyers provide detailed examples of key concepts in audiovisual format. You'll have access to free videos from a number of chapters of the book, with an option to purchase Mike's complete video training series.

TotalSims Simulations

Click the Mike Meyers' TotalSim link on the main menu. The link will take you to the Total Seminars Training Hub. Select the TotalSims for CompTIA Security+ (SY0-501). The simulations are organized by chapter, and there are free simulations available for reviewing topics covered in the book, with an option to purchase access to the full Total-Sims for CompTIA Security+ SY0-501.

Mike's Cool Tools

Mike loves freeware and open source networking tools. Most of the utilities can be downloaded from the Internet. Click the Intro Videos & Cool Tools link, which will open a submenu containing the link to Mike's Cool Tools page.

 CAUTION Although all of the tools are "Mike Meyers Approved," there is no guarantee they will work for you. Read any and all documentation that comes with each utility before using that program.

Technical Support

Technical Support information is provided in the following sections, by feature.

Total Seminars Technical Support

For questions regarding the TotalSims, the Mike Meyers video training, and the Total Tester software or operation of the CD-ROM, visit **www.totalsem.com** or e-mail **support@totalsem.com**.

McGraw-Hill Education Content Support

For questions regarding the introduction videos or the PDF copy of the book, visit **http://mhp.softwareassist.com** or e-mail **techsolutions@mhedu.com**.

For questions regarding book content, e-mail **hep_customer-service@mheducation .com**. For customers outside the United States, e-mail **international_cs@mheducation .com**.

802.1X A port-based authentication mechanism for networks; it usually requires authentication from the connecting client, and sometimes even the user. 802.1X is very often seen in enterprise wireless solutions, as well as hardwired Ethernet infrastructures.

802.11 *See* IEEE 802.11.

802.11i A wireless standard that added security features; also known as *WPA2*.

AAA (authentication, authorization, and accounting) *See* authentication, authorization, and accounting (AAA).

acceptable use policy (AUP) Organizational policy that describes both acceptable and unacceptable actions when using organizational computing resources, as well as the consequences of unacceptable use.

access control All-inclusive term that defines the degree of access granted to use a particular resource, data, systems, or facilities. That resource may be anything from a switch port, to permissions on a particular file, authentication methods, and even physical controls.

access control list (ACL) A clearly defined list of permissions that specifies what actions an authenticated user may perform on a shared resource. Access control lists are used on objects, such as files and folders, as well as on network devices, such as routers.

access log A log generated on a device, or manually, that gives details of a particular access event, such as a user name or ID, timestamp, and the object or resource that was accessed.

access point (AP) A network device that provides a connection point for hosts to enter the network; most often associated with wireless clients.

accountability The practice of holding users accountable for their actions; it involves conclusively tying a user account to any action performed.

accounting Keeping an historical record of what users do to shared resources.

Active Directory (AD) Microsoft's centralized authentication and directory services infrastructure, implementing the Lightweight Directory Access Protocol. *See also* Lightweight Directory Access Protocol (LDAP).

active reconnaissance   An information gathering technique in penetration testing where the pentester uses tools and techniques that may or may not avoid detection, but put the attacker at risk of discovery (for example, injection of packets directly onto the wire or purposefully walking up to a locked door to attempt entry).

ad hoc mode   A wireless networking mode where each node is in direct contact with every other node in a decentralized free-for-all. Ad hoc mode is similar to the *mesh topology*.

administrative control   One of the eight types of security controls; this includes administrative or managerial measures such as policies, procedures, standards, guidelines, and more.

administrator account   Credentials granted to a user that has complete power over the resource as well as the complete serving system. Windows calls this account *administrator*. In macOS and Linux/UNIX, this account is called *root*.

Advanced Encryption Standard (AES)   The official encryption standard for the U.S. government; it is based upon the Rijndael encryption algorithm, and uses key sizes of 128, 192, and 256 bits. It is a symmetric block algorithm, with 128-bit block sizes.

advanced persistent threat (APT)   When a threat actor gains control of a system and remains undetected for a long period of time, continually looking for new data to steal.

adware   A program or add-in downloaded from the Internet that monitors the types of Web sites you frequent and uses that information to generate targeted advertisements, usually pop-up windows.

Agile   A nonlinear software development lifecycle model.

air gap   Typically, the act of physically separating a network from every other network. This can apply to virtually any resource, even individual systems.

Aircrack-ng   An open source tool for penetration testing many aspects of wireless networks.

algorithm   A mathematical method used in the encryption process to convert plaintext into ciphertext.

allow action   The action of an access control that permits data or communication to pass through or to access a resource. Access control lists may use rules that allow or deny specific data or access to a resource.

annualized loss expectancy (ALE)   The expected loss of an asset determined over a period of one year. It is determined by calculating as follows: ALE = single loss expectancy (SLE) × annualized rate of occurrence (ARO).

annualized rate of occurrence (ARO)   The number of times a negative event is expected to occur on a yearly basis.

anti-malware   Software that attempts to block several types of software threats to a client, including viruses, Trojan horses, worms, and other unapproved software installation and execution.

antivirus   Software that attempts to prevent viruses from installing or executing on a client. Some antivirus software may also attempt to remove the virus or eradicate the effects of a virus after an infection.

application aware   Advanced feature of some stateful firewalls where the content of the data is inspected to ensure it comes from, or is destined for, an appropriate application. Application-aware firewalls look both deeply and more broadly to ensure that the data content and other aspects of the packet are appropriate to the data transfer being conducted. Packets that fall outside these awareness criteria are denied by the firewall.

application firewall   A type of firewall that inspects network traffic to determine if the traffic should be allowed or not. Application firewalls go beyond firewalls that filter based on network protocol or port. *See also* application aware.

Application layer   *See* Open Systems Interconnection (OSI) seven-layer model.

application log   A type of log that details application-specific events, such as when an application opens or closes. Different types of application logs record different events.

archive bit   An attribute of a file that shows whether the file has been backed up since the last change. Each time a file is opened, changed, or saved, the archive bit is turned on. Some types of backups turn off the archive bit to indicate that a good backup of the file exists on tape.

armored virus   A very sophisticated type of virus that has built-in protections to evade detection from antivirus solutions. Some of these protections include encryption or the ability of the virus to change its characteristics.

arp   Command-line utility used to determine the MAC address that corresponds to a particular IP address.

ARP cache poisoning   A type of attack where the attacker attempts to associate a false hardware or MAC address to her machine to fool victim clients into communicating with that machine rather than a legitimate device. This is often associated with man-in-the-middle attacks. CompTIA also calls this *ARP poisoning*.

asset   Anything that the organization values or that is important to its mission. Assets can be tangible, such as data, equipment, facilities, and people, or intangible, such as reputation, customer satisfaction, and so on.

asset value (AV)   A value assigned to an asset; usually expressed in terms of dollars. Asset value is used in quantitative risk calculations.

asymmetric cryptography   A form of cryptography that uses two separate, but mathematically related, keys for encryption and decryption; also called *public key cryptography*.

attack   An action where a threat actor actively attempts to take advantage of a vulnerability.

attack surface   All the vulnerabilities for a specific infrastructure item.

attribute-based access control (ABAC)   An access control model based upon identifying information about a resource, such as subject (like name, clearance, department) or object (data type, classification, color). Access to resources is granted or denied based on preset rules concerning those attributes.

auditing   The practice of recording events and analyzing them to detect negative events and determine patterns or trends. Auditing is usually performed through examination of manual and automatic logs.

authentication   The process that verifies the identity of the individual, an action traced to an individual or host, or traffic originating from a host. This process proves identity, and is associated with non-repudiation.

authentication, authorization, and accounting (AAA)   A security philosophy wherein a computer trying to connect to a network must first present some form of credential, have that credential verified, and then be subject to restrictive permissions within the network or on the resource.

authentication factors   Use of different characteristics of identification to identify a user and validate his or her credentials. These include knowledge (something you know); possession (something you have); inherence (something you are); action (something you do); and location (somewhere you are). *See also* multifactor authentication.

authentication server (AS)   A server that performs an authentication role at a network. In Kerberos realms, this is also the server that authenticates a user and provides a Ticket-Granting Ticket (TGT).

authorization   The step in the AAA philosophy during which a client's or user's rights or permissions are verified, based upon predetermined decisions. *See also* authentication, authorization, and accounting (AAA).

automation   The programming and sensing tools that enable compromised systems to use their non-persistence and redundancy to recover themselves with little or no human intervention.

availability   Ensuring that information and systems can be used for authorized purposes by authorized users whenever and however they need them.

back up   To save important data in a secondary location as a safety precaution against the loss of the primary data.

backdoor   A mechanism often built into a program or software application by its developers to facilitate quick and easy maintenance or to bypass security mechanisms.

banner grabbing The act of causing a server or other resource to give up information about its configuration, including its running software, version, and other information that could potentially lead an attacker to discover an attack vector.

baseline The state of a system when all required operating system software and applications, as well as configuration details, have been configured exactly according to a predetermined standard.

bastion host A single host that connects two separate networks and is used as a security device to filter network traffic through. Normally, a bastion host is seen only on very small networks and has very limited use and value.

behavior-based system A system that relies on an established pattern of behavior, typically through the establishment of a usage baseline, in order to detect unusual patterns, such as network attacks or misuse.

best evidence The original evidence obtained in an investigation. It is usually the preferred evidence and consists of *real evidence*, which comprises physical objects, and *direct evidence*, which is direct testimony from witnesses.

big data Large conglomerations of disparate datasets combined to create huge data warehouses.

biometric device A device that scans fingerprints, retinas, or even the sound of the user's voice to provide a more secure (though not foolproof) replacement for both passwords and smart devices.

biometrics Human physical characteristics that can be measured and saved to be compared as authentication in granting the user access to a network or resource. Common biometric factors used in access control include fingerprints, facial scans, retinal scans, voice pattern recognition, and others.

birthday attack A cryptanalytic technique that focuses on hash function collisions and the probabilities of birthday problem mathematics formulae.

black box test (or blind box test) A type of penetration test where the tester has no prior knowledge of the network they are targeting, and must discover details about the network through testing methodologies, which include reconnaissance and footprinting.

black hat hacker A hacker who uses his or her technical skills only for malicious purposes, usually with the goal of illegal access, data theft, or destruction.

blacklisting The process of detailing that an application or data is explicitly not allowed on the network or host. Blacklisting can include software, executables, disallowed Web sites, and even specific types of data.

block (action) Deny access to a resource, via either a firewall, an access control server, or other secure gateway. *See also* allow action.

block cipher (or algorithm)   A cryptographic algorithm that works on defined lengths of blocks of text.

Blowfish   A symmetric block algorithm invented by Bruce Schneier that uses 64-bit blocks, key sizes from 32 bits to 448 bits, and 16 rounds of encryption.

bluejacking   A type of Bluetooth attack in which a malicious user connects to an unsuspecting victim's Bluetooth device and sends unsolicited data to it, such as messages or media.

bluesnarfing   A type of Bluetooth attack in which a malicious user connects to an unsuspecting victim's Bluetooth device and steals information from it, such as contact information.

bot   In this context, a computer remotely controlled by a malicious operator.

botnet   A group of computers under the remote control of one malicious operator, used to further attack other hosts.

bring your own device (BYOD)   Mobile device environment in which employees are allowed to use their personally owned devices to access, store, and process data belonging to the organization.

brute-force attack   A type of attack wherein every permutation of some form of data is tried in an attempt to discover protected information. Most commonly used for password cracking.

buffer overflow attack   A type of attack in which the amount of system memory specifically allocated to an application is overflowed with either too much or nonstandard data, in an effort to cause the application to fail or be susceptible to arbitrary command execution.

business continuity planning (BCP)   The process of ensuring that a business can continue at some level of operation immediately following a disaster.

business impact analysis (BIA)   A type of assessment in which a business identifies and prioritizes its assets, processes, and other critical types of operations so that it may be able to determine which of these must be recovered first and foremost after a disaster, in order to ensure business continuity.

business partner agreement (BPA)   An agreement that specifies what type of business partnership two entities will have; often this dictates other considerations, such as interconnection requirements and security.

centralized authentication   A method of authentication in which a single set of authentication policies and mechanisms is used in the organization, and applies to all resources.

certificate   An electronic file used for a variety of purposes, most commonly to verify the identity of a resource (such as a PC, user, or service). A digital certificate stores a public key with a digital signature, personal information about the resource (URL, e-mail address, phone numbers, whatever), and (commonly) a second digital signature from a trusted third party. (A *self-signed certificate* lacks a third-party signature.)

certificate authority (CA)　An entity responsible for issuing and managing digital certificates throughout the certificate lifecycle.

certificate revocation list (CRL)　An electronic file, published by a certificate authority, that shows all certificates that have been revoked by that CA.

chain-of-custody　A process used to track the collection, handling, and transfer of evidence.

Challenge Handshake Authentication Protocol (CHAP)　A remote access authentication protocol in which the authenticating system challenges the remote client, which must provide the proper response, which is then compared by the authenticating server. If the server receives the answer it expects, the user is authenticated.

change management　The process of initiating, approving, testing, implementing, and documenting significant changes to the infrastructure.

change request　A formally documented request for a modification to some aspect of the network or computing environment.

cipher　A representation of text on a character-by-character basis. Enciphering converts a character of plaintext to ciphertext, and deciphering converts a character of ciphertext to plaintext.

cipher mode　Defined method that determines how a plaintext block is input and changed to produce ciphertext. Used in DES and other encryption standards. Examples include Electronic Code Book (ECB) mode, Cipher Block Chaining (CBC) mode, and more.

ciphertext　Plaintext that has been encrypted and converted to an unreadable format.

circumstantial evidence　Evidence that cannot necessarily prove a conclusion, but does support it.

clear text　*See* plaintext.

clear text credentials　User credentials that are sent over the network unencrypted, making them easily readable by anyone who could intercept them.

clickjacking　An attack where a malicious/compromised Web site places invisible controls on a page, giving users the impression they are clicking some safe item that actually is an active control for something malicious.

client　A computer program or host that uses the services of another computer program or host; software that extracts information from a server.

client-to-site   A type of VPN connection where a single computer logs into a remote network and connects to a larger network, as if it were internally on the network.

closed-circuit television (CCTV)   A self-contained, closed system in which video cameras feed their signal to specific, dedicated monitors and storage devices.

cloud computing service   A third-party service in which applications, and even services, are stored and executed by external resources, such as computing and storage infrastructure, usually not under control of the originating organization.

cloud provider   A third-party provider that provides cloud computing services.

clustering   A way of combining separate physical resources, such as servers, so that they appear as one logical resource and are able to service client requests even if one member of the cluster becomes unavailable.

code   In cryptography, a representation of an entire phrase or sentence.

codebook   A predefined dictionary that contains codes and the plaintext they represent.

cold site   A bare location that consists of essentially floor space of a building, facilities, desks, toilets, parking, and everything that a business needs, except computing equipment or utilities.

collision   The rare occurrence of two variable-length pieces of plaintext that, when hashed, produce identical message digests.

command injection   A type of Web-based attack where additional commands are injected into a user-fillable field in the hopes of causing an error or security issue within the Web application.

community cloud   A community cloud is made up of infrastructures from several different entities, which may be cloud providers, business partners, and so on. In this structure, common services are offered to all participants in the community cloud, to one degree or another. Community clouds are usually paid for and used by several like organizations, such as colleges or hospitals.

compensating control   A security control that temporarily compensates for a weakness in another control.

computer forensics   The science of gathering, preserving, and presenting (in a court of law) evidence that is stored on a computer or any form of digital media.

confidentiality   The security goal of protecting information and systems from unauthorized access.

configuration compliance scanner   A tool that scans critical systems to see if they meet the compliance standards set by IT security professionals in an organization.

configuration management A set of documents, policies, and procedures designed to help maintain and update the network infrastructure in a logical, orderly fashion.

connectionless A type of communication characterized by sending packets that are not acknowledged by the destination host. UDP is an example of a connectionless protocol in the TCP/IP suite.

connectionless protocol A protocol that does not establish and verify a connection between the hosts before sending data; it just sends the data and assumes that it is received without error. This type of communication is faster than communication using connection-oriented protocols. UDP is an example of a connectionless protocol.

connection-oriented Network communication between two hosts that includes negotiation between the hosts to establish a communication session. Data segments are then transferred between hosts, with each segment being acknowledged before a subsequent segment can be sent. Orderly closure of the communication is conducted at the end of the data transfer or in the event of a communication failure. TCP is the only connection-oriented protocol in the TCP/IP suite.

connection-oriented protocol A protocol that establishes a connection between two hosts before transmitting data and verifies receipt before closing the connection between the hosts. TCP is an example of a connection-oriented protocol.

containerization The practice of separating different types of data in a system, typically used on mobile devices in which personal and corporate data are kept separated.

contingency planning The process of creating documents that set forth how to recover quickly from an incident as well as protect lives and equipment.

continuity of operations (COO) A plan that ensures business or government has the appropriate systems, equipment, data, infrastructure, and, of course, people, to resume and maintain operations. The U.S. federal government adds a P to the initials, so you'll see COOP as well as COO for continuity of operations.

continuous monitoring A proactive way of ensuring that the network administrator receives all logs and data points throughout the network from all network devices and all systems, on a constant basis, to detect security issues.

control A security measure designed to protect an asset or make up for its security weakness.

cookie A small piece of text that contains information about a Web browsing session; it is stored on a user's computer, and is often used to enhance the Web browsing experience, although it can cause security issues if not properly controlled.

corrective control A type of security control that corrects an issue caused by an ineffective security control or security weakness. It is typically only temporary, until a more permanent solution can be found.

cross-site request forgery (XSRF)   A type of session hijacking attack that attempts to steal authentication information from session cookies during a user's current browsing session.

cross-site scripting (XSS)   A type of session hijacking attack in which malicious script content is injected into a vulnerable Web site, usually one that the client browser trusts.

cross-trust   A system in a public key infrastructure (PKI) whereby organizations typically have their own certificate authorities and issuing servers. Organizations have their root CAs trust each other to further business partnership arrangements.

cryptanalysis   The study of breaking encryption.

cryptography   The science of hiding information.

crypto-malware   Malicious software that uses some form of encryption to lock a user out of a system, often with a demand for payment—ransomware—to unlock the system.

cryptosystem   The total of the methods, techniques, algorithms, and keys used in a cryptographic process or system.

Data Encryption Standard (DES)   Older encryption standard that used a 56-bit key and a 64-bit block size; based upon the Lucifer algorithm.

Data Link layer   *See* Open Systems Interconnection (OSI) seven-layer model.

data loss prevention (DLP)   The combination of technologies, processes, and procedures used to prevent the release and loss of sensitive organizational data to unauthorized entities.

data sensitivity   The level of protection data requires based upon its criticality and the need to keep it from unauthorized access or modification.

data-at-rest   The state of data while it is in storage and not being processed or transmitted.

data-in-process   The state of data while it is being used.

data-in-transit   The state of data during transmission or reception.

deauthentication attack   Denial-of-service (DoS) strike that disconnects a wireless host from WAP, so that the victim is forced to reconnect and exchange the wireless key multiple times; an attacker can then perform an offline brute-force cracking of the password.

decentralized authentication   A method of authentication in which all hosts use their own authentication methods, databases, and policies to allow access to resources located on the host.

decryption   The process of converting ciphertext back into its original plaintext.

defense-in-depth   A concept that requires the use of multiple layers of security defenses and controls at various points, rather than relying on only a single control.

demilitarized zone (DMZ)   A network architecture that is situated between an untrusted network and a protected network and acts as a protective buffer zone between the two networks.

demonstrative evidence   Evidence that attempts to re-create an event in question.

denial-of-service (DoS) attack   An attack that floods a networked server with so many requests that it becomes overwhelmed and ceases to function, affecting availability. DoS attacks are designed to keep legitimate users from using their resources.

deprovisioning   The process of removing an application from a production environment.

detective control   A security control whose function is to detect illegal, unauthorized, or abnormal activities.

deterrent control   A security control designed to prevent someone from performing an unauthorized or illegal act. Deterrent controls rely on the fact that the user is aware that the control is in place.

DevOps   A cyclical software development lifecycle model. *Secure DevOps* integrates security into the toolchain.

Diameter   A proposed replacement for the RADIUS remote access protocol.

dictionary attack   A form of password cracking that relies on a text file—a dictionary file—that contains many common words and non-words used for passwords.

differential backup   A type of backup similar to an incremental backup in that it backs up the files that have been changed since the last backup. However, this type of backup does not change the state of the archive bit. This type of backup can be one of the slowest to perform, but the fastest to restore.

Diffie-Hellman   An asymmetric key exchange protocol, with several variations. It is used to negotiate a secret session key between two hosts, and securely exchange that key using public key cryptography.

dig   *See* Domain Information Groper (DIG).

digital certificate   A digital file containing the details of a certificate, including an individual's identity, the certificate's purpose, and the issuing authority. It is usually signed by the entity that issued it.

digital signature   A message that is signed (encrypted) by an individual's private key, which can only be decrypted by the public key in the pair. This assures that the message could have been sent or signed only by that individual, since they are the only one in possession of the private key.

direct evidence   A type of best evidence, usually in the form of written or oral testimony from people who actually witnessed an event.

directory traversal   A Web-based attack in which an attacker is able to browse different directories and their contents on the Web server, including those that would normally be restricted to authorized users. It is conducted by entering different directory levels into a URL or user input field, causing the Web application to change directories and sometimes display the contents of a directory.

disaster recovery   The process of reacting to an incident or disaster and recovering an organization, its personnel, and its systems to a functioning state.

discretionary access control (DAC)   An authorization model based on the idea that there is an owner of a resource who may, at his or her discretion, assign access to that resource. DAC is considered much more flexible than mandatory access control (MAC).

distributed denial-of-service (DDoS) attack   A DoS attack that uses hundreds or thousands of computers under the control of a single operator to conduct a devastating attack against other hosts or networks.

DNS amplification   A form of distributed denial-of-service (DDoS) attack that attacks a Web application's DNS server instead of the Web app itself.

DNS Security Extensions (DNSSEC)   A suite of security extensions proposed and used by the U.S. government and other entities that allows for secure Domain Name System (DNS) queries and zone transfers. DNSSEC provides the capability to authenticate DNS information from known and trusted servers.

documentary evidence   Evidence that directly supports or proves a definitive assertion; documentary evidence could be written or in the form of computer-generated data.

documentation   A collection of artifacts that supports a security assertion.

domain   A grouping of users, computers, and/or networks. In Microsoft networking, a domain is a group of computers and users that shares a common security accounts database and a common security policy. For the Internet, a domain is a group of computers that shares a common element in the computers' DNS hierarchical name.

domain controller   A Microsoft Windows Server system specifically configured to store user and server account information for its domain. Often abbreviated as "DC." Windows domain controllers store all account and security information in the *Active Directory* distributed directory service.

domain hijacking   Attack that takes control of a legitimate domain registration in some way that the actual owner does not desire.

Domain Information Groper (DIG)   Command-line tool in non-Windows systems used to diagnose DNS problems.

Domain Name System (DNS) The service and protocol associated with resolving Internet Protocol addresses to human-recognizable domain names; DNS uses TCP and UDP ports 53.

domain validation (DV) certificate Lowest level of Secure Sockets Layer (SSL) certificate issued by CAs; DVs have no verification check. *See also* extended validation (EV) certificate.

double-blind test A type of penetration test in which neither the testers nor the defenders are aware of aspects of the test; testers have no knowledge of the network they are attacking, and defenders have no knowledge of the attack itself. This test serves to provide valuable information on both attack methods and vulnerabilities, as well as the ability of network defenders to detect and defend against network attacks.

downgrade attack A legitimate request to a server to use a weak, deprecated algorithm that's easier to crack in hopes of then successfully getting keys, passwords, and so forth.

due care Performing all actions an organization or person could reasonably be expected to perform in order to prevent or reduce potential harm.

due diligence The act of fully investigating or researching potential issues, and being completely aware of the ramifications.

dumpster diving A nontechnical type of attack, classified as a social engineering attack, in which an attacker attempts to gain information about an organization by digging through its trash, hoping to find sensitive information.

Dynamic Host Configuration Protocol (DHCP) Service and protocol responsible for automatically providing IP addressing information to network hosts; it uses UDP on ports 67 and 68.

electromagnetic interference (EMI) A type of interference generated by any device or component that produces electrical or radio frequency signals.

electromagnetic pulse (EMP) The short release of electromagnetic radiation from a source, manmade (e.g., a nuclear bomb or a power line transformer exploding) or natural (a lightning strike). If concentrated (i.e., the source producing the blast is strong enough), it can have adverse effects on electrical circuits and communications.

electronic discovery The legal process of requesting and providing any data generated through the computer forensics process.

ElGamal Asymmetric algorithm used for both digital signatures and general encryption; based on Diffie-Hellman algorithms. It is also the basis for the U.S. government's Digital Signature Algorithm (DSA).

elliptic curve cryptography (ECC) Asymmetric algorithm based upon mathematical problems involving the algebraic structure of elliptic curves over finite fields; suitable for use in small mobile devices because of the low computing power requirements.

embedded system   A complete computer system—CPU, RAM, storage, operating system, drivers, etc.—whose only job is to perform a specific function either by itself or as part of a larger system.

encapsulation   The process of including encrypted data from one network, using encryption protocols such as IPsec, into a tunneling protocol, such as L2TP, for the purposes of sending it across an untrusted network.

encryption   The process of converting plaintext into ciphertext.

enterprise information security architecture (EISA)   An analysis of existing security systems, encompassing industry-standard frameworks and regulatory compliance.

environmental monitoring   Using devices and sensors in telecommunications rooms to monitor humidity, temperature, and more.

ephemeral key   A key that is generated for one immediate use only, and is never used again.

ethical hacker   Typically, a security professional who uses his or her security knowledge and abilities only for lawful purposes, to include assessing the security of a system or network to identify vulnerabilities and exploits that can be corrected.

evil twin   An attack that lures people into logging into a rogue access point that looks similar to a legitimate access point.

executable virus   A virus that is literally an extension of an executable and is unable to exist by itself. Once an infected executable file is run, the virus loads into memory, adding copies of itself to other executables that are subsequently run.

expert witness   A person who has the knowledge and skill necessary to testify in court that forensics procedures and processes were sound and followed accurately and closely. Expert witnesses must be formally recognized by the court, through various means, including years of experience, certification, education, professional status, and so on. It's really up to the court to decide if an expert witness is sufficient or not during the case, and if the court will accept their testimony. Expert witnesses normally have not witnessed the actual facts of the case; they merely testify as to the value of the evidence presented, and its potential accuracy. *See also* witness.

exposure factor (EF)   The level of loss that an asset may experience during a negative event, usually expressed as a percentage. It is used in quantitative risk calculations.

extended validation (EV) certificate   A Secure Sockets Layer (SSL) certificate issued by CAs that includes a rigorous verification process. Considered much more secure than domain validation (DV) certificates.

Extensible Authentication Protocol (EAP)   A flexible, extensible authentication framework that is capable of using different security protocols and authentication methods. It is widely seen in both wireless and remote communications.

external firewall   A firewall that is placed on the external perimeter of a sensitive or private network and serves to filter undesirable traffic from an untrusted network to a trusted network.

fail safe   Failure condition that occurs during an emergency, in which security mechanisms fail to a safe mode rather than a secure mode. An example of this would be a secure door lock that fails and is kept unlocked during an emergency situation so personnel could evacuate a facility.

fail secure   Failure condition that occurs during an emergency, in which the security mechanisms fail to a secure mode rather than a safe mode. An example of this would be a secure door lock that is kept locked during an emergency, ensuring that valuable assets and data are protected.

false acceptance rate (FAR)   The level of errors that the system may generate indicating that unauthorized users are actually identified and authenticated as valid users in a biometric system.

false negative   A term used to describe the condition where it is believed there is no vulnerability, but, upon further investigation, there is in fact a valid vulnerability.

false positive   A term used to describe the condition where a vulnerability may be shown to exist, when, upon further investigation, there is no vulnerability.

false rejection rate (FRR)   The rate of errors caused from rejecting someone who is in fact an authorized user and should be authenticated. This is also known as a *type I error*.

fault tolerance   The capability of any system to continue functioning after some part of the system has failed. RAID is an example of a hardware device that provides fault tolerance for hard drives.

federated system   A common authentication system shared by multiple separate entities that allows users to authenticate seamlessly among the different entities.

Fibre Channel (FC)   A self-contained, high-speed storage environment with its own storage arrays, cables, protocols, and switches. Fibre Channel is a critical part of storage area networking (SAN).

File Transfer Protocol (FTP)   An application-level protocol used to transfer files from one host to another. It is an unsecure protocol that does not encrypt its traffic, and it uses TCP ports 20 and 21.

File Transfer Protocol over SSL (FTPS)   A version of FTP made secure by tunneling it over a Secure Sockets Layer (SSL) or Transport Layer Security (TLS) connection. It uses TCP port 990 and should not be confused with either SFTP (which is a Secure Shell [SSH] implementation of FTP) or Secure FTP (which normally involves tunneling ordinary FTP traffic over an SSH connection).

firewall A device that restricts and filters traffic between two separate networks. Firewalls can be placed between the public Internet and a private network, or between two internal networks of different sensitivities.

first responder Any person who first notices, reports, or responds to an incident. The first responder's overall duties should be to secure the scene (if necessary), determine the scope of the incident, try to determine the seriousness and impact of the incident, and start the notification process for the incident management and response team.

flood guard A mechanism that automatically stops or prevents network attacks, such as ICMP or SYN floods, by disconnecting the network when these attacks reach a specified threshold.

forensics report A document that describes the details of gathering, securing, transporting, and investigating evidence.

full backup Captures all the data on a particular server, drive, or device and resets the archive bit to zero for all files, indicating that they have been backed up.

full disk encryption (FDE) Software or hardware function that scrambles contents of an HDD or SSD to make them unreadable without proper authentication. This protects data-at-rest; access to the contents of the drive only happens if the user can enter credentials before the operating system boots (pre-boot authentication). BitLocker in Windows is one tool that provides FDE.

fuzzing A type of assessment whereby random data is inserted into an application in hopes of generating and discovering errors or security issues. Fuzzing is a type of dynamic analysis of software in development.

geofencing A practice where mobile devices are configured to alert the administrator if they are removed from a particular area, such as the business campus.

geotagging The practice of ascertaining geolocation data from a device based upon characteristics of its phone calls, text messages, pictures, and video content. Called *GPS tagging* by CompTIA.

governance Overarching rules and requirements applied to an organization that dictate how it conducts business, protects data, and obeys the law. Governance comes in the forms of laws, regulations, internal rules, and industry standards.

gray box test A type of penetration test where the tester has some limited information regarding the target network, possibly including IP address space and other limited details about the target.

gray hat hacker A hacker who sometimes uses his or her abilities and knowledge for good purposes and other times for evil purposes.

group A collection of network users or computers that share similar characteristics and need similar permissions or security settings; groups are created to make administrative tasks more efficient.

group policy   A feature of Windows Active Directory that allows an administrator to apply policy settings to entire groups of computers and users within the domain. Generically, in the non-Windows context, group policy refers to a policy of managing users in a defined logical group, by functional, geographical, or security requirements.

Group Policy Object (GPO)   A set of configuration settings that enables network administrators to define multiple security configuration settings to very particular sets of users and computers within a Windows Active Directory domain.

guest   In terms of virtualization, an operating system running as a virtual machine inside a hypervisor.

guest network   A logically separated network that can contain or allow access to any resource the organization provides to insecure hosts or unauthenticated users.

guidelines   Suggested methods of performing actions or securing data and systems. Guidelines are typically not mandatory, but offer general assistance and advice.

hacker   Term popularized by the media used to describe a person who breaks into computer systems and networks. Hackers can be categorized as white hat hackers (ethical hackers or security professionals), gray hat hackers (hackers who use their abilities for both good and evil purposes), and black hat hackers (malicious hackers).

hacktivist   A hacker and an activist. These threat actors have some form of agenda, often political or fueled by a sense of injustice.

hardening   Locking down the security configurations of hardware and software to a very secure or restrictive degree.

hardware security module (HSM)   A hardware device, sometimes physically separated from other devices, that provides security services, such as encryption and key management or storage.

hash   The fixed-length cryptographic sum that represents a variable-length piece of text. Also called a *message digest*.

Hash Message Authentication Code (HMAC)   System used in conjunction with a hashing algorithm and symmetric key in order to both authenticate and verify the integrity of a message.

Hash Message Authentication Code (HMAC)-Based One-Time Password (HOTP)   A form of one-time password authentication that uses a hash value combined with a symmetric key.

hashing   The process of creating a fixed-length message digest that represents a variable-length piece of text.

header manipulation   Process of injecting additional information into a URL or Web page header to cause a Web application to produce abnormal data or perform actions unintended by the developer.

Health Insurance Portability and Accountability Act (HIPAA)   United States law enacted in 1996 to provide data privacy and security provisions for safeguarding medical information.

heating, ventilation, and air conditioning (HVAC)   All of the equipment involved in heating and cooling the environments within a facility. These items include boilers, furnaces, air conditioners and ducts, plenums, and air passages, as well as their monitoring and control devices.

heuristic system   A system that "learns" network traffic and usage patterns by observing and recording normal behaviors.

hex (hexadecimal)   Hex symbols based on a numbering system of 16 (computer shorthand for binary numbers), using ten digits and six letters to condense 0's and 1's to binary numbers. Hex is represented by digits 0 through 9 and alpha *A* through *F*, so that 09h has a value of 9, and 0Ah has a value of 10.

hierarchical trust   A system in a public key infrastructure (PKI) whereby intermediate certificate authorities trust the root certificate authority.

high availability (HA)   A term used to describe a system or network that must be kept at a significantly high and reliable level of availability for its users; typically measured as some form of a precise decimal percentage, such as 99.999 percent availability. It is the measure of the tolerance a business has for downtime with critical systems or processes.

hoax   A social engineering attack that uses a lie or false story to lead one or more people to believe something is true that is very much not true.

honeynet   An entire network of honeypots on their own network segment, used to get a hacker bogged down in a decoy network while the administrator locks down and secures the sensitive network and records and tracks the actions of the hacker.

honeypot   A network host that an administrator sets up for the express purpose of attracting computer hackers, usually so that their attack methods can be recorded and analyzed.

host   A single device (usually a computer) on a TCP/ IP network that has an IP address; any device that can be the source or destination of a data packet. Also, a computer running multiple virtualized operating systems.

host-based anti-malware   Anti-malware software that is installed on individual systems, as opposed to the network at large.

host-based firewall   A software firewall, such as Windows Firewall, that is installed on a host device to provide firewall services for just that machine.

host-based intrusion detection system (HIDS)   Software installed on a computer that can detect patterns of malicious traffic, such as those that may target certain protocols or services that appear to cause excessive amounts of traffic, or other types of intrusion.

host-based intrusion prevention system (HIPS)   Software installed on a computer that can stop malicious traffic, such as those that may target certain protocols or services.

hot and cold aisles   Design and layout of equipment racks in a data center, such that hot air and cold air are alternately forced through the front and back of the aisles so that hot air is drawn away from equipment and cold air is pushed into equipment, assisting in maintaining the optimum operating temperature.

hot site   A complete backup facility to continue business operations. It is considered "hot" because it has all resources in place, including computers, network infrastructure, and current backups, so that operations can commence within hours or even minutes after a disaster renders the primary site nonoperational.

hybrid cloud   A conglomeration of public and private cloud resources, connected to achieve some target result. There is no clear line that defines how much of a hybrid cloud infrastructure is private and how much is public.

hybrid cryptography   Using both symmetric and asymmetric cryptography together in order to make up for each type's disadvantages and leverage each type's advantages.

hygrometer (or hygrothermograph)   A device used to monitor and control environmental conditions, particularly humidity, within a data center or equipment room.

Hypertext Transfer Protocol over SSL (HTTPS)   A protocol to transfer hypertext data from a Web page to a client in a secure and encrypted fashion. Secure Sockets Layer (SSL) and Transport Layer Security (TLS) are used to establish a secure communication connection between hosts. All HTTP data sent through this encrypted communications tunnel is protected between client and server.

hypervisor (virtual machine monitor)   In virtualization, a layer of programming that creates, supports, and manages a virtual machine. A hypervisor can be either Type 1, which is a specialized operating system itself (also called *bare-metal hypervisor*), or Type 2, which is an application that resides on a host OS.

identification   The act of presenting credentials to a system for authentication.

identity management system (IMS)   Tool used to simplify secure access to multiple Internet-based services via single sign-on.

IEEE 802.11   IEEE subcommittee that defined the standards for wireless communications in the 2.4 and 5.0 GHz frequency ranges.

ifconfig   A command-line utility for Linux servers and workstations that displays the current TCP/IP configuration of the machine, similar to ipconfig for Windows systems. The newer command-line utility, ip, is replacing ifconfig on most systems.

imaging   The process of creating an exact forensic duplicate of a storage media.

impact   The degree of harm to or effect on an asset or the organization when a threat exploits a vulnerability in the asset.

impersonation   The act of pretending to be someone else, or even another host, in order to wage an attack on a victim system, network, or person.

implicit deny   The process of denying access to network traffic, or actions, due to the fact that that access has not been explicitly allowed.

inbound traffic   Network traffic coming into the network.

incident response   Response and reaction to any potential negative events that take place within an organization. The incident response process is preparation, identification, containment, eradication, recovery, and lessons learned.

incremental backup   Type of backup that backs up only the files that have been changed since the last full backup; this usually backs up only the files with the archive bits turned on. This type of backup also resets the archive bits to off.

industrial control system (ICS)   A system that controls other systems, typically manufacturing or utility systems (versus end-user types of systems).

infrastructure mode   Mode in which wireless networks use one or more wireless access points to connect the wireless network nodes centrally. This configuration is similar to the *star topology* of a wired network.

infrastructure-as-a-service (IaaS)   Cloud service that provides infrastructure, such as servers and network devices, to process, transfer, and store business data in a third-party environment. *See also* cloud computing service.

inheritance   A condition in which user permissions assigned to an object automatically flow from higher-level (parent) objects to lower-level (child) objects, such as folders and files.

initialization vector (IV) attack   A type of attack that focuses on the weakness of the initialization vector of a security key, such as a Wired Equivalent Privacy (WEP) key.

injection attack   A type of Web-based attack where additional characters, commands, or other data is injected into a user-fillable field or a URL, in the hopes of causing an error or security issue within the Web application.

input validation   The mechanisms used to ensure that any input into a Web field form meets strict criteria.

integer overflow attack   A type of attack where input numerical information exceeds the bounds or ability of variables to process it. This attack may come in the form of numbers outside of a specified range or length.

integrated development environment (IDE)   A programming tool available in most programming languages that supports code writing through real-time features that continually check the source code, as the programmer is writing the code, for items such as proper syntax.

integrity   The goal of security that ensures that data has not been subjected to unauthorized change or modification.

interconnection service agreement (ISA)   An agreement between two parties, usually either two businesses or two providers, that specifies the terms of connecting their respective private network infrastructures.

internal connections   The connections between computers within the internal boundaries of a network.

internal network   A private LAN, with a unique network ID, that resides behind a router.

internal threats   Threats that originate from inside an organization or network. These threats could include malicious users, misuse of resources, and accidents or unintentional actions.

Internet Control Message Protocol (ICMP)   A TCP/IP protocol used to handle many low-level functions such as error reporting. ICMP messages are usually request and response pairs such as echo requests and responses, router solicitations and responses, and traceroute requests and responses. There are also unsolicited "responses" (advertisements) that consist of single packets. ICMP messages are connectionless.

Internet Engineering Task Force (IETF)   An international organization that develops Internet standards, particularly those associated with the TCP/IP suite of protocols.

Internet Group Management Protocol (IGMP)   A protocol that routers use to communicate with hosts to determine a "group" membership in order to determine which computers want to receive a multicast. Once a multicast has started, IGMP is responsible for maintaining the multicast and terminating it at completion.

Internet Message Access Protocol (IMAP)   A client e-mail protocol that is an alternative to POP3. Currently in its fourth revision, IMAP4 retrieves e-mail from an e-mail server like POP3, but has a number of features that make it a more popular e-mail tool. IMAP4 enables users to create folders on the e-mail server, for example, and allows multiple clients to access a single mailbox. IMAP uses TCP port 143.

Internet of Things (IoT)   The idea that everyday objects could be capable of communicating with each other via the Internet. Although this capability certainly exists to an extent now, the future of this technology has much greater implications. Specialized devices connected to the Internet of Things are referred to as *static hosts*.

Internet Protocol (IP)   A protocol in the TCP/IP suite that is responsible for logical addressing and routing packets to different subnetworks; IP resides at the Network layer of the OSI model.

Internet Protocol Security (IPsec)   A Network layer encryption protocol that is used to encrypt data and transport it either internally between specified hosts (called *transport mode*) or externally between networks, over an unsecure method, using a tunneling protocol (called *tunnel mode*).

Internet Protocol version 4 (IPv4)   Older version of the Internet Protocol in which addresses consist of four sets of numbers, each number being a value between 0 and 255, using a period to separate the numbers (often called *dotted decimal* format). No IPv4 address may be all 0s or all 255s. Examples of IPv4 addresses include 192.168.0.1 and 64.176.19.164.

Internet Protocol version 6 (IPv6)   Newer version of the Internet Protocol in which addresses consist of eight sets of four hexadecimal numbers, each number being a value between 0000 and FFFF, using a colon to separate the numbers. No IP address may be all 0s or all FFFFs. An example of an IPv6 address is FEDC:BA98:7654:3210:0800:20 0C:00CF:1234.

Internet Small Computer System Interface (iSCSI)   A protocol that enables the SCSI command set to be transported over a TCP/IP network from a client to an iSCSI-based storage system. iSCSI is popular with storage area network (SAN) systems.

intranet   A private TCP/IP network inside a company or organization.

intrusion detection system (IDS)   A system designed to detect network intrusions based upon traffic characteristics. *See also* network-based intrusion detection system (NIDS).

intrusion prevention system (IPS)   A system that not only is responsible for detecting network attacks based upon certain traffic characteristics, but also has the ability to prevent and stop the attacks upon detection. *See also* network-based intrusion prevention system (NIPS).

ip   A command-line utility for Linux servers and workstations that displays the current TCP/IP configuration of the machine; similar to ipconfig for Windows systems.

IP address   The numeric address of a computer connected to a TCP/IP network, such as the Internet. IPv4 addresses are 32 bits long, written as four octets of 8-bit binary. IPv6 addresses are 128 bits long, written as eight sets of four hexadecimal characters. IP addresses must be matched with a valid subnet mask, which identifies the part of the IP address that is the network ID and the part that is the host ID.

IP filtering   A method of filtering or checking network traffic based on source and destination IP addresses.

IP spoofing   An attack that replaces a legitimate IP address with another and fools the system to send data to that other IP address. The same type of attack directed to MAC addresses is *MAC spoofing*.

ipconfig   A command-line utility for Windows that displays the current TCP/IP configuration of the machine; similar to UNIX/Linux's ifconfig.

jamming   The act of causing intentional radio frequency interference on a wireless network.

job rotation   A personnel security concept that involves periodically moving employees to different job positions in order to facilitate training and prevent fraud or improper acts.

Kerberos   An authentication standard designed to allow different operating systems and applications to authenticate each other. Kerberos uses timestamps and a Ticket-Granting System as mechanisms to provide authentication and access to different resources.

Kerckhoffs's principle A cryptography principle that states that the algorithm should not be the secret part of the cryptographic process or method used; the principle states that the key should be the secret part of the cryptosystem.

key A secret piece of information, such as a password, passphrase, or passcode, that is used along with an algorithm to convert plaintext and ciphertext; also called a *cryptovariable*.

Key Distribution Center (KDC) A designated system in a Kerberos realm that generates keys and provides for authentication. In a Windows Active Directory domain, this function is typically performed by a domain controller.

key escrow Practice of allowing a third party to maintain knowledge or copies of encryption or decryption keys.

key exchange The process used to exchange keys between users who send a message and those who receive it. Keys can be exchanged in-band (using the same system that other communications use) or out-of-band (using an alternate means of communication to prevent interception of the key).

key management The process of generating, issuing, managing, revoking, and disposing of encryption and decryption keys throughout their lifecycle.

key pair Name for the two keys generated in asymmetric key cryptography systems. One key in the pair is always a private key, and one key is always a public key. The keys in a pair are not identical; however, they are mathematically related.

key stream An input of random bits used with an algorithm and inserted into the encryption process, which assists in changing plaintext to ciphertext.

key stretching Various efforts and processes used to strengthen otherwise weak keys, including multiple rounds of encryption and padding.

keylogger Malware or physical device that records keystrokes.

LAN Manager (LANMAN) An older, proprietary authentication protocol used in earlier versions of Microsoft Windows.

layer 2 switch Any device that filters and forwards frames based on the MAC addresses of the sending and receiving machines. An ordinary "switch" is typically considered a layer 2 switch.

Layer 2 Tunneling Protocol (L2TP) A VPN protocol developed from two proprietary protocols, Layer 2 Forwarding (L2F) by Cisco, and Point-to-Point Tunneling Protocol (PPTP) from Microsoft. LT2P has no authentication or encryption, but uses IPsec to provide for its security mechanisms.

layer 3 switch A switch that also functions as a router, allowing routing between different logical subnets, and eliminating broadcast domains.

legal hold   Requirement for an organization anticipating litigation or government investigation to retain all electronic and physical records.

Lightweight Directory Access Protocol (LDAP)   A protocol that is used in distributed directory services networks, such as Active Directory, to assist hosts in locating network resources. LDAP replaced the older X.500 directory services protocol and uses TCP port 389 by default. A secure version of LDAP, called LDAP over SSL (LDAPS), used TCP port 636; deprecated with LDAP version 2 (version 3 is current version at the time of this writing).

Lightweight Directory Access Protocol (LDAP) injection   An attack in which malicious LDAP queries and commands are injected into a Web site that has access to an LDAP database. The objective of the attack is to gain user information or even create objects, such as user accounts, in the database.

Lightweight Extensible Authentication Protocol (LEAP)   A proprietary version of EAP used almost exclusively by Cisco wireless products. LEAP uses MS-CHAP authentication between a wireless client and a RADIUS server.

likelihood   The level of possibility of a negative event, such as a threat exploiting a vulnerability.

Linux   The popular open source operating system, derived from UNIX, that has a command-line interface as well as many different graphical user interface options.

load balancing   The process of taking several servers and making them appear to network users as a single server, balancing the workload of processing and supporting heavy bandwidth needs.

local user account   A user account that is unique to a single host or system and stored in the local system's files.

log file   An audit trail produced automatically from the system, or manually by a human being. Log files contain information about system events, security events, and various types of performance information.

log management   The process of providing proper security and maintenance for log files to ensure they are protected from unauthorized access or modification. Log management can be centralized (managed across all devices in the enterprise) or decentralized (managed on a per-host basis).

logic bomb   A malicious script planted in a system or network, designed to perform an adverse action, such as deleting sensitive data or rendering a system inoperable. Logic bombs are not malware per se, and are usually intended to execute at a certain time or after a given set of actions or circumstances occurs.

logical address   A network address that is assigned automatically by the DHCP service or manually by an administrator (unlike a physical address that is burned into the network interface card).

MAC (media access control) address   Unique 48-bit address assigned to each network card. IEEE assigns blocks of possible addresses to various NIC manufacturers to help ensure that each address is unique. The Data Link layer of the OSI seven-layer model uses MAC addresses to locate machines.

MAC address filtering   A method of limiting access to a wireless network based on the physical addresses of wireless network interface cards (NICs). Also called *MAC limiting*.

MAC time   In the field of computer forensics, the timestamp metadata contained in a file that indicates when the file was modified, accessed, or created (MAC).

macro   A specially written collection of application-level commands that can be programmed to perform the same functions as a virus. Malicious macros normally automatically start when the application is run and execute malicious actions.

malicious user   A user who consciously attempts to access, steal, or damage resources.

malware   Any program or code (e.g., macro, script, virus, Trojan, worm, or spyware) designed to perform malicious actions on a system.

mandatory access control (MAC)   A security model in which every resource is assigned a label that defines its security level. If the user lacks the security level assigned to a resource, the user cannot get access to that resource. MAC is typically found only in highly secure systems.

mandatory vacations   A personnel security concept that requires employees to take vacations so that their actions while holding a particular position can be extensively investigated and audited while they are absent.

man-in-the-middle (MITM) attack   Attack in which a third party surreptitiously inserts him- or herself into a network conversation between two hosts and covertly intercepts traffic thought to be only between those other people.

mantrap   An entryway into a secure facility with two concurrently locked doors and a small space between them, providing one-way entry or exit. This is a security measure taken to prevent tailgating and provide positive authentication for individuals.

mean time between failures (MTBF)   A numerical estimate for a piece of hardware or equipment that indicates how much time likely will pass between major failures of that hardware or equipment.

mean time to failure (MTTF)   A numerical estimate for a piece of hardware or equipment that indicates the length of time the hardware or equipment is expected to last in operation before it needs to be replaced.

mean time to recovery (MTTR)   A numerical estimate for a piece of hardware or equipment that indicates the likely time between the point a component fails and the time it can be recovered, either through repair or replacement.

memorandum of understanding (MOU) A document that defines an agreement between two parties in situations where a legal contract is not necessary or appropriate, such as where both parties work for the same overall organization.

message digest *See* hash.

Message Digest 5 (MD5) Hashing algorithm used to compute fixed-length message digests of variable-length pieces of texts, developed by Ron Rivest. It generates a 128-bit hash that is 32 hexadecimal characters long. Although MD5 is still widely used, it has been deprecated due to the potential for collisions, and is currently considered unsuitable for modern hashing applications.

mobile application management (MAM) Management structure and technologies used to centrally manage which types of apps can be installed and used on mobile devices.

mobile device management (MDM) The management structure and technologies used to centrally manage all aspects of mobile devices for an organization.

MS-CHAP Microsoft's variation of the CHAP protocol that uses a slightly more advanced encryption protocol. MS-CHAPv2 is most often seen in earlier versions of Windows.

multifactor authentication A form of authentication where a user must use two or more factors to prove his or her identity.

multi-person control A form of control in which a sensitive task requires more than one person to perform it; this practice prevents collusion, fraud, and unauthorized access.

Multipurpose Internet Mail Extensions (MIME) Protocol built into every e-mail client that enables users to make e-mail attachments.

near field communications (NFC) A technology recently implemented in mobile devices that enables the devices to communicate with each other within very close proximity or when touching each other. NFC is becoming popular in commercial device payment systems and file exchange applications.

need-to-know The requirement that an individual must have a valid reason, based upon their job or position, for accessing systems or data.

Nessus A popular and extremely comprehensive vulnerability testing tool. Previously an open source tool, it has now become a widely used enterprise-level commercial product.

NetBIOS An older application programming interface that provides services to the Session layer of the OSI model. It stands for Network Basic Input/Output System, and was primarily used in earlier versions of Windows to transition to using full TCP/IP protocols.

netcat (nc) An extremely versatile Linux command-line utility that reads and writes data across TCP/IP connections; can be used as a tunneling protocol, a scanner, and an advanced hacking tool. It's frequently nicknamed the *Swiss Army knife of hacking tools.*

netstat   A universal command-line utility used to examine the TCP/IP connections open on a given host.

Network Access Control (NAC)   Methods and technologies used to impose security and configuration settings on a device before it is allowed into the corporate network. NAC is usually implemented through a hardware device or associated technologies.

network access policy   A set of rules that defines who can access the network, how it can be accessed, and what resources in the network can be used.

network address translation (NAT)   A method used by various network and security devices to translate an organization's public IP addresses to its private IP address space.

network attached storage (NAS)   A dedicated file server that has its own file system and typically uses hardware and software designed for serving and storing files.

network scanner   A program that probes ports on a remote system, logging the state of the scanned ports and assisting in determining whether a port has a vulnerability that can be exploited.

network time protocol (NTP)   A protocol that is used to contact authoritative time servers in order to establish a synchronized time source within the network.

network-as-a-service (NaaS)   A cloud service that provides various infrastructure services to businesses, including network, server, and security services. *See also* cloud computing service.

network-based firewall   A network-based device that filters traffic coming into and out of the network, based upon different characteristics. Firewalls use rulesets that dictate what type of traffic is allowed and what type will be blocked or denied.

network-based intrusion detection system (NIDS)   A system that detects network attacks based upon certain traffic characteristics. *See also* intrusion detection system (IDS).

network-based intrusion prevention system (NIPS)   A system that not only is responsible for detecting network attacks based upon certain traffic characteristics, but also has the ability to prevent and stop the attacks upon detection. *See also* intrusion prevention system (IPS).

Nmap   A network utility designed to scan a network and create a map. Frequently used as a vulnerability scanner.

nonce   An arbitrary value, usually created by the application or operating system storing passwords, added to the end of a password before it is hashed to prevent replay attacks.

non-disclosure agreement (NDA)   A legal document that prohibits the signer from disclosing any company secrets learned as a part of his or her job.

non-persistence   A method to bring a system back quickly to its pre-attack state without needing a fixed set of hardware, OS, or configuration. Used to enhance resiliency.

non-repudiation   The process of ensuring that a person or entity cannot deny that they took an action, such as sending a message.

NoSQL   A type of database that is typically used in big data applications but does not necessarily rely on Structured Query Language to create or retrieve data. The lack of a standardized structure makes NoSQL difficult to secure.

nslookup   A once-handy tool that advanced techs used to query the functions of DNS servers. Most public DNS servers now ignore all but the most basic nslookup queries.

NT LAN Manager (NTLM)/NTLM v2   Replacement for Microsoft's earlier LAN Manager authentication protocol; version 2 can still be found on Windows systems, and is typically only used when the system is not part of a domain or cannot use Kerberos for authentication purposes. Both are very unsecure protocols.

NTFS permissions   Specific resource permissions found in Windows-based networks.

offboarding   The process of orderly separating an employee from the organization, including termination letter, exit interview, return of all company equipment, and transfer of knowledge for subsequent hires.

onboarding   The process of giving a new hire the knowledge and skills he or she needs to do the job, while at the same time defining the behaviors expected of the new hire within the corporate culture.

one-time password (OTP)   A system-generated password that is used to authenticate for one session only. Examples include token-based authentication and the type of authentication used for personal e-mail accounts through mobile devices.

Online Certificate Status Protocol (OCSP)   A security protocol used by an organization to publish the revocation status of digital certificates in an electronic certificate revocation list (CRL).

Open Systems Interconnection (OSI) seven-layer model   An architecture model based on the OSI protocol suite that defines and standardizes the flow of data between computers. The following lists the seven layers:

- **Layer 1**   The *Physical layer* defines hardware connections and turns binary into physical pulses (electrical or light). Repeaters and hubs operate at the Physical layer.
- **Layer 2**   The *Data Link layer* identifies devices on the Physical layer. MAC addresses are part of the Data Link layer. Bridges operate at the Data Link layer.
- **Layer 3**   The *Network layer* moves packets between computers on different networks. Routers operate at the Network layer. IP and IPX operate at the Network layer.
- **Layer 4**   The *Transport layer* breaks data down into manageable chunks. TCP, UDP, SPX, and NetBEUI operate at the Transport layer.

- **Layer 5** The *Session layer* manages connections between machines. NetBIOS and Sockets operate at the Session layer.

- **Layer 6** The *Presentation layer*, which can also manage data encryption, hides the differences among various types of computer systems.

- **Layer 7** The *Application layer* provides tools for programs to use to access the network (and the lower layers). HTTP, FTP, SMTP, and POP3 are all examples of protocols that operate at the Application layer.

order of data volatility The order in which data should be obtained from a system during a forensics investigation, based on its perishability. The order of data collection and volatility is typically the contents of RAM first, which includes running processes and open network connections, and then more traditional permanent storage devices, such as hard drives, CDs, DVDs, and removable media.

outbound traffic Packets leaving the network from within it.

packet filtering A mechanism that filters (examines) any incoming or outgoing network traffic from a particular IP address or range of IP addresses to see if the traffic matches specific rules, and then allows or denies the traffic based upon those rules. Also known as *IP filtering*.

packet sniffer *See* protocol analyzer.

pass the hash Very old attack that takes advantage of weak points in the NT LAN Manager (NTLM) and LANMAN protocols. Modern operating systems do not have this vulnerability.

passive reconnaissance An information gathering technique in penetration testing where the pentester uses tools and techniques that make detection of activity difficult. The information is gathered without the target's knowledge and usually consists of open, available, and legal-to-acquire sources.

password A series of secret characters that enables a user to gain access to a system or resource.

Password Authentication Protocol (PAP) An older form of authentication protocol that sends all information in clear text by default.

password cracker Type of tool used by bad actors to read ciphertext or hashes and try to extract a plaintext key or password; also called *password recovery tool*.

patch management Process of updating—automatically or manually—programming that makes a computing device function securely. Windows Update, an automatic feature of Microsoft Windows, is a typical example.

Payment Card Industry Data Security Standard (PCI-DSS) Standard that should be adopted by everyone who processes credit card transactions; provides for a dozen highly detailed security controls to mitigate credit card fraud.

penetration testing   A controlled, authorized attempt to intrude into a network or system and exploit any found vulnerabilities, in order to improve the security of the system.

perfect forward secrecy   Concept of cryptography in which any key generated by another key cannot be used to reverse engineer the process and discover the original key.

perimeter   The outer boundaries of a network, usually delineated by external security and traffic devices, such as routers, firewalls, demilitarized zones, and so on.

permissions   Sets of attributes that network administrators assign to users and groups to define what they can do to resources.

personal identification number (PIN)   A numerical password or passcode commonly used with ATMs and smart cards.

personal identification verification card   A type of smart card commonly used in two-factor authentication schemes. It may contain electronic chips storing personal digital certificates, and it serves to identify a user and grant access to various resources.

personally identifiable information (PII)   Information that is unique to an individual and may serve to identify that individual. Examples include (but are not limited to) Social Security numbers, bank account numbers, names and addresses, and birthdates.

personnel management policy   Defines the way a user works within the organization, including standard operating procedures, mandatory vacations, job rotation, and more.

phishing   A social engineering technique where the attacker poses as a trusted source in order to obtain sensitive information; this attack is typically carried out via e-mail and fake Web sites.

physical address   An address burned into a ROM chip on a network interface card. A MAC address is an example of a physical or hardware address.

physical control   A type of control that covers physical and operational security measures. Examples include guards, gates, cipher locked doors, fences, evacuation procedures, and so on.

ping (Packet Internet Groper)   A small network message sent by a computer to check for the presence and response of another system. A ping uses ICMP packets. *See also* Internet Control Message Protocol (ICMP).

ping -6   A switch for the Windows version of ping that specifies that the host under test has an IPv6 address.

ping6   Linux command-line utility specifically designed to ping hosts with an IPv6 address.

plaintext   Ordinary human- or machine-readable unencrypted text.

platform   Specific type of hardware and software environment that supports various computer systems. Examples of different platforms include operating systems, such as

Microsoft Windows and macOS, and hardware platforms, such as Intel and the older PowerPC platforms.

platform-as-a-service (PaaS)   A cloud-based service that provides hardware, operating system, and development platforms for its users. *See also* cloud computing service.

Point-to-Point Protocol (PPP)   An older protocol used to connect remote hosts to networks, typically via a modem connection.

Point-to-Point Tunneling Protocol (PPTP)   A Microsoft protocol that works with PPP to provide a secure data link between computers using encryption.

polyalphabetic substitution cipher   A type of cipher that uses multiple alphabets to substitute individual characters for other characters.

polymorphic malware   A type of malware that is designed to change characteristics, including signatures, making it harder to detect by anti-malware solutions.

port (logical connection)   In TCP/IP, a 16-bit number between 0 and 65535 assigned to a particular TCP/IP process or application. For example, Web servers use port 80 (HTTP) to transfer Web pages to clients. The first 1024 ports are called *well-known ports*. They have been pre-assigned and generally refer to TCP/IP processes and applications that have been around for a long time.

port address translation (PAT)   A common implementation of NAT where the internal client's source port is kept in a table and used in the translation process. When external communications are returned for that client, the device handling NAT knows the intended client.

port authentication   A function of many advanced networking devices that authenticates a connecting device at the point of connection. IEEE 802.1X is an example of a port authentication method.

port blocking   Preventing the passage of any TCP segments or UDP datagrams through any ports other than the ones prescribed by the system administrator.

port number   A number used to identify the requested service (such as SMTP or FTP) when connecting to a TCP/IP host. Some example port numbers include 80 (HTTP), 20 (FTP), 69 (TFTP), 25 (SMTP), and 110 (POP3).

Post Office Protocol version 3 (POP3)   One of the two client-level e-mail protocols that receive e-mail from SMTP servers. POP3 uses TCP port 110. *See also* Internet Message Access Protocol (IMAP).

Presentation layer   *See* Open Systems Interconnection (OSI) seven-layer model.

Pretty Good Privacy (PGP)   Cryptography application and protocol suite used in asymmetric cryptography. PGP is proprietary, but it also has an open source equivalent, Gnu Privacy Guard (GPG). Both use the web-of-trust model rather than a public key infrastructure.

preventive control A security control that serves to prevent undesirable actions. Unlike a deterrent control, users do not require knowledge of a preventative control for it to be effective.

principle of least privilege Security principle that states that users should receive only the privileges that they need to do their jobs, and no more than that.

privacy impact assessment (PIA) Part of a business impact analysis, a report that determines the impact on the privacy of the individuals whose data is being stored, and ensures that the organization has sufficient security controls applied to be within compliance of applicable laws or standards.

private cloud Software, platforms, and infrastructure, delivered via the Internet or an internal corporate intranet, which are solely for the use of one organization.

privilege creep The process that occurs over time, as personnel are transferred or moved within an organization, that leads to individuals accumulating privileges they no longer require. Privilege creep is prevented by auditing an individual's necessary rights, permissions, and privileges periodically, and when they are transferred or moved within the organization.

privilege escalation The process of accessing a system at a lower authentication level and upgrading (escalating) authentication to a more privileged level to present attack opportunities.

privileges Assigned rights to perform specialized actions on systems and within the network.

probability The likelihood—over a defined period of time—of someone or something damaging assets.

procedures Formally documented step-by-step processes that detail how to perform a particular task. Procedures are usually mandatory and support an organization's policies.

promiscuous mode A mode of operation for a network card in which an attacker can detect and capture all traffic on a network, rather than only the traffic that is intended for its host. Also called *monitor mode* in Linux.

Protected Extensible Authentication Protocol (PEAP) An authentication protocol that uses a password function based on MS-CHAPv2 with the addition of an encrypted TLS tunnel similar to EAP-TLS.

protected health information (PHI) Specific information related to an individual's healthcare that is protected by law, both as individual data elements and in aggregate. PHI includes any information that could be connected back to an individual, including medical diagnosis, conditions, or treatment, as well as billing or insurance information.

protocol An agreement that governs the procedures used to exchange information between cooperating entities; usually includes how much information is to be sent, how often it is sent, how to recover from transmission errors, and who is to receive the information.

protocol analyzer A software or hardware tool that has the capability to collect and analyze network traffic information. Also sometimes referred to as a *packet analyzer* or *packet sniffer*.

protocol suite A set of protocols that are commonly used together and operate at different levels of the OSI seven-layer model.

provisioning The process of moving an application from a development environment to a production environment. Also, creating and establishing a user account, along with its related rights, privileges, and permissions. May also refer to the initial configuration of a mobile or computing device.

proximity reader A system that detects a token, smart card, or other security device when the device is within a specific physical range of distance from the reader. Proximity readers typically use radio frequency (RF) signals to detect devices, which commonly have specialized active or passive RF signal chips embedded in them.

proxy server A network security device that acts as an intermediary between internal client devices and an external untrusted network, such as the Internet. The proxy makes requests on behalf of the client and services those requests as they come back from the untrusted network. External resources are not given any information about the client.

public cloud A cloud environment in which a third-party provider delivers software, platforms, or infrastructure via the Internet to customers for a fee.

Public Key Cryptographic Standards (PKCS) A set of proprietary standards developed by RSA Security that dictates types and formats of different digital certificates and files.

public key cryptography A method of encryption and decryption that uses two different keys: a public key for encryption and a private key for decryption.

public key infrastructure (PKI) The formal system used for creating, using, and managing digital certificates throughout their lifecycle.

qualitative assessment A risk assessment method that uses informed but subjective information and produces descriptive values for likelihood and impact.

quantitative assessment A risk assessment method that uses numerical or other non-subjective data to provide estimates for likelihood and impact values.

quarantine network An isolated network in which non-secure hosts that do not meet network standards are placed until they meet security standards and can be connected to the normal network.

RACE Integrity Primitives Evaluation Message Digest (RIPEMD) Hashing algorithm developed as an open standard; it comes in 128-bit, 160-bit, 256-bit, and 320-bit versions.

radio-frequency interference (RFI) The phenomenon in which a wireless signal is disrupted by a radio signal from another device.

RAID   *See* Redundant Array of Independent Disks (RAID).

rainbow table   A binary dictionary file that also includes hashed entries; used in password cracking scenarios.

ransomware   A specific type of malware in which the computer user is forced to pay a sum of money to the malicious attacker in exchange for decrypting and restoring the user's important data.

real evidence   A type of best evidence usually characterized by physical objects.

recovery agent   A designated person or entity who has the authority to recover lost keys or data in the event the person holding the keys is not available.

recovery control   A type of control used to recover systems or data. Restoration of a backup could be considered a recovery control in the event of a data loss, just as the use of an alternate processing site could be used to recover operations in the event of a disaster. Recovery controls are typically temporary or one-time requirements until other controls that are normally used are back in operation.

recovery point objective (RPO)   The maximum amount of data that can be lost for the organization, after which the business cannot recover or would suffer significant loss.

recovery site   As part of a disaster recovery plan, a location for relocating an organization. *See* cold site, hot site, warm site.

recovery time objective (RTO)   The maximum amount of time that a resource may remain unavailable before an unacceptable impact on other system resources occurs.

redundancy   To have more than one of some functioning feature of a system or even another complete system. Used to enhance resiliency.

redundant array of independent disks (RAID)   A way to create a fault-tolerant storage system that uses multiple hard disks configured in an array. RAID has six levels. Level 0 uses byte-level striping and provides no fault tolerance. Level 1 uses mirroring or duplexing. Level 2 uses bit-level striping. Level 3 stores error-correcting information (such as parity) on a separate disk and data striping on the remaining drives. Level 4 is level 3 with block-level striping. Level 5 uses block-level and parity data striping.

refactoring   Reprogramming a devices driver's internals so that the device driver responds to all of the normal inputs and generates all the regular outputs, but also generates malicious output.

Registration Authority (RA)   An additional element often used in larger organizations to help offset the workload of the certificate authority. The RA assists by accepting user requests and verifying their identities before passing along the request to the certificate authority.

regulations   Rules of law or policy that govern behavior in the workplace, such as what to do when a particular event occurs.

remote access   The capability to access a computer from outside the physical facility in which it resides. Remote access requires communications hardware, software, and network connections. Examples of remote access include access through a remote access server or through a VPN connection.

Remote Access Service (RAS)   Hardware and software that allows remote users from outside the network to connect into the internal network, as if they were physically located inside the network. Remote access service handles connection, identification, authentication, and authorization processes.

remote access Trojan (RAT)   A remote administration tool maliciously installed as a Trojan horse to give a remote user some level of control of an infected system.

Remote Authentication Dial-In User Service (RADIUS)   An AAA standard created to support ISPs with hundreds if not thousands of modems in hundreds of computers to connect to a single central database. RADIUS consists of three types of devices: the RADIUS server that has access to a database of user names and passwords, a number of network access servers that control the modems, and a group of systems that dial into the network.

Remote Desktop Protocol (RDP)   A protocol used to access the graphical desktop on a remote host, typically a Windows computer. RDP uses TCP port 3389.

remote lock   A security feature that enables an administrator to remotely lock a mobile device in the event of its loss or theft, in order to prevent unauthorized access to the device.

remote wiping   A security feature that enables an administrator to remotely wipe a mobile device in the event of its loss or theft, in order to prevent unauthorized access to the data on the device.

replay attack   An attempted attack in which user credentials are intercepted and retransmitted to the receiving end in order to authenticate to a network or resource.

rights   Abilities or privileges to perform certain actions on a host, system, or network. Also sometimes referred to as *privileges*.

RIPEMD (RACE Integrity Primitives Evaluation Message Digest)   *See* RACE Integrity Primitives Evaluation Message Digest (RIPEMD).

risk   The possibility of a negative event occurring that will impact or harm an asset or an organization.

risk assessment   A comprehensive assessment of the risk posture of a system or organization; typically involves formulation of threats, assets, impacts, and likelihood. A risk assessment often uses threat and vulnerability assessments, as well as penetration testing, to gather data on risk to the asset or organization.

risk factors   Elements that contribute to risk; risk factors can be either external to the organization or internal.

risk management   The process of how an organization evaluates, protects, and recovers from threats and attacks that take place on its networks.

risk management framework (RMF)   The major steps and flows of the complex process of applying security controls in an organized and controlled fashion.

risk response   The reaction an organization has to particular risk; the four general risk responses are risk mitigation, avoidance, transference, and acceptance.

Rivest Cipher 4 (RC4)   Symmetric streaming cipher popularly used in WEP, SSL, and earlier versions of TLS. It uses key sizes that range from 40 to 2,048 bits in length.

Rivest-Shamir-Adleman algorithm (RSA)   Widely used asymmetric algorithm used for generating the public and private key pairs used in public key cryptography.

rogue access point (rogue AP)   An unauthorized wireless access point (WAP) installed in a computer network.

role-based access control (RBAC)   An access control model based upon the definition of specific roles that have specific rights and privileges assigned to them. Rights and permissions are not assigned on an individual basis; rather, individuals must be assigned to a role by an administrator.

root account   Credentials granted to a user that has complete power over the resource as well as the complete serving system. Windows calls this account *administrator*. In macOS and Linux/UNIX, this account is called *root*.

rootkit   Type of malware that is hidden in operating system files and functions, typically by replacing those files and functions with files that can perform malicious or unknown actions. It is normally able to evade most common antivirus solutions.

round   An iteration of the cryptographic process used by algorithms during the encryption and decryption process.

router   A hardware device used to connect physically separate local area networks together. Routers direct traffic based upon logical Internet protocol addresses, and also eliminate broadcast domains, since broadcasts cannot normally cross router connections to different networks.

rule-based access control   An access control model in which access to different resources is strictly controlled on the basis of specific rules configured and applied to the resource. Rules may entail time of day, originating host, and type of action conditions. Rule-based access control models are typically seen on network security devices such as routers and firewalls.

rule-based system   A system that uses a preconfigured set of rules to allow or disallow access to other systems, networks, or resources.

salt   An arbitrary value, usually created by the application or operating system storing passwords, added to the end of a password before it is hashed.

sandboxing   The practice of keeping applications running in their own separate memory, storage, and program space, preventing their interaction and sharing of data or resources.

Sarbanes–Oxley Act (SOX)   United States law enacted in 2002, part of which requires private businesses to retain critical records for specific time periods.

scalability   The capability to support future network growth beyond its current needs.

script kiddies   Derogatory term for poorly skilled threat actors who take advantage of relatively easy-to-use scripts or programs developed by others to carry out attacks.

scytale   A baton or stick, used in Roman times, that used a strip of parchment wound around it several times, upon which writing was placed to ensure its confidentiality. The parchment would then be unreadable unless wound around an exactly sized similar baton.

Secure Copy Protocol (SCP)   A utility in the Secure Shell (SSH) suite of secure utilities that allows the user to copy files between two hosts.

Secure FTP (SFTP)   A secure version of the File Transfer Protocol used over SSH; it is primarily used for more permanent solutions rather than simply copying a few files between two hosts.

Secure Hash Algorithm (SHA)   A series of hashing algorithms developed by NIST and the NSA, which include SHA-1, SHA-2, and most recently SHA-3 (based upon the Keccak hash function).

Secure MIME (S/MIME)   Secure version of the Multipurpose Internet Mail Extensions (MIME) protocol built into every e-mail client that enables users to make e-mail attachments.

Secure RTP (SRTP)   A secure Real Time Protocol extension that enables protected voice and video communication.

Secure Shell (SSH)   A secure remote connection/terminal emulation program that is not only a protocol but also a suite of secure utilities. SSH uses TCP port 22 and is found natively on UNIX and Linux systems. It can also be ported to Windows systems.

Secure SMTP (SSMTP)   An implementation of the Simple Mail Transfer Protocol (SMTP) that is sent over an SSL connection to provide authentication and encryption services; it uses TCP port 465.

Secure Sockets Layer (SSL)   A secure Application layer protocol that relies on digital certificates and public/private keys to set up authentication and encryption services between two hosts. SSL is used to provide security services for various unsecure protocols, such as HTTP, SMTP, and FTP.

Security Assertion Markup Language (SAML)   A format for a client and server to exchange authentication and authorization data securely. SAML defines three roles for making this happen: principle, identity provider, and service provider.

security control   A policy, action, or safeguard, usually defined by an authoritative security agency (e.g., NIST), designed to mitigate security risks in the environment as much as possible. Controls are usually characterized in *families* and are audited annually for compliance.

security guard   A person who is responsible for controlling access to physical resources such as buildings, secure rooms, and other physical assets.

security ID (SID)   A numerical identifier in Windows systems used to identify a specific account or group. Similar to the concept of user IDs (UIDs) in UNIX- and Linux-based systems.

Security Information and Event Management (SIEM)   Refers to the technologies and products used to integrate security information management and security event management information into a centralized interface, providing real-time event correlation and analysis.

security log   A log that tracks anything that affects security, such as successful and failed logons and logoffs. It can be manually or automatically generated. Also referred to as an *audit log*.

security policy   Internal organizational governance that directs how security will be addressed regarding people, systems, and data.

security token   Physical device that enables authentication to a resource. In an online IMS, a device such as a smartphone can receive authentication prompts via an app, like you find with Steam games. This authentication prompt is a security token that enables a user to access restricted resources. Also called a *secure token*.

separation of duties   A personnel security concept that states a single individual should not perform all critical or privileged-level duties.

service level agreement (SLA)   A contractual agreement, signed by an organization and a third-party provider, that details the level of security, data availability, and other protections afforded the organization's data held by the third party.

service set identifier (SSID)   A basic network name for a wireless network, including both basic service set (BSS) networks, which use single access points, and extended service set (ESS) networks, which use multiple access points.

session   A particular communications session between two hosts or programs communicating via a network.

session hijacking   The interception of a valid computer session to get authentication information or other sensitive data.

Session layer   *See* Open Systems Interconnection (OSI) seven-layer model.

shared account (or generic account)   An account commonly used by more than one person, where all the users know its user name and password. Shared accounts should be avoided when possible, since they provide no accountability or non-repudiation services for actions taken on a system or network.

shoulder surfing   Social engineering attack whereby the attacker surreptitiously views what a victim is typing by looking over the victim's shoulder or passing by the victim.

signature   A specific pattern of bits or bytes that is unique to a particular virus. Virus scanning software maintains a library of signatures and compares the contents of scanned files against this library to detect infected files.

signature-based system   A system that uses signatures to scan for attacks or viruses, and then alerts the administrator.

Simple Mail Transfer Protocol (SMTP)   An unsecure messaging protocol used to send e-mail messages to other hosts. It uses TCP port 25 by default.

Simple Network Management Protocol (SNMP)   A protocol used to manage network devices. It uses ports 161 and 162.

single loss expectancy (SLE)   The loss incurred when an asset has been affected by a negative event. It is calculated as follows: SLE = asset value (AV) × exposure factor (EF).

single point of failure   A system component that has no backup, redundancy, or fault tolerance, such that if that component fails, the entire system fails.

single sign-on   A security mechanism whereby a user needs to log in only once and their credentials are valid throughout the entire enterprise network, granting them access to various resources without the need to use a different set of credentials, or continually re-identify themselves.

single-factor authentication   A form of authentication that uses only one of the following authentication factors: something you know, something you are, something you have, somewhere you are, or something you do.

site survey   A process by which an administrator determines all of the potential issues and problems that may be associated with installing or upgrading a wireless network. Site survey considerations include distance limitations, electromagnetic interference, power output levels, and so on.

site-to-site   A type of VPN connection that uses two concentrators, placed in separate locations. All of the hosts in each location go through their own respective VPN concentrator to contact the distant-end VPN concentrator, thus allowing them access into the other network.

small office/home office (SOHO)   *See* SOHO (small office/home office).

SMTP (Simple Mail Transfer Protocol)   *See* Simple Mail Transfer Protocol (SMTP).

smurf attack   A type of hacking attack in which an attacker floods a network with ping packets sent to the broadcast address from a spoofed source address. All hosts that receive this ICMP message will respond to the spoofed address, flooding the victim with replies and possibly causing a denial-of-service condition on the host.

snapshot   A point-in-time backup of the system state of a virtual machine. A snapshot allows an administrator to restore the virtual machine's operating state in case of a system crash or failure. It should not be considered a complete backup of a virtual machine.

sniffer   A piece of software or hardware that intercepts network traffic. Also referred to as a *protocol analyzer*. Wireshark is a popular network sniffer.

SNMP (Simple Network Management Protocol)   *See* Simple Network Management Protocol (SNMP).

social engineering   The process of using or manipulating people inside an organization to gain access to facilities or network infrastructures.

software-as-a-service (SaaS)   A third-party, cloud-based service that offers outsourced use of software by an organization; this allows an organization to use licensed software at a lower cost than buying, installing, and maintaining software. *See also* cloud computing service.

SOHO (small office/home office)   A classification of networking equipment, usually marketed to consumers or small businesses, that focuses on low price and ease of configuration. SOHO networks differ from enterprise networks, which focus on flexibility and maximum performance.

SOHO firewall   A simple firewall designed for a SOHO environment, often built into the firmware of a SOHO router.

spam   Unsolicited, and potentially harmful, e-mail. May be used to launch phishing or other malicious attacks.

spear phishing   A phishing attack that targets very specific users in an organization, such as network administrators or security personnel.

spim   A type of phishing attack that is similar to spam but takes place over instant messaging applications and systems.

spoofing   The act of impersonating a host, usually through impersonating its IP or MAC address.

spyware   Any program that sends information about your system or your actions over the Internet.

SQL (Structured Query Language)   A language created by IBM that relies on simple English statements to perform database queries. SQL enables databases from different manufacturers to be queried using a standard syntax.

SQL injection   An attack using malformed SQL statements input into a Web form to cause a database to give up more information than the user is authorized to view or to cause it to execute commands, potentially resulting in unauthorized modification, creation, or deletion of data.

SSH File Transfer Protocol (SFTP)   One method for sending FTP traffic over a Secure Shell (SSH) session using native SSH commands and methods. Note that this is not the same thing as *tunneling* regular FTP traffic over SSH (referred to as *FTP over SSH*, which is called *Secure FTP*).

SSID broadcast   A wireless access point feature that announces the WAP's SSID to make it easy for wireless clients to locate and connect to it. By default, most WAPs regularly broadcast their SSID. For security purposes, some entities propose disabling this broadcast.

SSL (Secure Sockets Layer)   *See* Secure Sockets Layer (SSL).

SSL VPN   A type of VPN that uses SSL encryption. Clients connect to the VPN server using a standard Web browser, with the traffic secured using SSL. The two most common types of SSL VPNs are SSL portal VPNs and SSL tunnel VPNs.

standard   A formally documented level of performance or process that supports security policies.

standard operating procedures (SOPs)   Usually a written document depicting the procedures and actions taken for a variety of circumstances that is provided to new hires to read.

static code analyzer   A debugging tool that reads the source code but does not run the code.

static host   A nonstandard device that uses Internet-based services and receives an IP address on a network. Examples include household appliances, automotive equipment, and game consoles. Commonly part of the concept of the Internet of Things.

steganography   The science of hiding information in other data.

storage area network (SAN)   A server that can take a pool of hard disks and present them over the network as any number of logical disks.

stream cipher (or algorithm)   An encryption method that encrypts a single bit at a time. Streaming ciphers are much faster than block ciphers. RC4 is an example of a streaming cipher.

subnet   An independent network in a TCP/IP internetwork.

subnet mask   The value used in TCP/IP settings to divide the IP address of a host into its component parts: network ID and host ID.

subnetting   Taking a single class of IP addresses and dividing it into multiple smaller groups.

substitution cipher   Type of cipher that substitutes different letters of the alphabet for other letters.

succession planning The process of identifying people who can take over certain critical positions (usually on a temporary basis) in case the people holding those positions are incapacitated or otherwise unavailable.

Supervisory Control and Data Acquisition (SCADA) A system that has the basic components of a distributed control system (DCS), yet is designed for large-scale, distributed processes and functions with the idea that remote devices may or may not have ongoing communication with the central control.

supplicant A client computer in a RADIUS network.

switch A network device that offers multiple client connections to a network and has the added capability to limit collision domains. Some switches also offer the capability to create virtual LANs (VLANs), segmenting traffic by logical subnet and eliminating broadcast domains.

symmetric cryptography Form of cryptography that uses only a single key for both encryption and decryption.

SYN flood A network attack in which an attacker continually sends the first sequence (SYN) of the TCP three-way handshake but never completes the handshake process, causing the victim host to have to repeatedly acknowledge traffic and use up resources.

syslog A logging facility often found in UNIX or Linux systems; it can collect logs from multiple systems at once for ease of administration.

System (or Software) Development Life Cycle (SDLC) A framework describing the entire useful life of a system or software, which usually includes phases relating to requirements definition, design, development, acquisition, implementation, sustainability, and disposal. CompTIA refers to SDLC as the *software development life cycle*, which narrows in on the development of an application.

system log A log file that records issues dealing with the overall system, such as system services, device drivers, or configuration changes.

system resiliency Adding technologies and processes to computing equipment and networks that don't stop attacks, but enable the equipment and networks to recover easily. Methods to increase resiliency include non-persistence, redundancy, and automation.

tabletop exercise A type of group review to measure the effectiveness of a business continuity plan or other security procedure.

tailgating An attempt by an unauthorized person to physically access the facility by closely following an authorized person into it.

TCP three-way handshake A three-segment conversation between TCP hosts to establish and start a data transfer session. The conversation begins with a SYN request by the initiator. The target responds with a SYN response and an ACK to the SYN request.

The initiator confirms receipt of the SYN ACK with an ACK. Once this handshake is complete, data transfer can begin.

TCP/IP model An architecture model that is based on the TCP/IP protocol suite and defines and standardizes the flow of data between computers. The following lists the four layers:

- **Layer 1** The *Link layer (Network Interface layer)* is similar to OSI's Data Link and Physical layers (Layers 1 and 2). The Link layer consists of any part of the network that deals with frames.

- **Layer 2** The *Internet layer* is the same as OSI's Network layer. Any part of the network that deals with pure IP packets—getting a packet to its destination—is on the Internet layer.

- **Layer 3** The *Transport layer* combines the features of OSI's Transport layer. It is concerned with the assembly and disassembly of data, as well as connection-oriented and connectionless communication.

- **Layer 4** The *Application layer* combines the features of the top three layers of the OSI model. It consists of the processes that applications use to initiate, control, and disconnect from a remote system.

TCP/IP suite The collection of all the protocols and processes that make TCP over IP communication over a network possible.

technical control A type of control characterized by all of the technical configuration options needed to protect a device or system. Also sometimes referred to as a *logical control*.

Telnet An older, nonsecure program that enables users to remotely access systems.

temperature monitor A device used in monitoring and maintaining data center temperatures.

TEMPEST The NSA's security standard that is used to prevent radio frequency emanation by using specialized enclosures and shielding.

Temporal Key Integrity Protocol (TKIP) The encryption mechanism used with Wi-Fi Protected Access (WPA). Each transmitted packet is sent with a different key, making it difficult to conduct an initialization vector attack on the protocol.

Terminal Access Controller Access Control System Plus (TACACS+) A proprietary protocol developed by Cisco to support AAA in a network with many routers and switches. It is similar to RADIUS in function, but uses TCP port 49 by default and separates authorization, authentication, and accounting into different parts.

threat A negative event or occurrence that exploits a vulnerability in an asset.

threat agent Any entity that initiates a threat; also called a *threat actor*.

threat assessment   A form of assessment that identifies all potential threats and threat actors that may affect the system or organization.

threat vector   A particular method used by a threat actor to initiate a threat against a vulnerability.

Ticket-Granting Ticket (TGT)   A ticket that is issued to a client by an authentication server in a Kerberos realm and is later used by the client to gain a service ticket with which to access a resource.

time-based one-time password (TOTP)   A one-time use only password used to authenticate one communications session; not only can it be used only one time, it also has a very short lifespan and cannot be used outside of that time period.

tracert (also traceroute)   A command-line utility used to follow the path a packet takes between two hosts.

tracert –6 (also traceroute6)   A command-line utility that checks a path from the station running the command to a destination host. Adding the –6 switch to the command line specifies that the target host uses an IPv6 address. tracerout6 is a Linux command that performs a traceroute to an IPv6 addressed host.

transitive trust   A trust between multiple systems or networks, such that if system A trusts system B, then system A will also automatically trust system C if system B also trusts system C.

Transmission Control Protocol (TCP)   A transport-layer protocol that establishes a defined connection with the sending and receiving hosts before a data segment transmission session begins. TCP also manages segment sequencing and retransmission of lost segments through the use of sequence numbers.

Transmission Control Protocol/Internet Protocol (TCP/IP)   A set of communication protocols developed by the U.S. Department of Defense that enables dissimilar computers to share information over a network.

Transport layer   *See* Open Systems Interconnection (OSI) seven-layer model.

Transport Layer Security (TLS)   A more secure update to the SSL protocol that works with almost any TCP application. It also uses TCP port 443, as does SSL.

transposition cipher   A type of cipher that transposes or changes the order of characters in a message using some predetermined method that both the sender and receiver are aware of.

trap   An alert sent to an administrative station, due to an unusual event that occurs on a SNMP-managed device. A trap is a specific event configured with a certain threshold. If a configured threshold is reached for a particular event, the trap is triggered and the notification or alert is sent to the management console.

trend analysis   The process of collecting information from various sources over time and analyzing it for patterns or trends relating to resource access or network traffic.

Triple DES   An algorithm that is viewed as a replacement for DES and essentially puts plaintext blocks to the same type of encryption processes three distinct times; it uses three separate 56-bit keys.

Trojan horse   A form of malware that masquerades as a program with a legitimate purpose, so that a user will be tempted to run it, but performs malicious actions on the system when executed. The name is derived from the famed Greek Trojan horse.

trust relationship   An established security relationship between two entities or systems, such that they trust each other's user accounts database and allow unfettered authentication and authorization to each other's resources.

trusted OS   A specialized version of an operating system, created and configured for high-security environments.

Trusted Platform Module (TPM)   A hardware chip embedded in a device that provides for cryptographic key generation and storage functions. It is often used in computers for drive encryption and authentication processes.

trusted user   A user that is trusted to the extent that they may be allowed higher-level privileges on a system or with a resource.

tunnel   An encrypted link between two systems, regardless of the network they reside on, that protects traffic between those systems from interception or modification.

two-factor authentication   A method of security authentication that requires two separate means of authentication; for example, some sort of physical token that, when inserted, prompts for a password.

Twofish   A symmetric block algorithm that was one of the five finalists in the competition to become AES. It uses 128-bit block sizes, 16 rounds of encryption, and 128-bit, 192-bit, and 256-bit key sizes.

typosquatting   A method of attack in which a malicious actor purchases a similar sounding or slightly misspelled domain name that's a close match to a legitimate organization, in an effort to trick a user into visiting that domain instead of the legitimate one.

unencrypted channel   Unsecure communication between two hosts that pass data between them in unencrypted form, or clear text. HTTP, FTP, and the Telnet protocols are examples of connections that use unencrypted channels.

Unified Threat Management (UTM)   The concept of implementing multipurpose security devices that perform a wide variety of functions, including firewall, proxy, VPN, and data loss prevention functions.

uninterruptible power supply (UPS)   A device that supplies continuous clean power to a computer system, and protects against power outages and sags.

UNIX   A popular computer software operating system used on many Internet host systems.

unsecure protocol   A protocol that transfers data between hosts in an unencrypted, clear text format. HTTP, FTP, and Telnet are examples of unsecure protocols.

URL hijacking   Type of attack similar to typo squatting (using misspelled domain names), where an attacker uses a fake URL to lure users to a non-legitimate Web site.

user account   A logically created system identifier that binds to a particular individual and is used to tie a user to a particular action or allowed actions.

User Datagram Protocol (UDP)   A Transport layer protocol that is used to carry datagrams between two hosts; it does not rely on established connections, nor does it manage data sequencing or retransmission of lost data.

user identifier (UID)   Identifies a particular user in UNIX and Linux operating systems. It is very similar to the concept of a security identifier (SID) used in Windows systems.

user-level security   A security system in which each user has an account and password for a resource, and access to resources is based on user identity on that particular system. Also called *peer* or *workgroup-level security*, it is a decentralized security model.

virtual local area network (VLAN)   A subnet of a LAN that has been logically created on a switch device. VLANs are used to separate hosts in two logical networks, eliminate broadcast domains, and allow for better management and segregation of hosts by function, location, or security requirements.

virtual machine (VM)   A virtual computer accessed through a program called a *hypervisor* or *virtual machine manager*. A VM runs *inside* an actual operating system, essentially enabling you to run two or more operating systems at once.

virtual machine manager (VMM)   *See* hypervisor.

virtual private network (VPN)   A technology used to securely connect to an organization's internal network by tunneling unsecure protocols and data over a secure connection through an unsecure external network, such as the Internet, to a secure device known as a *VPN concentrator*.

virus   A piece of malicious software that must be propagated through a definite user action.

virus definition (or signature) files   Data file updates that enable virus protection software to recognize the viruses on a system by their characteristics and remove or quarantine them. Virus definitions should be updated often. Also called *signature files*, depending on the virus protection software in use.

vishing   An attack method that uses Voice-over-IP (VoIP) telephone systems to carry out phishing attacks.

Voice over IP (VoIP)   A set of technologies used to send telephony and voice services over standard Internet Protocol networks.

vulnerability   A potential weakness in an infrastructure, network, host, or even a person or organization that a threat might exploit.

vulnerability assessment   A type of security assessment in which vulnerabilities for a system are discovered and documented.

vulnerability scanner   A tool that scans a network for potential attack vectors.

walkthrough test   A type of group review to measure the effectiveness of a business continuity plan or other security measure; more thorough than a tabletop exercise.

warchalking   An older, obscure practice of secretly marking the location of unsecured wireless networks by drawing specialized symbols on sidewalks and walls with chalk to let others know about the wireless network.

wardriving   The practice of driving through an area and scanning for unsecured wireless networks with the intention of connecting to them for free wireless access or hacking into them.

warm site   A facility with all of the physical resources, computers, and network infrastructure needed to recover from a primary site disaster. A warm site does not have current backup data, and it may take a day or more to recover and install backups before business operations can recommence.

waterfall   A linear software development lifecycle model.

watering hole attack   Type of social engineering attack that targets a group within an organization based on patterns in Web usage.

Web services   Applications and processes that can be accessed over a network through a Web server, rather than being accessed locally on the client machine. Web services include things such as Web-based e-mail, network-shareable documents, spreadsheets and databases, and many other types of cloud-based applications.

web-of-trust   A model used between users of digital certificates and key pairs to trust each other's keys. This model is primarily used in small groups of users, and instead of using a centralized certificate issuing authority, it relies on the trust that individual users have in each other. PGP, when used in small groups, typically uses this model.

whaling   A specific phishing attack targeted at large targets, such as senior executives. This attack normally is more complex and makes more use of specific information gathered through social engineering.

white box test   A penetration test in which the tester has full knowledge of the target systems and network through information provided by the network administrator. This test is usually conducted to verify known vulnerabilities, as well as to discover potentially unknown vulnerabilities and exploit them.

white hat hacker   A security professional who uses his or her abilities and knowledge to help secure networks; also known as an *ethical hacker.*

whitelisting   The practice of allowing only specifically allowed programs, applications, executables, and files, from only allowed providers, into a network or system.

Wi-Fi   The name given to the consumer and commerce wireless technologies that use the Institute of Electrical and Electronics Engineers (IEEE) 802.11 wireless standards; "Wi-Fi" is a trademarked name belonging to the Wi-Fi Alliance.

Wi-Fi analyzer   Any device that finds and documents all wireless networks in the area. Also known as a *wireless analyzer.*

Wi-Fi Protected Access (WPA)   A wireless security protocol, developed by a consortium of vendors, that addresses the weaknesses of Wired Equivalent Privacy (WEP). WPA offers security enhancements such as dynamic encryption key generation (keys are issued on a per-user and per-session basis), an encryption key integrity-checking feature, user authentication through the industry-standard Extensible Authentication Protocol (EAP), and other advanced features that WEP lacks. WPA was intended as a temporary measure while awaiting the adoption of the official IEEE 802.11i standard, also known as *WPA2.*

Wi-Fi Protected Access 2 (WPA2)   The common name for the official IEEE 802.11i standard, which includes the use of the Advanced Encryption Standard as the de facto encryption algorithm. It is also backward-compatible with the WPA standard in most cases, since it can fall back to using the Temporal Key Integrity Protocol (TKIP), the standard encryption mechanism in WPA.

Wi-Fi Protected Setup (WPS)   Automated and semi-automated process to connect a wireless device to a WAP. The process can be as simple as pressing a button on the device or pressing the button and then entering a PIN code. WPS has several security issues, and was later proven to be ineffective in establishing a secure wireless network.

wildcard certificate   Certificate issued by a CA that applies to a domain rather than an specific URL. Subject Alternate Name (SAN) extensions to X.509 reduce the risk involved with wildcard certificates by listing supported URLs.

Windows Firewall   The firewall that has been included in Windows operating systems since Windows XP, through Windows 8.1. Originally named Internet Connection Firewall (ICF), Microsoft renamed it Windows Firewall in XP Service Pack 2.

Wired Equivalent Privacy (WEP)   The first attempt at wireless security protocols, introduced in the older IEEE 802.11b standard, which uses RC4 as its encryption algorithm. It is susceptible to many attacks, including initialization vector attacks and weak keys attacks.

wireless access point (WAP)   A network device that connects wireless network nodes to other wireless or wired networks. Many WAPs are combination devices that act as high-speed hubs, switches, bridges, and routers, all rolled into one.

wireless analyzer   *See* Wi-Fi analyzer.

Wireshark   A popular network protocol analyzer; it can be used on either wired or wireless networks.

witness   A person who sees an event. In computer forensics, the term "witness" takes on a different meaning. While people can testify that they visually saw someone enter data into the system or remove hardware, for example, most computer transactions that occur are "witnessed" by computers and equipment, not actual people. A person can witness a printout or what's shown on the screen of a computer, but data can be altered before it is printed out, or shown on the screen, so the value of an actual physical witness to an event in a computer forensics case may be limited. *See also* expert witness.

workgroup   A method of organizing computers, users, and resources in a small environment; does not require an Active Directory domain. A workgroup configuration uses decentralized user-level security, where resources are located on individual hosts, and the user of each computer decides how other users access those resources.

worm   A very special form of malware that can replicate itself to other systems on a network by taking advantage of security weaknesses in networking protocols. Unlike a virus, a worm does not require user action or intervention to infect other files.

WPA2-Enterprise   A version of WPA2 that is used in large enterprise environments and typically uses more advanced authentication technologies, such as IEEE 802.1X port authentication, and a RADIUS server for authentication.

X.509   A popular standard for the format, creation, use, and management of digital certificates.

XMAS attack   A network-based attack in which specific TCP flags are set to the "on" position; many hosts are not configured to properly deal with the specific combination, and it may cause a denial-of-service attack on the host.

XML injection   A specific type of injection attack that injects malformed XML into a Web application, causing data modification or destruction or the execution of arbitrary code on the system.

XOR function   Mathematical function that looks at each bit of plaintext and performs a mathematical eXclusive OR operation on it.

zero-day attack   A new attack that uses a vulnerability that has yet to be identified, and for which no known mitigation or patch exists.

zombie   A single computer that is under the control of an operator and is used in a botnet attack. *See also* botnet.

INDEX

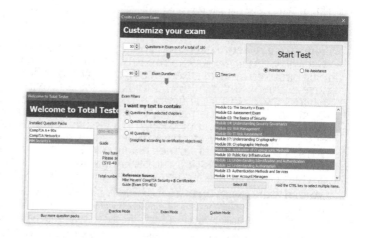